Joseph Addison Alexander

The Acts of the Apostles

Vol. 1

Joseph Addison Alexander

The Acts of the Apostles
Vol. 1

ISBN/EAN: 9783337398040

Printed in Europe, USA, Canada, Australia, Japan

Cover: Foto ©Lupo / pixelio.de

More available books at **www.hansebooks.com**

THE

ACTS OF THE APOSTLES

EXPLAINED

BY

JOSEPH ADDISON ALEXANDER

IN TWO VOLUMES

VOLUME I

THIRD EDITION.

NEW YORK:
CHARLES SCRIBNER, 124 GRAND STREET,
CORNER OF BROADWAY.
1860.

PREFACE.

THE materials of this book were collected in a course of academical instruction, and prepared for publication, in the first instance, with a view to the peculiar wants of ministers and students. But after the first chapter was in type, the writer was induced to recommence the work upon a new plan, in the hope of making it more generally useful, by the reduction of its size, and the omission of all matter supposed to be interesting only to professional or educated readers. This will account for the prominence given to the English version, the exclusion (for the most part) of the Greek text, and the absence of any detailed reference to other writers. It will be found, however, that the constant subject of the exposition is the inspired original, and that one of its main objects is to perfect the translation, so as to place the English reader as nearly as possible on the same footing with the student of the Greek text. In attempting to effect the change of form already mentioned, it has sometimes been difficult to obliterate all trace of the original design; but this, it is hoped, will be considered rather a literary blemish than a practical inconvenience. The numerous citations have been carefully selected, for the benefit of those who wish to master the analogy and usage of the Scriptures; and the frequent reference from one part of the commentary to another is intended to fit it for occasional consultation as well as for continuous perusal. It may not be superfluous to add, that the purpose of the work, as indicated by the title, is simple explanation of the sense and illustration of the history, leaving all further uses, and among the rest all practical improvement, to those who may avail themselves of its assistance, and especially to such as may employ it in historical as well as exegetical instruction.

PRINCETON, *June* 1, 1857.

INTRODUCTION.

THE Biblical History consists of two great parts, contained in the Old and New Testaments respectively. The New Testament portion naturally falls into two divisions; the Gospel History, or Life of Christ, from his birth to his ascension; and the Apostolical History, from his ascension to the close of the canon. The Apostolical History may again be subdivided into two parts; a connected narrative, extending from our Lord's ascension to the second year of Paul's captivity at Rome; and a body of detached and incidental statements, scattered through the other books of the New Testament.

The materials of this last class may be used to illustrate and complete the other, but are not to be confounded or incorporated with it. This is forbidden, first, by the uncertain chronological relations of these insulated data to the formal history recorded in the Acts of the Apostles. For example, the account of Paul's visits to Jerusalem and Corinth, as given in the Acts and in his own Epistles, although no doubt perfectly consistent, cannot be reduced to one harmonic view, except by probable approximation, quite sufficient for all necessary uses, whether exegetical or apologetical, but not for a precise specification of the corresponding points in the collateral or parallel authorities. The same thing is still more emphatically true as to the dates of Paul's Epistles, some of which are still disputed, and the rest, though commonly agreed upon, are still not so absolutely certain as to justify their being made a part of the authoritative narrative, and put upon a level with the facts there positively stated.

Another objection to the actual insertion of these supplementary details into the history is the violence done to its integrity and unity, as being not a mere collection of materials but a regular historical composition, the plan and character of which depend as much on the omission or exclusion as upon the introduction, both of general topics and minute particulars. The choice between these rests exclusively with the historian, and any foreign interference, though it may enrich the composition as a storehouse of materials, must impair its oneness, as an intellectual creation, and the realization of a definite idea. The omissions in any of the sacred histories are not inadvertent or fortuitous, much less the fruit of ignorance or want of skill, to be supplied by subsequent interpolation, but belong to the original design and must be left untouched, excepting in the way of illustration and interpretation. This is the use which it is here proposed to make of the detached and incidental facts found elsewhere, in explaining the Acts of the Apostles, as a complete and independent history, constructed on a rational, consistent plan, designed to make a definite impression and to answer a specific purpose.

This description can be fully verified by nothing less than a detailed examination of the book itself; but a compendious statement of the grounds on which it rests will be given in its proper place below, as a part of this general introduction. In the mean time its truth may be assumed and used to prove that the book is not a mere farrago of heterogeneous fragments, or a collection of independent documents, or a series of anecdotes or desultory recollections, but the continuous and systematic product of a single mind. The conclusion thus drawn from the unity of purpose traceable throughout the book is confirmed by its marked uniformity of style and manner. While the Greek of this book is comparatively classical and pure, it has peculiarities of language, not the less real because slight and unimportant in themselves, distinguishing its style from every other except that of the third Gospel, which, besides a general resemblance not to be mistaken, coincides with it in some of its most striking singularities of thought and diction. This remarkable coincidence creates of course a strong presumption that the two books which exhibit it are works of the same author. This presumption is still further strengthened by the fact, that the two together make up an unbroken history, the one beginning where the other ends, to wit, at the Ascension. It is further strengthened by the later book's purporting on its face to be the sequel or continuation of another, the contents of which, as there described (Acts 1, 1), exactly correspond to those of the third gospel. It is still further strengthened by the circumstance that both books are inscribed to the same man (Theophilus), and seem to have been primarily meant for his instruction. All these considerations go to confirm, and are themselves confirmed by, the unanimous tradition of the ancient church, that the third Gospel and the Acts of the Apostles are works of the same author.

In attempting to determine who the author was, we find that this, like all the other histories of Scripture, is anonymous. Even the titles of the Pentateuch and Gospels, though correct, are traditional, and form no part of the text itself. This usage is the more remarkable because the contrary is uniformly true as to the prophecies, in all of which the writer's name is given, not excepting the Apocalypse, in which John names himself repeatedly, although he never does so in his Gospel, nor in either of his three Epistles.

When we look into the Acts for some internal indication of its origin, we find in certain parts (ch. XVI. XX. XXI. XXVII.

xxviii) the first person plural (*we* and *us*), implying that the writer was an eye-witness of the circumstances there recorded, which in all such cases are detailed with an unusual precision and minuteness as to times and places, showing that the form of speech in question is not merely accidental or unmeaning, but expressive of a personal and lively recollection on the part of the historian.

Some have attempted to account for this phenomenon by supposing that these portions of the narrative were taken from the notes or journals of those actually present, and incorporated without change into the history. But this is to get rid of a supposed improbability by means of one still greater, since the supposition of two writers is less obvious and natural than that of one. For if we may assume without proof that the historian derived this part of his materials from one who witnessed the events, much more may we assume that the historian witnessed them himself. It may be said, indeed, that if this were the case, the same form of expression would have been employed throughout. To this it may be answered, in the first place, that the writer, although constantly present, might refer to himself only when directly acting or concerned in the events related; and in the next place, that he may not have been always personally present, which, as we shall see, is probably the true solution.

Another objection to the supposition of incorporated documents from other sources is, that a writer who was capable of planning and composing such a history as this, would be incapable of thus inserting extracts from the manuscripts of others in their crude state, without either intimating that they were so or assimilating them in form to his own context.

The only remaining supposition is, that the writer of the history was at least occasionally one of Paul's travelling companions. Now of these we know that some of the most eminent, particularly Silas and Timothy, were present upon some of the occasions here recorded, and we therefore naturally think of them, or one of them, as probably the writer. But to this there are objections both internal and external. The use of the first person begins at Troas and ceases at Philippi (16, 10. 18); but Silas and Timothy had joined Paul long before (15, 40. 16, 3), and were with him in Thessalonica and Berea (17, 1. 14), and afterwards rejoined him in Corinth (18, 5.) Yet in all these movements, there is no indication of the writer's presence by the use of the first person. And when this peculiar form of speech does re-appear, it is so employed as to distinguish Timothy at least from the historian, by expressly saying, "these (among whom he is by name included) going before, waited for us at Troas" (20, 4. 5.) Another objection, both to Timothy and Silas, as the author of the history, is that so eminent a name would have been perpetuated by tradition, which is only too apt to connect such names with famous writings and achievements, as for instance to make all the persons mentioned in the Acts and Apostolical Epistles bishops of the places where they seem to have resided. In the present case it would be wholly unaccountable, that such names as those of Timothy and Silas should be dropped or exchanged for one otherwise unknown.

This is the name of Luke, whom an ancient and uniform tradition recognizes as the author, both of the third Gospel and the Acts of the Apostles. The only supposition that accounts for the origin of this tradition is the simple supposition of its truth. It may therefore be added to the internal evidence already stated, as a ground for the conclusion that the writer of both books was Luke, who is three times named in Paul's epistles, once as a companion (2 Tim. 4, 11), once as a fellow-labourer (Philem. 24), and once as a beloved physician (Col. 4, 11.) This is absolutely all the information with respect to Luke afforded directly by the books of the New Testament, though other facts have been deduced from these by inference and combination. The name, in its original form (*Lucas*), is most probably contracted from Lucanus, Lucius, or Lucilius, this termination (*as*) being commonly used in such abbreviations, as in Demas from Demetrius, Silas from Silvanus, Antipas from Antipater, &c. On the ground that such contracted names were often borne by freedmen or emancipated slaves, and that Greek slaves were in that age the physicians of their Roman masters, Grotius builds the fanciful hypothesis that Luke was a freedman of the Lucian or Lucilian family. A less extravagant but still precarious conjecture would identify him with the *Lucius* of Acts 13, 1 and Rom. 16, 21. Connected with the former name, perhaps, is the old tradition of his being born or resident at Antioch, and there first introduced to Paul's acquaintance. From the way in which he is supposed to be distinguished from the "circumcision" (in Col. 4, 11), some infer that he was certainly a Gentile, which is also thought to be confirmed by his apparent reference to Gentile rather than to Jewish readers. The notion that he was a painter is comparatively recent and perhaps occasioned by a misconstruction of some reference to his graphic or descriptive mode of writing history. Some have imagined that Paul calls him a physician in a metaphorical or spiritual sense, as Christ called his first disciples "fishers of men." But even this description presupposes that they had been literally fishermen, and no good reason can be given for the special application of this name to Luke's spiritual ministry, unless it was descriptive of his secular profession. It is probable, however, from Philem. 24, that he exercised the cure of souls as well as bodies. The traces of his medical profession, found by many in his writings, although faint and doubtful, will be noticed as they present themselves in the progress of the exposition.

This remarkable dearth of information as to Luke, beyond his name, profession, and the general fact that he was one of Paul's most intimate associates, and perhaps for many years his medical attendant, gives the more importance to the uniform tradition of the early church, not only that he wrote these books, but that he wrote them under Paul's direction and control, thereby imparting to them, in addition to the common seal of inspiration, the specific stamp of apostolical authority. Another tradition represents the second Gospel as sustaining a similar relation to Mark as its immediate author, and to Peter as its apostolical endorser, and the source from which some of its most interesting statements were directly drawn. These traditions, though intrinsically not improbable, may possibly have sprung from the supposed necessity of giving to the second and third gospels, though not written by apostles, an equality of rank and honour with the first and fourth, which were so written.

However this may be, the canonical authority of Acts has never been disputed in the church at large, the book having always formed a part of the New Testament Canon, as far back as its history can now be traced. It was rejected by some ancient heretics for obvious reasons, as opposed to their peculiar notions; by the Manichees, because it represents the Holy Spirit (and not Manes) as the promised Comforter; by the Encratites, because it showed their meritorious abstinences to be inconsistent with the doctrine and the practice of the early church; by the Ebionites, because it proved the ceremonial law to be a temporary institution; by the Marcionites, because it recognized it, while it lasted, as divine and sacred. On the other hand, the book is found in all the ancient catalogues of orthodox or catholic authority, and quoted (or referred to) by the earliest Christian writers, from Clement of Rome in the first century to Irenæus at the close of the second, in whose extant works a modern writer has discovered more than thirty citations from the Acts of the Apostles. That the book was not received from the beginning as canonical, has been inferred by some from an expression of Chrysostom, that many in his day were not aware of its existence. But this, if genuine, which has been doubted, is a mere rhetorical hyperbole, intended to rebuke in strong terms the neglect of this important part of Scripture. The same thing might be said now, in the same sense, as to other books, the canonicity of which has never been disputed.

It is no doubt true, that certain parts of the New Testament, in ancient as in modern times, were more read and therefore better known than others. It must be remembered that the books of the New Testament were separately written, and originally circulated one by one, but gradually gathered into groups or classes, and eventually into one complete collection. One of the earliest divisions of the canon, which we know to have prevailed before the time of Origen, was into two unequal parts called GOSPEL and APOSTLE; the first containing the four Gospels by themselves, not as superior to the rest in inspiration or authority, but only in dignity of subject, as exhibiting the Life of Christ, and also as the chronological basis of the whole, corresponding to the Books of Moses in the Hebrew Canon. The other division, being not only larger but more miscellaneous, was familiarly subdivided into several, one containing Paul's Epistles, another the Apocalypse, another the Acts of the Apostles, and another the Catholic Epistles, the two last, however, being often joined together, that is, written in one volume.

That these conventional divisions of the Canon were not transcribed with equal frequency, we learn from a comparison of extant manuscripts. Of those collated by the modern critics (excluding *Lectionaries*, or selected lessons used in ancient worship) it may be stated in round numbers, that the Gospels are found in above five hundred, the Epistles of Paul in about three hundred, the Catholic Epistles and the Acts in above two hundred, and the Book of Revelation in about one hundred. Of the two hundred manuscripts (or more) containing Acts, eight or nine are of the Uncial or most ancient class, written in capital letters, for the most part without accents, breathings, stops, or even spaces between the words, the common use of all which is a sign of later date. Among these are the four oldest copies of the Greek Testament known to be extant, and distinguished in the latest critical editions by the four first letters of the alphabet. A. The Codex Alexandrinus, in the British Museum. B. The Codex Vaticanus, in the Papal Library at Rome. C. The Codex Ephraemi, in the Imperial Library at Paris. D. The Codex Bezæ, in the University Library at Cambridge. The precise date of these manuscripts is still disputed, but is now commonly agreed to range from the fourth to the sixth centuries inclusive. From this it follows that, although the extant copies of the Acts are far less numerous than those of the Gospels or of Paul's Epistles, they include the very manuscripts whose aid is most important in determining the true text even of those other books.

Besides the preservation of the Greek text in these copies, the book has also been preserved in several ancient versions, the most important of which are the Syriac Peshito, made in the third if not the second century, and the Latin Vulgate, made by Jerome, on the basis of an old Italic version, near the close of the fourth century. Other early versions, from the third to the ninth century, are the Egyptian in two dialects, the Ethiopic, Gothic, Armenian, Georgian, Arabic, and Slavonic. Occasional reference will be made, in the following exposition, to some modern versions, more especially to Luther's, and the six old English versions, those of Wiclif (1380), Tyndale (1534), Cranmer (1539), the Geneva Bible (1557), the Rhemish Version (1582), and King James's Bible (1611), the last of which is still in common use. Two of these, Wiclif's and the Rhemish, are translations of the Vulgate; Cranmer's is little more than a reprint of Tyndale's, with a few unimportant variations; the same is true, but in a less degree, of the Geneva Bible; while the common version, though to some extent influenced by all the others, is founded mainly upon Tyndale's, with occasional changes for the worse and for the better, but a frequent adherence to him even when in error.

Besides mere versions or translations, this book has been a favourite subject of interpretation, more or less minute and thorough, from the earliest to the present times. In addition to the interest belonging to it as part and parcel of the sacred history, it possesses great importance in connection with the most exciting questions of Ecclesiology, as furnishing the sole authentic record of the primitive church-government and organization. Hence it has been interpreted in every variety of form, from the most elaborate and learned to the most popular and practical, as well in general expositions of the Bible, or of the New Testament, as in special works on this book in particular. Besides formal commentaries on the text, this part of Scripture has received much illustration from a class of writers who have sought rather to present the substance of the history in popular and interesting forms. Among the latest and best specimens of this kind may be named the Apostolical History of Baumgarten, and the Life and Letters of St. Paul by Conybeare and Howson, and as a masterly elucidation of a single passage, the Voyage and Shipwreck of St. Paul by Smith of Jordanhill. The plan and limits of the following exposition forbid particular citation of the many works consulted in preparing it.

The oldest known division of the Greek text, by Euthalius, who lived in the sixth century, was into forty chapters. The present division into twenty-eight was made by Cardinal Hugo, in the thirteenth century, to facilitate the use of his Concordance to the Latin Vulgate, and was not adopted in the copies of the Greek text till the fifteenth century. The division into verses first appears in the margin of Stephens' edition (1551), and is said to have been made by him during a journey between Paris and Lyons. The actual separation of the verses, by printing them in paragraphs, appears for the first time in Beza's edition (1565), and although discontinued in the latest publications of the Greek text, still prevails in most editions of the English Bible and of other modern versions. The history of these divisions should be clearly understood, not only to prevent their being thought original, or even ancient, but also to deprive them of an undue influence upon the exposition of the text itself. The distinction of the chapters in this book is often injudicious and unskilful, and at best, these conventional divisions are mere matters of mechanical convenience, like the paragraphs and pages of a modern book.

But while we make use of these mechanical contrivances

for ease of reference and consultation, they must not be suffered to usurp the place of a more rational division growing out of the relations of the history itself, as a methodical and systematical whole, designed to answer a specific purpose. The ideas of most readers as to this point are derived from the familiar title, ACTS OF THE APOSTLES. But this title is regarded by the critics as traditional, and forming no part of the text, but added by a later hand. It is, however, very ancient, being found in all the oldest copies, though with some variety of form. That the book appeared at first without a title, or that its title has been lost and another substituted for it, seem to be equally improbable hypotheses, unless it be assumed that it was first sent, as a sort of historical epistle, to Theophilus, and afterwards provided with a name when brought into more general circulation.

Even this title does not mean, however, nor is the book in fact, a history of the twelve apostles, most of whom are barely named in the first chapter. It is not the biography of Peter and Paul, as Apostles by way of eminence; for each of them is prominent in one part only, and the whole life of neither is recorded in detail. It is not a general history of the Apostolical period, as distinguished from the ministry of Christ himself; for many interesting facts belonging to that subject are omitted, some of which have been preserved in the Epistles. BUT THE BOOK BEFORE US IS A SPECIAL HISTORY OF THE PLANTING AND EXTENSION OF THE CHURCH, BOTH AMONG JEWS AND GENTILES, BY THE GRADUAL ESTABLISHMENT OF RADIATING CENTRES OR SOURCES OF INFLUENCE AT CERTAIN SALIENT POINTS THROUGHOUT A LARGE PART OF THE EMPIRE, BEGINNING AT JERUSALEM AND ENDING AT ROME. That this is really the theme and purpose of the history, any reader may satisfy himself by running through it with this general idea in his mind, observing how the prominent points answer to it, and that as soon as this idea is exhausted the book closes, in a way that would be otherwise abrupt and harsh. The same thing may be ascertained in more detail by using this description as a principle or method of division, without any forced or artificial process, simply letting the history divide and subdivide itself in reference to its subject and design, as these have been already stated. Such an analysis, though presupposing a detailed examination of the book, may be presented here as a preliminary basis of the exposition.

The whole book naturally falls into two great parts, each of which may be grouped around a central figure. The subject of the first part is the planting and extension of the Church among the Jews by the ministry of Peter. The subject of the second is the planting and extension of the Church among the Gentiles by the ministry of Paul. It is not as individuals, nor merely as Apostles, that these two men occupy so large a space and a position so conspicuous, but as the chosen leaders in these two distinct but harmonious movements. We have therefore no details of their biography except so far as these are needed to illustrate this important period of church-history. It may also be observed that neither is presented, even in his own sphere, to the absolute exclusion of the other; but the spheres themselves are so connected as to show that both belong to one great system. Peter, the Apostle of the Circumcision, introduces the first Gentile to the Christian Church. Paul, the Apostle of the Gentiles, preaches always " to the Jew first" when he has the opportunity, not only in the opening of his ministry at Damascus and Jerusalem, but down to its very close at Rome. With this important qualification, the first part of the history (ch. I–XII) may be described as that of Peter and the Church among the Jews, and the last (ch. XIII–XXVIII) as that of Paul and the Church among the Gentiles.

Looking now at the first of these divisions (I–XII), in which Peter is the central figure, and the Church among the Jews his field of labour, we can almost see it subdivide itself into two successive processes or series of events, distinctly and successively exhibited. The first is the formation and maturing of a mother-church and model-church within the precincts of the holy city, nurtured and trained by apostolic care to be not only the beginning or the germ, but for a time, and in a certain sense, the representative of all the other churches in the world, or rather of the one undivided body, to which all other churches are related, not as separable portions, but as living members. This original and normal church is here presented in its unimpaired, undivided state, from its inception to its temporary dissolution and the wide dispersion of its members and materials on the death of Stephen (I–VII). This affords a natural transition to the second process here recorded (VIII–XII), that of sudden, simultaneous radiation from the central point in various directions, spreading the light, which had been hitherto confined, to other regions, and accomplishing the purpose revealed centuries before, that the law should go forth from Zion, and the word of the Lord from Jerusalem (Isaiah 2, 4).

Let us now for a moment fix our eye upon the former of these subdivisions (I–VII), and allow it, as it were, to fall apart, without mechanical contrivance or coercion, into topics or historical phenomena, precisely as they lie upon the surface, or succeed one another in the progress of the narrative. The whole book opens with two preliminary incidents, by which the way is prepared for the organization of the church and the commencement of its history. The first is the Ascension of our Lord, connecting this whole narrative with that of which it is the sequel (Luke 24, 51), and at the same time opening the way for the effusion of the Spirit, which was not to be expected till the Son had returned to the bosom of the Father (John 14, 26. 15, 26. 16, 7.) The other is the choice of an Apostle to supply the place of Judas, that the theocratical or patriarchal form of the new organization might be perfect when the Spirit came to give it life (ch. 1).

These preliminary incidents are followed by the great events of Pentecost, the birth-day of the Christian Church, the outpouring of the Spirit, and the gift of tongues, Peter's sermon and the baptism of three thousand, with a picture of the social and the spiritual state of the newly organized community (ch. 2).

Then follows a succession of vicissitudes, by which the infant church was purified and hardened, an alternate series of disturbances and trials from without and from within, which at the time of their occurrence may have seemed fortuitous, but which can now be seen to form a chain of disciplinary providences, all preparatory and conducive to intended changes (ch. III–VII).

First, a miracle of healing gives occasion to another public exhibition of the Gospel, and this to an attack upon the Church by the authorities, resulting in a triumph of the truth, increased zeal and boldness in its propagation, and more rapid growth of the new body both in numerical and spiritual strength (ch. III–IV).

But to warn the Church of other dangers from a very different quarter, which had hitherto perhaps been unsuspected, God permits her purity and peace to be disturbed by a commotion from within, the first appearance of hypocrisy and secular ambition in the infant body, but immediately disarmed of its pernicious influence on others by a signal indication of divine displeasure, which not only punished the original offenders, but deterred all like them from presumptuous imitation. By another alternation, too exact to be fortuitous, the next disturbance is again *ab extra*, a concerted movement of the High Priest with the Sadducean party, to suppress the preaching of the resurrection, and by that means of the new religion; a proceeding only saved from being murderous by Pharisaic policy or wisdom, and resulting, as before, in the triumphant propagation of the new faith, in defiance of the Jewish rulers (ch. V).

The next vicissitude presents a second movement from within, but wholly different from the first, and owing not to false profession or corrupt ambition, but to jealousy of races and administrative discontents, allayed by the erection of a new church-office, and the consequent appearance of a new and interesting character, whose preaching, miracles, and controversial triumphs over Jewish bigotry and prejudice, result in his arrest and accusation at the bar of the great national consistory, before which he concisely recapitulates the history of Israel as the chosen people, shows the temporary nature of their cherished institutions, and unmasks their national apostasy and treason, with a clearness and a pungency which rouses them to madness, and precipitates the terrible but glorious translation of the first Christian martyr (ch. VI–VII).

The death of Stephen is the signal for a general persecution, which at first appears to threaten the complete extinction of the Church, but in fact only changes its condition from a local and confined to an expansive and aggressive one. This great disaster, like a terrible explosion, served to scatter the materials and seeds of fire into distant regions, where they kindled many shining lights and opened many sources of congenial heat, to warm and illuminate the nations. This radiating process is the subject of the second subdivision which, beginning where the other closes, with the martyrdom of Stephen, in a series of contemporaneous views exhibits the extension of the Church in various directions, still returning at the close of each description to the point of original departure, thus disclosing at the same time the relation of the incidents themselves and the peculiar structure of this portion of the history, as not consecutive but parallel (ch. VIII–XII).

From the centre of the movement and the highest point of observation in Jerusalem, we first see Philip on his mission to Samaria, followed by two Apostles, introducing to the Church the excommunicated heretics of that despised and hated region; then proceeding with a new commission to the south, receiving the first-fruits of Ethiopia, and acting as a pioneer until he reaches Cesarea, where the history leaves him for the present (ch. VIII).

Looking back to the scene of Stephen's martyrdom, we see the young man at whose feet the actors in the tragedy deposited their garments, setting out as a fanatical persecutor to Damascus, but arriving there an humble convert, then appearing as a champion of the faith which he had once sought to destroy, forced to flee for his life, but repeating the same process at Jerusalem, and finally returning to his native land and city, not now as a destroyer, but a founder and a builder of the church there (ch. ix).

Returning once more to the starting point, the history exhibits Peter on an Apostolic visitation of the churches, working miracles at Lydda and at Joppa, disabused by vision of his Jewish prepossessions in relation to the Gentiles, and then called to Cesarea, where he openly receives into the church a Roman officer and his dependants, as the pledge and foretaste of a glorious harvest to be reaped by other hands, but as yet requiring to be justified before it can be sanctioned by the brethren in Judea (ch. ix–xi).

Looking forth for the last time from Jerusalem, we see a nameless company of Cyprians and Cyrenians preaching Christ, not only to the Jews, but to the Gentiles of the Syrian metropolis; their efforts seconded by Barnabas from Jerusalem and Saul from Tarsus; the new name of Christian first applied at Antioch, destined now to be a secondary centre to the Gentile world, and yet maintaining its own filial relation to her mother at Jerusalem, by sending help for the approaching famine by the hands of her two most honoured ministers (ch. xi).

The institution of this radiating centre for the heathen world concludes the first division of the history, the transition to the second being furnished by a narrative, connected equally with both, of what befel the mother Church while Barnabas and Saul were on their mission of mercy in Judea; the Herodian persecution at Jerusalem, the death of James the Elder, the imprisonment of Peter, his miraculous deliverance and departure from Jerusalem, the dreadful end of the persecuting Herod, the return of Barnabas and Saul to Antioch, in order to be ready for the opening of the second act of this grand drama, in which both for a time and one of them throughout had to act so conspicuous a part (ch. xii).

In the second great division of the book (ch. xiii–xxviii)

Paul is the central figure, and the Gentile church his field of operations. It divides itself without constraint into two parts, corresponding to two different conditions under which the great Apostle laboured, which may be distinguished as his Active and Passive Ministry, or less equivocally as his Apostleship at large and his Apostleship in bonds, the turning point or bounding line being fixed by his arrest at Jerusalem and subsequent captivity.

The former of these subdivisions, Paul's active ministry, or his Apostleship at large (ch. xiii–xxi), may be resolved into Missions, and the Missions classed as Foreign and Domestic; not of course in the familiar sense of this distinction, but employing the second of these terms as a convenient designation of his official journeys to Jerusalem; the other, as usual, denoting visits to the heathen with a view to their instruction and conversion. The two sorts of missions thus distinguished are not entirely separate in the history, but intermingled, no doubt in the order of their actual occurrence (ch. xiii–xxi).

We have first the solemn separation, by express divine authority, of Barnabas and Saul to this important work; their setting out from Antioch, and sailing from Seleucia to Cyprus; their preaching in the synagogue at Salamis, and journey through the isle to Paphos; the hostility and punishment of Elymas the sorcerer and false prophet, and the conversion of the Roman Proconsul. At this juncture Saul assumes a new position, as Apostle of the Gentiles, takes the place of Barnabas as leader of the mission, and is thenceforth known exclusively as Paul. From the native land of Barnabas, they now proceed to that of Paul, where Mark, their minister, forsakes them. From Pamphylia they pass into Pisidia, at the capital of which province Paul delivers his first apostolical discourse on record, and announces to the unbelieving Jews his mission and commission to the Gentiles. Being driven to Iconium, he there renews the same experience. At Lystra, by a miracle of healing, he excites the heathen population to do sacrifice, but by a sudden change of feeling, owing to the machinations of the Jews who had pursued him, he is stoned and left for dead, but soon proceeds to Derbe, where his mission terminates. Returning as he came, he organizes churches in the cities previously visited, and coming back to Antioch, the point from which he had set out, he reports his proceedings to the church there and resumes his former labours (ch. xiii–xiv).

This mission to the Gentiles in their own lands, naturally raises the question whether they must first be Jews before they can be Christians. The affirmative, maintained by certain teachers from Judea, gives occasion to a warm dispute at Antioch, in consequence of which Paul and Barnabas are sent up to consult the mother Church in its representative character, maintained by the continued presence and co-operation of Apostles. The decision of this body in favour of Paul's conduct, at the instance of Peter and James, is reduced to writing and sent back to Antioch, where Paul and Barnabas now again resume their labours. While they are thus employed, Paul proposes to revisit the field of their first mission, to which Barnabas consents, but on condition that John Mark shall again attend them. Paul's refusal, with the sharp dispute arising from it, leads to their temporary separation, which is overruled, however, as a means of multiplying labourers; for while Barnabas and Mark proceed to Cyprus, Paul revisits Asia Minor, having filled their places with two new associates, Silas, a leading member of the mother church, and Timothy, a convert of his own in Lycaonia (ch. xv).

This second mission seems to have been undertaken without any express intimation of the divine purpose; for we find them vainly trying to effect an entrance into several provinces of Asia Minor, and from some peremptorily excluded by the Holy Spirit. This mysterious failure and repulse are not explained until they come to Troas, near the site of ancient Troy, and opposite to Greece, whence the hosts of Agamemnon came against it. From this memorable battle-field a very different war is to be carried into Europe, which is now for the first time to receive the Gospel. At this interesting juncture, Paul is warned in vision to go over into Macedonia, where so many of his triumphs were to be achieved, and where he proceeds, in the face of the most violent resistance, both from Jews and Greeks, to lay the foundations of those Macedonian churches, now immortalized by intimate and indestructible association with his three canonical epistles to the Philippians and Thessalonians (ch. XVI).

Having fixed these central points of influence in Northern Greece, and one perhaps less lasting at Berea, he proceeds to Athens, the most famous seat of ethnic art and science. Here he shows his versatility of talent and his apostolical wisdom by his formal and colloquial discourses in the synagogue, the market, and the areopagus, adapting his instructions, with extraordinary skill, to the capacities and wants of those whom he addressed. Although apparently without effect on the philosophers who heard him, his appeals at Athens were responded to by some, including one at least of high rank, and he left behind him even there the germ or the basis of a Christian church. At Corinth, the chief city of Achaia, he stays longer and accomplishes more visible results by founding that important Church to which he afterwards addressed two of his longest and most interesting letters (ch. XVII).

Having thus, as it were, taken possession of the most important points in Greece, he turns to Ephesus, the influential capital of Asia Proper, as another fortress to be won and occupied for Christ. At present he attempts only to reconnoitre the defences of the enemy while on his way back to the east, reserving his attack upon them as the work of his third mission. This design he is enabled to accomplish, in a residence of three years, during which, by teaching and by miracle, he not only gained the respect and esteem of the most enlightened classes, but drew off many thousands from the worship of Diana and the practice of the occult arts. "So mightily grew the word of God and prevailed" (ch. XVIII–XIX).

This triumph over heathenism, in one of its impregnable strongholds, seemed to leave but one great post unoccupied, the citadel of Rome itself, to which accordingly, while still at Ephesus, he turned his thoughts, saying, "I must also see Rome." But here a most extraordinary part of the divine plan or purpose is disclosed. Instead of sailing from Ephesus to some Italian port, as he no doubt might have done with ease, he first revisits Greece, and then, accompanied by seven representatives of Gentile Christianity, as well as by his beloved physician, who seems now to have rejoined him, he deliberately sets his face, not to the west but to the east, performs a miracle of healing or resuscitation at the place where he had seen his Macedonian vision, puts an end to his third mission by a solemn and affecting valedictory address to the Ephesian elders, and then journeys towards Jerusalem, though warned at every step, and sometimes by inspired men, of the danger there awaiting him (ch. xx–xxi).

This persistency in rushing upon certain peril, in the face of such dissuasives, is entirely unaccountable except upon the supposition of an express divine command, requiring it for some mysterious and momentous purpose. And accordingly, on putting all the facts together, it becomes quite certain that instead of journeying at once to Rome, and there establishing the last great centre of his operations, he was secretly directed to revisit Palestine, and there make a last appeal to his own countrymen, by whom it was foreseen that he would be rejected and delivered to the Gentiles, thus prefiguring or symbolizing, in his own experience, the transfer of the Gospel from the one race to the other, and arriving at his final destination, not as he once expected, in the use of his own freewill and discretion, but as a prisoner, accused by his own people, and removed by his own appeal to the tribunal of the emperor. We have here then the transition from his active to his passive ministry, or rather from his free and unconfined apostleship to that which he so long exercised in bonds (ch. xxi–xxviii).

As Paul is still the central figure of the history, this last division may be readily resolved into Apologies, defences of himself and of the Gospel, upon various occasions providentially afforded, and to various auditories both of Jews and Gentiles, who are brought into a remarkable and interesting juxtaposition both with him and with each other, as accusers, persecutors, judges, and protectors. His first Apologies are to the Jews, but in the presence of the Romans; one to the people from the castle-stairs adjacent to the temple, and the other at the bar of the great national council. His third and fourth defences are addressed to Roman Governors, but in the presence of a Jewish delegation from Jerusalem, the former before Felix and the latter before Festus, both as it would seem in the Prætorium at Cesarea. His fifth Apology was to Agrippa, representing both the Jewish and the Roman power, and contained a fuller statement of his true relation to the old religion, and his claim to be regarded as a genuine and faithful Jew (ch. XXII–XXVI).

His extraordinary mission being thus accomplished, he again turns his eyes to Rome, as the distant but conspicuous goal of his career, which he at length attains, but as a prisoner, and after having suffered shipwreck by the way, a sort of symbol representing the vicissitudes through which the Church was to attain her ultimate and universal triumphs. Having made one more appeal to unbelieving Israel, as represented by the Jews at Rome, and having finally abandoned them to their judicial blindness, he turns wholly to the Gentiles, and establishes the last great radiating centre from which light was to be shed upon the world, until the light itself was turned to darkness (ch. XXVII–XXVIII).

Whether the view, which has been now presented, of the history considered in its internal structure and its mutual relations, is a true and natural or false and artificial one, can only be determined by a patient process of detailed interpretation.

THE ACTS

OF

THE APOSTLES.

CHAPTER I.

This chapter contains the preliminaries of the Apostolical Church History, which does not properly begin until the day of Pentecost. The time included in the chapter is a period of nearly fifty days, divided into two unequal intervals. The two main incidents recorded are our Lord's Ascension and the designation of a new Apostle. The book itself purports to be the sequel of Luke's Gospel (1), and begins where that ends, at our Lord's Ascension (2); but first tells how the interval of forty days was spent (3), and more particularly, what passed at the final meeting between Christ and his Apostles (4—8). Then follows an account of the ascension itself (9), and the heavenly assurance of Christ's second coming (10, 11), the return of the eleven to Jerusalem (12), with a list of their names (13), and some account of their associates and employments (14). During the interval between Ascension Day and Pentecost, Peter addresses an assembly of disciples (15), representing the apostasy and death of Judas as events predicted in the ancient scriptures (16-20), alleging the necessity of filling the vacated place, and stating the necessary qualifications (21, 22). Of the two thus eligible (23), after prayer for the divine decision (24, 25), one is chosen by lot to be the twelfth Apostle (26).

1. The former treatise have I made, O Theophilus, of all that Jesus began both to do and teach.

This verse describes the whole book as the sequel or continuation of another, by the same writer, and containing the history of our Saviour's personal ministry on earth. *Former treatise* might be more exactly rendered *first book* or *discourse*. Herodotus applies the same Greek word (λόγοι) to the divisions of his history. It is not so much a *former treatise*, or distinct work, that is here referred to, as a first instalment of the same that is continued in the book before us. *Have I made*, or, more definitely, *did make, made*, at a particular time, well known to the person here immediately addressed. As to this person, we have no historical or certain information, although various conjectures are proposed respecting him. The name, according to its Greek etymology, denotes a Friend of God, and has by some been taken as an epithet, equivalent to "Christian Reader" in a modern preface. But besides being in itself improbable, this notion is refuted by the reference to his previous acquaintance with the history, in Luke 1, 4, as well as by the honorary title there applied to him. As that title is repeatedly applied in this book (23, 26. 24, 3. 26, 25) to the Roman governors or procurators of Judea, some have hastily concluded, that the person here addressed was one of high official rank. This, though possible, is not susceptible of proof from such imperfect data; and the same thing may be said of the attempt to prove that he was resident in Italy, because the writer seems to presuppose a knowledge of that country, while, in writing of others, he often gives minute geographical details. The tradition that he was a high priest mentioned by Josephus, rests upon a mere coincidence of names, and is intrinsically most improbable. The most that can, with any plausibility, be gathered from the book itself, is that Theophilus may have been a Christian resident at Rome, at whose request the book was originally written. The whole question is of less importance, as the inscription of the history to this man has probably affected its contents and form as little as a modern dedication. *Of all*, i. e. *about, concerning all*, thus pointing out the subject of *the former treatise*, or earlier division of the history. *All*, in the original, is plural, and means *all things.* It is not a hyperbole or exaggeration, but a relative expression, meaning all that was included in the writer's plan or necessary to his purpose. *Began* is not a pleonastic or superfluous expression, but emphatic, and suggestive of two important facts. The first is, that what our Saviour did, he did for the first time; no one ever did it before him. The second is, that what he thus began in person upon earth was afterwards continued by his Apostles, under the influence and guidance of his Spirit. *Both* seems to make a marked distinction between doing and teaching; but the one may be understood as comprehending all official acts not included in the other. Thus explained, the verb *to do* refers especially, but not exclusively, to our Saviour's miracles. The *first book,* or *former treatise,* thus described, is no doubt the Gospel according to Luke, which is addressed to the same person, written in the same style, and exactly corresponds to this description.

2. Until the day in which he was taken up, after that he through the Holy Ghost had given commandments unto the Apostles whom he had chosen.

As the first verse represents this book to be the sequel or continuation of another, so the second draws the line between them, or defines the point at which the one closes and the other opens. This point of contact and transition is afforded by our Lord's ascension, which is really recorded in both narratives. (See Luke 24, 50. 51.) *Until the day,* the very day, a form of speech implying a precise chronological specification. *In which,* on which or during which, the preposition not being expressed in the original, which simply means *the day which,* or still more exactly, *what day,* a construction not uncommon in old English, and still used in poetry. *Taken up,* and *taken back,* i. e. to heaven, both which ideas are suggested by the Greek verb (ἀνελήφθη), which moreover has peculiar force from its position at the end of the sentence, *until the day in which, after* etc., *he was taken up.* The second clause describes what Christ had done before he was taken up. The six words, *after that he had given commandments,* correspond to one in Greek (ἐντειλάμενος), a past participle, the exact sense of which is, *having charged* or *commanded.* This may refer, either to the whole period of forty days mentioned in the next verse, or to the last interview between our

Lord and his Apostles, on the very day of his ascension. The latter is more probable, because, in the original, the verse before us closes with the words *taken up*, and the next verse seems to go back to the previous interval of forty days. The reference may then be specially, though not perhaps exclusively, to the great apostolical commission recorded by Matthew (28, 18–20) and Mark (16, 15. 16), as well as to the specific charge recorded in Luke 24, 49, and in v. 4 below. *The apostles* are here mentioned as a well defined and well known body of men, whose vocation and mission had already been recorded by this writer (Luke 6, 12–16), though their names are afterwards repeated for a special reason. (See below, on v. 13.) *Had chosen*, more exactly, *did choose*, chose out for himself, which is the full force of the Greek verb (ἐξελέξατο). *Through the Holy Ghost:* these words, in the original, stand between the verbs *commanded* and *chose*, and are by some connected with the latter, *whom he chose through the Holy Spirit*. But although there is, in either case, a transposition foreign from our idiom, the usual construction is more natural and yields a better sense, as the interesting question here is, not how he had chosen them at first, but how he charged them and instructed them at last. The words, thus construed, may denote either the spiritual influence under which our Saviour's mediatorial acts were all performed, or the influence by which his last instructions were accompanied, and by which the apostles were enabled to obey them. Here again, the second explanation is more obvious, and better suited to the context, which would lead us to expect, not a mention of the spiritual gifts which our Saviour had received, but of those which he bestowed on this occasion.

3. To whom also he showed himself alive after his passion, by many infallible proofs, being seen of them forty days, and speaking of the things pertaining to the kingdom of God.

Before proceeding to describe our Lord's ascension, Luke reverts to the long interval between that event and his resurrection, showing how it had been spent, and what important purposes it answered. The first of these was, that the minds of the apostles were convinced of his identity, and of his having actually risen from the dead. *To whom* refers, of course, to the apostles, who had just been mentioned, and who not only witnessed his ascension, but saw and conversed with him for many days before it. *Also* is not unmeaning or superfluous, but marks the recurrence to a time preceding that referred to in the second verse. As if he had said: although this was his last meeting with them after his resurrection, it was not the first; for besides this final charge immediately before ascending, *he also showed himself*, etc. This last verb (παρέστησεν) strictly means *presented, placed before* or *near one* (23, 33), and is elsewhere used in reference to resurrection or resuscitation (9, 41); but besides this physical and strict sense, it sometimes means to place before the mind or prove (24, 13). Both these ideas may be here suggested, that of sensible exhibition as the means, and that of rational conviction as the end. *Showed himself* is therefore a felicitous translation, as the same double sense belongs to the usage of the English verb, *show* being often equivalent to *prove*. *Alive*, literally *living, after his passion*, literally *after suffering*, or *after he had suffered*, i. e. suffered death. This absolute use of the verb *to suffer* in the sense of dying, is a common idiom in the Greek of the New Testament. (See Luke 22, 15. Acts 3, 18. 17, 3. Heb. 9, 26. 13, 12. 1 Peter 2, 21. 3, 18. 4, 1.) What he showed in this case was that he was living after being dead, not only *vivus* but *redivivus*. (See Rev. 1, 18. and compare Rom. 11, 15.) The proofs of this were not only *many* but *infallible*, conclusive or convincing. This epithet is not expressed in Greek, but is really included in the meaning of the noun (τεκμηρίοις), which is used by Plato and Aristotle to denote the strongest proof of which a subject is susceptible. The particle before it properly means *in*, i. e. in the use of such proofs, and is therefore an emphatic equivalent to *by*, which only denotes instrumental agency or means to an end. *Being seen of them*, or more exactly, *appearing to them*, i. e. from time to time, not constantly seen by them, as before his passion. This distinction is suggested not only by the participle here used (ὀπτανόμενος), but also (according to Chrysostom) by the preposition (διά) before *forty days*, which is not expressed in the English version, but which means *through*, during, in the course of, any given time. According to this view, every *appearance* of our Saviour, in the interval between his resurrection and ascension, was an *apparition*, not in the sense of an optical illusion or a superstitious fancy, but in that of a miraculous or preternatural manifestation of his person on particular occasions, as a proof of his identity and resurrection. *Forty days*, the length of the interval just mentioned, and known to us only from this passage, which enables us moreover to determine the interval between the Ascension and the day of Pentecost. (See below, on 2, 1.) The other use to which our Saviour put the longer of these intervals was that of conversation and instruction. *Speaking*, not merely talking, but authoritatively teaching and declaring. *Of* is not in the original, and is superfluous in the translation. He not only *spoke of* or *about the things*, etc., but he uttered or declared the things themselves. *Pertaining to*, concerning, is expressed in the original, and indicates the subject of our Lord's authoritative declarations. This was *the kingdom of God*, denoting in its widest sense the Church under all its forms and dispensations, and including therefore the Theocracy or Jewish Church, but here referring more especially, no doubt, to the Messiah's kingdom, or the new form under which the Church, or chosen people, was about to be re-organized. It is worthy of remark, that the last days of our Lord on earth were still employed in words and acts relating to the great end of his mission, and in strict accordance with his words and acts in early childhood. *Wist ye not that I must be about my Father's business?* (Luke 2, 49.) In this he furnishes a model and example to his people, not only in their last days, but throughout their lives.

4. And being assembled together with them, commanded them that they should not depart from Jerusalem, but wait for the promise of the Father, which (saith he) ye have heard of me:

This is the command, or one of the commands, referred to in v. 2, as given on the day of the ascension, at the last meeting between Christ and his disciples. *Assembled together*, or more simply, *met*, having (or being) met with them, not accidentally or unexpectedly, but most probably by previous appointment. The translation, *lodging with them*, rests upon a different reading (συναυλιζόμενος), that of *eating with them*, on an ancient but erroneous explanation of the common text (συναλιζόμενος), perhaps suggested by the analogy of Luke 24, 43. John 21, 13. Acts 10, 41. The active construction, *having assembled* (or *assembling*) *them*, gives a good sense, but is less agreeable to Greek usage. *Commanded* is a different verb from that in v. 2, and denotes a peremptory order, such as a military word of command. *That they should not depart*, literally, *not to be parted* or *divided*, either by physical or moral force. This is the meaning of the Greek verb (χωρίζεσθαι) for the most part in the classics, and always in the Scriptures. See 1.8, 1. 2, where it seems to imply self-constraint or effort, and compare Rom. 8, 35. Heb. 7, 26. I Cor. 7, 10. 11. 15. Philem. 15. There is no need of diluting it in this case, so as to mean mere departure. The expression seems to have been chosen for the very purpose of conveying the idea, that they must not allow themselves to be either drawn or driven from Jerusalem, until the time prescribed had fully come. The original order of the words is, *from Jerusalem not to be parted*. Wiclif's version of the next clause is, *abide the behest of the Father*. The promise of the Father was the promise given by him, not merely in the prophecies of the Old Testament (such as Joel 3, 1. Zech. 2, 10), all which were summed up in that of John the Baptist, mentioned in the next verse; but through our Lord himself, as he expressly adds. (See Luke 24, 49. John 14, 16. 15, 26. 16, 7. 13, and compare Matt. 10, 20. John 20, 22.) The promise is here put, by a natural metonymy, for its fulfilment. *Heard of me* is ambiguous in English; but the context here determines it to mean *heard from me*. This abrupt transition from the indirect to the direct form of expression, by the substitution of the first for the third person, is not uncommon in the best Greek writers, and a favourite idiom of the historians, both Greek and Latin. For scriptural examples of the same thing, see Gen. 26, 27. Deut. 21, 3. Ps. 2, 3. 6. 91, 14. Luke 5, 14. Acts 17, 3. 23, 22. Most modern versions preclude all ambiguity by the insertion of the words *said he*.

5. For John truly baptized with water, but ye shall be baptized with the Holy Ghost, not many days hence.

This verse assigns the reason for the command in v. 4, namely, because it was necessary to the execution of the divine purpose, as revealed by John the Baptist, when he taught that the rite which he administered was only a precursor, pledge, and type of that extraordinary influence, for which they are commanded·here to wait, as for something that must necessarily precede the renovation of the Church and the commencement of their own official functions. (See

Matt. 3, 11. Mark 1, 8. Luke 3, 16. John 1, 33. Acts 11, 16.) But had not the Spirit been already given? Yes, to individual believers, and indeed to the apostles in a body (John 20, 22); but not in such a mode or measure as was necessary, both for themselves and for the church at large. *Truly*, or *indeed*, is the inadequate equivalent in English of a particle (μέν), which, with its correlative (δέ) in the next clause, gives the verse an antithetical or balanced form extremely common in Greek prose. This relation of the clauses may be otherwise, but still imperfectly, expressed in English. '*As* John baptized with water, *so* ye shall be baptized etc.' '*Though* John baptized with water, *yet* ye must be baptized' etc. The extraordinary influences of the Holy Spirit are repeatedly described, both in the language and the types of the Old Testament, as *poured* on the recipient. Thus the standing symbol of official gifts and graces is the rite of unction or anointing, as described or referred to, in the Law (Lev. 8, 12), the Psalms (133, 2), the Prophets (Isai. 61, 1), and the Gospel (Luke 4, 18). The official inspiration of Moses was extended to the seventy elders by being *put upon them* (Numb. 11, 17. 25. 26. 29), and the highest spiritual gifts are promised in that exquisite expression, "until the Spirit be *poured upon us* from on high." (Isai. 32, 15.) This effusion is the very thing for which they are here told to wait; and therefore, when they heard it called a baptism, whatever may have been the primary usage of the word, they must have seen its Christian sense to be compatible with such an application, particularly as they must have known it to be used in Hellenistic Greek to signify a mode of washing where immersion was excluded, such as that of tables or couches, and the customary pouring of water on the hands before eating, as still practised in the East. (See Mark 7, 4. 8. Luke 11, 38.) With their fixed Old Testament associations, when assured that they were soon to be *baptized with the Holy Ghost*, they would naturally think, not of something into which they were to go down, but of something to be *poured upon them from on high*. The indefinite expression, *holy spirit*, might without absurdity be taken as a parallel to *water* in the first clause, each then denoting a baptismal element or fluid. But the personal sense of *Holy Spirit* is so frequent and predominant in Scripture, that the presumption must be always in its favour; and that presumption is confirmed in this case by the very absence of the article in Greek, which may be understood as implying that the phrase had come to be regarded as a personal or proper name. *With*, literally *in, the Holy Spirit*, which may either be a synonymous expression, or expressive of more intimate relation, and perhaps of the essential difference between a mere material element and one not only living but divine. *Not many days hence*, literally, *not after these many days*. All the old English versions, from Wiclif's to the Rhemish, have either *after* or *within these few days*.

6. When they therefore were come together, they asked of him, saying, Lord, wilt thou at this time restore again the kingdom to Israel?

The construction of the first clause is ambiguous, as it may also be translated, *they then* (or *so then they*) *who had come together asked* etc. This makes it doubtful whether vs. 4 and 6 refer to different meetings or the same. In favour of the former supposition is the circumstance that otherwise the mention of their having come together is superfluous, unless we understand it of their gathering around him, to propose the question; and this is hardly consistent with the usage of the Greek verb (συνελθόντες). On the other hand, the natural impression made by the whole context is that of one continued conversation. The question happily is one of little exegetical importance. *Asked of him*. Here, as in v. 3, *of* seems superfluous, at least in modern English. The Greek verb is a compound one, perhaps denoting to interrogate or question, with formality and earnestness. *Wilt thou restore*, or more correctly, *art thou restoring*, or about to restore? The precise form of the original is foreign from our idiom, though not unusual in Greek. *Lord, if thou art restoring*, i. e. (tell us) if thou art restoring, etc. The verb itself is applied both to physical and moral changes, as for instance to the healing of a withered limb (Matt. 12, 13), the miraculous recovery of sight (Mark 8, 25), and the revival of the old Theocracy, to be effected by Elijah at his second coming (Matt. 17, 11. Mark 9, 12). The essential idea is that of return to a previous state, which had been lost or interrupted. The question shows, neither an absolute misapprehension of the nature of Christ's kingdom, nor a perfectly just view of it, but such a mixture of truth and error as might have been expected from their previous history and actual condition. That the kingdom of Israel was to be restored, they were justified in thinking by such prophecies as Isai. 1, 26. 9, 7. Jer. 23, 6. 33, 15. 17. Dan. 7, 13. 14. Hos. 3, 4. 5. Amos 9, 11. Zech. 9, 9. They were only mistaken, if at all, in expecting it to be restored in its primeval form. Some have understood them as protesting against its restoration to the people who had so lately put our Lord to death. His reply shows, however, that the gist of the inquiry was not *Israel*, but *at this time*.

7. And he said unto them, It is not for you to know (the) times or (the) seasons, which the Father hath put in his own power.

This is our Lord's answer to their curious inquiry as to the time fixed for the erection of his kingdom. The first word answers to the continuative particle in Greek (δέ), which may be rendered either *and* or *but*. *It is not for you*, literally, *it is not yours*, i. e. your province or your privilege, your duty, or your share in the great work now going forward. *Times* and *seasons* are not synonymes, but generic and specific terms, the one denoting intervals and periods, the other points and junctures, like *era* and *epoch* in modern English. By supplying the article, our version puts a limitation on the words, which may be true, but is not found in the original. It was not *the times or seasons* of this one case merely, but *times or seasons* generally, that they were forbidden to pry into. *Father* may here be put for God, as opposed to creatures, without regard to the distinction of persons; or for the Father, as distinguished from the Son. (See Mark 13, 32. and compare Matt. 20, 23.) Perhaps our Lord here speaks of the Father's knowledge rather than his own, in order to divert the minds of his disciples from the subject. *Put in his own power* seems to mean that they were not so of necessity, but made so by an arbitrary act of will. This is not only an incongruous idea in itself, but would have been otherwise expressed in Greek. The verb (ἔθετο) has no doubt the same meaning as in 19, 21, viz. *determined* or *resolved*, and the next phrase (ἐν ἐξουσίᾳ) the same as in Matt. 21, 23. 27. The whole clause will then mean, *which the Father hath fixed* (or *settled*) *in* (the exercise of) *his own power* (or *authority*, both physical capacity and moral right). This is a general reproof of all excessive curiosity in reference to such times or seasons as have neither been explicitly revealed, nor rendered ascertainable by ordinary means. (See Deut. 29, 29.)

8. But ye shall receive power, after that the Holy Ghost is come upon you, and ye shall be witnesses unto me, both in Jerusalem and in all Judea, and in Samaria, and unto the uttermost part of the earth.

This verse contrasts what they were not to know with what they might know, as a sort of consolation or compensation for the repulse which they had just experienced. They were not to have the knowledge which they sought, but something better for themselves and others. The knowledge which they needed was rather knowledge of the past than of the future. The prophetic gift is not excluded, but implicitly denied to be the primary function of the Apostolic office, which was testimony, not prediction. He cures their morbid curiosity (says Calvin) by recalling them to present duty. If they really expected to be kings, at once and in the worldly sense, these words must surely have sufficed to disabuse them. *Power* may here be either a cause or an effect: the power of the Holy Ghost exerted on them, or the power wrought in them by the Holy Ghost. In favour of the latter is the parallel expression in Luke 24, 49, "until ye be *endued with power* from on high," which could not have been said of a divine perfection. The *power* then is their extraordinary preparation for their work, including the gifts of tongues, of teaching, and of miracles. The margin of our Bible gives a different construction of this first clause, *ye shall receive the power of the Holy Ghost coming upon you.* There are two grammatical objections to this syntax; the absence of the article before the noun (*power*), and the position of the participle (*coming*). The modern philological interpreters prefer the absolute construction of the genitives, *the Holy Spirit coming,* i. e. by his coming, at his coming, when he comes, or as the text of our translation has it, *after that the Holy Ghost is come upon you.* The same verb is applied elsewhere to the divine agency in the miraculous conception of our Saviour (Luke 1, 35). Instead of *witnesses unto* or *for me* (μοι), some of the oldest manuscripts have *my witnesses* (μου), without material effect upon the sense. They were to be witnesses of all that they had seen and heard from the beginning of their intercourse with Christ (John 15, 27. Luke 24, 18), his doctrines, miracles, life, death, resurrection, and ascension. (See below, v. 22. ch. 2, 32. 10, 39. 41. 22, 15. 26, 16.) The Greek word for *witness* (μάρτυς) is not here used in its later sense of *martyr* (see below, on 22, 20), as the grand function of the apostolic office was no more martyrdom than it was prediction. The gradation in the last clause corresponds to the great periods of the history recorded in the book before us. *Both in Jerusalem and all Judea*, not merely in the capital, as might perhaps have been expected, but throughout the country. *All Judea* may mean all the rest of that province besides the capital (as in Isai. 1, 1. 2, 1. 3, 1), or Judea in the wide sense, as denoting the whole country. This last is not forbidden by the mention of Samaria, the inhabitants of which were not considered Jews (John 4, 9), and which is here introduced as a sort of neutral ground or frontier between Jews and Gentiles. This wider sense is also favoured by the circumstance that Galilee is not named, although some have thought it to be mentioned in the last words, which must then be rendered, *the uttermost (part) of the land*. But this limitation of the sense is forbidden by the obvious climax, or progressive enlargement of their field of labour to its utmost limits, as well as by the clear analogy of other places, where any but the strongest sense is inadmissible. (See below, on 13, 47, and compare Isai. 49, 6.) *Uttermost (part)*, or *extreme (point), of the earth*. This and other kindred phrases are employed in the Old Testament, to signify all nations, not excepting the remotest. (See Ps. 2, 8. 19, 4. 67, 7. 72, 8. Isai. 48, 20. Zech. 9, 10.) *Unto* does not fully represent the Greek preposition (ἕως), which can only be expressed in English by such strengthened forms as *out to, even to, as far as*, all suggesting the idea of great distance. Chrysostom hints at the remarkable contrast between this charge and their original commission (Matt. 10, 5). "Go not into the way of the Gentiles, and into (any) town of the Samaritans enter ye not." (Compare Matt. 15, 24.) The time of this restriction had expired, and the last great apostolical commission is entirely catholic and œcumenical.

9. And when he had spoken these things, while they beheld, he was taken up, and a cloud received him out of their sight.

The preliminaries of our Lord's ascension having been

described, the historian now records the Ascension itself. *When he had spoken*, literally, *having spoken*. The past participle (εἰπών) implies that his discourse was finished, not interrupted by his disappearance. *While they beheld*, literally, *they beholding*. It was not behind their backs, or while they were looking in a different direction, but in full view, and as an actual object of their vision, that our Lord ascended. *Taken up* would be a perfectly correct translation, if it did not seem to make the verb (ἐπήρθη) coincide exactly with the one in v. 2 (ἀνελήφθη), as descriptive of the whole transaction, beginning on earth and ending in heaven; whereas it signifies the first stage or incipient act of the Ascension, that of rising, or rather being raised, above the surface of the ground. The nearest equivalent in English would be, *he was lifted*. By *a cloud* some understand a dark or thunder cloud, like that at Sinai (Exod. 19, 16); others a luminous or bright cloud, such as that which overhung the transfiguration (Matt. 17, 5.) The intervention of a cloud may have been designed to answer two important purposes; first, that of making our Lord's transit from earth to heaven more distinctly visible; and then that of recalling to the minds of the spectators the awful but familiar symbol of Jehovah's presence under the Old Testament (Exod. 16, 10. 19, 16. 24, 15. 18. 33, 9. 10. 40, 34–38.) *Received* is a very inadequate translation of the Greek verb (ὑπέλαβεν), which primarily means to raise a thing by getting under it, and then to catch up or raise suddenly, as a wind or storm does. This sense, which is common in the classics, is entirely appropriate here, and marks the second step or stage of the Ascension. *A cloud caught him up* (and away) *out of their sight*, or, more exactly, *from their* (*very*) *eyes*. Here again we are reminded, that they were actually looking on and saw the whole proceeding, till the object passed the natural and necessary boundary of vision. This distinguishes the case from every other like it; not only from the fabled apotheosis of Hercules amidst the smoke of his own funeral-pile, and that of Romulus during an eclipse, with the addition, in both cases, of a preternatural and fearful storm; but also from the fiery translation of Elijah (2 Kings 2, 11), the difference between which and our Lord's ascension has been thought to prefigure that between the spirit of the old and new economy, or of the Law and Gospel. (Compare Luke 9, 52–56.) It is characteristic of the sacred history, that Luke's whole narrative of this astonishing occurrence, in the book before us, is confined to this one verse, the context having reference to what occurred before and afterwards. And yet it is not a mere reiteration of his previous account, which is also comprised in a single sentence. (See Luke 24, 51, and compare Mark 16, 19.) From Luke's mention of *the eleven and them that were with them* (Luke 24, 33), and the unbroken narrative that follows there, it has been inferred that there were many witnesses of the Ascension; but the narrative before us makes the natural impression, that this grand sight was confined to the Apostles.

10. And while they looked stedfastly toward heaven, as he went up, behold, two men stood by them in white apparel.

They looked stedfastly, or rather, *they were gazing*. The Greek verb strictly denotes tension or straining of the eyes. The word translated *while* corresponds to our *as*, and like it may express either time or resemblance. If the latter meaning is assumed here, the sense of the whole clause will be that *they were like* (*men*) *gazing*, or *were as* (*if*) *gazing, into heaven*. But the temporal meaning (*when* or *while*) is preferred by almost all interpreters. *Toward heaven* might be more correctly rendered *into heaven*. They gazed not only at but into heaven, as if to penetrate its secrets and discern their now invisible Redeemer. *As he went up*, literally, he advancing or proceeding, the direction of his course being not expressed but suggested by the context. All this is intended to evince more clearly, that our Saviour did not vanish or miraculously disappear (compare Luke 24, 31), but simply passed beyond the boundary of vision. *Behold*, as usual, introduces something unexpected or surprising. While they were gazing into heaven, *two men stood*, or rather *had stood* (or *taken their stand*) *beside them*. *White apparel*, or *white garments*, as in such connections elsewhere, seems to signify not colour merely, but a preternatural effulgence. (See Matt. 17, 2. Mark 9, 3. Luke 9, 29.) This has led to the conclusion that the *men* here mentioned, though in human form, were *angels*, like the strangers who appeared at the resurrection, and to whom both designations are applied by different evangelists. (Compare Matt. 28, 2. John 20, 12, with Mark 16, 5. Luke 24, 4.) Some have thought it not unlikely, that the same two angels reappeared on this occasion; but a still more striking supposition, which I owe to the suggestion of a friend, is that these two men were Moses and Elijah, who had been present at the transfiguration, and there talked with Jesus of his *exodus* about to be accomplished at Jerusalem (Luke 9, 31.) There is something sublime in the idea, that the great prophetic Legislator and Reformer, who had come from heaven to be present at the momentary anticipation of the Mediator's glory, now appeared again as witnesses of his departure to take final and perpetual possession of it. This hypothesis may help us to account for the abruptness and conciseness of the narrative, as if the writer, for the moment, thought of the Transfiguration and Ascension as immediately successive, losing sight of all that intervened, and therefore introducing the same persons without naming them again. It also gives unspeakable authority and interest to the promise in the next verse, as proceeding from two most illustrious prophets of the old economy. After all, however, this idea, fruitful as it is, must be regarded as a mere conjecture.

11. Which also said, Ye men of Galilee, why stand ye gazing up into heaven? This same Jesus, which is taken up from you into heaven, shall so come in like manner as ye have seen him go into heaven.

Here, as in v. 2 above, the *also* is by no means superfluous, but adds to the simple meaning of the verb, that they did not merely take their stand by the disciples, which was sufficient of itself to awe them, but also audibly addressed them. *Men of Galilee*, or *Galilean Men*, or still more closely, *Men, Galileans*, that is, *Men* (who are also) *Galileans*. This designation, which was afterwards derisively applied to Christians, can of course have no such meaning here, but is rather a respectful recognition of those present, as the countrymen and tried friends of the person who had just ascended. The same idea is suggested by the use of the word translated *men* (ἄνδρες), which, in ancient usage, approaches to the modern sense of *gentlemen*, in this and other like combinations. (See below, v. 16. 2, 14. 22. 17, 22, etc.) *Why stand ye*, or, adhering closely to the form of the original, *why have ye stood* (or *been standing*, so long) *looking into heaven?* The word *gazing*, which is here used by four of the old English versions, would have been more appropriate in v. 10, where they all have *looked*. The question of the two men seems to involve an indirect reproof of their forgetfulness or unbelief of what their Lord himself had told them. This was betrayed by their excessive and continued wonder at his disappearance, as if they had expected him to stay on earth for ever, though the promise of the Paraclete, which he had just renewed to them, was formally suspended on his own departure, and return to the bosom of the Father (John 16, 7.) Their astonishment, moreover, seems to show that they despaired of ever seeing Christ himself again; whereas he had repeatedly declared that he would come again (John 14, 3), and in the very way that he had now departed, i. e. *in a cloud* (Luke 21, 27), or as it is variously expressed by the Evangelists, *in clouds, on the clouds*, or *with the clouds of heaven*. (See Mark 13, 26. 14, 62. Matt. 24, 30. 26, 64, in several of which places, the English versions have gratuitously changed the preposition.) The question of the two men was intended therefore to recall them to themselves, and to remind them that, instead of stupidly and idly gazing after one who was no longer visible, they should rather show their love to him by instantly obeying his farewell commands, and trusting his repeated promise to return, which they accordingly repeat, as if to show their own implicit confidence in its fulfilment. *In like manner*, literally, *what manner*, an expression similar to *what day* in v. 2 above. The Greek phrase (ὃν τρόπον) never indicates mere certainty or vague resemblance; but wherever it occurs in the New Testament, denotes identity of mode or manner. (Compare Matt. 23, 37. Luke 13, 34. Acts 7, 28. 2 Tim. 3, 8.) *Have seen*, or more exactly, *saw*, the form of the original implying that the sight was over when these words were uttered. The verb itself is not the ordinary verb *to see*, but one implying some unusual or striking spectacle, the root of our word *theatre* and all its cognate forms. We read nothing more of the *two men*, who may have disappeared as suddenly as Moses and Elijah at the Transfiguration (Mark 9, 8.) It would seem, at least, perhaps from the conciseness of the narrative, that the Eleven thought no more of them, but in their eagerness to do as they were bidden, turned their backs on those by whom the admonition was conveyed to them, without inquiring whence they came, or what was now become of them. (See below, on 8, 39.)

12. Then returned they unto Jerusalem from the

mount called Olivet, which is from Jerusalem a sabbath-day's journey.

This verse and the two following furnish the transition from the first to the second principal event recorded in the chapter. We have here the return of the Eleven from the place of the Ascension to the Holy City. *Unto*, or more exactly, *into Jerusalem*, denoting not mere approach or arrival, but actual entrance, as appears from the verse following. In the next clause the original construction is peculiar—*from a mount, the* (*one*) *called Olivet*—as if he had said, 'they returned from a mountain where all this occurred, and which, it may be added, was called Olivet.' This name is borrowed from the Vulgate (*Oliveti*) and is found in all the English versions, except that of Geneva, which has *Olive Hill*. The Latin word is used by Cicero, and means an oliveyard or orchard. The Greek word occurs only here in the New Testament, but often in the Septuagint version, with a similar form meaning *vineyard*. The name is given here, and sometimes by Josephus, to the high ridge on the east side of Jerusalem, beyond the Kedron, elsewhere called the *Mount of Olives* (Zech. 14, 4. Matt. 21, 1. Mark 11, 1. Luke 19, 29. John 8, 1.) The English Bible also uses the form *Olivet* in 2 Sam. 15, 30, where the Hebrew, Greek and Latin have the Mount of Olives. It still bears the tree from which it takes its name, but not in such abundance as of old. The old tradition, mentioned by Eusebius in the early part of the fourth century, that Christ ascended from the summit of the mountain, seems to contradict the statement in Luke 24, 50. 51, that *he led them out as far as Bethany*, which was on the eastern side of Olivet, and fifteen furlongs from Jerusalem (John 11, 18); whereas the distance of the mount itself is here described as little more than half as great. The *sabbath-day's journey*, or as it might be more exactly rendered *sabbath's way* or *walk*, was not a long one, as the use of the word *journey* has led many English readers to imagine, but a space of two thousand cubits, between seven and eight furlongs, the extent to which the Jews were allowed, by the tradition of the elders, to leave home upon the sabbath. The measure is supposed to have been borrowed from the space between the people and the ark, when they passed over Jordan (Josh. 3, 4.) The distance seems to be here stated only for the purpose of conveying the idea, that the Mount of

Olives was not far from the city. This idea is, besides, expressed in Greek by a word omitted in the common version, namely, *near* (ἐγγύς). The literal translation of the clause is, *which is near Jerusalem, having a sabbath's walk* (between them.) The word *having* (ἔχον) is also omitted in the English version, by a double inadvertence, with which our translators are not often chargeable. Some take the Greek word in the sense of *distant*, which belongs however only to the compound form (ἀπέχον). There is no allusion to the customary sabbath promenade of the inhabitants, but only to a measure of distance, with which all Jewish readers were familiar.

13. And when they were come in, they went up into an upper room, where abode both Peter and James and John and Andrew, Philip and Thomas, Bartholomew and Matthew, James (the son) of Alpheus and Simon Zelotes, and Judas (the brother) of James.

The entrance mentioned in the first clause may be either that into the city or that into the house. *An upper room*, not any room above the ground-floor, which would be otherwise expressed in Greek; much less a garret or inferior apartment; but a comparatively spacious room reserved, both in Greek and Jewish houses, for the use of guests or for unusual occasions. (See below, on 9, 39. 20, 8.) The original expression has the article (*the upper room*), which may mean the only one belonging to the house; but as no house is specified, it seems rather to refer to something previously mentioned or already known. This is altogether natural if we suppose them to have still frequented the same upper room, in which they had partaken of the Passover, and which had been designated by the Lord in a remarkable manner (Matt. 26, 18. Mark 14, 15. Luke 22, 12.) This is much more probable than that they had procured another place for their assemblies, either in a private house or in the precincts of the temple. Even supposing that they could have been accommodated in one of the chambers or small houses which surrounded the courts of the temple, they could have had no reason for preferring it to one already consecrated by th presence and the farewell words of their ascended Master It is probable, indeed, that strangers, who continued in Jerusalem from Passover to Pentecost, commonly retained the same rooms during the whole interval. Besides, an apartment belonging to the temple would hardly have been simply called an *upper room*. The statement in Luke's Gospel (24, 53) that after their return from the Ascension, "they were continually in the temple, praising and blessing God," means nothing more than our familiar phrase, that any one is always at church. To the argument derived from the propriety or fitness of the first Christian meetings being held within the precincts of the Jewish sanctuary, it has been replied, that there was nothing more distinctive of the new dispensation than its freedom from the local and ritual restrictions of the old. Though neither of these reasons can be deemed conclusive, they may serve at least to neutralize each other. *Where abode*, or literally, *were abiding*, a form of expression which implies continued, but not necessarily a constant residence. The Greek verb is promiscuously used to signify both permanent and temporary occupation. The requisitions of the text and context are quite satisfied by the assumption, that they daily assembled in the upper room, or at the most spent a large part of their time there, in the acts and services described below. We have then a catalogue of the Apostles, introduced, as some suppose, because they were now re-assembled and re-organized after their dispersion (Matt. 26, 56. Mark 14, 50.) But besides that they had several times met since that defection (Matt. 28, 16. Mark 16, 14. Luke 24, 36. John 20, 19. 26. 21, 14), a distinct enumeration of their names would have been natural, not to say necessary, as an introduction to the apostolical history. This is the fourth list contained in the New Testament (compare Matt. 10, 2–4. Mark 3, 16–19. Luke 6, 14–16), and in some points different from all the rest. Although no two of these catalogues agree precisely in the order of the names, they may all be divided into three quaternions, which are never interchanged, and the leading names of which are the same in all. Thus the first is always Peter, the fifth Philip, the ninth James the son of Alpheus, and the twelfth Judas Iscariot. Another difference is that Matthew and Luke's Gospel give the names in pairs, or two and two, while Mark enumerates them singly, and the list before us follows both these methods, one after the other. A third distinction is that this list adds no titles or descriptions to the leading names, but only to those near the end. *Both Peter*, like a similar expression in v. 8, means not only Peter but the others also. This, with his uniform position at the head of the list, marks distinctly his priority, not as a superior in rank and office, but as a representative and spokesman of the rest, like the foreman of a jury or the chairman of a large committee. This priority, which often incidentally appears throughout the Gospel History (e. g. Matt. 15, 15. 16, 16. 17, 24. 18, 21. 19, 27. Mark 10, 28. 11, 21. Luke 8, 45. 12, 41. 18, 28. 22, 32. 33. John 6, 68. 13, 24), so far from amounting to a primacy or permanent superiority, was less an advantage to himself than a convenience to his brethren, and indeed occasioned some of his most serious errors and severest trials. (See Matt. 16, 16. 22. 26, 33. 51. 58. Mark 8, 32. 14, 29. 47. 54. 66. Luke 22, 34. 50. 55. John 13, 8. 36. 37. 18, 10. 11. 16.) It is now a very general belief, that the affecting scene in John 21, 15–17, was Peter's restoration to the apostleship, from which he had fallen for a time by the denial of his master; the three questions and injunctions there recorded corresponding to his three acts of apostasy. Be this as it may, we find him here resuming the position which he occupied before and is to occupy throughout a large part of the present history. The other names are all familiar from the Gospels. *James and John*, the sons of Zebedee, and Sons of Thunder, early called to be disciples and apostles (Matt. 4, 21. 10, 2. Mark 1, 19. 29. 3, 17. Luke 5, 10. 6, 14), and with Peter frequently distinguished from the rest as confidential servants and companions of our Saviour (Matt. 17, 1. Mark 5, 37. 9. 2. 13, 3. Luke 8, 51), while John was admitted to a still more intimate and tender friendship (John 13, 23. 19, 26. 21, 7. 20.) Traits of their character appear in Mark 10, 35–41. Luke 9, 52–56. *Andrew*, the brother of Simon Peter, and placed next to him by Mark, but here postponed to the two sons of Zebedee. On one or two occasions in the Gospel history, we find him incidentally referred to, as attending on the Master and conversing with him (Matt. 4, 18. 10, 2. Mark 1, 16. 29. 3, 18. 13, 3. Luke 6, 14. John 1, 40. 44. 6, 8. 12, 22.) The same thing may be said of *Philip*, his townsman and associate (Matt. 10, 3. Mark 3, 18. Luke 6, 14. John 1, 44–49. 6, 5–7. 12, 21. 22. 14, 8. 9.) It is worthy of remark, that these two apostles are known only by Greek names, though, according to the custom of the age, they may have had Hebrew ones besides. *Thomas*, elsewhere surnamed *Didymus* (the Twin, a Greek translation of his Aramaic name). He also appears now and then in close attendance on his master and peculiarly devoted to him, although chiefly remembered for refusing to believe that Christ was risen from the dead, until assured of it by ocular inspection (John 11, 16. 14, 5. 20, 24–29. 21, 2.) *Bartholomew* is commonly supposed to be the same with the *Nathanael* of John's Gospel, chiefly because it seems improbable that one so highly honoured by the Saviour, and so intimately known to the Apostles, should be excluded from their number, while a person otherwise unknown was admitted to it. (See John 1, 46–50. 21, 2.) *Matthew* the Publican, also called Levi and the Son of Alpheus, whose vocation and first intercourse with Christ are recorded by himself and others. (See Matt. 9, 9. 10, 3. Mark 2, 14. 3, 18. Luke 5, 27–29. 6, 15.) *James of Alpheus*, i. e. as is commonly supposed, his son, while, on the other hand, *Judas of James* is no less generally understood to mean his brother, although some assume the same ellipsis in both places, and make Jude the son of a James otherwise unknown. By comparing the evangelists, it seems that Jude, or Judas not Iscariot, was also called Lebbeus and Thaddeus. (See Matt. 10, 3. Mark 3, 18. Luke 6, 16. John 14, 22.) Between James and Judas appears the name of *Simon*, surnamed here *Zelotes*, in reference either to his ardent temper, or to his previous connection with the party of the Zealots, whose fanatical zeal ultimately caused the downfall of the Jewish state, and of whose organized existence there are traces even in the book before us. *Zelotes* seems to be the Greek translation, as *Cananites* is the Greek form, of an Aramaic name denoting Zealot. The Greek word for *Canaanite* is altogether different. The meaning *Canaïte* (inhabitant of Cana) rests upon another reading. (See Matt. 10, 4. Mark 3, 18. Luke 6, 15.)

14. These all continued with one accord in prayer and supplication, with (the) women, and Mary the mother of Jesus, and with his brethren.

To the names of the Apostles is now added an account of their employments during the interval between Ascension Day and Pentecost. *These*, whose names have just been enumerated. *All*, without exception, none of the eleven being absent at this interesting juncture. *Continued*, literally, *were continuing* (or *persevering*), a construction similar to that in the preceding verse, *were dwelling* (or *abiding*). The Greek verb here used strictly denotes personal attendance, sticking close to any thing or person, particularly that of a superior, and is then transferred to perseverance in duty, such as that of public worship, and particularly prayer. *With one accord*, or *one mind*, as the Greek word properly denotes, implying unanimity of sentiment and concert or agreement, as well as mere coincidence of time and place. *Prayer and supplication*. The last word is omitted in the Vulgate, and in several of the oldest manuscripts and latest critical editions. It is not a mere tautology, however, as the word translated *prayer* originally signifies the votive or promissory part of worship, that which man presents to God; while the one translated *supplication* properly means want, then desire, and then the expression of it, whether addressed to God or man. The two (if both be genuine) are here joined to express the whole idea of devotional address to God. *With the women*, or, as Calvin and some others understand it, *with their wives*. But this, according to Greek usage, would require the insertion of two words, to wit, the article and pronoun (*with the wives of them*), neither of which is found in the original. The strict translation is, *with women*, i. e. with women as well as men; these services were limited to neither sex. There is no express reference to those particular women who accompanied our Lord from Galilee, witnessed his crucifixion, watched his burial, and rejoiced in his resurrection (Luke 8, 2. 3. 23, 55. 24, 1. Matt. 27, 55. 56. Mark 15, 47. 16, 1. John 19, 25.) Some of these were no doubt present; but the fact is explicitly asserted only of his mother. This is her last appearance in the history, a striking comment on the false position which the church of Rome assigns to her, and from which, if it were well founded, she might be expected to fill much the largest space in all that follows. According to one old tradition, she died early in Jerusalem; according to another, she accompanied John to Ephesus and lived to an advanced age. *With his brethren*, or *his brothers*, probably the same who accompanied his mother upon several remarkable occasions in the Gospel History (John 2, 12. Matt. 12, 46-50. Mark 3, 31-35. Luke 8, 19-21), and would therefore seem to have been members of her household. Beyond this, who his brethren were, has been a subject of dispute for ages. The bearing of this question on the personal identity and apostolical authority of James, the so-called bishop of Jerusalem, will claim attention in its proper place. (See below, on 12, 17. 15, 13. 21, 18.) In the case before us, it is of little exegetical importance, whether we suppose *his brethren* to have been the sons of Joseph and Mary, or her nephews, or the nephews of her husband, or his children by a former marriage; all which opinions have been plausibly defended. The only fact certainly revealed here is, that among those who united in the prayers of the Apostles at this interesting juncture, were the nearest relatives of Christ himself.

15. And in those days, Peter stood up in the midst of the disciples and said—the number of names together were about an hundred and twenty—

Here begins the second topic or occurrence recorded in this chapter, the election of a new Apostle. We have first the proposition made by Peter (15–22), and in this verse a specification of the time and place. *In those days*, an indefinite expression elsewhere used with great latitude, but here restricted by the context to the ten days, which constitute the difference between the forty mentioned in the third verse and the fifty denoted by the name of Pentecost. (See below, on 2, 1.) We have no means of determining at what part of this interval the occurrence here recorded took place. It seems most natural however to suppose that it happened near the end of the ten days, and perhaps on the very eve of Pentecost. *Peter*, as might have been expected, takes the lead on this occasion, in the exercise of that representative priority, with which he had so long been invested, and to which he had been recently restored. *Stood up*, or *arose*, implying more publicity and form than belongs to a mere conversation. *In the midst of the disciples*, i. e. among them, or surrounded by them, without any reference to exact position. After writing the word *said*, but before recording the words uttered, the historian guards against the error of supposing that this speech was made to a small or select audience. *The number of names together were* might have been more exactly rendered, *there was a crowd of names together*. The first Greek noun (ὄχλος) does not mean mere number; nor a very great absolute number, which a hundred and twenty is not; but a promiscuous assemblage, as distinguished from a corporate or official body, such as that of the Apostles. (See below, on 19, 26. 33. 35.) *Names* is not synonymous with *persons*, either here or elsewhere (Rev. 3, 4. 11, 13), but implies registration, and that again supposes some degree and kind of organization. The distinction here suggested is not that between males and females, only the former being registered in ancient times; nor that between distinguished names and unknown persons; but the word is meant to qualify the one before it, by suggesting that although the meeting was promiscuous rather than official, it was not a nameless rabble, but a gathering of persons known by name, and therefore one by one, to be disciples. Whether these were all Galileans, or all Presbyters, or Presbyters and Bishops, or representatives of congregations, there is nothing in the text or context to determine. It is highly improbable, however, although frequently asserted, that this meeting comprehended the whole body of believers, even in Jerusalem. (See John 2, 23. 3, 26. 7, 31. 11, 45. 48.)

16. Men (and) brethren, this scripture must needs have been fulfilled, which the Holy Ghost by the mouth of David spake before concerning Judas, which was guide to them that took Jesus.

Peter begins by showing that the apostasy and death of Judas had been long before predicted, and could not therefore fail to happen. *Men (and) brethren* is a combination similar to that in v. 11, although very differently rendered. While *men* has the same respectful import as in that case, the use of the word *brethren* recognizes them as fellow Christians. The singular form *scripture* does not necessarily denote a single passage (as in Luke 4, 21), but here includes the two quotations in v. 20 below. *Must needs have been*, or it was necessary (ἔδει) that it should be fulfilled, as it has been, in the death of Judas. (Compare the present of the same verb in v. 21 below.) The prediction here referred to is not only spoken of as *scripture*, i. e. written by divine authority, but expressly ascribed to the Holy Spirit, as its ultimate author, and to David only as the vehicle or channel of communication. We have thus the testimony, both of Peter and of Luke, to the inspiration and Davidic origin of the psalms in question. *Spake before*, not merely spake of old or formerly, but foretold or predicted long before the event, an act necessarily implying inspiration and prophetic foresight. *Concerning Judas* cannot be grammatically construed with *fulfilled*, so as to mean that although spoken of another it was verified in him. This is forbidden by the collocation of the words and by the preposition (περί), which can only indicate the theme or subject of the prophecy itself. *Which was guide*, or more exactly, *who became a guide*, implying defection and apostasy; he had been a friend and an apostle, but he afterwards became a guide to those who seized him. In both these clauses, the original construction has a participial form, *the (one) becoming guide to the (men) seizing him*. The reference is of course to the arrest of Jesus in the garden of Gethsemane (John 18, 2. 3). One of the oldest commentators (Chrysostom) directs attention to this mild and almost negative description of the crime of Judas, and ascribes it, not improbably, to Peter's painful recollection of his own denial of his master, which had only been prevented by that master's intercession (Luke 22, 32) from being equally complete and fatal. This is certainly more natural and candid than the charge, which some have brought against Peter, of uncharitable harshness, in referring to Iscariot at all, when his own analogous but temporary fall was still so recent.

17. For he was numbered with us, and had obtained part of this ministry.

This verse assigns a reason why the prophecy and its fulfilment concerned them especially, to wit, because Judas had been one of them, not only in appearance or in name, but by actual and personal participation. *Numbered with us* implies, not only registration or enrolment, like the use of the word *names* in v. 15, but also a definite and well-known number, namely, that of twelve, which was by no means arbitrary or unmeaning, as we shall see below. As if he had said, 'he helped with us to make up that significant and sacred number, which has now been broken and must be restored.' Or the word may be referred, in a less emphatic sense, to the whole body of believers, and the mention of his apostolic office be restricted to the last clause. *Part of this ministry* might seem in English to denote a portion as distinguished from the whole. But both the verb and noun (*obtained part*) have reference in Greek (ἔλαχε τὸν κλῆρον) to the ancient practice of distributing by lot, though secondarily applied to any allotment, or appointment not dependent on the will of the recipient, whether the bestowing power be divine or human. The clause might be more exactly rendered, *shared the allotment of this ministry.* The ministry in question is of course the apostleship, to which the same word is applied by Paul (Rom. 11, 13.) Both the Greek and the English word strictly denote *service*, although commonly suggestive of official *power*. It is a fine remark of Æschines, that office, when conferred by an election, is not a lordship (ἀρχή) but a service (διακονία).

18. Now this (man) purchased a field with the reward of iniquity, and falling headlong, he burst asunder in the midst, and all his bowels gushed out.

Having mentioned the treachery of Judas, and his long connection with the college of Apostles, Peter reminds his hearers of his frightful end; not as something new to them, or something which they had forgotten, for the facts were too recent and notorious to be so presented; but to impress upon their minds the actual and terrible fulfilment of the divine threatening. There is no need, therefore, of regarding this verse as a parenthetical remark of the historian, which indeed is forbidden by the form of the original, where *now* is not a single but a double particle (μὲν οὖν), employed to mark the interruptions and resumptions of a continuous discourse, like *so then* in the pauses and transitions of a narrative. Such an expression would be wholly out of place in the beginning of an insulated note or comment, interrupting the thread of the discourse. *This* may be regarded as contemptuous, a meaning which it sometimes has in Classical as well as Hellenistic Greek. Peter is here speaking, not as a historian but as an orator, to those already well acquainted with the facts, and therefore in no danger of misapprehension. He contrasts the loss and gain of the betrayer; he had lost his office and his soul, and he had gained—a field, a piece of ground, which only served to perpetuate his infamy! The disproportion here suggested is still greater than the one involved in our Saviour's awful question, What is a man profited if he gain the whole world and lose his own soul? *Purchased* is not so good a version of the Greek verb as *acquired* or *gained*. There is therefore really no disagreement between Peter's oratorical and Matthew's plain historical account of the same matter, according to which it was the priests who bought the Potter's Field with the betrayer's wages after he was dead (Matt. 27, 7.) Nor is it even necessary to apply the legal maxim, *qui facit per alium facit per se*, or to cite the universal practice of describing one as building, planting, saving, or destroying, when he only uses means or instruments. In all such cases there is a conscious purpose, and at least a mediate or indirect co-operation, on the part of the prime agent, which is here entirely wanting. *A field*, or literally, *a place*, but like the latter word, applied familiarly to landed property, estates, or residences. *With the reward*, or rather, *out of, from, the wages of iniquity*, not merely as the means of acquisition, but the source, the fountain, of his infamous celebrity. *Iniquity*, injustice, with particular allusion to our Saviour's lawless condemnation, but including also the more positive idea of corruption and malignity, as causes and occasions of the treachery of Judas. *Falling headlong*, literally, becoming prone or prostrate, an expression often used by Homer in connection with verbs of falling, which completely justifies the common version from the charge of introducing an idea not contained in the original. *Burst asunder:* the original verb primarily signifies a bursting noise, but secondarily, the rupture which occasions it. *In the midst*, not of us, or of a circle of spectators, as the common version might suggest to English readers, but as Wiclif has it, *in the middle*, i. e. of his body. *Gushed out*, or rather, as the form is passive, they were spilt, poured out, or shed forth. This shocking description of the death of Judas may be reconciled with Matthew's simple statement that *he hanged himself* (Matt. 27, 5), by merely supposing what is constantly occurring in such cases, that the rope or branch from which he was suspended broke, and he was violently thrown upon the ground, with the effect above described. As no one can deny that the two statements are compatible, the only difficulty is that the two Apostles should record entirely different parts of the transaction. The solution is afforded by the difference of the circumstances under which the two accounts were given, and which has been already mentioned. Matthew wrote as a historian, for a wide circle of readers, many of whom had no previous knowledge of the case; he therefore states the main fact, and according to his usual custom passes over the minute details. Peter, orally addressing those who knew the facts as fully as himself, and less than six weeks after their occurrence, and upon the very spot, assumes the main fact as already known, and naturally dwells upon those very circumstances which the Evangelist, many years later, no less wisely and naturally leaves out altogether. However this may seem to others, there is scarcely an American or English jury that would scruple to receive these two accounts as perfectly consistent, if the witnesses were credible, and any cause could be assigned for their relating two distinct parts of the same transaction.

19. And it was known unto all the dwellers at Jerusalem, insomuch as that field is called in their proper tongue, Aceldama, that is to say, the Field of Blood.

We here learn from Peter himself, that what he is relating is no news or fresh discovery to his hearers, but a fact notorious to all Jerusalem, and already perpetuated by a descriptive and commemorative name. *It was known*, or rather *it became known* or notorious, i. e. from the very time of the occurrence, and of course had so continued till the time of Peter's speaking. *Insomuch as* is an awkward and obscure expression, found in none of the older English versions, most of which have *insomuch that*, while the oldest of all (Wiclif's) gives the simple and exact translation, *so that*. The common version must not be confounded with the similar phrase *inasmuch as*, which is equivalent in meaning to *because*. *In their proper tongue*, i. e. their own language or peculiar dialect, an Aramaic modification or corruption of the Hebrew, spoken by the Jews from the time of their captivity in Babylon, and often called by modern writers *Syro-Chaldaic*, which is apt however to suggest the false idea of a compound language formed by the mixture of two others, rather than that of a correlative or parallel derivative from a common source. As Peter seems to speak of the language as a foreign one, some understand by it the dialect of Judea or Jerusalem, as distinct from that of Galilee. But although there was certainly a perceptible difference (Matt. 26, 73. Mark 14, 70), it was probably not greater than that which now distinguishes the English from the Scotch and Irish, and would scarcely have been made so prominent by Peter, even if his hearers were all Galileans like himself, which is by no means certain. Some have inferred, therefore, that these cannot be the words of Peter, and that this verse, at least, if not the one before it, must be a parenthetical addition by the hand of the historian. But the utmost that can be inferred is that the clause immediately before us was so added, which may be admitted without any derogation from the credit of the narrative or the authenticity of the discourse. If a French orator should allude to the original meaning of the word *tuileries* in speaking of the famous palace, an English reporter of his speech could scarcely fail to add, "which in French means a brick-kiln," without dreaming that the reader would suppose these words to have been uttered, or that their insertion would impair the credibility of the report. *Aceldama* is easily reducible to two words (חקל דמא), of frequent occurrence in the ancient Aramaic versions, and equivalent in meaning to Luke's Greek translation, *Field of Blood.* This name would readily suggest two ideas, that of our Lord's judicial murder, to which he was betrayed by Judas, and the subsequent suicide of Judas himself. (See Matt. 27, 8.)

20. For it is written in the book of Psalms, Let his habitation be desolate, and let no man dwell therein: and, His bishopric let another take.

In the preceding verses (17–19) the Apostle seemed to have lost sight of his main purpose, as propounded in v. 16; but he now returns to it, in such a way that the apparent interruption fortifies his argument. Having stated in general, that the apostasy of Judas was the subject and fulfilment of a prophecy, and having dwelt upon the fearful circumstances of his death, he now shows what particular predictions had been terribly verified in these events. The logical connection is with v. 16. The scripture concerning Judas must be fulfilled—and there is such a scripture—*for it is written*, etc. But the intervening verses, though in form a digression, have prepared the mind for the citation, and so make it more impressive than it could have been, if immediately subjoined to the general proposition in v. 16. As if he had said, 'these are awful realities, still fresh in every memory, and yet they were predicted many centuries ago, *for it is written*, etc.' The original expression is still stronger, *for it has been written* (γέγραπται). The *Book of Psalms* is here distinctly recognized, as a collection well known to his hearers, and acknowledged by them as a part of the divine revelation comprehended in the Hebrew Canon. The indefinite term *scripture*, used in v. 16, is here defined, not only by the mention of the book, but by the actual quotation of two passages, the first from Ps. 69, 25, the other from Ps. 109, 8. They are not combined through inadvertence or mistake, as some have foolishly alleged, but from a clear and profound view of their mutual connection, as belonging to the same class, and admitting of the same interpretation. This is not to be regarded as a mere *accommodation* of the language to a subject altogether different from that at first intended, which is inconsistent, not with inspiration only, but with common sense, especially as these alleged predictions are here made the ground and warrant of an important public measure. Those, however, who reject the notion of accommodation, are by no means agreed as to the principle, on which the cited passages may be applied to Christ and Judas. Some regard the whole of both psalms as exclusively and strictly Messianic, and explain the confession in Ps. 69, 5, as relating to imputed sin. Others suppose one part to relate to the Messiah and his enemies, while the remainder in both cases has respect to David or some other ancient sufferer. A third hypothesis applies the whole to David and his adversaries in a lower sense, but in a higher sense to Christ and Judas. To avoid the inconveniences attending all these exegetical hypotheses, some modern writers make the subject of these Psalms, and others like them, a generic or ideal person, representing a whole class, to wit, that of the righteous under persecution, and apply them to Christ, not exclusively but eminently, as the highest and most perfect representative of that class, although some strokes of the description are true only of inferior examples. The quotations, as recorded, are taken from the Septuagint version, with a few slight variations. *Habitation*, in Hebrew, an enclosure or encampment; in Greek, a shelter for the night, with special reference to shepherds and their flocks, and thence transferred to farm or country houses, but here used in the generic sense of home or dwelling. *Bishopric*, though in itself correct, because a mere corruption of the Greek word, suggests foreign ideas by its modern usage and associations. The marginal translation in our Bible (*charge* or *office*) is not only free from this objection, but much nearer to the meaning of the Greek and Hebrew words, which both denote official visitation and inspection.

21. 22. Wherefore, of these men which have companied with us, all the time that the Lord Jesus went in and out among us, beginning from the baptism of John, unto that same day that he was taken up from

us, must one be ordained, to be a witness with us of his resurrection.

This is the practical conclusion of the argument, the proposition with which Peter closes his address. The first word indicates the logical connection. *Wherefore*, or *therefore*, i. e. since the apostolical office is ordained of God, and this first breach in it was foreseen and predicted by the Holy Spirit centuries ago, it must be the divine will and purpose, that its integrity should be preserved. In the English version of this sentence, there is an unusual departure from the original order of the words, a change not only needless, as in multitudes of other cases, but in this case really injurious to the force and clearness of the passage. Thus the word *must*, in the middle of v. 22, stands in Greek at the beginning of the whole sentence, which is its natural and proper place, as it contains the sum of the conclusion drawn from all that goes before. *It is necessary therefore* (δεῖ οὖν) that the place of Judas should be filled, as afterwards expressed. The necessity alleged was proved, but not created, by the prophecy, which was a mere announcement of God's will and purpose. Peter then proceeds to state the necessary qualifications, or to define the class from which the new Apostle must be taken. The grand qualification was familiar intercourse with Christ and his immediate followers throughout his public ministry, and a consequent capacity to bear witness of his words and actions. *Men* (ἀνδρῶν), not in the vague sense of persons or human beings, but in the distinctive sense of males, or men not women. *Which have companied with us*, or more literally, *those going* (or *who went*) *with us*. As the Greek verb really answers both to *come* and *go* in English, it might here be rendered *coming and going*, i. e. moving about, or in various directions. The essential meaning, although not the form of the original, is well expressed by *companied with us*. The idea evidently is, that the candidate must not only have believed Christ's doctrines and submitted to his teaching, as a disciple in the widest sense, but formed a part of that more permanent body, which appears to have attended him from place to place, throughout the whole course of his public ministry. This last idea is expressed in a peculiar idiomatic form, *all the time that* (or more exactly, *in which, during which*) *the Lord Jesus went in and out among us*. To *go* (or *come*) *in and out* is a Hebrew phrase, denoting constant and habitual movement, sometimes applied to the whole course of life (Deut. 28, 6. 19. John 10, 19), sometimes restricted to official action (1 Sam. 18, 13. 16. Acts 9, 28.) *Among us* does not fully reproduce the sense of the original expression, which, according to the usage of the Greek words, rather means *upon us*, i. e. *over us, above us*, as our head and leader. This important idea of superiority is merged, by the English version and most others, in the minor one of mere association or companionship. But how was this period to be computed or defined? By fixing its extremities, as Peter does in v. 22. The construction of *beginning* is ambiguous in English; but in Greek, its very form shows that it must be construed with *the Lord Jesus*, and denotes the beginning of his active ministry. The starting point was *the baptism of John*. This does not mean the baptism of our Lord himself by John, which would be otherwise expressed, and which throws the *terminus a quo* too far back, as the public ministry of Christ did not begin as soon as he had been baptized; nor would it have been possible to find men who had constantly attended him from that time to the day of the election; so that this construction would make the prescribed condition an impossible and therefore an absurd one. The *baptism of John* no doubt means his entire ministry, so called from the peculiar rite by which it was distinguished, just as *the circumcision* means the Jewish church or party, and *the cross* is often put for the Gospel or the Christian religion. The precise point indicated is not the beginning but the close of John's preparatory ministry, with which the beginning of our Lord's is explicitly connected by the statement in the Gospels, that "after John was put into prison, Jesus came into Galilee, preaching the gospel of the kingdom of God." (Mark 1, 14, compare Matt. 4, 12. 17.) *Unto that same day* is a strong but not inaccurate translation, as the Greek preposition (ἕως) is the same used in a local sense above (v. 8), and here means *quite to*, or until the very day in question. *Taken up from us* suggests two ideas, that of their own loss, and that of their own presence as eyewitnesses. *Ordained*, like *bishopric* (in v. 20), has acquired a fixed ecclesiastical meaning, wholly foreign from the Greek word here used, which means simply *to become*, or more emphatically, *to be made*. *A witness of his resurrection*, the great key-stone of the Christian system, presupposing his life and death as necessary antecedents, and implying his ascension and exaltation as necessary consequents. Hence the extraordinary prominence given to this fact in the first preaching of the gospel (2, 32. 3, 15. 4, 10. 5, 30. 10, 40. 13, 33. 17, 18. 31. 25, 19. 26, 23), and in the doctrinal parts of the New Testament. (See particularly 1 Cor. 15, 12–20.) *With us*, not by himself, or independently of those already constituted witnesses, but as a member of that organized and indivisible body, to which this great trust had been jointly committed. The end, as well as the beginning, of this long and pregnant period, differs very much in the translation and original. As the first word in Greek is (δεῖ) *must*, or *it is necessary*, so the closing words are *one of these*. Although our idiom would hardly have admitted of this collocation, yet it ought to be observed that by connecting this phrase with the word *men* in the first clause of verse 21, the English version unintentionally suggests an idea, which, although it may be true, is not expressed in the original, to wit, that the choice was to be made from among those actually present; whereas *these*, in its original position, does not mean those now before you, but these whom (or such as) I have now described.

23. And they appointed two, Joseph called Barsabas, who was surnamed Justus, and Matthias.

This verse records the execution of the plan proposed by Peter. The act described has been referred by some to the eleven, and by others to the whole assembly of an hundred and twenty. In the absence of any thing to solve this doubt, and in accordance both with Greek and Hebrew usage, the verb may be indefinitely construed, as equivalent in meaning to a passive, *they were set up* or *appointed*. The process itself seems identical with that called in modern parlance *nomination* as distinguished from *election*, i. e. the propounding of a limited number, out of which the choice is to be made. But a difficulty here arises, as to the authority, by which this preliminary step was taken. If the apostles or disciples were competent to choose two, why not to choose one? If, on the other hand, the ultimate decision was necessarily referred to God himself, what right had this assembly to restrict his choice to two whom they had previously fixed upon? The only escape from this dilemma is afforded by a supposition, in itself entirely natural, that these two were the only persons present or within reach, who possessed the necessary qualification. It is by no means probable that many could be found, who had companied with the disciples during the whole period of Christ's ministry, and who were therefore competent to act as his official witnesses. Some have imagined, it is true, that the whole body of believers present upon this occasion were thus qualified; but this is a gratuitous assumption, and intrinsically most improbable. The explanation just proposed may seem to be at variance with the fact that these two persons were *appointed;* but this is equally at variance with the subsequent divine decision. To appoint two new apostles and then ask God to choose one of them, would certainly have been both foolish and irreverent. The truth is that the Greek verb (ἔστησαν) simply means *they placed* (or *set up*) these two men as duly qualified, and then left the decision to their Lord and Master. The part performed by the apostles or disciples in this grave transaction was entirely ministerial, and consisted in ascertaining who were eligible, on the principles laid down by Peter, and then placing the men thus selected in the presence of the multitude, or rather before God, as objects of his sovereign choice. *Joseph called Barsabas,* a name very similar to two others which occur below, *Joses surnamed Barnabas* (4, 36), and *Judas surnamed Barsabas* (15, 22.) Some have regarded the three forms as accidental variations of the same name; but the difference, though slight, is sanctioned by the highest manuscript authority, as well as by the fact that in the later cases there is no allusion to the earlier, nor any intimation that the persons were identical. The name *Barsabas* is of doubtful etymology, but is commonly explained to mean a *son of swearing* (or *an oath*). His third name is a Latin one, and may have been imposed by Romans, as a testimony to his character. It was not uncommon with the Jews of that age to have Gentile names as well as Jewish ones. (See below, on 12, 12. 13, 6. 8. 9.) From the triple name of this man, and his being named first, it has been inferred that he was the choice of the apostles, and that Matthias was put forward only *pro forma* or in obedience to express command. If so, their expectations were defeated, and from this imaginary disappointment Calvin draws the lesson, that the favourites of men are not necessarily the favourites of God; a wholesome doctrine, but one resting on a firmer basis. One of the names must of necessity stand first, and all of Joseph's are recited for the same reason, no doubt, that he bore them, namely, to distinguish him from other Josephs.

24. And they prayed and said, Thou, Lord, which knowest the hearts of all (men), show whether of these two thou hast chosen.

The presentation of the candidates is now followed by an appeal to the divine decision. *Prayed and said*, or more exactly, *praying said;* the acts were not successive but coincident. (See below, on 16, 25.) It has been disputed whether this prayer was especially addressed to Christ. In favour of that supposition is the uniform usage of the word *Lord* in the New Testament, together with the obvious propriety of leaving the selection of a new apostle to him by whom the twelve had been originally chosen. (See above, on v. 2.) The ascription of omniscience to the Saviour is in perfect keeping with such passages as John 2, 24. 25. 21, 17. Rev. 2, 23, and entirely consistent with the application of the same term to God in ch. 15, 8 below. *Which knowest the hearts* is a necessary but enfeebling paraphrase of one Greek word (καρδιογνῶστα) meaning *heart-knower*, and resembling in form Homer's favourite epithet of Zeus or Jupiter, *cloud-gatherer* or *cloud-compeller* (νεφεληγερέτα), but how much more sublime and worthy of a spiritual being! *Whether* is here used in its old English sense, as a pronoun, equivalent to *which* or *which one*. The word translated *show* has a peculiar propriety, because used in Attic Greek to signify the public announcement of the result of an election. It is altogether different from the verb so rendered in v. 3 above. *Hast chosen*, already, for thyself, which accessory ideas are suggested by the tense and voice of the original verb (ἐξελέξω.)

25. That he may take part of this ministry and apostleship, from which Judas by transgression fell, that he might go to his own place.

Even in the act of asking the divine decision, they distinctly state for what end they desire it, or for what specific purpose one of these two men was to be chosen. *That he may take part* might have been more simply and exactly rendered *to take part*, i. e. to take his share, or lot, or his allotted share. The Greek noun is the same as in v. 17 above; but some old manuscripts have *place* (τόπον). *Ministry and apostleship* is not a mere hendiadys meaning *apostolical ministry*, but a generic and specific term combined, the one denoting service in general, the other a particular office. (See above, on v. 17.) *By transgression fell* is a paraphrase rather than a version, and introduces a new figure, that of falling, which is not in the original. A close translation would be, *from which Judas transgressed* or *apostatized*. *That he might go*, like *that he might take part* above, is a needless departure from the infinitive construction, which is equally correct and more concise, *to go to his own place*. Various efforts have been made to escape from the obvious but fearful sense of these words. Some refer them, not to Judas, but to the new apostle, who was chosen *to go into his own place*, a most superfluous addition, and still more so if we understand by *own place* that which Judas had left vacant. Who is ever chosen to supply his own place, or to fill the own place of his predecessor? Both these constructions are objectionable also on account of the harsh syntax which they both assume, and the unusual sense put upon the Greek verb (πορευθῆναι), which does not mean simply to go, but to go away, depart, or journey. (See above, on v. 10, where it is applied to Christ's ascension.) Another explanation grants the reference to Judas, but by his own place understands his house, his field, his new associates, or the scene of his self-murder. All these are ingenious but unnatural expedients to avoid the plain sense of the words, as substantially synonymous with what is elsewhere called *the place of torment* (Luke 16, 28.) The same sense is put by the rabbinical interpreters on Num. 24, 25, *Balaam rose up and went and returned to his* (*own*) *place;* and similar expressions are applied by Plato to a future state of retribution. The essential idea may be that of fitness and condignity, including, in the case before us, by a sort of fearful irony, a contrast or antithesis between the place, of which Judas had proved so unworthy, and the place for which he had exchanged it, and which suited him exactly.

26. And they gave forth their lots, and the lot fell upon Matthias, and he was numbered with the eleven apostles.

We have here the conclusion of the whole matter by the final designation of a new apostle. It has been disputed whether it was only the eleven, or the whole assembly, that *gave forth their lots*. The very question assumes, either that this was an election, in the ordinary sense of the expression, and that *lots* means *votes* or *ballots*, which is utterly at variance with the usage of the word and with the circumstances of the case; or that *their lots* means the lots of the apostles or assembled brethren; whereas it means the lots of the two candidates, i. e. the lots which were to choose between them, and were probably inscribed with their respective names. Especially must this be the sense if we adopt the reading of the oldest manuscripts and latest editors, which changes *their lots* into *lots for them*. This makes it wholly unimportant who performed the mere external act of drawing, shaking, or the like, which seems to be intended by the phrase *they gave lots*, an expression also used in the Old Testament, though sometimes confounded in our version with the more familiar formula, *to cast lots*. The precise mode in which the lots were used can only be conjectured, or inferred from analogous cases in the classics, as for instance in the third book of the Iliad, where the lots were cast into a helmet, after prayer for the divine direction, and the one that first came out when shaken was decisive of the question. The same thing is here expressed by the figurative phrase, *the lot fell upon Matthias*, perhaps with some allusion to the maxim of the wise man, that " the lot is cast into the lap, but the whole disposing thereof is of the Lord." (Prov. 16, 33.) The validity of this whole proceeding has been questioned, upon several grounds; because there is no express command recorded; because Peter was habitually rash and forward; because the Holy Ghost was not yet given to qualify them for such functions; because we read nothing more of Matthias in the history; and lastly, because Paul is thus excluded from the number of the twelve apostles. To these specious arguments it may be answered, that a command is often left to be inferred from the recorded execution, and vice versa; that this, although proposed by Peter, was no more his act than that of the whole body; that the choice was really the act of neither, but of God himself; that the history is equally silent as to most of the apostles; and that Paul might with more probability be reckoned the successor of James the Son of Zebedee than of Judas Iscariot; or rather that he was not one of the twelve at all, but an additional apostle for the Gentiles, as the twelve were the apostles of the circumcision.

Add to all this, that they who had been called *the eleven* since the death of Judas, are afterwards called *the twelve*, and that while Saul was still an enemy of Christ; and consider the extreme improbability that so much space would have been given, in so brief a history and at such a juncture, to an unauthorized proceeding of this nature, not omitting even the accompanying prayer, and yet without the slightest intimation of its being uncommanded, and consequently null and void. But apart from these considerations, the whole question, if there is one, seems to be determined by the last words of the narrative itself, which admit of but one natural interpretation, namely, that Matthias was now reckoned, by divine right, as the twelfth apostle. (Compare Matt. 28, 16. Mark 16, 14. Luke 24, 9. 33, with Acts 2, 14. 6, 2.)

CHAPTER II.

Here begins the Apostolical Church History, to which the events recorded in the preceding chapter were preliminary. The two topics first presented are the events of Pentecost (1–41) and the condition of the infant Church (42–47.) Under the first head are described the gift of tongues (1–4), with its effect upon the foreign Jews who witnessed it (5–12), the frivolous or malignant charge of drunkenness (13), and Peter's Pentecostal sermon (14–36), in which he first repudiates the odious charge (14), and then declares what they beheld to be the very effusion of the Spirit promised by the Prophet Joel (15–18), as a part and token of a great revolutionary change (19. 20), which would be ruinous to all who did not trust in the appointed Saviour (21), whom he shows to be no other than the man whom they had crucified but God had raised (22–24), as David had predicted in the sixteenth psalm (25–28), in terms which could not be applied to David himself (29), but must refer to the Messiah (30. 31), and had been fulfilled in Jesus (32), who was really the author of the present miracle (33), being now exalted, according to another prophecy of David (34. 35), which was also inapplicable to himself, and had only been fulfilled in Jesus, whom he therefore concludes to be the true Messiah (36.) Then follows the effect of this discourse upon the hearers (37), and Peter's further exhortations and instructions in reply to their inquiries (38–40), with the consequent addition of three thousand converts to the church by baptism in that single day (41.) The remainder of the chapter is occupied with a description of their social state and mode of life, from that day onward (43–46), and of their steady growth in popularity and numbers (47.)

1. And when the day of Pentecost was fully come, they were all with one accord in one place.

The writer here begins his account of the reorganization of the church by an exact specification of the time when it occurred. The day selected for this great event was one of the three yearly festivals prescribed in the Mosaic Law. It is one of the most interesting features of that system, that these annual observances were not mere arbitrary institutions, but connected, in the minds of those observing them, with three distinct sets of associations, the first derived from nature, the second from experience, the third from the promises of God and the expectations of his people. Thus the Passover, the first in time and dignity, was associated, in the revolution of the seasons, with the early harvest; in the national recollections of Israel, with the exodus from Egypt; and in his hopes, with the advent and sacrifice of the Messiah. The Feast of Tabernacles, or of Trumpets, had a like threefold association, with the vintage or ingathering of fruits, with the journey through the wilderness, and with the rest that remaineth for the people of God. These two great feasts were placed at the beginning and the end of the half-year, to which the annual solemnities of the ceremonial system were confined. Between them was a third, but nearer to the Passover, from which it took its name, both in Hebrew and in Greek. It was celebrated at the end of seven weeks (or a week of weeks) from the second day of the Passover, or Feast of Unleavened Bread, i. e. the sixteenth day of the month Nisan (Lev. 23, 15. 16.) Hence it was called the Feast of Weeks (Ex. 34, 22. Deut. 16, 10.) From the Greek-speaking Jews of later times, it received the equivalent name of *Pentecost* or *Fiftieth*, i. e. the feast of the fiftieth day after the sixteenth of Nisan. The Greek adjective thus used became a substantive, and is so employed in the verse before us, where it is not to be construed with *festival* or *day* understood, but taken as the proper name of the festival or day itself. It might have been expected from analogy that this anniversary, like the other two, would have its threefold associations, natural, historical, and typical or prophetical. It is remarkable, however, that only one of these can be distinctly traced in the Law itself. This is the first, as we know that Pentecost occurred at the completion of the harvest or cereal ingathering, and was therefore sometimes called *the feast of harvest* (Ex. 23, 16), and *the day of the first fruits* (Num. 28, 26), because its distinctive rite was the oblation of two loaves, as a sample and acknowledgment of the harvest (Lev. 23, 17.) But with what historical event was it associated, past or future? That it had no such association, like the Passover and Feast of Trumpets, is antecedently improbable; but none such is recorded. Jewish tradition has filled the chasm, as we learn from the Talmud and Maimonides, by affirming that the Pentecost, or fiftieth day after the sixteenth of Nisan, was the very day on which the law was given from Mount Sinai. This ingenious combination, if it be not rather a collateral tradition, is entirely consistent with the facts and dates of the Mosaic record, and may therefore be allowed to supply the omission, though we cannot account for the omission itself. If this be granted, as to the historical significance of Pentecost, its typical significance will be found in the passage now before us, that is to say, in the selection of this day for the reorganization of the church, which may be said to have been organized at first, or at least to have received its ceremonial form, on the same day many centuries before. It is no trivial result and recommendation of this view, that it completes what seems (but only seems) to be imperfect in the ceremonial calendar, by clothing this third feast with the same threefold associations, which the Law expressly, or by necessary implication, has attached to the other two. Why this day was chosen is perhaps sufficiently explained by the coincidence or correspondence between these two great acts of organic legislation. As additional reasons it may be observed that the selection of one of the great yearly feasts secured, not only a great concourse of the native Jews, but a full representation of the foreign Jews or Hellenists; and that the death and resurrection of our Saviour having been associated with the Passover, it was natural and convenient that the next great movement in the erection of his kingdom should be likewise associated with the next great annual observance of the Jewish church and the Mosaic Law. According to Chrysostom, another reason was, that the same persons might be witnesses of both events. That some importance and significance belong to the selection of the time, appears to be implied in the expression of the verse before us, *when the day of Pentecost was fully come*, or retaining the peculiar form of the original, *in the fulfilling (of) Pentecost*, i. e. when the appointed and therefore necessary interval had quite elapsed. The corresponding festival in Christian calendars is *Whitsunday*, which, although so called for a different reason, is the fiftieth day after Easter. In Luke 9, 51, the same Greek phrase is applied to the mere approach, and not the actual arrival, of a certain time; but there the time itself is more indefinite, being not the *day*, but the *days*, of his assumption. The plural form is also employed here, but inaccurately, by the Vulgate. On what day of the week this Pentecost occurred has been a subject of dispute for ages, but is happily a question of no moment. *All* is a strong, but not a definite expression, i. e. not one that determines what precise number, or what specific class of persons, were assembled upon this occasion. It must therefore be interpreted by the foregoing narrative, in which we read of two assemblages, the first of eleven (1, 4), and the second of a hundred and twenty persons (1, 15.) The proximity of this last, and the strength of the expression *all*, seem to forbid its restriction to the twelve, but not its extension to a greater number than a hundred and twenty. Indeed, as there is reason to believe that this last was a fortuitous assemblage, representing a much larger body of believers (see above, on 1, 15), it seems most probable that *all* here designates that body, and affirms its presence, not in all its individual members, nor in just the same who were convened before, but in such numbers that the crowd (ὄχλος 1, 15) was a full and fair representation of the aggregate body. The two phrases previously used to signify coincidence of place and purpose, are here combined, in order to express more fully the kindred but distinct ideas of local convention or assemblage, and of concert and intelligence as to its purpose. They were not merely *together*, or *in one place*, as they might have been without design, but they were there *with one accord* and by previous agreement.

2. And suddenly there came a sound from heaven,

as of a rushing mighty wind, and it filled all the house where they were sitting.

The effusion of the Spirit was preceded and accompanied by sensible signs addressed to the ears and eyes of those assembled. The first impression was that of an extraordinary noise, preparing them for the still more extraordinary sight that was to follow. This sound came *suddenly*, and could not therefore be referred to any natural external cause. It came *from heaven*, which may refer both to the sensible impression of a sound descending from above, and to its real supernatural origin, as caused by God himself. The natural sound which it resembled most was that of a strong wind; but it was something more, as appears from the comparative expression *as*, which would be otherwise superfluous. The word translated *rushing* is a passive participle, meaning *borne* or *carried*, and is properly descriptive of involuntary motion caused by a superior power, an idea not suggested by the active participles *rushing, driving*, or the like, which seem to make the wind itself the operative agent. The other epithet in Greek means more than *mighty*, being expressive not only of a quality but of an effect, *violent*, destructive. The noun itself, which these words qualify is not the ordinary term for wind, but a stronger one answering to *blast* or *gust*. The whole phrase therefore is descriptive of a powerful tempestuous commotion of the air by some extraordinary cause. (Vulg. *advenientis spiritus vehementis*.) Such a phenomenon was specially appropriate in this case, on account of the generally recognized analogy between breath or wind and spiritual influences, which may be traced in various languages, for instance in our own. The point of resemblance seems to be an invisible cause producing visible effects. *It filled all the house*, i. e. the sound, not the wind, which is only mentioned in the way of comparison. *The house where they were sitting* was no doubt the same in which they were accustomed to assemble (see above, on 1, 13.) The form of expression is far more natural in reference to a private dwelling or a hired lodging, than to the temple or any of its appurtenances. The supposed difficulty as to its capacity assumes that a private house could not be a large one, and is further removed by the obvious assumption that, although the commotion began in the house, the crowd may have assembled in the open air.

3. And there appeared unto them cloven tongues, like as of fire, and it sat upon each of them.

The audible sign was followed by one addressed to the sense of sight. *Appeared unto them*, or, as some explain the Greek words, *were seen upon them*, i. e. by others; but the common version is more agreeable both to the context and to usage. (See Matt. 17, 3. Mark 9, 4. Luke 1, 11. 22, 43. 24, 34. Acts 7, 2. 26. 30. 35. 9, 17. 16, 9. 26, 16.) The form of the original is passive and means strictly, *were seen by them.* *Cloven* should rather be *distributed*, so that one appeared on each. (Vulg. *linguae dispertitae*.) The common version, which implies that each tongue was divided into two or more, as represented in most paintings of the scene before us, is at variance with the usage of the Greek verb (διαμεριζόμεναι), which sometimes denotes moral separation or estrangement (Luke 11, 17. 18. 12, 52. 53), but never physical division. Its usual sense of distribution or allotment may be seen by a comparison of Matt. 27, 35. Mark 15, 24. Luke 22, 17. 23, 34, and v. 45 below. *Tongues* may be regarded as a metaphorical description of the natural appearance of all fire, as in Isai. 5, 24, from which comes the classical figure of a lambent flame; but here there is moreover an evident allusion to a special miraculous resemblance, prefiguring the extraordinary gift that was to follow. *Like as of fire*, or more exactly, *as if of fire*, i. e. the appearance of these tongues was the same as if they had been really composed of fire, but without forbidding the conclusion that they were so. This comparative expression, like the one in the preceding verse, leaves room for doubt as to the presence of material fire or of a real wind. A similar dubiety exists in Luke's account of the bloody sweat (Luke 22, 44), and of the visible descent of the Holy Ghost upon our Saviour at his baptism (Luke 3, 22.) The very frequency, however, of this form of speech in Luke's writings makes it proper not to press it, as a proof that the appearance was unreal. *It sat upon each of them.* The singular number has been variously explained, as referring to *Spirit* in the next verse, or to *fire* in this, or to the whole appearance (τὸ φαινόμενον) viewed as one, or to the distribution previously mentioned, which implied that *one* of the tongues sat on each. As this last is the preferable construction, it affords an additional objection to the version *cloven tongues*, which leaves the singular verb (*it sat*) without satisfactory solution. *Each of them*, i. e. of those assembled upon this occasion. There is nothing to restrict or qualify the wide expression used in v. 1, or to limit what is here said to the twelve apostles. The whole assembly was collectively a representation of the body of believers, now about to be reorganized upon a Christian basis, and perpetuated as the Christian Church. This representative character accounts for the want of precise specifications as to the names and number of those present, and precludes the necessity of trying to supply the omission either by reasoning or conjecture.

4. And they were all filled with the Holy Ghost, and began to speak with other tongues, as the Spirit gave them utterance.

The sensible signs of an extraordinary spiritual influence are followed by the influence itself, and this again by a sensible effect, affording external proof of its reality. The repeated use of the word *all* shows that this effect was not confined to the Apostles. No one could have been disposed to doubt that the extraordinary gift extended to *all the Apostles*, if vouchsafed to any; but the very feeling which leads us to doubt its further extension, shows the necessity of saying *they were all filled with the Holy Ghost*, if such were really the case. This expression is a favourite one with Luke (4, 8. 31. 6, 3. 5. 7, 55. 9, 17. 11, 24. 13, 9. 52. Luke 1, 15. 41. 67. 4, 1), and denotes a fresh illapse and extraordinary influence of the divine agent, not excluding previous communications, but always implying the reception of supernatural gifts or powers. (Compare Luke 24, 49. Acts 1, 8.) Here the precise nature of the gift is particularly stated; *they began to speak with other tongues*. *Began* is no more pleonastic here than in the first sentence of the book, but conveys, as it does there, the twofold idea, that what is here recorded happened for the first time, and that it was afterwards repeated or continued. *Other tongues* can only mean languages different from their own, and by necessary implication, previously unknown. (Vulg. *linguis variis*.) In our Saviour's promise of this gift before his Ascension (Mark 16, 17), he uses the equivalent expression, *new tongues*, i. e. new to them. The attempt to make these phrases mean a new style or a new strain, or new forms of expression, is not only unnatural but inconsistent with the following narrative, where every thing implies a real difference of language. Some have imagined that the miracle was wrought upon the ears of the hearers, each of whom supposed what he heard to be uttered in his mother tongue. But this is a gratuitous and forced assumption, and at variance with the fact that the use of other tongues appears to have preceded the arrival of the foreign witnesses, whose hearing is supposed to have been thus affected. The design of this gift was not merely to facilitate the preaching of the gospel. It is nowhere historically mentioned as contributing to that result. Its necessity for that end was in a great measure superseded, at least within the Roman Empire, by the general use of the Greek language. That it was not a permanent and universal knowledge of all the tongues spoken in the countries visited by the Apostles, is inferred by some from 14, 11, where the use of the vernacular language seems to be mentioned, as an explanation of the tardiness with which Paul and Barnabas rejected the idolatrous honours of the heathen Lycaonians. While the gift of tongues may, in particular emergencies, have answered this important purpose, it had other uses, even regarded as a transient or momentary inspiration. It served, like any other miracle, but with a special propriety and force, to prove the reality of an extraordinary spiritual influence, which might otherwise have been denied or doubted. And it served, as a symbol, to prefigure the vocation of the Gentiles, whose excision from the church or chosen people had been typified of old by a corresponding prodigy, the miraculous confusion of tongues at Babel. As the moral unity of mankind had been then lost, it was now to be restored, by the preaching of the Gospel to all nations. To this historical connection between diversities of language and the spiritual condition of the world, there seems to be allusion in the frequent use of the word *tongues* in prophecy to designate *nations*. (See Isaiah 66, 18. Dan. 3, 4. 7. Rev. 5, 9. 7, 9. 10, 11. 11, 9. 13, 7. 14, 6. 17, 15.) While the practical design of this gift, as an aid in preaching, would confine it to one sex and a small class of believers, its demonstrative and symbolical design made it equally appropriate to others. Its original exercise was not in mere talk, the generic Greek term (λαλεῖν) being qualified by one (ἀποφθέγγεσθαι) which primarily means to *speak out*, clearly or aloud, and secondarily, to utter something weighty or authoritative, in which sense it is the root of the word *apophthegm*. (Compare v. 14, 4, 18, 26, 25.) Even this utterance, however, was not left to their own choice or discretion, but directed by the same divine influence which enabled them to speak at all. They spoke *as the Spirit gave them utterance,* literally, *to utter* (Vulg. *dabat eloqui*), i. e. gave the capacity and right to do so. Cranmer and the Geneva Bible mark the identity of the divine agent by rendering, *the same Spirit.*

5. And there were dwelling at Jerusalem Jews, devout men, out of every nation under heaven.

Publicity was necessary to the effect of this great miracle, both as a symbol and a proof of special divine agency; and witnesses accordingly had been provided. The word translated *dwelling* does not of itself denote either permanent or temporary residence, but rather the act of settling or beginning to reside, as in Matt. 2, 23. 4, 13. 12, 45. Luke 11, 26. Acts 7, 2. 4, whether the subsequent abode be temporary, as in Heb. 11, 9, or permanent, as in Acts 9, 32. 17, 26, and often in the book of Revelation, where it is a favourite expression for the general idea of inhabitation. There is nothing therefore to confine the word here to Jews who had come to end their lives in Jerusalem, as they have done in all ages, or to such as had come merely to attend the feast. The special reference, if any, would be naturally to the latter. All that is expressly said, however, is that there were then present at Jerusalem, either as visitors or constant residents, representatives of *every nation under heaven.* This is a natural hyperbole belonging, not to artificial rhetoric, but to the dialect of common life. It loses something of its strength when compared with the statements of Philo and Josephus, that there were Jews then settled in every country upon earth. There is also an allusion to the language of Gen. 11, 4, confirming the assumed relation of the gift of tongues to the confusion there recorded. These representatives of all nations were themselves, as might have been expected, Jews, and of the serious or devout class, such as were believers in the prophecies and looking for the consolation of Israel. (Compare Luke 2, 25. 38.) The Greek epithet (εὐλαβεῖς) originally signifies cautious, timid, but in Hellenistic usage is applied to the fear of God. The Geneva Bible has expressly, *Jews that feared God;* Wiclif, after the Vulgate, *religious men.* Some have supposed it, like the similar phrase, *fearing God,* to be descriptive of proselytes from heathenism (10, 2. 22. 13, 16

26); but its application to Simeon, if not to Ananias (22, 12), shows it to be properly expressive of a certain type of Jewish piety. (See below, on 8, 2.) Its introduction here is not unmeaning, as it shows that the effusion of the Holy Ghost was attested by the most competent and trustworthy witnesses, Jews of the most serious and perhaps most bigoted character, who at the same time represented every nation under heaven. It is an admissible, though not a necessary supposition, that this concourse at Jerusalem had some connection with the general expectation of a great deliverer, which prevailed at this time, not in Israel only (Luke 2, 25. 26. 38. 3, 15. 19, 11. John 1, 20. 21), but among the Gentiles, as attested by Suetonius and Tacitus.

6. Now when this was noised abroad, the multitude came together, and were confounded, because that every man heard them speak in his own language.

The first clause is more literally rendered in the margin of the English Bible, *when this voice was made.* The exact form of the original is, *this voice having happened*, or come into existence, i. e. become audible. The common version seems to take *voice* in the sense of *rumour* or *report;* but there is no such usage either in classical or hellenistic Greek. Some identify it with the *noise* of v. 2, and *voice* is certainly applied elsewhere to inarticulate sounds, as that of the wind (John 3, 8), of a trumpet (Matt. 24, 31), of thunder (Rev. 6, 1), wings and chariots (Rev. 9, 9), waters (Rev. 14, 2), etc. But as it properly denotes the human voice, it seems best here to understand it of the voice of the disciples speaking in other tongues. The singular number (*voice* for *voices*) is collective, and as natural in this case as in 4, 24, and in the phrases, *voice of many angels, voice of harpers and musicians* (Rev. 5, 11. 18, 22.) The voice of the disciples would at first attract the notice of those near at hand, and then, by an influence of which we have continual examples, gather a still larger audience. *The multitude* is neither the multitude accustomed to assemble at the temple, from which some have drawn an inference as to the scene of these events; nor the multitude ready to assemble upon such occasions, or what we call 'the mob'; but the large body of foreign Jews described in the preceding verse, and providentially provided as witnesses of this great miracle. Having said that there were such men in the city, the historian now says that the whole mass of them (τὸ πλῆθος) came together, when these strange sounds became audible. He then describes the effect produced upon them by this singular phenomenon. *Confounded* means originally *poured together*, and describes the mixture of liquids, but is secondarily applied to any confused mixture, as of people in a tumult (19, 32. 21, 31), or of thoughts in the mind, as in 9, 22 and here. The Greek verb is peculiar to this book of the New Testament. The margin of our Bible has *troubled in mind;* the older English versions read *astonied, astonied in thought,* or *astonied in mind.* The cause of their confusion or perplexity is expressly stated. The form of the last clause in the original is, *because they heard, each one in his own dialect, them speaking. Dialect,* a kindred form to *dialogue,* originally means discourse or conversation; then mode of speech, style, or diction; then diversity of language, whether national or provincial. *Own* is emphatic; not merely in a language which he understood, but in his own particular, peculiar tongue. What could this possibly mean, if the *other tongues* were merely higher strains or singularities of diction? Some have strangely understood this clause to mean, that each of those who came together heard all the disciples speaking in his own tongue; and on this interpretation rests the notion that the miracle was not wrought on the tongues of the disciples, but the ears of those who heard them. This is certainly not the sense suggested by the words to an unbiassed reader. They evidently mean no more than that each of the witnesses heard his own language spoken, whether by one or more. Another objection to this view of the passage, as already stated, is, that the fact of their speaking in other tongues is distinctly mentioned, as something previous to, and therefore independent of, the concourse and confusion here recorded.

7. And they were all amazed and marvelled, saying one to another, Behold, are not all these which speak Galileans?

Amazed and *marvelled* are not descriptive of something subsequent to the confusion mentioned in v. 6, but either mere specifications of the term there used, or expressive of the inward state by which the outward confusion was produced. The verbs themselves are not synonymous in Greek, but generic and specific forms of the same idea. The first (ἐξίσταντο) means properly to be out of one's normal condition, and when applied to the intellect, to be beside one's self, with any strong emotion. It is the root of our word *ecstasy*, applied in English usage to extreme degrees of joy, whereas the Greek noun is appropriated, in the same way, to extreme degrees of wonder. As if he had said, they were beside themselves with wonder. This specific application of the term is then directly given by the second verb, *they marvelled*. Their wonder was expressed in mutual ejaculations; not that each of them uttered these precise words, but that this was the sum and substance of what they said to one another. (See below, on 4, 16. 24.) Their surprise is furthermore denoted by the particle *behold*. (See above, on 1, 10.) The particular description of the twelve as *Galileans* has been variously explained. Some take it as synonymous with *Christians*, which is both irrelevant and contrary to usage; irrelevant, because it mattered not of what religion the men were, to whom this power was imparted; it was no more wonderful in Christians than it would have been in Jews or Gentiles: contrary to usage, because *Galilean* had not yet become the designation of a sect or a religion. (See above, on 1, 11.) Others suppose the speakers to have reference to the ignorance and barbarism of the Galileans, and the consequent contempt with which they were regarded, even by the other Jews. (See John 1, 46. 7, 52.) Their very dialect seems to have been different from that of the Jews properly so called (Matt. 26, 73. Mark 14, 70); but this was a difference too slight to have attracted the attention of foreigners, and one which could not have increased their wonder at the gift of tongues. So far as education and learning were concerned, the Galileans were no doubt inferior to the other Jews, and this might seem to make the wonder greater, that they should now be heard speaking in tongues which they had never learned. But on the other hand, the Galileans were especially accustomed to free intercourse with foreigners; partly because their country was a thoroughfare between Judea and the countries to the north and east; partly because Galilee itself had a mixed population, especially that part of it called (it may be for that very reason) *Galilee of the Gentiles* (Isai. 9, 1. Matt. 4, 15.) In this point of view, it would be rather less than more strange that they should speak foreign tongues. The true solution seems to be, that Galileans here **means**

Jews or inhabitants of Palestine, the local designation being substituted for the general one, simply because it happened to apply; just as Frenchmen might express their surprise at the correctness with which French was spoken by a Scotchman or an Irishman, although his native tongue be neither Scotch nor Irish, but English. The strangers might have said, Are not these which speak all Jews or natives of Palestine? But as they saw them to be chiefly from one district, they naturally use the local or provincial name. Some have inferred from this expression, that all the followers of Christ were Galileans; others, that only the Apostles are referred to. But the language is sufficiently explained by the large proportion of disciples from that province, and by the prominence of the Apostles. It should also be observed, that the words are not affirmative but interrogative, and uttered not by those who knew the fact, but by a crowd of strangers, judging merely from appearances, and speaking from the impulse of the moment.

8. And how hear we every man in our own tongue wherein we were born?

The logical connection is more clearly indicated in the Geneva version, *how then?* i. e. if they are all Galileans, how is it that they speak our languages? The question is only an additional expression of surprise, an indirect assertion that the fact is unaccountable. The construction seems to be disturbed by the insertion of *every man* or *each one;* but without it, they might seem to have spoken all one language, and the writer seems resolved that the reader shall remember the diversity of dialect among these strangers. In order likewise to preclude all doubt as to the *other tongues* of v. 4, he not only here repeats the strong expression *own tongue* from v. 6, but adds the still stronger one, *in which we were born*, equivalent in meaning to the common phrase, *our mother tongue* or *native language*. This strange accumulation of terms necessarily denoting literal diversity of language, is not only unaccountable but perfectly unmeaning, if (as some allege) the wonder consisted merely in the use of unusual expressions or a style of extraordinary elevation. How could either of these modes of speech be called by any hearer his own dialect in which he was born? If the terms used in this narrative do not express diversity of language, in the obvious and proper sense, it is impossible for that idea to be clothed in words at all. Some complete the construction of the sentence by supplying (as the object of the verb *we hear*) *them speaking ;* but the true completion of the syntax is contained in v. 11 below, where the same verb (ἀκούομεν) is repeated and the sentence closed, after the long parenthesis in vs. 9, 10.

9. Parthians and Medes and Elamites, and the dwellers in Mesopotamia, and in Judea and Cappadocia, in Pontus and Asia ;

The sentence is continued from the foregoing verse. The long list of names which follows is a specification of the pronoun *we* in v. 8. 'We who are Parthians, etc.' As we have here recorded, not the very words of any individual speaker, but the sum and substance of what all said, we may suppose each man to have mentioned his own country, or one man to have mentioned several, without detracting in the least from the fidelity and fulness of the record. The names are neither chosen nor arranged at random, but follow each other in a certain geographical order, beginning at the north-east, and then proceeding to the west and south. The first three denote races adjacent to the Caspian Sea, and all belonging to the ancient Persian empire. During the interval between the Old and the New Testament, that empire had been partially resuscitated by the Parthians, who became a formidable hinderance to the progress of the Roman arms in Asia. From these north-eastern tracts he passes to Mesopotamia, so called from its position between the two great rivers, Tigris and Euphrates. There is here an apparently unnecessary change in the construction of the sentence. Instead of proceeding simply to enumerate the races or inhabitants of countries, he enumerates the countries themselves, prefixing the participle *dwelling* or *inhabiting,* until the end of the next verse, when the original construction is resumed. The only reason that can be suggested, even by conjecture, for this change of form, is that there was probably no gentile noun in use derived from *Mesopotamia* (and answering to *Mesopotamians*), and that having been obliged to use a circumlocution with respect to that name, Luke continued it through this verse and the next. From Mesopotamia he passes over to the peninsula of Asia Minor, and as Judea lay between, he introduces it, although not properly belonging to a catalogue of foreign countries represented at Jerusalem. It is then equivalent to saying, 'We, as well as those inhabiting Judea.' Some account for its insertion from the fact already mentioned, that the dialect of Galilee was different from that of Judea proper, and that Jews (in the local sense) might therefore join in the expression of surprise at hearing a Galilean speaking their own language. But this was nothing new to them, unless we arbitrarily assume that their provincialisms were miraculously rectified. Another explanation is that Luke, writing probably at Rome, surveys the countries rather from that point of view than from Jerusalem. At all events, there can be no ground for a change of text, by omitting *Judea* altogether, or by changing it to *Syria, Armenia, Bithynia, Lydia, India*, or *Idumea*, all of which have been suggested. Of Asia Minor five provinces are named, viz. *Pontus* on the north coast, *Pamphylia* on the south coast, *Cappadocia* and *Phrygia* in the interior, and on the west coast *Asia*, in its oldest and most restricted sense. Modern geography applies this name to one of the great primary divisions of the eastern hemisphere or old world, and, with the qualifying adjunct *Minor*, to the peninsula between the Black Sea and the Archipelago. But neither of these is its original and proper application, which was restricted to the provinces along the western coast of that peninsula. According to Pliny, it included Mysia, Lydia, and Caria, and nearly or exactly coincided with the Æolis and Ionia of still older geographers. Whatever doubt there may be as to its precise extent, there can be none as to its relative position, on the shore of the Egean Sea and opposite to Greece. In this ancient and restricted sense, *Asia* is used throughout the Acts of the Apostles, the alleged exceptions being more than doubtful. (See below, on 19, 26. 27. 21, 27. 24, 18. 27, 2.) In later times it was extended to the whole peninsula, and finally attained its present latitude of meaning, as a correlative of Europe, Africa, and America.

10. Phrygia and Pamphylia, in Egypt, and in the parts of Libya about Cyrene, and strangers of Rome, Jews and Proselytes;

From the central and southern provinces of Asia-Minor he crosses the Mediterranean to Africa, in which he singles out two well-known and adjacent countries on the northern coast. *Libya*, lying west of Egypt, was divided by the old geographers into three parts, one of which was called *Libya Pentapolis* or *Pentapolitana*, from its five noted cities. One of these was *Cyrene*, a Greek colony and seaport, from which the whole region was sometimes called *Libya Cyrenaica*. (See below, on 6, 9. 11, 20. 13, 1.) The periphrastic description, *Libya about* (or *towards*) *Cyrene*, is very similar in form to those which Dio Cassius and Josephus apply to the same country. From Libya Luke proceeds to Italy, as here representing the whole west. At this point the series of accusatives governed by the participle in v. 8 is concluded, and the original construction reappears. The irregularity of form is greater in English than in Greek, because the translators have gratuitously changed the participle (*inhabiting*) into a noun and preposition (*dwellers in*), which last they have omitted before some names and inserted before others, whereas the form of the original has no such inequality. *Strangers of Rome* does not mean, as some have imagined, *strangers at Rome*, which would be wholly out of place, as well as contrary to usage, but *strangers from Rome*, Roman strangers, at Jerusalem. Here again the Greek word is a participle and means sojourning, temporarily residing. The distinctive meaning of the Greek verb may be traced in its derivative *epidemic*, applied in medicine to the temporary prevalence of diseases, as distinguished from those which are *endemic* or at home, i. e. permanently established in particular localities. By *Jews* we are here to understand those born such, natural descendants of Abraham and Israel, as opposed to converts from the heathen, called προσήλυτοι, *advenae*, or *new comers*. Wiclif uses the word *comelings* to translate ἐπιδημοῦντες, though in etymology it seems to coincide exactly with προσήλυτοι. The latter is rendered by Tyndale *converts*, and paraphrased in the Geneva Bible, *those that were converted to the Jewish religion*. The combination of the two words here includes all sorts of Jews there represented. The position of the words is somewhat strange and has been variously explained. Some suppose that they were meant to apply only to the Romans; but for this no reason can be given. Others regard them as qualifying the whole catalogue; but this is not completed till the next verse. On the whole, perhaps, the best solution is, that the qualifying phrase, though really applicable to the whole, is introduced just here because it here occurred to the writer. As if he had said,

'Sojourners of Rome, including, as in all the other cases I have named, both native Jews and Gentile converts.'

11. Cretes and Arabians; we do hear them speak in our tongues the wonderful works of God.

The names here added do not violate the order previously followed, but complete the circle, as it were, by passing from the extreme west (Italy) to the extreme south (Arabia), between which two extremes the important island Crete (now Candia) lies in a direct line. This conclusion of the catalogue is followed by that of the whole sentence begun in v. 8, the connection being made clear by the repetition of the leading verb (*we hear*), of which the proper names preceding constitute the complex subject. *Our tongues* corresponds to *own tongue* (Gr. *own dialect*) in v. 8. *Wonderful works* is a correct paraphrase, but not an exact version, of the Greek word (μεγαλεῖα), which corresponds more nearly to *magnificent*, as an expression of the highest admiration. (Vulg. *magnalia*.) As the noun is not expressed, and as Xenophon repeatedly applies the adjective to words or sayings, it might here be understood as meaning that they heard the disciples speaking the *wonderful words* of God, i. e. words relating to him and inspired by him. But the reference to works or acts is favoured by the use of the Greek word, in the Septuagint version of Ps. 71, 19, to translate a Hebrew one (נִפְלָאוֹת), derived from a corresponding root and constantly applied in the Old Testament to the divine attributes and acts. (See Job 5, 9. 9, 10. 37, 5.) Still more decisive is the analogy of Luke 1, 49, the only other instance of its use in the New Testament, where it is joined directly with the verb *to do*. There is nothing in the text or context to determine what specific acts are here referred to; but it may be safely affirmed that the effusion of the Spirit upon this occasion was at least included. Some who deny the gift of tongues, in the sense of a plurality of languages, make this the emphatic word of the whole sentence, and suppose the wonder to consist in the greatness of the matter, and not in the mode of the expression. It was the glorious works of God, as uttered by the disciples under a special divine influence, that filled these Jews with wonder. But even granting this to be an adequate occasion of the feeling here expressed, how could it have been clothed in words by saying that each of the spectators heard them speak his language, his own dialect, his mother tongue? If these phrases, and the *other tongues* of v. 4, may be made to mean an elevated spiritual strain or style, the fruit of strong excitement, or even of a real inspiration, but without effect upon the dialect, then all interpretation is uncertain, and the most important end of language nullified.

12. And they were all amazed, and were in doubt, saying one to another, What meaneth this?

This may be taken either as an emphatic repetition of what had been already said, or as a direct continuation of the narrative. In the latter case, the meaning is, that their mutual interrogations led to no satisfactory result, for they were still astonished and perplexed. In addition to the verb explained above (on v. 7) and here repeated, Luke employs another very strong expression to describe the extent of their confusion. From a Greek noun meaning *passage* (πόρος) comes the adjective *impassable* (ἄπορος), or when applied to persons, having no passage, outlet, or way of escape. From this again is formed the verb (ἀπορέω) to be shut up or at a loss, and its emphatic compound (διαπορέω) to be utterly or wholly at a loss, which is the word here used. This continued uncertainty betrayed itself in further questionings, of which an example is here given in a very idiomatic form. *What meaneth this* is no doubt the correct sense, but the form of the original is, *what will* (or *would*) *this be?* Examples of the same mode of expression have been quoted from Herodotus, Anacreon, and other classics. The nearest approach to the original in any English version is by Wiclif, *what wole* (will) *this thing be?* Weaker and less exact is the Geneva version, *what may this thing be?* From this extended and minute description, it is clear that the historian considered it important for his purpose, that the reader should be strongly impressed with the helpless confusion and extreme astonishment of these beholders.

13. Others mocking said, These men are full of new wine.

Thus far the language and the conduct of the witnesses have been described as altogether serious and earnest. Now another and a very different tone is audible. The apparent inconsistency between the *all* of v. 12 and the *others* of v. 13 may be solved in two ways. One is by supposing that we here have an example of a form of speech common to all languages, but particularly frequent in the Greek and Hebrew, and consisting in the use of an absolute expression to be qualified immediately by one which follows. Resolved into our idiom, the sense would be, 'all were astonished and perplexed excepting some who mocked and said,' etc. But this solution, although perfectly admissible in case of exegetical necessity, is not imperatively needed here, as there is yet another, still more satisfactory. This consists in limiting the application of the word *all* in v. 12 to the foreign Jews and proselytes just mentioned, and applying the *others* of v. 13 to the natives of Judea or Jerusalem. The reason of this difference will appear below. *Mocking*, or making a jest of the whole matter. Some of the oldest manuscripts and latest critical editions have a stronger form than that in the received text (διαχλευάζοντες), which, without altering the sense, makes the expression more emphatic and intensive. *Full*, literally *filled*, saturated, sated, the idea of excess being necessarily suggested by the Greek word. *New wine* might be more exactly rendered *sweet wine*, as the Greek word properly denotes sweetness, and although sometimes applied in classic Greek to the fresh grape-juice before fermentation, is also used of those fermented wines, in which the sweetness was retained by a peculiar process, and some of which were unusually strong. The very phrase, *drunk with sweet wine*, is employed by Athenæus. The same Greek word is used in the Septuagint version of Job 32, 19, to represent the common Hebrew term for wine, in a connection where the reference to fermentation is not only certain but essential to the meaning. But apart from these authorities, the reference to new wine, in the sense of unfermented must or grape-juice, would be here a gross absurdity. The very nature of the case, as well as Peter's answer, shows the charge to have been not merely that of drinking but of being drunk. Some have used this as an argument against the actual diversity of languages, which could not (it is said) have been ascribed to drunkenness. But even supposing the charge to have been serious, what could more naturally have suggested it, than the very mixture of strange languages, which to the great mass of these native Jews must have been an unintelligible jargon? It is indeed a strong though incidental proof of authenticity, that this great miracle is represented as affecting these two classes in so different a manner, yet so perfectly in keeping with their situation. A fictitious writer might very naturally have described them as affected all alike, forgetting that while every additional diversity of dialect would furnish a fresh proof of divine agency to some among the foreign witnesses, the same cause would render the whole scene still more confused and apparently absurd to the resident or native Jews. This necessary difference between the cases would suffice to account for the levity with which the latter class regarded the whole matter, without referring it to any radical diversity of character, which cannot be historically shown to have existed. Language which conveys no meaning almost invariably excites a ludicrous emotion in the hearer. Another observation to be made upon this charge of drunkenness is, that it affords a further refutation of the notion entertained by Cyprian and Erasmus, that the miracle was wrought upon the ears of the spectators, so that each thought he heard his vernacular language. For in that case, these Jerusalemites would have understood what they heard, and could have had no pretext for the charge of drunkenness, unless it had reference merely to the excitement and enthusiasm of the speakers. It was this frivolous aspersion, rather than the serious inquiries of the devout Jews, that gave occasion to the great apostolical discourse which follows.

14. But Peter, standing up with the eleven, lifted up his voice and said unto them, Ye men of Judea, and all (ye) that dwell at Jerusalem, be this known unto you, and hearken to my words.

The Apostles repudiate the charge of drunkenness and explain the true nature of the whole occurrence. Peter, as usual, is the spokesman, acting no doubt by divine suggestion, and with the tacit acquiescence of his brethren. (See above, on 1, 15, and below, on 5, 3. 29.) *With the eleven*, himself being the twelfth. (See above, on 1, 26.) The meaning is not that they came together when they heard of the aspersion cast upon them, but that they repelled it on the spot, and as oon as it was uttered. *Standing up* is, in several of the lder English versions, rendered *stepped forth*, or came forward. But the proper sense is that of standing up or rising, as a preliminary to the act of public speaking. The particu lar mention of this gesture is a favourite idiom of Luke's. (See below, 5, 20. 11, 13. 17, 22. 25, 18. 27, 21, and compare Luke 18, 11. 40.) *With the eleven* naturally, though not necessarily, implies, that the eleven stood up with him. It may indeed mean only that they kept together as one body; but in either case, the idea of unity and concert is essential. They not only were, but were seen to be, governed by one purpose, acting under one commission. It was important that Peter should be recognized as not speaking in his own name, but as representing the whole body, which was itself the representative of Christ, in the organization and administration of his church or kingdom. That what follows was a speech or sermon, not a private and informal talk to a few chance hearers, is implied, not only in the act of rising, but in that of lifting up his voice, or speaking so as to be heard by a great number. There is no need of diluting the full import of the phrase, so as to mean merely, he began to speak. *Said* is a very feeble version of the Greek verb, which is the same with that employed at the end of v. 4, and there explained to signify the solemn and authoritative utterance of something weighty and important in itself. *Men of Judea* is a similar expression to *Men of Galilee* in 1, 11, and strictly means *Men Jews* or *Jewish Men*. It has here a local rather than a religious sense, and is correctly rendered in the common version. It is nearly equivalent to native Jews or Hebrews. That the foreign Jews, however, were included in the object of address, is intimated by the wider phrase, *and all inhabiting Jerusalem*, which does not mean the foreign Jews expressly or distinctively, but comprehends them with the natives under one generic formula. That the Greek verb does not of itself mean either permanent or temporary residence, see above, on v. 5. *Be this known unto you* is equivalent, in modern phrase, to saying, I have something to communicate or make known, with an implication that it is not without interest and importance to the hearers. The formula is found in this book only. (See below, 4, 10. 13, 38. 28, 28.) The remaining introductory phrase, *hearken to my words*, bespeaks attention to what follows, with a slight suggestion that it may prove to be something not only unexpected but unwelcome. Analogous, in this point, are the words which Shakspeare puts into the mouth of Brutus, when about to justify the death of Cesar. "Hear me for my cause, and be silent that you may hear." The word translated *hearken* (Vulg. *auribus percipite*) is a later Greek verb, unknown to the classics, and apparently formed in imitation of a Hebrew verb common in the Psalms, and usually rendered in our Bible, *give ear*. Both verbs are derived from the noun *ear*, which is probably the case likewise with the English *hear*. This introduction, though unstudied and entirely natural, is not without rhetorical merit and effect. The discourse itself, which follows, has peculiar interest, not only as the first in time, the earliest specimen of apostolical preaching, but also as a public exposition of the principles on which the church was to be organized, propounded at the organization itself. Though often repeated, and by some distinguished writers, it is far from being true, that this discourse consists simply and entirely of historical facts. How can this be a correct description of a passage, in which no less than three prophecies of the Old Testament are expounded and applied, with a formal refutation of a different exposition? The truth is that the mere historical facts, so far from making up the whole, are rather assumed or incidentally referred to, while the body of the discourse is argumentative and exegetical. In this, it resembles the first preaching generally, and is a model for our own, which ought not to be the telling of a story merely, but the logical and practical interpretation of the word of God. Another false view of this great discourse is that which makes it wholly desultory and even incoherent. Though informal, it is perfectly consecutive and even symmetrical in structure. It first repudiates the charge of drunkenness (14); then shows what had occurred to be the fulfilment of a signal prophecy (15–21); and then demonstrates the Messiahship of Jesus (22–36.) The details, as well as the transitions, of this scheme, and its coherent unity, will be pointed out as we proceed.

15. For these are not drunken, as ye suppose, seeing it is but the third hour of the day.

This is the negative part of the defence, or the denial of the false solution, which had been suggested, of the gift of tongues. Brief as it is, it includes three distinguishable points. The first is the categorical denial, or direct repudiation of the odious charge. *These men are not drunken*, i. e. *drunk*, the form of the adjective when absolutely used, while *drunken* is usually followed by the noun. The next point is an indirect suggestion that the charge was groundless and gratuitous, a mere assumption without proof or reason. This is the full force of the phrase, *as ye suppose*, or rather, *assume*, take for granted. For the primary meaning of the Greek verb, as applied to bodily motion, see above, on 1, 9. Its metaphorical or secondary sense of *taking up* an opinion, or *assuming* a fact, especially without proof, is of frequent occurrence in Herodotus, Xenophon, and Plato. The third point is an argument or proof, that they could not be drunk, drawn from the time of day. The ancient Hebrews reckoned the day from evening to evening (Gen. 1, 5. Lev. 23, 32), and are thought to have divided the day and night, i. e. the varying periods of light and darkness, each into three watches. (See Judges 7, 19. Ex. 14, 24. 1 Sam. 11, 11. Lam. 2, 19.) The later Jews adopted the Roman division of the night into four watches (Matt. 14, 25. Luke 12, 38. Mark 6, 48. 13, 35), and of the day into twelve hours (John 11, 9), reckoning from sunrise or, as an average, from six o'clock. The third hour, according to this computation, would fall between what we call eight and nine. At or about this time of day the effusion of the Holy Ghost took place, and from this circumstance Peter seems to argue that what they had now witnessed could not be the effect of intoxication. But wherein does the proof lie, or the argument consist? Who was to determine when intoxication could begin, or to forbid its being reckoned as the cause of its apparent effects? Some suppose an allusion to religious usage. The third hour, in the sense explained above, was the first of the three stated hours of daily prayer, observed by the Jews, without express divine command, but probably in imitation of David and Daniel (Ps. 55, 17. Dan. 6, 10. 13.) The other two hours of prayer are also mentioned in this book. (See below, 3, 1. 10, 9.) From this fact, and the alleged Jewish practice of abstaining from all food and drink until this hour, some explain the clause as meaning that the charge of drunkenness was inconsistent with their character and habits as devout Jews. But the charge itself virtually called in question their pretensions to this character, and could not therefore be disproved by claiming it. A much more obvious and simple explanation is that which supposes the third hour to be mentioned, not as an hour of prayer, but simply as an early hour of the day at which intoxication would imply the most intemperate and reckless habits. A striking parallel is furnished by a passage in one of Cicero's Philippics, where he characterizes the license practised at

Antony's villa by saying that they revelled there from nine o'clock. (*Ab hora tertia bibebatur, ludebatur, vomebatur.*) But still it may be asked, if such things were done, why might they not be done in this case; and how could a mere reference to the early hour be an answer to the implied charge of early revels? The answer to this question seems to be, that although such intemperance was possible, it was credible only in the case of habitual and reckless drunkards (1 Th. 5, 7), and the imputation of this character to Peter and his brethren carried its refutation with it. The clause may then be paraphrased as follows. 'As to the charge of drunkenness, it refutes itself; for unless you mean to class us with the lowest revellers and debauchees, which all who see us see to be absurd, it is inconceivable that all of us should be already drunk at this early hour of the day.' If to any the Apostle's reasoning, in answer to this charge, should still seem inconclusive, let it be observed that he does not undertake a formal refutation of so frivolous an accusation, which may not have been seriously intended even by its authors, but merely makes use of it in a single sentence, as an introduction or transition to the true solution of this wonderful phenomenon, contained in the next sentence. This view of the connection may be rendered clear by paraphrase as follows. 'Passing by the charge of drunkenness, as too absurd to be repelled except by simply reminding you how early in the morning it still is, I now proceed to tell you the true meaning of the strange things which you have just seen and heard.' Here again the transition is so natural and easy, yet so logical and suited to the speaker's purpose, that it does not more effectually clear him from the charge of rhetorical artifice or tricks of speech, than it does from the more common one of artlessness, not only in this good sense, but in that of rudeness and unskilfulness, a helpless incapacity to use language as the vehicle of thought with clearness and coherence. Let those who are continually thus describing the inspired writers learn to look at home.

16. But this is that which was spoken by the Prophet Joel.

The negative defence is followed by the positive; the false explanation by the true. The sum of it is: this is not intoxication, it is inspiration, and the fulfilment of a signal prophecy. In all such cases, it is necessary, first, to identify the passage; then, to ascertain the form of the quotation; and finally, to fix the sense in which it is applied. The first question is determined here, partly by the mention of the Prophet's name, omitted in some copies, manuscript and printed, but without sufficient reason; and more completely by the actual existence of the passage quoted in the text of the Old Testament. The Greek preposition (διά), more distinctly than the English (*by*), denotes the instrumental cause or agent, and might be correctly rendered *through*. 'Spoken by God through (or by means of) the Prophet Joel.' The whole form of expression implies, that Peter's hearers were familiar with the name of Joel, not only as a writer, but an inspired writer, or Old Testament Prophet. The personal history of Joel is unknown and unimportant with respect to the interpretation of this passage. The precise date of his writings is disputed, but the best authorities refer them to the reign of Uzziah, at least eight centuries before the date of these events. The passage quoted is the first five verses of the third chapter in the Hebrew text, corresponding to the last five verses of the second chapter in the Septuagint and English versions. The words are quoted from the former, but with several variations. Some suppose this passage to have formed a part of the temple-service on the day of Pentecost, and allege that it is still so used by the Caraites or anti-talmudical Jews. But this usage, even if sufficiently attested, may be of later date.

17. And it shall come to pass in the last days, saith God, I will pour out of my Spirit upon all flesh; and your sons and your daughters shall prophesy; and your young men shall see visions, and your old men shall dream dreams.

It shall be, happen, or come to pass, is the common mode of introducing a particular prediction in the Old Testament. The time of the event is indefinitely stated in the Hebrew, *afterwards*, here rendered somewhat more specific by the paraphrase, *in the last days*, i. e. in the days of the Messiah, or in the last days of the old dispensation, the very days of which we are now reading. *Saith God* is neither in the Hebrew text nor in the Septuagint version, but supplied by the Apostle, to remind his hearers who is speaking, not only as a means of making the words quoted more impressive and authoritative, but of making them intelligible, by supplying the subject of the sentence, which is here detached from its connection. For the use of pouring, as a figure for abundant gifts and influences, see above, on 1, 5, and compare Prov. 1, 23. Isai. 44, 3. Zech. 12, 10. Instead of the original expression, *pour out my Spirit*, the Septuagint, followed by Peter, has the partitive form, *of my Spirit*, intended to suggest, as some have thought, that the gift was not exhausted, that the residue of the Spirit was with God (Mal. 2, 15), and would still be bestowed upon the church. *All flesh* is an idiomatic Hebrew phrase, sometimes denoting the whole animal creation (Gen. 6, 17), but more usually all mankind (Gen. 6, 12.) To *prophesy* has here its usual sense, to speak by inspiration, or under a special divine influence. The idea of prediction or foretelling is not the primary etymological sense, nor even the prevailing one in usage. The collective or aggregate expression, *all flesh*, is defined and strengthened by the specific mention of both sexes, various conditions, and all ages. *Sons and daughters* is explained by some as a comprehensive description of the whole race, but there seems to be no reason for departing from its strict sense as denoting the two sexes, male and female offspring. Thus understood, the phrase would seem to confirm the previous conclusion, that the gift of tongues had been imparted to the whole assembly, including men and women. The objection that the gift could not be exercised by women, who are commanded to keep silence in the church (1 Cor. 14, 34. 35. 1 Tim. 2, 11. 12), applies only to the permanent use of this miraculous endowment in the service of the church, and not to its primary exhibition as a sign or as a symbol. (See above, on v. 4.) The next two clauses of the prophecy are inverted without any visible design, unless it be, as some have thought, to render prominent the case of the apostles, who were, for the most part, in the prime of life. If any distinction was intended to be made between the parallel expressions, *dreams* and *visions*, the latter may denote day-dreams, waking visions, and the former visions seen in sleep, or dreams properly so called. As we do not read of any such effects at Pentecost, the terms of the prediction must have been understood by the apostles as figures or types of extraordinary spiritual influence, and not as the precise forms in which the promise was to be fulfilled. The prominence given to miraculous endowments is to be explained by their peculiar fitness to evince the reality and designate the subject of the spiritual operation, and not by their intrinsic superiority to what are called the ordinary influences of the Spirit, and which are really included in the promise of the Prophet as here quoted.

18. And on my servants and on my handmaidens I will pour out in those days of my Spirit; and they shall prophesy.

This is a repetition of the promise in the verse preceding, with a simple substitution of male and female servants for sons and daughters. As the antecedent probabilities are adverse to a sheer tautology, without qualification or addition, we must look upon this verse as designed to add diversity of rank to that of age and sex. The word translated *and* at the beginning of the sentence, is not the simple copulative (καί), as in the Septuagint, but a strengthened form (καί γε), implying an emphatic addition to what was said before, q. d. nay more, not only sons and daughters but servants and handmaidens. Not only shall the weaker sex, but the humblest of both sexes, be admitted to participate in this great honour. The Greek words corresponding to *servants* and *handmaidens* are masculine and feminine forms of the word which properly denotes a slave. The repetition of the partitive form (*of my Spirit*) shows that it was not accidental or unmeaning in the verse preceding. The last clause, *they shall prophesy*, is added by the Apostle to remove all ambiguity and doubt as to the effusion of the Spirit promised. As if he had said: 'the Spirit which I thus pour out will be one of prophetic inspiration.' This precise specification, in a case where general and comprehensive terms might seem appropriate, arises from the fact that this was the precise form in which the promise was fulfilled at Pentecost. The gift of tongues was not a mere philological contrivance for the use of public speakers, but a real inspiration, extending to the matter as well as the expression, so that those who shared in it were heard, not only speaking foreign tongues, but in those tongues declaring the wonderful or glorious works of God. (See above, on v. 11.)

19. And I will show wonders in heaven above, and

signs in the earth beneath; blood and fire and vapour of smoke.

To the promise Peter adds the threatening which attends it in the prophecy, not merely for the purpose of rounding the period or completing the quotation, but as a solemn warning to his hearers that, as the promise had begun to be fulfilled, the execution of the threatening might be no less confidently looked for. Or perhaps the true view of the matter is, that this is not a threatening in the strict sense, as distinguished from a promise, but a prophecy of great revolutionary changes, clothed in familiar figures drawn from the prophetic dialect of scripture. (Compare Isai. 13, 10, 34, 4, etc.) The revolution thus foreshadowed was that through which Israel was to pass at the change of dispensations, and of which the outpouring of the Spirit at Pentecost was a certain premonition. *Wonders* and *signs* are absolute and relative expressions for the same thing, viz. miracles. The first word, both in Greek and English, represents them as they are in themselves, portents or prodigies (Vulg. *prodigia*). The other indicates their use or purpose, as signs or proofs of something else, the divine existence, will, or presence, the divine legation of the prophets and apostles, or the truth of their official teachings. The word translated *show* properly means *give*, and is so rendered by Wiclif and the Rhemish version.

20. The sun shall be turned into darkness and the moon into blood, before that great and notable day of the Lord come.

These are prophetic figures for great and sudden revolutionary changes. (Compare Isai. 13, 10. 34, 4, etc.) Before that day, the change shall be as great as the dissolution or extinction of the heavenly bodies would be in the frame of nature. *Notable*, remarkable, extraordinary, corresponds to a Greek word ($ἐπιφανῆ$) meaning manifest, conspicuous, illustrious, and that to a Hebrew one (נורא) meaning feared or fearful. *The day of the Lord* is not only the day appointed and foretold by him, but his own day, in a more emphatic sense, a day appropriated to himself, to the execution of his purpose and the vindication of his honour. (See Isai. 2, 12.) The day meant is that great day of judicial visitation, which may be said to have begun with the destruction of Jerusalem by Titus, and is to end in what we call the Day of Judgment. The portentous sights described by Josephus and Tacitus as seen both by Jews and Romans during the last siege of Jerusalem, may be regarded as among the outward *signs* foretold, but not as the main subject of the prophecy, which is symbolical.

21. And it shall come to pass, that whosoever shall call on the name of the Lord shall be saved.

The Apostle closes his quotation with the Prophet's cheering assurance of salvation to every one who looks to and confides in the true Saviour. *It shall come to pass*, literally, *t shall be*, as given in all the older English versions except Cranmer's and King James's. (See above, on v. 17.) Invocation is here mentioned as an act of worship. Even if the call meant be only a call for help, it implies omniscience and almighty power in the object of address. (See below, on 7, 59. 9, 14. 21. 22, 16.) The forensic usage of the same Greek verb to denote an appeal (as in 25, 11. 12. 21. 25. 26, 32. 28, 19) implies a recognition of judicial sovereignty. *Lord* corresponds, in the Septuagint version, to the Hebrew *Jehovah*, the incommunicable name of God, considered as the God of Israel. The constant application of the Greek equivalent (Κύριος) in the New Testament to Jesus Christ, is a strong proof of his divinity. For such an application of the prophecy this verse prepares the way, and at the same time for another great division of the apostolical discourse.

22. Ye men of Israel, hear these words. Jesus of Nazareth, a man approved of God among you, by miracles, wonders, and signs, which God did by him in the midst of you, as ye yourselves also know;

It is universally agreed that Peter here introduces a new topic, or in other words, that this is the beginning of a new division of his speech, namely that in which he asserts and proves the Messiahship of Jesus. It seems to be commonly assumed, however, that the transition is abrupt and arbitrary, as if he had merely taken advantage of the charge against him and his brethren, to bring forward an entirely different subject. This view of the passage, however it may favour the idea, that a rational coherence is not to be looked for in the sacred writers, may be easily refuted by a simple statement of the true connection. Having met the charge of drunkenness, first briefly and negatively, by a flat denial and the suggestion of a single reason why it could not possibly be true (v. 15); then fully and affirmatively by representing what was thus ascribed to wine as the work of the Spirit promised ages before by an inspired prophet (16–18), he quotes from the same context a warning and a promise well adapted to excite the fears and hopes of those who heard him, and to turn their thoughts upon the practical question of their own salvation (19–21.) *Whosoever shall call upon the name of the Lord shall be saved.* But what Lord? Not the absolute Elohim, or the half-revealed Jehovah, of the old economy, as they might naturally have supposed. What Lord was meant then? Why the very man whom they had crucified, and whom, in the remainder of this sermon, he proves to be the true Messiah. This analysis is certainly as simple and natural as any other, while it gives a perfect continuity and unity to the discourse. According to it, the leading thoughts of the Apostle are as follows. This is not drunkenness but inspiration—it was predicted centuries ago—on the fulfilment of that promise is suspended your personal salvation—and the promised Saviour is the man whom you have crucified. No wonder that in introducing such a doctrine, the apostle takes a new start, and conciliates afresh the indulgence of his hearers. *Men of Israel* is not a merely local or genealogical description, but a formal recognition of their national and ecclesiastical character as representatives of the chosen people. As if he had said: 'Thus far I have addressed you as natives of Judea and professors of the true religion; but I now appeal to you still more emphatically, as belonging so the Israel of God, and in that capacity entreat you still to hear me.' *Hear these words* is one of those expressions which are almost universally slurred over in the reading, as mere expletives, unmeaning forms of speech, affording a transition from one topic to another, or intended to impart a sort of finish and completeness to the composition. But in multitudes of cases, these neglected formulas are pregnant and emphatic clauses, upon which depends the force, if not the meaning, of the context. In the case before us, the Apostle again intimates (as in the opening of the whole discourse, v. 14) that he expected contradiction and impatience upon their part. 'Who then is the true and only Saviour, by invoking whom you may escape destruction? In answering this question, I am under the necessity of shocking your most cherished prepossessions and convictions; but nevertheless hear me, inasmuch as this is a matter, not of idle speculation, but of life and death, a question of salvation and perdition.' Having thus prepared them for the introduction of an unexpected or at least unwelcome topic, he delays no longer, but with fine rhetorical effect, if not design, immediately names *Jesus,* as the theme of what he further has to say. *Jesus of Nazareth* (or *from Nazareth*) is the literal translation of a phrase used by the same apostle on a subsequent occasion. (See below, on 10, 38.) But here, and in every other case where it occurs in this book (3, 6. 4, 10. 6, 14. 22, 8. 26, 9), the original expression, though equivalent in sense, is somewhat different in form, and might be more exactly rendered, *Jesus the Nazarene.* The avoidance of this form by our translators is without apparent reason, and, though unimportant in itself, has the unfortunate effect of hiding or obscuring from the merely English reader the direct and intimate connection of this title with a difficult but interesting statement of Matthew (2, 23), which seems most probably to mean, that all or many of the prophecies of Christ's humiliation were summed up, as to substance, in his reputed birth and real residence at an obscure town of a despised province, and as to form or expression, in his being habitually called *The Nazarene.* Some suppose that there can here be no allusion to its reproachful or contemptuous import, because used by an apostle. But even when employed by Christ himself (as in 22, 8), the allusion to this usage is not only evident but prominent. 'I am that Nazarene, whose very home is a reproach to him, and whom thou Paul hast often cursed and scoffed at, by that hated name.' Thus too it is used by the Apostles, who appear to have delighted in recalling this opprobrious description and applying it to their master's highest exaltation, so that he reigns and triumphs by the very name which was expected to consign him to eternal infamy. In the case before us, it is not to be lost sight of, that the great Apostle, in propounding the unwelcome theme of his remaining argument, propounds it under this offensive form, not merely *Jesus,* but *Jesus of Nazareth, the Nazarene.* As if he had said: 'I may well entreat you still to hear me while I name the true and only Saviour; for the one whom I intend to name, is he whose name is already a proverb of reproach among you, and whom perhaps you have this very day reviled and derided as *the Nazarene.*' Having named him, as a person whom they well knew, he describes him as one, with whose pretensions and credentials they were all familiar. He speaks of him, not as an adventurer, or one whose character was yet to be established, but as one already *proved (to be) from God.* This is most probably the true sense of the phrase ambiguously rendered in our Bible, *approved of God.* The word *approved,* like the *approbatum* of the Vulgate, from which it seems to have been copied, was once used as a synonyme of *proved.* Webster quotes two instances from one line of Milton. "Wouldst thou *approve* thy constancy? *Approve* first thy obedience." But this sense is now obsolete, and the only idea which the word conveys here to a modern reader, is a false one, namely, that of moral approbation or approval. The idea meant to be conveyed is that of proof or attestation. This is not essentially affected by the different grammatical constructions which have been proposed. 'A man from God, attested (or accredited) by miracles, etc.' 'A man accredited from (i. e. by) God through miracles, etc.' 'A man accredited (or proved to be) from God by miracles, etc.' The words *from God* do not refer to the divinity of Christ, which would be otherwise expressed, and would here be out of place, at the beginning of a series of expressions all relating to our Lord's humiliation. *From God* expresses his divine legation, the commission or authority under which he acted as the teacher of mankind and the founder of a new religion. This commission was attested by his miracles, to which, besides the two terms used in v. 19 (*wonders* and *signs*), the Apostle here applies one meaning *powers, forces,* i. e. exhibitions or exertions of a power above that of man. The translation *miracles,* although it designates the proper objects, fails to distinguish the three terms applied to them, expressive of their source, their use, and their intrinsic quality, as *powers, signs,* and *wonders.* These miracles are then ascribed to God as the efficient cause, and to Christ as the instrumental agent, *which God did by him.* For the true sense of the preposition (διά), see above, on v. 16. This representation is entirely consistent with the proper deity of Christ, since he is really included under both descriptions, his human instrumentality being subject to his own divine agency, as well as to the Father's. It is also in keeping with that true subordination of the Son to the Father, which the Scriptures teach, and which the Church has always held fast, even when tempted to abjure it by the hope of leaving heresy without excuse. It is rendered necessary, in the case before us, by the speaker's purpose to exhibit our Lord in "the form of a servant" and a messenger from God. Observe the confidence with which Peter here appeals to the knowledge and the memory of his hearers. The attestations or credentials of Christ's ministry and mission had not been presented at a distance, or in a corner, but *in the midst of you* (ἐν μέσῳ ὑμῶν), sent or addressed directly *to you* (εἰς ὑμᾶς), as the parties to be convinced and satisfied. This last idea is less clearly expressed in the common version, *among you*. It is again suggested in the last words of the verse, where the appeal is a direct one to themselves, *as ye yourselves do know* (or *also know*.)

23. Him, being delivered by the determinate counsel and foreknowledge of God, ye have taken and by wicked hands have crucified and slain.

Him, i. e. the person thus described; a method of resumption not unusual after so long an interruption of the syntax. *Delivered*, not bestowed, as some explain the Greek word (ἔκδοτον), but in violation of its usage, which requires the meaning *given up*, surrendered. Some refer this to the treachery of Judas, but most readers and interpreters suppose it to express the divine act of giving Christ up to the mercy of his enemies, or, in other words, permitting him to suffer. The word translated *counsel* properly means *will*, as appears both from etymology and usage. *Determinate* is not *determined*, in the moral sense of resolute, intrepid, but *determined*, in the physical or proper sense of bounded, defined, settled, as opposed to what is vague, contingent, or indefinite. The dative may be either one of cause, *by the will*, or of rule and measure, *according to the will*, most probably the latter. The same relation of Christ's death to the divine decree is formally asserted in the prayer of the Apostles (4, 28), and less distinctly by our Lord himself (Luke 22, 22), in both which cases the expressions, although not identical, are very similar to those here used. *Ye have taken* might be more exactly rendered *ye took*, or rather *ye received*, as the correlative of *given up*, and not as denoting the original or independent act of taking. God gave him and they took him. What God permitted they performed. *By wicked hands* might seem to mean no more than *with wicked hands*, i. e. your own, which adds no new idea to the general one of murder expressed in the next clause. But as the word translated *wicked* (ἀνόμων), and which properly means *lawless*, is applied by Paul (1 Cor. 9, 21), in its primary etymological sense, to the heathen as *without law* or a written revelation of the divine will, some have understood the phrase to mean either *lawless* (i. e. *Gentile*) *hands*, or *hands of lawless ones* (i. e. Gentiles.) It seems no sufficient reason for preferring this construction, that the language is otherwise too harsh for the Apostle's purpose of conciliation, if not inconsistent with his own concession in 3, 17 below. The main design of his discourse was to convince them of their own guilt, and nothing tending to promote that end can be inconsistent with it. But a stronger reason for referring these expressions to the Gentiles is afforded by the fact that the oldest manuscripts and latest editors read *hand* (χειρός) for *hands* (χειρῶν), thus requiring the construction, *by the hand of lawless men*, and suggesting the idea of some secondary agency, through which the malice of the Jews was gratified. Now such an agency was that of Pilate and the Roman soldiers, the use of which was certainly a fearful aggravation of the crime of Israel, because they not only rejected and murdered their Messiah, but gave him up to the power of the Gentiles. (See below, on 4, 27.) The word translated *crucified* means properly *transfixed*, and is applied in the classics to impalement and to the fastening of human heads on poles or stakes. It may here be understood in the specific sense of *nailing* to the cross, and is perhaps contemptuously used, to aggravate the suicidal folly of the Jews, who, instead of welcoming their long expected Prince, took him and nailed him to a tree. We have here a curious instance of the variations even in the authorized editions of the Latin Vulgate. Those published in the last years of the sixteenth century translate this word *affligentes*, while those of later date expunge the interpolated letter and read *affigentes*. The original construction is, *having nailed* (or *crucified*) *ye slew*. This last verb (ἀνείλετε, ἀνείλατε) is a favourite with Luke, occurring twenty times in his two books, and only twice in the rest of the New Testament. It does not mean directly to *kill*, but to *despatch*, to *make away with*, English phrases which are constantly applied to murder, though they do not necessarily express it. It is clear from this verse that the guilt of those who murdered Christ was neither caused nor nullified by God's determinate counsel and foreknowledge. Even Chrysostom refers to the analogy of Joseph's case (comparing Gen. 45, 8 with 50, 20), as showing how consistent, both in scripture and experience, are the doctrine of God's sovereignty and that of human freedom and responsibility.

24. Whom God hath raised up, having loosed th pains of death, because it was not possible that he should be holden of it.

With their treatment of the Saviour he contrasts that of God himself. When God gave him up, they took him; but when they crucified him, God raised him. This is a favourite antithesis with Peter, and repeatedly recurs in his discourses. (See below, on 3, 14. 15. 4, 10. 5, 30. 31. 10, 39. 40.) The Greek verb (ἀνίστημι), in its active tenses, always means to raise up; from what or to what is determined by the context. It is applied to raising from the dead by Homer in the last book of the Iliad (551). *Loosing pains* is an unusual combination, perhaps arising from the use of the second word (ὠδῖνας) in the Septuagint, to represent a Hebrew one, which has the double sense of *cord* and *sorrow*. (Compare Isai. 13, 8. with Ps. 18, 5.) Thus the two Greek nouns may have become associated, and their corresponding verbs convertible. The very combination here used appears also in the Septuagint version of Ps. 39, 2. It is the less unnatural because the verb to *loose* has a figurative sense (relax) no less appropriate to pains than its proper sense (untie) to cords. The Greek noun strictly means the pains of parturition, which are often used as figures of intense but temporary suffering. (See Isai. 26, 17. John 16, 21, etc.) *Impossible*, both physically, as a condition inconsistent with his deity, and morally, because the divine plan and purpose made his resurrection necessary. The verb (κρατεῖσθαι) which in classical Greek denotes conquest or superiority, in the New Testament always means to hold or to be holden fast, either in a literal or figurative sense, but never perhaps without some trace of its original and proper import, as for instance in the case before us, where the sense is that he could not be permanently held fast by death as a captive or a conquered enemy.

25. For David speaketh concerning him, I foresaw the Lord always before my face; for he is on my right hand, that I should not be moved.

The alleged impossibility is now confirmed by the testimony of David, which is also cited as a further proof of our Lord's messiahship. Besides the evidence afforded by his miracles (22) and resurrection (24), he was the only subject in which a certain signal prophecy had been or could be verified (25–32.) For the sake of the connection the Apostle quotes the entire passage (Ps. 16, 8–11,) but the proof of his position is contained in the last part of it. This may account for some apparent incoherence of the clauses beginning with the word *for*. The first of these, however, has respect to the assertion at the end of the preceding verse. It could not be, for he had said it should not be. The passage is quoted in the Septuagint version, almost without variation. The sixteenth Psalm, here ascribed to David, is so described also in the title of the Psalm itself, nor is there any internal evidence of later date. *Concerning him*, literally, *to* or *towards him*, i. e. in reference or relation to him. The Greek phrase (εἰς αὐτόν) has the same sense in Luke 19, 9. Eph. 5, 32. *Foresaw*, in English, has respect to time, and means *saw beforehand;* but the verb here has respect to place and means *saw before me*, which idea is also expressed by the next phrase (ἐνώπιόν μου.) This repetition is not found in the Hebrew, where the verb means to *set* or *place*. The general sense, in either case, is that of constant recognition or remembrance. *At the right hand* is not only a post of honour, but a position of defence or protection. (See Ps. 73, 23. 121, 5.) *That I should not be moved* is a slight modification of the simple future used in the original. The Greek verb (σαλευθῶ) is applied both to bodily and mental agitation (17, 13. 2 Thess. 2, 2.)

26. Therefore did my heart rejoice and my tongue was glad; moreover also, my flesh shall rest in hope.

Therefore, on account of this assurance of divine protection. *My tongue* corresponds to *my glory* in Hebrew, and may be regarded as a very ancient exposition of that phrase preserved in the Septuagint version, and according to which the tongue (i. e. the faculty of speech) is regarded as the glory of the human frame, or as the instrument of the divine

74 ACTS 2, 26. 27. 28.

praise. *Moreover also* introduces an emphatic addition, as in v. 18. Not only this, but more, my very flesh, etc. *Flesh* seems here to mean the body as distinguished from the soul. The verb translated *rest* originally means to pitch a tent, encamp, and then to sojourn for a time; that mode of life being constantly opposed to permanent abode in houses. *Hope* is hardly an adequate equivalent to the Hebrew word (בֶּטַח), which in this connection denotes confident security. The consecution of the tenses, *did rejoice, was glad, shall rest*, is closely copied from the Hebrew.

27. Because thou wilt not leave my soul in hell, neither wilt thou suffer thine Holy One to see corruption.

Because, or *that*, introducing the ground or subject of the confidence expressed in the preceding verse. *In hell*, literally, *to* or *into*, corresponding to a Hebrew phrase, which means not merely to *leave in* but to *abandon* or give up to. The Geneva Bible has *in grave*. *Hell*, in its old and wide sense of the unseen world (*hades*), the world of spirits, the state of the soul separated from the body, without any reference to happiness or misery. The essential meaning is, thou wilt not leave my soul and body separate. *Suffer*, literally, *give*, grant, permit, a use of the verb also found in Xenophon and Homer. (See below, on 10, 40.) *Holy One* answers to a Hebrew word which properly denotes an object of the divine favour, but suggests the idea of a corresponding character. In both senses, it is peculiarly appropriate to Christ. *See corruption*, or experience dissolution. Compare the phrase *see death*, Luke 2, 26. There are two Hebrew nouns of the same form (שַׁחַת) but of different derivation, one denoting the grave and the other putrefaction. The first would here be false, if not unmeaning.

28. Thou hast made known to me the ways of life; thou shalt make me full of joy with thy countenance.

The gist of the quotation was contained in the preceding verse. The conclusion of the psalm is added to express the same idea still more strongly by contrast. There is but one verb in the Hebrew of this verse, and that a future, *thou shalt make me know*. Instead of the second verb, the Hebrew has an abstract noun, *satiety* or *fulness*, which may either be governed by the verb at the beginning, or construed with the verb *is*, as in the English version (of Ps. 16, 11.) *With thy countenance* is a literal translation of a phrase which means, however, *in thy presence*. The last clause of the psalm is omitted, as unnecessary to the speaker's purpose. It is also to be borne in mind, that as all devout Jews were familiar with the passage, and could easily supply what was omitted, it mattered less to what length the quotation was extended.

29. Men (and) brethren, let me freely speak unto you of the Patriarch David, that he is both dead and buried, and his sepulchre is with us unto this day.

The respectful and conciliatory compellation, *men and brethren* (see above, on 1, 16), does not indicate a change of subject here, the connection with what goes before being as close and intimate as possible. But this form of address implies again that he had need of their indulgence, or had something to say which might offend their prejudices. The same thing is suggested by what follows, *let me speak*, or retaining the form of the original, (*it is* or *let it be*) *permitted* (lawful or allowable) *to say to you with boldness* (παῤῥησίας) or freedom of speech, implying that what he said might be considered too free, or not entirely consistent with becoming reverence for the *patriarch* or founder of the royal family. The same title is applied in the New Testament to Abraham (Heb. 7, 4) and to the sons of Jacob as the fathers of the twelve tribes (Acts 7, 8.) The Rhemish version of the next clause is much better, *that he died and was buried*. There is then no tautology in adding that *his sepulchre*, memorial or monument, *is with us*, or *among us*, i. e. in the city and not merely in the suburbs, or more generally, in the country, near us, and in our possession. It could be still identified in the reign of Adrian, if not in the days of Jerome, but has since been lost sight of. But wherein lay the boldness or presumption of asserting this familiar and notorious fact? How could any one deny, that David had died and been buried, or be shocked by hearing it affirmed? This question is connected with the drift and structure of the whole passage. It was not the fact of David's death and burial, at which Peter expected them to stumble, but at the conclusion which he meant them to draw from it, and which is not expressed. That conclusion was, that this remarkable prediction, which they were no doubt accustomed to apply to David, could not apply to him at all, but must have reference to another. This was a doctrine sufficiently at variance with their prepossessions to account for Peter's so respectfully asking leave to state it. But what is the reasoning by which he reaches this conclusion? It is this, that as the prophecy declares that the speaker's soul should not continue separate from his body, nor his body itself experience dissolution, it could not apply to David, *for he did die and was buried*, and had long since mouldered in the grave, still designated by a well-known monument among them. Precisely the same argument, but more concisely stated, is employed by Paul in his first apostolical discourse on record. (See below, on 13, 35–37.) This express and argumentative denial, that the words can be applied to David, excludes not only the typical but also the generic method of interpretation, which was adopted in 1, 20 above. At all events, the words cannot be understood of both in one and the same sense, consistently with Peter's declaration; and the only sense in which they are true of David, that of future resurrection, was wholly irrelevant to Peter's proof, that Jesus was the Messiah of the prophecies. In order to preserve what seems to be the obvious allusion of the Psalmist to his own case, some eminent interpreters suppose the words to be appropriate to David only as he was in Christ, represented by him and a member of his body. But how could it be said, even on this hypothesis, that David's soul and body were not permanently severed, and that his body did not see corruption? Whereas this, as Peter afterwards affirms, was literally true of Jesus and of him alone.

30. Therefore, being a Prophet, and knowing that God had sworn with an oath to him, that of the fruit of his loins, according to the flesh, he would raise up Christ to sit on his throne;

Since David, then, was not and could not be himself the subject of this prophecy, who was? A person altogether different and posterior by many ages. This of itself was not incredible to those who knew that David was a *Prophet*, in the strict as well as in the wider sense, i. e. endowed by inspiration with a knowledge of the future. This general description is then followed by a reference to a specific promise, that contained in 2 Sam. 7, 12–16, and repeated in Ps. 89, 3. 4. 132, 11, forming the basis of all the Messianic Psalms, and frequently referred to in the other prophecies. Its lowest sense is that of mere unbroken succession; but this is evidently not the whole, from the extraordinary gratitude expressed by David, and from his singular language in 2 Sam. 7, 19 (compared with 1 Chr. 17, 17), where it seems to be implied, if not expressed, that this was not a personal, nor even a national assurance, but a universal one concerning the whole race. The same thing is clear from the fact that this promise constitutes a link, which would otherwise be wanting, in the chain of Messianic Prophecies, by applying specifically to the house of David, what had been successively applied to those of Seth, Shem, Abraham, Isaac, Jacob, Judah. Several of the oldest manuscripts and latest critical editions omit the words, *according to the flesh would raise up Christ*, so that the clause reads, *knowing that God had sworn with an oath to him that of the fruit of his loins (one) should sit upon his throne*. Besides the external evidence in favour of this reading, it relieves the text from an enfeebling and embarrassing anticipation of what follows in the next verse. There the Apostle finally identifies the person of whom David wrote. Here he is only showing, in the general and in the way of introduction, that David might, without absurdity, be understood as speaking of a person different from himself and long posterior, because he was a prophet, and because he had received a most explicit promise, sanctioned by the oath of God, that he should have perpetual succession on the throne, a promise which had been already broken, if restricted to his natural descendants.

31. He seeing this before, spake of the resurrection of Christ, that his soul was not left in hell, neither his flesh did see corruption.

Having shown that David could not mean himself, and that he might mean one who was to live long after him, the Apostle positively and authoritatively tells them whom he did mean. He referred not to his own still future resurrection—the only sense in which he could have said this of himself—but to another resurrection, future when he wrote, but now already past, and therefore furnishing at once the explanation and fulfilment of the prophecy. This was the resurrection of *Christ*, not as a personal but as an official title, *the Messiah*, the Anointed One, the Prophet, Priest, and King of Israel, of whom the ancient prophets, priests, and kings were merely representatives, filling his place until he came, and for whose coming the whole race had been impatiently looking for a course of ages. Not content with saying simply that he spoke of the Messiah's resurrection, Peter shuts out all evasion and mistake by repeating the *ipsissima verba* of the prophecy in question and applying them to Christ, of whom alone it was predicted, and of whom alone it is historically true, that his soul was not left disembodied after death, and that his body, though it died, was not corrupted.

32. This Jesus hath God raised up, whereof we are all witnesses.

But one more step was wanting to complete this process of triumphant argument, and that step is here taken. It was not enough to show, as Peter had done, that the prophecy could not relate to David, or that it might relate to one long after him, or even that it did relate to the Messiah, unless he could identify the individual. The importance of distinguishing between our Lord's personal name and his official title is peculiarly apparent here, where the neglect of it converts into a mere tautology the last link of a concatenated argument. What he said in the preceding verse was, that David spake of the Messiah's resurrection. What he here says is, that this *Messiah* was no other than the *Jesus* whom they crucified. Why so? Because in him, and him alone, the prophecy has been fulfilled. The Messiah was to rise from the dead—Jesus of Nazareth has risen from the dead—therefore the two must be identical. But where is the proof that Jesus rose? The evidence is twofold, human and divine. God bore witness in the very act of raising him. *This Jesus hath God raised up.* We bear witness of the same thing, not only the Apostles, whose primary function was to testify of this event (1, 8. 22), but a multitude of others who had seen him since his resurrection (1 Cor. 15, 6.)

33. Therefore, being by the right hand of God exalted, and having received of the Father the promise

of the Holy Ghost, he hath shed forth this which ye now see and hear.

Having thus identified the subject of the sixteenth psalm, first negatively with a person different from the writer, then positively with the Messiah, and then personally with the Nazarene whom they had crucified, he now describes the present state and employments of the glorious though despised Redeemer. His humiliation being past, and its design accomplished, he is now *exalted*, lifted up, or raised on high, both in a local sense, i. e. in heaven, and in the sense of freedom from all suffering and superiority to all created powers, whether friendly or adverse. Compare the same Apostle's language in 1 Pet. 3, 22, and that of Paul in Eph. 1, 20–22. The *right hand* is a scriptural figure for active power. In a local sense, it is the post of honour. Either of these ideas would be here appropriate, exalted *by* God's right hand, as the instrument, or *to* his right hand, as the place of exaltation. In favour of the former is the Greek usage of the dative case (δεξιᾷ) which rarely denotes place, but often means or instrument. In favour of the other is the use of *right hand* in the passage quoted in the next verse. After all that has been said against the assumption of a double sense, as contrary to nature and the very use of words, there are multitudes of phrases in all languages which, though intended to convey one idea directly, not only may but must suggest another. Thus the hearers of Peter, upon this occasion, could not, without a process of reflection, separate the two familiar senses of *God's right hand* from each other. The only question is, which is the primary and which the secondary meaning; and this question is of little exegetical importance here, because both are so agreeable to fact and to the context. It was *by* as well as *to* God's right hand that our Lord had been exalted, i. e. by the exertion of divine power, and to the enjoyment of divine honours. Besides this general participation in the honours of the Godhead, Peter mentions a specific gift bestowed by the Father on the Son as Mediator, and by him upon his Church. The *promise* may be put for the thing promised, as in 1, 4, but with this distinction, that the genitive in that case indicates the giver, but in this the gift itself. Or *promise* may be taken in its proper sense, and the performance sought in the ensuing clause. In favour of the first construction, though apparently less simple, is the fact that the Son, and not the Father, is the agent in the last clause. *Having received of the Father the Holy Spirit previously promised, he has shed forth,* i. e. poured out, a figure implying both abundance and descent from above, *this* (*Spirit*), or more probably, *this* (*gift*), as Cranmer renders it, *this* (*influence*), *which ye now see and hear.* The Rhemish version marks the reference to the Spirit by the singular combination, *this whom,* copied from the Vulgate (*hunc quem.*) Some refer the two verbs to the acts and gestures of the disciples and to the gift of tongues respectively. But why should the sight of the fiery tongues be excluded, which in all probability was not confined to the disciples? On the whole, however, such exact distinctions are superfluous, the two senses or perceptions being mentioned simply to include all that they had witnessed. Instead of *now,* some manuscripts and editors read *both,* without a change of sense. By thus ascribing the phenomenon, which had occasioned his discourse, to Jesus, Peter completes the picture of his master's exaltation, and at the same time, comes back to the point from which he started, by a natural yet masterly transition, showing any thing but want of skill or helpless incoherence.

34, 35. For David is not ascended into the heavens, but he saith himself, The Lord said unto my Lord, Sit thou on my right hand, until I make thy foes thy footstool.

Having shown the resurrection of Christ to be the subject of an ancient prophecy, he now proves the same thing of his exaltation. The argument is rendered still more parallel and uniform by drawing the proof from the same part of the Old Testament. The passage cited is the first verse of Psalm 110, which, like Psalm 16 above, is declared to be inapplicable to David. The same thing had been previously affirmed by Christ himself (Matt. 22, 41–46), but on a different ground, to wit, that David calls him Lord or Sovereign. Here the ground is the same as in the previous exposition of Ps. 16, to wit, that the prophecy never was fulfilled in David. It could only be fulfilled in one who had ascended into heaven and sat down on the right hand of God. But no one pretended or imagined that David had so done; whereas Christ did thus ascend and reign, as the Apostle had affirmed in the preceding verse. Here then were two signal Messianic Prophecies, universally recognized as such and universally ascribed to David, neither of which could be applied to David as its subject, both of which must have respect to the Messiah, and both of which had been fulfilled in Jesus! The apparent play upon words in the phrase, *The Lord said to my Lord*, is found only in the Greek and other versions. The original expression is, *Jehovah said to my Lord*. The strong expression in the last clause of v. 35 for total subjugation may be borrowed from an actual usage of ancient warfare. (See Josh. 10, 24.) The exact form of the original is copied in the Rhemish version, *the footstool of thy feet*.

36. Therefore let all the house of Israel know assuredly, that God hath made that same Jesus, whom ye have crucified, both Lord and Christ.

This is the conclusion which the speaker draws from his whole argument, or rather which he leaves the house of Israel to draw for themselves. (See above, on v. 29.) The prefatory formula is not to be neglected, any more than in v. 22 above. It refers the decision of the question to the Jewish Church itself, but, by the use of the phrase, *let it know*, suggests that all dispute is at an end, that nothing now remains but to accept the only possible conclusion. This is indicated also by the qualifying adverb, *assuredly*, or *most certainly* (Wiclif), or *for a surety* (Tyndale). According to strict rule and usage, the phrase translated *all the house* means rather *every house* (or *family*) *of Israel*. But as there is great license with respect to the insertion of the article, which constitutes the difference of meaning here, the common version is substantially correct. The Greek word ($\mathit{\dot{\alpha}\sigma\varphi\alpha\lambda\tilde{\omega}\varsigma}$) corresponds in etymology, and partly in its usage, to *infallibly*, i. e. without the fear or possibility of error. The common version follows Tyndale and Cranmer in a transposition of the last clause, which is not only needless, but injurious to the emphasis and beauty of the sentence. The Greek collocation, as retained by Wiclif, the Geneva Bible, and the Rhemish version, closes the sentence with the words, *this Jesus whom ye crucified*, which has been quaintly but expressively described as the sting in the end of the discourse. Besides the loss of this peculiar beauty, the inversion has occasioned the omission of a pronoun in the clause immediately preceding. The literal translation is, *God made him Lord and Christ*, or still more closely, *both Lord and Christ him,hath God made—this Jesus whom ye crucified.* The *him* is commonly assumed to be superfluous (as in the Greek of Matt. 8, 1. 5.) But this is an hypothesis, seldom adopted now by the best writers, and only admissible in case of urgent exegetical necessity. Others go to the opposite extreme by making it mean *Lord himself* in allusion to the double *Lord* of v. 34 and Ps. 110, 1. 'The Lord who said to David's Lord, Sit thou, etc. has made Jesus *himself* to be that Lord.' But this construction seems too artificial. A much more simple one, and intermediate between the omission and exaggeration of the pronoun, supposes the sense to be grammatically complete without the words *this Jesus,* etc., and these words to be superadded as an emphatic supplement or afterthought. *God hath made him (to be) both Lord and Christ—this Jesus whom ye crucified.* Here, as in v. 27 and elsewhere, it is important to take *Christ* in its official pregnant sense, as distinguished from a mere name or personal designation. In the latter sense, it would have been absurd to say that *God had made Jesus to be Christ,* i. e. to be himself; but it is highly significant, and expressive of a most important fact, to say that *God made Jesus to be the Christ* or *the Messiah.* The verb *made* in this clause may be understood in two ways; as expressing the divine decree or constitution, which attached the office of Messiah (as explained above on v. 31) to the person of Jesus the Nazarene; or as a declaratory act, that of setting forth, exhibiting our Lord in this high character. While the latter is undoubtedly implied, as an actual effect of the Saviour's exaltation, the former seems to be the thing immediately expressed, both by the verb *made,* which is never a mere synonyme of *showed, declared,* and by the whole connection, which requires that Peter should conclude by affirming, not only the divine attestation of our Lord's Messiahship, but also its divine authority and constitution. If this be the correct construction, *Lord* cannot mean a divine person, in allusion to the first *Lord* (or *Jehovah*) of v. 34, for the Father did not make the Son to be God, but must mean a mediatorial sovereign. This Christ was made to be, as well as the Messiah, and because he was Messiah, the two characters or offices being indivisible. The second person, *whom ye crucified,* especially in Greek, where the pronoun (ὑμεῖς) is peculiarly emphatic, carries home the fearful charge of having disowned and murdered the Messiah to his hearers, both as individuals, so far as they had taken part in that great crime, and as the representatives of Israel, the ancient church, or chosen people. If those critics who consider it their duty to exalt the inspiration of the sacred writers, by denying them all intellectual and literary merit, can improve upon the logic or the rhetoric of this great apostolical discourse, or even on the force and beauty of this peroration, let them do it or forever after hold their peace.

37. Now when they heard this, they were pricked in their heart, and said unto Peter and to the rest of the Apostles, Men (and) brethren, what shall we do?

The personal bearing of the whole discourse, but more particularly of its close, was not without effect upon the hearers. This effect is described by a strong but intelligible figure. *They were pricked*, pierced, perforated, not in body, but *in heart*, i. e. mind or soul, as distinguished from the body. The specific reference to the conscience is not suggested by this word, but by the context. Nor is that reference an exclusive one, the effect described extending to the whole mind, in the way of rational *conviction* no less than in that of *compunction*, a word of Latin origin, analogous in figurative import to the one which Luke here uses. Peter's argument, unanswerable on their own avowed and cherished principles, must have convinced them that the man whom they had crucified was the Messiah, and that if so they had been guilty, not only of judicial murder, but of blasphemy and treason to their rightful sovereign. Their desperate perplexity was well expressed by the question, *what shall we do?* i. e. what ought we to do, as a matter of duty, and what must we do, as a means of safety? Their putting this question *to the other* (or *remaining*) *apostles*, does not imply that these had also spoken, but only that Peter was considered as the spokesman of them all, and that they concurred in what he said, as well as that the twelve were still together and collectively accessible. It may also show the eagerness with which the awakened hearers crowded round these witnesses of the Messiah, repeating and reciprocating Peter's compellation, *Men and brethren*, as if conscious of some new and intimate relation, over and above that of mere Judaism, civil or religious.

38. Then Peter said unto them, Repent, and be

baptized, every one of you, in the name of Jesus Christ, for the remission of sins, and ye shall receive the gift of the Holy Ghost.

Although the question was addressed to all the Apostles, Peter again answered for the rest, in the language both of exhortation and of promise. Two distinct acts are required, one inward and one outward. The first verb, according to its etymology and classical usage, denotes afterthought, reflection, and then, by a natural association, change of mind, including both the judgment and the feelings. In the Greek of the New Testament, it is applied to change of mind in reference to moral good and evil, and more especially to one's own character and conduct. Regret or sorrow is only one of its ingredients. Evangelical repentance, in its widest sense, is an entire revolution of the principles and practice, of the heart and life. Nothing less than this, or what directly led to it, could be required of these Jewish bigots who had murdered Christ. The Geneva version, *amend your lives*, is too restricted and one-sided; that of Wiclif and the Rhemish, *do ye penance*, now conveys a false idea, but was originally only a close copy of the Vulgate (*pœnitentiam agite*), which was no doubt intended to convey precisely the same sense with the original. (See below, on 3, 19.) The change of mind required was to be attested by an outward act: *repent and be baptized*. Even granting that this Greek verb originally meant to immerse, i. e. to dip or plunge—a fact which is still earnestly disputed—it does not follow that this is essential to its meaning as a peculiar Christian term. On the contrary, analogy would lead us to suppose that, like other Greek terms thus adopted, it had undergone some modification of its etymological and primary import. As *presbyter* no longer suggests personal age, nor *deacon* menial service, nor *supper* a nocturnal meal, as necessary parts of their secondary Christian meaning, why should this one word be an exception to the general rule, and signify a mere mode of action as no less essential than the act itself? Even if it could be shown that immersion was the universal ancient practice, both of Jews and Christians, it would prove no more than the universal practice of reclining at meals and mixing wine with water. Least of all can it be shown that Peter, in requiring this vast crowd to be baptized upon the spot, intended to insist on their complete submersion under water as the essence of the rite prescribed. Besides the arbitrary character of such a supposition in itself, it is forbidden by the obvious analogy between water baptism and the baptism of the Holy Ghost, which, as we have already seen (on 1, 5), from the time of Moses to the time of Christ, had always been conceived of, not as an immersion, but as an affusion or effusion, an abundant pouring from above. With such associations, when the multitude were told to *be baptized*, they would of course think, not of the depth of the water, or their own position with respect to it, but of the water itself and of its application, as a well known token of repentance on the one hand, and of regeneration on the other. The first of these associations had already been established in most Jewish minds, if not by the baptism of proselytes, the antiquity of which is still disputed, yet by that of John the Baptist, which is expressly called the *baptism of repentance.* (Mark 1, 4. Luke 3, 3. Acts 13, 24. 19, 4.) The other association, that of baptism with regeneration, was of older date, having its origin in natural relations, and confirmed by the significant ablutions of the ceremonial law, which were designed to keep this very doctrine in connection with the doctrine of atonement, as displayed in the sacrificial ritual, before the minds of all devout believers in the law of Moses. *In the name of Jesus Christ* is not the formula by which they were to be baptized, and therefore different from the one prescribed by Christ himself (Matt. 28, 19), but a description of the rite as Christian, and not merely Jewish, much less heathen, baptism, or an unmeaning form, connected with no religious creed whatever. (See below, on 8, 16. 19, 5.) *In the name of Christ,* i. e. by his authority, acknowledging his claims, subscribing to his doctrines, engaging in his service, and relying on his merits. The beneficial end to which all this led was the *remission of sins*. The first Greek noun (ἄφεσιν), derived from a verb (ἀφίημι) which means to *let go*, is applied by Plutarch to divorce, by Demosthenes to legal discharge from the obligation of a bond, by Plato to the emancipation of a slave, and to exemption from punishment, which last is its constant use in the New Testament. The whole phrase, *to* (or *towards*) *remission of sins*, describes this as the end to which the question of the multitude had reference, and which therefore must be contemplated also in the answer. To this implied promise of forgiveness, Peter adds an express one, that they should *receive the gift of the*

Holy Ghost. It has been disputed whether this denotes participation in the miraculous endowments just imparted to the twelve, or only those internal influences which we are accustomed to call spiritual in a special sense, and which the scriptures represent as absolutely indispensable to all regeneration and salvation. But as these were only different operations of one and the same Spirit (1 Cor. 12, 4–12), the assurance may be understood both as a promise of his ordinary sanctifying agency, to be experienced by all believers now and for ever, and also as a promise of extraordinary, temporary gifts, to answer a specific end, on this occasion.

39. **For the promise is unto you, and to your children, and to all that are afar off, even as many as the Lord our God shall call.**

This verse contains an explanation of the promise just promiscuously made to the whole multitude. Spiritual influence, the great gift of Christ to his church, was not confined to his immediate followers or their first converts, but intended to embrace all classes and all generations of those whom God should *call,* i. e. choose, designate, and actually bring into communion with his Son through faith. The promise was addressed to themselves and to their children, as in the covenants of the Old Testament, an expression favouring the supposition that their children were to be baptized with them, but not necessarily requiring it, as some, though less naturally, understand these words of later generations. But Peter is here dealing with the contemporary race, as represented by his hearers, and would therefore seem to mean by their children those already in existence, and especially those present upon this occasion. *All afar off* is likewise a disputed phrase. Some would refer this also to succeeding generations; but this is forbidden by the usage of the Greek word ($μακράν$), which relates to space, not time. Others apply it to the Jews dispersed in distant countries; but all Jews were so accustomed to equality of privileges in their own religion, that such an assurance would have been superfluous. Besides, the greater part of those whom he addressed belonged to his class, and could not therefore be distinguished from the *you* ($ὑμῖν$) of the first clause. A third opinion is, that *all afar off* denotes Gentile converts. It has been objected that Peter himself was not initiated into this great doctrine till long after. (See below, on 10, 28. 34.) Some have endeavoured to evade this objection, by admitting that Peter did not fully understand his own words. But both the objection and the answer rest upon a misconception, as to Peter's views at different periods of his history. He never could have thought that the Gentiles were excluded from the church or from salvation. There was no such exclusion, even under the restrictive institutions of the old economy. All the Gentiles in the world might have shared the privileges of the Jews, by complying with the prescribed conditions. Peter's error consisted in believing that these conditions still existed under the gospel, or in other words, that Gentiles must become Jews before they could be Christians. Of this error he was not yet disabused; but there was nothing in it to prevent his applying the expressions here recorded to the Gentiles. The only condition which he recognizes is the call of God, without regard to difference of rank or nation. In the first clause of this verse, the older English versions supply *was made* after *promise*.

40. And with many other words did he testify and exhort, saying, Save yourselves from this untoward generation.

We have here an interesting intimation both as to the quantity and quality of Peter's apostolical instructions on the day of Pentecost. As to the first, we learn that all his words are not recorded, but that *with many other* (literally *more*) *words he did testify*, etc. (Vulg. *aliis verbis plurimis*.) This admits of several suppositions, as to what is given in this chapter. It may be regarded as a summary or abstract of all that the Apostle said, or as a full report of one discourse, besides which others were delivered, but have not been left on record. The first is the more natural hypothesis, because it is not easy to conceive of what material the others were composed, or why they were considered requisite, as every thing essential seems to be included in the one here given, and the terms of the narrative are satisfied by simply supposing, that the ideas here recorded were expressed at greater length, and with such repetitions and amplifications as were suited to render them universally intelligible. As to the quality or character of Peter's preaching, it is indicated by two verbs, *testify* and *exhort*. The first expresses the complex idea of testimony, argument, and solemn affirmation, and is therefore frequently applied in this book to the preaching of the Gospel. (See below, 8, 25. 10, 42. 18, 5. 20, 21. 23. 24. 23, 11. 28, 23.) The other verb is also one of comprehensive import, including the ideas of summoning, commanding, and persuading. As the first describes the theoretical or doctrinal part of the apostolical preaching, so this may be regarded as expressive of its practical and hortatory element. They testified to what men should believe, and exhorted them to what they ought to do. As a sample or a summary of these exhortations, we are told that Peter said, *Save yourselves*, etc. The Greek verb (σωθῆτε) is a passive form, and although there are some instances, in which this aorist seems to have the meaning of the middle voice, there can be no reason for departing from the strict sense, when it suits the context better, as in this case. Such a departure is the more gratuitous, because the reflexive meaning (*save thyself*) is elsewhere expressed by an entirely different form of the same verb (σῶσον σεαυτόν). (See Matt. 27, 40. Mark 15, 30. Luke 23, 37.) The sense of the form here used is, *be saved*, i. e. consent that God shall save you, *from* (the character and destiny of) *this untoward generation*. The English word *untoward* is defined by its opposite, *toward*, and its cognate adjective, *towardly*, the first of which is used by Shakspeare, and the last by Bacon, in the sense of docile, manageable, tractable. The negative form, therefore, means perverse, intractable, and is no inaccurate translation of the Greek word here used, which means *crooked*, both in a physical and moral sense. (See Luke 3, 5. Phil. 2, 15. 1 Pet. 2, 18.) Its application here is founded on the description of Israel by Moses in Deut. 32, 5, where the Septuagint version has this very phrase. The *crooked generation* is the mass of unbelieving Jews, not considered as a race or nation, which is not the usage of the Greek word (γενεᾶς), but as a contemporary generation, out of which the penitent are urged to extricate themselves by consenting to be saved.

41. Then they that gladly received his word were baptized, and the same day there were added (unto them) about three thousand souls.

The Apostle's exhortation meets with a prompt and general response. There is the same ambiguity of construction in the first clause as in 1, 6. The common version, *they that gladly received his word*, seems to draw a distinction between two classes, those who did, and those who did not, gladly receive the Apostle's word. It seems more natural, however, to understand this clause as relating to the whole body of those mentioned in v. 37, as asking what they should do. *They then gladly received his word*, etc. The idea of cheerfulness and joy is twice expressed, being really included in the verb, according to Greek usage, and then separately indicated by an adverb. To the supposition that these converts were baptized by immersion, it may be objected, besides the greatness of the number and the shortness of the time, that Jerusalem has always been remarkably destitute of water, the fountain of Siloam being its only constant source. That the three thousand went out in procession to this fountain, or that many were baptized in swimming-baths or cisterns belonging to public establishments or to private dwellings, or that these difficulties were miraculously overruled for the occasion, are conceivable hypotheses; but whether they are probable or preferable to the simple supposition that the water, like the Holy Ghost in spiritual baptism, and the blood in ceremonial purifications, was poured or sprinkled—every reader must determine for himself. *The same day* evidently qualifies *baptized* as well as *added*, because it was by baptism that the additions were effected. *Added unto them* seems to mean to those mentioned in the first clause, but these were themselves the persons added. It is better, therefore, with the Geneva Bible, to supply *unto the church* from v. 47, i. e. to the previously existing body of believers, amounting, as some think, to a hundred and twenty, but probably a much larger number. (See above, on 1, 14. 2, 1.) *About*, literally *as, as if*, implies that the following number is a round one. (See above, on 1, 15.) The use of the word *souls* for *persons* in enumeration is an idiom, not only of the Hebrew (Gen. 46, 27) and the Hellenistic Greek (v. 43. 3, 23. 7, 14. 27, 37), but of many other languages.

42. And they continued stedfastly in the apostles' doctrine and fellowship, and in breaking of bread, and in prayers.

The history of Pentecost may be said to close with the preceding verse, what follows being an account of the condition of the infant church, from that day onward. *Continued stedfastly*, or as the Rhemish version more exactly renders it, *were persevering*. For the exact sense of the Greek verb, see above, on 1, 14. Here, as in many other cases, *doctrine* does not mean the truth taught, but the act or mode of teaching. (See Matt. 7, 28. 29. 22, 33. Mark 1, 22. 27. 4, 2. 11, 18. Luke 4, 32. 1 Tim. 4, 13.) What is here affirmed is not their adherence to a certain system of belief, but their personal attendance on the actual instructions of the twelve. Thus instruction followed, if it did not precede, baptism; or rather it both followed and preceded, for these converts were not heathen, but religiously trained Jews, and Peter had instructed them, before they were baptized, *in many words*, besides those here recorded. (See above, on v. 40.) But even if they had been received without instruction, that would be no warrant for a similar proceeding now, when there are no apostles and extraordinary gifts have ceased. The *teaching* here meant, however, is not merely that of catechumens, to prepare them for admission to the church, but that which is essential to the Christian life, and for the sake of which the convert is admitted to the church, as to the school of Christ. The word translated *fellowship* is very comprehensive in its import and various in its applications, corresponding, more or less exactly, to our words *community, communion*, and *communication*. Its rarest sense, at least in the New Testament, is the vague one of society or social intercourse. It might be applied, with strict propriety of language, to the community of goods described in the ensuing verses; to mutual participation of the same food, whether social or sacramental; and to the interchange of charities by alms or any other species of beneficence. All these are so appropriate and essential to the Christian character, that it is desirable to comprehend as much of them as possible in this description. We may therefore understand the historian as saying that the infant church was constantly engaged in mutual communion, both by joint repasts and sacramental feasts and charitable distribution. This last is, in actual usage, the prevailing application of the word in the New Testament. (See Rom. 15, 26. 2 Cor. 8, 4. 9, 13. Heb. 13, 16.) But the fact is that the three senses run into each other, as the three practices were really inseparable in the primitive or infant church. Its whole organization and condition was as yet that of a family, so that all their acts performed in common partook more or less of a religious character. It was at their social meals that their charities were dispensed; it was at these same meals that the eucharist was administered; so that all these elements must be combined to make up the full sense of apostolical communion (κοινωνία.) According to the common version, this word, as well as doctrine, is dependent on *apostles;* 'they adhered to their teaching and continued in communion with them.' But in Greek, *communion* is a separate and independent item in the catalogue. They continued, first, in the apostles' doctrine; then, in communion, not with them alone, but with the body of believers. The general idea of communion is then rendered more specific by the mention of the *breaking of bread*. As this was the beginning, or the initiatory act, of an ancient Jewish meal, it may be put for the repast itself, or for the eucharist that followed, or for both, as being then inseparable. The devotional character of all these services is shown by the addition, *and in prayers*. Such was the social state, and such were the employments, of the church, as reorganized at Pentecost and in Jerusalem. The whole might be summed up as consisting in apostolical teaching, mutual communion, common prayer.

43. And fear came upon every soul, and many wonders and signs were done by the Apostles.

While their internal state was such as has been just described, their outward state was one of safety under the divine protection. This safety was secured by a prevailing sentiment of awe (φόβος), not alarm or dread of injury, inspired originally, no doubt, by the great events of Pentecost, but afterwards maintained by miracles, here as in vs. 19. 22, described as *signs* and *wonders*, wrought by the Apostles. This connection of the clauses may be made clear by supplying between them, 'and in order to maintain this fear.' *Came* in the first clause, and *were done* in the second, are translations of the same Greek verb (ἐγίνετο), which strictly means became, came to pass, or happened.

44. And all that believed were together, and had all things common.

Such was the unity of feeling and affection in the infant church that, notwithstanding their numerical increase, they seemed to constitute a single household, with identity of interest, and even of possession. *All that believed*, those believing, the believers. This is one of the names given in the history to those who followed Christ and were professors of the new religion. The phrase is elliptical for those who believed in Jesus as the true Messiah. *Were together* does not mean that they assembled or resided in one place, for their numbers rendered this impossible; nor that they now began to meet in stated but distinct assemblies, an idea which the words do not express. The sense of unity in heart and purpose, which the word has elsewhere (see above, on 1, 15. 2, 1, and compare the Septuagint version of Ps. 133, 1), is perfectly appropriate here, and better suited to the context, both before and after, than that of outward local convocation. As one specification of this general description, it is added, *they had all things common*, i. e. no one regarded his possessions as belonging absolutely to himself, but as a trust for the benefit of others also.

45. And sold their possessions and goods, and parted them to all men, as every man had need.

The proof of this disinterested spirit was afforded by the fact that, when there was occasion, they actually sold such of their possessions as were necessary for the comfort and relief of others. *Parted*, divided, distributed, allotted. The words necessarily denote nothing more than what is often exemplified at present, except so far as this ancient liberality was modified by the more intimate relation which existed among Christians then, as members of one family or household. There is nothing said of a compulsory renunciation of all individual property, either as a divine institution or a voluntary self-denial. Such a renunciation is indeed at variance with facts recorded in the later history. (See below, on 5, 4.) Of those who understand it to be here meant, some regard it as a normal and commanded state, which ceased on the departure of the church from its primitive simplicity, and will return when that returns. Others make it a divine but temporary constitution, suited to the infant stage of Christianity, but not required, nor even possible, in its maturity. A third view is, that it was a mistaken though well meant attempt to continue in the church at large the mode of life adopted by our Lord and his Apostles. Whether the fact assumed in all these hypotheses is really recorded, either here or in the parallel passage at the end of the fourth chapter, is a question which will there present itself again. (See below, on 4, 32. 34.) The distinction sometimes made between the words translated *possessions* and *goods*, as denoting what is now called *real* and *personal* property, has no more foundation in Greek usage than the one made by Wiclif, who, instead of *goods*, has *cattle*. The second Greek word corresponds to our word *substance*, as applied to wealth. (Vulg. *possessiones et substantias*.) So far is κτήματα from meaning real or immovable estate, that in Homer it almost always denotes jewels or other hoarded treasure, and the Attic writers sometimes put it in antithesis to *land* (ἄγρος), sometimes to *money* (χρήματα). The two words are substantially equivalents, here put together to express more fully the one idea of property or wealth. Here, as often elsewhere in the English Bible, the words *man* and *men*, though not distinguished by italics, are supplied by the translators, who appear to have considered them essential to the meaning, although modern usage would allow the *man* to be replaced by *one*, and the *men* to be omitted altogether: *and parted them to all, as every one had need*. This insertion of the word *man*, as a sort of pronoun, is a favourite idiom of the old English versions. That it had a pronominal force, analogous to that of the same word in German, may be inferred from 1 Cor. 2, 11, where it is applied to God.

46. And they continuing daily with one accord in the temple, and breaking bread from house to house, did eat their meat with gladness and singleness of heart.

The writer here returns to his description of their daily habits and religious spirit, which he interrupted at the close of v. 42, to mention the effect produced on others (43), and the means of their subsistence (44. 45.) Their religious life is here presented under its two aspects, public and private. For the sense of *continuing with one accord*, see above, on 1, 14. This daily attendance at the temple is referred by some to meetings of their own within the sacred enclosure. This opinion seems to be confined to those who understand *the house where they were sitting*, in v. 2 above, to be a chamber of the temple. By others, what is here said is referred to the daily temple service, or at least to public prayer, in the appointed place, and at the stated hours. If this be the correct interpretation of the passage, we have here the first intimation of the singular fact, that although the ceremonial law, of which the temple was a part, had been abrogated by the advent and sacrifice of Christ, the apostles considered themselves bound, or at least authorized, to treat it with respect, so long as it was suffered to continue in existence. Some have explained this as an act of mere political obedience; but its combination, here and elsewhere, with their spiritual worship and their whole religious life, without a trace of any such distinction between secular and sacred as the one alleged, appears to show that their attendance at the temple was as really a part of their religion as their meeting elsewhere. The probable design of this paradoxical arrangement was to shield the new religion from the charge of being hostile to the old, or essentially distinct from it, and to show the identity of the church under both dispensations, by allowing one, as it were, to overlap the other, or the two to coexist for a time, instead of establishing the Christian church on ground left absolutely vacant by the total destruction of the ancient system. A precisely similar relation had subsisted for a time between the ministry of John the Baptist and the public ministry of Christ himself, and may be said indeed to have prefigured the one mentioned in the case before us. The evils, which might easily have sprung from this arrangement, if continued longer, were prevented by the speedy and entire destruction, not only of the temple and the ceremonial system, but of the civil organization, with which the Jewish church had for ages been identified. One incidental evil, which did really arise from this peculiar providential constitution, was the state of uncertainty and strife, in which the Jewish Christians long continued, with respect to the observance of the law, and the way in which the Gentiles should be brought into the church, until all reasonable doubt was ended by the great ecclesiastical and national catastrophe. Of these unhappy errors and disputes we shall have instances enough in the ensuing history. (See below, on 10, 1. 15, 1. 18, 18. 21, 20. 21.) *From house to house* is Cranmer's version; Tyndale has *in every house;* the Vulgate, *circa domos.* Compare *in every city* (κατὰ πόλιν) Tit. 1, 5. But the best authorities are now in favour of explaining it to mean *in the house* or *at home*, as distinguished from the foregoing phrase, *in the temple.* This philological decision is confirmed by the repeated use of the same Greek words in Paul's epistles, to describe a church, or stated meeting of believers, in a private dwelling. (See Rom. 16, 5. 1 Cor. 16, 19. Col. 4, 15. Philem. 2.) The whole clause then describes the two great parts of their religious life, public and private, or as Jews and Christians. *Breaking bread at home,* or *in private houses,* as we have already seen (in v. 42), exclusively denotes neither social repasts nor sacramental services, but both, in that most intimate conjunction, which was one of the characteristic features of the infant church, but which can no more be revived by us, than the innocent simplicity of childhood, or the habits of a father's house, can be continued in mature age and in distant homes. That the reference to the eucharist is at least not exclusive, may be seen from the ensuing phrase *they took their meat,* or more exactly, *they partook of nourishment.* The remainder of the verse describes the temper or the spirit, in which all these acts and duties were performed, viz. *with gladness,* or rather *exultation,* the Hellenistic word here used being one of great strength, and *with singleness* (Tyndale), or *simpleness* (Wiclif), or *simplicity* (Rheims), which seems to be the corresponding negative expression, by which every feeling is excluded, that could mar this picture of exquisite but childlike happiness. The quality described is not mere sincerity, or freedom from hypocrisy, but singleness of purpose, aim, and motive, as opposed not only to deceit, but to complexity of mind and character. This, too, in its perfection, or its highest measures, appertains peculiarly to the early stages both of individual and social progress. It is therefore eminently well-placed in this portrait of the primitive or infant church.

47. Praising God, and having favour with all the people. And the Lord added to the church daily such as should be saved.

The first words, *praising God,* close the description of their spiritual state and mode of life. He winds up all by saying that they praised God. This evidently means something more than that praise formed a part of their worship. The phrase is obviously intended to describe their whole life as a life of praise to God. It is not so much an additional particular in the description as a pregnant summary of the whole. As if he had said, 'In a word, they only lived to praise God and glorify their master.' The effect produced by all this upon others had before been represented as religious awe, maintained by a succession of miraculous performances. But this might have seemed to imply that the popular feeling towards the new society was one of distance, if not of aversion. It is therefore added here, that *they had favour with the people*, not with one class merely, *but with all the people*, as a whole, and as a body. There is obvious allusion to the constant use of this expression (τὸν λαόν) to denote *the people* by way of eminence, the chosen people, the people of God. The Jews collectively, no doubt with individual exceptions, favoured them. This state of public feeling is remarkable, and seems to be recorded, on account of the unhappy and inexplicable change which afterwards took place. But as yet, they enjoyed popular as well as divine favour. This last was manifest in their increase, not merely by great sudden movements, such as that of Pentecost, but also by constant though insensible accretion, thus exemplifying, in the experience of the infant church, both the great methods of advancement by which she has since been growing, culture and revival. This daily increase is described as a divine work and the work of Christ himself. The sudden change from *God* to *Lord*, in this short verse, can only be explained by supposing that the writer intended to describe the Great Head of the church as personally adding to its numbers. This is the first historical use of the word *church* (ἐκκλησία) in application to the body of believers after its reorganization. In the gospel of Matthew it is twice applied to the same body by our Lord himself (Matt. 16, 18. 18, 17), but in the way of anticipation. The Greek word, which expresses the idea of evoking, calling out, also suggests that of convoking, calling together, and is therefore most appropriate to the Christian church, as a select organic body, called out by divine choice from the mass of men, and called together by divine authority as a spiritual corporation. The Greek word was familiar to the Jews, not only as applied to the political assemblies of the Grecian states, in which sense it occurs below, 19, 39, but also as applied in their own Septuagint version to the host or congregation of Israel. Having thus been used for centuries to designate the ancient Jewish Church, it was peculiarly appropriate as an expression for the Church of Christ. To this body, now possessing an organic constitution, the Lord added daily *such as should be saved.* This awkward periphrasis, borrowed from the Vulgate (*qui salvi fierent*), has occasioned no small stir among the Calvinists and their opponents in the Church of England, who have warmly disputed whether it should be translated, those who had been saved, or those who were in the act of being saved, or those who were in the way of salvation; whereas Luke simply says *the saved*, as an additional description of the same class whom he calls *believers* in v. 44. It might as well be queried whether that expression denotes those who had believed, or would believe, or were believing. Men are said to be saved in reference not only to the final consummation but to the inception of the saving work. Of every penitent believing sinner, we may say, with equal truth, that he will certainly be saved, and that he has been saved already. There is therefore no occasion for doctrinal dispute afforded by the simple statement, that *the Lord daily added saved* (or *saved ones*) *to the church*, which is the order, as well as the true sense, of the original. The Vulgate adds to this verse an apparently unmeaning phrase (*in id ipsum,*) which is retained by Wiclif (*in the same thing,*) and is really the first words of the following chapter.

CHAPTER III.

Thus far the infant church had enjoyed the favour both of God and man. But this state of things was not designed to last. Opposition, and even persecution, were essential to the execution of the divine purpose, not only as a means of moral discipline, but also as a means of outward growth. The new religion was not to be a national or local one, but catholic and ecumenical. In order to attain its end, it must be spread; and in order to be spread, it must be scattered; and in order to be scattered, it must undergo strong pressure, from within and from without. The history now presents to us the series of providential causes by which these effects were brought about. The subject of the next two chapters is the first attack upon the church, occasioned by a signal miracle and apostolical discourse. Chapter III relates to the occasion, **Chapter IV to the attack itself.** At a certain time and place, distinctly specified (1), Peter and John perform a miracle of healing (2—8), which attracts attention and occasions a great concourse (9—11), of which Peter takes advantage to disclaim the honour of the miracle (12), and give it all to Christ, whose treatment at their hands he sets forth with several aggravating circumstances (13—15), and contrasts with the evidence of his divinity afforded by this miracle which they had witnessed (16.) Then, with a sudden and affecting change of tone, he represents their great crime as the fruit of ignorance (17), and as the execution of a divine purpose (18), not to extenuate their guilt but to encourage their repentance (19), which he also urges by the promise of Christ's coming (20, 21) as the Prophet of his people foretold by Moses (22, 23), Samuel and the other prophets (24), in whose predictions, as well as in the patriarchal promises (25), and in Christ himself as their fulfilment, the children of Israel had a primary interest and right, but only on condition of personal repentance and conversion (26.)

1. Now Peter and John went up together into the temple, at the hour of prayer, (being) the ninth hour.

Out of the multitude of miracles performed by the apostles after Pentecost (2, 43), Luke singles one, not merely on account of its intrinsic magnitude and great publicity, but chiefly on account of its connection with the progress of events and the condition of the infant church, as having furnished the occasion of a new apostolical discourse, and of the first hostile movement from without. This first verse specifies the place, the time, and the performers of the miracle. There is something striking in the mutual relations of Peter and John, as they may be traced in the history. After their joint mission to prepare for the last passover (Luke 22, 8), they seem to have been inseparable, notwithstanding the marked difference in their character and conduct. Peter alone denied his master; John alone continued with him to the last. (See John 18, 15. 19, 26.) Of Peter's fall John would seem to have been the only apostolical witness. Yet we find them still together at the sepulchre, and in Galilee after the resurrection (John 20, 2. 21, 7.) It is an observation of Chrysostom, that Peter's question (John 21, 21), *Lord, what shall this man do?* was prompted rather by affection than by curiosity. Here again we find them still *together* (ἐπὶ τὸ αὐτό), an expression implying not mere coincidence of place but unity of purpose. (See above, on 1, 15. 2, 1. 44.) *Went up* is the appropriate expression for the physical and moral elevation of the temple. *At the hour* (ἐπὶ τὴν ὥραν) might perhaps be more exactly rendered *towards* (i. e. just before) *the hour*. All the English versions, prior to king James's, have the strange expression, *the ninth hour of prayer*, which may however mean no more than the paraphrase given in our Bible. The ninth hour of the day, corresponding to our three o'clock in the afternoon, was the third stated hour of prayer, according to the Jewish custom, being probably the hour of the evening sacrifice. (See above, on 2, 15.) Here, as in 2, 46 above, there is nothing in the text or context to determine for what purpose the Apostles visited the temple, or rather nothing to determine whether, in addition to their private devotions, they took part in the ceremonial service. For the reasons in favour of supposing that they did, see above, on 2, 46.

2. And a certain man, lame from his mother's womb, was carried, whom they laid daily at the gate of the temple which is called Beautiful, to ask alms of them that entered into the temple.

To show the certainty, as well as greatness, of the cure effected, the case is here described as one of long standing and of general notoriety. It was not a case of lameness by disease or accident, but one of congenital infirmity. It was also one with which the people were familiar, from its daily exhibition in one of the most public situations of the city. The practice of placing objects of charity at the entrances of temples, both on account of the great concourse and the supposed tendency of devotional feelings to promote those of a charitable kind, was common among Jews and Gentiles, and is still kept up in some parts of the Christian world. No antiquarian research has yet succeeded in determining which gate of the temple or its area is here meant, or in accounting for the name here given to it. As the Greek adjective (ὡραίαν) was not commonly employed to express the general idea of beauty, but rather that of youthful bloom and freshness, which seems wholly inappropriate to such an object, it has been explained as the corruption of some oriental name, no longer ascertainable. But the wider Hellenistic usage of the word is clear from its being applied to feet (Rom. 10, 15) and whited sepulchres (Matt. 23, 27.) The more common opinion is, that the gate meant is the great eastern gate of the temple-enclosure, corresponding to the entrance of the temple itself, and described by Josephus as superior in size and decoration to all the others, being wholly covered with Corinthian brass. The material fact here implied, if not expressed, is that this was the most frequented entrance to the temple, and was therefore chosen by the cripple or his friends, as his place of habitual solicitation. Here, as in many other instances, the Rhemish version (*Specious*) violates our idiom, by closely copying the mere form of the Vulgate (*Speciosa*), even where it makes no sense in English. Wiclif, although equally a copyist of the Vulgate, had shown far more taste, as well as knowledge of the language, by his simple Saxon version (*Fair*). The word translated *alms*, like *charity* in English, denotes a feeling or a principle, but is secondarily applied to its outward manifestation or effect. The two verbs *laid* and *carried*, although similar in form, must be carefully distinguished, as relating to distinct times. *They* (i. e. others, or his friends) *laid* (*him*) *daily at the gate of the temple*, and had probably been doing so for many years. But *he was carried*, or in modern phrase, *was being carried*, to the customary place, on this occasion, just as Peter and John were going in.

3. Who, seeing Peter and John about to go into the temple, asked an alms.

About to go is expressed in Greek by a participle and infinitive, the first of which (μέλλοντας) has no equivalent in English, the verb denoting merely the idea of futurity, *to be about to do* the act expressed by the dependent verb. The Vulgate version (*incipientes*), copied by Wiclif (*beginning to enter*), goes as much too far in one direction as *intending* or *designing* in the other. Tyndale and Cranmer have the singular and now obsolete ellipsis, *would into the temple*. There is another verb in the last clause not expressed in the English version. *Asked*, in the original, is *asked to receive*, a pleonasm even in Greek, but one of which there are examples, after verbs of asking, both in Classical and Hellenistic writers.

(See below, on 7, 46.) *An alms* has been regarded by certain hypercritics as a solecism or a blunder. The final letter is not here the sign of the plural number, but one of the consonants of the Greek word (ἐλεημοσύνη) of which the English is a mere corruption, like *palsy* of *paralysis*. (See above, on v. 2.)

4. And Peter, fastening his eyes upon him, with John, said, Look on us.

Fastening his eyes is the same verb with *looked stedfastly* in 1, 10 above. Here too it might be rendered *gazing into him*. This act, though formally affirmed of Peter only, the Greek participle (ἀτενίσας) being singular in form, is ascribed to both Apostles by the words, *with John*, which indeed may be said of both the verbs, between which this parenthetic phrase is placed. It was Peter that looked and Peter that spoke, but he performed both acts *with John*, i. e. John looked and spoke at the same time, or Peter looked and spoke for both. The latter is more probable, at least in reference to the act of speaking. The intent look may have been designed in part to ascertain the man's condition and to verify his story; but also, no doubt, to arrest his own attention and prepare him for what followed, which was likewise the design of the command, *look on* (or *at*) *us*.

5. And he gave heed unto them, expecting to receive something of them.

The literal meaning of the first clause is, *he fixed* (or *kept fixed*) *on them*. We may supply either *mind* (as in Luke 14, 7. 1 Tim. 4, 16) or *eyes*, more probably the latter, as the verse describes his obedience to the previous command of the Apostles, *look on us*. The original order of the last clause is, *expecting something from them to receive*. This graphic yet natural account of the successive steps, by which the cripple was restored, imparts to the whole narrative a life-like character of authenticity, which can neither be mistaken nor assumed.

6. Then Peter said, Silver and gold have I none, but such as I have give I thee. In the name of Jesus Christ of Nazareth, rise up and walk.

Then, in the original, is nothing but the usual continuative particle (δέ) translated *and* at the beginning of v. 5. *Silver and gold* are put for money, the kind of alms which the lame man had asked (3), and was expecting to receive (5.) *Have I none*, literally, *is not* (or *exists not*) *to me*. It might be supposed that we have here a literal Greek version of what Peter said in Aramaic, as this is the usual periphrasis for the verb *to have*, which is unknown to the Semitic family of languages. But this supposition seems to be forbidden by the occurrence of that verb in the next clause. *Such as I have* might have been more briefly and exactly rendered, *what I have*. This may refer specifically to the gift of healing which he was about to impart, or more generally to the power of working miracles with which he was entrusted. But as this power does not appear to have been constant or unlimited, the first construction seems entitled to the preference. *Give I thee*, or retaining still more closely the original arrangement, *what I have, this to thee I give*. The demonstrative pronoun (τοῦτο) is omitted in our version, but adds something to the force of the expression. These authoritative words might seem to arrogate an independent power to the speaker, but for what directly follows. The apostolical miracles were all performed in the name of Christ, according to his own command and promise (Mark 16, 17. 18. John 14, 12.) This fact is expressly mentioned in some cases (see below, on 9, 34. 16, 18), and sufficiently implied in others (see below, on 9, 40. 14, 9. 10. 28, 8.) Our Lord's own miracles were not wrought even in the name of God, but by his own authority, and yet in intimate conjunction with the Father (John 11, 41. 42.) *In the name* here means by the authority of Jesus, 'as his representative and in his behalf I command thee.' The form of expression in 2, 38 is somewhat different. The preposition there used (ἐπί) suggests the additional idea of dependence or reliance. *Jesus Christ of Nazareth*, in Greek, *the Nazarene*, with an allusion to the contemptuous usage of the name. (See above, on 2, 22.) The combination thus arising is remarkable, and represents our Lord as being at once the Saviour of his people from their sins (Matt. 1, 21), the Messiah of the prophecies (Acts 2, 31), and yet an object of contemptuous neglect (Matt. 2, 23.) The command, *arise and walk*, is rendered still more laconic and abrupt by the omission of the first verb in some ancient manuscripts and late editions. *In the name of Jesus Christ the Nazarene, walk!*

7. And he took him by the right hand and lifted him up, and immediately his feet and ancle-bones received strength.

In this, as in many of our Saviour's miracles, the healing word was attended by an outward act or gesture, serving to connect the miraculous effect with the person by whom it was produced. (See Matt. 8, 15. 9, 25. 14, 31. 20, 34. Luke 7, 14.) *Immediately*, on the spot, or on the matter, as the Greek word (παραχρῆμα) might be etymologically rendered. The common word for *feet* is not here used, but one which properly means *steps*, and is then transferred from the effect to the cause. Both senses of the word are found in Sophocles. The two words *ancle bones* are used to represent one (σφυρά) simply meaning *ancles. Received strength*, literally, *were strengthened* or *made firm*. The particularity of this description is among the traces, found by some in Luke's writings, of his medical profession.

8. And he, leaping up, stood and walked, and entered with them into the temple, walking and leaping and praising God.

His *leaping up* or *out* (ἐξαλλόμενος) is understood by some as a spontaneous sign of joy, which is undoubtedly the meaning of the uncompounded verb (ἁλλόμενος) in the other clause. But this very fact seems to show, that the compound form rather denotes the act of leaping up from his recumbent posture, or the incipient attempt to walk. We have then a regular gradation in the cure; his limbs were strengthened; he sprang up; he walked, or in Wiclif's antique English, *wandered*. The mention of the fact, that he entered with them into the temple, reminds the reader that all this occurred between the arrival of the two apostles at the gate of the temple and their passage through it. The acts described in the last clause were, at the same time, proofs of his real restoration, and expressions of his gratitude and joy. *Walking*, or as the Greek word properly denotes, *walking about*, walking freely, without help or hinderance, as a man would naturally do, who had been thus restored, as if to satisfy himself that the change was real, and to try the extent of his recovered powers. That the man who had been healed was not without religious feeling, is evinced by the additional words, *praising God.*

9. And all the people saw him walking and praising God.

The repetition in this verse is not a mere tautology, but doubly emphatic, as implying, on the one hand, that the miracle was public and notorious, and on the other that it gathered a great multitude, to whom Peter presently addressed himself. Here, too, as in 2, 47, *all the people* does not mean a promiscuous rabble accidentally assembled, but the chosen people, the Jewish church or nation, represented by the worshippers then gathered at the temple. As if he had said, 'this miracle was not done in a corner, but in the holy place and in the presence of the people, who distinctly saw, walking about the sacred courts, and loudly praising God for his recovery, the very man whom they had seen for many years lying daily at the entrance of that very enclosure, a cripple and a beggar.'

10. And they knew that it was he which sat for alms at the Beautiful Gate of the temple, and they were filled with wonder and amazement at that which had happened unto him.

The material point here is the unquestioned identity of him who had experienced the cure. Had the miracle been wrought upon a stranger, its moral effect upon others would have been far less than it was, when the people universally recognized him as the crippled beggar, whom they were accustomed to see lying helpless in a certain spot, and that one of the most public and frequented in the city. Luke says, not only that it was the same man, but that *they knew* or *recognized* him (ἐπεγίνωσκον) as the same. The other clause describes the natural effect of this unhesitating recognition. The sight of this man walking, in the free use of his limbs, and loudly thanking God for his recovery, excited feelings of the highest wonder, not unmixed with awe, at this indication of God's special presence and activity among them. The word rendered *amazement* is the noun corresponding to the verb employed in 2, 7 above, and there explained. The word translated *wonder* is confined, in the New Testament, to Luke's writings (Luke 4, 36. 5, 9), though the verbal root is also used by Mark (1, 27. 10, 24. 32.) Though not so stated in the lexicons, it seems, at least in Hellenistic Greek, to have combined the primary idea of wonder or astonishment with that of fear or awe, especially in such a case as this, and others just referred to, where the wonder was excited by a special indication of the divine presence. The strongest English version is the Rhemish, *exceedingly astonied and aghast*. *What had happened* or *occurred to him*, the change which he had suddenly experienced, and which could not be referred to any natural or ordinary cause.

11. And as the lame man which was healed held Peter and John, all the people ran together unto them, in the porch that is called Solomon's, greatly wondering.

The six words, *the lame man which was healed*, correspond to three in Greek (τοῦ ἰαθέντος χωλοῦ), which might be more concisely rendered, *the healed cripple*. Instead of these words, some of the critical editions have the simple pronoun (αὐτοῦ) *he*. The original construction is, *he* (or *the healed cripple*) *holding Peter and John*. The idea that he was afraid of a relapse is much less natural than that he clung to them with thankfulness and admiration as the human instruments of his deliverance and restoration. In strict agreement with the language of v. 4, John is here not only said by the historian, but acknowledged by the man himself, to have joined in the performance of the miracle; whether by word or deed, or simply by his silent presence and concurrence, must be matter of conjecture. It is a natural, though not a necessary supposition, that this holding fast was subsequent in time to the acts mentioned in the foregoing verses. After proving the reality of his recovery by walking and leaping, and his gratitude to God by vocal praise, he may have run back to his two benefactors and embraced them in the manner here described This fact may be mentioned to account for the great concourse which immediately ensued, and which perhaps would have been less, if the lively gestures of the restored cripple had not partially diverted the attention of the people from himself to the Apostles. It was *to them*, i. e. to Peter and John, that *all the people*, in the same emphatic sense as in v. 9 above, *ran together in* or *to* (ἐπί) *the porch, the* (one) *called Solomon's*, a form of expression which implies that there were others, but that this was the most noted and frequented. The word translated *porch* (στοά) means a piazza or a colonnade, such as were attached to the Greek temples, and employed as places of instruction by the Greek philosophers, to one of whose sects or schools (the *Stoics*) this very word has given name. Several such porticoes or colonnades surrounded the courts of Herod's temple at Jerusalem, and one of them is described by Josephus as "the work of Solomon." This would account for the name and the pre-eminence of this particular piazza, as implied here and in John 10, 23, where we learn that Christ himself was accustomed to frequent it. It also enables us to fix in general its relative position, which, according to Josephus, was upon the eastern side, or, as some understand him, at the eastern end of the south side of the area of the temple. It is an old opinion that the wing or pinnacle (πτερύγιον) mentioned in the history of our Lord's temptation (Matt. 4, 5. Luke 4, 9), was some elevated point of this same structure. *Greatly wondering* is, in Greek, a single word, and that an adjective (ἔκθαμβοι), emphatic or intensive in its form, and corresponding in its etymology and meaning to the verb and noun explained above, on the preceding verse. Placed at the close of the whole sentence, it describes the crowd as still *amazed* or *awestruck*, and implies that the effect, at first produced by the miracle itself, so far from being weakened or effaced, was at its height, when Peter entered on the following discourse.

12. And when Peter saw (it), he answered unto the people, Ye men of Israel, why marvel ye at this? or why look ye so earnestly on us, as though by our own power or holiness we had made this man to walk?

With the wisdom, by which the Apostles after Pentecost were characterized, Peter, who now re-appears alone as their spokesman, when he saw what is recorded in the foregoing verse, to wit, the concourse of the people and their even more than natural amazement, instantly embraced the opportunity again to preach Christ to a portion of the multitude by whom he was betrayed and murdered. *Answered* is explained by some as a pleonastic synonyme of *said*, or *began to speak;* by others as relating to their thoughts or looks. But although there are examples of the latter usage elsewhere, there is no need of resorting to it here, where the strict sense is so perfectly admissible; the verbal expression of their wonder, although not recorded, being almost necessarily implied. 'When Peter saw the concourse of the people and their wonder, as expressed by looks and words, he answered.' His reply was addressed to *the people*, not as a mere mob, but as *men of Israel*, assembled at the sanctuary and representing the whole Jewish nation. *Why marvel ye at this* (*man*), or *at this* (*thing*) which has happened to him, either of which constructions is admissible. The question does not mean, that there was nothing wonderful in what had happened, but that their surprise was either excessive in degree, or of the wrong kind, i. e. disposed to rest in the mere instruments, without looking beyond them to the efficient cause, which last idea is expressed in the remainder of the verse. *Look earnestly* is still the same verb as in 1, 10. Instead of *power and godliness*, some versions have two synonymes, *strength and power*. But extraordinary piety (εὐσεβεία) was commonly associated with the idea of peculiar divine favour, both being expressed in Hebrew by the same word (see above, on 2, 27); and this idea was near akin to that of superhuman power. *As though we had made*, literally, *as having made* (i. e. caused or enabled) *this man to walk*.

13. The God of Abraham and of Isaac and of Jacob, the God of our fathers, hath glorified his son Jesus, whom ye delivered up, and denied him in the presence of Pilate, when he was determined to let (him) go.

The miracle which so amazed them was not wrought by magic, or by any unknown power, but by that of Jehovah, their own God, and the God of their Fathers. To express this idea more emphatically, he employs the customary formula, in which the three first patriarchs are separately named. (See Ex. 3, 6. 15. Matt. 22, 32.) He thus reminds them that the new religion was essentially identical with the old, and that God had himself done honour to the man whom they had crucified; the same contrast as in 2, 24 above, and v. 15 below. *Glorified*, by this extraordinary miracle, performed in Christ's name, and by his authority. The word translated *son* is not the one commonly so rendered (υἱός), but another (παῖς) used both for son and servant (Matt. 8, 6. 8. 13. 14, 2. Luke 12, 45, etc.) In this dubious or double sense, it is applied to David and to Israel collectively (Luke 1, 54. 69), as sustaining both a servile and a filial relation to Jehovah, and as representatives of the Messiah, to whom the title therefore belongs by way of eminence. (Compare Matt. 12, 18, and see below, on v. 26. 4, 25. 27. 30.) *Delivered up*, abandoned, to his enemies or executioners. The idea of treacherous betrayal, though not necessarily included in the meaning of the verb, may be suggested by it, as in its application to Judas Iscariot (Matt. 10, 4. 26, 16. 21. 46. 27, 3. etc.) The essential idea is that of putting into the power of another, whether by treachery or force (Matt. 5, 25. 10, 17. 19. 21. 18, 34. 24, 9. 10, etc.) The gross injustice of this treatment to an innocent man was, in their case, aggravated by peculiar circumstances, which the Apostle now proceeds to specify. The first was that it involved a formal rejection of their own Messiah. *Ye denied him* to be what he was, and what he claimed to be, the Prophet, Priest, and King of Israel. This was in fact disowning and renouncing all for the sake of which the Jews existed as a nation. The second aggravating circumstance suggested is, that this rejection, ruinous and wicked as it was in itself, was rendered still more heinous by its having been committed in the presence of a heathen ruler, representing the great dominant power of the Gentile world. *Ye denied him in the presence of Pilate*. (See John 19, 15.) But even this was not all. They rejected their Messiah, not only before Pilate, but against his will and better judgment. This idea might seem to be expressed by the words translated *in the presence*, which may also be rendered *to the face*; but Greek usage is in favour of the former sense. The aggravation now in question is expressed in the last clause, *when he was determined to let him go*, or as Tyndale has it, *judged him to be loosed*. The original construction is, *he* (or *himself*) *determining*, etc. It is a slight coincidence, but not unworthy of remark, that the Greek verb here used (ἀπολύειν) is the very one which Luke elsewhere puts into the mouth of Pilate himself (Luke 23, 16.)

14. But ye denied the Holy One and the Just, and desired a murderer to be granted unto you.

There is a double antithesis here, tending to aggravate

their guilt still further. They had not only demanded the condemnation of the innocent, but also the acquittal of the guilty. But more than this: they had rejected the Messiah and preferred a murderer! (See Matt. 27, 21. John 18, 40.) *Holy and Just* are epithets expressive not only of his innocence before the law (Matt. 27, 19. 24), but in a higher sense, of his peculiar character and mission as the Holy One of God (Mark 1, 24. Luke 1, 35), whom the Father had sanctified and sent into the world (John 10, 36.) *The Just* or (*Righteous*) *One* is a common description of our Lord in the New Testament. See below, on 7, 52. 22, 14, and compare 1 John 2, 1. *Murderer*, in Greek, *a man, a murderer*, the last noun having all the force of an adjective, a murderous man, i. e. one guilty of murder. Compare the phrase, *men, brethren*, in 1, 15 above. *Granted*, not as an act of justice, but of favour. (See below, on 25, 11. 16. 27, 24, and compare Philem. 22.)

15. And killed the Prince of Life, whom God hath raised from the dead, whereof we are witnesses.

Nay, they had preferred a murderer, not only to an innocent or just man, not only to their own Messiah, but to the prince of life himself. The word translated *prince* (ἀρχηγός) is so translated also in 5, 31 below, but in Heb. 2, 10, it is rendered *captain*, and in Heb. 12, 2, *author*. This example may suffice to show the want of perfect uniformity even in the best translations, and the inexpediency of urging the mere language of such versions, without reference to the original. The figure used is no more regal here, or martial in Heb. 2, 10, than in Heb. 12, 2, where there seems to be no trace of either. Most interpreters prefer the Vulgate version here (*auctorem*), as better suiting the antithesis between the giver of life and its destroyer. (See John 1, 4. 5, 25. 10, 28.) This climax of antitheses and aggravations is rhetorically striking and effective. Having brought it to its height in the first clause of this verse, Peter reverts to the old contrast between Christ's treatment by divine and human hands. (See above, on 2, 23. 24.) They killed him and God raised him. Instead of the ambiguous term (ἀνέστησεν) used in 2, 32, we have here the unequivocal though figurative phrase, *awakened* (ἤγειρεν) *from* (*among*) *the dead*, but with the same addition as in that case, *of which* (or *of whom*) *we are witnesses*.

16. And his name, through faith in his name, hath made this man strong, whom ye see and know; yea, the faith which is by him hath given him this perfect soundness in the presence of you all.

This verse assigns a cause for the effect which they had witnessed. The effect was that the infirm man had been *made strong*, and restored to *perfect soundness*. The Greek word (ὁλοκληρία) originally means an undivided or entire inheritance, but by the later writers is applied to bodily integrity and soundness. The causes to which this effect is ascribed are the *name* of Christ and *faith*, each of which is mentioned twice, with a singular complication of the two together. In the first clause it is expressly said that the *name* of the Lord of Life had strengthened the infirm man. If the following words are exegetical of these, the meaning is, *his name*, that is, *faith in his name*. But as the order of the clauses is inverted, and the preposition (ἐπί) cannot mean *that is*, the second clause (in English) must be understood as pointing out the means by which, or the reason for which, the name of Christ had wrought this wonder. His name, by means (or on account) of faith in that name, had restored this man to perfect soundness. This studied repetition of the word *name* shows that it cannot be a mere periphrasis for himself. (See above, on 1, 15.) It must either mean the invocation of his name, the fact that the miracle was wrought avowedly by his authority and delegated power; or the actual exertion of that power, as the *name of God* in the Old Testament so often means the manifestation of his attributes, especially in outward act. The first explanation is more simple and agrees better with what follows, *through faith in his name*, i. e. through faith in him whose name had been invoked, or in whose name, and by whose representative, the miracle had been performed. (See below, on 19, 17. 26, 9.) The preposition here translated *through* is not the one commonly so rendered (διά), but another (ἐπί) which, in such connections, properly means *on* or *for*. Some here explain it, *for faith*, i. e. for the purpose of producing faith; but this is unexampled in the Greek of the New Testament; whereas the preposition often signifies *by means of* or *because of* (e. g. Matt. 4, 4. 19, 9. Mark 3, 5. Acts 4, 9. 21. 26, 6.) On the whole, the meaning seems to be, that the perfect restoration of the cripple was the work of him in whose name and by whose authority the miracle was wrought, and that the condition upon which he acted, was that of faith in himself as thus invoked. But this faith is furthermore and otherwise described as *the faith which is by* (or *through*) *him.* The only natural interpretation of these words is that which makes them represent Christ as the author or procuring cause, as well as the end or object, of the faith in question. (Compare Heb. 12, 2.) But by whom was this faith exercised, or whose faith was it that had wrought such wonders? The most obvious answer to this question would be, faith on the part of the man healed. Nor is there any thing to contradict or peremptorily exclude this answer. Some of the Fathers, followed by some modern writers, have alleged that in their early miracles, both Christ and his Apostles dispensed with faith in the recipient as a previous condition of relief, although they afterwards required it. But this is a mere conjecture founded on the silence of the narrative in certain cases. We have every reason to believe that their practice was consistent if not uniform, nor can any reason be imagined why they should require faith afterwards and not at first. Interpreters, however, have been commonly disposed to understand by faith, in this place, that of the Apostles themselves, which we know to have been necessary, from the words of Christ on a remarkable occasion (Matt. 17, 20.) Three circumstances are insisted on, in this verse, as enhancing the proof of Divine agency, to wit, the notoriousness of the man's previous condition (*whom ye see and know*), the completeness of his restoration (*this perfect soundness*), and its publicity (*in the presence of you all.*)

17. And now, brethren, I wot that through ignorance ye did (it), as (did) also your rulers.

And now is a common formula, denoting a transition to some other topic, or the application of what has been already said. (See below, on 10, 5. 13, 11. 20, 22. 22, 16. 26, 6.) It may here be regarded as equivalent to saying, 'and now, since you are guilty of this, what hope remains?' The appellation *brethren* indicates his fellow-feeling and desire for their welfare. (See above, on 1, 16. 2, 29. 37.) Of the verse itself two very different views may be taken. The more obvious and common one regards it as a merciful concession on the part of the Apostle, an extenuation of his hearers' guilt.

This is not only a natural explanation of the language, but one recommended by the striking analogy of Christ's prayer for his murderers (Luke 23, 34), and Paul's declaration with respect to himself (1 Tim. 1, 13. Compare 1 Cor. 2, 8, and see below, on 13, 27.) To meet the objection, that whatever palliation might exist in the case of the multitude, there could be none in the case of their rulers, it has been proposed to construe the words thus, *that through ignorance ye did as your rulers did*, thus making a most marked distinction between these two classes. But this construction, though ingenious, is forbidden by the phrase *as also* (ὥσπερ καί), which indicates comparison, not contrast. If then the verse contains a concession or extenuation, it must comprehend the rulers no less than the people. Some deny, however, that there is any such extenuation, and suppose the ignorance here mentioned to be merely that of God's design in suffering all these things to happen. 'I know that you acted in ignorance of God's design, and so did your rulers; but this only aggravates your guilt without retarding the complete execution of his plan; he has effected his own purpose, and now calls you to repentance.' This view of the passage avoids the difficulties of the other, and agrees well with the next verse, which undoubtedly describes what had taken place as the fulfilment of prophecy. The principal objections are the restricted sense of *ignorance*, which it assumes, and the parallel passages before referred to. *Wot* is the old English verb to *know*, of which *wist* and *to wit* are other forms, *unwitting* and *unwittingly* derivatives. *Through ignorance*, or more literally, *according to* (or in proportion to) *your ignorance*. *Rulers* is Cranmer's version; Wiclif has *princes*, Tyndale *heads*, the Geneva Bible *governors*.

18. But those things, which God before had showed by the mouth of all his prophets, that Christ should suffer, he hath so fulfilled.

The death of Christ, although a crime on your part, was the execution of a divine purpose, as predicted by the ancient prophets. *Before had showed* is more exactly rendered in the Rhemish version, by a single word, as in Greek, *foreshowed*. The Greek verb, however, does not mean to show, but to announce beforehand. *By the mouth*, a common phrase for instrumental agency, when exercised in words, as *by the hand* is, where the reference is to act. (See above, on 1, 16. 2, 23.) *All his prophets*, i. e. the whole series of Old Testament Prophets, viewed as one organic body or official corporation. Whether each particular book contains such a prediction, is a question of no more importance than the question whether one is found in every chapter or on every page. The ancient prophets constitute one great representative body (see below, on v. 22), whose utterances are not to be viewed as merely those of individuals. The obvious meaning is that the point, to which the whole drift of prophetic revelation tended, was the death of Christ. For the New Testament usage of the verb to *suffer*, see above, on 1, 3. *So fulfilled*, in the original, *fulfilled so*, or as Tyndale has it, *thuswise*, i. e. in the great events which you have lately witnessed.

19. Repent ye, therefore, and be converted, that your sins may be blotted out, when the times of refreshing shall come from the presence of the Lord;

The first verb is here exactly rendered by the Vulgate (*poenitemini*), and somewhat less so by its English copyists (*be repentant, be penitent*), and yet the Greek word (μετανοήσατε) is identical with that in 2, 38. The exhortation to repent is here accompanied by one to *be converted*, or literally to *turn*, the Greek verb being of the active form. It may either be taken as the same thing with repentance; or as the outward change of life corresponding to the inner change of mind; or as a generic term, denoting the entire moral revolution, of which repentance is a necessary part. (See above, on 2, 38.) Instead of *remission*, we have here the stronger figure of abstersion or obliteration. The Greek verb is applied by Xenophon to the erasure of a name from a catalogue or roll. It may here denote the cancelling of charges against any one, and thus amounts to the same thing with the remission of 2, 38. The metaphor of blotting out occurs several times elsewhere (e. g. Ps. 51, 9. 109, 14. Isai. 43, 25. Jer. 18, 23. Col. 2, 14.) The word translated *times* is the same that is so rendered in 1, 7. It may here denote, still more specifically, set times or appointed times. The Greek word for *refreshing* admits of a twofold derivation (from ψυχή and ψύχω), according to which it properly denotes either cooling and relief from heat, or the recovery of breath after exhaustion. In either case, the essential meaning is the same, although the first is the idea naturally suggested by the English word *refreshing*. What is here meant is relief from toil or suffering, not without an implication of more positive enjoyment. What *times* are thus described depends upon a previous question as to the connection of the clauses and the grammatical construction of the sentence. *When* corresponds to a compound particle in Greek (ὅπως ἄν), which always elsewhere (Matt. 6, 5. Luke 2, 35. Acts 15, 17. Rom. 3, 4), like the uncompounded form (ὅπως), when followed by the same mood (Matt. 2, 8. 23. 5, 45. 6, 4. 16. 18. 8, 17), denotes the final cause or the effect (*so that, in order that*.) This gives a perfectly good sense, so far as this verse is concerned, to wit that their repentance would be followed by relief from the sense of guilt and God's displeasure. But this reference to personal experience may seem to be excluded by the promise of Christ's coming in the next verse, which can hardly be applied to any thing internal. In order to harmonize the two expressions, our translators make the particle a particle of time, showing *when* their sins were to be blotted out. But this, besides its violation of a uniform and constant usage, has the grave inconvenience of postponing their repentance, or at least their absolution, to some future time, if not to what we are accustomed to call Christ's second advent. How could the Apostle urge them to repentance by a promise that their sins should be cancelled as soon as the times of refreshing were come? Even if the interval were very short, this limitation of the offer of forgiveness is entirely at variance with the whole analogy of faith and scripture. This translation, therefore, which has been copied from the Vulgate into all the English versions, must be set aside upon a double ground; because it violates the usage of the language to obtain a sense which in itself is not a good one. If the stress of exegetical necessity were such as to justify a forced interpretation of the particle (ὅπως ἄν), it would be better to take it in the sense of *now that*, and refer it to the present or the past, and not the future. 'Repent and be converted to the blotting out of your sins, now that times of refreshing (i. e. the long expected times of the Messiah) are come from the presence of the Lord, and (now that) he has sent, etc.' This would render the whole passage clear and coherent, if it could be philologically justified. But as our task is to interpret what is written, in accordance with the general laws and usages of language, we are bound to reject every explanation which supposes ὅπως ἄν to be a particle of time, until some clear example of that sense can be discovered. Coming back, then, to the only sense justified by usage, we must understand the *times of refreshing* (or *relief*) to be in some way suspended upon their repentance as a previous condition. *From the presence of the Lord* (i. e. of God in Christ) denotes the source of the refreshing to be heavenly and divine, and the authority, on which the promise rests, to be absolute and sovereign. The divine face or presence, in such cases, may suggest the idea of his court or royal residence, from which his messengers go forth to execute his orders. (Compare Mattt. 18, 10. Luke 1, 19. 16, 22. Heb. 1, 14.) Looking simply at this verse, the *times of refreshing*, as observed already, might denote nothing more than the relief from pain, and other pleasurable feelings, which accompany repentance and conversion. Whether any other meaning is required by the context, is a question which can be solved only by determining the sense of the next verses.

20. And he shall send Jesus Christ, which before was preached unto you.

The objections to this version have been already stated, as well as to the version, *now that he has sent*, etc., which last would otherwise afford the best sense. The only grammatical construction, as we have already seen, is *so that* (or *in order that*) *he may send Jesus Christ*, here presented as a motive or a reason for repenting now. But to what sending do the words refer? Not to our Lord's first advent or appearance as a Saviour, which had already taken place, but either to his visible return hereafter, or to his presence in the hearts of individuals. The last agrees best with the context, as a motive to immediate personal repentance, but the first with all analogy and usage, as the Father is not elsewhere said to send the Son, as he is said to send the Spirit, into the hearts of men, as a matter of inward and invisible experience, but into the world, as a literal external fact of history. (Compare Gal. 4, 4 and 4, 6. See also Luke 4, 43. John 1, 10. 16. 17. 3, 34. 5, 36. 6, 14. 8, 42. 9, 39. 10, 36. 11, 27. 42. 12, 46. 16, 28. 17, 3. 8. 18. 21. 23. 25. 18, 37. 20, 21. 1 John 4, 9. 10. 14. 1 Tim. 1, 15. Heb. 10, 5.) Whatever be the sense of the particular expressions, it is clear from the whole drift of the discourse, that Peter here connects the times of refreshing and the mission of the Saviour, as identical, or at the least coincident events, with the repentance and conversion which he urges on his Jewish hearers. This being held fast, as undoubtedly involved in every possible, that is to say, grammatical construction of his language, some latitude of judgment, if not license of conjecture, may be tolerated as to the question wherein the connection of these things consists. In this sense, and to this extent, the passage may be paraphrased as follows. 'I exhort you to repentance and conversion, and I hold up, as inducements to these necessary acts, the delightful feeling of refreshment and relief, which has been rendered possible by God's gift of his Son to be a Saviour, and of his actual appearance for that purpose, in accordance with a previous divine appointment' or divine announcement, according as the common text (προκεκηρυγμένον, preached or proclaimed before), or that of the old manuscripts and latest editors (προκεχειρισμένον, appointed or ordained before) may be preferred.

21. **Whom (the) heaven must receive, until the times of restitution of all things, which God hath spoken by the mouth of all his holy prophets, since the world began.**

That the times in question were still distant, is implied in the account here given of Christ's local habitation during the interval. *The* before *heaven*, although not so distinguished in the English Bible, is supplied by the translators, not only without reason, but almost in violation of our idiom, which prefixes the article only to the plural number of this noun (*the heavens*.) Its insertion here would scarcely deserve notice, if it did not, by its very singularity, occasion a false emphasis, of which the original knows nothing. The construction of this first clause is ambiguous, as *heaven* may be either the subject or the object of the verb *receive*. The latter is preferred by Luther, Tyndale and Cranmer, *who must receive heaven*, i. e. take possession of it, occupy it, hold it. But the Greek verb (δέξασθαι) does not mean actively to take or seize, but passively or simply to *receive* or *accept* what is given by another. This sense though not irreconcilable with Luther's explanation, agrees much better with the one now commonly adopted. 'In the mean time, i. e. until God shall send Christ and the times of refreshing from his presence, he is committed to the heavens as a sacred trust to be delivered up hereafter.' The present tense (δεῖ) denotes an actual necessity already in existence, and arising from God's settled and avowed plan of procedure. (See above, on 1, 16. 21.) By *heaven* we are here to understand that place, or portion of the universe, where God manifests his presence to glorified saints and holy angels. Beyond this relative description, we have no account, and can have no conception, of its locality. To true believers the most interesting attribute of heaven is the one here specified, to wit, that the incarnate Son of God resides there. He then adds a third description of the times, to which he had directed their attention. Besides being times of refreshing (19), and of the Saviour's mission (20), they are also to be *times of restitution.* The Greek word is the noun corresponding to the verb explained above, on 1, 6. The indefinite expression is defined by the specification of the things to be restored, namely, *all things which God hath spoken*, etc. This has led some to take *restitution* in the sense of *fulfilment* or *accomplishment*, as being more appropriate to prophecy. But this, besides being destitute of all authority from usage, does not even suit the context; for the things to be restored or reinstated are not the predictions but the things predicted. As to the phrases, *by the mouth* and *all the prophets*, see above, on v. 18. They are here called *holy*, not so much in reference to personal as to official character. As Aaron, in his character of High Priest, was the saint or holy one of God (Ps. 106, 16), notwithstanding his infirmities and errors, so the Prophets are collectively described as *holy*, not as having all been eminently pious, but as having all been consecrated, set apart, devoted, to a special service, in discharge of which, and not as individuals, they uttered the predictions here referred to. Or rather, to retain the Apostle's strong and favourite expression, it was by their mouth that God spoke. *Since the world began* is not a version but a paraphrase. *Of old* or *from eternity* would be more faithful to the form of the original (ἀπ' αἰῶνος), which is found only in Luke's writings (see below, on 15, 18, and compare Luke 1, 70), as the correlative phrase (εἰς τὸν αἰῶνα) is a favourite idiom of John's (see John 4, 14. 6, 51. 58, and passim.) But the first is too weak, and the last too strong, in this connection. The Greek noun means duration, and especially indefinite duration, sometimes rendered more specific by the context in particular cases, which require the sense of age, lifetime, dynasty, or other great but variable periods (Matt. 12, 32. 13, 39. 40. 49. 24, 3,

Mark 10, 30. Luke 16, 8. 18, 30. 20, 34. 35.) Sometimes, on the other hand, the absence of all limitation, if not something still more positive, imparts to it the full sense of eternity (Mark 3, 29. Rev. 1, 6. 18, and passim.) In this case it may either be indefinitely taken as equivalent in meaning to our legal phrase, *from time immemorial,* or as a relative expression having more specific reference to the αἰών or cycle of the old economy, already virtually at an end and now fast verging to a visible conclusion. *All the holy prophets from* (the beginning of the prophetic) *period* or *dispensation,* which is tantamount to saying, ever since there were prophets in existence. This is clearly the opposite extreme to the final restitution mentioned just before, which does not therefore mean the restoration of all moral agents to a state of perfect holiness and happiness, but simply the completion or the winding up of that stupendous plan which God is carrying into execution, with a view to his own glory and the salvation of his elect people. This consummation may be called a *restitution,* in allusion to a circle which returns into itself, or more probably because it really involves the healing of all curable disorder and the restoration to communion with the Deity of all that he has chosen to be so restored. Till this great cycle has achieved its revolution, and this great remedial process has accomplished its design, the glorified body of the risen and ascended Christ not only may but must, as an appointed means of that accomplishment, be resident in heaven, and not on earth.

22. For Moses truly said unto the fathers, A prophet shall the Lord your God raise up unto you, of your brethren, like unto me: him shall ye hear in all things, whatsoever he shall say unto you.

The *for* connects this with the 20th verse, and verifies the statement there made, that Jesus Christ had been foreordained of God. The intervening verse is a digression or parenthesis relating to his present and future abode. This is the fourth prophecy expounded in this book by Peter; so far was he from dealing in mere narrative or exhortation. (See above, on 1, 20. 2, 16. 25. 34.) It is also his third exegetical argument in proof of the Messiahship of Jesus. The passage quoted is still found in Deut. 18, 15. 19. The omission of the words *to the fathers* in the oldest manuscripts is therefore of no moment. The quotation is made, with scarcely any variation, from the Septuagint version. The substitution of the plural (*you*) for the singular (*thee*) not only leaves the sense unaltered, but is fully justified by a similar change in the original. The truth is that the singular form there has reference to Israel, as a collective or ideal person. The objection to the application here made of this prophecy, derived from the original connection, may be obviated by extending it to the whole series or succession of prophets, representing Christ and terminating in him. The correctness of the Messianic application, here and in 7, 37 below, is confirmed by the historical fact, that this prophecy was never understood to be fulfilled in any intervening prophet, and that when John the Baptist came, he was asked, not only whether he was Christ, i. e. the Messiah, or Elijah his forerunner, but also whether he was "the prophet," or, as the English versions render it, "that prophet," the august but nameless subject of this very promise. (See John 1, 21. 25.) The resemblance between Christ and Moses, as prophets, mediators, legislators, founders of new dispensations etc. is obvious enough. The superiority of Christ is argumentatively urged in the epistle to the Hebrews (3, 3–6.) It may be doubted, however, whether *like me*, in the prophecy, was not designed to qualify the words immediately preceding, 'one of yourselves, belonging to your own race and lineage, as I do.' (*Truly* (μέν), as in 1, 5.)

23. And it shall come to pass that every soul, which will not hear that Prophet, shall be destroyed from among the people.

This is merely the conclusion of the passage, the essential part of which was quoted in the verse preceding. (See above, on 2, 25.) At the same time, it served to remind the hearers, that this question of Messiahship was no vain speculation, but a practical question of the utmost moment to themselves. (See above, on 2, 19–21.) *That prophet* is, in this case, the exact translation of the Greek words (τοῦ προφήτου ἐκείνου.) The phrase with which the quoted passage closes, *I will require it of him*, is a pregnant one, and means far more than strikes the eye at once. To express this latent meaning, the Septuagint version, *I will take vengeance*, is by no means too strong. In the verse before us, the Apostle brings it out still more emphatically, by employing the customary legal formula for the highest theocratical punishment, that of excision from the church or chosen people. (See Ex. 12, 15. 19. Lev. 7, 20–27.)

24. Yea, and all the prophets, from Samuel and those that follow after, as many as have spoken, have likewise foretold of these days.

It was not Moses only that predicted the times of the Messiah, but the whole series of the Hebrew prophets. This idea is expressed in a peculiar but intelligible manner, *all the prophets from Samuel and those that follow after.* Placing Moses by himself as the Prophet by way of eminence, he sums up all the rest as Samuel and his successors. Samuel is mentioned (here and in Ps. 99, 6) as the next great prophet after Moses, the first who remarkably resembled him in personal character and official position, and whose delegated work was to bring back the theocracy, as near as might be, to the ground where Moses left it, and from which it had declined during the agitated period of the judges and the interruption of prophetic inspiration (1 Sam. 3, 1.) The words *and (from) those that follow after* seem to express no more than had been expressed already in the words *all the prophets from* (or *after*) *Samuel;* but this redundancy rather makes the meaning clearer than obscures it.

25. Ye are the children of the prophets, and of the covenant which God made with our fathers, saying unto Abraham, And in thy seed shall all the kindreds of the earth be blessed.

But why should he refer to prophecies so ancient? What had the contemporary race to do with the old prophets and the Abrahamic covenant? The answer to this question, which might readily arise in any mind not thoroughly imbued with the true theocratical spirit, was exceedingly important, to define the scope of the Old Testament economy, as temporary in its own duration, but tending to ulterior and general results. The Apostle teaches them that they (and those who should come after them) were included in the scope of the old prophecies and the stipulations of the patriarchal covenant.

This is expressed, in a peculiar oriental form, by calling them *the sons of the prophets*. This cannot mean literal descendants, which could be true of only some among them, and is wholly inapplicable to the next phrase, (*sons* or *children*) *of the covenant*. The only sense that will apply to both is that of a hereditary interest and intimate relation to the promises and prophecies. (Compare Matt. 8, 12. Heb. 6, 17. Gal. 3, 29.) The form of expression may have been suggested by the mention of Samuel, and the historical association between his name and the prophets over whom he presided (1 Sam. 10, 5. 10), and who seem to have been afterwards called *sons of the prophets* (1 Kings 20, 35. 2 Kings 2, 3. 4, 1. 5, 22. 6, 1. 9, 1), an expression commonly supposed to denote pupils (whence the common though not scriptural phrase, "schools of the prophets,") but admitting also of a very different interpretation, namely, that of adherents to the prophets of Jehovah under the schismatical kingdom of the ten tribes. With the same essential meaning, that of intimate relation and hereditary interest, the Jews whom Peter was addressing might be justly called sons of the prophets and of the Abrahamic covenant. This wide scope of the promise he establishes by citing the assurance three times made to Abraham (Gen. 12, 3. 18, 18. 22, 18), and repeated successively to Isaac and Jacob (Gen. 26, 4. 28, 14), that in their seed all the nations of the earth should be blessed. The substitution of kindreds or families for tribes or nations, has of course no effect upon the sense. As to the seeming inconsistency of these views with Peter's scruples at a later period, see above, on 2, 39, and below, on 10, 34. 35.

26. Unto you first God, having raised up his Son Jesus, sent him to bless you, in turning away every one of you from his iniquities.

As the large views opened in the foregoing verse might seem to reach beyond the case of those to whom he now addressed himself, the Apostle here returns to his immediate subject, by adding to the certain truth, that the promise was to all the nations of the earth, the no less certain truth, that it was first to Israel. The expression is the same that Paul employs in teaching the same doctrine, *to the Jew first and also to the Greek* (Rom. 1, 16. 2, 9. 10.) *Raised up* is an ambiguous Greek verb (ἀναστήσας), which sometimes means to bring into existence, sometimes to raise from the dead. (For examples of both senses in the same context, see above, on 2, 30–32.) If the former meaning be adopted here, the next clause (*sent him*, etc.) must relate to our Lord's first advent; if the latter, to his coming by his Spirit after his ascension. It is not impossible that here, as in multitudes of other cases, both ideas were meant to be suggested, but with different degrees of prominence. (See above, on 2, 33.) The meaning of the verse will then be, that what God had promised to the fathers he had performed to the children by the advent, death, and resurrection of his Son in the form of a servant, whose original appearance was for their salvation, and although rejected and despised by many, was renewed in what they had so lately witnessed, the offer of forgiveness being still made on the same conditions to all who would consent to turn away from their iniquities. The Vulgate and some other versions make the verb (ἀποστρέφειν) reflexive or intransitive, *in every one's turning* or *converting himself*. But the common version, which makes *every one* the object, not the subject of the verb, is simpler and in keeping with the uniform doctrine of the Scriptures as to God's efficiency in man's conversion. (For a like ambiguity of syntax, see above, on v. 21, and for the pregnant sense of παῖδα, on v. 13.) This last clause is intended to preclude the favourite and fatal Jewish error, that the patriarchal promises and covenants would be fulfilled to Abraham's descendants, irrespective of their personal repentance and conversion. If saved at all, it must be from their sins, not in them. God had sent his Son to bless them, not by conniving at their guilt or leaving it unpunished, but by turning every one away from his iniquities. *To bless you*, literally, *blessing you*, in the very act of executing this commission. A comparison of this discourse with that recorded in the second chapter will disclose that mixture of variety and sameness, which is the surest test of authenticity. Had both discourses been identical in sentiment and structure, or had both been utterly unlike, the case would have been equally suspicious. But when both agree and differ, just as any speaker may agree and differ with himself on different occasions; when we find the same unstudied but effective rhetoric and logic, the same mode of interpreting the prophecies, the same mode of appealing to the conscience, yet without a trace of studied repetition, and with marked peculiarities of thought and style, distinguishing the two discourses from each other, not as incompatible or uncongenial, but as harmonious products of the same mind acting under varied circumstances and excitements; the hypothesis of forgery or fraudulent imitation becomes vastly more incredible than that of genuineness, oneness, and identity of authorship. And this again creates a general presumption in behalf of Luke's habitual fidelity as a reporter.

CHAPTER IV.

As the foregoing chapter describes the occasion of the first assault upon the church from without, so this describes the assault itself (1–22) with its effects (23–37.) The discourse of Peter, occasioned by the healing of the lame man, rouses the jealous indignation of the Jewish rulers, and especially the party-spirit of the Sadducees (1, 2), in consequence of which the two Apostles are imprisoned (3), but a multitude again embrace the new religion (4.) Being questioned by the Sanhedrim (5–7), Peter ascribes the miracle to Christ (8–10), the Messiah whom they had rejected, but whom God had exalted (11) and revealed as the true and only Saviour (12.) Astonished at their boldness (13), and embarrassed by the presence of the man who had been healed (14), the rulers, in a private conference (15), confess the fact of the miracle (16), but determine to arrest its effects (17), by forbidding them to preach Christ (18.) Peter and John, leaving the rulers to judge for themselves, announce their own determination to obey God rather than man (19. 20.) The rulers threaten but dare not punish them, on account of the publicity and popularity of what had happened (21. 22.) Reporting all this to their brethren (23), Peter and John unite with them in prayer to God, as the Creator (24), and as the author of an ancient prophecy (25), in which the rulers of the earth are represented as arrayed against the Lord and his Anointed (26), and which they acknowledge to have been fulfilled by the enemies of Christ (27), who thus unintentionally executed the divine plan (28.) The petition of the prayer is, that God would embolden them (29) and glorify their Master, by continued tokens of his favour and his presence (30); which petition was granted, both by sensible signs and spiritual influences (31.) After this triumphant issue of the first trial through which the infant church was called to pass, the historian describes her as still perfectly united and inspired with love (32), sustained by apostolical testimony and divine grace (33), sharing each others' secular advantages (34), under the guidance and control of the Apostles (35.) This general description is exemplified by two particular cases, one of which illustrates the reality and power of the ruling principle (36. 37); the other, of an opposite description, is recorded in the following chapter.

1. And as they spake unto the people, the Priests, and the Captain of the Temple, and the Sadducees, came upon them —

It was not to be expected that the freedom of speech exercised by Peter, in addressing the multitude assembled at the temple, would be suffered to continue undisturbed by the authorities. *Came upon them* (ἐπέστησαν), implying sudden movement or appearance, is a favourite verb of Luke's, occurring only thrice in any other part of the New Testament. (See below, 6, 12. 10, 17. 11, 11. 12, 7. 17, 5. 22, 13. 20. 23, 11. 27. 28, 2, and compare Luke 2, 9. 38. 4, 39. 10, 40. 20, 1. 21, 34. 24, 4.) *The priests*, i. e. those then on duty in the temple, who were bound *ex officio* to prevent all disturbance in the sacred precincts. This was especially incumbent on a certain body of Levites, whose commander is called in the Apocrypha the *prefect* (προστάτης) *of the temple*. A similar office may be traced in the Old Testament. (See Jer. 20, 1. 1 Chron. 9, 11. 2 Chron. 31, 13.) The term used here (στρατηγός) is a military one, from which some have inferred, that the person meant was a Roman officer, the commander of the garrison stationed in the castle of Antonia, at the northwest corner of the temple-area. (See below, on 21, 31.) But in the latter chapters of the book, this officer is repeatedly designated by another title (χιλίαρχος), which is also applied by John (18, 12) to the leader of the Roman detachment that arrested Jesus. Nor is it probable that the religious scruples of the Jews, which were always respected by their conquerors, would have suffered a heathen soldier to act as the guardian of their temple. The application of the title *general* or *captain* (στρατηγός) to officers not strictly military is justified, not only by the authority of Josephus, who uses it to designate the levitical officer described above, but also by classical usage. Having been extended from the generals, properly so called, to the ministers of war in Athens, it was afterwards applied to other public functionaries, and is used by Polybius to describe the Roman Consuls. As there may have been several such officers, who served at the temple in turn, there is no need of putting a different sense on the plural form in Luke 22, 4. 52. Some have attempted to distinguish the several motives of the parties joining in this opposition, by supposing that the officer of the watch objected merely to the breach of order in the sacred place, the priests to the assumption of the teachers' office by unauthorized persons (Matt. 21, 23), and the Sadducees to the doctrine taught by the Apostles, as described more particularly in the next verse. The Sadducees were not merely a religious sect, but a political party. They differed from the Pharisees, not only as to certain doctrines and the obligation of the oral law, but also in their national and patriotic feelings, and their greater disposition to assimilate themselves to the surrounding nations. The very name *Pharisee* most probably means *Separatist*, not in the modern sense, nor in allusion to their personal strictness and austerity, but rather as defining the position which they occupied in reference to other nations, by insisting upon every thing peculiar and distinctive, and affecting even to exaggerate the difference between the Gentiles and themselves. This, which was at first, i. e. after the return from exile, and even later, under the first Maccabees or Hasmonean princes, the true national and theocratical spirit, by degrees became corrupt, by losing sight of the great end for which the old economy existed, and worshipping the Law, with its traditional additions, as a system to be valued for its own sake, and designed to be perpetual. The opposition to this great national party arose chiefly from the *Sadducees*, a name of doubtful origin, but commonly traced, either to the name of a founder (Zadok), or to a Hebrew word denoting *righteous* (צדיק). At first, they seem to have objected merely to the narrow nationality of their opponents, and to have aimed at smoothing down, as far as possible, the points of difference between Jews and Gentiles, combining the Mosaic faith with the Greek philosophy and civilization, and renouncing whatever, in their own manners and religion, appeared most offensive or absurd to cultivated Gentiles. But this dangerous process of assimilation could not be carried far without rejecting matters more essential; as we find that the Sadducees did, not only with respect to the oral law or Pharisaical tradition, but also with respect to several important doctrines, and, as some think, to the greater part of the Old Testament; but this point is disputed. The Sadducees here mentioned may have been private individuals, but were more probably in public office, as we know from other parts of this same history, that the power was divided between these two great parties. (See below, on 5, 17. 23, 6.)

2. Being grieved that they taught the people, and preached through Jesus the resurrection from the dead.

This verse assigns the motive for the attack mentioned in the one preceding. It has been disputed whether two distinct subjects of complaint are here assigned, or only one; and also whether the whole verse relates to all the parties named before, or the first clause to the Priests and the last clause to the Sadducees. According to the latter view, the Priests were offended that the Apostles should presume to teach at all, the Sadducees only that they taught a certain doctrine. The principal objection to this view of the passage is, that it assumes an artificial structure of the sentence, and distinguishes too narrowly between the Priests and Sadducees as independent agents, whereas they may have been to some extent identical. (See below, on 5, 17.) *Being grieved*, or, as Tyndale has it, *taking it grievously*, though not an incorrect, is an inadequate version of the Greek word (διαπονούμενοι), which has the same sense here as in the classics, namely, *hard-worked*, exhausted by labour, and then, by a natural transition, wearied, out of patience, from the long continuance or frequent repetition of the cause, whatever it might be. In this case, they were tired of hearing the Apostles, and resolved that they should teach no longer. (See below, on 16, 18, and compare the Septuagint version of Gen. 6, 6. Ecc. 10, 9.) *The people*, i. e. the chosen people, the people of God, as in 2, 47. 3, 9. 11. 12. 23. 4, 1. What offended them was not the simple act of popular instruction, but the assumption of a right to be *masters of Israel* (John 3, 10) or the Jewish Church. *Preached* is too specific, from its familiar associations, to convey the exact sense of the Greek verb (καταγγέλλειν), which means simply to announce or proclaim. *Through Jesus* seems to mean that they proclaimed a general resurrection, to be effected or obtained through him. But this, though true and sufficiently taught elsewhere (e. g. 1 Cor. 15, 21. 1 Thess. 4, 14), is not the meaning of the words here used, but rather that they taught the doctrine of a resurrection, as proved and exemplified in that of Christ. So Paul says (1 Cor. 4, 6), "that ye might learn *in us*," i. e. by our example. The double article in Greek, before and after *resurrection*, has a force entirely lost in the translation, as implying that the noun is ambiguous, and that its sense must be determined by what follows. Like its verbal root (explained above, on 2, 24), it may be applied to any rise, or any act of raising; as it is by Plato to the act of rising up before one as a token of respect; by Sophocles to rising out of sleep; by Demosthenes to the rebuilding of a wall. It is true that in the Greek of the New Testament, it always means the resurrection from the dead; but it is not surprising that Luke, who wrote for Gentile readers, should preclude mistake by this express specification, both here and in Luke 20, 35, where the use of the article is precisely similar. As if he had said: 'they taught the doctrine of a *rising*, not from sleep, or from a low condition, or the like, but *from the dead.*' This last is not an abstract term, as it seems to have come to be in English, and as Tyndale formally translates it (*death*), but strictly means, *from* (*among*) *the dead*, from their society, or from a share in their condition. The very fact which they proclaimed, to wit, that Christ had risen from the dead, was fatal to one favourite dogma of the Sadducees (Matt. 22, 23. Mark 12, 18. Luke 20, 27. Acts 23, 8.) This accounts, not only for their wrath on this occasion, but for the general and otherwise inexplicable fact that, while the Pharisees are most conspicuous and active in the Gospels, as the opponents of our Lord himself, the Sadducees became so in the history before us, as the enemies and persecutors of his servants. They had little fault to find with the new doctrine, so long as it denounced the pharisaical traditions and corruptions, but as soon as the hated doctrine of the resurrection had been practically verified by that of Christ, they lost all patience with the men who preached it, and became, for a time at least, the most malignant of their persecutors. (See below, on 5, 17. 23, 6.) Less obvious and certain, although not entirely destitute of truth, is the distinction, made by some, between the Sadducees as more disposed to quarrel with Christ's doctrine, and the Pharisees with his morality, especially his treatment of themselves and their pretensions.

3. And they laid hands on them, and put (them) in hold unto the next day ; for it was now eventide.

Their first step was to arrest and imprison the two Apostles, not as a punishment, but *for safe-keeping*, which would not be an erroneous translation of the Greek phrase (εἰς τήρησιν), although most interpreters prefer the local sense of *prison*, on account of the parallel expression in 5, 18, where this sense is supposed to be required by the addition of the epithet *common* or *public*. The English version there has *prison*, but here *hold* (Wiclif, *ward*), which corresponds almost exactly to the strict sense of the Greek word. *Unto the next day*, or *the morrow*. The original expression is an adverb (αὔριον, *to-morrow*) used to qualify the word *day* understood. *Eventide* is a fine old English word, now obsolete in prose, equivalent to *evening-time*. This last clause may imply that it was either unlawful or unusual, or more probably than either, inconvenient to assemble the Sanhedrim at night, or on so short a notice. As they entered the temple at the ninth hour (v. 1), i. e. about three in the afternoon (see above, on 3, 1), and as Peter's discourse was probably much longer than the report of it here given (see above, on 2, 40), it must have been near evening, in the strict sense of the term, as denoting dusk or twilight. There is no need, therefore, of resorting to its wider usage, as denoting the whole afternoon, or to the Hebrew reckoning of a double evening (הָעַרְבַּיִם) between noon and night. See Ex. 12, 6. 16, 12. 29, 39. 41. 30, 8. Lev. 23, 5. Num. 9, 3. 28, 4, in all which places the phrase translated *in the evening* or *at even*, literally means, *between the (two) evenings*.

4. Howbeit many of them which heard the word believed; and the number of the men was about five thousand.

The preachers were arrested, but as Paul expresses it, (2 Tim. 2, 9), the word of God was not bound. In order to bring out this antithesis more clearly, the translators have employed the strong adversative *howbeit*, i. e. notwithstanding or in spite of all this, to express the continuative particle (δέ), which is not always even rendered *but*. (See above, on 1, 7.) *The word* is a phrase several times used in this book for the Gospel, the doctrine of Christ, the new religion. (See below

6, 4. 8, 4. 11, 19, 14, 25. 16, 6. 17, 11.) Still more frequent are the phrases *word of God* or *of the Lord*, of which this is an abbreviation, (See below, v. 31. 6, 2. 7. 8, 14. 25. 11, 1. 12, 24. 13, 5. 7. 44. 46. 48. 49. 15, 35. 36. 16, 17, 13. 18, 11. 19, 10. 20.) Other forms, occasionally used in the same sense, are *word of salvation* (13, 26), *word of grace* (14, 3. 20, 32), *word of the Gospel* (15, 7.) This sense is perfectly appropriate here, but less specific, and perhaps less natural, than that of *speech*, discourse, which also occurs elsewhere. (See below, 6, 5. 14, 12. 20, 7.) The effect here spoken of is not ascribed to the hearing of the Gospel elsewhere or before, but to the hearing of it as it had been now proclaimed by Peter. (See above, on 2, 41.) *Believed*, i. e. received it as true, and trusted in the Saviour whom it offered. This is one of the standing scriptural expressions for the saving change described in modern religious phraseology as getting religion, becoming pious, becoming a Christian, or obtaining a hope, with respect to all which harmless but needless innovations on the primitive church dialect, it may well be said, "the old is better" (Luke 5, 39.) Two questions have been raised, as to the number stated in the last clause of the verse. The first is, whether it includes the three thousand of 2, 41, or is to be added to that number, making a total of about eight thousand. The former is more probable, for two reasons; first, because the sentence otherwise contains an enfeebling tautology, which ought not to be assumed without necessity. The first clause is then unmeaning and superfluous—'many believed, five thousand believed'—whereas, upon the other supposition, the two clauses are alike essential to the meaning—'many were added upon this occasion, so that the whole amounted to five thousand.' Another reason for preferring this construction is derived from the Greek verb (ἐγενήθη), which does not mean simply that the number *was*, but that it *became* (or *came to be*) *five thousand*, a distinction often overlooked in the immediate English versions. (See above, on 1, 16. 19.) Those founded on the Vulgate, such as Wiclif's and the Rhemish, here as elsewhere, copy it almost too closely (*factus est, was made*.) There is less force in the argument, which some have urged, that Solomon's porch (3, 11) could not probably contain more than five thousand persons. It is equally improbable that it could contain so many, and still more so, that the crowd was compressed into the porch itself, instead of filling the vast court into which it opened. (See above, on 2, 2.)

Another gratuitous assumption in this argument is, that all the previous converts were still present in Jerusalem and at the temple, whereas many of the foreign Jews had probably gone home; unless we add a third assumption, namely, that what is here recorded took place immediately after Pentecost, if not in the evening of the day itself. But this, besides being perfectly gratuitous, and therefore just as easily denied as affirmed, is hardly consistent with the general description above given (2, 42–47) of the condition of the church, not merely on the day of its erection, but from that day onward, during a time long enough at least for the display of benevolent affections there described, as well as to justify the use of the expression that "the Lord added *daily* to the church" (2, 47.) A more legitimate though not conclusive argument, additional to those drawn from the language of the verse is, that if five thousand were converted by this one discourse, its effect far transcends that of the one at Pentecost, which nevertheless seems to be recorded as a signal and unique result, intended to do special honour to the organization of the Christian Church. The second question in relation to this number is, whether it includes both sexes, or is limited to males. In favour of the latter supposition is the uniform Greek usage, in which the generic and specific terms for *men* (ἄνθρωποι and ἄνδρες) are seldom interchanged. The absolute force of this consideration is impaired by the occurrence of exceptions, some of which are very doubtful, in the Greek of the New Testament (e. g. Matt. 14, 35. Luke 11, 31. 32. Rom. 4, 8. James 1, 12. 20. 23), as well as in the classics (e. g. in the favourite Homeric phrase, ἀνδρῶν τε θεῶν τε, and the no less favourite Platonic one, πᾶς ἀνήρ, in the sense of *every one* or *every body*.) This usage, although rare, is sufficient to destroy the necessity of holding fast the strict sense here, if exegetically inconvenient. Of those who so explain it, some understand it as implying what is expressed in Matt. 14, 21, "five thousand men *besides women and children*" (compare 15, 38), which would raise the aggregate much higher. Others, with far less probability, assume that the first converts may have been literally all men in the strict sense, especially if Solomon's porch, as some allege, was not accessible to female worshippers, who were restricted to the Court of the Women, as they are at this day to the latticed galleries of the synagogues. The ambiguous term *souls* in 2, 41, and the explicit ones, *both men and women* in 5, 14, have been used as arguments on both sides of the question; some alleging that the very mention of both sexes in the latter case shows clearly that the verse before us has respect to only one, while others no less plausibly contend, that the laconic and ambiguous expression here must be explained by the unequivocal language of the parallel passage. The whole question is more curious than important, as we know that there were multitudes of female converts not long after (5, 14); and even on the lowest computation of the numbers in the case before us, the increase of the Church was wonderfully great and rapid. The insertion of this parenthetical statement, in a narrative of suffering and persecution, suggests in a most striking and exhilarating manner God's sovereign independence, even of his chosen and most highly honoured instruments.

5. And it came to pass on the morrow, that their rulers and elders and scribes—

The sentence is completed in the next verse. The first phrase (*it came to pass*), as common in history as the future (*it shall come to pass*) in prophecy (see above, on 2, 17), here indicates the resumption of the main subject, after the brief digression in v. 4. *On the morrow*, a similar expression to the one in 3, 1, might be rendered *towards the morning* or *the next day*, implying that the Sanhedrim sat very early, but is usually understood as referring merely to the day and not the hour. *Their rulers* may, without the least absurdity, refer to the apostles or disciples, who were still subjects of the Jewish government; but most interpreters assume a prolepsis or anticipation of something mentioned afterwards. But as the Jews are not particularly named there, it is better to assume a free construction with a reference to the people generally, or their representatives mentioned in the first verse. A similar use of the same pronoun (αὐτῶν) without an expressed antecedent, occurs in Matt. 4, 23. In the use of the third person (*their rulers*) some find an indication, that Luke wrote, in the first instance, not for Jews but Gentiles. *Rulers* is best explained as a generic term, including the two clauses mentioned afterwards, *elders and scribes*. These are two of the orders represented in the national council, which is said to have been composed of seventy-one persons in imitation, if not in actual continuation, of the seventy elders who assisted Moses (Num. 11, 16.) From

Synedrion, the Greek word meaning *Session* or *Consistory*, and frequently applied to this later council (v. 15. 5, 21. 27. 34. 41. 5, 12. 15. 22, 30. 23, 1. 6. 15. 20. 23. 28. 24, 20), comes the Hebrew or Aramaic form *Sanhedrim*, by which it is now usually designated. The High Priest was the President of this assembly. (See below, on 7, 1. 23, 2.) By *elders* some have understood the rulers of the synagogues (Mark 5, 22. Luke 8, 41, 49. 13, 14. See below, on 13, 15. 18, 8. 17.) But this was only a later designation, or perhaps a real modification, of an older institution, that of the theocratical eldership, composed of the hereditary chiefs of tribes and heads of families, the natural as well as legal representatives and rulers of the people under the patriarchal system, which seems to have survived all changes in the Hebrew state from its foundation to its downfall, and may still be traced in other nations, being nothing more than an extension of domestic government, and therefore scarcely more destructible or mutable than the family relation upon which it rests. The elders, who composed a part of this great council, sat there as the proper representatives of Israel, considered as the church or chosen people. The *Scribes* of the New Testament are sometimes said to have been clerks or secretaries to the magistrates, appointed to assist them in the administration of the laws. But this was a Roman custom, rendered necessary by the military profession of most provincial governors; whereas among the Jews no such necessity existed. The more common explanation is that they were copyists or transcribers of the law. To this it has been objected, that the copies of the law in circulation were scarcely numerous enough to occupy so large a body of Scribes as seems to have existed in our Saviour's time (Luke 5, 17.) It is also objected that this theory leaves unexplained the authority evidently exercised by these men (Matt. 23, 2), which was far too great to be wielded by mere copyists, even of the Scriptures. It is said, in reply, that they were also expounders of the law; but this (it is alleged) has no necessary connection with the business of transcription. The truth lies, not between the two contending parties, but on both sides. The Scribes were copyists, but they were more. They were official guardians or conservators of the sacred text, in which work they succeeded Ezra, the first Scribe, in this sense, upon record (See Ezra 7, 6. 10. 11. 12. 21. Neh. 8, 4. 9. 13. 12, 26.) As he was commissioned to complete the canon of the Hebrew Scriptures, so the later Scribes were to preserve it unimpaired from generation to generation. This could only be secured by the most scrupulous transcription, and accordingly the care which has been exercised in this way by the Jewish Scribes is utterly unparalleled. Even what seems to be their superstitious and absurd excess is only the exaggeration and abuse of a most wise precaution. The severe rules by which new Hebrew manuscripts are still judged, and even the most beautiful condemned if blemished by a few mistakes, are relics of an immemorial custom, and bear witness to the care with which the Hebrew text has been preserved for ages. Thus a transcriber of the law, or he who officially had charge of its transcription, was something very different from an ordinary copyist. His work was not mechanical but critical, analogous to that which now engrosses some of the most learned men of modern times. The qualities required for this work were at the same time qualifications for the work of exposition. Thus the Scribes were naturally the interpreters, as well as the conservators of Scripture, and are therefore frequently called *lawyers* (νομικοί), not in the modern sense of advocates or aids in litigation, but in that of *jurists*, men officially employed about the law, and sometimes *doctors* (i. e. *teachers*) *of the law*, (νομοδιδάσκαλοι), both which expressions, chiefly used by Luke, would seem to be convertible with *Scribes*. (Compare Matt. 5, 20. Mark 2, 16. Luke 5, 30 with Luke 5, 17. 7, 30. 14, 3, and see below, on 5, 34.) Now as the Jewish state was a theocracy, in which law and religion were identified, these lawyers and doctors of the law were at the same time theologians and religious teachers. That this important office or profession should be represented in the Sanhedrim, is far less surprising than that English prelates should be members of the House of Lords. Such being the office of the Scribes, even on the supposition that its primary function was the preservation and perpetuation of the sacred text, there can be no need of discarding the common derivation of the name, in Hebrew, Greek, and Latin, from the verb *to write*, in order to derive it from a noun denoting *scripture* (ספר, γράμματα), and so to make it mean directly *scripturist* or *biblist*, an idea necessarily suggested by the nature of the office, as we have already seen, but not necessarily included in the meaning of the name. These two classes, the *elders* or hereditary representatives, and the *scribes* or spiritual guides of Israel, are here put for the Sanhedrim, of which they formed a necessary part. The omission of the priests, as a class, in this description, may be explained from their having been already mentioned as prime movers in this whole transaction (v. 1), whose presence therefore would be taken for granted as a matter of course; or from the fact that many of the Scribes were priests, as the same essential functions were discharged, in ancient times, by the sacerdotal tribe of Levi (Deut. 33, 10. 2 Chron. 17, 8. 9), and Ezra himself was both a Priest and Scribe (Ezra 7, 11. 12.)

6. And Annas the High Priest, and Caiaphas, and John, and Alexander, and as many as were of the kindred of the High Priest, were gathered together at Jerusalem.

Having described the Sanhedrim in general terms, by naming two of its constituent orders, Luke mentions separately several of its most distinguished members present upon this occasion, beginning with the High Priest, as the President. But a difficulty here arises from the fact, that Caiaphas, who is known, from Josephus as well as from the Gospels (Matt. 26, 3. 5. John 11, 49. 18, 13. 24), to have been the actual high priest at this time, is named in the second place without a title, while his predecessor Annas is named first, and expressly called High Priest. The confusion, which undoubtedly exists in relation to this matter, is not the fault of the historian but of the times, and corresponds exactly to the actual condition of the Jewish priesthood under the Roman domination. While the office was continued and regarded in its true light, as the representative of the theocracy, its authority and sanctity were greatly lessened in the eyes of all devout Jews, by the arbitrary interference of the Romans with its constitution and succession. According to the law, there could be only one High Priest, and he the hereditary representative of Aaron (Ex. 9, 44.) The office therefore was for life, and the incumbent immovable by any but divine authority. To this part of the system, with an inconsistency not easily accounted for, the Romans seem to have paid no respect whatever, but to have deposed and appointed the High Priest at pleasure, only limiting their choice, so far as now appears, to the sacerdotal race and lineage. Some idea of the length to which they pushed this license may be gathered from the fact recorded by Josephus, that no less than five sons of the Annas here named were High Priests successively, besides himself and his son-in-law Caiaphas. In consequence of this usurped authority and flagrant violation of the Law, there were sometimes several men living who had been High Priests, a thing unheard of and impossible in better times. The effect of this was twofold; first, to weaken and confuse the feeling of allegiance to these titular heads of the theocracy; and secondly, to introduce great latitude and looseness in the use of the official title. Those who still held fast to their integrity as Jews, could not acknowledge more than one High Priest, or recognize the claims of any man whose predecessor was still living. Thus he whom a Roman or Herodian called High Priest, might have no such character in the estimation of a Zealot or a Pharisee. This state of things may throw some light upon the passage now before us. Annas, who was probably a man of energy and talent, had been High Priest, and although displaced by secular authority, was still the only High Priest in the eyes of any strict or conscientious Jew. Even if his first appointment was irregular, he probably had no predecessor living, and being of the sacerdotal race, was the nearest representative of Aaron. But the title and the actual authority were now in the possession of his son-in-law Caiaphas, or, as Josephus calls him, Joseph. By some, the one would be regarded as the true High Priest, by some the other, by a third class neither. As the older and most probably the abler man, as well as the earliest incumbent, and perhaps the legitimate successor of Aaron, Annas would necessarily retain a large, if not the largest share of influence, through all the changes that succeeded his removal, especially as several of his successors were his own sons, and the one who held his place at this time was his son-in-law. Under such circumstances, nothing but prejudiced or morbid skepticism can discover inconsistency or error, either in the language of this passage, or in Luke's mention of these two men in his gospel (3, 2) as being both High Priests at once, which, in the sense above explained, was literally true. *John and Alexander*, from the position here assigned them, were no doubt well known members of the priestly race. Some have attempted to identify them with historical persons of that age; the first with Johanan Ben Zaccai, mentioned in the

Jewish traditions as an eminent contemporary priest; the other with a brother of the famous Jewish writer Philo, who was Alabarch or chief of the Jews at Alexandria. But no conclusion can be drawn from the names, which were both extremely common; the Hebrew name Johanan, on account of its meaning (*Jehovah favours*); the Greek name Alexander on account of the kind treatment of the Jews by the Macedonian conqueror, in consequence of which his name is said to have been given to all the males, at least of the sacerdotal race, who were born during the year, or on the anniversary, of his visit to Jerusalem. There can be no doubt, however, that the persons here meant were well known to Luke and to many of his early readers. The next clause has been variously explained, as denoting the chiefs of the twenty-four courses, into which the family of Aaron was divided; or the lineal descendants of his eldest son; or the various persons who had filled the office of High Priest. If another conjecture is worth stating, it may be that the words are intended to describe the family of Annas, so remarkable as having furnished half a dozen High Priests without lineal succession, and therefore worthy to be called *that archisacerdotal* (or *high-priestly*) *race*. This distinction, it is true, was acquired chiefly after these events, but might be generally known when Luke recorded them. *At Jerusalem*, according to the latest critical editions, *in* (ἐν) *Jerusalem*. The common text has *to* or *into* (εἰς) *Jerusalem*, which some explain as a mere interchange of prepositions, but which rather implies, that all the members of the Sanhedrim were not residing, or at least not actually present, in Jerusalem. (See a similar expression in 1, 12 above.)

7. And when they had set them in the midst, they asked, By what power, or by what name, have ye done this?

After the constitution of the court we have the formal arraignment of the prisoners. *In the midst* is by some understood to mean in the exact centre of the circle, or the semicircle, in which the members of the Sanhedrim are represented by tradition as habitually sitting. But it much more probably has the same sense as in 1, 15 above, where no such formal arrangement can be thought of. The essential meaning, although in a loose form, is conveyed by Tyndale's version, *set the others before them*. Then follows the judicial interrogation, no doubt conducted by the High Priest, as in 5, 27, and 7, 1, below. The question is similar to that put to Christ himself (Matt. 21, 23), but with a difference entitled to attention. Instead of asking, as in that case, by what *authority* (ἐξουσίᾳ), i. e. moral or legal right, they ask by what *power* (δυνάμει), i. e. physical capacity or force, and by what *name* (ὀνόματι) they had done this. The preposition before all these words is *in*, i. e. in the use or exercise of what power etc. (See above, on 1, 3.) *Name* seems here to have the same sense as in 3, 6. 16, although some suppose a reference to the magical use of the divine and other names by the exorcists and enchanters of that day. (See below, on 19, 13, and compare Matt. 12, 27.) The question then implies a suspicion of some occult and forbidden means in the performance of the miracle; for to that the pronoun *this* must be referred immediately, if not exclusively. To refer it, as some do, to the speech of Peter, or as others, to the speech and miracle together, is less natural. The question then is, 'in the use of what mysterious power, and as whose representatives, or by the invocation of whose name, have you effected this extraordinary cure?'

8. Then Peter, filled with the Holy Ghost, said unto them, Ye rulers of the people, and elders of Israel!

Peter again speaks for himself and John. This is his fourth speech recorded in the book before us. (See above, 1, 15. 2, 14. 3, 12.) What was before said, as to sameness and variety, might be here repeated. (See above, on 3, 12.) *Filled with the Holy Ghost,* not only by a previous or constant inspiration, but by an immediate and peculiar impulse, having special reference to this occasion. (See above, on 2, 4, and compare the promise, Mark 13, 11.) Under this influence, he not only addresses the assembly with respect, but recognizes its members in their official character and dignity. *Rulers of the people* and *elders of Israel* may be taken as equivalent descriptions of the whole body, since the rulers of the chosen people, under the patriarchal system (see above, on v. 5), were not elective but hereditary magistrates. Or the two titles may be so distinguished, that the last shall be descriptive of these natural representatives, and the first of persons holding office, independently of this hereditary rank, or in addition to it.

9. If we this day be examined of the good deed (done) to the impotent man, by what (means) he is made whole —

The sentence is completed in the next verse. This exordium, like those of Peter's previous discourses (see above, on 2, 15. 3, 12), although perfectly unstudied, and suggested by the circumstances under which he spoke, is, even rhetorically, striking and effective. The one before us is distinguished from the others by a tone of irony resembling and perhaps directly copied from our Lord's memorable saying to the Jews (John 10, 32), "Many good works have I showed you from my Father; for which of those works do ye stone me?" *If* (εἰ) does not always imply doubt, but is sometimes equivalent to *since*, or, as the Geneva Bible here translates it, *forasmuch as*. (See below, on 11, 17, and compare John 7, 4.) In this case, however, it is better to retain the proper sense, not only on the general principle of always giving it the preference, but because it strengthens the expression, by representing what was done as something strange and scarcely credible, as though he had said, 'if it can be true that you arraign us for this act of kindness.' The Greek verb (ἀνακρινόμεθα) is confined, in the New Testament, to Luke and Paul, who use it frequently, and almost always in the sense of judicial investigation, literal or figurative. (See below, on 12, 19. 17, 11. 24, 8. 28, 18, and compare Luke 23, 14. 1 Cor. 2, 14. 15. 4, 3. 4. 9, 3. 14, 24.) As it implies accusation and authority, *examined* is too weak here, unless understood to mean called in question, called to account, required to explain and justify one's conduct. The cognate noun (ἀνάκρισις) is used in like manner. (See below, on 25, 26.) *This day, to-day*, adds point and force to the hypothetical expression *if*, etc. 'Have we lived to see the day when men are called in question for their good deeds?' The effect is further heightened by the Greek noun (εὐεργεσία), which, both in etymology and usage, has the general sense of good conduct or behaviour, and the specific one of active kindness or beneficence. The English versions are weakened by the needless introduction of the definite article, "*the* good deed done to *the* impotent man," instead of "*a* good deed done to *an* impotent man," which is the form of the original. Another less gratuitous departure from that form is the insertion of the participle *done*, to represent a simple genitive construction (εὐεργεσίᾳ ἀνθρώπου), which could not have been retained in our idiom, but might have been more closely copied by simply substituting *to* for *of*. A third addition in the version, of which the English reader has no intimation, is that of the word *means*, which may be justified by the analogy of Matt. 5, 13, where the same phrase (ἐν τίνι), although not so translated, must be so understood. But the context here rather favours the translation *in whom*, i. e. in whose name, as in vs. 7 and 10. (For a similar construction of the preposition in a similar connection, compare Luke 11, 19.) *Impotent*, or more exactly, *weak*, *infirm*. *Is made whole*, literally, *has been saved*, which, in its widest sense, means saved from all evil, natural and moral (see below, on v. 12), but is sometimes used specifically to denote deliverance from bodily sufferings considered as effects of sin. (See Matt. 9, 21. 22. 27, 42. Mark 5, 23. 6, 56. 10, 52. Luke 8, 36. 50. 17, 19. 18, 42. John 11, 12.) In many of these places our translators use the verb *to heal* or *make whole;* whereas Wiclif even here translates *made safe*.

10. Be it known unto you all, and to all the people of Israel, that by the name of Jesus Christ of Nazareth, whom ye crucified, whom God raised from the dead, (even) by him doth this man stand here before you whole.

The exordium or preamble, which may almost be described as sarcastic or ironical in tone, is followed by a formal and most solemn answer to the question of the Sanhedrim, addressed not merely to themselves, but through them to the people of Israel, the chosen people, whom they represented. This implies that the fact declared was one of national concern, and less directly that the crime of crucifying Christ was that of Israel as a nation. The formula, *be it known*, occurs repeatedly in this book. (See above, on 2, 14. 36, and below, on 13, 38. 28, 28.) The Greek adjective (γνωστόν) is one of Luke's favourite expressions, being used only thrice in other parts of the New Testament. If *we* (ἡμεῖς) in v. 9 is emphatic, as it is in v. 20, there may be the same antithesis in this case as in that. 'If *we* must listen to your questions and reproofs in relation to this good deed, *you* must listen in your turn to us. Be it known, etc.' *By the name*, literally, *in the name*, as in the question of the Sanhedrim. (See above, on v. 7.) The accumulation of descriptive terms in this verse is remarkable. Jesus (the Saviour), Christ (the Messiah), the Nazarene (as such an object of contempt, but a subject of prophecy), the Crucified (by the hands of men), the Risen (or raised by the power of God.) The same contrast between Christ's treatment at the hands of God and man, is here presented as in both the previous discourses. (See above, on 2, 23. 24. 3, 14. 15.) The design, in all three cases, is to bring this great personal and public crime home to the consciences of those who heard him. The *even*, supplied in the beginning of the last clause, is intended to identify the subject of the sentence, still more clearly than it is in Greek by the repetition of the particle. *By him*, literally, *in this*, which may be referred directly to the person of the Saviour, or still more naturally to his name, which makes the parallelism of the clauses more exact. *In what name?* . . . . *in the name of Jesus* . . . . *in this* (*name*) etc. So much is comprehended in the name, as here used (see above, on 3, 16), that nothing is lost, but something gained, by this construction. *Here*, though not expressed in the original, is no gratuitous addition, being really included in the verb (παρέστηκει), which means to *stand by* or *near*. (See above, on 1, 10.) The same idea is expressed by the addition of the words *before you*, in your sight, in which he appeals to their own senses as eye-witnesses. From this we learn that the man who had been healed was also present, either of his own accord as a spectator, or cited by the council as a witness, or as a prisoner with the two apostles. *Whole*, not only as opposed to mutilation or the loss of limbs, but in the sense of *sound* or *healthy*. If the question of the Sanhedrim (v. 7) contains, as some suppose, a tacit reference to the law in Deut. 18, 19–22, where so much is said of speaking in the name of God, as opposed to that of other gods, it is remarkable that Peter, in reply, speaks only *in the name of Jesus*, which was either a direct violation of that law, or an indirect assertion of the deity of Christ. It is highly probable indeed that the continual reiteration of this phrase by the Apostles has some reference to its emphatic repetition in the passage of the law just cited. An old Greek manuscript, supposed to have been used by the Venerable Bede, and now deposited at Oxford, adds, *and in no other.*

11. This is the stone which was set at nought of you builders, which is become the head of the corner.

There being no formal reference to scripture here, as there is in several previous cases, some have supposed the words here quoted to be merely a proverbial expression of the fact that what men slight and overlook is often afterwards exalted. But although the saying may have been proverbial likewise, yet since Christ himself had quoted the same words as "written" (Luke 20, 17), and as something which his hearers must have "read in the scriptures" (Matt. 21, 42), and since they are still extant in the Book of Psalms (118, 22), there can be no doubt that this is a sixth (if not a seventh) prophecy, expounded and applied by Peter since the opening of this history. (See above, on 1, 16. 20. 2, 16. 25. 34. 3, 22.) The form is substantially that of the Septuagint version, but with the substitution of the stronger term (ἐξουδενηθείς), *nullified*, made nothing of, treated as nothing, for the more exact but weaker one (ἀπεδοκίμασαν) *rejected* or repudiated. Tyndale adapts it to the figure of a building by translating *cast aside.* The idea no doubt is that of a stone thrown aside as worthless or unfit by the builders of a house, but afterwards selected as the *head* (not the top-stone, but the chief foundation) *of the corner*, where the strength of the structure is supposed to reside in the juncture of the walls. Its appropriateness to Christ has never been denied, but only its original reference to him as its immediate subject. Besides those who find here another case of mere accommodation (see above, on 1, 20), some who grant the correctness of the application, grant it only in a typical or secondary sense, while others make the whole psalm a direct and exclusive prophecy of Christ. Intermediate between these two, but nearer to the first, is the hypothesis, that this psalm was first sung at the laying of the corner-stone of Zerubbabel's temple, as described in the third chapter of Ezra; that the immediate reference is to that structure, which however was itself a type, not only of the church or chosen people, in whom God resided, but of Christ, in whom he was to dwell in a far higher and yet stricter sense, and by whose advent the material temple would be superseded. This symbolical relation of the ancient sanctuary to the person of our Lord is not an exegetical expedient for the explanation of this passage, but the only hypothesis by which that feature of the ceremonial law can be accounted for, or Christ's own language on the subject vindicated from the charge of fanciful caprice. It was because the tabernacle and temple were designed to teach the doctrine of divine indwelling, by giving God a home among his people, similar to theirs, until he should take up his permanent abode in human nature by the incarnation of his Son; it was only for this reason, and on these conditions, that the Son himself, without a mere play upon words, or an evasion utterly unworthy of him, could say, "Destroy this temple, and in three days I will raise it up," when in fact he only "spake of the temple of his body" (John 2, 19–21.) Since then the temple was intended to prefigure Christ, there can be nothing fanciful or forced in applying what was said, in the first instance, of that temple to "the temple of his body" or his theanthropic person. That such an application was not altogether novel, we may learn from the hosannas of the multitude in honour of our Saviour's Messianic entrance to the Holy City (Matt. 21, 8. 9. Mark 11, 8–10. Luke 19, 36–38); the expressions there used being taken from this very Psalm (118, 26), which must therefore have been commonly regarded as in some sense a Messianic prophecy. The very word *Hosanna* is the *Save now* (or *I pray*) of Ps. 118, 25, almost as nearly as the Hebrew words could be expressed by the Greek alphabet. There is peculiar beauty in the application made by Peter, since it raises the image of Messiah's kingdom, as a palace or a temple still unfinished, and the very men whom he addresses as the regularly constituted builders (*you builders*, more exactly, *you the builders*) who, with fatal blindness, had rejected the chief corner-stone of the whole structure, and were now confounded because God, in spite of them, had set it in its proper place. It would be hard to frame a figurative exhibition of these great events, more striking in itself or more appropriate to those whom the Apostle was addressing, than the one furnished ready to his hand in the Old Testament, and already used for the same purpose by his Lord and Master. The same application is implied in Paul's description of the church, or the body of believers, as "built upon the foundation of the apostles and prophets, Jesus Christ himself being the chief corner-stone" (Eph. 2, 20.) A kindred prophecy, referring more exclusively to the Messiah, is that in Isai. 28, 16, twice explicitly applied to Christ by Paul (Rom. 9, 33. 10, 11), and once by Peter in his first epistle (2, 6.) In reference to both these passages it might be said, as Peter here says with respect to one of them, " this is the stone," i. e. 'this man, whom you crucified but God raised from the dead, is the very stone, of which you have so often read or heard in your own scriptures, as a stone rejected by the builders, but replaced by God himself at the foundation of his spiritual temple, i. e. of his church or kingdom.'

12. Neither is there salvation in any other, for there is none other name under heaven, given among men, whereby we must be saved.

The Apostle, here as elsewhere, brings his reasonings and expositions to a practical conclusion. (See above, on 2, 38–40. 3, 26.) He gives them solemnly to understand, that the mistake which they, as builders of the temple, had committed, was not merely theoretical or exegetical, but practical and, if persevered in, fatal, to themselves and others. He reminds them that the character ascribed to the Messiah was not merely one of dignity and honour to himself, but of vital interest to others also. The system, of which he was the corner-stone, was a system of salvation, and the only one which God had sanctioned or revealed. *Name* is here used in allusion to its frequent repetition in the foregoing context, and of course with the same latitude of meaning. No other person, no other authority, no other invocation, etc. may be all included. *Under heaven,* i. e. in the world, or on the earth. (See above, on 2, 5.) *Given,* i. e. by authority, bestowed by God, from whom all saving methods must of course proceed. *Among men* is not simply *to men,* as the objects of the favour, but among them, with a reference to its diffusion. 'No other method of salvation has been made known and diffused among mankind by God's authority.' *Whereby,* or more exactly, *wherein, in which,* not only by it as the means, but in the possession, use, and application of it. (See above, on v. 7.) *Must be saved,* not only may, as a matter of option or of right, but must, as a matter of necessity, if saved at all. This text is often weakened in quotation by the change of *must* to *may* or *can.* Because the verb *saved* is applied in the original of v. 9 to corporeal healing, some insist upon the same interpretation here, as if Peter meant to say that there was no other name, the invocation of which could effect a miraculous cure. But apart from the unworthiness and incongruity of this interpretation in itself considered, and the absence of all usage or analogy to recommend it, an argument against it may be drawn from the obvious parallelism or correspondence of the verb *to be saved* and the noun *salvation*, which is never, in the Greek of the New Testament, applied to the healing of disease, whereas it is the standing, not to say, the technical expression for the whole remedial work, which the Messiah was expected to accomplish, and of which his personal name (*Jesus*) was significant (Matt. 1, 21), the great salvation (Heb. 2, 3), which was to go forth from the Jews (John 4, 22), and which the Apostles preached to Jews and Gentiles (13, 26. 47), the greatest gift of God to man, and so described both here and elsewhere (Isai. 9, 6. 2 Cor. 9, 15. Eph. 1, 22. 2 Tim. 1, 9.) This salvation, although something infinitely more than bodily relief or healing, comprehends it, as the whole includes the smallest of its parts, and as the least effect must cease with the cessation of its cause. Even on earth, especially when Christ was personally present, the restoration of health was often but the outward and accompanying sign of spiritual healing, or at least the type and pledge to others of a blessing not immediately experienced. And in the case of all who shall be ultimately saved, the lower sense of this expression will be certainly included in the higher, not by an arbitrary constitution, but by a natural and rational necessity. "The inhabitant shall not say, I am sick, (because) the people that dwell therein shall be forgiven their iniquity." (Isaiah 33, 24. See also Rev. 21, 3. 4.)

13. Now when they saw the boldness of Peter and John, and perceived that they were unlearned and ignorant men, they marvelled, and they took knowledge of them, that they had been with Jesus.

Now is not an adverb of time, but a continuative particle (δέ), which might as well be rendered *and* or *but*. (See above, on v. 4.) It is remarkable that, although the effect of this discourse is here distinctly stated, as in the case of Peter's Pentecostal sermon (2, 37), the effect itself was altogether different. We read here of no compunction or alarm, no inquiry what they must do, and therefore no additional instructions as to that point. The only impression here described is that of wonder and perplexity. Looking at these two cases by themselves, we might be led to the conclusion, that the Gospel prevailed only in the humbler classes, and that the rulers were beyond its reach. Such a distinction seems in fact to have been made by the leading enemies of Christ themselves. "Have any of the rulers (ἀρχόντων) or of the Pharisees believed on him? As for this rabble (ὄχλος), who know not the law, they are accursed" (John 7, 48. 49.) But this proud boast, if not false when originally uttered, was afterwards falsified by the event. It would even seem that this relation of the rulers and the rabble was reversed; for we read in the same Gospel (12, 37. 42), that "although he had done so many miracles before them, they (the ὄχλος of v. 34) believed not in him . . . . nevertheless even of the rulers (καὶ ἐκ τῶν ἀρχόντων) many believed on him, but because of the Pharisees did not confess him, lest they should be put out of the synagogue." Of this class some, we know, did afterwards confess him, such as Nicodemus and Joseph of Arimathea (John 19, 38. 39), and the same was probably the case with others. Whether these were present on the occasion now before us, we have no means of determining. It is most probable that they were not, since no dissent or opposition is recorded, as in John 7, 50. 51; but even if they were, being already converts, they had no cause for compunction, and the rest remained insensible, not because they were Pharisees or rulers, but because they were abandoned to themselves, by that mysterious but not unjust discrimination, which may still be traced in the dissimilar effects produced by the same truth, from the lips of the same preachers, upon different companies or individuals. The verb translated *saw*, though not the same with that in 1, 11, has much of the same force, denoting not mere sight but contemplation, the act of viewing as a spectacle or show. The idea is, not simply that they *saw* the boldness of the two Apostles, but that they *surveyed* it for some time before they could account for it. One of the latest writers on this passage understands it as ascribing their wonder to the boldness of these men who had so lately left their master and been scattered (Matt. 26, 56. Mark 14, 50.) But this puts too confined a sense upon the word (παῤῥησίαν) translated *boldness*, which signifies not merely, nor according to its derivation mainly, bravery or courage, but freedom and readiness of speech, as opposed to hesitation and reserve, no less than to timidity or cowardice. See above, on 2, 29, and below, on vs. 29. 31. 28, 31. With respect to the joint mention of the two Apostles, as concurring in the words and deeds recorded, see above, on 3, 4. 11. There is, however, a distinction in the Greek, which is entirely lost upon the English reader. Not only is the name of John postponed to that of Peter, but also to the noun which governs it. The nearest English imitation would be, *seeing Peter's boldness and John's*. *Perceived*, or more exactly, *apprehending*, the latin etymology of which corresponds to that of the expression here used (καταλαβόμενοι), i. e. forming a conception of something not known or correctly understood before. Some understand it to mean *having learned* (or *ascertained*) by information from others; but it rather signifies perceiving, apprehending, from their own observation of the prisoners' appearance, language, and deportment. *Unlearned*, or, adhering more closely to the form of the original (ἀγράμματοι), *illiterate*, *unlettered*. It does not necessarily imply gross ignorance, or inability to read, since the Greek root (γράμματα) means something more than *letters* in the lower sense of alphabetical characters, namely, *letters* in the higher sense of learning, literature, education. Among the Jews it had particular reference to scriptural or sacred learning, as the only kind much cultivated by them, so that the adjective here used is virtually the negative or opposite of the noun (γραμματεύς) translated *scribe* (see above, on v. 5), and means without scholastic or rabbinical training. *Ignorant* seems simply an equivalent expression, but the Greek word (ἰδιῶται) has a different derivation and a marked significancy of its own. Its primary sense is that of *private persons*, as opposed to kings by Homer, to rulers by Herodotus, to military officers by Xenophon, and to the state or body politic by Thucydides. A secondary sense is that of one without official or professional knowledge, in which sense Thucydides opposes it to the physician, and Plato to the poet and musician. This approaches very nearly to the wider use of our word *layman*, which is perfectly consistent with its derivation (from λαός, *people*), its specific opposition to the clergy (κλῆρος, see above, on 1, 17) being merely conventional and matter of usage. Accordingly the oldest English versions, made directly from the Greek, translate the phrase, *unlearned men and lay people* (Tyndale), *unlearned and lay men* (Cranmer.) The same is probably the sense of Wiclif's version, *unlettered and lewd men*, the bad moral sense of *lewd* belonging to a later usage. By a further change the Greek word (ἰδιώτης) came to have the general sense of ignorant, uneducated. If this wide meaning be preferred here, the two epithets are nearly synonymous, as in the Geneva version, *unlearned men and without knowledge.* (Compare 2 Cor. 11, 6, where ἰδιώτης τῷ λόγῳ is translated *rude in speech*, the very phrase which Shakspeare puts into the mouth of his Othello, "Rude am I in speech, etc.") From the sense of *ignorant* arises, by a natural association, that of imbecile or foolish, which belongs however only to the modern derivative form (*idiot* or *ideot*), and not at all to the original Greek usage; so that Matthew Henry undesignedly misleads the English reader when he says, "they were *idiots* (so the word signifies); they looked upon them with as much contempt as if they had been *mere naturals*, and expected no more from them, which made them wonder to see what freedom they took." This is a gross exaggeration of the feeling here imputed to the rulers, and one founded solely on the version; for "so the word signifies" only in the modern tongues. Even the milder and better authenticated sense of *ignorant* is not entitled to the preference in this case, on account of the tautology which it produces, and because, according to a recognized hermeneutical principle, the presumption is always in favour of the primary or strict sense, in the absence of specific reasons for departing from it. The best sense, therefore, of the whole descriptive phrase is that of uneducated men and private individuals or laymen, with an implication of obscurity and want of experience as public speakers. (The Rhemish version has *unlettered men and of the vulgar sort.*) *Marvelled*, wondered, were astonished and unable to account for what they saw. (See above, on 2, 7, where the same verb is used, both in Greek and English.) *Took knowledge of* is an unusual expression, here employed to represent a Greek verb (ἐπεγίνωσκον), which, though sometimes only an intensive, meaning to know fully (Luke 1, 4. 1 Cor. 14, 37. 2 Pet. 2, 21), or to receive information (Luke 7, 37. 23, 7), is also used in the New Testament (e. g. Matt. 14, 35. 17, 12. Mark 6, 33. 54. Luke 24, 16. 31), as well as by the best Greek writers, in the specific sense of recognizing, knowing again, a thing or person known before. (See above, on 3, 10.) The choice lies here between this sense and that of learning, ascertaining, from others; but as no such source of information is referred to in the text or context, the former meaning seems entitled to the preference. 'They recognized them as men whom they had seen with Jesus.' There is no improbability in this, since *rulers* are particularly mentioned in some cases as attending on our Lord's instructions. (See Matt. 21, 23. Luke 18, 18. John 12, 42.) It is not, however, necessary to restrict the recognition here described to recollection of their persons. It is equally natural, and may be more so, to explain it of an inference drawn from the matter or the manner of their preaching, as sufficient to show that they had kept the company of Jesus. The pluperfect form, *they had been*, is substantially correct, though not an exact copy of the Greek, which strictly means, *they were*, i. e. they were (once) with Jesus as companions, or were (still) with Jesus as disciples or adherents; most probably the former, the idea of discipleship or partisan attachment being rather implied than expressed, both here and in Mark 14, 6. There still remains a question of some moment with respect to the connection of the clauses. Some understand this last clause as a part of what they wondered at, or as their reason for considering them ignorant unlearned men. 'They marvelled at their readiness of speech, recognizing them as former associates of Jesus, and therefore of course ignorant and common men.' But this construction is at variance with the natural consecution of the sentence, which first describes the Sanhedrim as struck with the Apostles' freedom of speech, then as noting or observing their illiterate and low condition, and finally as recognizing or recalling their connection with Jesus. The only natural interpretation of this last particular is that which understands it, not as a reason for their wonder but a remedy, the means by which they finally accounted for what seemed to them at first so unaccountable. While the form and manner of the men's discourse betrayed their want of education, and especially of rabbinical training, its substance and its spirit seemed to indicate a higher source, and this could be found only in their intercourse with Jesus, whose extraordinary wisdom and authority in teaching could not be disputed, even by his enemies. (See Matt. 7, 29. 22, 16. Mark 1, 22. 12, 14. 32. John 7, 15. 46.) The peculiar copulative (τε), which some would render, *they both marvelled and took knowledge* (see above, on 1, 1. 13), is compatible with both constructions, and cannot therefore help us to decide between them.

14. And beholding the man which was healed

standing with them, they could say nothing against (it).

This verse describes the embarrassing position of the Sanhedrim, produced not merely by the eloquence or reasoning of the Apostles, but by the miracle, which served as a divine attestation to the truth of their pretensions and their doctrines. This they would gladly have denied or called in question; but how could they, with the man himself before their eyes, perhaps brought thither by themselves as a prisoner or a witness? (See above, on v. 10.) *The man which was healed*, in Greek, *the healed (man.)* The word *standing* seems to be emphatic. It was not his simply being *with them*, in their company, that silenced these grave rulers, but his standing there, erect like other men, a sight which every moment must recall to mind the miracle just wrought. A beautiful parallel has been cited from the Gospel History (Mark 5, 15), where the same stress may be laid upon the act of *sitting*, i. e. sitting in an orderly and decent manner, or sitting at all, instead of roving and raving, as a proof that the maniac had been suddenly restored to reason. *Could say nothing against (it)* is a free translation, in which the last word, although not so distinguished in the English Bible, is supplied, in order to complete the construction, but without a grammatical antecedent. The literal version is, *they had nothing to reply*, or still more closely, *to say back*, in the way of contradiction or denial. That the verb *to have* ever means *to be able*, is a common but precarious assertion, insufficiently supported by such passages as Matt. 18, 25, where the strict sense is properly retained in our translation, and Mark 14, 8, where the exact sense is, *what she had she did*, meaning no doubt what she had at her command or in her power; but this ellipsis does not change the meaning of the verb itself. The other verb is common in the classics, although rare in the New Testament. The only other instance of its use is in a promise of our Lord, which may be said to have received its first fulfilment in the case before us. " Settle it therefore in your hearts (i. e. when delivered into synagogues and prisons, and brought before kings and rulers for his name's sake) not to meditate before what ye shall say in your defence (ἀπολογηθῆναι); for I will give you a mouth and wisdom, which all your adversaries shall not be able to gainsay (ἀντειπεῖν) or withstand." (Luke 21, 14. 15.)

15. **But when they had commanded them to go aside out of the council, they conferred among themselves.**

Unwilling to commit themselves by rash concessions in the presence of the prisoners, they first confer among themselves, respecting what they are to say and do. *But*, and, or so then. (See above, on v. 13.) *When they had commanded* is a periphrastic version of the participle, *having commanded*. *To go aside*, or more exactly, *to withdraw* or *go away* (ἀπελθεῖν). The exclusion of the prisoners was not an act of violence, or even of contempt, but like that of ambassadors from the Greek assemblies after they had spoken, a custom often mentioned by Thucydides, and not without its counterparts in modern usage, as for instance in the practice of courts martial and the trial of impeachments. *Conferred* or as the Greek word *threw* (or *laid*) *together*, i. e. compared opinions on a given subject. *Among themselves*, literally, *to each other*.

16. **Saying, What shall we do to these men? For that indeed a notable miracle hath been done by them, is manifest to all them that dwell in Jerusalem, and we cannot deny (it.)**

We have here, not the very words of any individual, but the sum and substance of what all said. (See above, on 2, 7.) The question has been idly raised, how Luke became acquainted with these secret consultations. To the obvious answer, that he wrote by inspiration, it has been objected, not without some truth, that inspiration was intended to supply the deficiencies of knowledge otherwise obtained, but not gratuitously to replace it. What was known, however, from other sources, if incorporated in a revelation by divine command, has all the authority of an original divine suggestion. There is no need therefore of attempting to discriminate between these elements of revelation. If Luke had human sources of intelligence, he doubtless drew upon them, by divine permission or command; but if he had not, this is so far from impairing the credit of his narrative, that on the contrary, it adds to it, by making the divine authentication of his statements more exclusive and direct. To the unbeliever in his inspiration, it may be a question of some interest and moment, whether he was personally present upon this occasion, or received his information, *viva voce* or in writing, from converted priests or rulers who were members of the Council. But to those whose judgments are convinced and satisfied by overwhelming evidence, that this whole history is more than a mere human composition, these inquiries must be matters of comparative indifference, because neither needing nor admitting of a certain answer. The form of the question in the first clause is precisely similar to that in 2, 37, that is according to the common text, for several of the oldest manuscripts, instead of *shall we do* (ποιήσομεν,) read *may* or *can we do* (ποιήσωμεν), both here and in 2, 37 above. *Indeed*, not *in fact, in truth*, or *really* (see below, on v. 27), but simply the continuative particle (μέν), usually answering to *but* (δέ), and really without an equivalent in our idiom. (See above, on 1, 3, where it is translated *truly*.) *Notable* is not a happy version, either here or in 2, 20, where it answers to a Greek word altogether different in form and meaning. The expression here used (and explained above, on v. 10) strictly means *well known*, familiar, and implies unquestionable certainty; a miracle *known* to have been wrought, and therefore undeniable. The other adjective means nearly the same thing, namely, *manifest* or *evident*, but instead of being applied to the miracle itself, is applied to the fact of its occurrence, as something visible and clear to all Jerusalem. The word here put for *miracle* is that which strictly means a *sign* or proof of something else. (See above, 2, 19. 22.) This is therefore a concession, not only of the fact, but of its logical consequences and results. This nice distinction is observed in the Rhemish version (*a notorious sign*.) *Them that dwell in*, literally, *those inhabiting*. (See above, on 2, 5.) *Can* is not a mere auxiliary, but an independent verb, *we are not able*. *It* is again supplied, as in v. 14, but its antecedent is in this case obvious, to wit, *sign* (or *miracle*) immediately preceding.

17. But, that it spread no further among the people, let us straitly threaten them, that they speak henceforth to no man in this name.

This verse records the poor expedient, to which they were reduced in their perplexity. The words are still those of the Sanhedrim in private consultation. The word translated *but* is not the copulative particle (δέ) so rendered in v. 15, but the proper adversative (ἀλλά), corresponding to the previous concession. 'Though the miracle is perfectly notorious, and it were folly to deny it, *yet* let us do what we can to hinder its effect.' *Spread no further*, (literally, *more*, or *to a greater degree*) is commonly explained, as in the Vulgate (*ne divulgetur*), of the miracle, 'that it may be no further known or heard of.' To this, though perhaps the obvious construction, there are grave objections. In the first place, what could they have gained by the suppression, in the country or the provinces, of what was already known to "all inhabiting Jerusalem?" If it be true that Paris is France, how much more true was it that Jerusalem was Jewry, as being not merely its political centre, but the seat of the theocracy, the chosen and exclusive sphere of the ceremonial law, in which alone its most important rites could be performed, and from which, as the heart of the whole system, vital influences not only did but were intended to go forth to the extremities. If the fact in question was notorious in Jerusalem, to foreign no less than to native residents, it mattered little whether it spread further in Judea and Samaria and Galilee or not. But even if it had been never so desirable to check the spread of this report, how could it be accomplished? And especially, how could it be accomplished by the means here proposed, i. e. by threats and prohibitions, not to state this fact, but to speak in this name, i. e. to preach Christ? The entire irrelevance and insufficiency of this expedient to prevent all further knowledge of the miracle, evinces that the end which they proposed to gain was something else; and as the end may be determined by the means, it seems to follow that, unless they were bereft of reason, their forbidding them to speak in Christ's name was intended, not to stop the news of what had lately happened, but to stop the progress of the new religion. The grammatical objection to this explanation, that the nearest antecedent is not *doctrine* but *miracle*, is very feeble, as the tacit change of subject in successive sentences is one of the most natural and common licenses in any language, and particularly frequent in the Scriptures. An example is afforded by this very context, vs. 10, 11, where a rigid application of the rule contended for would make the corner-stone to be not Christ but the recovered cripple! The force of this objection may be further weakened by observing that the miracle is called a *sign*, i. e. a proof or attestation of the truth of the new doctrine. There is therefore scarcely even a grammatical irregularity in making the new doctrine itself the subject of the verse before us. As a positive argument in favour of this view, it may be stated that the primitive form (νέμω) of the Greek verb (διανεμηθῇ) rendered *spread*, was familiarly applied to the eating of a cancer or malignant sore, and that Paul uses the derivative noun (νομήν) as a figure for doctrinal and moral corruption (2 Tim. 2, 17.) What could be more natural than such a figure, as applied to the new doctrine by its virulent opposers? This explanation agrees well too with the phrase *among the people*, or more accurately; *into the people;* 'lest it eat into the body of the church or chosen people, as a gangrenous ulcer.' *Straitly threaten*, literally, *threaten with a threatening*, which is often represented as a peculiar Hebrew idiom, although examples may be found in every language. Some of the oldest manuscripts and latest editors omit the noun; but Luke employs a similar combination elsewhere (Luke 22, 15.) The double negative in Greek (*no more to speak to no man*) does not cancel the negation as in Latin, but enforces it. *Threaten them that they speak* (or more exactly, *to speak*) is a pregnant phrase meaning *to forbid with threats*, as the means employed to make the prohibition effectual. *In this name* is not the phrase so rendered in v. 10, and in 3, 6 above, and meaning *by the authority*, or *as the representative*, but that employed in 2, 38 above, and strictly meaning either *for* or *on the name*, i. e. for its sake, or in reliance on it. Some suppose the omission of the name itself to be either superstitious or contemptuous; but see the next verse.

18. And they called them, and commanded them not to speak at all nor teach in the name of Jesus.

We have here the execution of the plan proposed in the preceding verse. It is remarkable how frequently the participial construction is resolved by our translators into finite tenses, as if foreign from our idiom, although to modern ears there is nothing offensive in the literal translation, *having called them they commanded*. (The second *them* is omitted by the latest critics, as not found in the oldest manuscripts and versions.) *Commanded*, peremptorily required or ordered. (See above, on 1, 4, where the same verb is employed, and below, on 5, 34.) *At all*, in the translation, seems to qualify the first verb only, but in Greek it stands before both negatives, and therefore qualifies both verbs. The Greek phrase (τὸ καθόλου) properly means *wholly, altogether* (corresponding to the Latin *omnino*), but in negative constructions must be rendered *not at all, by no means*, or, with the older English versions, *on no manner* (Wiclif), *in no wise* (Tyndale). The distinction made by some between *speak* and *teach* as denoting private talk and public speech respectively, is not consistent with the usage of the first Greek verb (φθέγγεσθαι), which, although not so strong as its compound (ἀποφθέγγεσθαι) used above in 2, 4. 14, still denotes the act of *speaking out* or speaking loud, and is therefore more appropriate to public than to private talk. The true distinction is that, while both verbs here refer to public speaking, the first relates more to the sound or utterance, the second to the matter uttered or the subject of discourse. The common version therefore, with a slight transposition, is correct, *not at all to speak or teach. In the name* is precisely the same phrase as in the verse preceding. The addition of the name itself refutes the notion that it was suppressed through fear or in contempt, unless we arbitrarily suppose it to be added here by the historian, or assume a difference between what they proposed to say and what they did say.

19. But Peter and John answered and said unto them, Whether it be right, in the sight of God, to hearken unto you more than unto God, judge ye!

The same remarkable conjunction of the two Apostles, which has run through the entire previous narrative, here occurs again, perhaps because the words recorded are a summary of what both said at greater length, although this is by no means a necessary supposition. (See above, on 3, 1. 4. 11. 4, 1. 13.) *Answered* is never wholly pleonastic (see above, on 3, 12), and has here its full force, as the words that follow are a direct reply to the command recorded in the verse preceding. The same remark applies to *if* (εἰ) or *whether*. (See above, on v. 9.) As *right* (Wiclif, *rightful*) by itself might have been understood to mean only *lawful*, in a lower sense, i. e. allowed by human laws, they add *before* (or *in the sight of*) *God*, i. e. in his estimation, or according to his judgment; which is the meaning of the Greek phrase elsewhere. (See below, on 8, 21, and compare Luke 1, 6. Rom. 3, 20.) *Hear* or *hearken* never of itself means to *obey*, but that idea is often necessarily implied, as in 3, 22. 23 above, Luke 10, 16. 16, 31. John 5, 24. 8, 47, and in the dialect of common life, where men are said to hear or not to hear advice or instruction, by a natural figure, without any reference to Hebrew usage. The word, however, suggests more than obedience, namely, attention and intelligence, as necessary antecedents. *More* is by some translated *rather*, on the ground that *more* implies mere difference of degree, whereas the question was not which should be obeyed the most, but which should be obeyed at all. The parallel cited in support of this correction (Luke 18, 14) is not entirely in point; for there, from the nature of the case, the denial of the Pharisees' justification must be absolute; whereas the Apostles cannot mean to say that men are not bound to obey human magistrates at all, but merely put the question, whether they are bound to give those magistrates the preference, when their authority conflicts with God's. Another difference, of no small moment, is that in the Gospel, the word ($\mu\hat{a}\lambda\lambda o\nu$) here translated *more* does not occur at all, but merely the conjunction ($\mathring{\eta}$) *than*, or according to the oldest text, its strengthened form ($\mathring{\eta}$ $\gamma\acute{a}\rho$), leaving the term of comparison itself to be supplied from the connection. There is no objection, therefore, to the version *more*, even considered as expressing a mere difference of degree, although it may, agreeably to English usage, have precisely the same sense that is proposed to be expressed by *rather*. The concluding words, *judge ye*, admit of two interpretations somewhat different, in emphasis and force, if not in their essential import. One meaning, and perhaps the one most commonly attached to them, is, 'you may judge for us; we are willing, in a case so clear, to abide by your decision.' The other, and to my mind the most striking and impressive, is, 'you may judge for yourselves, and take the consequences of your own decision; but as for us, we cannot but speak, etc.' (See below, upon the next verse.) The noble principle implied, if not expressed, in these words, was not wholly unknown, even to the more enlightened heathen. Parallels, more or less exact, have been cited from Herodotus and Livy; but by far the nearest and most striking is one found in Plato's Defence of Socrates, where the philosopher is made to say, "You, oh Athenians, I embrace and love, but I will obey God ($\mu\hat{a}\lambda\lambda o\nu$) more (or rather) than you."

20. For we cannot but speak (the things) which we have seen and heard.

This verse must be read in the closest connection with the one before it, on account of the antithesis between the first and second person, indicated by the pronoun *we*, which in Greek is not necessary, as it is in English, to distinguish the person of the verb, and therefore when inserted is most commonly emphatic. (See above, on v. 10.) This affords another argument in favour of the explanation just proposed of the words *judge ye*. '*You* may judge for yourselves; *we* have already judged for ourselves.' The meaning then is, not that the Apostles ask the council to judge for them, what they ought to do, but quite the contrary. In v. 19, they express their indifference to the judgment of the rulers; in v. 20, their own settled resolution. The true connection may be made clear by a paraphrase. 'Whether God would approve our listening to your commands in preference to his, you may determine for yourselves; but whatever your determination may be, our course is clear, WE *cannot but*, etc.' This last is an idiomatic English version of a Greek phrase strictly meaning, *we are not able not to speak*. The first verb is the same as in the last clause of v. 16. *Cannot but* is not yet obsolete in English, but is often erroneously replaced by the correlative expression, *can but*, which is altogether different in meaning. In the present case, *we can but speak* would mean 'we can only speak, we can do no more than speak,' whereas *we cannot but speak* means 'we must speak, we cannot avoid speaking.' An additional argument in favour of the view which has been taken of v. 19, may be drawn from the remarkable analogy of Josh. 24, 15, where the very same antithesis occurs, but unambiguously stated. "Choose you this day whom ye will serve . . . . . . but I, and my house, we will serve the Lord." (See below, on 6, 4.) *The things*, though wanting in the Greek, is not distinguished by italics in the English Bible, no doubt because it was considered as essential to the translation of the plural pronoun (ä) *which* or *what*. The things meant are of course the works and words of Jesus, of which they were the witnesses, appointed by himself (see above, on 1, 8. 22. 2, 32. 3, 15), a trust which would have been betrayed if they had ceased, as required by the council, "to speak or teach in the name of Jesus." The verbs are aorists and properly refer to time already past, *what (things) we saw and heard*, while Jesus was on earth, and we were his companions. There is some loss of emphasis, though not of clearness, in the English version, from the necessary change of collocation in accordance with our idiom. The original order of the sentence is, *not able are we, what (things) we saw and heard, not to speak.*

21. **So when they had further threatened them, they let them go, finding nothing how they might punish them, because of the people; for all (men) glorified God for that which was done.**

The construction in the first clause is similar to that at the beginning of 1, 6. 2, 41, except that one continuative particle (δέ) is substituted for another (μὲν οὖν). There is here, however, no such ambiguity as in those cases, since the subject of the sentence must be the magistrates, to whom the answer in the two foregoing verses was addressed. Here again the participial construction is avoided in the English version, although perfectly agreeable to modern usage and retained in the next clause. A more exact translation would be, *they then* (or *they however*) *having further threatened them. Further*, or *more*, or *in addition*, is expressed in Greek, not by an adverb, but by a compound verb, in which the particle prefixed (πρός, *to*) joins to the meaning of the verb itself the idea of addition or repetition. The power thus to modify the radical idea of a word, without the addition of another, is one of the chief excellencies of the Greek language, and enhances the difficulty of exact translation into English, which possesses the same power in a far inferior degree. Examples of the same thing may be found in Luke 10, 35, where the words *thou spendest more* correspond to a single word in Greek, compounded with the same preposition; and in Luke 19, 16, where the verb translated *gained* is of the same form and means gained besides or in addition to the capital. *Further threatened*, i. e. in addition to the threats proposed in v. 17, and no doubt actually joined to the commands in v. 18, though not particularly mentioned. *Let them go*, released them, or discharged them, no doubt by a formal and judicial act, whereas the English version rather suggests the idea of informally allowing their escape. (See above, on 3, 13, where the same Greek verb is used in reference to Christ and Pilate.)

The use of the verb *finding* is like that in Luke 5, 19, implying, in both cases, previous search and effort. Some would supply *fault* or *charge* from Luke 23, 14, but that introduces an idea not necessarily suggested here, where *not finding* rather signifies discovering no means or way of doing what they wished. Another singular Greek idiom, entirely foreign from our own, and therefore not apparent in the version, is the use of the article to qualify a whole clause or member of a sentence, where to us it seems entirely superfluous, and indeed would, without explanation, convey no idea to an English reader. Thus in the verse before us, the exact form of the middle clause is, *not finding the how-they-might-punish-them*, the last five words (corresponding to three Greek ones) being treated as a noun, with which the article agrees, and which the participle governs. The nearest approach, of which our idiom admits, is by the use of a demonstrative, *not finding this* (namely) *how they might punish them*. This peculiar form of speech is particularly frequent in Luke's writings (see below, on 22, 30, and compare the Greek of Luke 1, 62. 9, 46. 22, 4. 23. 37), but is also used by Mark (9, 23) and Paul (Rom. 8, 26. 13, 9.) The reserve here mentioned did not spring from any equity or moderation in the rulers, but was practised *on account* (or *because*) *of the people*. These words, from their position, both in Greek and English, might appear to qualify the verb immediately preceding; but as this construction would destroy the sense (how they might punish them because of the people), it is another illustration of the fact that there are exceptions to all rules, and that a most important function of sound exegesis is to ascertain them, without unduly multiplying or reducing the amount of such grammatical irregularities, if such they may be called. (See above, on v. 17.) The common sense of every reader leads him here to overleap the nearest antecedents, and connect this qualifying clause with one of the remoter verbs, 'they let them go (not finding, etc.) on account of the people'—or, 'not finding (how, etc.) on account of the people.' The fact in either case remains the same, that they were hindered from punishing the two Apostles, by the state of public feeling, which must therefore have been clear and unambiguous. How did they know it? *Because all were glorifying God for what had happened*. The use of the imperfect, not regarded in the English versions, adds to the essential meaning the accessory notion of continued action. They not only did so when they saw the miracle, but now, upon the next day, they were still employed in the same manner, while the Sanhedrim was sitting, and most probably within hearing of the praises of the multitude. The word translated *glorified* is sometimes used in that sense by the best Greek writers, but most commonly in that of thinking or opining, being of opinion. Both these senses, although seemingly remote, may be reduced to the same radical idea (δόξα, an opinion), in its two distinct phases, that of the opinion entertained by a person upon any subject, and that of the opinion entertained of him by others, more especially when this is highly favourable, and thus the same word which denotes opinion may be used to denote fame or glory. Tyndale has *lauded*, Cranmer *praised*, and Wiclif *clarified*, a curious example of the gradual restriction to material processes of words which once expressed intellectual and spiritual acts; unless the supposition be preferred, that the Reformer simply copied too closely the mere letter of his Vulgate (*clarificabant*), thus committing the same error which he shunned in 3, 2, while the other English copyist of Jerome (the Rhemish version), which was there betrayed into the solecism of a *specious gate*, has here the same form with King James's Bible, *glorified*. (For the meaning of the preposition *for* (ἐπί), see above, on 3, 16. 4, 17.) *That which was done*, or more exactly, *for the* (thing) *happened*, *come to pass*, or, as the Rhemish version has it, *chanced*. This refers of course to the miracle of healing, which had given occasion to the whole proceeding. We learn from this verse, that the opposition of the rulers to the infant church had not yet extended to the body of the people. (See below, on 5, 13.)

22. For the man was above forty years old, on whom this miracle of healing was shewed.

The length of time during which he had been crippled is not mentioned to enhance the miracle itself, as if a case of shorter standing might have been more easily restored, but to show the notoriety, both of his previous condition and of the sudden change which had been wrought, precluding all possibility of error or deception, and accounting for the popular effect described in the preceding verse. 'All were still glorifying God for such a signal and unquestionable miracle, in which there could be no suspicion of illusion or collusion, as the subject of the cure had been born a cripple and was now more than forty years of age.' *Above forty years old*, literally, *of more* (than) *forty years*. *On whom* is the version of a Greek phrase implying motion and rest over and upon an object (see above, on 1, 21), and suggesting therefore the idea of an influence or power from above, and at the same time of a permanent effect. *This miracle of healing,* Vulg. *signum istud sanitatis.* Tyndale's inexact translation of the last verb (*shewed*) is retained in our Bible. The Greek verb is one that has repeatedly occurred before (e. g. in vs. 4. 5. 11. 16. 21) and means *had happened*, come to pass, or been performed. Wiclif still adheres closely to the letter of the Vulgate, *the man in whom that sign of health was made.* The peculiar form of the original is, *on whom had come* (or *come to pass*) *the sign—this* (*sign*) *of healing.*

23. And being let go, they went to their own (company), and reported all that the chief priests and elders had said unto them.

And in this verse, *now* in v. 13, *but* in v. 15, and *so* in v. 21, are all translations of the same Greek particle (δέ); nor is there any reason for the variation but the taste of the translator. In the next phrase (*being let go*) the participial construction is retained in our version, although Tyndale has the usual periphrasis, *as soon as they were let go.* (For the meaning of the Greek verb, see above, on v. 22.) *Went*, or *came*, the Greek verb being used for both in different connections. (See above, on 1, 21.) There is nothing answering to *company* in Greek, nor is it necessary, either to complete the sense, or to accommodate the English idiom, as may be seen from John 1, 11. 13, 1, in which two places the translation has *his own* three times, without supplying any thing, while in Acts 24. 23, it is translated *his acquaintance.* The meaning here is *their own people, friends,* or as the oldest English versions have it, *fellows.* The Vulgate (*suos*) is much nearer to the Greek than its Rhemish copy (*theirs*.) The neuter (τὰ ἴδια) is used to signify one's home. (See below, on 21, 6, and compare John 16, 32. 19, 27.) Both forms are combined in that remarkable sentence, "he came unto his own (τὰ ἴδια) and his own (οἱ ἴδιοι) received him not" (John 1, 11.) As the language is designedly indefinite, it is wholly arbitrary to restrict it by conjecture. All that we can gather from the context is, that a particular assembly must be meant, and not a general visitation of the dispersed Christians. *Reported* (i. e. carried back) is an excellent translation of the Greek verb (ἀπήγγειλαν), which, though it may originally mean no more than to *announce*, is scarcely ever used in the New Testament, without some implication, more or less distinct, of previous intercourse between the parties. (See below, on 5, 22. 22, 26, and compare Matt. 2, 8. 8, 33. 11, 4. 28, 8. 10. Luke 7, 22. 14, 21, and many other places, where this special sense is not admitted by the lexicons, though no less natural than in the others.) Instead of *elders and scribes*, put for the whole Sanhedrim in v. 5, we have here *chief priests and elders*. As the first of these titles (ἀρχιερεῖς), though always rendered in the English version *chief priests*, is the plural of the one translated *high priest* in v. 6, and elsewhere (see below, 5, 17. 21. 24. 27. 7, 1. 9, 1. 22, 5. 23, 2. 4. 5. 24, 1. 25, 2), it becomes a question who are meant by *high priests* in the plural number. The principal opinions are, that it denotes the near relations of the High Priest (see above, on v. 6); or the heads of the twenty-four courses into which the priesthood was divided by David (1 Chron. 24, 1–19. Luke 1, 5); or the natural elders and hereditary chiefs of the house of Aaron; or priests appointed over certain parts of the temple service; or finally several of these combined. As all these explanations are conjectural, and none of them entirely accounts for the extension to these priests of a title properly belonging to the one High Priest; it may be worthy of consideration, whether this usage, at least in the book before us, may not have arisen from the strange confusion in the high priesthood which has been described above (on v. 6); so that *chief priests* really means *high priests*, i. e. all such as had been high priests *de facto* under the Roman domination, however small their number may have been at this time, since the two who are expressly mentioned (Annas and Caiaphas, see above, on v. 6) are sufficient to explain and justify the plural form. The question is of less importance here, because the phrase *high priests* is evidently joined with *scribes*, to designate the Sanhedrim, by naming two of its component classes, whether few or many. What the two Apostles now reported to their brethren was not so much the violence which they had suffered as the words of their oppressors. The Greek word (ὅσα) rendered *all that* is applied in the classics both to magnitude (*how great*) and to number (*how many*); but according to the lexicons, the latter sense predominates in the Greek of the New Testament. Our version uses great and somewhat arbitrary license in translating it *which* (John 21, 25), *what* (Mark 6, 30), *whatsoever* (Luke 4, 23), *all that* (Acts 14, 27), *all things that* (15, 4), *how many things* (2 Tim. 1, 18), *how great things* (Mark 5, 19. 20), *what great things* (Mark 3, 8.) If it ever has the more emphatic meaning, a specific reason must be given for diluting it, and no such reason can be given here. The best sense seems to be *how great things*, as expressed by Wiclif, and referring to the threatenings of v. 17. (See below, on v. 29.)

24. And when they heard that, they lifted up their voice to God with one accord and said, Lord, thou (art) God, which hast made heaven and earth, and the sea, and all that in them is —

The effect of their threatenings, as reported by the two Apostles, was to call forth so remarkable a prayer from the assembled brethren, that it has been left on record, in its substance, if not at full length. (For the meaning of the phrase *with one accord*, see above, on 1, 14. 2, 1. 46.) *Lifted up their voice*, or prayed aloud, not merely in their hearts, but with their lips and tongues. But how could all do this at once, and in the same words? This question has been variously answered. Some suppose a special inspiration, prompting the same thoughts and words in all who were assembled. There is nothing incredible in this to those who admit the possibility of inspiration. But the case supposed is certainly so rare, that we are not bound to assume it, if the words admit of any other explanation, without violence either to the text or context. Some accordingly suppose that this was a liturgical form, already introduced into the infant Church, and used on this occasion as peculiarly appropriate to the existing juncture or emergency. It is worthy of remark that this very singular opinion has found more favour, at least recently, with German than with Anglican interpreters. To the obvious objection, that the prayer is here recorded as a sudden outburst of devout emotion and desire, provoked by what the worshippers had just been told, it is replied, that there is nothing in the prayer exclusively relating to its proximate occasion, or forbidding its repeated use in other like emergencies. Another objection, not so easily disposed of, is that this hypothesis assumes the existence of a certain practice in the infant Church, not only without definite authority from Scripture, but in opposition to its whole drift and tenor. For whatever use ingenious theorists may make of insulated terms or passages, a thousand unsophisticated readers might peruse the whole New Testament, without once thinking of a form of prayer, any more than of a rosary or a crucifix. Besides, if Christian forms of prayer had been already introduced—and no one will contend that this was borrowed from the Jews—how does it happen that we have but this one specimen preserved to us? Whereas its preservation becomes altogether natural when we regard it, not as the recital of a form, however earnest and devout, but as the fruit of sudden and spontaneous impulse, growing out of the history, and therefore forming just as much a part of it as Peter's Pentecostal sermon, or his answer to the arrogant injunction of the Sanhedrim, recorded in this chapter. The only other argument that need be urged against this paradoxical interpretation, is that according to the warmest friends and most accredited historians of Liturgies in our day, they were not forms concocted and prescribed at once, but gradual collections and notations of such prayers as had first been orally repeated until they became the natural expression of religious feeling to the multitudes who used them, and were finally reduced to writing, not as something new but something old, not as a cause but an effect of devotion in the Church, developed and matured by the experience of generations, or perhaps of ages. If this be the true genesis of liturgies, on which some of their highest claims to admiration are now founded, there is something ludicrous in the idea of a peculiar Christian liturgy so early introduced and established at Jerusalem, that the disciples, upon this unexpected and remarkable occasion, could express their strongest feelings and desires in a form already known to all of them. At all events, it may be safely said, that neither the hypothesis of a special revelation, nor that of a familiar written form, is so self-evidently true as to preclude all possibility or need of a more natural interpretation. Two still remain to be considered, one of which appears to have commanded the assent of most interpreters in all times and churches. This is the simple supposition, that they are all said to have lifted up their voices with one accord, because they all united in the prayer of one, just as we now speak of a whole congregation praying, when a single voice is audible, whether the prayers be written or unwritten. This expression becomes still more natural if we assume that the whole company gave audible assent to the expressions of their spokesman, which we know to have been the ancient practice, both of the Jewish and the Christian Church. (See Deut. 27, 15–26. 1 Chron. 16, 36. Ps. 106, 48. 1 Cor. 14, 16.) The remaining explanation is, that all did actually pray aloud, and each one for himself, and that Luke here gives, not the exact words of any one among them, but the substance of the spirit of the prayers of all, clothed in expressions of his own, or rather in words taught by the Holy Ghost (λόγοις διδακτοῖς πνεύματος, 1 Cor. 2, 13). The advantage of this explanation is, that it enables us to take the words, *they lifted up their voice with one accord*, in their most natural and proper sense. The advantage of the other is, that it enables us to look upon the words here recorded as those actually uttered. Both are in strict accordance with the usage of this book, as the eleven are said to have prayed (1, 24) when every thing in the connection would lead us to regard the words as those of Peter; and in another case, where this is also the most probable assumption, both his words and actions are ascribed equally to John (compare vs. 18 and 13 of this chapter, and see above, on 3, 4. 11.) On the other hand, there are repeated instances, in the foregoing context, where the words ascribed to a plurality of persons seem to be a summary or abstract of what all said in another form and at greater length (compare v. 16 of this chapter, and see above, on 2, 7–12.) Each of these two hypotheses will probably commend itself to some minds as entitled to the preference, while most unbiassed readers will agree that both are more entitled to belief, than either of the two first mentioned, as requiring less to be assumed, and offering less violence to usage and analogy, but at the same time meeting all the requisitions of the narrative. The form of the prayer itself is worthy of particular attention. The petition occupies the smallest part (vs. 29, 30), being added, as a sort of supplement or afterthought, to the invocation of the Most High as Creator of the Universe (v. 24), and to an exposition of the second Psalm as a prophecy of Christ (vs. 2–28), the large space occupied by which makes it still more improbable, that this was a prescribed form of devotion in the infant Church. The address to God in this verse has a peculiarity of form not visible in the translation. The word here rendered *Lord* is not the common one (Κύριε, 1, 6. 24), but the Greek term for a *master* as distinguished from his *slaves*, and is repeatedly so used in the New Testament (1 Tim. 6, 1. 2. Tit. 2, 9. 1 Pet. 2, 18.) In its wider application by the classical writers, it denotes any one possessed of absolute authority or power; hence our English *despot*, with its odious associations. In a good sense, Euripides and Xenophon apply it to the gods; and this religious use has been retained in several passages of the New Testament, where the full force of the original expression is not felt in the translation (e. g. Luke 2, 29. Jude 4. Rev. 6, 10.) Paul and Peter both apply the term to Christ (2 Tim. 2, 21. 2 Pet. 2, 1.) In the case before us, it has reference to God's creative power, and his sovereign authority over his creatures thence arising, as appears from the remainder of the verse. The word *God* is omitted in the oldest manuscripts and latest critical editions. The word *art* is supplied in our translation, although not distinguished by italics. Most interpreters omit it and regard this verse, not as a complete proposition, but as a description of the being here addressed. *Oh Lord, who didst make* (or according to the common text, *the God who made*) *heaven and earth and sea*, with their contents, here put for the whole frame of nature or material universe. Here again the Greek verb has a participial form, and strictly means *the (one) making or having made*. The article should either have been inserted or omitted before all the nouns. The inequality, in this respect, belongs entirely to the version; in the Greek the words all have the article, though our idiom does not require it. This address to God as the Creator, and by necessary consequence the providential ruler of the world, prepares the way for another description in the next verse.

25. Who by the mouth of thy servant David hast said, Why did the heathen rage, and the people imagine vain things?

This is the eighth prophecy expounded in this book (see above, on v. 11), a sufficient commentary on the notion that it is a desultory series of anecdotes or reminiscences. *Servant* is the word translated *son* in 3, 13 above. As there explained, it really expresses both relations, but with different degrees of emphasis. When applied to Christ, the prominent idea is that of son; when applied to David, that of servant. (See below, on v. 27.) The Vulgate here has *pueri*, but its English copyists have not ventured to write *boy*. Wiclif indeed has a different reading, also found in some Greek manuscripts, *our father David*. The quotation is from the second Psalm (vs. 1. 2), which is explicitly declared to be the inspired work of David and a prophecy of Christ. The first of these descriptions is confirmed by the relation of the psalm to those which follow, and which are all acknowledged to be David's, as well as by the internal structure of the psalm itself. The imagery of the scene presented is evidently borrowed from the warlike and eventful times of David. He cannot, however, be himself the subject of the composition, on account of the universal dominion there ascribed to the king, and the general revolt of subject nations, the solemn declaration of his filial relation to Jehovah, and the absence of any thing answering to the whole description in the history of David, or of any other earthly sovereign. These considerations exclude David, even as the primary or inferior subject of the psalm, a complex and unnatural assumption here, which can only embarrass the interpretation. Even those writers, who give to other prophetic psalms a more generic meaning (see above, on 2, 25), are disposed to regard this as an exclusive Messianic prophecy. As such it was explained by the oldest Jewish interpreters, and as such it is repeatedly applied in the New Testament; the seventh verse by Paul (13, 33. Heb. 1, 5); the ninth by John (Rev. 2, 26. 27. 12, 5. 19, 15.) *Who hast said*, literally, *the (one) saying* (or *having said*), corresponding to the similar construction in v. 24, and giving an additional description of the being here addressed, as the God of revelation no less than of nature, as the God who made the world and who inspired the prophets. This passage was correctly used by Irenaeus and Theophylact, against those Gnostics who denied that the Supreme God was the author of the Scriptures or the maker of the universe. The Septuagint version, which is closely adhered to, is peculiarly expressive in the verse before us. The Greek word here translated *rage* originally signifies the neighing and snorting of a spirited horse, but is figuratively used for any noisy or obtrusive indication of self-confidence. The other verb properly denotes solicitous and anxious forethought (Mark 13, 11. 1 Tim. 4, 15.) The most expressive, although not the most exact, of the English versions here is Wiclif's, *heathen men gnashed with teeth together*. Two of the most familiar names applied by the Jews of that time to the great deliverer whom they expected, are derived from this psalm, namely, *Christ* (or *Messiah*) and *Son of God*. (See John 1, 49. Matt. 26, 63. Mark 14, 61.)

26. The kings of the earth stood up, and the rulers were gathered together, against the Lord and against his Christ.

The quotation from the second psalm is still continued. *Stood up*, or as Wiclif more exactly renders it, *stood nigh*. The Greek verb, which occurs above in v. 10, like the Hebrew one to which it corresponds, does not of itself denote hostility, but simply the act of appearing in one's presence, or approaching him, for any purpose. The idea of enmity and opposition is suggested by the context, and particularly by the preposition twice used in the last clause. *Gathered together*, implying coincidence of time, place, and purpose. (See above, on 1, 15. 2, 1. 44. 3, 1.) The Hebrew verb originally means to sit together, but with special reference to taking counsel. *The Lord and his Christ*, is, in the Hebrew, *Jehovah and his Messiah*. *Christ* (Χριστός), from the verb (χρίω) *to anoint*, is used in the classics only as an adjective, and only of the substance so applied. Its higher sense and personal application are peculiar to the Hellenistic Greek. The Septuagint constantly employs it to translate (מָשִׁיחַ) the Hebrew for *Anointed*. *Messiah* and *Christ* are therefore Hebrew and Greek equivalents, and are so explained in the New Testament itself (John 1, 42. 4, 25.)

27. For of a truth, against thy holy child Jesus, whom thou hast anointed, both Herod and Pontius Pilate, with (the) Gentiles, and the people of Israel, were gathered together —

This verse justifies the application of the prophecy to Jesus, by showing the agreement of the circumstances. *For* is therefore to be taken in its strict sense as a logical connective. 'This is really a prophecy of him, for, etc.' *Of a truth*, not merely *doubtless*, as the Geneva Bible has it, but *in fact*, literally, really, as opposed to a mere verbal correspondence or a fanciful accommodation. The Greek phrase is used four times besides by Luke and twice by Mark. It is once translated *truly* (Luke 20, 21), once *in truth* (Mark 12, 14), and once *the truth* (Mark 12, 32), but in all the other cases *of a truth* (10, 34. Luke 4, 25. 22, 59.) In this part of the sentence, several of the oldest manuscripts and versions, followed in quotation by some early Fathers, introduce the words, *in this city* (or, according to the Codex Alexandrinus, *in this thy city*), which is accordingly adopted as the true text by the latest editors. It is supposed to correspond to the words, *upon my holy hill of Zion*, in the second psalm. *Against* is not the same preposition that is twice used in the foregoing verse, but that employed in v. 22 and 1, 21, denoting motion over and upon an object. Its true equivalent is *on*, as in our phrase to make an attack or assault *on* one. *Holy*, as here applied to Christ, denotes not only character but office, not only his exemption from all moral taint, but his peculiar consecration to the work which his Father gave him to do (John 10, 36. 17, 4. 18. 19. See above, on 3, 14. 21.) *Child* is the word translated *son* in 3, 13, and *servant* in v. 25 above, where its twofold usage is explained. *Hast anointed*, didst anoint, i. e. when he was sent into the world. This denotes not merely consecration in general, but special preparation for his work by the influences of the Holy Spirit, of which unction is a symbol in the Old Testament. (See above, on 1, 2. 5. 2, 30. 31. 36. 38. 3, 6. 18. 20. 4, 10, and compare Isai. 61, 1. Luke 18, 21.) There is also an allusion to the use of the word *Christ* in the preceding verse. As if he had said, 'whom thou didst consecrate by unction to the office of a Prophet, Priest, and King, and who is therefore the Anointed One foretold in this and other ancient scriptures.' *Both Herod and Pontius Pilate*, not only one or separately, but both together by a remarkable conjunction, making the fulfilment still more striking. *With the Gentiles*, or *with nations*, as the article is not expressed in Greek, although the sense of Gentiles is required by the obvious antithesis with *peoples*. This plural, which has never obtained currency in English, although used by Lowth and other writers of authority, is not so necessary here as in a multitude of other cases, where the idea of plurality is an essential one, and yet unsuspected by the English reader. So impossible did such a plural seem to our translators, that at least in one case, they avoid it by a circumlocution, which is not only awkward but conveys a wrong idea. (See Gen. 25, 23, where the words *two manner of people* are a mere periphrasis for *two peoples*, the Hebrew phrase being similar in form to that preceding it, *two nations*.) The plural form is not so necessary here, because it seems to have been chosen merely as a parallel to *nations*, while it really agrees in sense with the usual expression *people*, as applied to Israel (see above, on 2, 47. 3, 9. 11. 12. 23. 4, 1. 2. 8. 10. 17. 21); whereas in v. 25, it denotes the Gentiles, or perhaps all nations, comprehending both. Another explanation of the plural form here is, that it denotes the *tribes* of Israel, which composed the nation, and are sometimes used to designate it, even when there is no reference to any separate or local action of the tribes as such. (Compare Ps. 105, 37. 122, 4. Isai. 49, 6. 63, 17, and see below, on 26, 7.) The main idea here is, that the prophecy had been fulfilled in its widest sense, for the nations had combined against the Christ, both Jews and Gentiles. Some suppose Herod to be mentioned as belonging to the latter, on account of his Idumean lineage and irreligious character. It seems more natural, however, to regard him as the representative of Israel, at least in this affair, as Pilate represents the Roman Empire or the Gentiles. The idea is at least as old as Chrysostom, that in the Greek verb (συνήχθησαν), which was also used in v. 26, and literally means *they were brought together*, there is an allusion to the ominous reconciliation of these two men, at the time, if not by means, of their concurrence in the unjust condemnation of our Saviour (Luke 23, 12.) The Herod meant is Herod Antipas, a younger son of Herod the Great (Matt. 2, 1. Luke 1, 5), who became tetrarch of Galilee and Perea on his father's death, and is often mentioned in the Gospels, especially in the history of John the Baptist, whom he put to death. (See Matt. 14, 1–12. Mark 6, 14–29. Luke 3, 1–19. 9, 7–9. 13, 31. 23, 7–15.) His elder brother Archelaus having been removed from the ethnarchy of Judea (Matt. 2, 22), it was annexed to the great Roman province of Syria, the governors of which ruled it for some years by their deputies (*procuratores.*) Of these procurators Pontius Pilatus was the sixth, on whose recall it was attached to the kingdom of Herod Agrippa (see below, on 12, 1), and after his death fell again into the hands of procurators, among whom were the Felix and the Festus of this history. (See below, on 23, 24. 24, 27.) It is somewhat curious that the first word in the Greek of this long verse (συνήχθησαν) stands last in the translation. For a similar but more important change of collocation, see above, on 1, 21. 22. The Greek order is, " they were gathered of a truth (in this city) against thy holy child Jesus, whom thou hast anointed—(namely) Herod, etc." Wiclif's antique version of the last clause is, *Eroude and Pounce Pilat with heathen men*, etc. He elsewhere calls the procurator *Pilate of Pounce*.

28. For to do whatsoever thy hand and thy counsel determined before to be done.

Here, as in 2, 23 above, the guilt of those who put our Lord to death is brought into the closest juxtaposition with the divine purpose, which it was the means of carrying into execution; another proof of the compatibility, assumed rather than affirmed in scripture, between God's sovereignty and man's responsibility. *For* is not the logical connective (γάρ) used at the beginning of v. 27, but a pleonastic sign of the infinitive, still sometimes heard in English as a colloquial or provincial idiom, and retained in French (*pour faire*) as a correct and elegant expression. So much less do some distinctions between good and bad grammar depend upon any law of mind or language, than on accidental usage and association. The Greek verb (ποιῆσαι) is dependent, not on *anointed*, which, although preferred by some, is an impossible construction, on account of the intervening words, but upon *assembled* or *brought together*, which, although still more remote in the original, is separated from the verb *to do* only by its own nominatives and qualifying phrases. (For the true sense of the words translated *counsel* and *determined*, see above, on 2, 23. For that of *hand* in such connections, see above, on 2, 33, and below, on 11, 21, and compare Luke 1, 71. 74.)

29. And now, Lord, behold their threatenings, and grant unto thy servants, that with all boldness they may speak thy word —

The first phrase in Greek (καὶ τὰ νῦν) is an instance of as singular an idiom as that in v. 21 above, and like it consisting in a use of the neuter article, which cannot be retained or reproduced in English. Mechanically copied it would be, *and the* (*things*) *now*, which may be an elliptical expression meaning, 'and now (as to) the things which have been mentioned.' The addition of the article distinguishes this phrase from that in 3, 17, where *now* is rather logical (*these things being so*) than temporal in meaning (*at this time*.) Precisely the same words that are here used occur also in 20, 32. 27, 22, below, and without the *and* in 17, 30, in all which cases they contrast past time with the present or the future. So here, the disciples, after speaking of what had been said and done, in a kind of historical preamble, now present their petition or prayer in the strict sense of the term. It is worthy of note, that though they pray for personal protection, it is only as a means to the discharge of their official functions, and is really postponed to their petition for the moral gift of boldness and fidelity. *Behold*, or *look upon* (ἔπιδε or ἔφιδε), in the only other place where it occurs (Luke 1, 25), implies a favourable look or visitation, which idea may, however, be suggested by the context. Or if it be inherent in the verb itself, it may be here referred, not to the threats or their authors, but to those against whom they were uttered. 'Look with favour on (the objects of) their threatenings.' It is much more natural, however, and affords a more emphatic sense, to give the verb its strict and simple meaning, and to understand the clause as signifying 'keep thine eye upon their threatenings,' that they may not be accomplished. The *threatenings* are those of vs. 17 and 21 above. *Grant* is in Greek the ordinary verb to *give*. *Thy servants*, literally *slaves*, the Greek word (δούλοις) being the correlative of *lord* or *master* (δέσποτα) in v. 24. The two together are descriptive of absolute authority on one hand and of absolute subjection on the other, but without implying either tyranny or slavish fear, for these are not essential but accessory ideas, superadded to the strict sense by the habitual abuse of power and submission to it. The word *slave*, therefore, can no more be used in actual translation here than *despot* in v. 24, or *idiot* in v. 13, though the reason is not perfectly the same in all three cases. It is indispensable, however, to the emphasis or full force of the passage, that we understand both *lord* and *servants* in the very strongest sense that can be called a good one, i. e. free from every implication of either oppression or of degradation. The infinitive construction in the last clause (*with all boldness to speak thy word*) is again exchanged for a subjunctive one (*that with all boldness they may speak thy word*), not without some loss, both of conciseness and of force, from the suggestion of contingency or mere possibility, rather than of certain and direct results. (For the true sense of *boldness* or *freedom of speech*, see above, on v. 13, and 2, 29.) The meaning of *all boldness* may be either absolute, *entire, perfect*, the highest possible degree of boldness; or it may be relative, every kind and all degrees of boldness that can be required for the performance of our ministerial work. This work is itself described as the speaking of God's word, i. e. acting as an organ of communication between God and man, or more precisely, preaching Christ, and thereby making known the new religion. (See above, on v. 4.)

30. By stretching forth thine hand to heal, and that signs and wonders may be done, by the name of thy holy child Jesus.

This verse defines the way in which they desire their petition to be granted. The boldness of the servants was to be secured by displaying the power of their master. To the figure of a hand, employed above in v. 28, is now added that of stretching it out, or exerting the power which the hand denotes. The nearest approach in English to the form of the original is, *in stretching* (or according to the common text, *in thy stretching*) *out thy hand* (Rhemish, *in that thou stretch forth ;* Tyndale, *so that thou stretch forth.*) Their demand is not now for miracles of vengeance or destruction, such as fire from heaven (Luke 9, 54), but for miracles of mercy. *To heal*, literally, *for healing*. (Compare *sign* or *miracle of healing* in v. 22, and for the sense of *signs and wonders*, see above, on 2, 19. 22. 43.) The verb of the second clause (γίνεσθαι) depends on the verb *give* in v. 29. 'Grant miracles to take place, or to be performed.' The first clause merely qualifies or amplifies the previous petition, 'give us boldness by performing miracles of healing.' The addition of the words *signs and wonders* may appear to indicate some other kinds of miracles than those of healing; but as the clauses are co-ordinate and not successive, this is really another way of saying the same thing, or rather an express specification of the figurative terms preceding. 'Stretch out thy hand for healing, i. e enable us to work miracles of that kind.' *By the name* is not the phrase so rendered in v. 10, nor that translated *in the name* in v. 18, but still a third (διὰ τοῦ ὀνόματος), strictly meaning *through*, by means of, *his name* (see above, on vs. 16. 25), and therefore really including both the others. *Holy child Jesus* has precisely the same meaning as in v. 27 above.

31. And when they had prayed, the place was shaken where they were assembled together, and they were all filled with the Holy Ghost, and they spake the word of God with boldness.

This verse contains the answer to the prayer immediately preceding, first in a momentary sensible manifestation of God's presence, then in the permanent moral effect which they had asked, secured by a new or greater spiritual influence. *When they had prayed* is in Greek a participial and absolute construction, *they having prayed*. The common version, though it does not reproduce this form, is more correct than Tyndale's, *as soon as they had prayed*, there being nothing to determine the precise length of the interval between the prayer and the response; and although they were probably immediately successive, it is not so said, and we have no right to insert it. *The place where they were assembled* (or *brought together*, the same verb as in vs. 26, 27), though as usual not further specified, was probably *the house where they were sitting* on the day of Pentecost (see above, on 2, 2), of which scene this was a partial repetition, on a smaller scale and in a narrower circle, but with precisely the same spiritual and an analogous sensible effect. As there the sound of wind filled the house, so here the place itself was shaken. The sign here given of God's presence was familiar to the saints of the Old Testament (Ex. 19. 18. Ps. 68, 8), and it is not perhaps surprising that the same belief prevailed among the heathen, whether from tradition or a natural association. The example usually cited is a well known passage in the third book of the Æneid, which certainly does bear a remarkable resemblance to the words before us. The permanent effect, prefigured by this sign, and produced by the spiritual influence that followed, was that according to their own petition, *they did speak the word of God with boldness*, sustained internally by new illapses of the spirit, and externally by new miraculous performances, attesting the divine presence and protection (see above, on 2, 43.) This triumphant issue of the first persecution, which the Church sustained, prepares the way for another description of its social state, or it may be more correct to say, for the resumption of the previous description (2, 42–47), which was dropped or interrupted, to relate this first attack, and now that this is seen to have had no injurious effect upon the Church, is resumed and continued in the remainder of the chapter.

32. And the multitude of them that believed were of one heart and of one soul, neither said any (of them) that ought of the (things) which he possessed was his own, but they had all things common.

A characteristic feature of this history of the infant church is the repeated alternation of particular narratives and general descriptions, suggestive and illustrative of one another. The detailed account of what occurred upon a single day, the day of Pentecost, is followed by a picture of the condition of the church for an undefined period ensuing. (See above, on 2, 42. 4, 4.) This again is interrupted by the account of a particular occurrence, filling the whole of the third chapter and a large part of the fourth, but near the close of the latter, passing again into the form of a more general description, not relating to a single day or point of time, but to a period of some length, although not defined, being no doubt the whole time, whether long or short, during which the Church continued undivided and restricted to Jerusalem; a period the history of which is contained in the first seven chapters of the book before us. Due attention to this structure of the narrative would have saved the world many crude suggestions, as to the total want of plan and method in the Acts of the Apostles. We have here the second alternation of the kind just mentioned, the remainder of this chapter corresponding to the last six verses of the second. It is, in fact, the same description, interrupted and resumed, with some repetitions and some new additions. The earlier passage (2, 42–47) is not to be considered as relating to an earlier period and the later (4, 32–37) to a later; but both are synchronous or co-extensive as to time, including the whole history of the primitive or infant church, as it existed at Jerusalem. While the sameness of the two accounts is quite sufficient to sustain this view of their relation to each other, they are far from being mere reiterative duplicates, the passage now before us adding several new points, both of fact and of expression. The original form of the first clause is still more beautiful and striking. *Of the multitude* (or *mass*) *of those believing* (or *believers*) *was the heart and the soul one.* (For the meaning of τοῦ πλήθους, see above, on 2, 6; for that of τῶν πιστευσάντων, on 4, 4.) Strongly analogous to this is the Greek proverb (δύο φίλοι ψυχὴ μία) "two friends, one soul," and the definition of friendship ascribed to Aristotle by Diogenes Laertius (μία ψυχὴ δύο σώμασιν ἐνοικοῦσα), "one soul residing in two bodies." There could scarcely be a stronger expression of the unity prevailing in the infant church, and not confined to sentiment or language merely, but extending to the interchange of social advantages and legal rights. *Neither said any of them* is still stronger in the Greek, *not one said*, or still more exactly, *was saying, used to say*, the form of the verb denoting not a single but habitual action. *Ought of the (things) which he possessed*, or, *any of the (things) belonging*, (literally *existing*) *to him*. (See the same verb in 2, 30. 3, 2. 6.) The infinitive construction is, as usual, avoided in our version; the exact translation is, *to be his own* (ἴδιον, as in 1, 7. 19. 25. 2, 6. 8. 3, 12. 4, 23), or as the Romans called it, his *peculium*, from which comes our adjective *peculiar*, properly descriptive of exclusive rights or property. But if all were required, or expected as a thing of course, to throw what they possessed into a common fund, what was there meritorious or remarkable in no man's calling what he had his own, i. e. no man's saying what every body would have known to be untrue? It is vain to urge that this is unfairly pressing the expression *said;* for if it means no more than that the case was so in fact, there is an end of argument from words or phrases. If it be said, that it relates to language, but to language used before the surrender of the property, and indicating the spirit by which it was prompted, there is still something strange in the expression, 'no one said that his possessions were his own,' when he was under the necessity (legal or moral) of abjuring them. This argument may seem to apply only to compulsory abandonment of property, and not to voluntary self-impoverishment or assimilation to the general condition. But if this voluntary act was universal and without exception, it is still, to say the least, a strange expression, that of all who thus renounced their property, not one *said* it was his own, either before or after he renounced it. It is not contended that the language is unmeaning, or even unintelligible, but only that it is unnatural, and not what might have been expected, in describing a complete and universal abjuration of all individual property by these believers. 'Not one spoke of any of the things belonging to him as his own.' How much simpler to have said, 'no one retained them, or continued to make use of them.' But on the other hand, how apt and how expressive is this language on the supposition that, while every man who had possessions still retained them, he was so inspired, not with mere philanthropy or pity, but with a sense of Christian oneness, that he did not speak of his possessions as his own, but as belonging to the church at large. It may be laid down as a law of sound interpretation, that where one view of a passage makes its terms unmeaning, and another gives them a peculiar emphasis and point, then, other things being equal, i. e. both being grammatical and philologically unexceptionable, the last is necessarily entitled to the preference. The conclusion thus reached helps us to another in relation to the last clause, which is repeated from 2, 44, with the unimportant change (not regarded in our version) of a Greek idiom (*they had all things common*) into a Hebrew one (*all things were common to them*.) (See above, on 3, 6.) If these expressions may, without violence, be used to describe either an absolute community of goods arising from the personal renunciation of all property, or a virtual community of goods arising from the practice of the most disinterested and self-sacrificing Christian love; and if the terms immediately preceding are, as we have seen, far more appropriate and significant upon the latter supposition; then we need resort to none of the hypotheses already stated (see above, on 2, 44), to account for a literal or absolute community of goods, which really had no existence. Both these conclusions have been drawn from these two passages exclusively, without regard to the corroborative evidence supposed to be contained in other places, yet to be considered. (See below, on vs. 34–37, and on 5, 4. 12, 12.)

33. And with great power gave the Apostles witness of the resurrection of the Lord Jesus, and great grace was upon them all.

Such was the social and spiritual state of the church, both before and after the first onset from without, which seems to have had no effect upon it, but for good. In the mean time the Apostles did not suffer any thing to divert their minds from their great official function, that of testifying to Christ's resurrection, which, for reasons before given, may be understood as comprehending the whole work of preaching Christ and making known the new religion. (See above, on 1, 22. 2, 32. 3, 15. 4, 2.) This they did *with great power*, not merely force of argument or eloquence, but in the exercise of that extraordinary spiritual power, with which they were invested for this very purpose, and by which they were enabled, both to testify of Christ, and to confirm their testimony by the evidence of signs or miracles. (See above, on 2, 43.) All this may be considered as included in the *great power* here ascribed to the Apostles. The verb translated *gave* often means *to give back*, pay or repay (e. g. Matt. 21, 41. 22, 21. Mark 12, 17. Luke 20, 25. Rom. 13, 7, in which places it is translated *render*); and this, though given in some lexicons as a secondary sense to that of *giving out* or *away*, appears to be the primary and proper one in Attic and Homeric usage. Here, however, the idea seems to be that of *giving forth* or *uttering*, with or without an implication of freeness and completeness. As our version sometimes introduces the article without necessity (see above, on 1, 7. 14. 4, 9), so here (as in 1, 13, and elsewhere) it omits it. There is force, if no additional idea, in the definite expression, *the testimony of the resurrection*, i. e. not a mere spontaneous attestation which they volunteered upon their own authority, but that formal and official testimony, which they had been chosen and commissioned to present. The English word *witness*, which was once equivocal, is now used chiefly of the person testifying, the sense of testimony being confined, perhaps exclusively, to one phrase, that of *bearing witness*. *The Lord Jesus*, as in 1, 21, the only other case where we have met with it in this book, is a pregnant combination of the Saviour's personal designation with that descriptive title, which exhibits him not only as the mediatorial sovereign (see above, on 2, 36), but as the *Jehovah* of the old economy and Hebrew scriptures. (See above, on 2, 21.) To the *great power* of the first clause corresponds the *great grace* of the second. This word, which means *favour* in the general, though commonly applied to that of God, and therefore properly translated *grace*, is also used to denote human favour or good-will, as in the only place where we have previously met with it, to wit, in the parallel description to the one before us. (See above, on 2, 47.) This might seem decisive here in favour of that sense, or rather application, of the word; but it is better still to comprehend them both, as perfectly compatible and perfectly appropriate.

The old cry against a double sense, besides its emptiness in general, may here be met by an appeal to Luke's expressions elsewhere, "Jesus increased in wisdom and stature, and in favour (χάριτι) with God and man" (Luke 2, 52.) If the same word may be thus used expressly to denote both kinds of grace or favour, why may it not be used elliptically, i. e. by itself, to suggest the same ideas? Had Luke, in that place, left the word to explain itself, it might have been as plausibly asserted as in this place, that it could not be intended to denote the favour both of God and man; and yet we now know from his own authority that this assertion would have been a false one. *Upon them* is the right translation, not *in them* Wiclif) or *with them* (Tyndale), but *upon them*, as descending from above, in reference to the grace of God, which may be regarded as the primary though not the only meaning. For reasons, which have been already given (see above, on 2, 1), *all* does not mean all the Apostles, which would be a most superfluous specification, but all the believers, whom they represented, who are the subject of the verse preceding, and to whom the writer now returns in the verse following. It is not unworthy of remark, that the retention of the Greek collocation in the English version of this sentence, to a greater extent than usual, not only makes the copy more exact and faithful, but by a slight inversion common in our older writers, improves its beauty to the eye and ear.

34. **Neither was there any among them that lacked; for as many as were possessors of lands or houses sold them, and brought the prices of the things that were sold —**

The sentence is completed in the next verse. There is certainly some harshness and irregularity in this abrupt return to the community of goods, which seemed to have been finally disposed of, in the verse preceding. But the fault is that of the translation, which omits the very word indicative of the connection. *Neither was there* should have been *for neither was there*, or still better, *for there was not*, as the particle (οὐδέ) can here have no effect but that of simply negativing the idea of the verb that follows. The omitted *for* (γάρ) shows that this is the reason or the explanation of something that precedes, not necessarily the nearest antecedent (see above, on v, 21), although that must always be entitled to the preference, where other things are equal. The only choice in this case lies between v. 32 and v. 33. If the former be preferred, the latter must be read as a parenthesis. 'They had all things common (and with great power the Apostles, etc.) for there was no one, etc.' To this construction there are two objections. In the first place, it leaves wholly unexplained the introduction of the facts recorded in v. 33, which is then not only parenthetical in form, but foreign from the context and an awkward interruption of the sentence. In the next place, the logical connection between vs. 32 and 34 is only apparent and not real; for how could it be said that *they had all things common because* (or *for*) *there was no one destitute among them*, unless we arbitrarily give *for* the sense of *so that*, and confound cause and effect by a preposterous inversion. It is vain to say that this and other particles are often used with great latitude; for besides the gross exaggeration of the general fact alleged, it cannot justify the preference of the lax use to the strict one, when the latter may be held fast, and a better sense obtained, by a different construction. Such a construction is the other above mentioned, which supposes *for* to introduce the reason of the statement immediately preceding: 'great grace was upon them, for (or because) there was no one destitute among them.' Besides the two advantages of giving *for* its proper sense and getting rid of the parenthesis, the sense evolved by this construction is a good one. They enjoyed both divine and human favour, the one as the cause, and the other as the consequence, of their extraordinary freedom from distress. The favour of God was evinced by there being no distress among them, and the same thing gave them popularity and credit, as a people freed from poverty and all its evils through the favour of their God, not by enriching them, but by disposing every one among them to regard what he possessed as the property of others also, and to deal with it accordingly. The verb translated *was* is not the common verb *to be*, but one originally meaning to *begin*, and then to come into existence, but most frequently employed without any perceptible allusion to this origin, as in 2, 30. 3, 2. 3, 6, above. If any such allusion should be here assumed, the meaning might be, that no one after this became poor, which, however, is at variance with the known facts of the history. (See below, on 11, 29. 24, 17, and compare Rom. 15, 26.) *Any that lacked,* literally *any poor* or *destitute (person.)*' The Greek adjective which occurs only here in the New Testament, properly means *wanting* or *deficient* in any thing, but is absolutely used to signify without the means of subsistence or the necessaries of life, by Xenophon and in the Septuagint version of Deut. 15, 4. 7. The condition here described is not one of affluence or wealth, but one of freedom from distress and want. The second *for* is unambiguous, and evidently indicates the ground or cause of this surprising absence both of poverty and riches. (Compare Prov. 30, 8.) It was because those who had lands or houses sold them and distributed to those who had not. *Lands*, literally, *places*, grounds, the same noun that is translated *field* in 1, 18, above. *As many as* (ὅσοι) is the masculine form of the word translated *all that* in v. 23. It does not necessarily mean *all*, as that word is occasionally added to strengthen it (see above, 3, 22. 24, and below, 5, 36. 37); but neither is the idea of totality excluded, as appears from its use in 2, 39. 4, 6. 23. In this respect, it approaches very nearly to our English *such as*, which may be applied to all or less than all, according to the context. Even the absolute term *all* (πάντες) must be restricted in the parallel passage (2, 44. 45), or we are brought to the conclusion, that *all who believed* sold their goods and distributed to *all*. But if all had property to sell, the sale itself was nugatory and superfluous, unless the object had been simply to put all upon a level by a common sustentation fund; and this idea is excluded by the words, *as each had need*, implying something more than inequality, to wit, the existence in some cases of actual necessity. In the case, however, more immediately before us, no restriction is required, as the adjective has reference not to all believers (as in 2, 44), but to all proprietors of lands or houses. Thus the parallel passages explain each other. Perhaps the best translation here would be, *for as many owners of lands or houses as there were*, or as existed in the infant church. We thus retain, not only the original arrangement, which is always an advantage, unless purchased at the cost of something more important, but a certain shade of difference between the two verbs of existence, not unlike that between our expressions *were* and *there were*. *Sold them and brought* is another departure from the Greek participial construction, *selling brought*. The word translated *price* commonly means *honour* (e. g. John 4, 44. Rom. 2, 7. 1 Pet. 1, 7, and throughout the writings of John, Paul, and Peter), but in this book always *cost* or *value* (see below, on 5, 2. 3. 7, 16. 19, 19) with the single exception of 28, 10, which is disputed. Both senses are reducible to one radical idea, that of *worth ;* whether that of persons, as acknowledged by respectful words and actions, doing *honour* to the object ; or that of things, as estimated and expressed in *price* or *value*. The latter sense is here determined by the qualifying genitive, *of the (things) sold*, another participial construction and another resolution of it in our version, *of the things that were sold*.

35. And laid them down at the Apostles' feet ; and distribution was made unto every (man), according as he had need.

- The sentence is continued from the verse preceding. It was the owners or proprietors there mentioned who performed this act. *Laid them down* is in Greek simply *placed* (or *put*) *them*. *At the feet* (i. e. by or near the feet) is as close an approximation to the Greek as our idiom permits. The Vulgate version (*ante pedes*), copied of course by Wiclif and the Rhemish (*before the feet*), is not a mere capricious variation, but a classical expression of the same idea. Thus Cicero (for Flaccus) speaks of a certain weight or sum of gold as having been paid "before the feet of the prætor in the forum" (*ante pedes prætoris in foro expensum*.) That *feet* are here put for the person, *the Apostles' feet* for the Apostles themselves, is a sample of the same kind of interpretation which makes *names* mean persons likewise, and affirms *began* and *answered* to be always pleonastic. (See above, on 1, 1. 15. 2, 4. 3, 12.) The examples cited in the present case prove nothing, namely, 5, 9 and Rom. 10, 15, in both which cases the feet are mentioned, not for the whole body, but as organs or instruments of locomotion. Some have inferred from 7, 58, that the idea meant to be conveyed is that of a deposit for safe-keeping ; but there is surely an important difference between laying clothes at a man's feet and laying money there. That it is not a mere figure, but expresses what was actually done, may be inferred from the repetition of the words in the next verse and in 5, 2 below. In the absence of explicit information and analogy or usage, we may lawfully resort to natural association, for the probable design of this proceeding. Viewed in this light, it would seem to imply, first, the presence and the presidence of the Apostles in the meetings of believers ; next, their great superiority in rank and authority to all the others, even though invested with high office; then, the fact that these pecuniary gifts had a religious character, or were regarded as oblations, votive offerings; and last, not least, that this whole work of relieving the necessitous, although sustained by private contribution, was considered not a personal affair, but a public or ecclesiastical proceeding, and was therefore metaphorically placed at the Apostles' feet, i. e. implicitly subjected to the apostolical control and management, just as the proceeds of the sales were literally placed there, not for convenience or safe-keeping merely, for the hand would then have served a better purpose, but as a sort of emblematical acknowledgment of what has now been stated as the natural import of the act itself. The last and most important of these implications, namely, that the distribution of the sums contributed was regulated, not by the contributors but the Apostles, may be gathered, partly, from the order of this sentence, in which the statement of the fact in question is immediately followed by the act of distribution; and partly from the narrative contained in the sixth chapter, where the whole proceeding presupposes such authority in the Apostles. (See below, on 6, 1.) The rule or principle of distribution is the same precisely as in 2, 45. The only difference of form is in the use of the words *all* and *each* or *every one*. The word *man*, which to some may seem exclusive, as it is in 1, 21 and elsewhere (see above, on v. 4), corresponds to nothing in the Greek, but is the pleonastic noun or pronoun, so profusely used by our translators. (See above, on 2, 45.) Another seeming difference, but confined to the translation, is the change of *as* (2, 45) into *according as*. The latter is the more exact translation of the Greek phrase, which is identical in both the places. Both in its simple and augmented form (καθότι and καθότι ἄν), it is peculiar to Luke's writings. (Compare Luke 1, 7. 19, 9, and according to the latest critics, 17, 31 below, where the common text has διότι.) Etymologically, as compounded of a preposition and a pronoun, it means *after* or *according to what*, while the addition of the particle (ἄν) imparts to it a doubtful or contingent character, like *ever* in the English word *wherever*, i. e. 'be it where it may.' So here, the rule of distribution is the need of the recipient, be it what it may, implying both contingency and inequality in different cases.

36. And Joses, who by the Apostles was surnamed Barnabas, which is, being interpreted, the Son of Consolation, a Levite, and of the country of Cyprus —

The sentence is completed in the following verse. We have here exemplified again that feature in the structure of this history, described above (on v. 32) as a frequent alternation of particular narrative and general description. Having fully described the spirit of self-sacrifice and mutual benevolence pervading the whole body of believers at this period, Luke illustrates this description by the statement of two cases, one of a favourable and the other of an opposite description. The first, being simply intended to illustrate, by an eminent example, what had just been said of the whole church, is briefly stated in a single sentence (vs. 36, 37.) The other, being introduced, not merely for the sake of the antithesis or contrast, but as introductory to further changes, is described more fully, but thrown, in the conventional division of the text, into another chapter (5, 1–11.) The first or favourable case is that of *Joses* or, according to the reading of the oldest manuscripts and versions, *Joseph*, of which some regard the first form as a familiar Jewish variation. He is further distinguished, not by an ordinary surname, but by one derived from the Apostles (according to the latest critics, ἀπὸ τῶν ἀποστόλων), which seems clearly to imply that the name given had respect to some official gift or quality. The Hebrew or Aramaic etymology of *Barnabas* has never yet been satisfactorily ascertained. The form most commonly assumed (בַּר־נְבוּאָה) denotes a *son of prophecy* or *inspiration;* and as one important function of the New Testament Prophets (or inspired teachers) was persuasive exhortation, as a means of enforcing doctrinal instruction (see above, on 2, 40), it is not improbable that in the author's Greek translation of the name, the last word (παρακλήσεως) has its primary sense of *exhortation* (or *persuasion*, 13, 15. 15, 31. Rom. 12, 8. 1 Cor. 14, 3. 2 Cor. 8, 4. 1 Tim. 4, 13. Heb. 12, 5. 13, 22), rather than its secondary sense of *consolation* (9, 31. Luke 2, 25. Rom. 15, 5. 2 Cor. 1, 3. 6. 7. 7, 4. 7. 13. Phil. 2. 1. 2 Thess. 2, 16. Philem. 7. Heb. 6, 18.) It will then describe him as a zealous and successful preacher or exhorter, which agrees well with his character and conduct as described in 11, 23. 24. The natural import of the words is, that he had already been thus surnamed when he made his gift; but all that they necessarily imply is that he was so distinguished before this history was written. (See above, on v. 6.) He is still further described as a *Levite,* or as paraphrased by Wiclif, *of the lineage of Levi.* As some Levites formed a part of the Diaspora, or general dispersion of the Jews among the nations, after the Babylonish conquest, and even after the return from exile, Barnabas is furthermore distinguished as a *Cyprian by birth* or *by descent* (γένει), which is better paraphrased in Tyndale's version (*a Cyprian born*) than in King James's (*of the country of Cyprus.*) That this is the same Barnabas, who acts so conspicuous a part in the sequel of this history (see below, on 9, 27, and compare 1 Cor. 9, 6. Gal. 2, 1. 9. 13. Col. 4, 10), has probably never been disputed. As to his connection with Cyprus, see below, on 13, 4. 15, 39. As to the identity of *Barnabas* and *Barsabas,* see above, on 1, 23, and below, on 15, 22.

37. Having land, sold it, and brought the money, and laid it at the Apostles' feet.

The sentence is continued and completed from v. 36. It represents a single individual as doing what was said in v. 34 to have been done by all proprietors of lands and houses. *Having land,* literally, *a field being* (or *belonging*) *to him.* The word translated *land* is different from that in v. 34 and 1, 18, and is the common Greek term for a *field.* Some have thought this statement inconsistent with the law (Num. 18, 20–24. Josh. 18, 7), excluding the Levites from a share in the land of Canaan. To this it has been variously answered, that he may have abandoned it for that very reason; that the law did not extend to Cyprus, where the land may have been situated; that it did not extend to individuals, but only to the tribe as such, which is inferred from Jer. 32, 9. It may be added that the tribe itself was excluded only from a continuous and compact portion of the promised land, but not from holding cities and their suburbs and adjacent pastures for their flocks and herds. (See Numb. 35, 1–5. Josh. 21, 1–42.) For *prices* (v. 34) we here have *money,* (χρῆμα), elsewhere written in the plural number (Matt. 10, 23. 24. Luke 18, 24. Acts 8, 18. 20. 24, 26), although the same use of the singular is found in Herodotus and other classics. The word for *selling* is also different from that before used, though substantially synonymous. If the distinction made by lexicographers be just, to wit, that the verb employed in v. 34 originally signified traffic beyond seas, it might seem more appropriate to this case, especially on the supposition that the land sold lay in Cyprus. But why was this case singled out and placed on record, while so many others were passed by in silence? Some have answered, as the first case of the kind that happened; others, as the case of one so highly honoured and so eminently useful. As if he had said, 'among the many who thus showed their benevolence and zeal, was one, with whose name you have long been familiar, or are yet to meet repeatedly in this same history.' Now both these explanations—and there seems to be no other worthy of attention—presuppose that there was something remarkable in what is here ascribed to Barnabas. But if all were required to abandon their possessions, or if all did in point of fact abandon them, wherein lay the distinction of this single case, or what mattered it who did first what all did as a matter of course afterwards? To say that this case set the fashion or example, is not only a gratuitous assertion, but supplies by mere conjecture what would no doubt have been clearly and emphatically stated, as the most important part of the transaction. The only satisfactory solution is the one already given (see above, on v. 34), to wit, that these were voluntary acts of genuine benevolence, among which that of Barnabas, though not more meritorious than others, was more interesting to Luke's readers, for one of the two reasons which have been suggested, either as the first in time, or far more probably, because of his subsequent celebrity. This then may be reckoned as a further proof, that the community of goods, described above, was not a social regulation or an article of primitive church polity, but the natural and necessary acting out of the principle of oneness, or identity of interest among the members of Christ's body, arising from their joint relation to himself; a principle expressly taught in scripture and received by all believers, and though far less operative than it should be, no less capable, when nurtured and developed, of producing such fruit now, than in the first church at Jerusalem, where every thing external helped to foster and mature it.

CHAPTER V.

This conventional division of the text contains the first recorded case of hypocritical profession in the infant church (1–4), with the severe but necessary means used to prevent its repetition (5–11), and the consequent increase of true conversions, and of popular respect and faith in the miraculous gifts of the Apostles, leading to innumerable cures (12–16), but also to a new attack upon the church (17–32), which seemed about to end in the death of the Apostles, when prevented by the interposition and advice of a distinguished Pharisee (33–39), in consequence of which they were subjected to a minor though disgraceful punishment, but joyfully continued to assert, both in public and in private, the Messiahship of Jesus (40–42.)

1. But a certain man named Ananias, with Sapphira his wife, sold a possession:

To the eminent example of self-sacrificing charity, exhibited by Barnabas (4, 36. 37), the history now adds, by way of contrast, one of a very different description, yet springing from the same peculiar state of things, and showing the abuses to which it might afford occasion, by converting into a mere form or fashion, what was at first, and continued still to be in most, the spontaneous impulse of a genuine affection. Such perversions are continually taking place wherever there are zealous and extensive efforts to do good in any way. The real charity and zeal of some are copied outwardly by others, not always with deliberate hypocrisy, but often from a superficial short-lived sympathy. From this, as well as other evils since prevailing, the primitive church, even under the control of the Apostles, was not wholly free; and her experience is here left on record "for our learning" (Rom. 15, 4), and "for our admonition, upon whom the ends of the world are come" (1 Cor. 10, 11.) The excessive regard paid to the division of the chapters, although often infelicitous and injudicious, hides from many readers the most intimate connection between this narrative and the conclusion of the fourth chapter; an effect not wholly counteracted by the melancholy *but* (as Matthew Henry calls it) which stands at the beginning of this verse, and which, in Greek, is nothing more than the continuative particle (δέ) so constantly employed throughout this history. The antithesis is indicated not so much by this as by the whole connection when continuously read. *A certain man* is an idiomatic English phrase, often applied to cases where there is no certainty at all, and simply meaning *somebody* or *some man* (Lat. *quidam*.) Here, where the noun *man* is expressed, the indefinite pronoun (τίς) merely intimates, that he was otherwise or previously unknown to the reader. *Named*, literally, *by name*. *Ananias* is the Greek form corresponding, in the Septuagint version, both to *Hananiah* (Dan. 1, 6) and *Ananiah* (Neh. 3, 23), which are more unlike in Hebrew than in English letters. Both were auspicious names, one denoting the favour, and the other the protection, of Jehovah (see above, on 4, 6) which accounts for the repeated occurrence of the Greek form, even in this history, as the name of different persons. (See below, on 9, 10. 23, 2.) The other name, which is variously written in the manuscripts (Sappheira, Sapphira, Saphphira, Saphphura), is commonly identified with the Hebrew and Greek words for a *sapphire* (Ex. 24, 10. Rev. 21, 19), but by some with an Aramaic adjective denoting *fair* or *beautiful* (Dan. 4, 9. 18; in the English Bible, 4, 12. 21). In either case, the names (as Bengel hints) were too good for their owners. *With* here implies what is expressed in the next verse, not mere joint action, but preconcert and conspiracy. It really means, therefore, in the closest and most intimate conjunction with her. *Possession*, although afterwards defined (see v. 3), is correctly rendered here as an indefinite expression, the plural of which occurs above (2, 45.) The specification is needlessly anticipated here by the Vulgate (*agrum*) and its Rhemish copyist (*a piece of land*.) The verb in this clause, and the act which it expresses, are the same as in the case of Barnabas, and other "owners of lands or houses," mentioned at the close of the last chapter (4, 34. 37.)

2. And kept back (part) of the price, (his) wife also being privy (to it), and brought a certain part, and laid it at the Apostles' feet.

The sentence is continued from the first verse. *Kept back*, literally, *set apart, appropriated*, but with special reference, in classical usage, to embezzlement or peculation. The old Greek lexicographers (Hesychius and Suidas) define it by a compound verb (ἰδιοποιέω) meaning *to make one's own*, not in a good sense, but in that of stealing (κλέπτω) or embezzling. The only other instance of its use in the New Testament, besides the next verse, is in Titus 2, 10, where it is translated *purloining*, and relates to the dishonest practices of slaves or servants. The whole phrase might be here expressed in English, *he abstracted from the price*, without supplying *part*, which is implied but not expressed in the original. (Wiclif, *defrauded of.* Whitby, *defalked from.*) The word for *price* is the same that was explained above, on 4, 34. *His wife*, or less respectfully, *the woman*, as the pronoun is suppressed. (See above, on 1, 14.) *Being privy*, literally, *being conscious* or *aware*, or, as the Greek verb primarily signifies, *knowing* (the same thing) *with him.* (See below, on 12, 12. 14, 6, and compare 1 Cor. 4, 4, where the sense of *consciousness*, or *conscience*, is determined by the pronoun, *by* or *to myself.*) In the rest of the verse, the terms used in 4, 34. 35, are studiously repeated, as if to show how perfectly the cases were alike in mere external form and circumstances. To the eye of uninspired man, Ananias did precisely what was done by Barnabas and many others. The essential difference between the cases is expressed by the addition of the words, *a certain part*, another instance of the English idiom which occurs at the beginning of v. 1. The Greek phrase (μέρος τι) might be more exactly rendered, *some part*, suggesting, although not directly expressing, the idea of a small part, which is also implied in the whole context, as the reservation of the larger share seems to assign a more adequate motive for reserving any. This explanation of the phrase gives a peculiar aggravation to the sin of Ananias and Sapphira, and to that extent assists us in explaining the severity with which they were punished.

3. **But Peter said, Ananias, why hath Satan filled thine heart, to lie to the Holy Ghost, and to keep back (part) of the price of the land?**

Peter again acts as the representative and spokesman of the twelve, whose presence, however, is implied in the plural form (*apostles*) at the end of the preceding verse. (*But*, as in v. 1.) *Satan* is a Hebrew word, meaning an adversary or opponent, whether in war (1 Kings 5, 4) or litigation (Ps.

109, 6), often applied to human enemies, but in one place to an angel (Num. 22, 22), and with the article (2 Sam. 24, 1), or as a proper name without it (1 Chron. 21, 1), to the Evil Spirit, or the Prince of fallen angels, as the adversary and accuser of mankind (Job. 1, 7. 2, 2. Zech. 3, 1. 2. Compare Rev. 12, 9. 10.) In this sense and application, it is nearly equivalent to the Greek Διάβολος (Rev. 12, 9. 20, 2) and Latin *Diabolus*, meaning slanderer, informer, false accuser, to which the English *Devil* may be easily traced back, through the intermediate forms of the French (*Diable*) and Italian (*Diavolo*). As the same being is the *tempter* of our race from the beginning (2 Cor. 11, 3), the name *Satan* sometimes has that special meaning (Matt. 4, 10. 16, 23. Mark 8, 33), and is so used here. But while the sin of Ananias is referred to this Satanic influence, the question (*why?*) represents it as a voluntary act, thus as it were making both agents jointly responsible. *Filled thy heart* is not so strong an expression as the one applied to Judas (John 13, 27), although the influence described may be the same. This influence is never represented as coercive, but as persuasive and resistible (James 4, 7.) To *fill the heart*, however, must mean something more than to suggest or to encourage. Taking *heart* in the generic sense of *mind* or *soul* (see above, on 2, 37), the idea seems to be that of occupying or engrossing the whole man with some particular desire or purpose. *To lie*, or as the Greek verb with the accusative is used by the purest Attic writers, *to deceive*, which is the marginal translation in our Bible. The verb is the same as in the next verse, but the syntax different. The verb itself does not mean to *belie*, as some would here explain it (i. e. to belie the Holy Spirit, either in himself by false profession, or in the Apostles by questioning their inspiration), but to cheat by lying. Some refer the act to Ananias, some to Satan, a difference of little exegetical importance, on account of their inseparable union in responsibility and guilt. There is no need of giving to the verb a merely tentative meaning (*sought* or *attempted to deceive*), as it does not here express the actual result, but the desire or purpose, with which Satan filled the heart of Ananias. The intimate grammatical connection of the two verbs shows that one is a specification of the other, or that the way in which he sought to deceive the Holy Ghost, was by keeping back, etc. This last verb (explained above, on v. 2), with the same preposition (ἀπό), occurs in the Septuagint version of Josh. 7, 1, in reference to the sin of Achan, between which and that of Ananias some of the older writers have discovered even too great a resemblance. The generic term *possession* (in v. 1) is now defined or specified as *land*, literally, *place* (see above, on 1, 18. 4, 34.) Tyndale uses here the old word *lyvelod*, which seems to be identical with *livelihood*, i. e. subsistence, or the source from which it is derived, namely, property or income.

4. **Whiles it remained, was it not thine own? And after it was sold, was it not in thine own power? Why hast thou conceived this thing in thine heart? Thou hast not lied unto men, but unto God.**

Whiles is an antiquated form of *while* or *whilst*. There is nothing corresponding to it here in Greek. The literal translation of the clause is, *remaining did it not remain to thee?* (Wiclif, *whether it unsold was not thine?*) So in the next clause, *being sold* (or *having been sold*) *was it not?* etc. This shows conclusively, that no compulsory abandonment of property, or absolute community of goods, existed in the primitive church. (See above, on 2, 44. 45. 4, 32.) The sentence, it is true, is interrogative, not affirmative (see above, on 2, 7); but the form of interrogation (with οὐχί) is one used when an affirmative answer is expected. (See Matt. 20, 13. Luke 12, 6. John 11, 9. Rom. 3, 29.) *Was* (ὑπῆρχεν), existed or subsisted (see above, on 4, 34. 37), has here very nearly the force of *continued* or *remained*, as in the first clause. *Power*, not physical but moral, authority, discretion. (See above, on 1, 7. 3, 12. 4, 7.) The sin of Ananias was therefore perfectly spontaneous and gratuitous, without coercion or constraint *ab extra*. He was not required to sell his land, or having sold it, to devote the proceeds to a public use. His freedom from all antecedent obligation so to do, is the very soul of this expostulation, robbed of which it becomes utterly unmeaning. If Peter knew that Ananias had no choice, but was compelled to give up all that he possessed when he became a Christian, these upbraiding questions would have been a cruel mockery. *Why* is not the same Greek form as in the verse preceding. There the words mean strictly, *for* (or *on account of*) *what?* (διὰ τί;) here (and in Luke 2, 49), the expression is elliptical and seems to mean, *how* (*is it*) *that*, as Tyndale here translates it, or *what (is the reason) that?* (τί ὅτι;) or the full form may be that in John 14, 22 (τί γέγονεν ὅτι;) *what has happened that? Conceived*, literally *put* or *placed*. A similar Hebrew phrase is used to denote purpose (Dan. 1, 8) or serious consideration (Mal. 2, 2.) See below, on 19, 21, and compare Luke 1, 66. *This thing*, or retaining the original and full force of the Greek word (πρᾶγμα from πράσσω, *to do*), *this deed* or *action*. *Lied* is here construed, not with the accusative, as in v. 3, and in the classical Greek usage, but with the dative. Some regard this as a mere dialectic variation, belonging to the Hellenistic Greek, but identical in sense with the accusative construction. It seems hard, however, to account for both forms being used in two successive sentences, unless there is some difference of meaning. If there is such a difference, it is probably that between *deceiving*, as the end, and *lying*, as the means of its accomplishment. (See above, on v. 3.) *Not unto men*, so much as unto God, as some explain it; or *not unto men* at all, since all regard to them is swallowed up in that due to God (compare Ps. 51, 4); or *not unto* (us as) *men*, but as the vehicles and organs of the Holy Ghost. (See Matt. 10, 20. Acts 13, 2. 15, 28.) The reference is then not merely to the presence and inhabitation of the Holy Ghost in all believers (1 Cor. 3, 16. 6, 19), but to his special and authoritative acting through the Apostles; so that disobedience to their rightful apostolical authority is represented as resistance to the Holy Ghost. (See 7, 51 below, and compare 1 Thess. 4, 8.) The use of the terms *God* and *Holy Ghost*, in these two verses, as convertible expressions, has always and most justly been regarded as a strong proof both of the personality and the divinity of the Spirit. In allusion to this doctrine, and to one of its heretical opponents in the early church, the Venerable Bede says, the Scripture here condemns the heresy of Macedonius before Macedonius was born. The sin of Ananias is so clearly and precisely said to have been that of lying to and trying to deceive the Holy Ghost, that it is strange men should ever have disputed whether it was sacrilege or avarice, ambition or vainglory. All these were undoubtedly included; but the grand specific charge against him, twice alleged by Peter, is that of lying to the Holy Ghost. The interpretation of the passage has been hindered and embarrassed, from the earliest times, by the neglect of this obvious and simple fact, and the attempt to make the guilt of Ananias and Sapphira lie in their violation of a vow, by which they had consecrated all their property to God, so that in withholding what they did, they were not only guilty of the crime of sacrilege, but (as one of the Fathers here observes) of self-robbery or stealing their own money! Such refinements are often handed down from age to age, in the tradition of the pulpit, or by one interpreter transcribing others, till the true sense, obvious and simple though it be, is supposed to be condemned by the judgment of the church, or lost sight of and forgotten. However complicated the offence of Ananias may have been, the head and front of his offending, as declared by the Apostle, was his lying to the Holy Ghost.

5. And Ananias, hearing these words, fell down and gave up the ghost; and great fear came on all them that heard these things.

Gave up the ghost is not, as the English reader might suppose, a Greek or Hebrew idiom, introduced into our language by too servile a translation, but an idiom of our own, retained in all the English versions subsequent to that of Tyndale. Wiclif's simple but expressive words are, *fell down and was dead*. The Greek verb (ἐξέψυξε) means *breathed out*, i. e. his life or soul, as the ellipsis is supplied by Euripides and Virgil. Our word *expire* (from the Latin *exspiro*) originally means the same. The phrase employed in the translation is one of the very few, in which the word *ghost* still retains its strict sense as a synonyme of *spirit*. The other forms in which it lingers are *Holy Ghost* and *ghostly*, as applied to spiritual guides or teachers. With these exceptions, English usage now restricts the word to the supposed return of disembodied spirits. As to the immediate cause of the death of Ananias there are various opinions. The earlier neologists of Germany, belonging to the so-called natural (or naturalistic) school of exegesis, in their eagerness to get rid of one miracle, almost assumed another, by ascribing the sudden death to fright or apoplexy, not perceiving that its occurring when it did, and in the case of man and wife, is enough to render even such a death miraculous. One writer of the same class, but more bold and reckless, alleges or insinuates that Peter actually killed him with a concealed weapon, and that Luke relates merely what was seen by the spectators. Apart from these monstrosities of exposition, there is a question, even among those who are agreed in considering the death of Ananias as a signal act of the divine justice, namely, whether this act was performed through Peter, or without his knowledge and co-operation. It is commonly assumed, as a matter of course, that Ananias was destroyed by a judicial word or act of the Apostle, as the representative of God or Christ. But there is no such intimation in the narrative itself, the terms of which are perfectly consistent with the supposition or conclusion, that the sudden death of Ananias was as much a matter of surprise to Peter as to others, and that his first knowledge of the divine will upon this occasion was derived from the appalling sight of the dissembler lying lifeless at his feet. We have no right to affirm this as unquestionably true; but we have still less right to affirm the contrary, and thus give colour to the charge of cruelty and rash vindictiveness against the great Apostle. False as such charges are, on any exegetical hypothesis, it is not wise to give them even an occasion or a pretext, by gratuitously representing as his own act, what the language of the narrative allows us to regard as the immediate act of God. If the writer had intended to exhibit the Apostle as a minister of wrath or vengeance, would he not have left on record some judicial sentence, some express premonition of the stroke that was to follow, such as Paul uttered in the case of Elymas the sorcerer (see below, on 13, 11), or at least such a warning and exhortation as Peter himself addressed to Simon Magus (see below, on 8, 20–23?) But whether used directly against Peter, or indirectly against God himself, the charge of rashness and undue severity may be repelled, without resorting to the ultimate unanswerable plea of the divine infallibility and sovereignty, by the complex aggravations of the sin committed, as embracing an ambitious and vainglorious desire to obtain the praise of men by false pretences; a selfish and avaricious wish to do this at as small expense as possible; a direct falsehood, whether told by word or deed, as to the completeness of the sum presented; but above all, an impious defiance of God the Spirit, as unable to detect the imposture or to punish it; a complication and accumulation of gratuitous and aggravated crimes, which certainly must constitute a heinous sin—if not the one unpardonable sin—against the Holy Ghost (Matt. 12, 31. 32. Mark 3, 29.) That Ananias had a view to his support from the common fund, while secretly retaining something of his own, presupposes a more literal and strict community of goods than we have found recorded. If the property sold by Ananias was so valuable that he could hope to gain a name by giving it away, and yet reserve a portion for himself, the hope of sharing in a common sustentation-fund could hardly have been much of a temptation. As additional reasons for inflicting so severe a stroke, it has been said, that an example of severity was specially required in the beginning of the Christian dispensation, analogous to those of Nadab and Abihu under Moses (Lev. 10, 1–3) and to that of Achan under Joshua (7, 1–26.) That the punishment, though just in itself, was specially intended to deter men from repeating the offence, is rendered probable by its actual effect, as here recorded. *Great fear* (both terror and religious awe) *came* (i. e. came to pass or happened) *upon all them that heard* (literally, *those hearing*) *these* (*things*.) The last word (ταῦτα) is omitted by the oldest manuscripts and latest editors, without effect upon the meaning. The only question is, whether the clause describes the impression made by the death of Ananias upon those who witnessed it, or on a wider circle who were reached by the report of it. The objection to the latter, which is certainly the natural import of the words—since the persons present would be rather spoken of as *seeing* than as *hearing* what had happened—is that such a statement seems misplaced between the death of Ananias and that of his wife, which happened so soon afterwards. But this may be explained in either of two ways. The first is by supposing a prolepsis or anticipation, which is altogether natural in such a case, the writer going on to tell what impression this fearful stroke eventually made, and then returning to complete his narrative of what occurred at once. 'This sudden death of Ananias caused a universal dread in all who heard it, and so did that of his companion in wickedness, which I shall now relate.' The other method of solution is to understand the language of this verse, without prolepsis, as describing the immediate effect produced by the news of Ananias's death, which, as in all like cases, would be spread with great rapidity, especially if the event took place in an assembly of disciples, as to which point, see below, on v. 7.

6. And the young men arose, wound him up, and carried (him) out, and buried (him.)

Some understand by *the young* (or more exactly, *younger*.)

men, a class of officers or servants in the primitive church, chiefly on two grounds; first, that the correlative term *elders* (πρεσβύτεροι) is so used, and sometimes contrasted with (νεώτεροι) the one which here occurs (1 Tim. 5, 1. 1 Pet. 5, 5. Tit. 2, 6): and secondly, that the word here has the article and therefore must denote a well-defined and well-known class. As to the first of these reasons, it would serve as well to prove that because the English *elder* is a title of office, there must be a corresponding class of officers called *youngers*. It may also be observed that the alleged opposition between the two Greek words occurs chiefly where presbyter or elder has its natural or personal, and not its technical official sense. As to the other reason, it is difficult to see in what respect an order of church-servants would be any more entitled to a definite description than *the younger men* of the community, or rather of the company present upon this occasion, who might naturally be expected, with or without an order or a sign from the Apostles, to perform the unpleasant duty here assigned to them. The main fact is, however, that the word in question never occurs again as an official title. *Wound him up*, wrapped him in his own clothes, or shrouded him in graveclothes. The last is not so probable, considering the haste with which the burial was performed. *Carried out* might seem to refer merely to the house, but the analogy of Luke 7, 12. John 11, 31, and the well-known usage of the Jews, seem decisive in favour of referring it to the city. From the ancient sepulchres still extant in the Holy Land, it would seem that the usual mode of burial was in lateral excavations, either in the hill-sides or in artificial vaults and natural caverns.

7. And it was about the space of three hours after, when his wife, not knowing what was done, came in.

It is not an improbable conjecture, that Ananias and Sapphira are described as coming into the Apostles' presence at two successive hours of prayer, the interval between which was three hours. (See above, on 2, 15. 3, 1.) This would imply that the incidents recorded here took place in a meeting for worship. But see what is said above (on 2, 42. 46) as to the mode of life among the primitive Christians. The first clause admits of two grammatical constructions. The simplest is the one adopted in our version, which makes *space* (or *in-*

terval) the subject of the verb at the beginning. 'There was (or there elapsed) an interval of about three hours, and (then) his wife, etc.' The other, which is harsher, but preferred by the highest philological authorities, gives to the first verb (ἐγένετο) its frequent sense of *happened*, came to pass, and construes the following words absolutely, as in Matt. 15, 32. 'And it came to pass—a space of about three hours (later)— that (literally, and) his wife, etc.' This use of *and*, in the last clause of a sentence, especially after a specification of time, is a common Hebrew idiom, and as such often used in the Greek of the New Testament. (See for example Luke 9, 28, where the structure of the sentence is the same as here.) *What was done*, or rather, *what had happened*, i. e. to her husband. How she had remained so long in ignorance of what must have been generally known, is not revealed, and it is idle to conjecture. Such exceptions are not only possible, but familiar matters of experience.

8. And Peter answered unto her, Tell me whether ye sold the land for so much? And she said, Yea, for so much.

Answered, not merely *said* (see above, on 3, 12), but replied, as some think, to her salutation, or, as others, to her looks or to her thoughts. *Tell me* is in Wiclif's version, *Woman, say to me*. The word translated *sold* here and in 7, 9 below, is the middle voice of the verb rendered *gave* in 4, 33 above. It has been disputed whether *so much* represents a specific sum which Peter named, or the money lying at his feet at which he pointed, or whether it here means *so little*, which, however, is at variance with usage. *Yea*, yes, the usual Greek particle of affirmation.

9. Then Peter said unto her, How (is it) that ye have agreed together, to tempt the Spirit of the Lord? Behold, the feet of them which have buried thy husband (are) at the door, and shall carry thee out.

Then is not an adverb of time, but the conjunction (δέ), translated *and* at the beginning of the three preceding verses. *How is it that*, the very phrase translated *why* in v. 4. These variations in the version, though intrinsically unimportant, are occasionally noticed, lest the English reader should suppose a difference of meaning, where there is not even one of form, in the original. *Ye have agreed together*, literally, *it was concerted by you* (or *between you*.) It is plain that this preconcert or conspiracy was viewed by the Apostle as a serious aggravation of the sin committed; not only because each was bound to hinder or dissuade instead of helping and encouraging the other; but because this previous agreement showed the sin to be deliberate and presumptuous, and cut off all excuse or palliation that might otherwise have been derived from haste, ignorance, or inconsideration. The sin itself is here described as that of tempting God, i. e. trying his patience, or putting to the test, and thereby impiously questioning, not merely his omniscience, but his veracity and power to punish. The term is repeatedly applied to God (Deut. 6, 16. Matt. 4, 7. Luke 4, 12. Heb. 3, 8. 9), and once to Christ (1 Cor. 10, 9), but here to *the Spirit of the Lord*, i. e. of God, or according to the prevalent New Testament usage, of Christ himself. See above, on 1, 24. 2, 21, and compare *the Spirit of his Son*, Gal. 4, 6. See also John 14, 26. 15, 26, where the Spirit is said to be sent, not only in the Son's name by the Father, but from the Father by the Son himself. The same relation of the divine persons is expressed in 2, 33 above. Ananias and Sapphira had conspired to tempt the omniscient Spirit, by agreeing to practise a deception on the men, in whom he manifestly dwelt in an extraordinary manner, and through whom he now spoke and acted, as the ruler and the guardian of his infant church. The connivance, or rather the complicity of Sapphira in her husband's sin—for she is evidently treated, both by Peter and by Luke, not as a mere accessory, but as a co-ordinate and independent party to the whole transaction—was so clear to her own conscience, and to others from her prompt and categorical reply to the judicial question put to her by Peter, that he thinks no further trial necessary, but contents himself with simply announcing her participation in the punishment, as well as in the sin, of her husband. Some have argued from the sentence here pronounced by Peter on Sapphira, that he must have acted likewise as a judge in the case of Ananias. (See above, on v. 5.) The conclusion might be valid if the premises were true, i. e. if what is here recorded were a formal and authoritative sentence, instead of being, as it is, a mere prediction. Even the word *shall*, used by our translators, conveys too strong a sense to modern readers. There is nothing to show that the Greek verb means more than that *they will* (or *are about to*) *do* for her what they have just done for her husband. *Carry out*, i. e. for burial, from the house, and probably from the city also, as in v. 6. This was known to Peter, not by mere conjecture, nor by reasoning from analogy, but no doubt by express revelation, which is perfectly consistent with the view already taken of his agency in executing the divine will upon Ananias. Although it may have pleased God, in the first instance, to effect his purpose without any previous intimation to his servant, in order to disburden him of all responsibility for so severe and sudden an infliction; yet as soon as the divine will had been made known by the death of Ananias, it seems altogether natural that Peter should resume his ordinary functions as a Prophet and Apostle. *Behold* (or *lo*), as usual, announces something unexpected and surprising (see above, on 1, 10. 2, 7), as this declaration must have been to her whom he addressed, and who had just come in, " not knowing what had happened " (v. 7.) The idea that *feet* may be put for the whole person (see above, on 4, 35–37), seems to be favoured here by the construction of that word as the subject of the verb in the last clause, 'behold their feet are at the door, *and shall carry thee out*,' which could be said only of the *hands*, if particular members, in the strict sense, were intended. But the true construction is, *and they* (not the feet, but their owners, who had buried Ananias) *shall carry thee out*. *At the door* has by some been regarded as a figure for *at hand*, within reach, and the whole clause as meaning, that death and burial were as near to her as they had been to her husband. But this sense may be obtained, and in a much more striking form, without departing from the literal interpretation of the clause as meaning, that the young men who had buried Ananias were returned, and either waiting at the door or in the act of entering. If the former, there is no need of assuming a long interval between their going and returning; if the latter, it is easily explained by the necessity of burying the dead without the city. Some preparation also for the burial may have been required, although not as much as usual, and not including (as some interpreters suggest) the digging of a grave, which is a transfer of our own associations to a very different mode of burial. (See above, on v. 6.) According to the literal interpretation of this clause, Peter's knowledge of the fact, that they were at the door, may have been derived from a divine suggestion, or from hearing their approach, or from both, as in the case of Abijah, who was warned of a visit from the wife of Jeroboam, and yet "heard the sound of her feet as she came in at the door" (1 Kings 14, 5. 6.) *Them which have buried* is in Greek *those burying* (or *having buried*.)

10. Then fell she down straightway at his feet and yielded up the ghost; and the young men came in and found her dead, and carrying (her) forth buried (her) by her husband.

Peter's prophetical announcement to Sapphira is instantaneously fulfilled. *Then*, see above, on v. 9. *Straightway*, the same word that is rendered *immediately* in 3, 7, and there explained. *At his feet*, in evident allusion to the fact mentioned in v. 2 (compare 4, 27.) As the money had been laid at the Apostles' feet, so now the deceivers fell down dead upon the same spot; for the same thing, although not distinctly mentioned, was no doubt true of Ananias also. *Yielded up the ghost* may seem to be a stronger expression than the one in v. 5; but in Greek they are identical. So too is the *carrying forth* of this verse with the *carried out* of that. *The young men*, namely, those who had removed Ananias (v. 6.) The argument derived from the analogy of the comparative forms (πρεσβύτεροι, elder, and νεώτεροι, younger) in favour of regarding both as technical official titles (see above, on v. 6), is considerably weakened by the *younger* being here called simply *young* or *youths* (νεανίσκοι). On the other hand, supposing these expressions to be used in their popular and simple sense, there is not only nothing strange in the promiscuous use of the comparative and positive degree, but an obvious significancy in the former where it stands (see v. 6), as suggestive of the reason for their undertaking this unpleasant duty, namely, that it would have been unbecoming to devolve it on their elders. In any civilized society or company, *the younger men* would feel themselves in honour bound to act in such emergencies, without official right or obligation, not merely on account of their supposed strength and activity, but also from a natural and reasonable disposition to relieve or spare, not only women and children, but *the older men*. Where the line between the ages should be drawn, is a question theoretically difficult enough, but one which would not give the slightest trouble in a practical emergency. *Came in and found her dead*, though not decisive, seems to favour the opinion that the foregoing verse relates to their actual return from the place of burial. The Codex Beza and the Syriac version here repeat the word which means to shroud or wrap up in v. 6 above. Though no part of the text, it may be supplied or understood, like the expression *at his feet* in the preceding clause. *By her husband*, literally, *to* (i. e. close to) *her husband*, implying proximity and juxtaposition. The Greek word (πρός), with the accusative, strictly denotes motion to or towards an object, and may here be used because the verb includes the idea of removal. The same preposition is substituted here, in what is now regarded as the true text, for another (παρά) meaning *by* or *at*, in the phrase *at his feet*, repeated from v. 2 above. The same idea (*by* or *at*) is expressed by still a third preposition (ἐπί) in v. 9, as well as in 3, 10. 11 above. The speedy burial of this unhappy pair has been often cavilled at, and variously justified. The naked reference to divine authority, without a positive command on record, is a virtual concession that the act admits of no excuse on ordinary principles, and also fails to guard against untimely imitation. The alleged practice of the Jews, from the time of the Captivity, to bury on the day of death, is historically doubtful, and by no means an example for the Christian world. The physical necessity, arising from the climate, is also doubtful, or at least exaggerated and at variance with scriptural examples. The true explanation seems to be, that the usual reason for delaying burial did not exist in this case. That reason is the propriety of ascertaining that the death has taken place before the body is interred. But here there was neither doubt as to the fact nor interment in the proper sense. The bodies were most probably deposited uncoffined in the horizontal niches of an open sepulchre above ground (see above, on v. 6.) But it matters little whether this were so or not, as the Apostles, who presided at this awful scene, must certainly have known that Ananias and Sapphira were completely dead.

11. And great fear came upon all the church, and upon as many as heard these things.

The effect of these judgments was an universal sense of awe and dread. The first and last words of the verse agree exactly with the second clause of v. 5; the change of *all that* to *as many as* existing only in the English version. This coincidence of form seems to favour, though it cannot of itself establish, the opinion that v. 5 is a prolepsis or anticipation of the statement here made in its proper place. The only difference between the two is that the general expression, *all those hearing these things*, is preceded, in the verse before us, by the more specific phrase, *the whole church*. This is the second instance of the use of this word in the book before us, or the first, according to some ancient manuscripts and recent critics, who omit the word (ἐκκλησία) in 2, 47. It may here mean either the assembly in whose presence these events took place, or the whole body of believers. But at this stage of the re-organization, there is reason to believe that the two ideas were coincident, that is to say, that those who met, especially for worship, were in fact the whole body or its standing representatives. Whether Tyndale and Cranmer, in translating the word *congregation*, meant to put the more restricted sense upon it, may be doubted, as this English word had once a wider usage. Thus Knox calls the Church of Christ his "Congregation," and the same name was long borne by the whole body of the Reformed in Scotland. Besides the general objection to the punishment of Ananias and his wife as cruel, it has been accused of undue relative severity compared with that of Elymas the Sorcerer (see below, on 13, 11), and with the supposed impunity of Simon Magus (see below, on 8, 24.) In explanation of this seeming disproportion, it has been suggested, that such rigour was particularly needed at the very outset (see above, on v. 5); and that Ananias and Sapphira had most probably experienced the extraordinary influences of the Holy Spirit, and having "fallen away," could no more be "renewed to repentance" (Heb. 6, 4–6), having really committed the unpardonable sin (Matt. 12, 31. 32. 1 John 5, 16.) The same considerations have been used to justify the sudden death of these two persons without previous notice, and without opportunity or space for repentance (Heb. 12, 17.) It is worthy of remark that such apologies are called for, only where the Scriptures are concerned, and that no man thinks it needful thus to "vindicate the ways of God to man," in reference to the multitudes of cases, in which unconverted sinners are continually swept into eternity without immediate warning and without repentance.

12. And by the hands of the Apostles were many signs and wonders wrought among the people; and they were all with one accord in Solomon's porch.

As the impression made by the events of Pentecost was strengthened and maintained by a succession of miraculous performances (2, 43); so now, the effect of the tremendous judgment upon Ananias and Sapphira was continued or increased in the same manner. The terms used in the two places are almost identical. As to the additional expression, *by the hands*, implying instrumental agency, see above, on 2, 23. 3, 18, and below, on 7, 25. As to the other phrase here added, *in* (or *among*) *the people*, see above, on 2, 47. 3, 9. 11. 12. 4, 1. 2. 21. The last clause has reference to neither of the nearest antecedents, *the Apostles* or *the people*, but to the whole body of disciples. (See above, on 2, 1. 4. 4, 31.) This clause has been understood to mean, that as the number of disciples had become too great to be accommodated elsewhere, their religious services were now held in the spacious portico, where Peter had addressed the people in relation to the healing of the lame man. But whatever acts of worship or instruction may have been performed there, it is more natural to understand the words here used in a wider sense, as meaning that Solomon's Porch, at all times, doubtless, one of the most public places in Jerusalem (see above, on 3, 11), now became the favourite resort and promenade of the disciples, as it may have been of Christ himself (see John 10, 23), which would give it, in their eyes, a kind of consecration, similar to that of "the upper room," where they had last eaten with him (1, 13) and "the house where they were sitting" on the day of Pentecost (2, 2.) The clause does not refer to a particular assemblage on a certain day, but to their habit of convening there by common consent (ἦσαν ὁμοθυμαδόν), though not perhaps by any formal rule or resolution. Here again, the record of particular occurrences is gradually merged in a description of what took place during a longer and less definite interval of time. (See above, on 2, 42. 3, 1. 4, 32. 36.)

13. And of the rest durst no man join himself to them; but the people magnified them.

The relation of *the rest* to *all* in the preceding verse is like that of *others* to the same word in 2, 12. 13. Here it only shows, however, that the *all* of v. 12 is a relative expression, meaning all the disciples, and not all the people. The word translated *join themselves* originally means to be glued or stuck fast; then, as a neuter verb, to cleave or adhere to any thing or person. It is almost confined, in the New Testament, to Luke and Paul, being once used by Matthew (19, 5) and once in a doubtful text of the Apocalypse (18, 5.) Its strength of meaning is evinced, not only by its primary usage, as above described, and as exemplified in Luke 10, 11, but by its application to the most intimate of all personal relations, that of marriage (Matt. 19, 5, compare 1 Cor. 6, 16), and by the words to which it is opposed (as in Rom. 12, 9.) Even where it seems to have a weaker sense, the stronger is admissible, and therefore, upon general principles, entitled to the preference. (See below, on 8, 29. 9, 26. 10, 28. 17, 34, and compare Luke 15, 15. 1 Cor. 6, 17.) We are bound, therefore, to explain it here, not merely of association or familiar intercourse, but of conjunction and adhesion, either in the literal and local sense of personal contact, or in the metaphorical and moral sense of joint profession and organic union. This usage of the word suffices to exclude some of the many explanations of the first clause of the verse before us; such as Lightfoot's notion, that the twelve Apostles were henceforth regarded with more deference by the hundred and eight presbyters (12+108=120, see above, on 1, 15); and that of other writers, that the same thing is affirmed as to the body of disciples. That these, or any part of these, should not have dared to come in contact or associate with the twelve, is altogether inconsistent with the general impression made by this whole narrative, or rather by the whole New Testament, in reference to the social relations of the infant church. (See above, on 2, 42–47. 4, 32. 33.) The same objection does not lie against the old and prevalent opinion, that *the rest* here means the unconverted multitude, who were deterred by what had taken place from either joining or assailing the disciples. But this last sense (assailing) is entirely foreign from the usage of the Greek verb, and the other (joining) makes the clause directly contradictory to what is stated in the next verse, namely, that great multitudes did join them, both of men and women. Two evasions of this argument have been attempted; one by making this verse and the next successive as to time—'the rest were at first afraid to join them, but the people still admired them, and by degrees the number of believers multiplied, etc.'—a construction which supposes the decisive terms, "at first" and "by degrees" or "afterwards," to be omitted, which can never be assumed except in case of exegetical necessity, that is, when it enables us to clear up what is otherwise hopelessly obscure; and this is not the present case, as we shall see. The other evasion is by making a distinction between *joining* (13) and *believing* (14), so as to restrict the latter to the faith of miracles, or faith in the power of the Apostles to perform them; a distinction wholly arbitrary in itself, and directly contradicted by the fact that these believers *were added to the Lord* (14). As another sample of the singular diversity of judgment in relation to this clause, it may be added, that some eminent interpreters suppose *the rest* to be contrasted, not with *all* (12), but with *the people* (13), and therefore to denote the rest of the wealthy and superior class, who were deterred by the fate of Ananias and Sapphira, as well as by the proofs of superhuman power afforded by the miracles of the Apostles, from uniting themselves with them, as they would otherwise have done. This is commonly rejected as a forced interpretation, and is justly liable to such a censure, on account of the antithesis which it assumes, and on which it appears to rest. But this antithesis is not essential and may easily be modified in such a way as to entitle this interpretation to the preference over every other, except one which will be afterwards presented. The modification consists in making *the rest* refer, not to *the people* in the next clause, but to *Ananias and Sapphira* in the foregoing context. *The rest* will then mean others of the same class, or rather the same character, i. e. ambitious, worldly, and dishonest people, who might otherwise have joined the church as hypocritical professors, under some momentary impulse, or with some corrupt design, sufficient to outweigh the fear of persecution, which indeed at this time must have been extremely slight, but who were now deterred, by a regard to their own safety, from incurring even the remote risk of a fate like that of Ananias and Sapphira. This agrees well with the foregoing context, in which Luke has been describing the effect produced by that catastrophe and afterwards maintained by other miracles, to all which it is certainly a natural conclusion or appendix, that the salutary fear thus engendered was the means by which it pleased God to preserve the church, in this its infant state, from the intrusion of impure and hypocritical professors. The only objection to this view of the passage is its not accounting for the local specification which immediately precedes, and seems to separate the cause and the effect from one another in a very unusual and puzzling manner. 'The fear produced by this event was heightened by the miracles which followed—and the disciples now habitually occupied the porch of Solomon—and no more hypocrites, like Ananias and Sapphira, dared to join them.' This is certainly no natural association of ideas, although not absolutely fatal to the exposition which involves it, if no other can be found that is not open to the same objection, and at least as satisfactory in other points. The question then is, whether the first clause of v. 13 can be so explained, that the last clause of v. 12 shall not be an abrupt interpolation or parenthesis, but a natural and necessary member of the sentence. This can only be effected by supposing that the writer, in the first clause of v. 13, instead of reverting, as the other exegetical hypothesis assumes, to the moral effects, which he had been describing, when he paused to speak of the locality in question, is still speaking of that same locality, as now by common consent given up to the disciples, and generally recognized as their appropriated place of meeting. The whole connection, thus explained, may be paraphrased as follows. 'The death of Ananias and Sapphira filled the public mind with awe, and this was afterwards maintained by a continued series of miracles, in consequence of which the disciples were allowed to constitute a body by themselves, without molestation or intrusion from without; and as they had now gradually formed the habit of assembling daily in the porch of Solomon, no others ventured to mix with them there, but the people were contented to look on as mere spectators from the courts adjoining, and continually *magnified* (i. e. admired and praised) them, as a company among whom God was present in a new and most extraordinary manner.' Besides the difference between these two interpretations, with respect to the connection of v. 13 with v. 12, they also differ as to the precise sense of the verb *to join themselves;* the one referring it to union with the church by profession, the other to mere external contact or joint occupation of the same place. But as both these meanings are legitimate deductions from the etymology and usage of the Greek verb, as explained above, the choice between the two constructions cannot rest upon this difference, but must be decided by a view of the whole context. And as the one last stated is the simplest and, without departing from the natural import of the words, gives clearness and coherence to an otherwise perplexed and interrupted context, it appears, upon the whole, to be the true interpretation.

14. And believers were the more added to the Lord, multitudes both of men and women.

Believers is in Greek a participle and means *believing* (men or persons.) Some connect it with *the Lord* (believing in or on him), which is a possible construction; but the one given in the version is not only simpler and more obvious, but also recommended by its unambiguous occurrence elsewhere. (See below, on 11, 24.) On the other supposition, *added* means *added to the church*, as in the common text of 2, 47. The ellipsis is the same as in 2, 41. *Added to the Lord*, i. e. to Christ, as the Head of the Church, which is his body, and of which all converts become members. Some of the oldest writers on the passage have observed, that Luke no longer gives specific numbers, an omission which enhances the idea of increase. As to the mention of both sexes, see above, on 4, 4. The distinct mention of female converts, for the first time, may have been occasioned by the melancholy end of Sapphira, as if the writer had intended to suggest, that the place left vacant, not only by the husband but the wife, was speedily supplied by many true believers of the same sex. It is plainly implied that these accessions took place, not at once, but during an indefinite period. (See above, on v. 12.) The statement here made has already been referred to, as a proof that the first clause of the preceding verse cannot mean that the people were deterred by fear from joining the disciples, as professors of the new religion. On the other hand, it is entirely reconcileable with either of the two interpretations of that clause, which were left to the decision of the reader. According to the one first stated, the idea is, that although no more Ananiases or Sapphiras joined the church, it was replenished with a multitude of true converts; according to the other, that although the unconverted mass remained aloof as admiring spectators, many were continually passing from their ranks to those of the believers, and the numbers thus subtracted from the adverse party were of course added to the host, the household, and the body of the Lord. There is a subtle difference, in English usage, between *more* and *the more.* 'Believers were more added' would mean simply more than ever, or continually more and more. 'Believers were the more added' means that the addition was greater on account of something previously mentioned, and which might have seemed to threaten diminution. In the other places where the Greek phrase (μᾶλλον δέ) is used, it is translated *but rather* (1 Cor. 14, 1. 5. Eph. 4, 28. 5, 11), *or rather* (Gal. 4, 9), and might have been so rendered here, 'but believers (instead of being lost or lessened) were rather added to the Lord, etc.' In this case, however, there is not, as in the others, any reference to what immediately precedes, namely, *the people magnified them*, but either to the first clause of v. 13, or to some remoter antecedent, as for instance to the death of Ananias and Sapphira, which, instead of diminishing the number of conversions, caused them to abound *the more*. The simplest syntax is to make this clause a part of the preceding verse. 'None dared to join them, but the people magnified them and believers were more and more added to the Lord.'

15. Insomuch that they brought forth the sick into the streets, and laid (them) on beds and couches, that at the least the shadow of Peter passing by might overshadow some of them.

The original construction of the first clause, *so as to bring out the sick*, etc. connects it still more closely with what goes before than in the common version, where *they brought* might seem to be indefinite, and to mean nothing more than that *the sick were brought forth* (see above, on 1, 23); whereas the literal translation above given identifies the subject of the verb with persons previously mentioned. But with whom? Or on what preceding verb is the infinitive dependent? Few questions of construction in the whole book have been more disputed. The older writers, with surprising unanimity, pass over the immediate context, to discover a remoter antecedent, throwing what is thus passed over into a parenthesis. But as to the extent of this parenthesis, they disagree among themselves. Some begin it in the middle of v. 12, and read, *by the hands of the Apostles many signs and wonders were performed among the people . . . . . . so that they brought*, etc. This is the arrangement of the text in the Geneva Bible, copied by King James's version. Others, regarding such a long parenthesis as neither natural nor needful, place the beginning at the end of v. 13, and read, *the people magnified them . . . . . . so that they brought out the sick*, etc. The current of opinion among modern critics and philologists is adverse to the assumption of parentheses at all, especially in plain historical prose, without some urgent exegetical necessity. Such a necessity, indeed, is here assumed by those who plead for the constructions above given, and who seem to be agreed, however much they differ otherwise, that the last words of v. 14 and the first words of v. 15 cannot possibly belong together. It is hard, however, to perceive the ground of this grammatical assumption. What better reason, than the multitude of converts, could be given for the multitude of cures performed? Without insisting that *believers* in v. 14 simply means believers in the wonder-working gifts of the Apostles—which indeed, as we have seen above (on v. 13), is inconsistent with the fact that they were *added to the Lord*—and without insisting that the passive faith of miracles was always accompanied by saving faith; we know that the converse of this proposition must be true, or in other words, that saving faith included that of miracles, or trust in the miraculous endowments of Christ's servants; so that the multiplication of believers would be naturally followed by more numerous applications for miraculous relief. There is nothing therefore to forbid the obvious construction of the clauses as immediately successive, without any parenthesis at all, *and believers were more added to the Lord, multitudes both of men and women, so as to bring* (or *so that they brought*) *forth the sick*, etc. The sense obtained by this construction is indeed much better than the one afforded by assuming a parenthesis; for the apostolical miracles were rather the effect than the cause of this great concourse, and the people's magnifying them (13) is not so good a reason for that concourse as the increase of faith and the multiplication of true converts. This view of the passage has moreover the advantage of confirming what we know in other ways, that the miracles of Christ and his Apostles were not always the prime motive of the multitudes who followed them, but often secondary to the craving for instruction and salvation. (Compare Luke 5, 1.) *Into* hardly expresses the full force of the Greek particle (κατά) which sometimes means *along* (8, 26. 25, 3. 26, 13) or *through* (8, 1. 11, 1. 15, 23. 24, 12.) The sick were laid along the streets, throughout their whole length, to await the approach of the Apostles. *Streets*, literally, *broad (ways)*, in the singular denoting the main street of a town or city (Rev. 11, 8. 21, 21. 22, 2. Judg. 19, 15. 20. LXX), and in the plural its thoroughfares or wide streets, as contrasted with its narrow streets or lanes (Luke 14, 21), and especially considered as public places of resort (Matt. 6, 5. 12, 19. Luke 10, 10. 13, 26.) *And laid*, literally, *and to put* or *place*, the infinitive construction being still continued. The word translated *into* properly means *down to*, i. e. from the houses, or *along*, implying that they lay there and awaited the approach of the Apostles, which agrees exactly with the intimation in the other clause, and dependent upon *so as* (or so *that*) in the beginning of the sentence. *Beds and couches*, so that even the most helpless and bedridden were included in this dispensation of healing power. In the oldest manuscripts, the first word is diminutive in form (κλιναρίων), as well as in the Vulgate (*lectulis*), denoting small beds that were easily carried. *Beds* may either have its proper sense or that of *bedsteads*, which, though no longer used in the East, were well known to the ancients. The oldest and the latest writers are agreed in supposing, that the two words here used were intended to describe the couches of the rich and poor, a distinction countenanced, if not required, by a phrase of Cicero's (*non modo lectos verum etiam grabbatos*), from which some have inferred that the second noun (κραββάτων, κραβάτων, or κραβάττων) is of Latin origin, whereas the modern Greek philologists describe it as a Macedonian word, used only by the latest writers. (Tyndale's translation here is, *beds and pallets*.) The original construction in the last clause is, *that*, *Peter coming, the shadow might*, etc. *At the least* (Tyndale, *at the least 'way*) is in Greek a compound or contracted particle (κἄν for καὶ ἐάν), meaning originally *and if*, and repeatedly so used (Mark 16, 18. Luke 13, 9. James 5, 15), but sometimes more emphatically, *even if* (Matt. 21, 21. 26, 35. John 8, 14. 10, 38. 11, 25), or *if even* (Heb. 12, 20), and then absolutely or elliptically, *if but* or *if only* (2 Cor. 11, 16), which is the meaning here and in a passage of the gospels, where precisely the same thing is said, in reference to the fringe or border of our Saviour's garment (Mark 6, 56.) The crowd was so great and so incessant, that many could do nothing more than place themselves, or their afflicted friends, under the shadow of the Apostles, and especially of Peter, as the most conspicuous and active, as he came by or along (ἐρχομένου.) But this was in itself as powerless, and by divine appointment as effectual, as any word or deed, by which the miracle was commonly connected with the person of the thaumaturge or wonder-worker. (See above, on 3, 7.) Far from being superstitious, it was rather a strong proof of the people's faith, analogous to that which Christ commended in the woman with the issue of blood (Matt. 9, 22), but especially in the centurion (Matt. 8, 10), who believed that Christ could heal his servant without personal contact or even being present. In order that these miracles of healing might extend to all who sought them, and yet be visibly connected with the persons who performed them, it pleased God that their shadow should, in this case, answer the same purpose with the words and gestures used on other occasions. This seems much more natural than the supposition, that the writer pauses here to mention a pitiable superstition which had no effect whatever, or was mercifully made effectual in spite of its absurdity and sinfulness. As to the Popish argument in favor of the primacy of Peter, from the virtue here ascribed to his very shadow, this is an error in the opposite extreme, but one refuted by the great Apostle's representative position, and by the similar statement elsewhere with respect to Paul. (See below, on 19, 12.) *Some of them*, i. e. some one of them, the first pronoun (τινί) being singular in Greek. This qualifying phrase has reference rather to the hopes of the recipients than to the actual effect, as appears from the last clause of the next verse. The Codex Beza and another uncial manuscript make an addition to this verse in somewhat different forms, one of which is copied by the Vulgate and its followers (*et liberarentur ab infirmitatibus suis.*)

16. There came also a multitude out of the cities round about unto Jerusalem, bringing sick folks, and them which were vexed with unclean spirits; and they were healed every one.

The concourse and the miracles, described in the preceding verse, though locally restricted to Jerusalem, were not confined to its inhabitants. The idea of confluence or concourse is more clearly expressed in the original, which means, *there came together*. *Also* represents a double particle in

Greek (δὲ καί), which, although strictly meaning nothing more than *and* (or *but*) *also*, has in usage an emphatic sense, equivalent to 'nay more' or 'besides all this.' (Compare καί γε, 2, 18 above, and the remark there.) *A multitude*, or more exactly, *the multitude*, a much stronger expression, meaning the whole mass of the people (see above, on 2, 6), which was no doubt literally true, though not without individual exceptions. The impression made by this as well as by the Gospel History, is that these great movements comprehended the whole body of the population, which was thus made thoroughly acquainted with the claims of Jesus and the doctrine of his servants. Another variation from the form of the original consists in the insertion of the small word *out*, which materially modifies the meaning. 'A multitude out of the surrounding cities' is a very different thing from 'the multitude (or mass) of the surrounding cities.' The former might have come and left the vast majority at home; but no such sense can be attached to the exact translation. *Round about* is in Greek a single word (πέριξ), a rare and strengthened form of a common preposition (περί), here used as an adverbial adjective (τῶν πέριξ πόλεων), and therefore well expressed in English by *surrounding*. The noun which it qualifies would here be more exactly rendered by the generic term *towns*, in its proper English sense, as including villages and cities. It is no doubt put for the whole country; partly because the population lived almost entirely in towns great or small; partly because these towns represented the more rural districts, which were civilly dependent on them. The omission of the preposition (εἰς) before *Jerusalem*, in some old manuscripts and late editions, can have no effect upon the sense, which must still be that of motion towards the holy city. The crowd are not described as merely *bringing* (ἄγοντες) but as *bearing, carrying* (φέροντες) *the sick*, literally, *strengthless*, weak, infirm, but applied, like the last English word, not only to debility, but to bodily disease. The word *folks* (or *people*) is not in the original, which might have been exactly rendered, *the infirm* (or *sick*.) Besides this general description of the objects upon which these healing miracles were wrought, the writer mentions a specific malady, because of its extraordinary prevalence at that time, its peculiarly distressing character, its strange complication of moral and physical disorder, and above all, its mysterious connection with the unseen world and with another race of spirits. These are called *unclean* or impure in a moral sense, essentially equivalent to *wicked*, but suggesting more directly the idea of corruption, as existing in themselves and practised upon others. These are the *angels* or ministering spirits of the Devil, who fell with him, or have since been added to him, as believers are added to the Lord (v. 14), and are co-operating with him as the tempters and accusers of mankind. (See above, on v. 3, and compare Matt. 25, 41.) To these fallen and seducing spirits our race has ever been accessible and more or less subjected; but when Christ was upon earth, they were permitted to assume a more perceptible, if not a more complete ascendency, extending to the body and the mind, and thus presenting the worst forms of insanity and bodily disease combined. That these demoniacal possessions are not mere poetical descriptions of disease or madness, but the real acts of spiritual agents, is apparent from the personality ascribed to them, as well as from their being so explicitly distinguished from all other maladies, as in the case before us; while the fact that they did really produce disease abundantly accounts for their being sometimes so described and constantly connected with corporeal illness. The extraordinary prevalence of these disorders in the time of Christ, while we scarcely hear of them in any other period of history, may be partly owing to the fact, that what is always going on in secret was then brought to light by his authoritative interposition; and partly to the fact, that the stupendous strife between the "seed of the woman" and the "seed of the serpent" (Gen. 3, 15), which gives complexion to all human history, then reached its crisis, and these demoniacal possessions were at once the work of Satan, as a means of doing evil, and of God, as a means of doing good, by glorifying him whom he had sanctified and sent into the world. (See John 10, 36. 17, 1. 5.) Every expulsion of a demon by our Lord himself, or in his name by his Apostles, was a triumph over his great enemy, not only in the unseen world but upon earth, in the sight of men as well as angels (Luke 10, 17. 18. John 12, 31. 16, 11.) This immediate relation of these strange phenomena to Christ's person and official work, accounts for their absence both before and since, as well as for the impotent resistance of the evil ones themselves, and their extorted testimony to the character and rank of their destroyer. (See Matt. 8, 29–32. Mark 5, 7. 9, 26. Luke 4, 33–35. 41. 8, 28. 29.) It explains likewise the distinct mention of this class of miracles, both here and elsewhere (e. g. Matt. 4, 24. 8, 16. 28, 33. Mark

1, 34. 6, 13. 16, 17. 18. Luke 8, 2. 36), as being in themselves the most surprising of all cures, and at the same time the most palpable of all attestations to the Messiahship and Deity of Jesus. *Vexed* (Wiclif, *travailed*), literally, *thronged* or *crowded*, the original expression being a derivative of ὄχλος (see above, on 1, 15), as our words *perturbed, disturbed*, etc., are of the synonymous word *turba*. As the Greek word, though employed by later writers in the vague sense of annoying or harassing, has in earlier usage, such as that of Herodotus and Æschylus, the specific sense suggested by its etymology, namely, that of harassing with crowds or mobbing, there is no absurdity in supposing, both here and in the other place where it occurs (Luke 6, 18), an allusion to the grand peculiarity and fearful aggravation of such sufferings, namely, the co-existence of two spiritual agents in connection with a single body, one the tyrant, one the slave; a state of things which could not better be expressed in one word than by saying they were *crowded*, *thronged*, by evil spirits. (See Mark 5, 9. Luke 8, 30. 11, 26.) But terrible as this condition was, we know that it was not incurable, and that although the Apostles had once failed, through want of faith, to work a dispossession (Matt. 17, 14–21. Mark 9, 18. 19. Luke 9, 40. 41), yet now, though the Master was no longer with them, when demoniacs were brought to them in crowds from the surrounding country, *they were all healed*, or retaining the emphatic collocation of the Greek text, *they were healed all*. The less exact but expressive version, *every one*, is that of Tyndale.

17. Then the High Priest rose up, and all they (that were) with him, which is the sect of the Sadducees, and were filled with indignation.

Here begins another alternation or transition from more general description to particular narration. (See above, on 2, 42. 4, 32. 36. 5, 12.) If *then* were an adverb, meaning *at that time*, (as in 1, 12. 4, 8), it might indicate a mere chronological connection between what is here related and what immediately precedes, as if he had said, 'about the same time other things occurred entirely distinct from these.' But as it is the usual continuative particle (δέ), by which the members of the previous narrative are linked together, it denotes a much more intimate relation, and suggests that this new attack upon the church was not only preceded but occasioned by the state of things described in vs. 12–16. It was not only when (or after) the believers were so greatly multiplied, and the people so impressed by the miracles of the Apostles, but for that very reason, that this new assault was made, which may be regarded as the second hostile movement from without, the first being that recorded in 4, 1–22, as the affair of Ananias and Sapphira was the earliest disturbance from within. (See below, on 6, 1.) In this, as in the former case (4, 1), the hostile parties are the Priesthood and the Sadducees; but here the movement has a still more national or public character, because the High Priest is particularly mentioned. As we have no clew whatever to the length of the interval between these several occurrences, the safest as well as the most natural presumption, is that Annas is the person here intended. (See above, on 4, 6.) *Rose up*, literally, *rising* or *having risen*. This is a neuter or intransitive form of the verb explained above, on 2, 24. 32. 3, 22. 26. It is a favourite of Luke's, and not unfrequent in the other books of the New Testament. In some cases, it has obviously the literal or local sense of rising from one's seat or bed (e. g. Matt. 9, 9. Mark 1, 35. Luke 4, 16, 29. 39. John 5, 8.) In a scarcely figurative sense, it is applied to resurrection from the dead (Matt. 17, 9. Mark 6, 14. Luke 9, 8. John 20, 9.) In other cases, it seems to have the vague sense of rousing or addressing one's self to action, without reference to actual corporeal movement (e. g. Mark 7, 24. 10, 1, 50. Luke 1, 39. 4, 29, etc.) As in many of these instances, however, the strict sense is admissible, or at least an allusion to it, that sense is of course entitled to the preference, without some reason for departing from it. (See above, on 4, 9.) This is peculiarly the case here, as the same word occurs twice in the Gospels (Matt. 26, 62. Mark 14, 60) in relation to public acts of the High Priest. Upon this ground, some understand it here as meaning, that the High Priest rose up from his seat in the Sanhedrim, or in some private consultation with his allies mentioned in the other clause. But this explanation overlooks a material difference between this case and the two last cited, namely, that in them the High Priest had been represented as presiding in the Council, whereas here there is nothing of the kind referred to in the previous context, but the act of *rising up* is introduced abruptly. Another explanation gives the verb the emphatic sense of rising up in opposition or against (Beza, *insurgens*,) which may seem to be sustained by the analogy of Mark 3, 26; but there the object is expressed, and the idea of hostility conveyed, not by the verb but by a preposition. Most interpreters have therefore acquiesced in the third meaning above given, namely, that of addressing one's self to action; which is certainly far better than the favourite notion of a certain school, that it is pleonastic, or in other words, means nothing at all. The additional idea which it here suggests is that of previous inaction. Since the first abortive effort to arrest the progress of the new religion (4, 18. 21. 31), the authorities would seem to have been passive or indifferent, but now aroused themselves again to action. *All they that were with him*, or more exactly, *all those with him*, is supposed by some to mean the other priests, or the other members of the Sanhedrim; but no such vague and loose description of official persons occurs elsewhere. Still more unlikely is the sense of relatives or private friends, which some support by a reference to 4, 6. 13. The only satisfactory interpretation is that which makes the clause mean, *those* (now acting) *with him*, in his opposition to the church, implying that it was not his own personal or party friends. This precludes the inference, which some have drawn from these expressions, that the High Priest was himself a Sadducee. We know from Josephus, that a son of Ananus (or Annas), bearing the same name, attached himself to that sect; but all our information on the subject tends to the conclusion, that both Annas himself and Caiaphas were Pharisees. (See below, on 23, 6.) What is here described is, therefore, not a party-organization, but a coalition of distinct and hostile parties for a special purpose, not unlike that of Herod and Pilate against Christ. (See above, on 4, 27, and compare Luke 23, 12.) *Which is the sect*, in Greek, *the sect being*, or *the existing sect*. The participle does not agree (as it appears to do in English) with the nouns preceding, but with that which follows (ἡ οὖσα αἵρεσις). This is explained by some as a case of the grammatical figure called *attraction*, and equivalent in meaning to (ὄντες ἡ αἵρεσις) *being the sect*, i. e. 'they who acted with the High Priest, upon this occasion, were the sect of the Sadducees.' But this, though true and necessarily implied, can hardly be the meaning of the words here used. The participle (*being*) seems intended, from its feminine and singular form, not to identify the allies of the High Priest with the Sadducees, but rather to describe the Sadducees themselves, as an existing, long established, well-known body. (See below, on 13, 1, where the same unusual expression is employed in reference to the church at Antioch.) The authors of the movement then are here described as the High Priest and those acting with him, the existing (i. e. previously existing, or perhaps still existing) party of the Sadducees. *Sect*, although now fixed by prescription, is not perfectly appropriate to these great Jewish parties. The Greek word (αἵρεσις) originally means the act of taking, then a choice, a preference, especially of certain views or principles, philosophical, religious, or political. Its nearest equivalents, as thus applied, are *school* and *party*, without any necessary implication of erroneous doctrine or improper practice. Thus the word is used in Greek to designate the Stoical *system* of philosophy; and Cicero, referring to a certain person's philosophical preferences, says, *in ea haeresi est*. Later ecclesiastical usage appropriated it to doctrinal departures from the orthodox or catholic faith, which is the only meaning of its English derivative (*heresy*.) But in the New Testament, the Greek word still retains its older application to the party holding an opinion, rather than to the opinion itself. Even in 1 Cor. 11, 19. Gal. 5, 20. Tit. 3, 10. 2 Pet. 2, 1, the immediate reference is rather to schismatical divisions than to doctrinal corruptions, although these are necessarily implied. In other parts of the book before us, it is applied to Pharisaism (15, 5. 26, 5,) and, in an unfavourable sense, to Christianity itself (24, 5. 14. 28, 22.) In all these cases, the word *heresy* is as inappropriate as *idiot* in 4, 13, or *despot* in 4, 24, though the three English words are not even corruptions of the Greek ones (like *alms, palsy, bishop*), but direct derivatives, formed by a simple change of termination. So far is mere coincidence of origin or form from proving words to be synonymous. There is not the same objection to the word *sect*, used by our translators here and elsewhere (15, 5. 26, 5,) and now established as a stereotyped technical expression in relation to the Pharisees and Sadducees. The word, however, should be carefully explained and clearly understood, as not implying what its general usage now includes, to wit, distinct organization and a separate worship, but merely a diversity, in certain points of theory and practice, between persons holding the same creed and joining in the same devotions. If a word were now to be selected for the first time, it is plain that this idea would be better expressed by the term *school*, when doctrinal diversities are specially in question, and the term *party*, when the reference is rather to practical matters of authority or discipline. Such were the relations of the Pharisees and Sadducees who, far from being independent sects or churches, in the modern sense, were two opposing factions in the same great church and body politic, continually striving, with alternate or variable success, for the predominance, and at this time probably sharing the great offices between them. As to their distinctive views and practice, and the motives of the Sadducees in persecuting the Apostles, see above, on 4, 1. They are here said to have been filled with jealousy or party-spirit. *Indignation* is a sense, of which there seems to be no clear example, either in classical or hellenistic usage. According to its etymology and primary usage, the Greek word (ζῆλος) denotes any warm affection or enthusiastic impulse, either in favour of or opposition to a given object, thus coinciding almost perfectly with its derivative in English (*zeal.*) But besides this wider sense, it has the more specific one of *jealousy*, which some high authorities pronounce a Hebraism, but which occurs, though rarely, in the purest Attic writers, and is really a slight modification of a meaning common in the best Greek usage, that of eager rivalry or emulation, whether good or bad, and therefore opposed by Plato to *envy* (φθόνος), while Hesiod confounds them. In the case before us, the word necessarily suggests the ideas of zeal, party spirit, and malignant jealousy or envy, all of which are perfectly appropriate.

18. And laid their hands on the Apostles, and put them in the common prison.

The first step of this movement is the same as in the former case, to wit, arrest and imprisonment, not as a punishment, but with a view to their arraignment and trial. (See above, on 4, 3.) The subject of the sentence is the same as in v. 17, the High Priest and the Sadducees who acted with him. *Laid their hands* is, in several of the oldest manuscripts, *laid hands* (or *laid the hands*) without the pronoun. This abbreviated form is very common (see Matt. 26, 50. Luke 20, 19. John 7, 30. 44. Acts 12, 1. 21, 27.) There is but one certain instance of the other (Luke 21, 12; in Mark 14, 46, the text is doubtful.) This is not a mere figure for arrest, but a literal description of the act by which it is effected. There is no ground whatever, in the text or context, for the supposition that *Apostles* here means Peter and John, of which restricted use there is no example elsewhere, unless it be in 14, 4. 14, where *Apostles*, as we shall there see, has itself a different meaning. In every other case, throughout this history, *the Apostles* means *the twelve* as a collective body. (See below, on v. 29.) *Prison* is the word translated *hold* in 4, 3, but in a different case, and preceded by a different preposition. The noun, according to Greek usage, is an abstract, meaning *custody* or *keeping*, and is so used in a moral sense by Paul (1 Cor. 7, 19.) The only classical example of the local meaning (*prison*) is said to be a dubious expression of Thucydides. That sense is thought to be required here by the adjective, which might however be applied to the confinement as well as to the prison. The adjective itself is apt to be misapprehended by the English reader, from the equivocal language of the version. *Common prison* naturally calls up the idea of promiscuous association between prisoners of various rank and character; and this has actually been insisted on by some interpreters, as an intentional insult to the twelve, or at least a serious aggravation of their sufferings. But the English word most probably, and the Greek word most certainly, means nothing more than *public*, belonging to the people (δῆμος) or the whole community, and not to any individual. Though common in the classics, it is found only in this book of the New Testament, and excepting in the case before us, only as an adverb (δημοσίᾳ), which is once translated *openly* (16, 37), and twice *publicly* (18, 28. 20, 20), but might have been still more exactly rendered by the corresponding English phrase, *in public*.

19. But (the) angel of (the) Lord by night opened the prison doors, and brought them forth, and said:

From this imprisonment they were delivered, not as before, through the fears or policy of their oppressors (4, 21), but by a divine interposition. (*But*, and, or then. See above, on v. 17.) *The angel of the Lord* is an expression used in the Old Testament to designate the Angel of Jehovah's presence, whom the church has commonly identified with the second person of the trinity. According to Greek usage, the words here employed denote *an angel of the Lord*, which may however be an imitation of the Hebrew idiom, in which a noun governing another does not take the article, however definite its sense may be. In this very title, for example, the word *angel* is without the article (מַלְאַךְ יְהֹוָה). But as the phrase itself, in this emphatic sense, belongs to the Old Testament exclusively, and as we have no reason to ascribe this deliverance to a personal appearance of the Son of God, the more indefinite or Greek construction of the words (*an angel*) seems entitled to the preference. The absence of the article before *Lord* rests upon a different usage, namely, that of its omission before proper names, to which class this word (Κύριος), as the Greek representative of the Hebrew *Jehovah*, may be properly considered as belonging. The deliverance took place *by night* (διά, through or in the course of, as in 1, 3), probably in order to increase the terror and surprise which it occasioned. It was effected, not by a miraculous suspension of the laws of nature, but by simply opening the doors of the prison, no doubt so insensibly as not to be perceived by those who guarded it, although there may have been a supernatural effect produced upon their senses, as in other cases. (See Matt. 28, 4. Luke 24, 16. John 20, 14.) The pretence that this is a poetical or oriental figure for the release of the Apostles by the jailor, or the guards, or any other human intervention, has been long since exploded as a sheer absurdity, or unmasked as an indirect denial of the truth of what is here recorded. By a strange revolution of opinion, many of the same class of unbelievers, who could once resort to such means of evasion, rather than abandon their old Sadducean error (see below, on 23, 8), now profess to be in actual and confidential intercourse with spirits in the other world. *Brought them forth*, literally, *bringing* (or *having brought*) *them forth*. This participial construction is extended, by some manuscripts and editors, to the preceding verb (*opening* for *opened.*) That this miraculous deliverance was not intended merely for their own relief, but for a higher end, appears from the instructions of the angel, given in the next verse.

20. Go, stand and speak in the temple to the people all the words of this life.

Go is not a mere expletive or pleonasm, as it often is in English, but has here its full sense, *go away*, depart hence, linger here no longer. (See above, on 1, 10. 11. 25.) As they had been released, not merely to enjoy freedom, but to exercise their ministry, the angel here exhorts them to renew it. *Stand and speak*, literally, *standing* (or *having taken your stand*) *speak*. (For the use of the verb *stand* in such connections, see above, on 2, 14.) *In the temple* (ἱερῷ) i. e. in the sacred enclosure, as distinguished from the edifice itself, which is denoted by another word (ναός, Matt. 23, 35.) They were to preach there the whole Gospel, *all the words of this life.* Most interpreters regard this as an instance of the figure called hypallage, equivalent in sense to *all these words of life*, i. e. living or life-giving doctrines. (Compare John 6, 68. Acts 7, 38. John 12, 50. 17, 3.) Other examples of the same construction are supposed to be found in 13, 26 below, and in Rom. 7, 24. But some deny the hypallage in any of these cases, or at least retain the obvious construction here, explaining *all the words of this life* to mean all the doctrines or instructions, which are necessary to make known to Israel this new form of their own religion, as a rule of life here, and a means of everlasting life hereafter. (For a like use of the word *way*, see below, on 9, 2. 19, 9. 23. 22, 4. 24, 14. 22, and compare the fuller forms, 13, 10. 16, 17. 18, 25. 26. 2 Pet. 2, 2. 15. 21.) Their angelic commission (see above, on 1, 11) was not merely to talk but to preach, not privately but publicly, not in the streets but in the temple, not to the rulers but the people, not a part of the truth necessary to salvation, but *all the words of this life.* (See below, on 20, 27.)

21. And when they heard (that), they entered into the temple, early in the morning, and taught; but the High Priest came, and they that were with him, and called the council together, and all the senate of the children of Israel, and sent to the prison, to have them brought.

When they heard that, literally, *hearing* or having heard; *that* is supplied by the translators. *The temple*, i. e. the sacred enclosure, as in the preceding verse. *Early in the morning*, just about (or just before) daybreak. The Greek noun sometimes means the dawn, sometimes the morning-twilight. The preposition *under*, both in Greek and Latin, is applied to time, when the idea to be expressed is that of indefinite nearness. *Taught*, i. e. preached, taught publicly, as the angel had directed them. *But* (δέ,) and, or then. *The High Priest and those with him* is exactly the phrase used above in v. 17, with the omission of the word *all*. Here again it means those acting with him upon this occasion, i. e. the Sadducees, as there expressed. It is rather implied that they were not, than that they were, his usual confederates or associates. *Came,* literally, *being* (or *becoming*) *near*, at hand, or present. The Greek word is seldom used in the New Testament, except by Luke, with whom it is a favourite expression. (See below, on vs. 22. 25, where it occurs again.) It is nearly equivalent, in this case, to our phrase, *being on the ground*, implying rather than expressing previous arrival. There is no need therefore of inquiring to what spot, or what apartment of the temple, they now came. That they were not in the same part of the vast enclosure with the Apostles, who were probably as usual in Solomon's porch (v. 12), is clear from what follows, but creates no difficulty, as the courts of Herod's temple were both large and many. *Senate,* or eldership, the Greek word bearing the same relation to (γέρων) *an old man*, that *senate* does to the corresponding word in Latin (*senex.*) Neither primitive nor derivative occurs more than once in the New Testament. (See John 3, 4.) The latter is applied in the classics to the highest council of the Doric States, particularly Sparta. In the Septuagint version, it is used, as a collective, to translate the plural *elders*, when considered as the representatives and rulers of the whole people (as in Ex. 3, 16. 18. Deut. 27, 1), or of any particular locality (as in Deut. 19, 12. 21, 2.) In the Apocrypha it signifies the Sanhedrim, and is so used also by Josephus. Luke elsewhere uses the synonymous term *presbytery*, from *presbyter* or *elder*. (See below, on 22, 5, and compare Luke 22, 66.) The Vulgate and the older English versions, have a plural form (*seniores, eldermen, ancients, elders.*) The only question here is whether it is merely a synonymous expression with the one before it (τὸ συνέδριον); or denotes the elders, as a part of the Sanhedrim; or a body of elders not included in it. Some infer from the use of the word *all,* that instead of a mere representation of the elders, as in ordinary cases, the High Priest and his associates, upon this occasion, summoned the whole eldership, so far as it was within reach. A striking analogy would then be furnished by the Great Consistory of the Reformed Dutch Churches. One thing is certain, that the body now assembled was a regularly constituted Sanhedrim, identical in law with that before which Peter and John had been arraigned (v. 6. 7), and as such, ordered the Apostles to be brought before it. The word translated *prison* is not that used above in v. 18, but a derivative of the verb (δέω) to bind, from which comes (δεσμός) a band or bond, from this (δεσμώτης) a bondman or prisoner, and from this (δεσμωτήριον) a place of bondage. *To have them brought,* or more exactly, *for them to be brought.* The unusual length of this verse, though admitting readily of subdivision, is probably a mere inadvertence of the learned printer, to whom we are indebted for this whole arrangement. (See the Introduction, p. xii.)

22. But when the officers came, and found them not in the prison, they returned and told:

But, as in v. 21. *Came* is the same verb as in that verse. *Officers,* civil not military. The Greek word originally means a rower, then any sailor, then any labourer, then any servant or dependent, in which sense it is applied to the attendant in a synagogue (Luke 4, 20), and still more frequently to officers of justice, the ministerial agents of a court or magistrate. The later Greek historians use it to describe the Roman lictors. It here denotes the officers attending on the Sanhedrim to execute its orders, precisely as in Matt. 26, 58. Mark 14, 54. 65. John 7, 32. 45, 46. 18, 3. 12. 18. 22. 19, 6. The older English versions here have *ministers*. *Prison* is still a third Greek word for that idea, entirely different in form from both the others, but resembling that in v. 18, as being properly an abstract (*guard* or *watching*), and almost exclusively so used in the classics. *Returned and told,* returning (or having returned) told, reported, brought back word, as in 4, 23 above.

23. Saying, The prison truly found we shut with all safety, and the keepers standing without before the doors; but when we had opened, we found no man within.

Prison, as in v. 21. *Truly* (μέν), as in 1, 5, here answering to *but* (δέ) in the other clause. *Shut,* i. e. shut fast or fastened, the Greek expression being stronger than our *closed,* as appears from John 20, 19. 26, where the mere closing or shutting of the doors would have been no protection. *With all safety,* in complete security or certainty. *All,* as in 4, 29. (Cranmer,—*with all diligence.* Tyndale, *as sure as was possible.*) *Without* (ἔξω) is omitted in the oldest manuscripts and latest critical editions. It was probably inserted as a counterpart to *within* (ἔσω). *When we had opened*, literally, *having opened*. *No man*, no one, nobody. (See above, on 2, 45.) They were, therefore, the only prisoners, unless *prison* here means *ward* or *cell*, or unless the others were set free at the same time. (See below, on 16, 26.)

24. Now when the (High) Priest, and the Captain of the Temple, and the chief priests, heard these things, they doubted of them, whereunto this would grow.

The *now* of this verse is the *but* of that before it. *When*, literally, *as*, the comparative particle being used, both in Greek and English, as a particle of time. (See above, on 1, 10.) *The High Priest* is in Greek simply *the Priest*, and even that is omitted in several of the oldest manuscripts and versions, but probably on account of the unusual expression. *The Priest*, i. e. by way of eminence, the High Priest. Or the title may be used generically, without reference to minor distinctions, as in Ps. 110, 4. Heb. 7, 17. Of the former usage there are some examples elsewhere. Thus in one of the Apocryphal books (1 Macc. 15, 1), Antiochus is said to have written to Simon, "the Priest and Ethnarch of the Jews;" whereas the letter itself, which immediately follows, is addressed to "the Grand or High Priest (ἱερεῖ μεγάλῳ)." The same use of the simple term occurs in Josephus. As to the *captain of the temple*, see above, on 4, 1. (Vulg. *magistratus templi*.) He is mentioned again here, because as the conservator and guardian of the sacred place, he shared in the solicitude of the national rulers. As to the *chief priests*, see above, on 4, 23. Cramner inverts the usual distinction and reads *Chief Priest* and *high priests*. Tyndale has *Chief Priest of all*. *Doubted* is not strong enough to represent the Greek verb, which means that they were utterly perplexed and at a loss. (See above, on 2, 12,) *Of them*, concerning or about them, is by some referred to things, but by most to persons, namely, the Apostles. They were wholly at a loss, and knew not what to think of them, or expect from them. *Whereunto this would grow*, literally, *what this would become*. It is different therefore from a phrase resembling it in form τί ἂν εἴη), *what it might be*, *what it was*, which is elsewhere used in connection with the same verb. (See above, on 2, 12, and below, on 10, 17.) The question here was not what it was that they beheld, but what it would be, if they failed to use preventive measures. This seems to be the meaning of the Vulgate version (*de illis quidnam fieret*), which is better imitated by the Rhemish (*what would befall*) than by Wiclif (*what was done*). Even some modern writers understand the words to mean, *how it had happened*, which is wholly ungrammatical.

25. Then came one and told them, saying, Behold, the men, whom ye put in prison, are standing in the temple, and teaching the people.

Then is the word translated *now* in the preceding verse. *Came*, coming, or having come, the same verb as in vs. 21, 22. *One*, some one, somebody. (See above, on v. 1.) *Told*, reported, brought back word, implying perhaps that he had been sent, or gone of his own accord, to bring intelligence. The verb *told*, and the noun *prison*, are the same as in v. 22. *Behold*, as usual, introduces something unexpected and surprising. (See above, on 1, 10. 2, 7. 5, 9.) *Are standing and teaching* is a better version than the older one of Tyndale, *stand and teach*. The original order is, *are in the temple, standing and teaching*, i. e. not in conversation merely, but in public discourse. (See above, on v. 20.) *The people*, in the usual emphatic sense, almost equivalent to *the church*. (See above, on 4, 1.)

26. Then went the captain with the officers, and brought them without violence, for they feared the people, lest they should have been stoned.

Then (not δέ but τότε) is the adverb of time, properly so rendered, and serving not merely to continue the narrative (like *then* in the preceding verse), but to mark the succession of events. It was after the report recorded in v. 25, and in consequence of it, that this step was taken. *Went*, literally, *going away*, as in 4, 15 above. *The captain*, i. e. of the temple, as the Geneva Bible adds, while Tyndale reads, *the ruler of the temple with the ministers*. The persons here described as acting are the commander of the Levitical guard (see above, on 4, 1), and the executive or ministerial servants of the Sanhedrim (see above, on v. 22.) *Without violence*, literally, not with violence (or by force), which implies that the Apostles offered no resistance. *Lest they should have been stoned* is Tyndale's awkward version, retained in King James's Bible. The exact translation is, *in order that they might not be stoned.* (*Ἵνα*, omitted in some ancient manuscripts, is retained as genuine by the latest critics.) The clause therefore cannot be dependent on the verb *feared*, which would require a different conjunction; although this construction is required by the parenthesis in most editions of the English Bible. The true parenthesis, if any be assumed, includes only the words, *for they feared the people*, and the true construction is, *not with violence, lest they should be stoned.* The stoning, so often mentioned in the New Testament, is not mere pelting, as an act of popular violence, but an ancient theocratical expression of abhorrence for some act of blasphemy or treason to Jehovah. This form of capital punishment, for such it was, had been preferred to others in the law, because it made the death of the offender, not the act of a hated executioner, but that of all the people who were present, and especially of those who had acted as informers and witnesses. From this arose the peculiar Jewish custom of taking up stones to stone one, as a sort of testimony against him. (See below, on 7, 58. 59. 14, 19, and compare John 8, 5. 10, 31–33. 11, 8. 2 Cor. 11, 25.) *To stone*, as a transitive verb, is Hellenistic; in the classics, it means *to throw stones*, and is followed by a preposition. Such was the popular regard for the Apostles, that the men sent to arrest them were afraid, not merely of bodily injury, but of being denounced and disowned by the people, as untrue to the theocracy and law of Moses.

27. And when they had brought them, they set (them) before the council, and the High Priest asked them:

And, but (22), now (24), then (25). *When they had brought*, having brought. *Set*, set up, presented, as in 1, 23. *Before* (literally, *in*) *the council*, i. e. in the place of their assembly (see above, on 4, 15), or still more naturally, in the midst (see above, on 4, 7), or in the presence, of the Sanhedrim itself. The High Priest presides in the assembly and conducts the judicial examination, as he afterwards did in the case of Stephen and of Paul. (See above, on 4, 5, and below, on 7, 1. 23, 2. 3.) This authority was not derived from the Sanhedrim, but inherent in the office of High Priest, in whom was concentrated and summed up the representation, not only of the family of Aaron and the tribe of Levi, but of Israel as a whole, and through it of all God's elect, or the invisible church, of which the chosen people was the type and representative; while on the other hand, he prefigured the Messiah. This official representation, both of the Body and the Head, made the High Priest at all times, but particularly when the royal and prophetical offices were in abeyance, the visible head of the theocracy, entitled, not by popular choice but by divine right, to preside in its most dignified assemblies.

28. Saying, Did not we straitly command you, that ye should not teach in this name? And behold, ye have filled Jerusalem with your doctrine, and intend to bring this man's blood upon us.

The reference is to the injunction upon Peter and John, recorded in 4, 18. The critical editions now omit the negative (*ou*), as does the Vulgate, so as to read, *we straitly commanded you*, etc. In favour of the common text is the expression *asked* (or *questioned*) *them*, in v. 27. *Straitly*, literally, *with commandment*, an expression similar to *straitly threaten* (threaten with a threatening) in 4, 17. The intensive force of the added noun may be variously expressed in English; strictly, expressly, absolutely, peremptorily, etc. Here, too, the suppression of Christ's name is commonly regarded as contemptuous; but see above, on 4, 18. It may be added that, according to Jewish notions and traditions, the suppression of a name is rather reverential than contemptuous, as appears from the immemorial refusal to pronounce the name Jehovah, and the singular interpretation of Lev. 24, 15. 16, upon which it rests. *And behold*, contrary to what we had expected, and to our surprise. (See above, on v. 25.) *Filled Jerusalem* is not a Hebraism but a natural hyperbole, common to all languages. It appears in a much stronger form in 2 Kings 21, 16, where we read that "Manasseh shed innocent blood very much, till he had filled Jerusalem from one end to another." *Doctrine*, i. e. teaching ('you have taught this new religion in all parts of Jerusalem') not belief ('you have converted all Jerusalem to your religion') a concession which would hardly have been made by the High Priest. (See above, on 2, 42.) *Intend*, literally, *wish*, but often with an

ACTS 5, 28. 29. 30.

implication of design and plan, as well as mere desire. (See below, on v. 33. 12, 4. 15, 37. 18, 27. 19, 30. 28, 18, and compare Matt. 1, 19. 2 Cor. 1, 15. 17.) *To bring blood upon the head* is a peculiar Hebrew idiom, meaning to make one answer for the death or murder of another. (See below, on 18, 6, and compare Ezek. 33, 4. Matt. 23, 5. 27, 25.) One of the Fathers here remarks that the High Priest had forgotten the fearful imprecation, by which he and his followers had assumed the very responsibility, which he charges the Apostles with desiring to fasten on them. The reference here, however, is not so much to the divine vengeance as to that of the people, whom the rulers had misled and urged on to this dreadful crime, but whose feelings had already undergone a violent reaction, which might well seem threatening to their faithless guides. (As to *this man*, see above, on *this name*.)

29. Then Peter and the (other) Apostles answered and said, We ought to obey God rather than men.

The original form of the first clause is peculiar, one verb agreeing with *Peter* in the singular, and the other with *Apostles* in the plural. This seems to mean that Peter alone spoke, but that all the Apostles spoke through him. (*Then*, as in v 25, not as in v. 26.) *We ought* should rather be *we must*, expressing not mere obligation but necessity. (See above, on 1, 16. 22. 4, 12.) The same principle is here avowed as in 4, 19. 20, but in a more positive and pointed form. Instead of the verb *hear* or *hearken* there used, we have here, not the ordinary verb *to obey*, but a compound form of it, denoting submission to government or constituted authority (ἀρχή). It is the word translated *to obey magistrates* in Tit. 3, 1. Besides the essential idea of obedience, it here suggests, that God is superior to man, not only in power, but in rightful authority. The translation *rather*, contended for by some in 4, 18, is here adopted by the translators themselves.

30. The God of our fathers raised up Jesus, whom ye slew and hanged on a tree.

Here again we have the favourite antithesis or contrast between Christ's treatment at the hands of God and man, which may be described as the key-note of this, as of the three previous discourses of Peter. (See above, on 2, 23. 24. 26. 3

13. 15. 4, 10.) *The God of our fathers*, our own national and covenant God. The *our* identifies the speaker and the hearers, as belonging to the same race and believing the same scriptures. *Raised up*, literally, aroused, awakened, i. e. from the sleep of death. (See above, on 3, 15. 4, 10.) *Slew* is none of the verbs commonly employed in that sense, but one strictly meaning to handle, manage, and applied by the later classics, like our *despatch*, both to the transaction of business and the destruction of life. (See below, on 26, 21, the only other place where it occurs in the New Testament.) *Hanged on a tree*, i. e. crucified. (See below, on 10, 39, and compare Gal. 3, 13. 1 Pet. 2, 24.) The word translated *tree* has no such usage in the classical Greek writers of an early date, but corresponds to *wood* in English. In the Hellenistic dialect it corresponds to the Hebrew word (עץ) denoting both. The contrary change has taken place in our word *tree*, which once had a wider meaning than it now has, as appears from such compounds as axle-tree, saddle-tree, gallows-tree. This ambiguity of the Greek and Hebrew words has some importance in connection with the fulfilment of prophecy. Crucifixion was a punishment unknown to the law of Moses or the practice of the Jews till introduced by foreign conquerors. The hanging mentioned in the law (Deut. 21, 22) is the posthumous exposure of the body after being otherwise put to death. And yet the curse pronounced on such is so framed as to be strictly applicable to the case of crucifixion, the terms *hanging on a tree* being appropriate to both, but only on condition that the word *tree* be considered as equivalent to *wood*. The ancient hanging was most probably on trees, in the literal sense of the expression; the later crucifixion was on wooden crosses framed expressly for the purpose.

31. Him hath God exalted with his right hand (to be) a Prince and a Saviour, for to give repentance to Israel, and forgiveness of sins.

Him, literally, *this (one)*, i. e. the very one whom you thus crucified. *Exalted*, or as Tyndale has it, *lift up*. *With his right hand*, by the exertion of his power, and *to his right hand*, i. e. to a share in that power and in the dignity connected with it. (See above, on 2, 33.) *To be*, or *as a Prince and Saviour* already, which last is preferred by some interpreters. (The Rhemish version is, *this Prince and Saviour hath God exalted.*) *Prince,* captain, author ; (see above, on 3, 15.) *For to give* (see above, on 4, 28.) *To give repentance* is not merely to give time for it (as Philo says, δίδωσι χρόνον εἰς μετανοίαν), or place for it (as Quintilian says, *detis locum pœnitentiæ,* compare Heb. 12, 17), but to give the grace of repentance, i. e. power and disposition to repent. The old sense of *penance* may be seen in Wiclif's version of this clause (*that penance were given*). *Forgiveness* is the word translated *remission* in 2, 38, and there explained. The express mention of Israel, as the object of this favour, is not intended to restrict it to the Jews; but either to intimate the priority of the offer made to them (see above, on 3, 26) ; or to embrace the spiritual Israel, the entire church of God's elect (see Rom. 9, 6) ; or more probably than either, to assure the contemporary Jews, who had been implicated in the murder of their own Messiah, that even this most aggravated sin was not beyond the reach of the divine forgiveness, if repented of; to bestow both which gifts, i. e. repentance as the means, and forgiveness as the end, was the very purpose for which Christ had been exalted as a Prince and Saviour.

32. And we are his witnesses of these things, and so is also the Holy Ghost, whom God hath given to them that obey him.

Some of the oldest manuscripts omit *his* before *witnesses,* without material effect upon the sense. *Things,* literally, *words* or *sayings.* It may be doubted whether the Greek word ever has the vague sense of *things,* without some reference to their being spoken, promised, or commanded. See below, on 10, 37, and compare Luke 1, 37. 2, 19. 51. In the last two places, our version renders the same word *things* and *sayings,* although the connection is precisely similar. Some suppose an allusion here to the *words of this life* in v. 20, where the same Greek word is used. They again assert their apostolical commission as witnesses for Christ (see above, on 1, 8. 22. 2, 32. 40. 3, 15), but with a remarkable addition, claiming to be joint-witnesses with the Holy Spirit, whom the Lord had promised (John 15, 26) in that very character. (See below, on 15, 28, and compare Heb. 10, 15.) The testimony of the Spirit, here referred to, is not that spoken of in Rom. 8, 16, as involved in the experience of all believers, but an outward testimony corroborating that of the Apostles. This could only be afforded by the miraculous endowments of the first disciples, who are here described as *those obeying God*, with manifest allusion to the principle avowed in v. 29, the Greek verb being the one there used and explained, as denoting obedience to the rightful authority and government of God.

33. When they heard (that), they were cut (to the heart), and took counsel to slay them.

The effect of this discourse was very different from that upon the day of Pentecost, although the terms used to describe it are somewhat similar. *When they heard that*, or more literally, *they hearing*. *Cut to the heart*, literally, *sawn through*. As the Greek verb is sometimes used with *teeth*, to signify the act of sawing, grinding, or gnashing them, some suppose that to be its meaning here. But besides the absence of the noun which indicates this meaning elsewhere, it is forbidden by the analogy of 7, 54, where the same verb is used, with the addition of the noun *hearts*, to denote that the effect was an internal mental one. The same noun is added in 2, 37, but to a milder verb (*pricked* or *pierced*). The effect here described is probably a mixture of conscious guilt with revengeful wrath, as expressed in the Geneva Bible, *they brast* (burst) *for anger*. (Vulg. *dissecabantur*. Wiclif, *were tormented*. Tynd. *they clave asunder*. Rhem. *it cut them to the heart*.) This feeling led to a new step in the march of persecution. Instead of idle threats and prohibitions (see above, on 4, 17. 18), they now conceived the thought of capital punishment and bloody persecution. *Took counsel*, deliberated, or consulted, denotes mutual conference and comparison of views, as in 4, 15. But the verb here used more probably means, *formed the plan* or *purpose*, nearly equivalent to *intended*. (See below, on 15, 37, where *determined* is too strong, as *consulted* is too weak in John 12, 10.) Tyndale's *sought means* is not a version but a paraphrase. Several of the oldest manuscripts and versions read (ἐβούλοντο) *they wished*, which, as explained above (on v. 28), amounts to nearly the same thing; but the common text (ἐβουλεύοντο) is retained by the latest critics. *Slay* is not the verb translated *slew* in v. 30, but the one used in 2, 23, and there explained.

34. Then stood there up one in the council, a Phari-

see, named Gamaliel, a doctor of the law, had in reputation among all the people, and commanded to put the Apostles forth a little space.

These sanguinary measures are prevented by the interposition of a new and interesting character. *Then stood there up* is Tyndale's version; a more literal translation would be, *and arising*. *One* (τις), some (one), a certain (man or person.) See above, on v. 1. *In the council*, and by necessary implication, a member of the body. In what capacity he sat there, is afterwards explained. *A Pharisee*, and therefore not one of the party which was acting in conjunction with the High Priest, and in opposition to the new religion. (See above, on v. 17.) *Gamaliel*, an old and honourable name in the tribe of Manasseh (Num. 1, 10. 2, 20.) There is no reason for disputing the identity of this man with the Gamaliel of the Talmud, a grandson of the famous Hillel, and a son of Simon (supposed by some to be the Simeon of Luke 2, 25), himself so eminent for wisdom, and especially for moderation, that his death is represented in the Jewish books, as the departure of true Pharisaism from Israel. Nor is there any ground for doubt, that this was the Gamaliel at whose feet Saul of Tarsus sat. (See below, on 22, 3.) *A doctor* (i. e. teacher) *of the law*, in Greek one compound word (νομοδιδάσκαλος), used only by Luke and Paul (Luke 5, 17. 1 Tim. 1. 7), and either convertible with *scribe* and *lawyer*, or a specific designation of those scribes and lawyers, who were recognized as public and authoritative teachers. (See above, on 4, 5.) It was in this capacity or character, no doubt, that Gamaliel acted as a member of the Sanhedrim. *Had in reputation* (Tyndale, *had in authority*) is a paraphrase of one Greek word (τίμιος from τιμή, *honour*, see above, on 4, 34), meaning honoured, highly valued, precious, dear (Wiclif, *worshipful*.) *To all the people*, as distinguished from the rulers or the higher classes. He might therefore be regarded as the leader of the opposition to the dominant party, which was now that of the Sadducees, or under Sadducean influence. *Commanded* is not the word so rendered in 1, 4. 4, 18, but the one used in 4, 15, in a precisely similar connection. This seems to favour the distinction made by some, but not recognized by others, between the first of these verbs (παραγγέλλω), as denoting an absolute or peremptory order, and the other (κελεύω), as denoting rather an authoritative exhortation, and applied by

Herodotus and Homer even to the petitions or requests of an inferior. In this connection, it approaches very nearly to the modern usage of *proposed* or *moved*, but with an implication of authority, official or personal, on the part of him who made the proposition. At all events, it furnishes no ground for the inference, which some have drawn, that Gamaliel was presiding in the Sanhedrim, a dignity belonging *ex officio* to the High Priest. (See above, on v. 27, and with respect to the exclusion of the prisoners, on 4, 15.) Some of the latest critics, following the Vulgate and several ancient manuscripts, instead of *the apostles*, read *the men*. *To put forth* is the English equivalent of an idiomatic Greek phrase (ἔξω ποιῆσαι) meaning literally *to make out* or *outside*. Tyndale and Cranmer have *aside*, as King James's version also has in 4, 15. Another idiomatic phrase follows (βραχύ τι), originally meaning *something short*, and then *some little*, whether applied to quantity (as in John 6, 7), or to distance (as in Acts 27, 28), or to time (as in Luke 22, 58), which last is here preferred by most interpreters, and may have been intended by our own translators, although they have retained Tyndale's ambiguous phrase, *a little space*, which rather seems to have a local meaning.

35. And said unto them, Ye men of Israel, take heed to yourselves, what ye intend to do, as touching these men.

Them is without a grammatical antecedent, as the same pronoun is in 4, 5 above. The application of a rigid rule would represent Gamaliel as addressing the Apostles. (See above, on 4, 17.) To supply this omission, one old version and one old Greek manuscript read, *said to the rulers and the counsellors*. Gamaliel's speech is interesting in itself, and on account of the effect which it produced, but also as a specimen of Jewish oratory, wholly distinct from that of the Apostles, and exhibiting just that degree of sameness and variety which might have been expected from the circumstances of the case. (See above, on 3, 26.) After a prefatory warning (35), he refers to two historical examples (36. 37), and then lays down and applies to the case before them an important principle of action (38. 39.) *Men of Israel* (as in 2, 22. 3, 12) reminds them that they are acting in a national or theocratical capacity, and may be likened to the warning given to our church-courts, when about to exercise judicial functions. *Take heed* is in Greek an elliptical expression, meaning *hold to* or *apply* (the mind), i. e. advert, attend. With the dative, it means to pay attention or regard (as in 8, 6. 10, 11. 16, 14); with a preposition (ἀπό), to beware of, to avoid (as in Matt. 6, 1. Luke 20, 46); with a reflexive pronoun (ἑαυτοῖς), to take heed to one's self, to be on one's guard (as in 20, 28. Luke 12, 1. 17, 3. 21, 34.) This is the meaning here, where the Sanhedrim are warned, not only of error, but of danger to themselves. The remainder of the verse admits of two constructions. One connects the words *as touching these men* (Tyndale's antiquated phrase for *as to* or *concerning them*) with the verb *to do*. 'Be careful (or consider well) what you are about to do to these men.' This, though natural enough in English, is in Greek made less so by the collocation of the sentence, in which the words, *ye are about to do*, come after *these men*, not before it. This inconvenience is avoided by the other syntax, which connects *concerning these men* with the words preceding. 'Take heed to yourselves, as touching these men, what ye are about to do.' *Intend* is not the verb so rendered in v. 28, but that employed in 3, 3, and there explained as signifying mere futurity, *to be about to do* the act denoted by the verb that follows.

36. For before these days rose up Theudas, boasting himself to be somebody, to whom a number of men, about four hundred, joined themselves; who was slain, and all, as many as obeyed him, were scattered and brought to nought.

In support of his advice, he adduces two historical examples, both familiar to his hearers, and perhaps still fresh in their recollection. *Before these days* is an indefinite expression, not so strong as that in 15, 17, and intended merely to suggest, that the case before them was by no means new. *Arose*, or *stood up*, does not mean *rebelled*, or made an insurrection (*insurrexit*), which is neither the classical nor scriptural usage of the Greek verb (see above, on v. 17), but *appeared*, came forward. (See below, on 7, 18, and compare Heb. 7, 15.) *Boasting*, literally, *saying*. *Somebody*, i. e. *some great one*, as it is more fully expressed in reference to Simon Magus. (See below, on 8, 9, and compare the well known phrase of Juvenal, *si vis esse aliquis*.) *Joined themselves*, a compound form of the verb used above in v. 13, and there explained. The latest editors adopt another reading (προσεκλίθη), which originally means *leaned towards* or *inclined to*, but in its secondary usage, coincides very nearly with the common text (προσεκολλήθη), both denoting adherence or adhesion. *Slain*, despatched, made away with, as in v. 33, and in 2, 23 above. *All as many as*, see above, on 4. 34. *Obeyed* is properly a passive, meaning *were persuaded*, and is never used to signify compulsory obedience. It is therefore peculiarly expressive of the voluntary deference paid to party leaders and religious teachers. *Scattered*, or rather, dissolved, disorganized. *Were brought to nought*, or came to nothing (see above, on 4, 11), in obvious allusion and antithesis to his thinking himself somebody or something. Josephus also gives the history of an impostor (γόης), by the name of *Theudas*, who drew a great part of the people after him, and promised to divide the Jordan, but was seized and beheaded by order of the Roman Procurator of Judea. But this was in the reign of Caligula or Claudius. The supposed anachronism has been variously solved, by dating the events here recorded several years later than the usual chronology; by charging the error on Josephus; by identifying Theudas with some one of the many such insurgents, whom Josephus mentions under other names; or lastly by supposing two of the same name, one recorded by Josephus and the other by Luke. This last, which has been the common explanation since the time of Origen, is favoured by the fact, that the Theudas of Josephus was beheaded, and could not therefore have been cited by Gamaliel, as a proof that such pretenders should be left to themselves, without official interference. Such a coincidence of names, though not to be assumed without necessity, is common enough in history and real life to be admissible where such necessity exists, especially in this case, where the name in question is said to have been common, even among Greeks and Romans. This explanation would be still more satisfactory if it could be shown, as some assume, that Theudas was the name of a father and a son, who successively excited insurrections. The essential point to be observed, however, is that there is no ground for charging Luke with ignorance or error. Such a charge is in the last degree improbable, considering how often such apparent inconsistencies are reconciled by the discovery of new but intrinsically unimportant facts;

and also that the error, if it were one, must have been immediately discovered, and would either have been rectified at once, or made the ground of argumentative objection.

37. After this man rose up Judas of Galilee, in the days of the taxing, and drew away much people after him: he also perished, and all, (even) as many as obeyed him, were dispersed.

This man is also mentioned by Josephus, once as a Gaulonite, but in several places as a Galilean, one name perhaps denoting his place of residence, the other that of his nativity. *In the days of the taxing*, or as Tyndale has it, *in the time when tribute began*, which seems to mean, at the beginning of the Roman domination. But this is a mere paraphrase, and most interpreters apply the words to a particular measure of the Roman government in Palestine, of such a nature as to furnish a convenient date or epoch. The word translated *taxing* primarily means *transcription*, then *inscription* or enrollment, both of things and persons, being applied by Plato to the registration of property, by Polybius to that of men liable to military duty, by Josephus to a census, both of citizens and their estates. In Luke 2, 2, it denotes such a census or assessment, taken with a view to taxation, under Cyrenius (the Greek form of Quirinus), Proconsul of Syria. This same Cyrenius is said by Josephus to have vanquished and destroyed the Galilean rebel *Judas*; a coincidence of much more weight in favour of the narrative before us, than any difference or doubt, as to minute chronology or other circumstances, ought to have against it. Tried by the rigid rule, which many would apply in this case, the most accredited historians, ancient and modern, might be constantly convicted of mistake or falsehood. It was against this census, or the taxation which it had in view, that Judas roused the people to resistance, as inconsistent with their national and theocratical immunities. Josephus mentions the destruction of his sons, but not his own, which is explicitly asserted here. That writer also represents him as the founder of a sect or party, which survived him. This is not inconsistent with the statement that his followers were *dispersed*, as the Greek verb here used properly denotes the scattering of individuals by sudden violence; whereas the verb of the preceding verse expresses rather the entire dissolution of an organized body, as for instance the disbanding of an army, to which Xenophon applies it. *Drew away*, incited to *apostasy*, a word derived from the Greek verb here used, as well as in the Septuagint version of Deut. 7, 4. 13, 10, where it denotes the act of turning others from the worship of Jehovah. For a very different use of the same verb as an intransitive, see the next verse.

38. And now I say unto you, refrain from these men and let them alone; for if this counsel, or this work, be of men, it will come to nought;

He here applies the principle, deducible from the cases which he had just cited, to the case in hand. *And now* marks the transition from the past to the present or the future in the speaker's mind. (See above, on 4, 29.) *I say unto you* is not an unmeaning or superfluous expression, but an indication of the speaker's earnestness, and of the importance he attached to what he was about to say. (See above, on 2, 22. 29.) *Refrain*, literally, *stand off*, stand aloof, a neuter or intransitive form of the verb used in the preceding verse. (For other examples of the same sense, see below, on 12, 10. 15, 38. 19, 9. 22, 29.) *Let them alone*, or more exactly, *suffer them*, permit them, i. e. to go on, to do as they are doing. The suppression of the second verb is not uncommon in the best Greek writers. The second clause assigns the ground or reason of the exhortation in the first. *Counsel* and *work* are related to each other as plan and execution; what they wish or purpose, and what they have actually done or are now doing. The principle here laid down is a general but not an universal one. Gamaliel could not mean to say that every human scheme must fail, which is notoriously false. His words may be qualified or limited in two ways. *Of men* (literally *out of*, i. e. arising or originating from men) may be understood to mean without regard to God or in defiance of him. But a still more natural and satisfactory solution is afforded by referring the entire proposition to such cases as the one in hand, i. e. attempts to introduce a new religion, or at least new modes of faith and practice. Of these it may be truly and emphatically said that if they are *of men*, i. e. of human origin, they must eventually *come to nought*. The Greek verb thus translated is a kindred form to one in v. 36, not that rendered *brought to nought*, but *scattered*. The essential meaning in both compounds is solution, dissolution, that kind of destruction which consists in or arises from internal separation or disintegration, such as the ruin of the temple, in which not one stone was to be left upon another, and to which this verb is applied by the evangelists. (See Matt. 24, 2. Mark 13, 2. Luke 21, 6, and compare Matt. 21, 61. 27, 40. Mark 14, 58. 15, 29. 2 Cor. 5, 1. Gal. 2, 18.) The expression is peculiarly appropriate to that internal dissolution which, even in the absence of all outward force, awaits every system of religious faith which has a merely human origin.

39. But if it be of God, ye cannot overthrow it, lest haply ye be found even to fight against God.

This is the alternative hypothesis, which he suggests, as no less possible than that propounded in the former verse. *Of God* corresponds exactly to *of men* in v. 38, and therefore means, proceeding from him, as its origin or source. *Cannot*, or according to the text adopted by the latest critics, *will not be able*, the future form suggesting still more strongly than the present, the idea of remote contingency. The parallelism of the verses, and of Gamaliel's suppositions, is partially hidden from the English reader, by a needless variation in the rendering of the same Greek verb, the *overthrow* of this verse being the same with the *come to nought* of that before it. Another various reading in the text is *them* for *it*, which seems sufficiently attested, but has no material effect upon the meaning, as it merely substitutes the men themselves for their work or counsel. Between the clauses some supply, as a connecting thought, 'and ye ought not to attempt it, lest etc.' *Ye be found*, i. e. prove unexpectedly to be so, as the same form of the same verb means in Matt. 1, 18. *To fight against God* gives the sense, but not the form or the peculiar force of the original, in which these four words are replaced by one, and that one not a verb, but an expressive compound adjective (*God-fighting*, or, taken absolutely as a noun, *God-fighters*.) It is unknown to the classics, but is used by one of the old Greek translators to represent a Hebrew word for *giants*, which he probably confounded with the Titans of the Greek mythology. A verb compounded of the same elements (θεομαχέω) is found in Euripides, and in the received text of 23, 9 below. Very extreme views have been taken of this speech and of its author's character and motives. The old opinion, found with various embellishments in several early writers, that Gamaliel was a Christian, of the same class with Nicodemus and Joseph of Arimathea, is inconsistent with the high position which he has maintained in the tradition of the Jews (see above, on v. 34), if not with Paul's allusion to him as his own instructor in the strictest form of Pharisaical religion (see below, on 22, 3.) That the speech itself is an authoritative statement of the true principle to be adopted and applied in all such cases, is as groundless an opinion as its opposite, to wit, that there is no truth at all in the doctrine here propounded, but only a sophistical apology for temporizing unbelief. The common sense of readers in all ages has avoided both extremes by regarding the speech as an argument *ad hominem*, designed to show, and actually showing, that his hearers, on their own principles, were bound to take the course here recommended, as a matter both of duty and of safety. If they, as conscientious Jews, believed the new religion to be altogether human in its origin, and utterly without divine authority, and yet could neither question nor explain away the miracles by which it was attested, they were bound to do precisely what Gamaliel here advises, i. e. nothing at all. The position of the rulers who continued to reject Christ had become extremely difficult and dangerous. Unwilling to acknowledge him as the Messiah, yet unable to refute his claims, or to deny the evidence by which they were attested, their only safety was to sit still and observe the progress of events. A resort to violence was full of peril to themselves, and yet on this the council seemed resolved. There could not, therefore, have been wiser counsel, under the circumstances of the case, than that here given by Gamaliel, whether prompted by habitual aversion to all rash and hazardous expedients; or by jealous opposition to the Sadducees, from whom the proposition came; or by a secret misgiving that the new religion might be true.

40. And to him they agreed; and when they had called the Apostles and beaten them, they commanded them that they should not speak in the name of Jesus, and let them go.

To him they agreed might seem to mean that they were previously of the same opinion, and therefore assented to it as it was pronounced by him. But the original expression means, *they were persuaded* or *convinced*, and implies a change of mind effected by Gamaliel's speech. This was the more remarkable because he seems to have been one of the minority. (See above, on vs. 34. 36.) *When they had called*, etc., literally, *having called the apostles, having beaten, they commanded them.* This cruel inconsistency shows the perplexity to which they were reduced. The scourging could not be intended as a means of inquisition or discovery (see below, on 22, 24), for there was nothing to discover; but only as a punishment, too light if they were guilty, too severe if they were innocent. This kind of punishment was common among the Jews, from the time of Moses (Deut. 25, 1–3) to the time of Paul (2 Cor. 11, 24), who seems to distinguish between different forms or methods of infliction. The word here used, which properly means *flaying*, denotes the severest kind of scourging. This punishment was also thought peculiarly disgraceful (τιμωρία αἰσχίστη, as Josephus calls it.) Their subjection to the scourge had been explicitly predicted by their Master (Matt. 10, 17), and was a necessary part of their conformity to his example (Matt. 27, 26. Luke 23, 6.) *Ordered not to speak*, as in 4, 18, where the terms here used have been already explained. This repetition of a measure, which before had proved entirely ineffectual, illustrates the degraded position of the rulers, while the scourging shows their impotent malignity.

41. And they departed from the presence of the council, rejoicing that they were counted worthy to suffer shame for his name.

So then (μὲν οὖν, 1, 6. 18. 2, 41) *they departed* (ἐπορεύοντο, 1, 10. 11. 25. 5, 20) *rejoicing from the presence*, etc. One of the Fathers notes it, as a characteristic of the first disciples, that they are so often represented as rejoicing under circumstances naturally suited to awaken opposite emotions (see below, on 13, 52, and compare Luke 24, 52.) *Counted worthy to suffer shame*, a beautiful antithesis (the honour to be dishonoured, the grace to be disgraced) far more pointed and expressive than the famous words of Seneca, sometimes quoted as a parallel. (*Digni visi sumus Deo in quibus experiretur quantum humana natura pati posset.*) *For his name*, not merely for being called by his name, but for the sake of all that it implies, his doctrine, his messiahship, his service, his divinity. The oldest manuscripts, and all the ancient versions, omit *his* (αὐτοῦ), not only without loss, but with advantage to the sense, or at least to the force and beauty of the passage. *The name* is then used absolutely, like *the word* (see above, on 4, 4), and *the way* (see below, on 9, 2), for the name above every name that is named, at which every knee must bow. (Phil. 2, 9. 10. Eph. 1, 21. Heb. 1, 4.)

42. And daily in the temple, and in every house, they ceased not to teach and preach Jesus Christ.

Besides the immediate and more personal effect of this maltreatment on the feelings of the sufferers, as described in the preceding verse, the historian records its permanent effect on their official conduct, namely, that they did precisely what they were commanded not to do. To make this prominent, the terms of the prohibition are repeated. (See above, on 4, 18. 5, 40.) *Every day, both in the temple and at home*, in private houses, not *in every house*, which would be an inappropriate and gratuitous hyperbole. (See above, on 2, 46.) *Ceased not*, as might have been expected, and as they had been explicitly commanded. *Teaching and preaching* are specifications of the *speaking* forbidden in v. 40. They may either correspond to the private and public ministrations previously mentioned, or be descriptive of all their ministrations, whether public or private, as instructive and yet cheering, communicating truth and at the same time joyful tidings or good news, which is the full sense of the verb here rendered *preach*, whereas the other verbs so rendered elsewhere simply mean to publish or proclaim. (See above, on 3, 24, and below, on 8, 5.) The one here used sometimes governs, as an active verb, the persons preached to (see below, on 8, 25. 40), a construction also used with its derivative in modern English (*to evangelize a country* or *the world*), but not when the accusative denotes the subject of the preaching, as in 8, 4. 12. 35, and in the case before us, where the Rhemish version violates our idiom by its slavish imitation of the Vulgate (*to evangelize Jesus Christ*). The last words of the verse are to be understood as in 2, 38. 3, 6. 20. 4, 10, not as personal names but as official titles, meaning *Saviour* and *Messiah;* or, as in 2, 36, where *Jesus* is the subject and *Christ* the predicate—'teaching as a doctrine, and proclaiming as good news, that Jesus is the Christ,' i. e. the anointed and predicted Prophet, Priest, and King of Israel.

CHAPTER VI.

To prepare the way for the extension of the Church, a difference is permitted to arise within it (1), in consequence of which the twelve assemble the disciples (2), and propose a cure for the existing evil (3. 4), which is accordingly applied by the appointment of seven men to dispense the charities of the church (5. 6.) A great addition, from the most important class of Jews, ensues upon this measure (7.) One of the seven is involved in a controversy with certain foreign Jews (8–10), who by false charges rouse the populace, and arraign him before the Sanhedrim as a blasphemer and a traitor to the Mosaic institutions (11–14.) All this, with the account of his extraordinary aspect at the bar (15), is introductory to his masterly defence, recorded in the following chapter.

1. And in those days, when the number of the disciples was multiplied, there arose a murmuring of the Grecians against the Hebrews, because their widows were neglected in the daily ministration.

Those days is an indefinite expression, sometimes relating to an interval of a few days (as in 1, 15), sometimes to one of many years (as in Matt. 3, 1), but always implying some connection between what precedes and follows. It may here be understood to mean, 'while they were thus engaged in preaching Christ' (see 5, 42.) *The disciples multiplying* is the literal translation. *Disciples*, not in the restricted sense of *apostles* (Luke 6, 13), but in the wider sense of *learners*, pupils in the school of Christ, a favourite expression for believers, converts to the new religion (see below, on 9, 26.) *Arose*, literally, happened, came to pass, or into existence; implying that the dissatisfaction was a new thing and subsequent to the increase just mentioned. *Murmuring* or *whispering*, any suppressed talking, sometimes indicative of fear (John 7, 12. 13), but commonly, as here, of discontent (Phil. 2, 14. 1 Pet. 4, 9.) *Grecians* (*Hellenists*), not *Greeks* (*Hellenes*), but Jews using the Greek language in their worship, and therefore applied to the whole class of foreign or Greek-speaking Jews, as distinguished from the *Hebrews*, or natives of Palestine and others, who used the Hebrew scriptures, and spoke the Aramaic dialect before described (on 1, 19.) Between these races there was no doubt constant jealousy or emulation, although no real difference of faith or practice; and this party-spirit many seem to have carried with them into the Christian Church on their conversion. *Widows* are often specified in Scripture, as particular objects of compassion, both divine and human, and therefore may be said to represent the whole class of helpless sufferers. (See Ex. 22, 22. Deut. 10, 18. 1 Tim. 5, 3. 4. 5.) But here no doubt, the complaint was a specific one respecting widows in the proper sense. *Neglected*, literally *overlooked*, not necessarily implying ill-will or contempt, but merely such neglect as might arise from their being less known than the natives. The jealousy of the races may have prompted the complaint, without affording the occasion for it. *Ministration*, dispensation, distribution, probably of food, to which the Greek word properly relates, and which agrees best with its being *daily*. The charities of the infant church were connected originally with its social meetings and repasts (see above, on 2, 42, and compare Neh. 8. 10), although no doubt afterwards extended, as occasion served, to domiciliary and pecuniary aid. This verse confirms the previous conclusion, that there was no absolute community of goods, or common sustentation-fund, from which all might draw alike.

2. Then the twelve called the multitude of the disciples unto (them), and said, It is not reason that we should leave the word of God, and serve tables.

Then, so, but, or *and*, as in v. 1. *The twelve*, now complete by the election of Matthias (1, 26), and acting as an organized and organizing body, evidently authorized to mature the constitution of the church, by providing for emergencies as they arose. The one before us being of a popular or social nature, they refer it to the aggregate body of believers, but themselves prescribe the mode of action; thus applying and exemplifying two great principles of apostolical church polity, the participation of the people in the government of the body, and its subordination to divinely constituted officers. *Calling* or *having called*, i. e. summoned or convened them in the presence of the twelve. *The multitude*, not merely a great number, but the whole mass or aggregate body of believers, as distinguished from its subdivisions and from the Apostles. *Disciples* has precisely the same meaning as in v. 1. *Not reason*, literally, *not pleasing*, acceptable, agreeable, i. e. to God or to Christ, and to us as his vicegerents. The idea of *right* or *proper*, although not expressed, is necessarily implied. *That we should leave . . . and serve*, literally, *for us leaving , . . to serve.* *The word of God*, i. e. the duty of dispensing and proclaiming it, the propagation of the new religion (see above, on 4, 4.) *Serve tables*, i. e. wait upon, attend them. The Greek verb is the one corresponding to the noun (*ministration*) in v. 1. Its being here combined with *tables* shows that the latter is not to be taken in the sense of money-tables, counters, banks (which it has in Matt. 21, 12. Luke 19, 23), but in that of dining-tables, boards at which men eat (as in 16, 34. Mark 7, 28. Luke 16, 21.) There is no reference to what we call communion-tables, except so far as sacramental and charitable distributions were connected in the practice of the infant church.

3. Wherefore, brethren, look ye out among you seven men of honest report, full of the Holy Ghost and wisdom, whom we may appoint over this business.

Wherefore, because the two employments are thus incompatible, and one of them has much the stronger claim on us. *Brethren*, not brethren in the ministry but in the faith (see above, on 1, 16.) *Look out*, literally, *look at*, visit, or inspect, for the purpose of discovering the necessary qualifications. *Among you*, literally, out of, from among you, of yourselves, belonging to your body (see above, on 3, 22.) *Men*, not in the vague sense of persons, but in the specific sense of males, not women (see above, on 4, 4.) *Seven* has been variously explained, as a number arbitrarily selected, or for some reason of convenience, now unknown; or because seven nations are supposed to have been represented; or because the church was now divided into seven congregations; or, most probably of all, because of its sacred associations.

which may all perhaps be traced back to the institution of the Sabbath, by the consecration of one day in seven to God's special service. (See Gen. 2, 3. 7, 2. 3. 8, 10. 12. 41, 2. Lev. 23, 15. 25, 8. Num. 23. 1. Josh. 6, 4. Job 5, 19. Prov. 9, 1. Mic. 5, 5. Zech. 3, 9. 4, 2.) This is sufficient to account for its selection, where any other number might have served as well, but not to prove it necessary, as it was considered afterwards, and formally declared by one of the early councils. Rome, at one time, we are told, had forty presbyters and only seven deacons. *Of honest report*, literally, *testified, attested*, i. e. certified by others to be what they ought to be (see below, on 10, 22. 16, 2. 22, 12.) *Full of the Holy Ghost*, both of his ordinary sanctifying influences, and of his extraordinary preternatural endowments. *Wisdom*, not merely practical skill or professional experience, but heavenly prudence, teaching how to act in all emergencies. *We may appoint* (or according to another reading, *will appoint*), place, constitute, establish. (See below, on 7, 10. 27. 35. 17, 15.) *Business*, literally, *need, necessity* (2, 45. 4, 35. 20, 34. 28, 10), or necessary business, implying a present and particular emergency.

4. But we will give ourselves continually to prayer, and to the ministry of the word.

But we, emphatically (see above, on 4, 20), we on our part, as distinguished from the persons thus selected. *Prayer*, not personal devotion merely, but the business of conducting public worship, as *the ministry* (or *dispensation*) *of the word* (see above, on v. 2), evidently means the work of preaching or public and official teaching. *Will give ourselves continually* corresponds to one Greek verb, the same that occurs above, in 1, 14. 2, 42. 46, and there explained, meaning to adhere to or attend upon a person or a duty. We have here the apostolical decision as to the relative importance of alms-giving and instruction, as functions of the ministry. Whether the Apostles had previously discharged both and now relinquished one, or whether they should here be understood as declining to assume a burden which they had not borne before, there is nothing in the text or context to determine. The first idea is perhaps the one conveyed by the language of the passage to most readers.

5. And the saying pleased the whole multitude: and they chose Stephen, a man full of faith and of the Holy Ghost, and Philip, and Prochorus, and Nicanor, and Timon, and Parmenas, and Nicolas a proselyte of Antioch;

Saying, word, discourse, or speech. The idea of *plan* or *proposition* is implied but not expressed. *Pleased*, literally, pleased before, or in the sight of, an imitation of the common Hebrew idiom, to be good or right in the eyes of any one (see Gen. 41, 37. 45, 16. 1 Sam. 29, 6. 2 Sam. 17, 4. 1 Chr. 13, 4. 2 Chr. 30, 4. Esth. 1, 21.) *The whole multitude*, apparently without exception or dissent, which seems to show the absence of malignant jealousy and party-spirit. *Chose*, or as the Greek verb properly denotes, *chose out for themselves*. (See above, on 1, 24, where the same form is applied to the divine choice.) *Faith* here takes the place of *wisdom* in v. 3, not because the words are synonymous or the things identical, but because the wisdom there meant is a fruit of faith, and therefore something more than secular prudence or skill in business. This description is not applied expressly to all the seven; for then it would have had the plural form and the last place in the sentence. But its limitation to Stephen does not imply, that the others were destitute of these gifts, which had been required in all (v. 3); nor even that they were inferior, for why should such inequality exist in men appointed at the same time to the same work? The true explanation is, that this whole narrative is simply introductory to Stephen's martyrdom, and he is therefore singled out and rendered prominent among the seven, not only in this general description, but in vs. 8–10. Hence it appears, moreover, that we have not here a formal history of the institution of an office in the church, but at most an incidental notice of it, as the occasion of a subsequent discussion, persecution, and diffusion of the gospel. (See below, on 8, 1. 4.) As all the names are Greek names, it is not improbable that these men were selected from among the Hellenists, to silence their complaints; either by a generous concession of the Hebrews, who agreed that this whole business should be managed by their foreign brethren; or by adding seven Grecians to the Hebrew almoners before existing, whose official action had been called in question. The inference from the Greek names is not conclusive, as many Jews had double names in that age (see above, on 1, 23. 4, 36); but this does not account for the concurrence of so many Greek names, without Hebrew equivalents, and in connection with a strife between the races. *Nicolas the proselyte of Antioch*, literally, *the Antiochean proselyte*, or convert from Heathenism to Judaism, and now to Christianity. Some have inferred from this description, that the other six were *Jews* by birth, although not *Hebrews*, in the sense explained above (on v. 1); others, that they were likewise proselytes, but of Jerusalem not Antioch. A third hypothesis, that three were Hebrews, three Greeks, and one proselyte, is purely conjectural and inadmissible, because no heathen converts had as yet been directly introduced into the church (see above, on 2, 39, and below, on 10, 34. 35.) The old opinion, that this Nicolas was the founder of the Nicolaitans, condemned in Rev. 2, 6. 15, seems to be a mere conjecture from the similarity of names, and in the absence of all proof, does gross injustice to one of the men chosen by the Church, approved by the Apostles, and described, at least by necessary implication, as full of wisdom and the Holy Ghost. *Philip*, not the Apostle (see above, on 1, 13), who was one of those to be relieved by this appointment, but another person of the same name, who becomes conspicuous in the sequel of the history. (See below, on 8, 5. 40. 21, 8.) *Prochorus, Nicanor, Timon*, and *Parmenas*, are names recorded only here.

6. Whom they set before the Apostles: and when they had prayed, they laid (their) hands on them.

Set, placed, caused to stand, the verb translated *appointed* in 1, 23. In both cases it denotes the presentation of the persons found to possess the prescribed qualifications. Election, in the proper sense, is not suggested by this word, but explicitly recorded in the context (v. 5.) The subject of this verb is the collective term, *the multitude*, but not of the verbs in the last clause; for if the people performed all the acts, the presentation was superfluous. *When they had prayed*, literally, *having prayed*, or *praying*, as the two acts were most probably performed at once. That of praying was a solemn recognition of their own dependence on a higher power. The imposition of hands is a natural symbol of transfer or communication, whether of guilt, as in the sacrificial ritual (Lev. 2, 2. 8, 13), or of blessing (Gen. 48, 14. Matt. 19, 13.) In the New

Testament, we find it accompanying certain signal gifts, as that of bodily healing (Matt. 9, 18. Mark 6, 5. 7, 32. 8, 23. 16, 18. Luke 4, 40. 13, 13), that of the Holy Spirit (Acts 8, 17. 19, 6), and in one case both together (Acts 9, 17.) In the case before us, it denotes, not only delegation of authority, but also the collation of the special gifts required for its exercise. This might seem to render doubtful the propriety of using it in modern ordinations, where no extraordinary gifts are thus imparted; but even when performed by the Apostles, it was only as a sign, without intrinsic efficacy of its own. In the case before us, it has even been disputed whether the act was that of ordination to a permanent office in the church, or only that of designation to a temporary service, like that of Barnabas and Saul in 13, 3 below. But although the title *deacon* is not used in this passage, nor indeed in this whole book, yet the judgment of the church has in all ages recognised this as the institution of that office, the continuance of which in other places and in later times is inferred from 1 Tim. 3, 8. 12. Phil. 1, 1. Rom. 16, 1. What were the functions of the office thus created, has also been a subject of dispute; some inferring from the circumstances of its institution, that its only work was that of charitable distribution, or at most of secular economy; while others argue from the fact that Stephen preached, and Philip both preached and baptized, that the seven deacons were already ministers when called to this work, or that the diaconate itself was only an inferior degree or order in the Christian ministry. To this it may be answered that the ministerial acts of Philip were performed, not as a deacon, but by virtue of another office, that of an evangelist (see below, on 21, 8); and that Stephen, if he really performed such acts at all, may have performed them in the same capacity. (See below, on 8, 5. 11, 30.)

7. And the word of God increased; and the number of the disciples multiplied in Jerusalem greatly; and a great company of the priests were obedient to the faith.

The word of God is here an elliptical expression for its effect upon the minds of men, in the way of conviction and conversion, and its *increase* is the growth or enlargement of the church. It seems to be implied, though not explicitly affirmed, that this effect was promoted by the measure just before described, the ordination of the seven almoners or deacons. It may have operated thus in two ways; first, by allaying the incipient divisions in the church itself, and thus removing one chief obstacle to its advancement; then, by bringing into public view and into contact with the foreign Jews especially, such men of their own kindred as the seven must have been. Besides the general description of increase here given, a particular accession is recorded, from the most important class of the community, the Priests. Some have thought this incredible, on two grounds; first, on account of their peculiar zeal and obstinacy as opponents of the Gospel; and secondly, because we find them subsequently active as its enemies and persecutors. But no degree or kind of opposition to the truth is inaccessible to saving grace; and if there were above four thousand priests at the return from the captivity, their number must have been so great now that a crowd might be converted, and yet leave enough to carry on the persecution. There is no need therefore of changing *Priests* to *Jews*, which makes the phrase almost unmeaning, or of adopting forced constructions, e. g. 'a multitude believed (and among them some) of the priests'—or 'a rabble of priests' (i. e. the lowest members of the priesthood.) *Were obedient to* (literally, *obeyed*) *the faith*, i. e. submitted to the Gospel, as a system of belief and practice. (Compare Paul's similar expression *for obedience to the faith*, Rom. 1, 5.) This was not the first time that great numbers of the most intelligent and influential Jews embraced the doctrine of the Saviour. (See above, on 4, 13.) It was no doubt one of the means used to prepare for the diffusion of the Gospel not long after. (See below, on 8, 1.)

8. And Stephen, full of faith and power, did great wonders and miracles among the people.

That the growth of the church mentioned in v. 7 was occasioned or promoted by the appointment of the Seven, is confirmed by Luke's returning here to Stephen and continuing his history. *Full of faith* (or according to the latest critics, *grace*) *and power* is a third variation of the same essential formula. (See above, on vs. 3, 5.) By *power* we are here to understand preternatural, extraordinary power, as appears from the remainder of the verse. *Wonders and miracles*, or *prodigies and signs*, are two of the descriptive epithets applied to miracles before. (See above, on 2, 19. 22. 43. 4, 30.

5, 12.) This is the first instance of miraculous performances by any one not an Apostle (see below, on 8, 6. 7), and may serve to illustrate the remarkable position occupied by Stephen, who was evidently more than a deacon in the strict and ordinary sense. *Among the people,* literally, *in the people,* not as mere spectators, but as subjects and recipients. The imperfect tense (ἐποίει) refers, not to a point of time, but to a longer though indefinite period.

9. Then there arose certain of the synagogue, which is called (the synagogue) of the Libertines, and Cyrenians, and Alexandrians, and of them of Cilicia and of Asia, disputing with Stephen.

Then arose certain, or more exactly, *and some arose,* i. e. appeared, came forward, and addressed themselves to action. (See above, on 1, 15. 5, 17. 34. 36. 37.) *Some of those of the synagogue.* This Greek word originally means *collection,* and is properly applied to things, but in the Hellenistic dialect to persons also, like our English *meeting.* It is frequently applied in the Septuagint version to the whole *congregation* of Israel, as an aggregate and corporate body. During the Babylonish captivity, it seems to have been transferred to the divisions of this body, in their separation and dispersion, and more especially to their assemblies for religious worship. After the second great dispersion of the Jews, occasioned by the Roman conquest and destruction of Jerusalem, the synagogues assumed the form of organized societies, with a peculiar constitution and discipline, from which that of the Christian Church is commonly supposed to have been copied. It is doubtful, however, whether synagogues, in this later sense, existed in the time of Christ and the Apostles, when the word, though sometimes, like the English *church, school, court,* etc. transferred to the place of meeting, properly denoted the meeting itself, not as an organic body, but as an assembly of the people for a special purpose. In Jerusalem, where multitudes of foreigners were gathered, to attend the feasts or as permanent settlers, it was natural that those of the same race and language should convene together, both for worship and for social intercourse; and this accounts for the extraordinary number of synagogues, alleged by the Jewish tradition to have existed in Jerusalem before its downfall (480), an incredible number if we understand by synagogues distinct organizations of a public and a formal nature, but possible enough if nothing more be meant than gatherings of the people, in larger or smaller circles, for religious purposes. Of such *synagogues* we have clear traces in the verse before us; but how many are here mentioned, is a subject of dispute. The ambiguous construction of the sentence allows us to suppose either one or five such bodies to be here referred to—i. e. the synagogue of the Libertines, Cyrenians, Alexandrians, etc.—or, the synagogue of the Libertines, and that of the Cyrenians, and that of the Alexandrians, etc. Between these extremes lie the possible hypotheses of three synagogues (1. of the Libertines, 2. of the Cyrenians and Alexandrians, 3. of the Cilicians and Asians)—or two (1. of the Libertines, Cyrenians, and Alexandrians; 2. of the Cilicians and Asians.) Still a different construction, and perhaps the simplest, is to connect *synagogue* only with the first name, and to understand the rest of individuals belonging to the nations mentioned. 'Some of the (members) of the synagogue called (that) of the Libertines, and (some) Cyrenians and Alexandrians, and (some) of those from Cilicia and Asia.' However the question of construction may be settled, the essential fact affirmed is still the same, to wit, that the opponents of the Gospel here described were chiefly or entirely foreign Jews, and from the two great regions of North Africa and Asia Minor. (As to *Asia* and *Cyrene*, see above, on 2, 9. 10.) *Alexandrians*, inhabitants of Alexandria, the great commercial city of Egypt, founded by Alexander the Great, and under his successors inhabited by a multitude of Jewish colonists, so that it became the chief seat of Hellenistic learning. *Cilicia* was the south-eastern province of what we call Asia Minor, and the native country of St. Paul, who was born at Tarsus, its chief city. (See below, on 9, 11. 30. 11, 25. 21, 39. 22, 3.) *Libertines* is understood by some to be a national or geographical name like the rest, either, put by an error of the copyist for *Libyans* (see above, on 2, 10), or denoting the people of *Libertum*, a city of Proconsular Africa. But as all the ancient manuscripts agree with the received text, and as Libertum, if it then existed, was too obscure to be largely represented in Jerusalem, the great body of interpreters identify the word with the latin *libertini*, meaning freedmen or the sons of emancipated slaves, and suppose it to denote here Roman proselytes of that class, whom Tacitus describes as numerous in Rome itself, or the sons of Jews carried captive into Italy by Pompey and afterwards set free. Either of these is much more probable than the opinion, that these *Libertines* were slaves set free by Jewish masters and residing at Jerusalem, where they formed a separate synagogue or congregation, either from necessity or choice. The moral sense of *libertine*, as meaning a licentious liver, is of later date. (Compare the corresponding difference of *idiot* and *despot*, in ancient and modern usage, as explained above, on 4, 13. 24.) *Disputing*, or, as the Greek word signifies according to its etymology and classical usage, *seeking* (or *inquiring*) *together*, but in the New Testament always with an implication of dissension and debate. *Arose disputing* may imply that the discussion, which at first was private, became generally known and public. *With Stephen*, not perhaps exclusively, but only as the first and best known of the seven; or his name may be particularly mentioned for the reason before given (on v. 5), that this whole account is introductory to that of Stephen's martyrdom and its effect on the condition of the church. It is no improbable conjecture, that his ministry among the Christian Hellenists may have brought him into contact and collision with their unbelieving relatives and friends. The subject of this controversy may be gathered from the following account of his arraignment and defence.

10. And they were not able to resist the wisdom and the spirit by which he spake.

Another fulfilment of the promise in Luke 21, 15 (see above, on 4, 14), and another variation of the formula employed above in vs. 3. 5. 8. The analogy of v. 3 here precludes the vague and somewhat modern sense of *spirit*, i. e. energy or vigour, as well as the more genuine but lower one of intellect or sense, and requires that of Holy Spirit, if not as a person, as an influence. The relative (*by which*) agrees in form with *spirit* only, but in sense with *wisdom* likewise, although our idiom would use different prepositions to denote the two relations. He spoke *with wisdom*, for he spoke *by inspiration*.

11. Then they suborned men, which said, We have heard him speak blasphemous words against Moses, and (against) God.

Then, in the proper sense, *at that time*, or after what had just been mentioned. *They*, the Libertines and Hellenistic Jews, whom Stephen had vanquished in debate. *Suborned*, i. e. procured indirectly or unfairly, but specially applied in English law to the procuring of false testimony. The Greek verb means both to *substitute* (e. g. a supposititious child), and to *suggest* or prompt, which is also appropriate to false swearing. *Which said*, literally, *saying*. The Greek idiom, which prefixes *that* (ὅτι) to the words quoted or repeated, cannot be retained in English. *Speak*, literally, *speaking, talking*. *Blasphemous*, in Demosthenes and later classics, means abusive or calumnious (as in 2 Pet. 2, 11. 2 Tim. 3, 2), but in the Greek of the New Testament, is specially applied to railing words when spoken of divine things or of God himself. (See 1 Tim. 1, 13, and compare the cognate noun and verb, *blaspheme* and *blasphemy*, which are of frequent use in the New Testament.) *Against*, literally, *to* or *towards*, a particle which indicates the subject of discourse, the idea of hostility being suggested by the context. (See above, on 2, 25.) The second *against* is supplied in the translation. *Moses and God* is not an irreverent or preposterous inversion, but a pregnant combination, which may be thus resolved and amplified, 'against Moses, our great legislator, and by necessary consequence, against the God, whose representative he was, and from whom all his legislative power was derived.' Compare the words, "it seemed good to the Holy Spirit and to us," in 15, 28 below.

And they stirred up the people, and the elders, and the scribes, and came upon (him), and caught him, and brought (him) to the council,

Stirred up, literally, *moved together*, agitated at the same time, in reference either to what goes before or follows. If the former, the verb must be construed with the remoter subject, those who procured the witnesses, and who are then described as adding popular agitation to subornation of perjury, as a means of destroying Stephen. If the latter, the subject of the verb may be the witnesses themselves, and the commotion mentioned the effect of their misrepresentations. *Both* (τε) *the people*, as an aggregate body, *and the elders and the scribes*, as its representatives and rulers. (See above, on 4, 5.) *Came upon him*, unexpectedly or suddenly (see above, on 4,

1), probably while engaged in teaching or discussion. *Caught him*, seized and carried him along with them, as the Greek verb properly denotes, being applied in the classics to an eagle and a storm. *To the council*, literally, *into* it, i. e. into the place where it assembled (see above, on 5, 27), or into the midst of the assembly itself.

13. And set up false witnesses, which said, This man ceaseth not to speak blasphemous words against this holy place, and the law.

And also (τε) *set up*, as in v. 6, and in 1, 23. *False witnesses*, not in the sense of mere inventors, fabricators, or gross liars, but in that of unfair and perverse reporters, who, even in repeating what he really had said, distorted it and caused it to produce a false impression. (Compare Matt. 26, 59–62. Mark 14, 55–60.) *Which said*, literally, *saying*, as in v. 11. *This man* is perhaps contemptuous; but see above, on 4, 17. 18. *Ceaseth not*, an evident exaggeration, intended to aggravate the charge which follows. *To speak*, literally, *speaking*. *Blasphemous* is omitted by the latest critics, as an interpolation from v. 11, not found in the oldest manuscripts. The sense is then to *utter words*, an emphatic equivalent to *speak*. Instead of *Moses and God* (v. 11), the objects of the blasphemy are here described as *this* (or according to the latest critics, *the*) *holy place*, i. e. the city of Jerusalem, or more precisely, the temple, *and the law*, i. e. the theocratical and ceremonial system, of which it was the visible heart and centre. (See above, on 4, 11. 5, 27.)

14. For we have heard him say, that this Jesus of Nazareth shall destroy this place, and shall change the customs (or rites) which Moses delivered us.

This is not a merely formal variation of v. 13, but a more precise specification of the general charge recorded there. 'He is guilty of that charge, *for* we have heard him saying thus and thus.' If *this* was contemptuous in the preceding verse, it is doubly so here, being joined with the derisive title, *Jesus the Nazarene*. (See above, on 2, 22. 3, 6. 4, 10.) *Destroy*, the same verb that is used above in 5, 38. 39, and there explained. *This place*, the temple and the city, as in v. 13, considered as the centre of the whole Mosaic system, the congeries of *customs* (ἔθη), *rites*, or rather *institutions*, which Moses *delivered*, revealed, communicated, by divine authority, to be *handed down* from one generation to another; which last idea would also be suggested by the Greek verb, as the root of the noun meaning *tradition*. (Compare Mark 7, 13, where both occur; and for a very different sense of the verb, see above, on 3, 13.) This charge was no doubt true so far as it related to the doctrine, that the new religion, or rather the new form of the church, was to supersede the old. Its falsity consisted in the representation of the two as hostile or antagonistic systems, and of the change as one to be effected by coercion or brute force.

15. And all that sat in the council, looking stedfastly on him, saw his face as (it had been) the face of an angel.

All that sat, literally, *all the* (persons) *sitting*. *In the council* itself, as members of the body, or in the council-chamber, as spectators; it is doubtful, however, whether any such were present. *Looking stedfastly on him* is in Greek still stronger, *gazing into him*, as if to read his very soul, an emphatic expression for the most intense and eager curiosity, the same phrase that is used above in 1, 10. 3, 4, and below, in 7, 55. 13, 9. This clause stands first in the original (*and gazing at him, all those sitting in the council saw*, etc.) *As it had been*, literally, *as if*, as though, without a verb expressed. In the history of David, he is four times compared by others to *an angel* (or *the angel*) *of God*, but always in reference to intellectual or moral qualities, his goodness (1 Sam. 29, 9) or his wisdom (2 Sam. 14, 17. 20. 19, 27.) An analogous comparison to that before us, but still stronger, is the one addressed by Jacob to Esau (Gen. 33, 10), "I have seen thy face, as though I had seen the face of God, and thou wast pleased with me." This is clearly a hyperbolical description of a friendly or benignant countenance, and many understand the words before us as a similar description of the calmness and serenity expressed in Stephen's looks. It seems more natural, however, to explain them of a preternatural glow and brightness, like the shining of the face of Moses when he came down from Mount Sinai (Ex. 34. 29.) In either case, the comparison with an angel is not intended to convey a definite idea of the actual appearance—as we know neither how an angel looks nor whether all angels look alike—but merely to suggest the thought of something superhuman and celestial.

CHAPTER VII.

This chapter contains Stephen's defence before the council (1–53) and his execution (54–60). His defence is drawn entirely from the Old Testament history, and is designed to show, that all God's dealings with the chosen people pointed to those very changes which Stephen was accused of having threatened. This he proves by showing, that the outward organization and condition of the church had undergone repeated change, under Abraham (2–8), Joseph (9–16), Moses (17–44), David (45–46); that the actual state of things had no existence before Solomon (47); that even this was intended from the beginning to be temporary (48–50); and lastly, that the Israelites of every age had been unfaithful to their trust (9. 25. 27. 35. 39–43. 51–53.) The remainder of the chapter describes the effect of this discourse upon the council (54), Stephen's heavenly vision (55. 56), and his death by stoning (57–60).

1. Then said the high priest, Are these things so?

The High Priest, as president of the council and chief magistrate of the nation, interrogates the prisoner, as when our Saviour was crucified (Matt. 26, 62. Mark 17, 60. John 18, 19.) The verse is connected in the closest manner with the one before it by the continuative particle ($\delta\epsilon$) here rendered *then*. *Are these things so?* literally, *whether these* (*things*) *so have* (themselves)? This idiomatic phrase, equivalent to *are*, occurs again below (17, 11. 24, 9.) *These things*, namely, those alleged by his accusers (6, 11. 13).

2. And he said, Men, brethren, and fathers, hearken. The God of glory appeared unto our father Abraham, when he was in Mesopotamia, before he dwelt in Charran,

To the phrase, *Men (and) Brethren*, used by Peter (1, 26. 2, 29), Stephen adds *Fathers*, either to distinguish his judges from the mere spectators, or as a twofold description of the former, first as his countrymen or fellow Jews, then as his superiors, the Senators or Conscript Fathers of his nation (see above, on 5, 21.) The same form of address is elsewhere used by Paul (22, 1), perhaps not without allusion to the speech before us, of which other recollections have been traced in the Apostle's writings. The exhortation to *hear*, found in both these places, and also in the introduction to Paul's speech at Antioch in Pisidia (13, 16), seems to imply that something might be said which would offend their prejudices, and that patience would therefore be required on their part. (See above, on 2, 14. 29.) After thus bespeaking their attention, he appeals at once to history, not for the information of his hearers, whose Jewish education and familiarity with Scripture he assumes, but simply for the purpose of his argument. As his first object was to show the outward changes, through which the church or chosen people had already passed, he begins with the event from which it derived its separate existence, the calling of Abraham. *The God of glory*, not merely the glorious God, or the God worthy to be glorified (Ps. 29, 1. Rev. 4, 11), but more specifically, that God who sensibly revealed himself of old, which is a standing sense of *glory* (כבוד, δόξα) in the Old Testament (e. g. Ex. 24, 16. Isai. 6, 3. Ps. 24, 7–10), here employed by Stephen in allusion to the charge of blaspheming Moses and Jehovah (6, 11.) For the same reason he calls Abraham *our father*, thus professing his adherence to the national traditions and associations with respect to their great founder. *Appeared*, was seen (see above, on 2, 3), may denote any special and direct divine communication, but is properly expressive of such as were conveyed by vision, or addressed to the sense of sight. *When he was*, literally, *being*. *Mesopotamia*, a term of physical rather than political geography, denoting the region between the Tigris and Euphrates. (See above, on 2, 9.) Like other ancient names of this kind, it is used with considerable latitude. Thus Ammianus Marcellinus mentions *Ur (of the Chaldees* or *Chaldea)* as a town of Mesopotamia, and Josephus makes it include Babylonia itself. So, too, the poet Lucan calls *Charran* (Haran) *Assyrius Currus*, the scene of the famous defeat of Crassus. This confusion of terms arose, no doubt, at least in part, from the want of definite boundaries. There is therefore no mistake here, either in geography or history, as some have alleged, because in Gen. 12, 1, Abram is said to have been called after his removal to Haran. But even admitting the pluperfect form of the English version there (*the Lord had said*) to be inexact, it is highly probable (and seems to be at least implied in Gen. 15, 7. Neh. 9, 7), that he had been called before, and thus induced to leave his native country. That such repetitions of the divine communications were not foreign to the patriarch's experience, we may learn from Gen. 12, 3. 18, 18. 22, 18. That the first call is not explicitly recorded in its proper place, is not surprising in so brief a history. Upon this obvious and natural interpretation of the narrative in Genesis, rests the Jewish tradition, preserved both by Philo and Josephus, that Abram was twice called, once in Ur and once in Haran. *Dwelt*, or more exactly *settled*, took up his abode (see above, on 2, 5.)

3. And said unto him, Get thee out of thy country, and from thy kindred, and come into the land which I shall shew thee.

These words are from the Septuagint version of Gen. 12, 1, the form in which Stephen seems to have adduced them, as he was probably a Hellenist or Greek Jew (see above, on 6, 5), and that language was no doubt familiar to his judges. The only variations from the Septuagint are, that he omits the phrase, *and from thy father's house*, as being really included in the more generic one, *and from thy kindred;* and also that the article before *land* is omitted in the common text, but not in the oldest manuscripts. *Come*, in the original, is properly an adverb (δεῦρο), meaning *here* or *hither!* sometimes coupled with a verb of motion (as in Matt. 19, 21. Mark 10, 21. Luke 18, 22), sometimes elliptically used without it or in place of it (as here and in John 11, 43. Rev. 17, 1. 21, 9.) *The land which I shall show thee* is too definite; the true sense is, *whatever land* (ἣν ἄν) *I show thee* (or *may show thee*), implying uncertainty, and therefore strong faith, upon Abram's part. A beautiful comment is afforded by the last clause of the parallel passage in Heb. 11, 8, "he went out not knowing whither he went."

4. Then came he out of the land of the Chaldeans, and dwelt in Charran: and from thence, when his

father was dead, he removed him into this land, wherein ye now dwell.

Then, in the proper sense, as a particle of time, meaning *afterwards* or *next*. *Came he out*, literally, *having come out*. (*Dwelt*, as in v. 1.) *When his father was dead*, or more exactly, *after his father died*. This seems to contradict the chronological statements of the Old Testament, that Terah was 70 years when he begat Abram (Gen. 11, 26); that Abram was 70 when he left Haran (Gen. 12, 4); and that Terah lived to be 205 (Gen. 11, 32), i. e. 60 years after the migration of Abram into Canaan. The difficulty has been variously solved; by reading (in Gen. 11, 32) 145 for 205, which seems to be a mere conjectural emendation of the Samaritan Pentateuch; or by understanding Stephen's words of Terah's spiritual death, according to an old tradition found in Philo, and probably founded upon Josh. 24, 2 (compare Judith 5, 6. 7), that Terah in his old age apostatized to idolatry, so that Abram was justified in leaving him, although he lived long after and died in Haran (Gen. 11, 32); or far more probably than either, that the age given in Gen. 11, 26, is that of Terah when he begat his eldest son, as in the preceding genealogies, and that Abram was not the eldest son, but put first on account of his great eminence, as Napoleon might be named first in a list of the Bonapartes, though not the eldest. This would enable us to fix the birth of Abram at such a distance from that of his elder brother or brothers, as would bring his seventy-fifth year after the natural death of his father. Either of these possible solutions is more probable than the supposition of so gross an error on the part of Stephen. *Wherein*, literally, *whereinto*, into which, the verb implying previous removal, not of themselves but of their fathers. (See the same construction in the Greek of 12, 19. Matt. 2, 23. Mark 1, 39.) *Ye* is emphatic (see above on 4, 20), as opposed, not only to their fathers, but to Stephen himself, as a Hellenist or foreign Jew.

5. And he gave him none inheritance in it, no, not (so much as) to set his foot on: yet he promised that he would give it to him for a possession, and to his seed after him, when (as yet) he had no child.

So far was the present complex and imposing system from

existing in the time of Abram, that he had not even foot-hold in the land as a possessor. *None,* or more exactly, *not. Inheritance,* property which he could transmit to his heirs. *In it,* this land, just mentioned in v. 4. *No not* is a single word in Greek, meaning simply *not* or *nor.* So *much as to set his foot on,* literally, *a foot-step,* or a stepping-place for his foot. The same phrase is used in the Septuagint version of Deut. 2, 5. (Compare Gen. 8, 9.) It is here put for the smallest space or quantity, without regard to any definite measure. (Tyndale, Cranmer, and Geneva, *the breadth of a foot.*) But how does this consist with Abraham's purchase of a hereditary burial place (Gen. 23, 20. 50, 13)? We may understand the words to mean that he *had not yet given him,* or still more exactly, *did not give him,* i. e. in the first years of his residence, the smallest portion of the land of Canaan. This is all that was necessary for Stephen's purpose, which was simply to show what changes had already taken place in the condition of the chosen people since the calling of Abraham. His later acquisition might be reckoned as one of these changes, and would therefore rather strengthen than impair his argument. *Yet,* literally, *and,* which is here equivalent, however, to *and* (*yet*). He gave him none of it at first, and but little of it afterwards, but promised him the whole for his descendants. *Promised,* insured, or assured, which is the full force of the original. *That he would give,* literally, *to give.* For *a possession,* a Greek word specially appropriated in the Septuagint version, to the occupation of the promised land. (See Gen. 17, 8. Num. 32, 5, and compare v. 45 below.) *When as yet he had no child,* literally, (*there*) *not being to him a child,* is added to enhance the faith of Abram, who believed a promise made expressly to his offspring, when as yet he had none.

6. And God spake on this wise, That his seed should sojourn in a strange land; and that they should bring them into bondage, and entreat (them) evil four hundred years.

Having given the substance of the promise, he now gives its form, or rather one of the forms in which it is recorded. The citation is made from the Septuagint version of Gen. 15, 13. 14, with a few unimportant variations, chiefly in the order of the words. *On this wise,* an old English phrase, synonymous with *in this way* or *manner.* The original is one word, meaning *so* or *thus*. *Seed*, offspring or posterity. *Should sojourn*, literally, *shall be sojourning*, or *a sojourner*, a temporary resident, as in v. 29 below (compare the verb in Luke 24, 18.) The future belongs to the direct form of quotation, in which the very words used are repeated, but the third person (*his seed*) to the indirect form, which only gives the substance. *A strange land*, not unknown, but foreign; not their own, belonging to others. *They*, i. e. the land, often put for its inhabitants. *That they should bring them into bondage* (Wiclif, *make them subject to servage*), literally, *and they shall enslave it*, (i. e. the seed of Abram, which is a collective.) *Entreat them evil*, or in modern English, *treat them ill*. Here again the original is one word, corresponding to *abuse* or *maltreat*. (See below, on v. 19. 12, 1. 18, 10. In 14, 2, it has an intellectual or moral sense.) *Four hundred* is a round number for four hundred and thirty, and is so used likewise by Josephus. In Ex. 12, 40. 41, it is expressly said that the sojourn of Israel in Egypt lasted 430 years, and that they came out on the very day when the 430 years were completed. But Paul speaks of the law (Gal. 3, 17) as having been given 430 years after the promise to Abraham. This might be understood to mean *at least* so long, because the longer the interval the stronger the Apostle's argument. But as this does not account for his using that specific number, and as the genealogical tables seem to indicate a shorter period, a better solution is to understand the 430 years of Ex. 12, 40 to include the previous residence in Canaan, as well as that in Egypt. The difference between these two sojourns being merely circumstantial, and the main idea being that of an expatriated, homeless state, it was more important to tell how long they were in such a state, than how much of this period was spent in Egypt. This is a possible, though not a very obvious, construction of the terms used in Exodus, which may be understood as meaning, that the whole period of exclusion from the actual possession of the promised land, including both their residence in Egypt and their previous nomadic life in Canaan, was 430 years, and that this period expired on the day of the exodus from Egypt. This solution is at least a very old one, being found not only in Josephus, but in the Samaritan text and the Septuagint version, both which add, "and in the land of Canaan," while the former, and a very ancient copy of the latter, insert after *Israel*, "and their fathers." These are not to be regarded as independent witnesses, nor as exhibiting the true text, which has no doubt been preserved in the Masora, or critical tradition of the Jews. But the emendation shows how early the difficulty was perceived, and this means used for its solution.

7. And the nation to whom they shall be in bondage will I judge, said God: and after that shall they come forth, and serve me in this place.

The quotation from Genesis is here concluded. *To whom*, literally, *to whomsoever* (ᾧ ἐάν), because it had not been expressly named. As if he had said, 'and that nation, whatever it may be, &c.' See above, on v. 3, where a similar expression (ἣν ἄν) is employed. *Shall be in bondage*, or *shall serve as slaves*, is the translation of a single Greek word, differing only in a single letter from the one just used in the transitive or active sense of enslaving or bringing into bondage. *Will I judge*, deal justly with, do justice to, and as a necessary consequence, implied but not expressed, condemn and punish. *Said God* is supplied, as in Peter's quotation from the Prophet Joel (see above, on 2, 17), to remind the hearers that these words were still those of a divine speaker and must therefore be fulfilled, and at the same time to relieve the syntax, which was somewhat embarrassed by the mixture (before mentioned) of direct and indirect quotation. *After that*, literally, *after these* (*things*). *They* refers to the remoter antecedent, the collective phrase, *his seed* (in v. 6). *Come forth*, or out of Egypt. *And shall serve* (or *worship*) *me in this place* is implicitly contained in Gen. 15, 16 (*they shall return hither*), though the form of expression is borrowed from a promise made to Moses, when about to carry into execution the one made to Abram. See Ex. 3, 12, *ye shall serve God upon this mountain*, i. e. Horeb (v. 1), for which Stephen substitutes *in this place*, an expression which may be applied to a whole country, as when Xenophon says, "this place was called Armenia."

8. And he gave him the covenant of circumcision: and so (Abraham) begat Isaac, and circumcised him the eighth day; and Isaac (begat) Jacob; and Jacob (begat) the twelve patriarchs.

Another outward change was the subjection of the chosen people to the distinctive rite of circumcision. Abram was called and justified while yet uncircumcised (compare Rom. 4, 10–12); but circumcision afterwards was peremptorily required. *He gave him*, i. e. God gave to Abram. *Gave*, not merely as a favor or a privilege, but as a duty to be done, a law to be obeyed. *Covenant*, originally, *disposition* or *arrangement*, commonly applied in the classics to a testamentary disposition of one's property, a last will, but in Scripture, with the probable exception of Heb. 9, 16. 17, to a mutual arrangement or agreement, binding on both parties. *A covenant of circumcision* may be either circumcision itself, as a covenanted, stipulated rite, or a covenant of which circumcision was the sign and seal. (See Gen. 17, 10. 11, where both these ideas seem to be expressed, and compare Gen. 9, 12.) *So*, i. e. in this new condition or relation, under this new covenant, not as an ordinary progenitor, but as one sustaining a peculiar federal relation, both to God and to posterity. This is much better than to make it a connective or continuative particle, equivalent to *so then* in colloquial narration, which is otherwise expressed in Greek. (See above, on 1, 6. 18. 2, 41. 5, 41.) The emphatic word is not *begat* but *circumcised*, as if he had said, 'all the other patriarchs were born under this covenant of circumcision.' This idea is obscured in our translation by repeating the first verb alone, instead of repeating both (*begat and circumcised*), or neither, leaving the reader to supply them from the first clause, as in the Rhemish version (*Isaac Jacob, and Jacob the twelve patriarchs*). The mere genealogy or lineal succession was entirely irrelevant to Stephen's purpose, as well as perfectly familiar to his hearers. The main idea of the verse is, that the patriarchs who followed Abraham were all born under a covenant or dispensation, which had no existence when he was himself called to be the Friend of God (Isai. 41, 8. James 2, 23) and the Father of the Faithful (Rom. 4, 11. 16.) The recital of these simple and familiar facts is perfectly unmeaning, unless intended to establish Stephen's proposition, that the outward condition of the chosen people had already undergone repeated changes, quite as great as those which he was charged with blasphemy for having threatened. *Patriarchs*, founders of distinct families or races. See above, on 2, 29, and compare the use of the primitive noun elsewhere (Luke 2, 4) to denote the lineage of David.

9. And the patriarchs, moved with envy, sold Joseph into Egypt; but God was with him,

The next important change in the condition of the chosen race was the migration into Egypt, providentially secured by the sale of Joseph as a slave there. Stephen dwells on the particulars of this change more than was absolutely necessary for his argument; partly, because of their extraordinary character, evincing the whole series of events to be the execution of a divine plan; but also for the purpose of suggesting an analogy between Joseph's treatment by his brethren and that of Christ by their descendants. Here then begins another thread of the discourse, running parallel to that which we have thus far traced, and adding to the proof that the existing state of things was not immutable, a proof derived from the same source that Israel had always been unfaithful to his trust and his advantages. This course of defection and rebellion is here tacitly traced back to the treacherous and cruel conduct of the sons of Jacob toward their innocent and helpless brother. The motive assigned is not *indignation* (Tyndale, Cranmer, and Geneva), nor mere *emulation* (Rheims), but *jealousy* and *envy*. (See the use of the kindred noun in 5, 17 above.) The original expression is a single word, *envying* or *having envied*. *Sold*, see above on 5, 8, where the same verb is employed, as well as in the Septuagint version of the history of Joseph (Gen. 37, 27.) *Sold into Egypt* is a pregnant construction, which implies (without expressing) motion or removal. The very same construction, both of verb and noun, occurs in the Septuagint version of the passage just referred to (Gen. 37, 36.) *But*, literally, *and*, but with a really adversative effect, producing an antithesis like that in 2, 23. 24. 3, 14. 15. 4, 10. 5, 30, between divine and human treatment of the same person, thus confirming the existence of a typical relation, or a recognised analogy, between the sufferings of Christ and Joseph. The suggestion of this parallel, however slight, was really equivalent to saying, 'As you have now dealt with the Saviour of the world, your fathers dealt with the deliverer of their nation, showing even then the same unthankful and rebellious disposition which we see in you.' *God was with him*, in a providential sense, as his protector and preserver, which is the lower of the two ideas conveyed by the prophetic name *Immanuel* or *God with us*

(Isai. 7, 14. Matt. 1, 23). What was true, in this lower sense, of Joseph, was true, and in the highest sense, of Christ.

10. And delivered him out of all his afflictions, and gave him favour and wisdom in the sight of Pharaoh king of Egypt; and he made him governor over Egypt and all his house.

This is a mere amplification of the last clause of the ninth verse, showing in what respect or what sense God was with him. *Delivered*, extricated, plucked out (Matt. 5, 29. 18, 9.) See below, on v. 34. 12, 11. 23, 27. 26, 17. *Afflictions*, literally, *pressures*, straits, distresses. See below, on v. 11. 11, 19. 14, 22. 20, 23. *Favour and wisdom*, i. e. gave him favour by giving him extraordinary wisdom, both as an interpreter of dreams and as a statesman. This wisdom was exhibited *before* (over against, opposite, in presence of) *Pharaoh*. The subject of the last verb may be either God or Pharaoh; but the former gives a more striking sense by making Joseph's exaltation altogether a divine act. *Made him governor* (Wiclif, *ordained him sovereign*). The verb means properly to *set down* in a place (see below, on 17, 15), then to *set up*, constitute, appoint (see above, on 6, 3, and below, on vs. 27, 35.) *Governor*, literally, *leader*, or still more exactly, *leading* (*man*), chief magistrate, prime minister (see below on 14, 12. 15, 22, and compare Matt. 2, 6, and the antithesis in Luke 22, 26.) This last idea is also expressed by his being placed over the royal household. (See below, on 8, 27. 12, 26.)

11. Now there came a dearth over all the land of Egypt and Canaan, and great affliction; and our fathers found no sustenance.

He now relates the other part of the strange providential scheme, by which Joseph was made the means of bringing his whole family to Egypt. *Now*, and, or but, the usual continuative (δέ). *A dearth*, a famine, a destitution or deficiency of food. *Came over*, or *upon*, implying not mere prevalence but judicial infliction by a higher power. The form of expression is closely copied from the original history (Gen. 41, 54. 42, 5), with which most of Stephen's hearers were as well acquainted as himself. *Our fathers*, here and in the next verse, has been thought to express a kind of sympathetic feeling for the sufferings of the patriarchs; but it is rather an assertion of the speaker's kindred or relation to his hearers, as descended from a common ancestry. (See above, on 3, 13.) *Found no* (literally *not*, or did not find) *sustenance*, provisions, victuals. The Greek word is plural and applied in the classics only to the food of cattle (fodder), which sense it also has in the Septuagint version (Gen. 24, 25. 32.)

12. But when Jacob heard that there was corn in Egypt, he sent out our fathers first.

But is the word translated *now* in v. 11. *Jacob hearing (of) corn being in Egypt* is nearer the form of the original. *Corn*, in the generic sense of grain or bread-stuffs, which is its proper English usage. The particular reference is no doubt to wheat, for which Egypt was famous in the ancient world, and with which it afterwards supplied Rome itself. (See below, on 27, 6. 38. 28, 11.) *Sent out*, sent off or away, the compound Greek verb being very emphatic and conveying, at least sometimes, the idea of an authoritative peremptory sending, almost equivalent to driving out or off (e. g. in Luke 1, 53. 20, 10. 11.) But in other cases it denotes a simple mission, or at most a distant one. (See below, on 7, 30. 11, 22. 12, 11. 17, 14. 22, 21.) *Our fathers*, see above, on v. 11. *First*, i. e. a first time, implying that they went more than once, and that nothing extraordinary happened till their second visit.

13. And at the second (time), Joseph was made known to his brethren, and Joseph's kindred was made known unto Pharaoh.

At the second (time), or *in the second (visit)* of the patriarchs to Egypt. *Was made known* occurs twice in this one verse, a repetition only found in the translation, the original expressions being altogether different. The first is a single word, the passive of a Greek verb used by Plato in the sense of knowing again, recognizing. (For another verb expressing that idea, see above, on 3, 10. 4, 13.) *He was recognized by* (or *again made known to*) *his brethren*. Although used in the Septuagint version (Gen. 45, 1) to translate a reflexive verb (*he made himself known*), it is not itself reflexive, but a simple passive. The other phrase translated *was made known* denotes strictly *became manifest*, i. e. was discovered or disclosed. *Joseph's kindred*, not his kinsmen, but his descent, extraction, race, or *family*, considered as an abstract not a concrete term, like that used in the next verse. (See above, on 4, 36.)

14. Then sent Joseph, and called his father Jacob to (him), and all his kindred, threescore and fifteen souls.

Then sent Joseph, Gr. *and Joseph sending*. *To him* is not expressed in Greek, but may be considered as included in the verb, which means *sent for*, while the middle voice has the usual reflexive meaning. (See below, on 10, 32. 20, 17. 24, 25.) *His kindred*, or according to the oldest manuscripts, *the kindred*, the family, in the concrete sense, as denoting persons. (For the corresponding abstract term, see above, on v. 13.) *Threescore and fifteen souls*, i. e. seventy-five persons. (See above, on 2, 41. 43. 3, 23). Omitted in our version is the preposition *in*, which stands before these words in Greek, both here and in the Septuagint version of Deut. 10, 22. Some suppose it to be put for a Hebrew prefix, corresponding both to *in* and *with*. Examples of the latter sense are found in Hellenistic Greek, not only that of the Apocrypha (1 Macc. 1, 17. 7, 28), but that of the New Testament (Luke 14, 31). But although Jacob might have been sent for *with* seventy-five others, how could this be said of *the whole family?* Another explanation gives to *in* the same sense as in our phrase *consisting in*, i. e. composed of seventy-five persons. But besides this grammatical question, there is one of more importance in relation to this clause. The number here given (75) is also found in the Septuagint version of Gen. 46, 27. Ex. 1, 5, and in some very ancient copies of Deut. 10, 22, whereas the Hebrew text, in all these places, has the round number (70). This difference has been variously explained, by supposing that though only seventy went down with Jacob, Joseph invited (*called for*) seventy-five, the supernumerary persons being three wives of Jacob and two sons of Judah, whom Joseph did not know to be dead; or that in addition to the 66 mentioned in Gen. 46, 26, Stephen reckoned the twelve wives of Jacob's sons, omitting Judah's, who was dead, and Joseph's, who was in Egypt, as well as Joseph himself, for the same reason; or lastly, that in Gen. 46, 20, the Septuagint adds the sons of

Ephraim and Manasseh, from the genealogy in 1 Chron. 7, 14–21, while the Hebrew text omits them, because not born until afterwards. In one of these three ways, the variation of the Septuagint from the Hebrew may be readily accounted for. Stephen's adhering to the former may be then explained, by supposing, either that he quoted the most current and familiar version without alteration, in a matter of so little moment in itself or in relation to his own immediate purpose; or that he spoke in the language of the country, and that the quotation was recorded in its present form by Luke. But this last would only shift the charge of error, not remove it; and that Stephen spoke most probably in Greek, see above, on v. 3 But either of these suppositions is more reasonable than that Stephen was himself mistaken, or that the Hebrew text is wrong, and that he meant to correct it.

15. So Jacob went down into Egypt, and died, he, and our fathers —

The sentence is completed in the next verse. Stephen now comes to the critical change in the condition of the chosen people, for which vs. 9–14 were a preparation. *So* is not the same Greek word as in v. 8 above, but merely the continuative particle (δέ), so constantly occurring and so variously rendered, *and* (v. 6), *now* (v. 11), *but* (v. 12), *then* (v. 14.) *Died*, literally, *ended* (sc. his life.) This elliptical use of the verb, which is the only one found in the New Testament, is sanctioned by the usage of the best Greek writers, from Herodotus to Xenophon. *He and our fathers* connects the verb *died*, which is singular in form, with Jacob's sons as well as with himself. A similar construction occurs in John 2, 12, and in the common text of Matt. 12, 3. The whole clause is equivalent to saying, 'Jacob went down into Egypt, and so did *our fathers*,' i. e. his sons, the *patriarchs*, or founders of the twelve tribes of Israel. (See above, on v. 8.) *Went down* sometimes denotes literal descent from a higher to a lower level, or at least from the interior to the sea-coast (as in 8, 26. 16, 8, below). In other cases, it is doubtful whether the expression is thus used, or with reference to the moral as well as local elevation of Jerusalem (see below, on 24, 1. 22. 25, 6. 7.) In the case before us, there may be allusion, either to the physical difference between Palestine and Egypt, as a hilly and a level land respectively; or to the moral difference between the Holy Land and any heathen country; or to both these points of dissimilitude together.

16. And were carried over into Sychem, and laid in the sepulchre that Abraham bought, for a sum of money, of the sons of Emmor, (the father) of Sychem.

Carried over, transferred, or removed; a compound form of the verb following, *laid*, put, or placed. *Sychem*, a Septuagint form of the Hebrew *Shechem* (Gen. 33, 18. 19. 34, 21). A later Aramaic form is *Sychar* (John 4, 5.) The Romans called the town *Flavia Neapolis*, of which the present name, *Nablus* or *Nabulus*, is an Arabic corruption. In the time of Christ, it was already a chief city of the Samaritans, and has so continued ever since. *Sepulchre*, memorial, monument (see above, on 2, 29). *A sum of money*, literally, *a price of silver* (see above, on 4, 34.) *Emor* or *Emmor*, the Greek form of the Hebrew *Hamor* (Gen. 33, 19. 34, 2.) The Vulgate and its followers supply *son* instead of *father*, but the latter agrees better with the narrative in Genesis (33, 19. 34, 2. 4. 6. 8. 13. 18. 20. 24. 26.) As Jacob was buried in the cave of Machpelah at Hebron (Gen. 49, 30. 50, 13), the first verb in this verse must refer to his sons, whose place of burial is not designated in the Old Testament. ('Jacob went down into Egypt and died there, and so did our fathers, and were removed to Shechem.') It is highly probable, however, that their bodies were transported, like their father's, into Canaan, except Joseph's, which would naturally be retained, as that of an Egyptian ruler, in the land of his adoption till the exodus. Another reasonable supposition is, that they were all removed together, but that Joseph's bones alone are mentioned (Ex. 13, 19. Josh. 24, 32), on account of the recorded oath (Gen. 50, 25.) It is far less improbable that these facts were omitted in the history, than that the remains of the eleven patriarchs were left to moulder in the land of bondage. This conclusion is confirmed by the tradition, both of the Jews and early Christians, that all the sons of Jacob were buried at Shechem. *Which Abraham bought of the sons of Emor*. But according to Gen. 33, 19, this purchase was made by Jacob; whereas Abraham had bought a place of burial near Hebron, from Ephron and the Hittites (Gen. 23, 3–20.) This apparent contradiction has been variously explained, by reading *Jacob* for *Abraham;* or by omitting *Abraham*, and construing the verb with *Jacob* in v. 15, or with an indefinite subject (*one bought it = it was bought*), both which emendations of the text are destitute of manuscript authority; or by supposing a concise and therefore an obscure allusion to both purchases—'which Abraham (and Jacob) bought of the sons of (Heth and) Emmor'—; or by admitting a confusion of the two transactions in the mind of Stephen, who was not an inspired historian. But as he was under an extraordinary influence, and endowed with extraordinary spiritual gifts, including that of wisdom (see above, on 6, 3. 5. 8. 10); and as Luke has preserved his words without correction, which, although it might evince his candor and veracity, is hardly consistent with his task as a historian; this last hypothesis (that Stephen erred), even if admissible in case of exegetical necessity, is far less natural and probable than either of the others. With respect to the concurrence or accumulation of supposed inaccuracies in this one verse (as to Jacob's burial, that of the Patriarchs, and Abraham's purchase), so far from proving one another, they only aggravate the improbability of real errors having been committed in such quick succession, and then gratuitously left on record, when they might have been so easily corrected or expunged. This circumstance, when duly weighed, makes the assumption, even of unusual constructions or of textual corruptions, however improbable on general grounds, comparatively easy. In all such cases, it is necessary to consider the difficulties which attend the supposition of mistake or contradiction, as well as that of truth and consistency, especially as skeptical critics and their Christian followers are accustomed to look only at one side of the question. In this case, for example, it is easy to cut the knot by assuming a mistake on Stephen's part, but not so easy to account for its being made by such a man, addressing such an audience, and then perpetuated in such a history, without correction or exposure, for a course of ages.

17. But when the time of the promise drew nigh, which God had sworn to Abraham, the people grew and multiplied in Egypt—

The sentence is completed in the next verse. We have here a transition from the times of Joseph to those of Moses, as the next stage in the progress of the chosen people. (*But = so* in v. 15.) *When*, lit. *as*, the Greek word being elsewhere always expressive of resemblance (see above, 2, 4. 22) not of time, as its primitive or uncompounded form sometimes is (see above, on 1, 10. 5, 24.) Here it probably means *in proportion* (or *according*) *as*, and intimates, not only absolute increase, but a progression in its rate or ratio, which agrees well with the obvious implication in the history (Ex. 1, 7. 12. 20), that the growth of Israel in Egypt was preternatural, if not miraculous. *The time of the promise* is the time that had itself been promised; or *the promise* may be put for its fulfilment. (See above, on 2, 33.) '*Sworn* (ὤμοσεν), or according to the latest critics, *promised*, *agreed* (ὡμολόγησεν). There is no oath mentioned in the passage more immediately referred to (Gen. 15, 13); but there is in the parallel promise (Gen. 22, 16). According to Maimonides, every divine assurance, such as that in Gen. 15, 13, is equivalent to an oath; and such a sanction is undoubtedly implied in every covenant or stipulation between God and man. *The people*, not yet organized as a nation, but preparing, by this very increase, to become one, *grew and multiplied*, or more exactly, *was multiplied*, the active and passive being probably combined, as an exhaustive or complete expression of the whole idea. Or perhaps the one may be intended to express spontaneous, natural increase, and the other that which was extraordinary, or produced by the immediate act of God. Here, and throughout this whole discourse, the speaker is not giving a historical lesson, but reminding his hearers of the most familiar facts, for a specific purpose. (See above, on v. 2.) Having shown the divine independence of all outward forms, by reciting the extraordinary changes which occurred in the experience of the Patriarchs, he proceeds to show the same thing, by exhibiting the still more startling contrast between Patriarchal freedom and Egyptian bondage on the one hand, and the Mosaic dispensation on the other. With a view to this, he mentions the condition of the people while in bondage, and the providential means by which the next change was prepared for and eventually brought about.

18. Till another king arose, which knew not Joseph.

The sentence is completed from the foregoing verse. *Until* is not to be interpreted exclusively, i. e. as meaning that the growth then ceased, but negatively, i. e. as meaning merely that it had not ceased before. 'This process of increase was still in operation, when a new king *arose*, etc.' This verb does not imply rebellious usurpation (see above, on 5, 17. 36. 37. 6, 9), nor even accession to the throne, which is suggested by the word *king* and the context, but appearance in the world or on the field of history. *Another king*, not only numerically different, but, as the Greek word sometimes means, diverse in kind or quality. (See above, on 2, 4, and compare 1 Cor. 14, 21. Mark 16, 12. Rom. 7, 23. Gal. 1, 6. James 2, 25. Heb. 7, 11, 15. Jude 7.) This may refer, either to his ignorance of Joseph, or to his being of another house or dynasty, as stated by Josephus. Various attempts have been made, both by ancient and modern writers, to identify this "new king" (Ex. 1, 8), but without success. *Who knew not Joseph* is by some supposed to mean, who did not love him or regard him, or remember his great public services, as reasons for kind treatment to his brethren and descendants. But no clear example can be cited of the Greek or Hebrew verb in this sense (the most plausible, 1 Thess. 5, 12, admitting of a strict interpretation), and the proper one is perfectly appropriate, to wit, that the new king was partially or wholly ignorant of Joseph and his public measures, either from lapse of time or intervening revolutions. The idea of indifference or enmity, at all events, is not expressed by this phrase (*knew not*), but suggested by the context.

19. The same dealt subtilly with our kindred, and evil entreated our fathers, so that they cast out their young children, to the end they might not live.

The same, or *this*, i. e. this king who knew not Joseph. The pronoun refers to the remoter antecedent, as in 4, 11. *Dealt subtilly*, outwitting, circumventing, by the use of indirect and crafty means to break the strength of Israel, both by excessive labor and by promoting the exposure of their children. The Greek verb is borrowed from the Septuagint version of Ex. 1, 10. *Our kindred*, family, or race, as in 4, 6 above, and 13, 26 below, where the same word is translated *stock*, as it is in the Rhemish version here (*circumventing our stock;* Wiclif, *beguiled our kin.*) *Evil entreated*, or in modern English, *ill treated*, maltreated, persecuted. (See above, on v. 6.) *Our fathers*, as in vs. 12. 15; compare v. 2. *So that they cast out* makes the infanticide the mere result of this atrocious persecution, while the Greek seems to make it the design of Pharaoh. *Cast out* (or *expose*), literally, *made exposed*, as we say, *made known* and the like (see Matt. 12, 16. John 7, 23.) *To the end*, in order that, implying purpose, either that of Pharaoh in oppressing them, or that of the oppressed, in their despair desiring to exempt their children from the sufferings which they felt themselves. *Might not live*, literally, be preserved alive (as in Luke 17, 33; compare Mark 8, 35), a common Hellenistic meaning of the verb, which in the Classics denotes procreation. (See the Septuagint version of Gen. 6, 19. Ex. 1, 17.)

20. In which time Moses was born, and was exceeding fair, and nourished up in his father's house three months.

As the word translated *time* does not denote a period but a juncture (see above, on 1, 7, and compare 3, 20), it might be better to translate the phrase here, *at which time*, i. e. when the crafty and cruel persecution of the Israelites by the Egyptians was at its height. It was at this crisis in the history of the chosen people, that their great deliverer came into the world. *Exceeding fair*, or as it is translated in the margin of the English Bible, *fair to God*, which is variously explained to mean *like God* (divinely fair), a common expression in the classics; or *through God* (made so by him); or *before God* (in God's sight or estimation); or simply *very fair*, as an idiomatic periphrasis of the superlative, of which other examples are supposed to occur in 1 Cor. 3, 6. 2 Cor. 1, 12. 10, 4. Col. 2, 19. The Greek adjective means *civic* as opposed to *rustic;* then *urbane* or polished; then *agreeable* or pleasant; and then *beautiful*, or rather (according to Aristotle) *pretty*, as applied to familiar and diminutive objects. In Heb. 11, 23, the same word is rendered *proper*, in the old English sense of fair or handsome. Some suppose this beauty of the child to have been supernatural, as an indication of what was in reserve for him, and the reason of his being concealed three months. Josephus describes him as "divine in form," and the Roman historian Justin also speaks of his extraordinary beauty. *The house of his father*, i. e. Amram (Ex. 6, 20.)

21. And when he was cast out, Pharaoh's daughter took him up, and nourished him for her own son.

When he was cast out (or *exposed*), in Greek, *him being exposed*, or according to several of the oldest manuscripts, *he being exposed*. One old version adds, *by his people*, another, *by his mother*, a third, *along* (or *in*) *the river*, which is also found in several Greek manuscripts, and is retained in Wiclif's English (*put out in the flood*.) *Pharaoh's daughter* is named by several of the ancient writers, but so discordantly as to evince that the names are fictitious or conjectural. *Took him up*, not out of the water, which would have been otherwise expressed in Greek, but rescued, saved him, as opposed to his exposure, the two Greek verbs being those employed in the classics to express the same two acts. *Nourished up*, nursed, brought up, the active form of the same verb that occurs in the preceding verse. *For her own son*, as (or to be) a son for herself. This last idea is also expressed by the middle voice of the Greek verb. (See above, on 1, 2. 24.)

22. And Moses was learned in all the wisdom of the Egyptians, and was mighty in words and in deeds.

The consequence of this adoption was an education such as Moses could not have received otherwise. *Learned* seems here to be not an adjective but a participle, in the old sense of *taught, instructed*, which is the meaning of the Greek verb. The wisdom of Egypt was proverbial in the ancient world, being rivalled, in the general estimation, only by that of the East, the region of the Tigris and Euphrates, which was regarded as the cradle of the human race, and the fountain-head even of Egyptian knowledge. In this oriental wisdom Daniel was instructed (Dan. 1, 4), and both are joined in describing that of Solomon, which "excelled the wisdom of all the children of the East country and all the wisdom of Egypt" (1 Kings 5, 10; in the English Bible, 4, 30.) Philo pretends to enumerate the branches of knowledge, in which Moses was instructed, including astrology and magic, but commits a gross anachronism when he adds that the rest of the encyclopedia (or circle of the sciences) he learned from Grecian teachers; whereas even Pythagoras and Plato are represented in the Greek tradition as disciples of Egyptian sages. The last clause describes the effect of this instruction upon Moses. *Mighty in words and deeds* (or as the oldest manuscripts and versions have it, *his deeds*), is supposed by some to be at variance with his own description of himself as "slow of speech" (Ex. 4, 10);

to remove which contradiction, *words* has been taken in the sense of writings, doctrines, laws, predictions, and *deeds* (or *works*) in that of miracles or military feats, such as Josephus ascribes to Moses when he makes him the conqueror of Ethiopia. Another solution is to give the whole phrase a proverbial sense, as meaning strong in every way, in theory and practice, in judgment and in action, as Thucydides describes Themistocles, "most able both to say and do." The necessity of all these explanations is removed by the simple observation that the passage in Exodus relates to readiness or fluency, but this to energy and force of speech.

23. And when he was full forty years old, it came into his heart to visit his brethren the children of Israel.

This is Tyndale's version; Wiclif gives the first clause more exactly (*when the time of forty years was filled to him.*) This chronological specification is nowhere else contained in Scripture, but agrees well with the old Talmudical tradition, that Moses was forty years in the Egyptian court, forty years in the land of Midian, and forty years with Israel in the desert. (See below, on v. 30, and compare Ex. 7, 7. Deut. 34, 7.) Another tradition, of inferior authority, assigns him twenty years of age at this time. *Forty years*, Gr. *a time of forty years*, or still more literally, *a forty-year time*. *When he was*, etc., Gr. *as* (*this time*) *was fulfilling*, or in modern phrase, was being fulfilled, i. e. was drawing to a close. The divine delay in fashioning such instruments has often been contrasted with the haste and impatience of corresponding human processes. *Came*, literally, came up, rose, ascended, a favourite expression in the Septuagint version (e. g. Isai. 65, 17. Jer. 3, 16. 32, 35.) The subject of the verb is not a noun understood (such as *plan* or *thought*, compare Luke 24, 38), but the verb *to visit*, which in the New Testament has a very pregnant meaning, as it almost invariably (the only exception being that in 6, 3,) means to visit for the purpose of assisting or relieving, whether the action be ascribed to God (Luke 1, 68. 78. 7, 16. Acts 15, 14. Heb. 2, 6) or man (Matt. 25, 36. 43. James 1, 27.) The unfavourable sense of visiting to punish prevails in the Old Testament (e. g. Ps. 89, 33. Jer. 14, 10.) The most appropriate sense in this place is the primary one of *looking after*, which implies that Moses now conceived the purpose, not of simply *going to see* his brethren, but of attending to their interests, becoming their protector; and that not merely as a scheme or notion of his own, but no doubt as a divine communication or suggestion, which "came up into his mind (or heart)."

24. And seeing one of them suffer wrong, he defended (him), and avenged him that was oppressed, and smote the Egyptian.

One of them, literally, *some* (*one*), or *a certain* (*man*), as the same pronoun is translated in 3, 2. 5, 1 above. That it was one of the Israelites themselves, is assumed as perfectly well known to Stephen's hearers, and also that the wrong-doer was an Egyptian. This confirms what was said above (on vs. 2, 17), that he is not communicating information, but reasoning from familiar facts. *Suffer wrong*, literally, *wronged* or *injured*. That the injury consisted in blows or other bodily violence, is probable, but not affirmed. *Defended*, literally, *warded off*, averted from one's self; but the use of the middle voice, in the sense of defending others, is found, though rarely, in the purest Attic writers. By inserting *him*, the English version seems, at first sight, to distinguish between *him that suffered wrong* and *him that was oppressed;* whereas the Greek construction is, *defended and avenged the oppressed* (*one*.) *Avenged*, however, is too strong a word, at least in modern English, to express the Greek phrase, which means properly *did justice to* (maintained the right of) *the oppressed*. Compare Luke 18, 7. 8, where *avenge* is equivalent to *vindicate* or *right*, as a judicial act. The strong sense of the same word in Rom. 12, 19. Heb. 10, 30, is determined by the context, both in the original and the quotation. *Oppressed*, literally, *worn out*, broken down by hard work (see a kindred form in 4, 2 above, and 16, 18 below), which may here refer, not merely to the struggle which Moses witnessed, but to previous maltreatment and oppressive bondage. *And smote*, not as an additional, distinct act, but *smiting*, as a simultaneous act, or rather as the mode in which the act of defence and vindication was performed. The Greek verb means properly to *knock* or *beat;* then to *wound*, and when emphatically used (like the corresponding Hebrew word) to wound mortally, to kill, which is expressly recorded by Moses himself (Ex. 2, 12.) It is an old and not improbable opinion, that *the Egyptian* was one of Pharaoh's overseers or taskmasters, by whom the

Israelites were driven to their work (Ex. 5, 6. 10. 14), and that the wrong or injury here meant was an aggravated case of their habitual severity.

25. For he supposed his brethren would have understood, how that God by his hand would deliver them; but they understood not.

By inserting *for* and the auxiliaries *would* and *would have*, the translation seems to limit what is here said to the single act of slaying the Egyptian, either as one justified by his official mission, or as a sign and symbol of the mission itself. But *supposed* or *thought* (Wiclif, *guessed*), being in the imperfect tense, denotes continued or habitual belief; he was thinking, or used to think, before he did this, that *his brethren* (or according to the latest critics, *the brethren*) *understood* (did actually know) *that God, by his hand* (i. e. the instrumental agency of Moses) not *would deliver*, but does deliver, i. e. is about, or has begun to do so, the speaker throwing himself into the time of which he speaks, and using such expressions as Moses himself might have employed. *Deliver them*, Gr. *gives to them deliverance* (or *salvation*.) Some suppose their not understanding this to be here represented as a fault or sin, since they had seen so many proofs of an extraordinary providence, and special divine purpose, in the life of Moses. Others suppose the fault to be upon the side of Moses, who, although divinely called to this great work, had prematurely entered on it, before the people had been made acquainted with his high vocation. A third opinion is that there was fault on both sides, rash zeal and revengeful ger on the part of Moses, unbelief and stupidity on that of Israel, to punish which their liberation was deferred for forty years, and Moses sent for the same term into such complete inaction and obscurity, that when God called him to the actual discharge of his important functions, he refused to undertake it (Ex. 3, 11. 13. 4, 1. 10. 13.) The allusion to the failure of the ancient Israel to recognize their temporal deliverer, no doubt involves one to the still more fatal error of their children in mistaking and disowning the Messiah. As if he had said, 'Your rejection of Christ proves nothing with respect to the truth of his pretensions; since your fathers for a time rejected Moses.' This parallel is afterwards suggested still more clearly (see below, on v. 35.)

26. And the next day, he shewed himself unto them as they strove, and would have set them at one again, saying, Sirs, ye are brethren; why do ye wrong one to another?

This is the proof of what had just been affirmed, to wit, that the people did not recognize him as the great deliverer whom they expected. *Next day*, literally, *coming* or *coming on*, ensuing, following (Wiclif, *the day suing*.) It is joined in like manner with *night* once below (23, 11), and several times used without a noun, but agreeing with *day* understood (16, 11. 20, 15. 21, 18.) The Hebrew text has *second day* (Ex. 2, 13), in reference to his first appearance as recorded in v. 25. (See above, on v. 13.) *Showed himself to them*, literally, *was seen by them*, the same form of expression as in 2, 3. The context shows that this was something more than a fortuitous appearance or encounter. It was rather a deliberate and formal presentation of himself in a public or official character. The common version therefore (*showed himself unto them*) is correct considered as a paraphrase. *As they strove*, literally, *to them striving* (*quarreling* or *fighting*.) The Greek verb is elsewhere used in the New Testament to signify a war of words, disputing, wrangling (John 6, 52. 2 Tim. 2, 24. James 4, 2.) But as the Septuagint frequently applies it to a bodily struggle or contention (e. g. Ex. 21, 22. 2 Sam. 14, 6), it is better so to understand it here. *To them* may refer to the "two men of the Hebrews," mentioned in Ex. 2, 13, and here assumed to be both well known and remembered by the hearers (see above, on v. 24); or it may be regularly construed with the nearest antecedent, *brethren*, and the combatants supposed to represent the whole mass, because suffered so to act without constraint and hinderance, or because they were in fact congenial spirits and fair samples of the general body. Here, as in v. 25, the *would have* of all the immediate English versions weakens the sense, which is, *he drove them together into peace*, i. e. he authoritatively required them to be at peace, by virtue of his office, either entered on before the time, or disowned by the people. (See above, on v. 25.) *Set them at one again*, i. e. reconciled or brought together. *Atonement*, in old English, denotes reconciliation (Rom. 5, 11.) Neither effort nor persuasion is expressed by the verb, but an act of authority. By a singular coincidence, the same verb is repeatedly employed by Homer (but without the addition of the words *to peace*) in the opposite sense of setting against each other or causing to fight. *Sirs*, literally, *men*, gentlemen (see above, on 2, 14); but some connect it with the next word, so as to mean *men–brethren*, i. e. men who are brothers, kinsmen, countrymen, and of the same religion. This was a reason both for not fighting and for not provoking others, as suggested in the following question. *Why* (the same word as in 4, 25 above) *do ye wrong* (or *treat unjustly*) *one another?* The passive participle of the same verb occurs in the first clause of v. 24.

27. But he that did his neighbour wrong thrust him away, saying, Who made thee a ruler and a judge over us?

The first words imply that one of the two was simply acting in self-defence like the Hebrew of v. 24 (compare Ex. 2. 11.) The original construction is, *the (one) wronging the neighbour*. This last word, which in Greek is properly an adverb meaning *near*, and with the article, *the (one) near* (or *next*), has here its Scriptural or Hebrew sense of fellow-man, but probably with some allusion to the more intimate relation of these combatants, expressed in the preceding verse by *brethren*. *Thrust him away*, or pushed him back, both in the literal and proper sense of a corporeal movement, and in the figurative one, which it suggests or symbolizes, of rejecting with disdain, a meaning found not only in the Septuagint version (e. g. Jer. 6, 19. Hos. 9, 17), and in the best Greek writers (such as Herodotus, Thucydides, and Plato), but also in the Greek of the New Testament (Rom. 11, 1. 2. 1 Tim. 1, 19), and in this very book (see below, on 13, 46.) In the last clause this expressive action is translated into words. The question is equivalent to a strong negation, or at least to a demand for his authority, like that addressed to Christ (Matt. 21, 23) and his apostles (see above, on 4, 7) by the rulers of Israel. The jealous feeling thus expressed is the same that was entertained towards Lot in Sodom (Gen. 19, 9), and seems to be referred to by our Lord in declining all judicial interference with men's property or secular affairs (Luke 12, 14.) *Made*, constituted, placed, appointed, as in v. 10 and in 6, 3. *Over us*, precisely the same phrase that occurs in 1, 23 above; but the latest critics change the case, though without a change of meaning. *Ruler and judge* may be generic and specific terms denoting the same thing, as in 4, 5, or distinctive terms for what would now be called judicial and executive authority. (Wiclif, *who ordained thee prince and doomsman on us?*) This taunting question shows that Moses was regarded, not as a mere intruder or officious friend, but as asserting some official right to interfere between them. And as this agrees exactly with the previous narrative, especially with vs. 23, 24, as we have just explained them, the reproaches cast by some interpreters upon the angry Hebrew, for putting so uncharitable a construction on an act of simple kindness, are entirely undeserved.

28. Wilt thou kill me, as thou didst the Egyptian yesterday?

So far from acknowledging this act of homicide as proving his official right to interfere, he taunts him with it as an act of lawless violence, and insinuates a charge that he was seeking to repeat it. The peculiar form of the interrogation ($μή$), and the emphatic introduction of the pronoun ($σύ$), make the original much stronger than the version, and almost equivalent to saying, 'Surely thou dost not mean to kill me, etc.' The verb repeated in this clause is the one translated *took up* in v. 21 above, but here used, as in 2, 23. 5, 33. 36, in the sense of despatching, making away with, or destroying. *As*, literally, *what manner*, the idiomatic phrase employed in 1, 11, and always denoting, not mere general resemblance, but specific similarity of form or circumstances; so that there is probably a covert and ironical allusion, not only to the fact that he had killed an Egyptian, but to the circumstances not here mentioned, though recorded in the Pentateuch by Moses himself (Ex. 2, 12), that he did it secretly and hid the body. As if he had said, 'Perhaps you mean to murder me and hide my body in the sand, as you did yesterday to the Egyptian.'

29. Then fled Moses at this saying, and was a stranger in the land of Midian, where he begat two sons.

Then, and, or but, as in the two preceding verses. The sense of *then* (immediately or forthwith) is sufficiently expressed by the following phrase, *at* (literally *in*) *this saying*, i. e. in the very act or time of hearing it. When it is said (Matt.

12, 41. Luke 11, 32), that the Ninevites repented *at* the preaching of Jonah, the idea may be likewise that of instantaneous or simultaneous action; but the form of expression differs more in the original than in the version. *Was a stranger,* literally, *became a sojourner,* implying change as well as actual condition, and suggesting what he left and lost, as well as what he found. The Greek noun, in the classics, means one who dwells or settles by another, but in Hellenistic usage is applied specifically to domesticated aliens (e. g. Gen. 15, 13. Ex. 2, 22), and in this place is synonymous with Moses's description of himself as "a stranger in a strange land." *The land (of) Madian,* being without the article, might seem to mean *a land (called) Madian,* but for the like expression in v. 36 (*land of Egypt*), where no such explanation is admissible. *Madian* is a sort of intermediate form or compromise between the Hebrew *Midian* and the Greek *Madiam,* the name of one of Abraham's sons by Keturah (Gen. 25, 2), also applied to his descendants, a nomadic tribe who roved about the desert between Moab, Sinai, and the Red Sea, and are therefore found in different and distant places. (Compare Ex. 3, 1. 18, 5. Num. 31, 2. Judg. 6, 1.) The last clause means that though he still felt himself a stranger, he was so far settled and domesticated among these people, as to be a husband and a father. (Compare Ex. 2, 21, 22. 4, 20. 18, 1–6.)

30. And when forty years were expired, there appeared to him, in the wilderness of Mount Sina, an Angel of the Lord, in a flame of fire in a bush.

This translation of the first clause is found in all the English versions except Wiclif's, who retains the true sense of the verb (*filled*), though not the original construction, which is that of the genitive absolute, *forty years having been fulfilled* (or *completed.*) See above, on v. 23, and 2, 1. This marks the close of another period of forty years in the history of Moses. *The wilderness of Mount Sinai* is the desert tract, through which extends the mountainous range of *Horeb.* This is the distinction made by the highest modern geographical authorities, although tradition recognizes Horeb and Sinai as northern and southern peaks of the same mountain. This tradition seems to have arisen from the fact that Moses, in his farewell discourse, no longer designates the scene of his divine legation by its proper name of *Sinai*, as he does in the earlier books, but applies to it the general name of *Horeb*. (Compare Ex. 19, 11. 18, 20. 23. 24, 16. 34, 4. 29. 32. Lev. 7, 38. 25, 1. 26, 46. 27, 34, with Deut. 1, 6. 4, 10. 15. 15, 2. 18, 16. 29, 1.) *Appeared to him*, literally, *was seen by him*, as in v. 26 and 2, 3. *An angel* (or according to the Hebrew idiom, *the angel*) *of the Lord*, see above, on 5, 19. This is explained by certain modern interpreters to mean some natural object, such as a bush struck by lightning and instantly extinguished; by some Christian writers, an extraordinary sensible impression of God's presence; by others a created angel; but by most interpreters in every age, the second person of the Godhead, even then appearing as the revealer of the Father (Matt. 11, 27. Luke 10, 22.) *A flame of fire* is in several of the oldest manuscripts, as in the Septuagint version of Ex. 3. 2, *a fire of flame*, i. e. according to a well-known Hebrew idiom, *a flaming fire*. *In a bush*, literally, *of a bush*, which gives the whole phrase an exceedingly peculiar form, although the sense is clear.

31. When Moses saw (it), he wondered at the sight, and as he drew near to behold it, the voice of the Lord came unto him.

The original construction is, *and Moses seeing . . . . and he approaching*. *Admired* (or *wondered at*) *the sight*, either in the simple sense, as denoting an object of vision, or in the stronger one of a supernatural spectacle, as in 9, 10. 12. 10, 3. 17. 19. 11, 5. 12, 9. 16, 9. 10. 18, 9, from which it will be seen that this is one of Luke's favourite expressions, being found elsewhere only in Matt. 17, 9. *To behold*, or rather *to observe*, i. e. more closely than he could while at a distance. (See below, on 11, 6. 27, 39, and compare Matt. 7, 3. Luke 6, 41. 12, 24. Heb. 3, 1. James 1, 23. 24.) *Came*, literally, became, or came into existence, became audible, precisely as in 2, 5 above.

32. (Saying), I am the God of thy fathers, the God of Abraham, and the God of Isaac, and the God of Jacob. Then Moses trembled and durst not behold.

Some of the oldest manuscripts and versions omit the name of *God* before *Isaac* and *Jacob*. The form is then the same as in 3, 13 above. In either case it is a solemn claim to be the God who covenanted with the Patriarchs, and according to our Saviour's own interpretation (Matt. 21, 32), was still their God as living spirits, one day to be reunited with their bodies. This was probably the first divine communication to Moses since his flight from Egypt. (See above, on v. 25.) *Trembled*, literally, becoming tremulous, a natural sign of fear. (See below on 16, 29, and compare Heb. 12, 21.) *Behold*, look, observe, as in v. 31.

33. Then said the Lord to him, Put off thy shoes from thy feet, for the place where thou standest is holy ground.

Then said, and said, so said, as in vs. 29. 32. *The Lord to him*, Gr. *to him the Lord*. *Put off*, lit. *loose*, untie (as in Mark 1, 7. Luke 3, 16.) *Thy shoes*, lit. *thy sole* (or *sandal*), any thing bound under the foot. The singular form is applied, as a collective, to both shoes, like the French *chaussure*, meaning shoes and stockings, or whatever is worn upon the feet. *From thy feet*, or rather, *of thy feet*, belonging to them, or now on them. The Syriac version has 'the land (or ground) on which thou standest is holy.' The holiness was moveable and temporary (except as a matter of memory), arising from the momentary presence of Jehovah. The expression of reverence or awe by uncovering the feet is very ancient, being enjoined by Pythagoras ("Unshod sacrifice and worship"), who had probably learned it in Egypt. (See also Josh. 5, 17.) The ground of it is not clear, as it can scarcely have been transferred, as some imagine, to God's presence from the floors of palaces or private houses, even supposing that the custom there existed. As the same thing is expressed among ourselves by uncovering the head, it may be a mere accidental habit or association. The most probable solution perhaps is, that it symbolized the putting away of all impurity, to which the feet are peculiarly exposed in walking (compare John 13, 10), more particularly in the East, where the Mahometans still leave their slippers at the entrance of their mosques. From Juvenal's alluding to this custom in connection with the Sabbath, it would seem to have been known to him only as a Jewish practice. Though not explicitly enjoined, it is implied in the silence of the law as to any covering of the feet, amidst such particular directions as to head-dress and other parts of the sacerdotal costume. Chrysostom points out Stephen's tacit argument against the perpetuity and absolute necessity of the temple, from the holiness ascribed to any place where God chose to reveal himself.

34. I have seen, I have seen, the affliction of my people which is in Egypt, and I have heard their groaning, and am come down to deliver them. And now come, I will send thee into Egypt.

The literal translation of the first words is, *Seeing I have seen*, a form of expression much more frequent in Hebrew than in Greek, though found in both, the very same verb being so used by Lucian (ἰδὼν εἶδον) and Arrian (ἰδὼν οἶδα.) It may either be intensive ('I have indeed seen'), or may suggest the additional idea of distinctness, frequency, duration, or the like. (See above, on 4, 17, where the form is similar, but not the same.) *Affliction*, or more exactly, *oppression*, maltreatment, the noun corresponding to the verb used in v. 6. 19 above, and in 12, 1. 18, 10 below. *My people*, belonging to me, although not yet formally organized as such, nor fully conscious of our mutual relation. *Which is in Egypt*, lit. *the (one) in Egypt*, as distinguished from all others. *Groaning* (or *sighing*) under their oppressions, whether addressed to God as a complaint, or uttered merely as a natural expression of distress. *Am come down*, or more exactly, *came down*, from heaven which is God's throne (Isai. 66, 1. Matt. 5, 34) i. e. became visible on earth. God is often represented as coming down to see for himself before he punishes. (See Gen. 11, 5. 18, 21, and compare Ps. 144, 5.) *To deliver*, see above, on v. 10, and below, on 12, 11. 23, 27. 26, 17, in all which cases the same verb is used. *And now*, since this is so, as in 3, 17 above, and 10, 5. 13, 11. 20, 22. 25. 22, 16 below. *Come*, or retaining the original adverbial form, *here! hither!* (See above, on v. 3.) *I will send*, or according to the oldest copies extant, *let me send*, the same form being used in the Septuagint version of Ex. 3, 10. The explanation of the aorist subjunctive as a future, although sanctioned by Greek usage, is unnecessary here, where a proposition is at least as natural as a peremptory order.

35. This Moses, whom they refused, saying, Who made thee a ruler and a judge? the same did God send

(to be) a ruler and a deliverer, by the hands of the Angel which appeared to him in the bush.

The repetition of the pronoun *this* is highly emphatic, both here and in the beginning of the next three verses; but it does not mean *this great man*, which is as arbitrary as to make it constantly expressive of contempt. (See above, on 6, 14.) *Refused*, denied to be what he was, i. e. a messenger from God (see above, on v. 27.) The refusal of the one man was virtually that of all; for all were of the same mind, and this was a fortuitous disclosure of the general feeling. *The same* (or this), i. e. the very same whom they rejected forty years before, (if not by word or deed, in thought and will,) and no one else. The question is repeated from v. 27, with the omission of *over us*, and even this is found in some old manuscripts. *Did God send*, or according to the latest critics, *has sent*. *To be* (or *as*) *a ruler*, see above, on 5, 31. Three of the oldest manuscripts read, *both a ruler and deliverer*, i. e. not only a ruler, which they had denied him to be, but a deliverer, which was vastly more. *Deliverer*, literally, *redeemer*, from a verb which means to buy back from captivity by payment of a ransom. The noun occurs only here; but the cognate forms, *redeem, redemption, ransom*, are repeatedly applied to Christ. (See Matt. 20, 28. Mark 10, 45. Luke 1, 68. 2, 38. 24, 21. Heb. 9, 12. 1 Pet. 1, 8.) As there is evident allusion to the parallel between Christ and Moses, and as the deliverance from Egypt was a type of that from sin, there is no need of diluting the expression so as to mean mere deliverance, without reference to ransom or redemption in the proper sense. Even in reference to this temporal salvation, if it could not be said of Moses, it could be said of God, whose messenger and instrument he was, that he had *bought* his people out of bondage, by a natural and not uncommon figure. (See Isai. 45, 13. 14.) *By the hands*, lit. *in the hand*, which may mean under the protection and control of the uncreated Angel who accompanied the chosen people. (See Ex. 14, 19. 32, 34. Isai. 63, 9.) But the five oldest manuscripts read *with the hand* (Vulg. *cum manu*), which may mean, 'clothed with the power of the Angel,' but more probably describes him as the organ of communication between God and Moses. (See the Septuagint version of Num. 15, 23. 2 Chron. 29, 25.) *The Angel who appeared* might also be grammatically rendered, *the Angel of him* (i. e. *of the God*) *who appeared to him in the bush*. But this construction is less obvious and altogether needless, as we read expressly, both in Ex. 3, 2, and in v. 30 above, that it was an Angel that appeared to him. Both readings, *in* and *with* (*the hand*), may have arisen from too close an imitation of the corresponding Hebrew phrase (בְּיַד), in which the preposition corresponds to several distinct particles in Greek; or it may be a pleonastic form for the dative of cause, manner, and instrument. (See above, on 1, 3. 5. 4, 7. 9. 10. 12.) Either is more probable than the supposition, that the *in* (ἐν) is merely the last two letters of the preceding verb, repeated by mistake. The meaning of the whole verse seems to be, that God had rebuked the incredulous and disobedient Israelites in Egypt, by sending the same man, whom they had taunted with aspiring to judicial authority, to exercise far higher functions, namely, those of a national liberator and protector.

36. He brought them out, after that he had shewed wonders and signs in (the) land of Egypt, and in the Red Sea, and in the wilderness, forty years.

This verse describes the third great period of forty years in the life of Moses. (See above, on vs. 23. 30.) *He brought them out* is not sufficiently emphatic, a defect which some versions, ancient and modern, have attempted to supply (Pesh. *this is he who brought them out.* Wicl. *this Moses.* Tynd. *and the same*). The full force of the clause is, *this* (same man) *did bring them out.* He not only received the commission, but he executed it. He was the actual leader of the Exodus, the great migration to which Israel owed its national existence. His divine legation was attested, not only by success, but by miracle. *After that he had* implies that all the signs and wonders were previous to the exode, which is inconsistent with the remainder of the verse. The aorist participle strictly means *having wrought*, but sometimes denotes a simultaneous action (Vulg. *faciens.* Tynd. *shewing ;* see above, on v. 14, and on 1, 24.) It may even mean *by working* miracles, as in 10, 39, *whom they slew and hanged*, i. e. slew by hanging, though the literal translation seems to imply that he was dead before his crucifixion. For *wonders and signs*, the Peshito has *signs and wonders and mighty deeds.* For *land of Egypt*, several of the oldest manuscripts have *the land Egypt*, others simply *Egypt. In the Red Sea* is by some translated *on* or *at the Red Sea ;* but the *in* refers to the miraculous change wrought upon the sea itself, to the passage of the Israelites through it, and to Pharaoh's destruction in it. *The Red Sea*, in the earlier Greek writers, is what we call the Indian Ocean, with its two great arms, the Persian and Arabian Gulfs, to the last of which the name is given in the Septuagint version. It was called Red, as some of the ancients thought, from the colour of the water; but even Quintus Curtius speaks of this as an ignorant mistake, and derives the Greek name from that of an old king (Erythra.) The moderns trace it to the colour of the sea-weed which abounds in it, and from which it was called in Hebrew (and in the Peshito here) *Yam Suph* (*Mare Algosum*) the Sea of Seaweed. The name Red Sea is still applied to the same narrow gulf between Arabia and Africa, about 1400 miles in length, through the northern extremity of which the Israelites passed (Ex. 14, 21. 22.) Local tradition still identifies the spot as the Bahr-al-Kolsum or Sea of Destruction, in allusion to the fate of Pharaoh's host (Ex. 14, 28.) The ancient Christian historian Orosius says that the traces of the chariot-wheels were visible in his time! All the miracles here mentioned are included in the forty years; the actual error in the wilderness, though often so described in round numbers (Num. 14, 33. Josh. 5, 6. Neh. 9, 21. Am. 2, 10), lasted only thirty-eight years (Deut. 2, 14.)

37. This is that Moses which said unto the children of Israel, A Prophet shall the Lord your God raise up unto you of your brethren like unto me; him shall ye hear.

This is the Moses presupposes their acquaintance with the history and prophecy, which last had been quoted and applied by Peter (see above, on 3, 22), and to this there may here be an allusion. As if he had said, 'this is the author of that prophecy so lately quoted and interpreted before you.' Moses was not only a type of the Messiah, but the author of one of the most striking testimonies to him. *The Lord* is omitted in the oldest manuscripts and versions (except the Peshito), and may have been inserted from the parallel passage (3, 22), for the purpose of assimilation. This may also be the case with *your*, which is omitted in several of the oldest manuscripts, while two read *our*. *Like unto me*, lit. *as me*, i. e. according to some, *as* (*he raised up*) *me*. Some copies of the Vulgate connect it with what follows (*tanquam me audietis*.

Wicl. *as me ye shall hear him.*) Most refer the *like me* to his dignity and rank (see Num. 12, 8. Deut. 34, 10) ; but it may relate to *from your brethren*, one of yourselves, *as I am* (see above, on 3, 22.) Some suppose it to describe Christ as the end of the law (Rom. 10, 4.) *Him shall ye hear* is omitted by the oldest manuscripts and fathers, and is regarded by some modern writers as another effort at assimilation on the part of the transcribers. The inference that Jesus was this prophet (John 1, 21. 25. 6, 14), Stephen leaves the Sanhedrim to draw for themselves (see above, on 2, 36), with its necessary consequence that they, not he, dishonoured Moses, by refusing to aknowledge and obey the Prophet whom he had so solemnly predicted.

38. This is he that was in the church in the wilderness, with the Angel which spake to him in the Mount Sina, and with our fathers; who received the lively oracles to give unto us.

There is here a contrast or antithesis (like that in 2, 23. 24. 3, 15. 4, 10. 5, 30) between the treatment of the same person at the hands of God and man. The Moses whom they so contemptuously slighted, was the chosen organ of communication between Israel and Jehovah, throughout the error in the wilderness. According to the best interpreters, *in the church in the wilderness* is a parenthetical specification of the time and place, and the main proposition is that Moses *was with the Angel* (then another parenthesis) *and with our fathers*, i. e. the mediator or interpreter between them. The idea of intimate and confidential intercourse with either party is rather implied than expressed. (See above, on 4, 13, and below, on 20, 18, and compare Mark 16, 10.) *Church* (Tynd. *congregation*, Rh. *assembly*) is by some understood to mean the actual assemblage at the giving of the law, because the next clause refers to a specific time and place ; but it does so only to identify the Angel, without necessarily restricting what precedes to that particular juncture. 'The Moses who communicated with the Old Testament church throughout the error in the wilderness, was the same who acted as the organ of the divine Angel at the giving of the law.' The last clause may then have reference either to the legislation or to the subsequent divine communications. *Oracles*, divine responses or authoritative declarations. The Greek word (λόγια) has been variously explained as a diminutive of (λόγος) *word*, meaning a brief, condensed, and pregnant utterance; or as the neuter of an adjective (λόγιος) meaning rational, profound, wise, and as a substantive, a wise saying. Herodotus and Thucydides apply it to the responses of the oracles (compare Rom. 3, 2. Heb. 5, 12. 1 Pet. 4, 11.) *Lively*, i. e. *living* or alive; not because uttered *viva voce*, which is both unworthy and at variance with usage; but either as the words of the living God, or as being in themselves efficacious and especially life-giving. (Compare John 6, 51. Heb. 10, 20. 1 Pet. 1, 23.) Even the law is such in its own nature (Rom. 7, 12.) The Vulgate and the oldest English versions have *the words* (Tynd. *word*) *of life. Lively oracles* is the Geneva version. Moses is here represented, not as the author, but as the recipient, of these authoritative revelations.

39. To whom our fathers would not obey, but thrust (him) from them, and in their hearts turned back again into Egypt.

The *to* at the beginning is a violation of the English idiom, copied from Tyndale by the other old translators, and arising from the needless substitution of *obey* for the original expression, *be* (or *become*) *obedient*, which is retained only in the Rhemish Bible. *Would not* is more than an auxiliary and means *were not willing*, did not choose. The repetition of the verb *thrust away* (from v. 27) suggests the idea that they still repeated or continued the same act which was at first performed by their representative on that occasion. As he refused the Prophet's mediation in the quarrel with his neighbour, so the people refused his mediation between them and God. *Turned back again into Egypt* does not refer to the attempt of the children of Israel literally to retrace their steps (see Num. 14, 4, and compare Ex. 16, 3. 17, 3), as may be inferred from Ex. 32, 1. 4. Neh. 9, 18, where they ask for the God who brought them out of Egypt, not for one who should conduct them back again. The reference is rather to their Egyptian spirit and propensities, their lingering attachment to the idolatries of their native country. (See Ezek. 20, 5–8. 24.) *In their hearts*, i. e. their thoughts and their desires, as distinguished from their outward movements.

40. Saying unto Aaron, Make us gods to go before

ACTS 7, 40. 41.

us; for (as for) this Moses, which brought us out of the land of Egypt, we wot not what is become of him.

This verse explains the statement in the one before it, that they turned back in (or with) their hearts to Egypt. How? By saying unto Aaron, &c. *Gods* might be taken as too close a translation of the plural *Elohim*, if the latter were not construed with a plural verb in the passage quoted (Ex. 32, 1, compare Gen. 20, 13. 35, 7.) It is variously explained as a categorical plural, denoting the whole class, though immediately referring to a single object; or by supposing that the people asked for a plurality of idols, but that Aaron made them only one. *To go before us*, literally, *who shall go before us*, as Jehovah had gone before them in the pillar of cloud (Ex. 13, 21), and as images were carried by the heathen in their marches. The meaning is not, who shall guide us back to Egypt? see above, on v. 39. The second clause assigns the ground of their request, to wit, the absence of Moses, not merely as a strenuous opponent of idolatry, but as the representative of Jehovah, whose place they proposed to fill by a visible representation of the divine being. *This* is commonly regarded as contemptuous; but in Hebrew and the Septuagint it is *this man*, and the Hebrew noun is one of a respectful import. Besides, how else could *this (man)* be expressed, if no contempt at all were intended? This consideration, with the opposite sense put by some upon the same pronoun in v. 35 above, shows how precarious such assumptions are, although sustained by the authority of eminent interpreters. *This Moses* has no verb agreeing with it, but is placed at the beginning of the clause as a nominative absolute, which some regard as a mere negligence of style, but others as intended to enhance the sarcasm, or at least the emphasis. Other examples of the same construction may be seen in Matt. 12, 36. John 15, 2. 7, 38. Acts 20, 3. Gal. 1, 20. *Wot not*, know not. Wiclif has a still more antiquated form (*we witten not*.) *What is become of him*, literally, what has happened to him.

41. And they made a calf in those days, and offered sacrifice unto the idol, and rejoiced in the works of their own hands.

The first verb in Greek occurs only here, and is supposed to have been coined by Stephen, or, if he did not speak in

Greek, by Luke. The nearest equivalent in English would be *calf-made*. *Offered*, literally, *led up*, i. e. to or upon the altar, or *caused to ascend*, which is the meaning of a Hebrew verb, from which comes the noun translated *burnt-offering*, but strictly meaning *what ascends*, i. e. upon the altar as a victim, or from the altar in the form of vapour. The Greek phrase here used occurs also in Herodotus, and in the Septuagint version of 1 Kings 3, 15. *The idol* (Wiclif, *mawmet*) i. e. the golden calf, designed no doubt, like the calves of Jeroboam (1 Kings, 12, 28), to represent Jehovah (Ex. 32, 4), but under a forbidden form, borrowed from the Egyptian worship of Osiris, one of their ancient kings, the reputed inventor of the plough, and tutelary god of agricultural labour, worshipped under the form of a bull, representing the productive power of nature, called Apis at Memphis and Mnevis at Heliopolis. Analogous appearances are furnished by the colossal bulls lately found at Nineveh, and by the ox as a cherubic symbol (Ezek. 1, 10.) *Rejoiced*, made merry (Ex. 32, 6), not as a mere fortuitous accompaniment, but as an essential part of the idolatrous service (see 1 Cor. 10, 7.) *Rejoiced in*, not merely on account of, or in reference to, but in the possession of, and in the closest union with, *the works of their own hands*, not the idol alone, called *works* for emphasis; or as the product of united labour; but the idol with all that appertained to it, the altar, implements of sacrifice, &c. Bengel observes that God alone has a right to rejoice in the work of his own hands; that man may rejoice in the works of God, but as soon as he begins to rejoice in his own works, he becomes an idolater.

42. Then God turned and gave them up to worship the host of heaven, as it is written in the book of the Prophets, O ye house of Israel, have ye offered to me slain beasts and sacrifices, by the space of forty years, in the wilderness?

Then, and, but, or so. *Turned and gave* is by some understood to mean *gave again*. But this, though a Hebrew idiom, is not a Hellenistic one, the first verb in all supposed examples which have been adduced, expressing a distinct and independent act. Another construction supplies *them*; he turned them from one form of idolatry to another. A third supplies his mind, his manner, or his hand. It is now commonly agreed, however, that the verb has here a reflexive meaning, as in English, and is equivalent to saying, *turned himself*, or *turned away* in anger, as Isaiah says (64, 10), "he was turned to be their enemy." A cognate verb is used below (15, 16), in the favourable sense of turning back or being reconciled. *Gave them up*, not merely suffered them, but condemned or punished by suffering them, as in Rom. 1, 24. 26. 28. *The host of Heaven* sometimes means the angels (as in 1 Kings 22, 19. Ps. 103, 21. 148, 2. Luke 2, 13), but more frequently the heavenly bodies (as in Deut. 4, 19. 2 Kings 17, 16. Isai. 34, 4. (Wiclif, the knighthood of heaven; Tyndale, the stars of the sky; Cranmer and Geneva, the host of the sky.) Because they chose to worship the true God under a forbidden form, he gave them up to Sabaism, so called from the Hebrew word for *host*. *The book of the Prophets*, i. e. either the twelve minor prophets, which were reckoned in the Jewish canon as a single volume; or in a wider sense, the whole body of the prophets, as the second great division of the Hebrew Scriptures. The quotation is from Amos 5, 25–27, in the words of the Septuagint version. The interrogation (with $\mu\dot{\eta}$) anticipates a negative answer ('you did not—did you?') and is therefore equivalent to a strong negation. This has been variously understood as meaning, that they literally offered no sacrifices in the desert, which is inconsistent with the plain terms of the history; or that their offerings were only occasional and few; or that the offerers themselves were few; or that they did not offer from right motives and in a right spirit; or that they sacrificed to devils, not to God (Lev. 17, 7. Deut. 32, 17.) As if he had said, 'Was it to me (or to your idols) that ye offered in the wilderness?' *Slain beasts* (or *victims*, Rhem. Vers. *hosts*) *and sacrifices*, i. e. offerings of all sorts, animal and vegetable, as the Hebrew words express, although the Septuagint version fails to make the distinction.

43. Yea, ye took up the tabernacle of Moloch, and the star of your god Remphan, figures which ye made to worship them; and I will carry you away beyond Babylon.

Yea, literally, *and*, as if he had said, 'and (while ye thus withheld from me the service which was due) ye took up &c.', *Took up*, i. e. as some explain it, carried in procession; but unless we refer the whole verse to the idolatry of later times, it cannot be supposed that Moses would have tolerated such unblushing heathenism in the camp of Israel, any more than he connived at the unlawful worship of Jehovah under the form of a golden calf. (See above, on v. 41.) Others, with more probability, assume a reference to the secret carrying about and worshipping of small shrines, similar to those of the Ephesian Artemis or Diana. (See below, on 19, 24.) *Tabernacle*, literally, *tent*, may then denote the shrine itself, as Diodorus Siculus, the Greek historian, mentions the "sacred tent" carried in the van of the Carthaginian army. At the same time, there is evident allusion to the tent or tabernacle of Jehovah; as if he had said, 'instead of carrying my tabernacle (or at the same time that you carried it), you took up that of *Moloch*.' The Hebrew name is *Molech*, an ancient form of the noun *melech* (*king*), sometimes written as a proper name, *Milcom* (1 Kings 11, 5. 33. 2 Kings 16, 3. 23, 13), which bears a strong resemblance to the word here used by Amos, and denoting properly *your king*. But as this idea is suggested or expressed by all the forms, there is no need of supposing that the Greek translator confounded any one of them with any other. Moloch was the national god of the Ammonites (1 Kings 11, 7), worshipped, according to the Rabbins, under the form of a brazen image with outstretched arms, into which, when heated, children were thrown as offerings and burnt alive. This horrid superstition was long practised in the valley of Hinnom on the south side of Jerusalem (1 Kings 11, 7. 2 Kings 23, 10); and that it was not unknown in the time of Moses, is clear from its express and repeated prohibition in the law (Lev. 18, 21. 20, 2. Deut. 12, 31. 18, 10.) The reference of *your king* to Moloch, therefore, is in perfect keeping with historical analogy. In the next clause there is a transposition of the Hebrew words, which does not necessarily affect the sense. *Remphan* is not in the original, unless it be identified with *Chiun* (כיון), which some interpreters explain as an appellative, denoting framework, stand, or pedestal, but which may also be so pointed as to read *Kevan*, and this, according to some eminent interpreters, might easily be changed, by successive transcription, into *Revan*, *Refan* (or *Rephan*), *Remphan*, as it is variously written in the manuscripts both of Acts and Amos. Another mode of reconciling the Greek and Hebrew forms, instead of assuming a corruption in the text, identifies the two as Semitic and Egyptian names of *Saturn*, both as a planet and a deity, which some go further and identify with Moloch, thus accounting for the human victims offered up to both, and for the mention of a star in the passage now before us, as well as of the heavenly host in the preceding verse. By Coptic scholars, *Remphan* is variously explained to mean "light-giver," "dweller in heaven," and "king of heaven," on which ground some suppose it to denote the sun. *Figures*, forms, or types, *which ye made*, Heb. and Sept. *for yourselves*, to which Luke or Stephen adds by way of explanation, *to adore* (or *worship*.) *And* (*therefore*, as expressed in the Geneva Bible), *I will remove you* (as the same version has it), i. e. make you migrate (as in v. 4 above). All the other English versions have *translate you*. *Beyond* (Wiclif, *into*) *Babylon* substituted for *beyond Damascus* (Am. 5, 27, Heb. and Gr.), which is not an error or an inadvertence, but designed to bring the prophecy, without any real change of meaning, into contact and agreement with the historical associations of the people in relation to the Babylonish exile.

44. Our fathers had the tabernacle of witness in the wilderness, as he had appointed, speaking unto Moses, that he should make it according to the fashion that he had seen.

The tabernacle of Moloch naturally suggests, by way of contrast, the *tabernacle of witness* or *testimony*. This is the phrase constantly employed in the Septuagint to translate a Hebrew one meaning the *tabernacle of congregation*, or rather of *appointment*, not the tent belonging to the congregation or host of Israel, nor the tent in which they were accustomed to assemble, but the tent where God appointed to meet with them, or the place of meeting between God and Israel, or Moses as their representative. (See Ex. 25, 22. Num. 17, 19, in the English Bible, 17, 4.) The Greek translators seem to have confounded this phrase with another, sometimes applied to the tabernacle, as a witness of the covenant between Jehovah and his people, or as containing the tables of the law, which were a divine testimony against sin. (See Num. 9, 15. 18, 2. 17, 22. 23, in the English Bible, 17, 7. 8.) The use of both names in the law makes the substitution in the case before us wholly unimportant. *Our fathers had*, literally, *was to our fathers*, which is the reading of the oldest manuscripts and latest critics. The common text is, *was in* (i. e. *among*) *our fathers*. *Appointed*, arranged, ordered, see below, on 18, 2. 20, 13. 23, 31. 24, 23. *Speaking*, more exactly, *the* (*one*) *speaking*, or as it is translated in the margin of our Bible, *he who spake*. The command referred to is the one recorded in Ex. 25, 9, 40. 26, 30. (Compare Heb. 8, 5.) While the preceding verse establishes one part of Stephen's argument, that founded on the national unworthiness, this verse establishes the other, that derived from the comparatively recent origin and frequent changes of the sanctuary. Not only the temple, but the tabernacle which preceded it, had no existence till the exodus from Egypt, the divine command to make it being still on record in the books of Moses. *Fashion*, type, or model, the same word that is rendered *figure* in v. 43.

45. Which also our fathers that came after brought in with Jesus into the possession of the gentiles, whom God drave out before the face of our fathers, unto the days of David.

The tabernacle thus planned and constructed lasted only till the time of David. *Which*, from its form in Greek, can have no antecedent except *tabernacle* in v. 44. *Also*, i. e. not only its origin, but its later history, is perfectly well known. *Our fathers* again identifies the speaker with the hearers, as belonging to the same race (see above, on vs. 2, 12, 15.) *That came after*, literally, *succeeding* (*one another*), or still more probably, *receiving* (*from each other*), and transmitting by succession, which approaches very nearly to the idea of *inheriting*. *Brought in*, i. e. into the promised land, or land of Canaan, which there was the less need of expressly naming, because Stephen was within its borders when he spoke. It is as if he had said, *brought in here* (or *hither*). *Jesus*, the Septuagint form of *Joshua*, occurs also in Heb. 4, 8, and in both cases creates some confusion in the minds of English readers. *With Jesus*, i. e. when they followed Joshua, or marched along with him, to conquer Canaan. *Brought in....into*, an inelegant if not ungrammatical construction, seems to mean that *the fathers brought the tabernacle into possession of the Gentiles*, which must either signify that they were in possession of the tabernacle, or it of them; but the former is untrue and the latter unmeaning. Still more incorrect and arbitrary is the explanation of *possession* as equivalent to *land possessed*, or *territory*, since the Greek word means the act of seizure or of taking possession. The true construction of the clause is, *which our fathers* (i. e. the younger race who came in under Joshua) *inheriting*, receiving by succession (from the older race, who came out of Egypt, and by whom it was constructed), *brought in* (to the land of promise, when they came themselves) *with Joshua, in* (or *at*) *the conquest* (forcible possession, capture) *of the nations* (who had previously occupied it.) This use of *possession* to mean *dispossession*, or the act of dispossessing, corresponds exactly to that of the Hebrew verb (הוֹרִישׁ) in speaking of this very matter. (See Ex. 34, 24. Num. 32, 21. Deut. 4, 38.) *Drave out*, literally, *pushed* (or *thrust*) *out*, is a very strong expression, near akin to those in vs. 27, 39 above. *Before the face*, literally, *from the face* (or *presence*), implying flight and total disappearance. In the famous inscription, which Procopius professes to have seen in Africa, recording the arrival and settlement of fugitives from Canaan there, a similar expression is employed ("who fled from the face of the robber, Joshua the son of Nun.") *Until the days of David*, if connected with the words immediately preceding, describes the expulsion of the Canaanites as gradual, and not completed till the reign of David. But this, although historically true, would not have been expressed by the aorist (ἔξωσεν), which denotes an act performed once for all. Nor is it relevant to Stephen's purpose to relate how the Canaanites were driven out, but rather to describe the condition of the sanctuary during that long interval. From Joshua to David, God abode among his people in a moveable tent, which was often shifted from place to place, and handed down from one generation to another.

46. 47. Who found favour before God, and desired to find a tabernacle for the God of Jacob; but Solomon built him an house.

A new era in the history of the sanctuary opens with "the days of David," which had just been mentioned (v. 45.) The repetition of the verb *to find* can hardly be unmeaning or for tuitous. He did find favour before God (i. e. in his presence or his estimation, as in 4, 19. 6, 5 above), as to many other matters, or in general; but this did not satisfy him, he desired to find something more, to wit, a dwelling for Jehovah. *De-*

sired (Cranmer, *would fain have found*), or more exactly, *asked* (as a favour) *for himself* (the idea suggested by the middle voice, as in 3, 14 above), asked permission, begged leave, which agrees exactly with the governing desire and cherished purpose of his life, so beautifully expressed in the 132d Psalm. *To find*, which occurs there also, and cannot therefore be a mere allusion to the same verb in the first clause, may refer to the discovery of the place where the temple was to be erected, which was made known to David by a special revelation (1 Chr. 21, 22. 26. 22, 1). The use of the word *tabernacle*, in all the English versions, makes a false antithesis between it and *house* in v. 47; as if David had only sought to pitch a tent, and Solomon had actually built a house; whereas the first word (not the same that had been used in v. 44, but a derivative or cognate form) means any shelter, being applied in classical usage to the cover of a wagon or a bed &c., and here denotes precisely the same thing with *house*. There is really a tacit contrast between David and Solomon, in favour of the former, which is apt to be neglected, but without which Stephen's words cannot be fully understood. Solomon, notwithstanding his wisdom and the splendour of his reign, holds a very inferior place to David in the Scriptures, being scarcely mentioned after the close of his own history, and only as a sort of executor to his father. This being well known to the priests and scribes whom Stephen was addressing, he employs it to enforce his argument, but tacitly and indirectly, lest he should appear to speak indecorously of so great and wise a king as Solomon. What is thus suggested or implied may be brought out more distinctly by a paraphrase. 'So far is a permanent and solid temple from being essential to acceptable worship, that even David, the favourite of Jehovah, the man after God's own heart, whose darling wish it was to find a shelter and a home for his divine protector, was not suffered to erect the house which he had planned, and for which he had collected the materials, but it was Solomon who built it!' (Wiclif, *Solomon builded the house to him*.) *God of Jacob* (in allusion to Ps. 132, 2. 5), i. e. the national and covenanted God of Israel, as the chosen people.

48. Howbeit the Most High dwelleth not in temples made with hands, as saith the Prophet:

The sentence is continued in the following verse, to which the last clause of this verse refers, and not to the preceding words, which are a summary or paraphrase of Solomon's own language at the dedication of the temple. "Will God indeed dwell on the earth? Behold, the heaven and heaven of heavens cannot contain thee; how much less this house that I have builded!" (1 Kings 8, 27. 2 Chron. 6, 1. 2. 18.) These words, considering by whom and in what circumstances they were uttered, cannot involve an absolute condemnation of material temples, but only of their abuse. Under the ceremonial law, the doctrine of God's presence with his people was symbolized by giving him a home among them, and resembling theirs, a tent while they were wandering, a solid house when they were permanently settled. But this was a temporary institution, and any attempt to prolong it, after the time set for its abrogation, was contrary, not only to the gospel, but to the spirit of the law itself. No stronger proof of this could be adduced than the testimony of Solomon, the very builder of the temple which they now almost worshipped as immutable; for the temples built by Solomon, Zerubbabel, and Herod, were regarded as historically and morally identical. That Solomon is not named, or his words exactly quoted, will appear less strange if this verse and the one before it are thrown together as a single sentence, which will also remove the inequality in the division of the text. As if he had said, 'Solomon indeed did build the temple; but you know who said, when it was dedicated, that the Most High dwelleth not &c.' *Howbeit*, copied by our version from three older ones (Tyndale, Cranmer, and Geneva), is in Greek the usual adversative (ἀλλά), properly answering to *but* in English, whereas *but* (δέ) in v. 47 might as well have been translated *and* or *then*. *The Most High* varies strangely in the old English versions; Wiclif has *the High God;* Tyndale and Cranmer, *he that is highest of all;* Geneva, *the Most Highest;* Rheims, *the Highest*, which is nearest to the form of the original. *Temples* is omitted by the oldest manuscripts and latest critics, having probably crept into the text, by assimilation, from 17, 24 below. The Rhemish version supplies *houses*, Wiclif *things;* the Vulgate nothing (*manufactis.*)

49. Heaven is my throne, and earth is my footstool; what house will ye build me, saith the Lord, or what is the place of my rest?

This is the saying of the Prophet cited at the close of the preceding verse. The unskilful division of the text throws the whole into confusion. The true division would have been as follows. '47. And Solomon built him a house, but (Solomon well knew and publicly declared that) the Most High dwelleth not in hand-made (temples). 48. As (likewise) saith the Prophet, Heaven is my throne, etc.' The quotation is made from the Septuagint, with few and unimportant variations. The Prophet quoted is Isaiah (66, 1. 2), and the passage that in which he winds up all his prophecies with an express prediction of the change of dispensations, of the time when Jehovah would no longer dwell in temples (v. 1) but in human hearts (v. 2); when the ritual, although divinely instituted, would be no less hateful than idolatry itself (v. 3), and they who still cling to it would be fearfully but righteously requited (v. 4.) This remarkable prophecy is doubly appropriate to Stephen's purpose; first, as a declaration of the general truth before affirmed by Solomon, and therefore showing that the same doctrine was maintained by the prophets between him and Christ; and then, as a pointed and direct prediction of the very changes that were taking place when Stephen spoke. A little amplified and paraphrased, the meaning of the sentence is as follows. 'The arbitrary unessential nature of all temples was affirmed by Solomon in dedicating his; a doctrine afterwards repeated by Isaiah in the very act of pointing out the temporary nature of the ceremonial law, denouncing the divine wrath upon those who should still cling to it, when abrogated by the same authority that first enacted it, and formally predicting the precise change, which I am charged with having blasphemously threatened!' *Throne*, in all the older English versions, is *seat*, which is the primary usage of the Greek word, with particular reference in Homer to a high seat with a footstool; in Herodotus (with *royal*) to a chair of state; and in Xenophon (without it) to a throne in the restricted sense, which is the one belonging to the word in the New Testament. *Will ye build* is the true sense of the Hebrew word, and therefore more correct than the common version of Isaiah. *Place of my rest*, i. e. my permanent abode after wandering so long without one, a frequent description of the temple as contrasted with the tabernacle which preceded it. (See 2 Sam. 7. 6. 2 Chron. 6. 41. Ps. 132, 8. 14.)

50. Hath not my hand made all these (things)?

The division of the verses here was probably made in imitation of the Hebrew, where this sentence is the first clause of the second verse, but forming only a small part of it, and as the rest is not here quoted, it would have been better to put all Isaiah's words with Stephen's prefatory formula together, instead of dividing them among three verses, thus obscuring the connection, and attaching the form of quotation (*as the Prophet says*), not to the language of Isaiah, but to that of Solomon or Stephen himself. We have here the most considerable variation from the form of the original, as well as of the Greek version, an interrogation (*hath not*, etc.?) being substituted for an affirmation (*all these hath my hand made*), but without a change of meaning, since the question admits only of an affirmative answer. The passage in Isaiah presents a striking climax. First, the temples made by men are contrasted with the great material temple of the universe; then this is itself disparaged by Jehovah as his own handiwork, and still more in comparison with a nobler temple of a spiritual nature, the renewed and contrite heart. (Compare Isai. 57, 15. Ps. 34, 18. 138, 6. 2 Cor. 6, 16.) A bare citation would of course suggest the whole connection to the minds of Stephen's judges.

51. Ye stiff-necked and uncircumcised in heart and ears! Ye do always resist the Holy Ghost: as your fathers (did), so (do) ye.

One of Stephen's lines of argument was now completed. He had shown, by a simple but masterly historical deduction, the temporary nature of the ceremonial law, and of the temple as a part of it, concluding with a reference to Solomon himself, and to Isaiah, who had foretold the same changes now foretold by Stephen. What link could have been added to this chain of proof? Had he pursued the history and multiplied quotations, as he might have done from Jeremiah (7, 4) and other later prophets, he would only have consumed time and patience without adding to the strength of an argument already finished and wound up by citing the great builder of the temple and the great evangelical prophet, as authorities to prove that the temple itself was designed to answer a temporary purpose, and that no sin or folly could be greater than that of trying to make it answer any other. All that was left then was to take up and complete his other line of argument, designed to show, by means of the same history which he had been expounding, that the Jews had always been unfaithful to their trust, and that the abrogation of the present system was not only necessary to the execution of God's purpose as revealed from the beginning, but a righteous retribution of the sins of those by whom the system was administered. Having prepared the way for this conclusion by referring to the sins of Joseph's brethren, and of the Israelites in Egypt and the wilderness, he now suggests the conclusion itself, not by a formal inference, but by a terrible invective, summing up all that he had said on this point in a brief description of the men whom he addressed, and of the nation which they represented. There is no need, therefore, of supposing any interruption in the thread of his discourse, much less a passionate excitement caused by an appearance of hostility or inattention in his hearers. Such an assumption is not only quite gratuitous, but does dishonour to the memory of Stephen, by ascribing to a sudden fit of anger what was really suggested by the Holy Ghost, besides the folly of supposing that a grave historian, and above all an inspired one, would leave on record an unfinished speech, which never reached the point (as some imagine) where it might have done some good to those who heard it. This whole idea of a sudden interruption and a violent apostrophe is founded on the notion, that this long discourse of Stephen is a rambling talk which never comes to any point, and therefore must have been unfinished; or at most a desultory incoherent compend of the national history, which could not be complete unless brought down to date; whereas the speech is a historical argument, in which the facts are rather presupposed than formally related; and as soon as it has reached the conclusion aimed at, it is instantly arrested. Thus understood, the meaning of the verse before us is that, as the ancient Israel had always, as a nation, been rebellious and unfaithful, so the present generation had exactly the same character, and therefore might expect the evils threatened to their fathers. To them the Prophets had applied the same reproachful epithets which Stephen here applies to his accusers and his judges. *Stiff-necked*, rebellious, like a stubborn ox, refusing to receive the yoke, is never said of individuals as such, but only of a race or a contemporary generation. (See Ex. 32, 9. 33, 3. 5. 34, 19. Deut. 9

6. 13.) In one place (Deut. 10, 16) Moses has connected it, as Stephen does in this place, with the figure of *a heart uncircumcised*. (See also Lev. 26, 41. Deut. 30, 6. Jer. 9. 26. Ezek. 44, 7.) That of an *ear uncircumcised* is also used by Jeremiah (6, 10.) These expressions denote far more than impurity or insensibility, however great. Whatever circumcision may have symbolized, or naturally represented, of a moral nature, it was chiefly regarded by the Jews as a distinctive sign of their relation to Jehovah as his people, and entire segregation from all other races. The thought most readily suggested by the epithet *uncircumcised*, so common in the Hebrew Scriptures (e. g. Gen. 34, 14. Ex. 12, 48. Judg. 14, 3. 15, 18. 1 Sam. 14, 6. 17, 26. 36. 31, 4. 2 Sam. 1, 20. 1 Chr. 10, 4. Isai. 52, 1. Jer. 9, 25. Ezek. 28, 10. 31, 18), is not that of personal uncleanness, whether physical or moral; but that of national and ecclesiastical exclusion from the favour of Jehovah and the privileges of his people. Its nearest equivalent, as here applied, is *heathenish*, the most insulting name that could be given to a Jew in any age or any country, as implying not merely social degradation and inferiority, but treason to Jehovah and unfaithfulness to Moses, by a violation of the most solemn and important trust that God had ever confided to a people. The compound terms, *uncircumcised in heart and ears*, mean therefore those who hear and think and feel like gentiles, like the heathen; and their sudden application to the Sanhedrim, instead of necessarily implying a departure from the theme of his discourse, is rather a tremendous summing of it up in the conclusion, that these proud representatives and rulers of the chosen people were in fact mere heathen. Some conception of the force of this concluding blow may be obtained by supposing one impeached among ourselves to describe the senate at whose bar he stands as slaves and negroes. Even this, however, is without the sting belonging to the charge, not only of political and social infamy, but of religious apostasy and reprobation. Far from being an ungovernable burst of passion, this was the other great conclusion at which Stephen had been aiming from the first, and which was now established by irrefragable proofs, not only with respect to the contemporary race, but also to preceding generations, whose accumulated guilt might justly be rewarded with the loss and abrogation of those very institutions which had been the object of their trust and worship. (See Matt. 23, 32, 35. 36. Luke 11, 50, and compare 2, 40.)

Resist, lit. *fall against*, implying active as well as passive opposition to the *Holy Ghost*, as the divine author of all revelation, whether history or prophecy, doctrine or precept, law or gospel. *Ye do always* is addressed to the whole race of Israel, past and present, as a collective or ideal person, as explained in the remainder of the sentence, which is greatly weakened in translation by supplying *did* and *do*, instead of construing all the nominatives with one verb. 'As your fathers so yourselves are ever resisting the Holy Ghost.' (Wicl. as your fathers, so ye. Rhem. as your fathers, so ye also.)

52. Which of the Prophets have not your fathers persecuted? And they have slain them which shewed before of the coming of the Just One, of whom ye have been now the betrayers and murderers.

It now becomes still more clear, that Stephen's speech is not unfinished, from the way in which he comes back to his starting-point, and makes a most effective application of the facts recited to his own case. The first clause is a specification of the sweeping charge, that both they and their fathers had constantly withstood the Holy Ghost, as he spoke to them, not only in the Law, but in the Prophets, who were really his messengers and spokesmen. The form is not affirmative but interrogative, and does not necessarily exclude a qualified or palliative answer. It is not therefore strictly hyperbolical; but even if it had been a direct assertion, that they had rejected and maltreated every prophet who had ever come to them, so natural a figure could be quarreled with by none but captious cavillers or hypercritical grammarians. (See above, on 3, 24, and compare Matt. 23, 34–36. Luke 13, 33.) There may seem to be a reference to two distinct classes in the two first clauses of this verse; but the second only gives a more particular description of the prophets who had just been spoken of, by mentioning their great official function, that of foretelling (*shewed before* is Tyndale's version) the Messiah, who is here, as in 3, 14 above, emphatically called *the Just* (*One*), that is, innocent before the law of what he had been charged with, and intrinsically righteous (Wicl. *the rightful man.* Tynd. *that just.*) The original construction is, *did not your fathers persecute and kill those foretelling*, etc. *Ye have been*, or more exactly, *have become*, by virtue of your late proceedings. *Betrayers*, (Wicl. *traitors*) is a term applied elsewhere (Luke 6, 16) to Judas Iscariot. *Betrayers and murderers* express two of the blackest crimes which one man can commit against another, both which are here charged home by Stephen on his judges, and through them upon the people whom they represented. *Now* and *ye* stand in emphatic opposition to the ancient times and former generations, which had just been mentioned. This antithesis, however, only serves to aggravate the guilt of those immediately addressed, in comparison even with the guilt of their progenitors; for these had only persecuted prophets, whereas those had both betrayed and murdered the Messiah, to predict whose advent the old prophets had been sent from God. Of this great personal and public crime he thus reminds them, with a view not only to their own conviction but to his defence, as showing that the mere fact of his prosecution no more proved him guilty of the crimes alleged, than the bloody persecution of the Prophets, and of Christ himself, could have a similar effect in their case.

53. Who have received the law by the disposition of angels, and have not kept it.

The obvious meaning of the verse is that the Jews, as a nation, had betrayed the highest trust, and proved themselves unworthy of the greatest honour ever granted to a people. They, the recipients and depositaries of an exclusive revelation, had themselves endeavoured to defeat the very end for which it was vouchsafed to them. Beyond this, accusation or invective could not well be carried. In point both of rhetoric and logic, Stephen could not have concluded more effectively. There is no ground, therefore, for the favourite idea of interpreters and editors, that his voice was here drowned by the cries of his infuriated hearers, and that not only the discourse but the sentence is unfinished, as indicated even to the eye, in some editions of the Greek text, by the mode of printing. *Who* ought rather to be *ye who*, as the form of the Greek relative is one employed, not merely to continue or connect the sentence, but to introduce a further description of its subject. As if he had said, 'and this has been done, not by Gentiles, but by you, the very people who received the law,' etc. Only the emphasis, and not the meaning, of the passage is dependent on the doubtful and disputed words translated *by the disposition of angels*. Whatever may be their specific meaning, they are evidently meant to aggravate the charge here brought against the Jewish nation, by exalting and ennobling that peculiar system, under which they lived, in which they trusted, and of which they boasted, but against which they were nevertheless guilty of the worst conceivable offence, to wit, that they refused to keep (i. e. observe, obey) it. Another undisputed fact is, that the aggravating circumstance suggested is the agency of angels in the giving of the law; the only question is, in what that agency consisted. The Greek noun (διαταγάς) rendered *disposition* (after the Rhemish Bible, whereas Wiclif, Tyndale, and Geneva have *ordinance*, and Cranmer *ministration*) occurs only once in the Septuagint version (Ezra 4, 11) and nowhere in the classics; but its general meaning is determined by its obvious deduction from the verb employed in v. 44 above, and by the usage of a kindred noun (διάταξις) to signify arrangement, disposition, applied by Herodotus to the drawing up of troops, and by Polybius to a will or testamentary order. In accordance with this usage, some would give it here a military sense, *among troops of angels*, in allusion to their presence on Mount Sinai, which, though not recorded in the history, appears to be implied in Deut. 33, 2. 3 (where the word *angels* is actually inserted by the Septuagint version), and still more clearly in Ps. 68, 17. Gal. 3, 19. Heb. 2, 2. The sense obtained by this construction is a good one in itself, and sufficiently sustained by the analogy of Scripture. The only objection, but perhaps a fatal one, is the meaning which it puts upon the preposition (εἰς) contrary to all Greek usage. The same objection lies, at least in some degree, against the common explanation, *by* (or *through*) *the ministration of angels*, which agrees well with Paul's language in the places above cited; but in both those places the preposition (διά) properly means *by* or *through*. The only meanings of the one here used that can be justified by usage are *at*, *upon*, in reference to time (as in Matt. 12, 41), and *as*, *for* (as in v. 21 above.) Assuming the latter, an old Greek interpreter explains the clause to mean, that they received the law *as* (or *for*) *angelic institutions*, i. e. such as, if observed, would have made them like or equal to the angels (Luke 20, 36.) Assuming the other, we obtain the much more natural and obvious idea of a law received *at the orders* (or *command*) *of angels*, not as its authors or as legislators, which is sometimes made an argument against this explanation, but as messengers or heralds, through whom the divine communications passed, as a military word of command does from rank to rank, or from officer to officer, until it reaches the whole corps or army. The silence of the history, as to any such proceeding at Mount Sinai, only raises a presumption, which can easily be set aside by countervailing evidence, and such would seem to be afforded by the passages already cited, and especially by Paul's repeated declaration, that it was *through angels* that God's *word* was *spoken* (Heb. 2, 2), and his *law enacted* or *ordained* (Gal. 3, 19), the very verb from which the noun before us is immediately derived. This explanation is moreover recommended by its really including the one first proposed (*among troops of angels*), but with an additional suggestion that they were not mere spectators, and without a violation of Greek idiom or usage. In comparison with this, no attention need be given to the many other senses which have been proposed; by Chrysostom, for instance, who refers it to the angel in the burning bush, and by Lightfoot, who takes *angels* in its primary sense (*messengers*) and then applies it to the prophets, as inspired expounders of the law. It is this angelic agency or ministration in the giving of the law that Stephen here employs to aggravate the guilt of those who had not kept it. At the same time, this allusion to a preternatural and superhuman incident in sacred history, as well as to a spectacle or scene of unexampled grandeur, and connected with the great transaction from which Israel derived his national existence and pre-eminence, imparts to the conclusion of this speech, which some regard as broken and unfinished, a rhetorical sublimity, which, added to its logical and moral force, entitles it to take rank with the noblest specimens of ancient eloquence.

54. When they heard these (things), they were cut to the heart, and they gnashed on him with their teeth.

When they heard is more exactly rendered in the Rhemish version, *and hearing.* *These* (*things*), i. e. the things uttered in vs. 51–53, if these are an abrupt apostrophe, and an expression of excited feeling, unconnected with what goes before (see above, on v. 51.) But according to the view which we have just been taking of the passage, there is nothing to prevent our understanding *these things* of the whole discourse, consisting, as it does, of a concatenated argument, whose logical conclusion is at the same time a powerful invective. The drift of Stephen's speech towards this conclusion must have been long suspected, if not clearly seen, by so attentive and intelligent an audience; but when it was actually reached and formally propounded, and in terms so terribly insulting, it is not to be considered strange, that even priests and scribes expressed their brutal spite by noises borrowed from the brutes themselves. The word translated *gnashed* originally means any audible but inarticulate outburst of pain or rage, such as groaning, roaring, bellowing, etc. Its specific meaning is determined here by the addition of the word *teeth*, even without which Homer uses it, according to some eminent philologists, in this sense, although others understand it of the cry uttered by the wounded warrior in the agony of death. *On him*, or *over him*, not merely *at him*, which they might do at a distance, whereas this implies a rushing movement towards him, which is afterwards expressed (in v. 57.) Wiclif has *grenneden* (grinned?) *with teeth on him*. The preceding clause is variously rendered in the older versions (Wicl. were diversely tormented. Tynd. their hearts clave asunder. Gen. their hearts burst for anger. Rhem. were cut in their hearts.) The Greek verb is the same with that in 5, 33, and there explained as literally meaning *they were sawn through*, here defined or specified by the addition, (*in*) *their hearts*. It evidently means more than rage or self-exasperation, as explained both by ancient and by modern lexicographers. The strength of the expression, and the obvious analogy of 2, 37 (they were pricked, or pierced, in their hearts), seem to indicate a more complex and violent emotion, which may be supposed to have consisted in the simultaneous combination of a strong conviction, both of mind and conscience, with unbending pride, vindictive spite, and furious anger, which together were no doubt sufficient to saw through their very hearts.

55. But he, being full of the Holy Ghost, looked up stedfastly into heaven, and saw the glory of God, and Jesus standing on the right hand of God.

Being, not the ordinary verb of existence, but one employed repeatedly above (2, 30. 3, 2. 6. 4, 34. 37. 5, 4), and originally meaning to begin, or to begin to be, but used as early as Herodotus and Æschylus in the general sense of being or existing (see above, on 4, 34.) If any accessory idea is suggested here, it is rather that of being still, or continuing to be (see above, on 5, 4.) The fact here mentioned is intended to explain the vision which follows as a special revelation. *Looked up stedfastly*, or more exactly, *gazing into heaven* (see above, on 1, 10. 3, 4. 12. 6, 15.) *Into heaven* does not necessarily imply that he could see the sky from where he stood, but merely that he looked up towards it; all the rest was preternatural, ecstatic vision. As such, the process was, of course, inscrutable and indescribable. In what sense, or in what way, Stephen *saw* this glorious sight, whether by a miraculous extension of his bodily vision, or by mere removal of all intervening obstacles, or by the presentation of a visionary object, or by a miraculous impression on his mind, there is no need of inquiring, as the actual effect must still have been the same, and must have seemed so even to himself. It is enough to know that this effect was supernatural and wrought upon him by the Holy Ghost, and also that it was confined to Stephen, as appears from the conduct of his judges, recorded in the next verse. *The glory of God*, i. e. a sensible manifestation of his presence. (See above, on v. 2.) *On the right hand of God*, as the post of honour and coequal power. (See above, on 2, 33. 34. 5, 31.) *Standing*, not sitting, as he is usually represented (Matt. 26, 64. Mark 16, 19. Eph. 1, 20. Col. 3, 1. Heb. 1, 3. 13. 8, 1. 10, 12. 12, 2.) Some regard this as an unimportant difference, not meant to be significant, as Paul and Peter elsewhere simply say that he "is at the right hand of God," without defining his position (Rom. 8, 34. 1 Pet. 3. 22.) But most interpreters, especially since Gregory the Great, explain the standing posture as implying, that he had risen from his throne to meet or to assist his servant. The local phrase, though uniformly rendered, for the most part, in the English Bible, is considerably varied in the Greek, *right* being sometimes in the singular (ἐν δεξιᾷ), and then agreeing with *hand* understood, and sometimes in the plural, either dative (as in Mark 16, 5), or genitive, (as in Matt. 27, 38. Mark 15, 27. Luke 23, 33, and here), in which cases it agrees, not with *hands*, but with *parts*, sides, or places. The particle prefixed is sometimes *in*, but here and often elsewhere *from*, an idiomatic equivalent to *at* or *on* in English. Wicl. *on the right half of the virtue of God*.

56. And said, Behold, I see the heavens opened, and the Son of Man standing on the right hand of God.

Behold, as usual, introduces something unexpected and surprising. (See above, on 1, 10. 2, 7. 5, 9. 25. 38.) *I see*, or rather, *I survey, contemplate*, implying something grand and solemn in the object. (See above, on 3, 16. 4, 13, and compare 1, 11.) *The heavens opened*, not merely *open*, as Tyndale and his followers have it, but just opened, i. e. to the view of Stephen. Some cite as a parallel a line from Virgil (*video medium discedere cœlum*) describing a flash of lightning; but no such idea is suggested by the Greek words here, any more than in the account of our Lord's baptism (Matt. 3, 16. Mark 1, 10. Luke 3, 21.) *The Son of Man*, which here replaces *Jesus* in the foregoing verse, is nowhere else in the New Testament applied to Christ, except by himself. Stephen's use of the phrase here is not sufficiently explained by the fact, that Jesus appeared in his human form and as the representative of mankind, unless we furthermore suppose a reference to his Messianic claims and honours. 'I see the heavens opened to my view, and him who used to call himself the Son of Man on earth, now standing as the Son of Man in the highest place of honour and authority.'

57. Then they cried out with a loud voice, and stopped their ears, and ran upon him with one accord.

Then they cried, literally, *and crying*. (Tynd. *then they gave a shout*.) One or two manuscripts have *crying* in the genitive singular, (*he*) *crying*, or (*Stephen*) *crying;* but Greek usage would require the noun or pronoun to be expressed. *Cried out with a loud* (literally, *a great*) *voice*, some understand to mean, that they called upon him to be silent; but it seems rather to denote a confused clamour, some crying one thing, some another, as expressly stated on a different occasion. (See below, on 19, 32.) *Stopped*, literally, held fast by pressing, as the same verb means in other applications. (Compare Luke 8, 45. 22, 63.) This act, which is a natural expression of unwillingness to hear, appears to have been practised both by Jews and Gentiles, as a special gesture of abhorrence, on the utterance of blasphemy or impious language. The tumultuous excitement here described may seem incredible in a grave national assembly, and especially in one of a religious character. But it is perfectly in keeping with the treatment of Paul, and of our Lord himself, before the same tribunal. (See below, on 23, 2, and compare John 18, 22.) It also agrees well with what we know, from other sources, of the growing fanaticism of the Zealots, which precipitated, if it did not cause, the final downfall of Jerusalem, and with it the destruction of the Hebrew state, and of the Jewish Church, in its legitimate and ancient form. (See above, on 1, 13.) *Ran upon him* is in Greek still stronger, the verb originally meaning to rouse, urge, drive, and then as an intransitive, to *rush*, which last is the most exact equivalent in this place. *With one accord*, not merely at the same time, but with one spontaneous impulse, as if the movement had been previously agreed upon. The original expression is a single word, which has occurred repeatedly before in this book. (See above, on 1, 14. 2, 1. 46. 4, 24. 5, 12.)

58. And cast him out of the city, and stoned him; and the witnesses laid down their clothes at a young man's feet, whose name was Saul.

The blasphemer in the wilderness was stoned without the camp (Lev. 24, 14), and the same form was observed in the case of Naboth (1 Kings 21, 13.) In the case of an idolater, the law explicitly requires, that "the hands of the witnesses shall be first upon him to put him to death, and afterwards the hands of all the people" (Deut. 17, 7.) This law was designed, no doubt, to regulate the zeal of informers and accusers, by requiring them to act so conspicuous a part in the execution of the sentence founded on their testimony. In order to perform this duty with convenience, as the stones first cast are said to have been very large, they were obliged to free themselves from the encumbrance of their long and flowing *upper garments*, which is the precise sense of the word here rendered *clothes*. *Laid down*, or as the Rhemish version more exactly renders it, *laid off*, the other idea being implied but not expressed, *at* (near or by) *the feet*, the same phrase that occurs above, in 4, 35. 37. 5, 2. 10. From the analogy of those passages, it might seem to denote here, not a mere deposit for safe-keeping, which would hardly have been mentioned, but the recognition of some official authority or dignity in the person mentioned. (See below, on 26, 10.)

But perhaps the true view of the matter is, that a circumstance, which in itself was wholly unimportant, is introduced into the narrative because of its connection with the first appearance of a person so illustrious, and so conspicuous in the sequel of this very history. *Young man*, youth, is used both in Greek and Hebrew, with great latitude, and therefore furnishes no certain measure of his age at this time. His description of himself to Philemon (v. 9) *as Paul the aged*, even on the largest computation of the interval consistent with known facts, would seem necessarily to show that at the time of Stephen's death, he had long passed the period of adolescence. It is by no means certain, therefore, that he was still sitting "at the feet of Gamaliel," (another instance of the phrase implying superiority of rank and office,) which some regard as highly improbable, because the conduct here described was so much at variance with Gamaliel's own advice (see above, on 5, 38. 39.) But disciples are not always as forbearing as their teachers; and in this fanatical excitement, even Gamaliel himself may have yielded to the torrent of ungovernable zeal. *Saul*, the same name with that of the ancient king, who was also of the tribe of Benjamin (see below, on 13, 21, and compare Rom. 11, 1. Phil. 3, 5), from which some have inferred that the Apostle was his descendant. The name is sometimes written in its original Hebrew form (as in 9, 4. 17. 22, 7. 13. 26, 14), but usually with a Greek termination (as in 8, 1. 9, 1. 11, 25. 13, 1, and here.)

59. And they stoned Stephen calling (upon God) and saying, Lord Jesus, receive my spirit.

The repetition of the statement, that *they stoned Stephen*, has been variously understood, as distinguishing the formal execution from rude pelting by the way; or the general stoning by the people from the preliminary stoning by the witnesses; or as a mere resumption and continuation of the narrative, after the parenthetical statement with respect to the witnesses and Saul. A more important question is, whether this was a judicial execution or an act of tumultuary violence. In favour of the former supposition are the facts, that Stephen was arraigned before a regular assembly of the Sanhedrim (6, 12. 15); that he and the witnesses had been judicially examined (6, 11. 13. 7, 1); and that the law of Moses was punctiliously complied with in the act of stoning

(v. 58.) It is objected, that we read nothing of a formal sentence; but the same omission is observed in cases where we know that all the legal forms were meant to be complied with, as in that of Naboth (1 Kings 21. 13.) A much stronger argument is that derived from John 18, 31, where the Jews themselves say, "it is not lawful for us to put any one to death." This is commonly understood to mean, that the Romans had deprived them of the power of life and death; and we find in the Talmud a tradition, that the Sanhedrim did lose this power about forty years before the destruction of the temple. But if this were so, how shall we account for Paul's repeatedly speaking of himself as having aided in persecuting the disciples *unto death?* (See below, on 22, 4. 26, 10.) Although this, and similar expressions in Josephus, may be explained upon the supposition, that the Jews could pass a sentence of death (Matt. 26, 66. Mark 14, 64), but could not execute it, some have preferred the explanation of John 18, 31, proposed by Cyril and Augustin, who suppose the incapacity alleged there to be merely ceremonial and temporary, arising from the sacredness of the season; so that being equally unwilling to defer their vengeance and to desecrate their feast, they asked Pilate to do for them what they did not feel at liberty to do for themselves. But even if the common explanation of that passage be adopted, it is not impossible that the persecution unto death, of which Saul speaks, was permitted or connived at by the Roman governor, and therefore not a violation of the rule which John records. As to the passionate and furious deportment of the judges, it has been explained already (on v. 58) as the effect of violent excitement acting on the growing fanaticism of the Zealots, and analogous to outbursts of vindictive feeling, which have sometimes accompanied the execution of not only regular but righteous sentences in modern times. There is neither necessity nor warrant, therefore, for assuming a distinction in the narrative between the judges and the populace, referring what was formal and judicial to the one class, and what was lawless and tumultuous to the other. From all that we know of these Jewish rulers, they were capable of any thing that could be perpetrated by the people, whose worst excesses upon previous occasions had been instigated by themselves. (See Matt. 27, 20. Mark 15, 11. Luke 23, 23.) *Upon God* is introduced by the Geneva version and King James's, no doubt with a good design, but with a very bad effect, that of separating Stephen's invocation from its object, and obscuring, if not utterly concealing, a strong proof of the divinity of Christ. *Calling*, not merely naming or addressing, but invoking, calling to one's aid, which is the meaning of the middle voice of this verb in the best Greek writers. The object of the invocation is apparent from the invocation itself which immediately follows. *Calling upon God and saying Lord Jesus* may have been intended by the translators to identify these objects in the strongest manner; but besides the impropriety of such interpolations, even for such a purpose, the actual impression is most probably the contrary, to wit, that there are two distinct acts here recorded, that of calling upon God, and that of saying Lord Jesus, whereas these acts are spoken of as one and the same, in the Greek and in several of the older versions. (Vulg. *invocantem et dicentem*. Tyndale and Cranmer, *calling on and saying*.) The religious invocation of our Lord was not only practised by the first disciples, but gave rise to one of their most common appellations. In this very book, they are repeatedly described as those who "call upon this name" (9, 14. 21), which can only mean the name of Christ, because the general invocation of the name of God was no distinction, being common both to Jews and Christians, and in a wide sense, to the heathen also. This usage makes it highly probable, that even the less definite expression, *calling on the name of the Lord* (2, 21. 22, 16. Rom. 10, 12. 13), was designed to have the same specific meaning. In the face of all this, it is folly to deny that invocation implies worship, and worse than folly to pretend that *Jesus*, in the last clause of the verse before us, is a genitive (*Lord of Jesus!*) Besides the grammatical objection, that this construction would require the article in Greek, it is condemned by the analogy of Rev. 22, 20, where no one can deny that the very same phrase means *Lord Jesus*, and involves a recognition of him in the twofold character of a Sovereign and a Saviour. The petition is not that he would take away his life or suffer him to die, as in the case of Elijah (1 Kings 19, 4) and of Jonah (4, 3), but that he would receive or accept his soul when separated from his body. This prayer of Stephen is not only a direct imitation of our Lord's upon the cross (Luke 23, 46), but a further proof that he addressed him as a divine person, since he here asks of the Son precisely what the Son there asks of the Father.

60. And he kneeled down and cried with a loud voice, Lord, lay not this sin to their charge. And when he had said this, he fell asleep.

He *kneeled down*, literally, *placing the knees*, i. e. upon the ground (as in 9, 40. 20, 36. 21, 5. Luke 22, 41.) Paul, in similar cases, speaks of *bending the knee*, as a preliminary act to that here mentioned. (See Rom. 11, 4. 14, 11. Eph. 3, 14. Phil. 2, 10.) In the case before us, this movement may have been, not merely an expression of religious feeling, but a symptom of exhausted strength (Rhem. *falling on his knees*), as in Luke 23, 34. Some with less probability suppose him to have *kneeled up*, or risen from a prostrate to a kneeling posture. This last prayer of the martyr is also copied from our Lord's upon the cross (Luke 23, 34.) *Lay not to their charge*, a correct paraphrase though not an exact version of the Greek, which strictly means *do not set* (or *place*), i. e. to their account, or, as some explain it, *do not fix* (or *establish*) this against them. Another sense is that suggested by the usage of this verb in Homer (and in Matt. 26, 15) to denote the act of *weighing* money, which was the most ancient mode of paying it. *Do not weigh their sin*, or reckon it, in dealing out to them what they deserve. The essential meaning of the prayer is still the same on all these suppositions. *He fell asleep* may simply mean *he died*, a figure common in the dialect of Homer, and perhaps in every other; but it more probably implies that the martyr died a peaceful death, notwithstanding the fury of his murderers and the violent means by which he lost his life. The same exquisite figure reappears in Paul's description of departed Christians as those who are *fallen asleep in Christ* (1 Cor. 15, 18), and those who *sleep in Jesus* (1 Thess. 4, 14.)

CHAPTER VIII.

From the history of the undivided Mother Church, we now pass to that of its extension in successive or contemporary radiations, occasioned by what seemed to be a great disaster, but resulting in the wide and rapid spread of the new doctrine, and in the formation of affiliated churches, at various central points of influence throughout the empire. The conventional division of the text has thrown into the chapter now before us the commencement of this process, beginning with its proximate occasion, in the persecution following the death of Stephen (1–3), and the consequent dispersion of believers (4), among whom the historian selects, as an eminent example, Philip and his mission to Samaria (5–8), with its remarkable success, both real and apparent (9–13), followed by an apostolical commission from Jerusalem (14–17), and the public conviction of a spurious convert (18–24). Before or after the return of the Apostles to the Holy City (25), Philip receives a new commission (26) to become the instructor and baptizer of an Ethiopian ruler (27–39), after which he preaches in a number of important towns, including Cesarea, where the history now leaves him (40), and where he reappears long after (21, 8.)

1. **And Saul was consenting unto his death. And at that time there was a great persecution against the church which was at Jerusalem, and they were all scattered abroad, throughout the regions of Judea and Samaria, except the Apostles.**

We have here one of the most striking instances of carelessness, or want of judgment, in the division of the chapters and verses. Not only is this first verse of unusual and needless length (see above, on 5, 21), but it is made so by annexing to it what would have sufficed to form another (*and they were all scattered*, etc.), and by prefixing to it what should have been the conclusion of the foregoing verse and chapter (*and Saul was consenting to his death.*) *Was consenting* is the true sense of the participial construction, which denotes not a momentary act (Tynd. *consented*), but continued or habitual action. (See above, on 1, 10. 13, 14.) *Consenting*, i. e. agreeing, acting in concert, with the murderers (Luke 11, 48. Rom. 1, 32. 1 Cor. 7, 12. 13), not merely approving or assenting to the murder. *Death* is too negative a version of the Greek word, which is the noun corresponding to the verb translated *slay* in 5, 33. 36, and *kill* in 7, 28, and here used in the active sense of killing, murder. (For Paul's account of his own share in this transaction, see below, on 22, 20, and compare 26, 10.) *At that time,* lit. *in that day,* which is sometimes used indefinitely by the Prophets (e. g. Isai. 2, 11. Jer. 39, 17. Ez. 29, 21. Hos. 2, 18), but in the New Testament always seems to mean *that very day,* whether spoken of the past (Matt. 13, 1. 22, 23. Mark 4, 35. John 5, 9. Acts 2, 41), or of the future (Matt. 7, 22. Mark 2, 20. 4, 35. Luke 17, 31. John 14, 20. 16, 23. 26); the more indefinite idea being expressed by the plural form, *in those days* (Matt. 3, 1. 24, 19. Mark 11, 9. 8, 1. 13, 17. 24. Luke 2, 1. 4, 2. 9, 36. 21, 23. Acts 2, 18.) It was therefore on the very day of Stephen's death and burial, and as an immediate consequence, that this persecution began. *There was,* or more exactly, *there arose,* began to be, or happened. (See above, on 7, 52.) For *church,* Tyndale, Cranmer, and the Geneva Bible have, as usual, *congregation.* (See above, on 5, 11.) *Which was at Jerusalem,* lit. *the (one) in Jerusalem.* The disciples, although now so numerous (see above, on 2, 41. 4, 4. 5, 14. 6, 1. 7), are spoken of as still constituting one body. *They were all scattered,* more exactly, *all were scattered,* as *they* is not expressed in Greek, and has no grammatical antecedent except *church. All* has been variously understood, as a natural hyperbole for *most* or *many;* as denoting all the preachers (see v. 4); or as strictly meaning all, with the exception mentioned in the last clause, many of whom, however, afterwards returned, so that the church did not become extinct, or require to be organized afresh, the presence of the twelve being indeed sufficient to preserve its existence and identity. *Throughout* is here the best equivalent for the Greek preposition, which means, in different connections, down, along, among, etc. (See above, on 2, 10. 5, 15.) Galilee is again omitted (as in 1, 8), perhaps because *Judea and Samaria* was a customary designation of the whole country (but see below, on 9, 31); or because something not recorded really prevented the dispersed from visiting that province, so highly honoured by the long-continued residence of Christ himself, and possibly for that very reason less in need of visitation now. *Except* (Wicl. *out-taken*) *the Apostles* seems to be at variance with our Lord's express command to them, "When they persecute you in this city, flee into another" (Matt. 10, 23.) This has been variously explained by supposing, that the twelve, from the awe with which they were regarded, or for some other reason now unknown, escaped the persecution; or, which is the simplest and most obvious solution, that the general rule, laid down in Matthew, was suspended or qualified by special revelation. Apart from the command in question, it is easy to imagine reasons why they should remain at the centre of operations, as the constituted organizers and administrators of the system which had just been set in motion, and as such imparting to the one church of Jerusalem a representative and normal character, in consequence of which its acts were binding on the whole body, when extended even into other countries. (See below, on 15, 2. 6, 22. 23. 16, 4.) According to an old tradition, which Eusebius has copied from an earlier writer, the Apostles were required to stay twelve years in Jerusalem; but this has no foundation in the history itself, nor any intrinsic probability to recommend it. The general dispersion here described may be regarded as the first fulfilment of the double or repeated promise, that the law should go forth from Zion and the word of the Lord from Jerusalem (Micah 4, 2. Isai. 2, 3.)

2. **And devout men carried Stephen (to his burial), and made great lamentation over him.**

After stating the general effect of Stephen's death, to wit, the persecution and dispersion, the historian, before following the exiles, as he does in this and several ensuing chapters, pauses to tell us what became of Stephen's body, and what Saul was doing in the mean time. Such interruptions and resumptions are so natural and common in all history, that it is hard to understand the objections made in this case, and the various propositions to amend, transpose, or strike out, as the only means by which the text can be made intelligible or coherent. There is no need even of assuming a double contrast or antithesis, between the persecution and the burial, and then between the devout men and Saul. The whole objection rests upon the prevalent but shallow notion, that the slightest deviation from the order of time, in the narration of events, if it does not vitiate the truth, at least impairs the form of history, whereas such deviations are continually practised by the best historians, as well as in the dialect of common life. There is indeed a certain beauty in these momentary pauses and returns to something previously mentioned, for the purpose of completing it before proceeding further, that is far more pleasing to a cultivated taste than inflexible adherence to a mathematically straight line, without looking to the right hand or the left. That the sequence of ideas in the narrative before us is entirely natural and easy, may be made clear by a paraphrase. 'The martyrdom of Stephen, in which Saul so heartily concurred, produced a general persecution and dispersion of believers from Jerusalem, none being left there for a time but the Apostles; and yet this did not deprive the martyr's body of religious burial, for devout men bore him to his grave and mourned for him, while Saul was actually ravaging the church and searching every house for Christians.' *Devout men*, a phrase used above (2, 5) in application to the foreign Jews who witnessed the effusion of the Spirit on the day of Pentecost. As in that case it denotes the serious and sincere, as distinguished from the frivolous and hypocritical, so here it seems to mean the just and conscientious, as distinguished from the bigoted and the fanatical. The objection to the explanation of these words as describing disciples of Christ, is not that they would not have been permitted to perform the act here mentioned, for they might have braved the prohibition, and thereby provoked the persecution; but it is that the epithet here used is nowhere else applied to Christians. (See above, on 2, 5, and below, on 22, 12.) *Carried*, literally, *gathered*, brought together, as applied to fruits by Xenophon, and in the Septuagint version of Job 5, 26, where it is also metaphorically used of burial, as it is by Sophocles, while Plutarch and Thucydides apply it to the literal collection of dead bodies on a field of battle to be burnt. The common version is derived from the Geneva Bible ("certain men fearing God carried Stephen among them to be buried,") whereas Tyndale and Cranmer render the verb *dressed*, perhaps confounding it with that used in 5, 6, and the Rhemish version has the singular periphrasis, *took order for Stephen's funeral*. The simplest, and perhaps the best, of all the English versions is the oldest (Wicl. *good men buried Stephen*.) *Lamentation*, literally, *beating*, in allusion to the ancient practice of beating the breast, as a sign of mourning. (Analogous, both in etymology and usage, is the Latin *planctus* from *plango*.) *Over*, not merely in the figurative sense of about, concerning, but in the literal and local sense, implying that they mourned while standing (or hanging) over the dead body. Some have made it an objection to the reference of this clause to devout Jews, that they could not be expected to express such sorrow as is here described. But why not, if they were his countrymen, his relatives, his private friends? Such ties are not necessarily destroyed by religious differences, however great; and this is a much more satisfactory solution than the one derived from the alleged custom of the moderate and pious Jews to bury those whom they regarded as unjustly put to death. This, if sufficiently attested, would explain the act of burial, but not the *great lamentation* over Stephen, unless that be ascribed to other mourners, i. e. the disciples, which, although a possible construction, is by no means obvious or natural. The case may seem analogous to that in 6, 6, where the subjects of the two successive verbs are different; but in that case, the subject of the last clause is expressly mentioned in the first. " Whom they (the people) set before the Apostles, and they (the Apostles) laid their hands upon them." But in the case before us the only subject named is the *devout men* of the first clause. It is better, therefore, on the whole, to understand this *great lamentation*, not as a public or sectarian, but as a personal or private mourning, perhaps made more intense by what they looked upon as Stephen's apostasy from God and Moses (6, 11.)

3. As for Saul, he made havoc of the church, entering into every house, and haling men and women, committed them to prison.

The connection between this and the preceding verse would be correctly indicated by translating (δέ), instead of *as for*, *while*, or *in the mean time*. The idea is, that all these things were going on at once, or nearly at the same time, devout men bearing Stephen to his burial, disciples flying from Jerusalem, and Saul still driving them before him. *Made havoc* (Tyndale, Cranmer, and Geneva), literally, *wasted* (Rhemish version), i. e. laid waste, ravaged, as a beast of prey does; then transferred to human tyranny and persecution. (Compare the similar expressions used in 9, 21 below, and in Gal. 1, 13.) *Into every house* (Tyndale, Cranmer, and Geneva), or *from house to house* (Rheims), should rather be translated *into houses*, as distinguished from more public places. (See above, on 2, 46.) *Haling* (in the first edition of King James's Bible written *hailing*) is an old English form of *hauling*, i. e. violently pulling, dragging. As the Greek verb is repeatedly applied by Luke (17, 6. 12, 58) to the bringing up of accused persons before magistrates, it may mean nothing more in this case; but the strict and strong sense is entitled to the preference, not only as such, but because proceedings of this kind must always be attended with some force or violence. Saul's agency in these imprisonments is more than once referred to by himself. (See below, on 22, 4. 5. 26, 10.) This form of persecution was expressly predicted by our Lord (Luke 21, 12.)

4. Therefore they that were scattered abroad went every where preaching the word.

Therefore (Cranmer and Geneva) should be *so then*, as a resumptive and continuative particle, the same that is used above, in 1, 6. 2, 41. 5, 41, and there explained. The writer, having paused to tell us what became of Stephen and of Saul, now resumes his narrative of the dispersion, not by repeating what he said in v. 1, but by advancing a step further. As he there said that all (except the twelve) were scattered, he now says that all who were thus scattered preached the word. Some would infer from this, that none but preachers were expelled; but it is far more natural to understand the verse as referring, not to preaching in the technical or formal sense, but to that joyful and spontaneous diffusion of the truth, which is permitted and required of all believers, whether lay or clerical, ordained or unordained. *Went every where* (Tyndale, Cranmer, Geneva), literally, *went through* (Rheims, *passed through*, Wiclif, *passed forth*), i. e. through the country, or its towns; but when absolutely used, it is nearly equivalent to *went about*. (See below, on v. 40, and 10, 38.) *The word*, a common abbreviation for *the word of God*, the Gospel, or the new religion. (See above, on 4. 4.) *Preaching*, proclaiming it, as good news or glad tidings. (See above, on 5, 42.) Here again the Rhemish version violates our idiom by the barbarous translation, *evangelizing the word*. We have here a signal illustration of the providential law, according to which what appears to be an irretrievable calamity, is not only overruled, but designed from the beginning, to promote the very cause which it seems to threaten with disaster and defeat.

5. Then Philip went down to the city of Samaria, and preached Christ unto them.

The general statement, that the dispersed disciples carried

with them the glad tidings of salvation, through whatever region they might pass, is now exemplified by one specific instance out of many, chosen either as the first in time, or as relating to a race who occupied a sort of intermediate position between Jews and Gentiles. (See above, on 1, 8.) The connection would have been better indicated by a simple copulative (*and*) than by an adverb of time (*then*). *Philip*, not the Apostle (see above, on 1, 13)—for he would then be an exception to the previous exception in the last clause of v. 1, but one of the Seven (6, 8), who may have been peculiarly exposed to persecution, as the colleagues of Stephen, or because their office brought them into frequent contact and collision with the unbelieving Jews. (See above, on 6, 9.) He is no doubt the same person described in 21, 8, as an Evangelist, perhaps from the circumstances here related. His being expressly so described relieves all difficulty as to a Deacon's preaching, without requiring us to grant that it belonged, as a necessary function, to that office. His being called a Preacher, or Evangelist, so late in the history, is no objection, as that description must be retrospective, and as Philip, if ever entitled to be thus called, must have been so when he *preached Christ* to the Samaritans. *The city of Samaria* can in English only mean *the city* (called) *Samaria*, the royal residence of the kings of Israel for two hundred years, from the time of Omri, by whom it was founded (1 Kings 16, 24. 2 Kings 17, 5. 6) on the summit of an insulated hill in the central plain or table-land of Palestine, a site described by travellers as unsurpassed in the whole country for combined richness, strength, and beauty. Nothing could seem more natural than that some of the dispersed disciples should visit the Samaritans, to whom their Master had himself done so much honour at an early period of his ministry (John 4, 40), and that in so doing they should make the ancient capital the centre of their operations. Yet to this obvious and in English only meaning of the passage there are several objections, some of which have little force, but others are less easily disposed of. One objection is, that the old city was no longer in existence; but we learn from Josephus, that although destroyed by Hyrcanus, it had been rebuilt by Gabinius, and beautified by Herod the Great. It is alleged, however, that this new or renovated city was not called *Samaria*, but *Sebaste*, the Greek equivalent of *Augusta*, in honour of Augustus Cæsar. This is true, but it is also true that old names seldom die in popular and local usage; and that this was not the case with the name *Samaria*, we know from its occasional occurrence in the writings of Josephus. But even granting that the place was in existence, and might still be called Samaria, its designation here by that name is less probable, because in every other passage where the name occurs, it means the province, not the city. (See Luke 17, 11. John 4, 4. 5, 7. Acts 1, 8. 9. 31. 15, 3.) It might still by possibility have that sense in this context; but in v. 9, the wide one is required by the use of the word *nation* (ἔθνος), which could not, in accordance with Greek usage, be applied to the population of a single city; and in v. 14, although the same doubt may exist as in the case before us, the wide sense is at least as natural as the restricted one. Strong as these reasons are against limiting the name to the city of Samaria, they are made still stronger by the genitive construction, which, though perfectly familiar to all English readers, occurs but rarely, if at all, in classic Greek, and only once besides in the New Testament (2 Pet. 2, 6), and even there admits of another explanation, as referring not to Sodom and Gomorrah alone, but to the towns dependent on them. If, in spite of all these arguments from usage, this should still seem to be the only natural import of *the city of Samaria*, it may finally be urged, that the original expression is indefinite, i. e. without the article, and strictly means *a city of Samaria*. The similar expression, *city of David* (Luke 2, 4), is not perfectly analogous, as we might call Bethlehem *David's city*, but could hardly call Samaria *Samaria's city*. The conclusion from all these considerations seems to be, that the historian here speaks, not of the city called Samaria, but of some other place belonging to that province; the distinction being just the same with that between "the city of New York," which is applicable only to one place, and "a city of New York," which is appropriate to many. To the question what town of Samaria is meant, if not the ancient capital, no certain answer can be given. It may still be the capital, though not expressly so described, just as "a city of New York" may vaguely designate "the city of New York," as well as any other. Or it may be some place unknown to history, and wholly unimportant in itself, perhaps the first town of Samaria to which Philip came, where he instantly preached Christ without delay, and where the general reception of the gospel might be justly represented (in v. 14 below) as the act of

Samaria, i. e. of the race or nation, represented by these early converts or first fruits of apostolic labour. Or, avoiding both extremes, the place meant may be Sychar, the ancient Shechem, a city famous in primeval history, more lately honoured by a two days' residence of Christ himself, and ever since, until the present day, the chief seat and centre of the Samaritan race and religion. (See above, on 7, 16.) That no good ground can be assigned for the suppression of the name is true, but as a purely negative objection or argument *a silentio*, can hardly neutralize the cumulative reasons for interpreting *Samaria* in a wide sense, and *a city* in a vague one. But whatever may be the particular place meant, the essential fact is still the same, that it belonged to the *Samaritans*, a mixed or, as some suppose, a purely heathen race, introduced by the Assyrians to supply the place of the ten tribes (2 Kings 17, 24), and afterwards partially assimilated to the Jews (ib. 25–41), by the reception of the law of Moses, and the professed worship of Jehovah on Mount Gerizim, involving a rejection of the sanctuary at Jerusalem, from the rebuilding of which, after the Babylonish exile, they were excluded by the restored Jews (Ezra 4, 1–3.) At the time of the Advent, they were expecting the Messiah, but only, it should seem, in his prophetic character (John 4, 25), for which reason, and because of their entire segregation from the Jews (John 4, 9), our Saviour did not scruple to avow his Messiahship among them (John 4, 26. 29, 42), and to gather the first fruits of an extra-Judaic church (John 4, 39), with the cheering promise of a more abundant harvest, to be reaped by his Apostles (John 4, 35–38.) Of this promise we have here the first fulfilment, and at the same time the incipient transition of the gospel from the Jews to the Gentiles, between whom the Samaritans might be regarded as a link, or as a frontier. (See above, on 1, 8.) To them Philip now *preached Christ* or *the Messiah*, i. e. proclaimed that he was come, and that Jesus of Nazareth was he. As all this had been taught by Christ himself at Sychar, that may be regarded as an argument, though far from a conclusive one, against supposing that place to be here particularly meant; since Philip is not said to have taught doctrines altogether new, and since just such a repetition or renewal of his work had been predicted by our Lord himself (John 4, 35–38.) *Unto them*, i. e. to the inhabitants, the grammatical antecedent being latent in the name or description of the place, as it is in *Galilee,* Matt. 4, 23, and *church* in v. 1 above.

6. And the people with one accord gave heed unto those things which Philip spake, hearing and seeing the miracles which he did.

The previous preparation of the ground, by the visit of our Saviour, may have contributed to the success of Philip's ministry. *The people,* literally, *the crowds* or *multitudes,* a word implying not mere numbers, many as opposed to few, but promiscuousness, masses as opposed to classes. (See above, on 1, 15. 6, 7.) *Gave heed,* lit. *applied* (the mind), i. e. attended, paid attention to his teaching. (See above, on 5, 35.) It may imply belief here, as it seems to do in vs. 10. 11, and in 16, 14. *The (things) spoken by Philip,* as described in the last clause of v. 5, i. e. the Messiahship of Jesus and the doctrine of salvation through him. The common version, perhaps in order to remove an ambiguity, transposes *unanimously,* or with one accord, from its original position, which is after *the things spoken by Philip,* both in Greek and in the old English versions. The Rhemish even joins it to the last clause, by its punctuation of the sentence (*with one accord hearing and seeing.*) For the meaning of the word itself, see above, on 1, 14. 2, 1. 2, 46. 4, 24. 5, 12. 7, 57. *Hearing and seeing* may either mean *hearing* (of the miracles) *and seeing* them, i. e. seeing some and hearing of others; or, *hearing* (*them*) *and seeing the miracles,* i. e. hearing the things spoken by Philip, and seeing the miracles which he performed. *Miracles,* literally, *signs;* see above, on 2, 19. 22, 43. 4, 16. 22, 30. 5, 12. 6, 8. 7, 36.) *Hearing and seeing,* literally, *in the* (act, or at the time of) *hearing and seeing,* not *in* (consequence of) *hearing and seeing,* i. e. because they heard and saw, which, though implied, is not expressed. (See above, on 7, 29.) As in our Saviour's day, so now in that of the Apostles and Evangelists, the masses were attracted and impressed, not merely by the miracles performed, but also by the truth proclaimed. (See above, on 5, 15, and compare Luke 5, 1.) The two inducements mutually fortified each other. The miracles of Christ and his Apostles were designed, not merely to relieve distress and prove their own divine legation, but to open men's hearts to instruction, and to serve as signs and pledges of a spiritual healing, with which bodily relief was often really connected. (See above, on 4, 12.) The possession of the same extraordinary powers by Philip and by Stephen (6, 5. 8) shows that the description there was only formally restricted to the latter.

7. For unclean spirits, crying with loud voice, came out of many that were possessed with them; and many taken with palsies, and that were lame, were healed.

Lest the incidental reference to Philip's miracles (in v. 6) should be overlooked or misconceived, the fact is now explicitly asserted, and with some minuteness of detail. As if he had said, 'I speak of miracles, for out of many of those having unclean spirits, etc.' As to the prominence given here and elsewhere to this class of miracles, see above, on 5, 16. The frequent mention of the demons as crying when they came out (Mark 1, 26. 3, 11. 9, 26. Luke 4, 41) may arise from the fact, that the cry was evidently not uttered by the patient, in the free use of his vocal organs, and therefore proved the reality of the possession. The construction of this verse is ambiguous, as *unclean spirits* may be either the object of the verb *had*, or the subject of the verb *came out*. In the former case, the literal translation is, (*from*) *many of those having unclean spirits, crying with a loud voice* (*these*) *went out;* in the other, (*from*) *many of those having* (*them*), *evil spirits, crying with a loud voice, went out.* The essential meaning is of course unaffected by this question of construction. The Vulgate and its followers read, 'many of those having unclean spirits, crying with a loud voice, went out,' which apparently absurd construction is found in the text of the three oldest manuscripts, and, if received as genuine, may be explained as an irregular expression of the same idea, the demoniac being substituted for the demon, either intentionally, on account of their intimate union, or by a natural and unimportant negligence of style. To this worst class of maladies are added two of the most common and severe, but not preternatural affections. *Taken with palsies*, literally, *paralyzed*, both English words being derived from the Greek one here used, which is almost confined to Luke (the only other instance being Heb. 12, 12), while the corresponding adjective (*paralytic*, never used in any of the English versions, but invariably expressed by a circumlocution) is found only in the other evangelists. (Compare the Greek of Matt. 4, 24. 8, 6. 9, 2. 6. Mark 2, 3. 4. 5. 9. 10, with that of Luke 5, 18. 24. 9, 33.)

8. And there was great joy in that city.

The happy effect of Philip's mission upon these Samaritans is beautifully set forth in this one short sentence, which is not, however, fully reproduced in English. *There was* (ἐγένετο), there came to be, began to be, arose, or happened, implying a great change and new occasion of rejoicing. (See above, on v. 1, and on 7, 29.) There seems to be allusion to the proverbial joy of harvest (Isai. 9, 3. 16, 9), as predicted by our Saviour, in relation to this very people (John 4, 35. 36.) *That city* is compatible with any supposition as to the particular place meant, but seems more natural if spoken of a town not named before, than if applied to the famous city of Samaria. For the wide sense of the word translated *city*, see above, on 5, 6 (p. 211.) The *joy* here mentioned is to be restricted, neither to the natural enjoyment of recovered health, in one's own person and in that of others, nor to the intellectual pleasure of acquiring knowledge and discovering truth, nor to the spiritual happiness arising from conversion and assurance of forgiveness, but must be understood as comprehending all these elements, and therefore justly called a *great joy*.

9. But there was a certain man called Simon, which beforetime in the same city used sorcery, and bewitched the people of Samaria, giving out that himself was some great one.

The field presented in this city, although highly promising, was not unoccupied when Philip entered it. *A certain man, by name Simon* (the precise form of expression used above in 5, 1), was there before him (προϋπῆρχεν), *using sorcery*, or practising the profession of a *Magus*. This word, of Persian origin, but found in the Old Testament (Jer. 39, 3), as well as in the Classics, is said to have been originally the name of a Median tribe, but was afterwards employed, like *Chaldee* or *Chaldean* (Dan. 2, 2. 4, 71), as a generic designation of the priests, philosophers, and men of science, in the Persian empire. Such, no doubt, were the Wise Men (*Magi*) supernaturally guided from the East to Bethlehem, to do homage to the new-born King of the Jews (Matt. 2, 1.) The connection which existed between ancient Oriental science and the occult arts, as for instance between astronomy and astrology, occasioned a lower application of the name to sorcerers and wizards, a secondary usage which may still be traced in our words *magic* and *magician*. Such pretenders to extraordinary power and knowledge appear to have been very numerous in the Apostolic Age, their influence arising, no doubt, in great measure, from their real science, as compared with the great mass of their credulous contemporaries. It is in this sense, and not in that of mere juggling, that Simon seems to be described here as (μαγεύων) practising magic, acting as a Magus, in this city of Samaria, not at a former time, as might seem to be the meaning of the English version, but immediately before Philip's appearance. *Simon was before* (*him*) *in the city, using sorcery*, etc. His success appears to have been very great, though not precisely such as might be gathered from the version, *and bewitched the people*, which implies the real exercise of some extraordinary physical power, whereas the Greek word only means *amazing* them, as in 2, 7. 12 above, and 9, 21 below, or at the most maddening, depriving them of reason, by excessive admiration and excitement, the idea conveyed by the Italian phrase, *far furore*. The subjects of this violent commotion were *the people* (or more exactly, *the nation*) *of Samaria*, not the mere population of one city, but the race inhabiting the whole province of that name, and who have been described already. (See above, on v. 4.) This may perhaps imply that he was an itinerant magician, like the "vagabond exorcists" of Ephesus (see below, on 19, 13), and like the other sorcerers of that day, as described by Josephus and the classical historians. We may then suppose him to have reached the city here in question upon one of his professional visits, just before Philip's arrival, although previously known to the inhabitants, as mentioned in the next verse. *Giving out* (an old English phrase for declaring or professing) *himself to be some great* (*one*), or rather *some great* (*being*), not merely a distinguished man, but something superhuman. The expression is the same as in 5, 36 above, with the addition of the epithet *great*.

10. To whom (they) all gave heed, from the least to the greatest, saying, This man is the great power of God.

They is superfluous, as in v. 1. *Gave heed*, as in v. 6, expressing only fixed attention, but implying faith or confidence in either case. *All*, as in v. 1, means the mass or body of the people, without reference to individual exceptions. *From the least to the greatest* (so in all the English versions) might be more exactly rendered, *from small to great*, a Hebrew idiom, or a natural expression, for all ranks and ages, which occurs again in Heb. 8, 11 (compare Jon. 3, 5.) *This man* (Tynd. *this fellow*) *is the power of God*, not only clothed with delegated power by God, but himself a divine person, or at least an emanation from the Godhead, in accordance with the favourite theosophy of that day, afterwards embodied in the Gnostic systems. Several of the oldest manuscripts and versions read, *the* (power) *called great*, which may either mean so called but not so really, or so called in some well known theory or doctrine, as in Simon's own description of himself. What he claimed to be precisely, we have no means of determining. According to different early writers, he professed to be the Logos, the Messiah, the Samaritan Archangel, and the Power of God personified, which last is a mere gloss upon the words before us. Jerome represents him as saying, "I am the Word of God, I am the Paraclete, I am the Almighty, I am all (or the whole) of God (*omnia Dei*.") But this is probably a figment of later Christian origin.

11. And to him they had regard, because that of long time he had bewitched them with sorceries.

This is not a mere repetition of the statement in v. 10, but assigns a reason for the fact there stated. The English reader would hardly suspect that *had regard* in this verse is identical with *gave heed* in the one before it. Some of the older versions go still further in these heedless variations. Tyndale, for example, renders the same Greek word *gave heed* (v. 6), *regarded* (v. 10), and *set much by* (v. 11), in all which changes he is closely followed both by Cranmer and the Geneva Bible. The reason that they paid him such attention is here said to be, that he had long bewitched, as in v. 9, i. e. astonished and confounded them by sorceries (μαγείαις) or magical illusions, perhaps the fruit of his superior scientific knowledge, but which these Samaritans could neither call in question nor account for, and were therefore, so to speak, obliged to submit to his pretensions, as incapable of refutation. There is no allusion to any physical effect, but only to this moral influence, exerted by his arts, whatever they may have been. (Wiclif, who had *deceived* in v. 9, here has *madded*.) All this, we here earn, was no new thing, but had continued *time enough*, a phrase used in Greek, as it might be in familiar English, for *a long time*, but without affording any definite measure of duration. (See below, on 9, 23. 43. 14, 3. 18, 18. 27, 7. 9, and above, on 5, 37, where the same term is applied to quantity or number.)

12. But when they believed Philip preaching the (things) concerning the kingdom of God and the name of Jesus Christ, they were baptized, both men and women.

This verse describes the striking change effected among Simon's dupes by Philip's preaching. The question whether *they believed* has reference to these alone, or to the people generally, is of no importance, as the context shows that these two classes were identical. It is plain, at all events, that what is here described was a general conversion of the people. One subject of the preaching which produced it is described as *the things concerning the kingdom of God*, the same expression that was used in 1, 3, with respect to our Saviour's conversations with the twelve before his ascension. The oldest manuscripts omit *the* (*things*), and read, *concerning the kingdom of God*, without material effect upon the sense, which is still, that Philip told them all about it, not the mere fact of its existence, but its history, doctrines, duties, hopes, yet all as good news (εὐαγγελιζομένῳ.) The other subject of his preaching was *the name of Jesus Christ*, i. e. all denoted by these names, one of which means the Saviour of his people (Matt. 1, 21) and the other their Messiah, or Anointed Prophet, Priest, and King. Into this name, i. e. into union with Christ, and subjection to him, in all these characters, the Samaritan believers were introduced by the initiatory rite of baptism, which, unlike that of Judaism, was administered alike to *both men and women*. The same minute exactness is observable in what is said above (v. 3), with respect to the extent and ruthlessness of Saul's persecution, in which neither sex was spared.

13. Then Simon himself believed also, and when he was baptized, he continued with Philip and wondered, beholding the miracles and signs which were done.

Then, not afterwards, but at the same time. *And* (δέ) *Simon also himself believed*, as well as his adherents, who had just been mentioned. Not only the followers, but the leader, believed. With what kind of faith, is an old subject of dispute, and various answers have been given to the question, chiefly in the form of technical distinctions, e. g. with a historical, speculative, temporary faith, etc. These designations may be all correct; but they throw little light upon the history, the most obvious sense of which is, that the sorcerer believed to all appearance as the rest did; he professed belief, became a convert in the view of others, and in the customary way, by submitting to the rite of baptism. If Philip was deceived, this only shows that he was not omniscient, or even competent to read the heart. If he was not deceived, his sufferance of Simon's false profession is analogous to that of Judas by our Lord himself (John 6, 64. 70. 71.) Simon's own motive has been variously explained and understood. Most probably he went at first with the multitude to hide the shame of his desertion and defeat. With this may have been combined a wish to know the secret of Philip's miraculous performances, and perhaps to add this higher magic to his own, so as to do really what he had before done only in appearance or pretence. For this purpose, having been baptized, and thus admitted to free intercourse with Philip, he not only *continued with him*, as the English versions somewhat feebly render it, but *was cleaving* (or *adhering*) *to him*, the intrinsic strength of the expression being heightened by the participial construction, which suggests the idea of continuance or perseverance in addition to that of sticking close to Philip. (Compare the use of the same verb in 2, 46. 6, 4, and of the same construction in 1, 14. 2, 42.) *Beholding*, as a curious spectator (see above, on 3, 16. 4, 13. 7, 56.) *Miracles*, literally, *powers*, i. e. exhibitions and exertions of divine or superhuman power. See above, on 2, 22, where the same word is joined with *signs and wonders*, to exhaust the idea of miraculous performances. The copies vary with respect to the order and grammatical form of these words, but without effect upon the sense, except that several of the oldest manuscripts and versions add the epithet *great*. *Which were done* is a single work in Greek, a participle, strictly meaning *happened*, come to pass. *Wondered*, which expresses the effect on Simon, is the last word in the original sentence, and might have been consistently translated, *was bewitched*, being simply the passive of the verb so rendered in vs. 9, 11. The absurdity of this translation here ought surely to have hindered its adoption there. The true sense in both cases is that of extreme wonder or amazement, which the Rhemish Bible labours to express here by translating, *was astonied with admiration*.

14. Now when the Apostles, which were at Jerusalem, heard that Samaria had received the word of God, they sent unto them Peter and John.

Now represents the same Greek word (δέ), and indicates the same connection, with the *and*, *but*, and *then*, of the three preceding verses. *When the Apostles heard*, Gr. *the Apostles having heard* (or *hearing*.) *Which were at Jerusalem*, Gr. *those in Jerusalem*, might seem to mean that some were absent, and thus to contradict the last clause of v. 1, or to imply an intervening change; but it really describes them as all there, and for that very reason calls them *the Apostles in Jerusalem*. *Samaria*, not the city, whose reception of the Gospel would have been a small thing in comparison with its reception by the "nation of Samaria," as it is expressed above in v. 9. In the one case, this great change is affirmed of the capital exclusively; while in the other case, that city, or some other, represents the whole, as being the first fruits of its conversion, and at the same time an important step towards the general and unrestricted preaching of the gospel. (See above, on v. 5.) It is not surprising, therefore, that the college of Apostles, when they heard (Tynd. *heard say*) that Samaria had received the word of God, should send a deputation to the place where the good work had begun, wherever it might be; not, as has been variously imagined, because Philip was only a Deacon, for he was more, as we have seen above (on v.

5); or because they were jealous or suspicious of him; or because they doubted the sincerity or depth of the Samaritan conversions; or to show that the Apostles, though this work began without them, still retained their old position; but because they were the constituted organizers of the church, and as such not only authorized but bound to enter every open door, whoever might have opened it. As in the original mission of the twelve (Mark 6, 7), and of the seventy (Luke 10, 1), two were sent together, and the two commissioned upon this occasion were the same whom we have seen before so constantly in company. (See above, on ch. 3, 1.) *Unto them*, i. e. to the Samaritans, the plural subject latent in the singular collective name *Samaria*, as in v. 5 above. *The word of God*, the new revelation or religion. (See above, on v. 4.) *Received*, not only in the passive sense of hearing, but in the active sense of believing and obeying. They not only had the opportunity of being saved through Christ, but they embraced it. The position here assigned to Peter, however honourable and important, is by no means that of a superior, much less of a primate.

15. Who, when they were come down, prayed for them, that they might receive the Holy Ghost.

Coming (or *having come*) *down*, see above, on 3, 1. 7, 15. The form of expression here employed, or rather the fact here recorded, shows that this gift was not bestowed, even mediately, by the Apostles, but by God directly, in answer to their prayers, and sometimes without even that degree of intervention. (See below, on 10, 44.) This by no means favours the opinion, that the Apostolical commission was sent down, simply because Philip, as a Deacon or Evangelist, could not impart the Holy Ghost. He certainly could pray for it, nor is there any intimation that his prayers would have been less effectual than those of the Apostles. The natural impression on the reader is, that John and Peter came down with a general commission to inspect and regulate, and afterwards report, and in the mean time to instruct the people; and that while engaged in executing this commission, they prayed, etc.

16. For as yet he was fallen upon none of them; only they were baptized in the name of the Lord Jesus.

As yet, literally, *not yet*, the Greek idiom admitting of a double negative for emphasis. *Only* implies that the two things were expected or accustomed to go together. (See below, on 9, 17. 18. 10, 47. 19, 5. 6.) But in this case, the baptism of water had not been followed by the spiritual baptism of which it was the sign, or rather by the visible witness of the Spirit which commonly attended it. (See above, on 5, 32.) *Into the name*, i. e. into union with him, and subjection to him, as their Sovereign and their Saviour. (See above, on v. 12.) Several of the older English versions, and a few Greek manuscripts, have *Christ Jesus*, others *Jesus Christ*, while the Codex Beza combines two of these readings, *Lord Jesus Christ*. *Fallen* is omitted in the Peshito, and exchanged for *come* in the Vulgate and the older English versions. This variation must be euphemistical or accidental, as it is not found in the Greek manuscripts. *Fallen* denotes the sudden illapse of a superior power or influence. (See below, on 10, 44. 11, 15.) The expression may be borrowed from Ezekiel 11, 5, "the Spirit of the Lord fell upon me, and said unto me, Speak." It is elsewhere in this book applied to other sudden seizures, both miraculous and natural, as wonder (10, 10), fear, (19, 17), blindness (13, 11.) It is evident from this verse, that the fact which it records was regarded as a strange one. *Were baptized* is not the full sense of the Greek phrase (βεβαπτισμένοι ὑπῆρχον), which suggests, if it does not express, the idea, that they still remained baptized and nothing more. (See above, on 5, 4.)

17. Then laid they their hands on them, and they received the Holy Ghost.

The obvious connection between this verse and the fifteenth (v. 16 being clearly parenthetical) shows that the touch of the Apostles' hands merely symbolized a spiritual gift which had been granted in answer to their prayers. (See above, on 6, 6.) The reception of the Holy Ghost here meant is doubtless that of his extraordinary influences, either in the way of inspiration, or in that of miraculous endowments, or of both combined, as in the case of the Apostles. That the gifts conferred were not merely moral or internal, but such as could be verified and brought to the test of observation, is clear from the effect which they produced on Simon, as recorded in the next verse. *Received*, in the imperfect tense, might seem to denote a repetition of the process here described, but that the other verb is in the aorist form, and therefore must relate to a specific time. The imperfect (*were receiving*) may possibly have reference to what follows, and denote that this solemnity was still proceeding, when the incident recorded in the following verse took place. The impression naturally made by these three verses is, that the baptism of these converts not being followed by the gift of the Holy Ghost, as on the day of Pentecost (11, 17), and probably on subsequent occasions, although not recorded (4, 4. 5, 14. 6, 7), the Apostles, who had come down to direct the whole proceeding, made it the subject of specific intercession, and by imposition of their hands, evinced that their prayers were answered.

18. And when Simon saw, that through laying on of the Apostles' hands the Holy Ghost was given, he offered them money —

The sentence is completed in the next verse. *When Simon saw*, Gr. *Simon beholding* (θεασάμενος, see above, on 1, 11), or according to the latest critics, *seeing* (ἰδών.) *Through*, denoting instrumental agency (see above, on 1, 16. 2, 16. 22, 23. 43. 3, 18. 21. 4, 16. 25, 30. 5, 12. 7, 25.) The epithet *Holy* is omitted by some manuscripts and editors. *Was given*, literally, *is given*, the present form bringing up the scene before us, as one actually passing. *Money*, literally *monies*, a plural common in old English, and still retained in certain forms of business. The Greek word is the plural of the one used in 4, 37 above, and there explained. *Offered*, literally, *brought to*, as in Matt. 22, 19. Mark 10, 13. Luke 18, 15, often used to signify religious gifts, oblations (as in 7, 42 above), but here in the intermediate sense of an offer made to men.

19. Saying, Give me also this power, that on whomsoever I lay hands, he may receive (the) Holy Ghost.

The sentence is continued from v. 18, and completed. *To me also*, not to me as well as others, but to me as well as yourselves. He asked not merely what he saw them give, but the power of bestowing it. *Power*, i. e. moral power, right, authority, not physical capacity or strength. (See above, on 1, 7. 5, 4.) *Holy Spirit*, being without the article, may mean *a holy spirit*, and imply the want of any definite conception as to a personal agent. What precise meaning he attached to the phrase, we have no means of determining. He may have used it merely as he heard it used by others, without knowing what it meant at all. Up to this point, the language used implies that both the apostles were distinctly recognized as acting jointly, and as equal in authority. *They* prayed (v. 15), *their* hands (v. 17), offered *them* (v. 18), give *ye* (v. 19).

20. **But Peter said unto him, Thy money perish with thee, because thou hast thought that the gift of God may be purchased with money.**

Peter now assumes his usual position as the spokesman. (See above, on 1, 15. 2, 14. 38. 3, 6. 4, 8. 5, 3. 9, 29.) Various attempts have been made to explain away the seeming imprecation in this verse. Some understand the words to mean, 'let thy money remain with thee for thy ruin' (compare Dan. 5, 17), which is neither perfectly grammatical nor any relief of the supposed difficulty. Others explain it as a mere prediction of the necessary consequence or tendency of that which he was doing. But the true solution seems to be, that Peter spoke by direct divine authority, and also that the wish is to be qualified by the exhortation in v. 22. As if he had said, 'Perish, if you will not repent.' The first *money* is not the word so rendered in the other clause and in v. 18 above, but the one employed in 7, 16, and strictly meaning *silver*, a usage perfectly coincident with that of the French *argent*. *Perish with thee*, literally, *with thee be for ruin* (or *unto perdition*.) *Hast thought*, or more exactly, *didst think*, i. e. just now, when he made his proposition. *The gift of God*, elsewhere called *the gift of the Holy Ghost* (see above, on 2, 38, and below, on 10, 45.) The very terms imply gratuity, the Greek noun being used in the accusative (δωρεάν) as an adverb corresponding to the Latin *gratis*. (See Matt. 10, 8. John 15, 25. Rom. 3, 24. 2 Cor. 11, 7. Gal. 2, 21. 2 Thess. 3, 8. Rev. 21, 6. 22, 17.) The sin and folly of the sorcerer's offer lay not merely in the thought of bribing God, but in that of purchasing what, from its very nature, could be only a free gift. *With money*, literally, through, by means of, as in v. 18. *Money*, literally, *monies*, as in the same verse. (The Syriac version here has *worldly wealth*, or *riches of the world*.) *May be purchased* is a single word in Greek, and the last one in the sentence. It is infinitive in form (κτᾶσθαι), but ambiguous in meaning, as it may be either active or passive. The latter sense, though common only in the later writers, is found in the Attic Greek of Thucydides and Euripides. The active meaning seems to be forbidden here by the construction, 'thou hast thought to obtain,' which, though correct enough in English, is not so good Greek as the passive sense, 'hast thought the gift of God to be obtained.' It is only by a figure of speech that *simony*, a term derived from this man's name, has been applied to the sale and purchase of ecclesiastical office, which, however heinous it may be, is something very different from offering to buy and sell the Holy Ghost.

21. Thou hast neither part nor lot in this matter, for thy heart is not right in the sight of God.

Not content with repelling his base offer, the Apostle now reveals to him his spiritual state, no doubt by special revelation and immediate divine authority. *Thou hast neither*, literally, *there is not to thee*. *Part* and *lot* are substantially equivalent, the first denoting any share or portion (see below, on 16, 12), the second one determined or assigned by lot (see above, on 1, 17. 25.) *In this matter*, literally, *in this word*, and so translated by the Vulgate and its English copyists. The immediate English versions, older than King James's, all have *business*. Modern philologists, however, question whether this sense of the Greek words (λόγος and ῥῆμα), which the old interpreters supposed to be derived from a peculiar usage of the Hebrew (דָּבָר), ever occurs in the New Testament at all. (See above, on 5, 32.) In Luke 4, 36, the common version is correct, namely, *word*, meaning word of command, and in Luke 2, 15, "this thing which is come to pass" means really "this word (or divine declaration) which has been fulfilled." So too in 15, 6, below, "this matter" properly denotes this question, or this point of doctrine. Accordingly, some understand it here as meaning, *this (new) doctrine* (or *religion*), a sense at least as old as the Peshito (*in this faith*), and much more natural than that adopted by some modern writers, *in this speech* (or *speaking*), with allusion to the gift of tongues, as one of those which Simon wished to buy the power of bestowing, but which is not mentioned in the text or context. *Right*, literally, *straight*, an epithet applied both to physical and moral qualities. (See below, on 9, 11, and 13, 10.) *Before God*, i. e. in his estimation (see above, on 4, 19. 7, 46), with a tacit reference, as some suppose, to Philip's error; but see above, on 4, 13.

22. Repent, therefore, of this thy wickedness, and pray God, if perhaps the thought of thine heart may be forgiven thee.

The exhortation to repent shows that the case was not entirely desperate, while at the same time it qualifies the terrible denunciation in v. 20. *Therefore*, because otherwise you can have no part in this salvation. *Of this*, literally, *from* (away from) *this*, implying not mere sorrow but conversion. *Wickedness*, literally, *badness*, the most general expression of that idea in the language, once applied even to mere physical evil (Matt. 6, 34), sometimes used in the specific sense of malice or malignity (e. g. Tit. 3, 3), but here most probably in that of moral evil, sin, depravity. *This* may either mean this specific act of sin, which he had just committed, or *this depravity of thine*, which thou hast just revealed to us. *Pray God*, or retaining the original construction, *ask, beseech of God*. (The oldest reading seems to be, *the Lord*.) *If perhaps* is exactly the expression used in Mark 11, 13, and in both places construed with the future, *if perhaps the thought of thy heart shall* (or *will*) *be forgiven*, or remitted, the verb corresponding to the noun employed in 2, 38, and there explained (see also 5, 31.) *If perhaps* (Wiclif, *if paradventure*) is a much more correct translation than Tyndale's (*that the thought*, &c.,) copied as usual by Cranmer, and also in the Geneva Bible, but with a qualifying phrase (*if it be possible*.) Some suppose the doubt implied in these words to be only a doubt of his repentance, to which others object that it would not then be placed between his prayer and his forgiveness, and refer it rather to his having possibly committed the unpardonable sin. *The thought of thy heart*, not merely thy opinion but thy purpose, the fruit not only of a darkened mind but of corrupt affection. It includes his false belief as to the gift of God, and his presumptuous effort to obtain it for himself, in a way at once unlawful and impossible. The specific idea of an *evil* thought or purpose is suggested by the context.

23. For I perceive that thou art in (the) gall of bitterness, and (in the) bond of iniquity.

As Simon had already been baptized (v. 13), the exhortation to repent might have seemed to have respect to this particular transgression, as a single act of disobedience. But the words of the Apostle show that the whole work of repentance and conversion was yet to be performed. The original order of the sentence is *for in the gall of bitterness and bond of iniquity I see thee being*. *Gall of bitterness*, like *gall and wormwood* (Deut. 29, 17), seems to mean an intense bitter, and this to be put for poison (see Job 20, 14), from some natural association, or perhaps from an opinion, which we find in Pliny, that the venom of serpents resides in their gall. The idea of moral corruption is conveyed by a kindred figure, *root of bitterness* (Heb. 12, 15.) *Bond of iniquity*, is by some translated *bundle of unrighteousness*, and instead of *being in* (ὄντα εἰς), *being for* (as in 7, 21. 53), i. e. being a mere bundle of unrighteousness, as Shakspeare says, "the lunatic, the lover, and the poet, are of imagination *all compact*," i. e. entirely and exclusively made up of it. The older and more usual interpretation gives the first noun the sense of bond or bondage, and the preposition (εἰς), its usual and proper sense of *into*, as if he had said, 'thou art (fallen into and remainest) in the bondage of unrighteousness.' Both figures, then, and especially the last, suggest the idea of a permanent and long continued state, and cannot therefore be applied to a relapse or fall from grace after his baptism. There is, however, still a third interpretation, of more recent date than either of the others, which applies these difficult expressions, not exclusively to Simon's own condition at the time when they were uttered, but to his future influence on others. 'I see thee (by the light of my prophetic inspiration) being or becoming (ὄντα εἰς, compare the Hebrew הָיָה לְ) gall of bitterness (i. e. a source of misery, or a deadly poison) and a bond (bond of union, see Eph. 4, 3. Col. 2, 19. 3, 14) of iniquity (a centre of corrupting influence to others.)' Whether this be regarded as a natural or even an admissible construction of the words or not, it is certainly entitled to the praise of ingenuity, and also of a singular agreement with the subsequent career and influence of Simon, as preserved in the traditions of the church. In any case, he is described by the Apostle, either expressly or by implication, as an extremely wicked man, who could be saved from condign ruin only by repentance and conversion or return to God.

24. **Then answered Simon and said, Pray ye to the Lord for me, that none of these things which ye have spoken come upon me.**

Then, as in vs. 5, 13, 17. *Answered,* literally, *answering. Ye* is emphatic. 'Pray yourselves; do you pray for me.' *The things which ye have spoken* seems to be a euphemistical periphrasis for the perdition threatened in v. 20. The plural form may represent the fulness or variety of evils which he understood to be included in that pregnant term. For *come upon me,* Tyndale and his followers gratuitously use the word *fall,* which they seemed to avoid in its proper place. (See above, on v. 16.) This request may have been prompted by mere dread of punishment, or it may be regarded as a proof of his compliance with the exhortation to repent. What became of Simon, we are not informed, as the narrative ends abruptly here. Tradition represents him as having persevered in his iniquity, and classes him among the heresiarchs of the apostolic age. Some regard him as the founder of the Simonians of the second century, who held a mixture of Jewish and Samaritan opinions, with certain oriental theosophic notions; while others deny all connection, even in the names. From ten to twenty years after these events, we meet with a Simon in Josephus, who describes him as a sorcerer from Cyprus, employed by Felix to seduce the affections of the Jewess Drusilla. (See below, on 24, 24.) The identity of name, and similarity of character, would leave no doubt that this was Simon Magus, but for a statement of Justin Martyr, that the latter was by birth a Samaritan. This is entitled to the more weight as Simon was himself a native of that country, and as he designates the town of Gitton or Gitta as the birth-place of Simon, which by some has been identified with Citium in Cyprus. Justin goes on to say, however, that he afterwards removed to Rome, where he was worshipped as a god, and had a column dedicated to him. By a curious coincidence, a fragment has been excavated there in modern times, inscribed to an Etruscan deity (*Semoni Sanco*), which some suppose to be a part of Justin's column, and as he was mistaken upon this point, they infer that his statement is entitled to no weight whatever. The decision of this question seems to be at once unimportant and impossible. The only certain trace of Simon in history is the use of the word *simony*, which has been already mentioned. (See above, on v. 19.)

25. And they, when they had testified and preached the word of the Lord, returned to Jerusalem, and preached the gospel in many villages of the Samaritans.

The preaching of the gospel among the Samaritans was not confined to the city where it had begun, but extended to many of the smaller towns, through which the Apostles passed on their return. For *villages*, Tyndale has *cities*, Geneva *towns*, Wiclif *countries*. *They*, i. e. Peter and John. *When they had*, literally, *having testified*. Here again the apostolical preaching is described as testimony (see above, on 2, 40.) *Preached* is repeated only in the English. The first of the two Greek verbs literally means *talking*, speaking, as in 3, 24. 4, 1. 17. 20. 29. 4, 31. 5, 20. 40. 6, 10. The other verb, translated *preached the gospel*, is the one employed above, in vs. 4, 12, and denoting the communication of glad tidings; but instead of governing the subject of the preaching, as it does there and in 5, 42, it is construed here with the places where they preached (*evangelizing the villages*) a construction which has been retained in modern English. (See below, on 14, 15. 21. 16, 10.) *Returned*, is one of Luke's favourite Greek expressions (see above, on 1, 12.) Both this and the last verb have the form of the imperfect tense in several of the oldest manuscripts, which may imply a similar connection with the following verse to that between vs. 17 and 18. The sense will then be, that while Peter and John were thus employed, Philip received his new commission.

26. And the Angel of the Lord spake unto Philip, saying, Arise, and go toward the south, unto the way that goeth down from Jerusalem unto Gaza, which is desert.

An angel of the Lord (see above, on 5, 19) cannot without absurdity be resolved into a suggestion of Philip's own mind. Although it is not said that an angel appeared (see below, on 12, 23), a personal agency, exterior to himself, is even more explicitly referred to here, than in v. 29 below. The command appears to have been given in Samaria. If it were said to have been given in a dream, *arise* might be understood to mean, arise from sleep or out of bed. (Compare Matt. 2, 13. 14. 20, 21, where the verb, however, strictly means to *awake*.) In the absence of any such intimation, it seems rather to mean, address yourself to action (see above, on 1, 15. 5, 17. 6, 9.) *Go, go away*, journey, travel (see above, on 1, 10. 11, 25. 5, 20. 41.) *Toward*, see below, on 27, 12, and compare Phil. 3, 14. *The south*, literally, *mid-day*, i. e. the place of the sun at noon. (Precisely similar, in etymology and usage, is the German *Mittag*.) He is not required to go to Jerusalem, but to get upon the road leading thence to Gaza. *Going down*, see above, on v. 5. Gaza is one of the oldest places mentioned in the Bible. It first occurs in Gen. 1, 19, as a frontier town of the Canaanites; in later history, as the southernmost of the five cities of the Philistines, to whom it really belonged, even after it was formally assigned to Judah (Josh. 15, 47. Judg. 1, 18.) It was the scene of one of Samson's most remarkable exploits (Judges 16, 3.) It was besieged by Alexander the Great, and destroyed by Alexander Jannæus, rebuilt by the Roman General Gabinius, and given by Augustus to Herod, after whose death it was attached to the province of Syria. *Which is desert*, literally, *this is desert*, forming an independent clause or sentence, but connected in the closest manner with what goes before. The demonstrative pronoun may refer grammatically either to the city or the road. According to some ancient writers, there was a new Gaza, distinct from the ruins of the old, destroyed by Alexander, and the words in question were intended to direct Philip to the latter, as if he had said, 'that is, the desert one.' But besides the want of satisfactory evidence in favour of the fact alleged, why should the places be distinguished here, unless they were so far apart, that different roads led to them from Jerusalem, in which case their identity would be destroyed. One ingenious modern writer understands the words as a remark of the historian, in reference to the town itself having been again destroyed during the Jewish war; but this would make the date of composition later than we have any other reason for believing it. For these or other reasons, most interpreters suppose the clause to be descriptive of the road, as Arrian speaks of a road desert for want of water. The words may then have been intended to guide

Philip to the least frequented of the roads which appear to have existed between these two places, or added by the writer (as in John 6, 10), to bring the scene more vividly before the reader. But according to Greek usage, the article is indispensable in distinguishing between two objects. Of those who refer it to the road, some suppose it to be indicated as a proper place for meditation, others as a sort of type or symbol of spiritual desolation, like the desert in Isai. 40, 3. Matt. 3, 3. But perhaps the simplest and most natural interpretation of the words is that which understands them as implying, that there was something strange in the command, and in the incident which followed its execution. As if Luke had said, 'an angel sent him to the road between Jerusalem and Gaza, which might well have seemed a singular direction, since it is a desert road, in which he was not likely to encounter travellers, much less to meet with such an adventure as did there befall him.' Any of these exegetical hypotheses is far more probable than that of a gloss or spurious addition to the text, the origin of which would be as unaccountable as it is destitute of all external evidence, the words in question being found apparently in all Greek manuscripts without exception.

27. And he arose and went, and behold, a man of Ethiopia, an eunuch of great authority, under Candace, queen of the Ethiopians, who had the charge of all her treasure, and had come to Jerusalem for to worship —

The sentence is completed in the next verse. We have here disclosed the purpose of the strange command recorded in v. 26. According to a very common scriptural usage, Philip's obedience is stated in the terms of the command itself, *he arose and went*. *Behold*, as usual, denotes something unexpected (see above, on 1, 10. 2, 7. 5, 9. 25, 28. 7, 56), and is peculiarly appropriate here, because the mission was itself a strange one. As if it had been said, 'he obeyed the angelic order, unaccountable as it appeared, and though the road, to which he was directed, was a desert one, he soon saw whom he had been sent to meet.' *A man of Ethiopia*, more exactly *an Ethiopian man*, or still more closely, *a man, an Ethiopian*. (See above, on 1, 11. 16. 2, 5. 14. 22. 29. 37. 3, 12. 14. 5, 35. 7, 2.) *Ethiopia* is the Greek name corresponding to the *Cush* of the Old Testament, but less extensive, being restricted to the country watered by the Nile, south of Egypt, corresponding to the Nubia of modern geography, with the adjacent parts of Abyssinia. *Eunuch* originally means a *chamberlain*, and is so translated here by Tyndale and Cranmer. Its secondary meaning is derived from the oriental practice of employing emasculated men as guardians of the harem. The wider meaning of the term, which is found in the Septuagint version of Gen. 37, 36. 39, seems to be required in the case before us by the prohibitory law of Deut. 23, 1 (2.) His office then would be the same with that held by Blastus in the court or family of Herod Agrippa (see below, on 12, 20.) In early times, offices of state were not so carefully distinguished as at present from those of the royal household. *Of great authority*, literally, *a dynast* or *potentate*, a term applied to princes (Luke 1, 52) and to God himself (1 Tim. 6, 15), but here denoting one in power, and especially in office, under a sovereign, as the word is also used by Xenophon and Plutarch. The plural is applied in the Septuagint version to the "house of Pharaoh" (Gen. 50, 4.) *Candace*, a common or hereditary title of the queens who for many years succeeded one another in the island of Meroe, belonging to the ancient Ethiopia, as we learn from Strabo, Dio Cassius, and Pliny. *Had the charge of all her treasure*, literally, *was over it*, a phrase corresponding to the Hebrew title, *over the house* or *palace* (Isai. 22, 15), and to the kindred Greek phrase, *over the bed-chamber* (see below, on 12, 20.) Both offices may have been united in this person, if *eunuch* has the wider sense above suggested. By a curious coincidence, the *chamberlain* of London, and some other cities, is the *treasurer*. *Treasure* is here used to translate a word said to be of Persian origin, and specially applied to royal treasure. (Thus Quintus Curtius says, *Pecuniam regiam gazam Persae vocant;* and Cornelius Nepos describes the office here in question by the title, *gazae regiae custos*.) *And had come*, more exactly, *who had come*. *To worship* is, in Greek, not an infinitive but a future participle, which occurs again in 24, 11 below (compare John 12, 20.) It is evident from this that he was either a Hellenist or foreign Jew by birth, or a proselyte from heathenism to the Jews' religion.

28. Was returning, and, sitting in his chariot, read Esaias the Prophet.

The sentence is completed from the verse preceding. *Returning*, a favourite Greek verb of Luke's (see above, on v. 25, and on 1, 12.) *Was returning* represents exactly the form of the original, which is the same as in v. 13 above. As he was no doubt returning to his own country by the way of Egypt, his first stage or journey was from Jerusalem to Gaza. *In* (literally, *on*) *his chariot* implies, in this connection, an equipage suited to his rank, including, no doubt, one or more attendants (see below, on v. 38.) *Read*, in the imperfect tense, *was reading*, i. e. at the time when Philip first caught sight of him. That this was in compliance with a Jewish maxim, extant in the Talmud, is not half so probable as that he was induced to search the Scriptures by what he had seen and heard while at Jerusalem. *Was reading*, probably aloud, which some regard as the precise sense of the Greek verb, and which is certainly its meaning in such places as 13, 27. 15, 21 below (compare 2 Cor. 3, 15. 1 Thess. 5, 27.) That the Ethiopian was attended, as the great men of that day often were, both on journeys and at home, by an *anagnost* or reader, is a perfectly gratuitous assumption, without any thing to countenance it in the text or context. *Esaias*, the Greek form of *Isaiah*, or rather of the Hebrew (ישעיהו), from which both forms depart so much, that it would have been better to use one exclusively in the translation of both Testaments. (See above, on 7, 45.) *The prophet*, not necessarily by way of eminence, but the well-known prophet of that name, implying the existence of his writings, and their general reception as a part of the Old Testament canon. Some interpreters assume that he was reading the original, and then infer from this assumption, that he was a *Hebrew* (see above, on 6, 1); but it is far more probable that he was reading it in Greek, as the Septuagint version had its origin in Egypt, through which country he had passed and was about to pass again, and was in common use among the Jews there, even in their synagogue service.

29. Then the Spirit said unto Philip, Go near, and join thyself to this chariot.

It is evident that Philip was to be gradually apprised of what he had to do on this remarkable occasion. An angel sends him to a desert road; he there sees a chariot; which he is now required to join. *The Spirit* of this verse, and the *angel* of v. 26, although coincident, are not identical, the Spirit being the divine authority or power, of which the angel was the instrument or agent. (See above, on 5, 19. 7, 30. 35. 38. 53.) *Go near*, literally, *go to*, the idea being not that of mere approach, but of actual arrival and immediate contact. (See below, on 9, 1.) *Join thyself* is not a mere tautology, but expresses something more, to wit, the act of sticking to the chariot, not losing sight of it or leaving it, until the divine purpose was accomplished. (For the usage of the Greek verb, simple and compound, see above, on 5, 13, and below, on 9, 26. 10, 28. 17, 34.)

30. And Philip ran thither to him, and heard him read the Prophet Esaias, and said, Understandest thou what thou readest?

In obedience to this order, the authority of which he seems not to have questioned for a moment, whatever may have been the mode of the divine communication, Philip takes the first step towards its execution, by hastening to place himself within the stranger's reach, and listening to him as he read aloud. *Ran thither* is the Geneva version; Tyndale and Cranmer render more exactly, *ran to* (*him*.) *Heard him read* (Wicl. more literally, *reading*) *the Prophet Isaiah*, and a passage so peculiarly important and obscure, that it prompted the abrupt inquiry, with which he accosted the traveller. The form of the original interrogation (ἆρά γε) seems to anticipate a negative answer; as if he had said, 'you surely do not know what you are reading,' perhaps with some allusion to the rapidity or seeming nonchalance, with which the Ethiopian pronounced the passage. The verb translated *read* is a compound form of that translated *know*, so that their combination (γινώσκεις ἃ ἀναγινώσκεις) gives a point to the original, which cannot be retained in any version. It is worthy of remark, as one of the resemblances in language between Luke and that Apostle, under whose influence an uniform tradition represents him as having composed both his books, that Paul has the very same *lusus verborum* in 2 Cor. 3, 2, (γινωσκομένη καὶ ἀναγινωσκομένη) *known and read of all men*. It is not necessary to suppose, that Philip listened for some time before accosting him, but that just as he came up to him, he heard enough of what he read to know that it was in a certain passage of Isaiah.

31. And he said, How can I, except some man should guide me? And he desired Philip that he would come up and sit with him.

The Eunuch's question may contain a gentle intimation that he thought the tone of the inquiry unbecoming or unreasonable. As if he had said, 'How can you expect a stranger without aid to comprehend what puzzles your most learned doctors?' *Some man*, some one, somebody; see above, on 2, 45. 4, 35. *Guide me*, a figure for instruction, used by Christ himself (see Matt. 15, 14. Luke 6, 39. John 16, 13, and compare Matt. 23, 16. 24. Rom. 2, 19.) The specific reference in all these cases is to the guidance of the blind. *How can I?* has a peculiar form in the original ($\pi\hat{\omega}\varsigma$ $\overset{\text{\textasciiacute}}{\alpha}\nu$ $\delta\upsilon\nu\alpha\acute{\iota}\mu\eta\nu$), which, according to the nice distinctions of the Greek idiom, expresses in a high degree the speaker's doubt, if not as to the absolute intrinsic possibility, at least as to the actual and present practicability of the thing in question. 'What reason have you to suppose me capable of understanding it without assistance?' Besides the modest self-depreciation of this answer, it implies a suspicion, if no more, that the stranger who thus suddenly accosted him was just such a guide and helper as he needed. This feeling he expressed still more clearly by inviting Philip to ascend the chariot. *Desired*, literally, called for, invited (as in 28, 20), or entreated (as in 16, 39.) This, which would have been an act of hospitable kindness, in any case whatever, to a solitary traveller on foot in that secluded road (v. 26), derives a higher character and meaning from the few words which had previously passed between them, and becomes expressive, not of mere compassion or a wish for company, but also for instruction in the word of God.

32. The place of the Scripture which he read was this, He was led as a sheep to the slaughter, and like a lamb dumb before his shearer, so opened he not his mouth. 33. In his humiliation his judgment was taken away, and who shall declare his generation? for his life is taken from the earth.

The particular *context* or *passage* ($\pi\epsilon\rho\iota o\chi\acute{\eta}$) *of the Scripture*, which the Ethiopian was reading when Philip interrupted him, is still extant in Isaiah 53, 7. 8. It is quoted by Luke, as it was no doubt read, in the Septuagint version, with a few unimportant verbal variations from the common text, such as the present participle for the aorist, the insertion of *his* before *generation*, etc. The second sentence quoted is among the most disputed and obscure in the Old Testament; but all that is necessary to the understanding of the narrative is what all interpreters admit, that like the verse before it, it describes the sufferings of an innocent and unresisting victim. Nothing here depends on the precise sense of the words, because they are quoted, not as the part which particularly exercised the Eunuch's mind, but as that which he happened to be reading aloud when Philip joined him; and also because, as afterwards appears, the question that perplexed him was not in reference to the sense of these words, but in reference to their subject, or the person of whom they were written. The solution of this question would not be promoted in the least by the most complete enumeration of the senses, which have been put upon the words themselves by different interpreters; because, on any exegetical hypothesis whatever, it might still be asked, to whom they were intended to apply. (Some account of the different interpretations may be found in the writer's notes upon the passage of Isaiah.)

34. And the Eunuch answered Philip and said, I pray thee, of whom speaketh the Prophet this, of himself, or of some other man?

This is a further answer to the question, with which Philip had begun the conversation (see above, on v. 30.) The answer is indeed itself a question, but this mode of reply is very frequent in the dialect of Scripture and of common life. At all events, there can be no sufficient ground for the jejune interpretation of *answered* as pleonastic, or in other words, as meaning nothing. The whole tendency of thorough and consistent exposition is to reduce the number of factitious and imaginary pleonasms. The Eunuch's question is an interesting one, as exhibiting, not only his own state of mind, but that of the contemporary Jews, the *status quæstionis* of the controversy then existing, as to the subject of this signal prophecy. Without attempting to determine whether all the views proposed by later writers, and recorded in the works upon Isaiah, had been broached so early, it is clear that one of the most plausible was known, or had at least occurred to this inquirer, although far more probably suggested by his intercourse with Jewish doctors, and perhaps with Christians, at Jerusalem. This was the doctrine, here proposed as an alternative, that Isaiah was speaking of himself, not as a private individual but as a prophet, or a representative of all the prophets as a class. This doctrine which, in one form or another, has found many advocates in later times, is here suggested, either as the only other known to the speaker, or as the only one entitled to be brought into comparison with the old and still prevailing application of the words to the Messiah, which probably would never have been called in question, if it had not become necessary as a means of combating the claims of Jesus. Perhaps this ingenious evasion had been recently invented or discovered, and the Ethiopian had heard the passage thus expounded at Jerusalem, but could not fully acquiesce in this interpretation. It was probably in this state of uncertainty respecting it, that he was reading it again when Philip first accosted him, and frankly owned his incapacity to solve the doubt, without assistance from some other quarter. He little dreamed, as we may well suppose, that such assistance was at hand, expressly furnished by an Angel (v. 26) and the Holy Spirit (v. 29.) There are no doubt many other cases, in which such help has been afforded no less opportunely, though without the same extraordinary circumstances.

35. Then Philip opened his mouth, and began at the same scripture, and preached unto him Jesus.

That the subject which engrossed the Eunuch's mind was not the exact sense of the verses quoted from Isaiah, is furthermore apparent from the fact that Philip, instead of dwelling upon that one passage, merely used it as the starting-point or text of a discourse on the Messiahship of Jesus. The idea of a regular discourse, as distinguished from a simple conversation, is suggested by the otherwise unmeaning statement, that he *opened his mouth*, i. e. began to speak with continuity and some formality of method. The wide scope of his argument is shown by his simply *beginning from this scripture*, i. e. the one which had been the occasion of his speaking at all. The subject and spirit of his sermon are denoted by the phrase inadequately rendered, *preached unto him Jesus*. The defect lies in failing to convey the full force of the verb, which, from its very form and derivation, must suggest to every reader of the Greek, the joyous and exhilarating nature of the truths taught, as good news or glad tidings of salvation, an idea not by any means inseparable from the simple act of preaching, either in its first sense of proclaiming, or in its secondary sense of exhortation and religious teaching. (See above, on v. 25.) This idea, so distinctly legible in the original, has been retained by some translations, e. g. in the Rhemish, with its usual violation of the English idiom (*evangelized unto him Jesus*), and by Luther (*preached to him the evangel of Jesus*.) There is also a meaning in the name itself, of which we are continually tempted to lose sight, by the inveterate habit of regarding it as a mere personal designation, no more distinctive or significant than those in common use among ourselves; whereas *Jesus*, as we have often had occasion to observe, was designed from the beginning to be, not a mere convenience like a label or a number, but a pregnant description of him to whom it was applied, before his birth, by an angel, as the Saviour of his people from their sins. (See above, on vs. 12. 16.) That he was such a Saviour, and the very one predicted in the Hebrew Scriptures, was the doctrine now propounded and established in Philip's exegetical and argumentative discourse to his companion.

36. And as they went on their way, they came unto a certain water; and the Eunuch said, See (here is) water; what doth hinder me to be baptized?

The effect of Philip's discourse is indirectly but expressively suggested by a little incident, recorded without comment and with perfect simplicity. The road, as we have seen above (v. 26), was desert, running probably along or through a dry and barren tract. Of this we are reminded by the statement, not that *they went their way*, which would be saying little, but that *they were travelling, along the* (same) *road*, when their attention was awakened by their coming, not to *a certain water*, which might seem to mean a well known lake or stream, of which the region seems to have been wholly destitute, but, as the Greek words properly denote, *to some water*, the indefinite expression, like that in 5, 2, suggesting naturally the idea of a small degree or quantity. The sudden and perhaps unexpected sight of this slight interruption to the dryness of the road, at once suggested to the Eunuch's mind the thought of baptism, and without deliberation or delay, he seems to have proposed it. *See*, lo, behold, (*here is*) *water*, where it might least have been expected. (See above, on v. 27.) The consecution of the clauses seems to show that he considered nothing but the want of water as a reason for delaying the profession of his faith. There could not be a stronger or more beautiful expression of the strength of his convictions or of Philip's argument by which it was effected. The readiness with which the Ethiopian made this proposition has been supposed by some to imply a previous familiarity with proselyte baptism as a Jewish practice. But besides the historical uncertainty which overhangs this custom, and the high authorities by which it is denied, it seems scarcely natural that one who had already been baptized at his reception into Judaism, should expect, as a matter of course, to be baptized again, when convinced of the Messiahship of Jesus; unless indeed he knew that this rite was an essential one, prescribed by Christ, himself; and if he did know this, there can be no need of resorting to the dubious assumption of a Jewish baptism, to explain what is as well or rather better understood without it. The most obvious and natural solution is, that Philip's argumentative discourse included and perhaps wound up with an explicit statement of the way in which new converts must profess their faith and be received into the church, and that the Eunuch, as the strongest possible expression of assent, proposed to do what he had just been told he must do, and for which the outward means were providentially presented, at the very moment when they could be used.

37. And Philip said, If thou believest with all thine heart, thou mayest. And he answered and said, I believe that Jesus Christ is the Son of God.

This verse is excluded from the text by the latest critics, because wanting in several of the oldest manuscripts and versions, while in many copies which contain it, there is a diversity of form, both in the words themselves and in their order, which is commonly considered a suspicious circumstance. The interpolation is accounted for, as an attempt to guard against the practice of precipitate admission to the church, in favour of which this verse might with some plausibility have been alleged. But on the other hand, it may be argued that the verse, though genuine, was afterwards omitted, as unfriendly to the practice of delaying baptism, which had become common, if not prevalent, before the end of the third century. It is moreover found in many manuscripts, including some of the most ancient, and is quoted as a part of this context, not only by Cyprian but by Irenæus. It is therefore one of those cases, in which the external testimony may be looked upon as very nearly balanced, and in which it is the safest course to let the scale of the received text and traditional belief preponderate. At the same time, let it be observed that even if the verse should be expunged, there would be nothing taken from the text that is not easily supplied from other places, and indeed implied in what immediately precedes and follows; not only in the act of baptism, but in the proposal of the Eunuch, as explained above, and really involving just such a profession of his faith in Jesus, as Philip, in the verse before us, more explicitly requires.

38. And he commanded the chariot to stand still, and they went down both into the water, both Philip and the Eunuch, and he baptized him.

The expression in the first clause shows that he was not driving it himself, but, as might have been expected from his rank, was accompanied by one or more domestics. That they went down *into the water*, can prove nothing as to its extent or depth. Without insisting, as some writers have done, that the Greek phrase (εἰς τὸ ὕδωρ) may mean nothing more than to the water's edge, its stronger sense is fully satisfied, if we suppose that they stood in it, which in any language would be naturally expressed by saying, *they went into it*. That the phrase does not necessarily imply submersion, is moreover clear from the consideration, that such an inference would prove too much for those who draw it, namely, that the baptizer must himself be totally immersed. For not only is there no distinction made, but it is twice said expressly, in two different forms, as if to preclude all doubt and ambiguity, that *both* (ἀμφότεροι) *went down into the water, both* (ὅ τε) *Philip and the Eunuch*. If the verb and preposition necessarily imply immersion, they imply it equally in either case. If they do not necessarily imply it in the one, there can be no such necessary implication in the other. This is not used as an argument to prove that there was no immersion here, but simply to prevent an unfair use of the expression, as conclusively proving that there was. The same negative effect may be promoted by a simple illustration from analogy. Suppose them to have stopped for a similar yet altogether different purpose, one requiring no complete immersion, such as that of washing the face or hands. How could this have been more conveniently accomplished, especially by orientals, travelling either barefoot or in sandals, than by simply standing in the water; and how could it be otherwise expressed by the historian, without gratuitous minuteness or circumlocution, than by saying just what Luke says here, that they stopped the chariot and "both went down into the water." All that is contended for is this, that terms which might be naturally used in cases where there is no immersion at all, cannot possibly be made to prove, in any one case, that there was immersion. To the very different question, in what character, or by what right, Philip administered the ordinance, the narrative itself affords no certain answer. All that it is necessary to insist upon, according to the principle just stated, is that it cannot be shown to have been done by Philip as a deacon, and as a necessary function of that office. This negative position may be fully justified by the existence of alternative hypotheses, either of which, to say the least, is as probable as that just mentioned. The fact that Philip is described below (21, 8), not only as "one of the Seven" (named in 6, 5), but first and most distinctively as "the Evangelist," if not enough to prove that he baptized in this capacity, is certainly sufficient to rebut the proof that he baptized as a Deacon. The lapse of time between the case before us and the place where he is called an Evangelist, creates no difficulty, since, as we have seen above (on v. 5), his previous labours in Samaria were precisely such as we should look for in this class of ministers, whether the title be explained to mean a Missionary, or a Preacher clothed with temporary and extraordinary powers. (See below, on 21, 8.) These two questions have been here discussed at some length, for the purpose of exemplifying an important principle, to wit, that while we have no right to draw positive conclusions, in defence of our own usages and doctrines, from passages admitting of a different interpretation, we are equally bound to resist all similar abuses, and to see, so far as in us lies, that others do not handle the word of God deceitfully (2 Cor. 4, 2.)

39. And when they were come up out of the water,

the Spirit of the Lord caught away Philip, that the Eunuch saw him no more, and he went on his way rejoicing.

The first words of this verse correspond to those used in the one before it, and must be explained accordingly. If *immersion* is described in one case, so is *emersion* in the other, but with equal reference, as before, to both the persons. If, on the other hand, *they went down into the water*, only so far as to stand in it, then their coming up out of the water means no more than that they ceased to stand there, whether the *up* and *down* have reference to the bank or to the chariot. *The Spirit of the Lord* cannot possibly mean less than a special divine influence exerted upon Philip's movements; nor is there any good ground for denying that it means a divine person. (See above, on 1, 5, and compare v. 29.) *Caught away* is often applied elsewhere to corporeal seizure (John 6, 15. 10, 12. Acts 23, 10. 1 Th. 4, 17. Rev. 12, 5), though sometimes with a figurative application (Matt. 11, 12. 13, 19. John 10, 28. 29. Jude 23), and in one case with unquestionable reference to a supernatural or spiritual rapture, "whether in the body or out of the body," he who experienced it could not tell (2 Cor. 12, 2. 4.) But it is never applied elsewhere to mere mental impulse, and has therefore been most commonly here understood of a miraculous removal of Philip from the place where he had just baptized the Eunuch, and of course from the sight of the Eunuch himself. Some deny, however, that the words necessarily denote more than the hurrying of Philip away by a divine communication, without any miraculous disappearance or passage through the air. *That the Eunuch saw him no more*, is Tyndale's inexact construction, implying that the reason of his seeing him no more was his having been miraculously snatched away; whereas the meaning of the Greek is, *and the Eunuch saw him no more*, for another reason, stated in the next clause. *And he went*, another inexact translation from the same source, the correct one being, *for he went*. The reason, therefore, given in the text for Philip's being seen no more by the Eunuch, is not the Spirit's catching him away, but the Eunuch's going on his way rejoicing. The sequence thus suggested by the Greek words or a close translation is, that the Spirit hurried Philip from the spot, and the Eunuch saw him no more, neither searching nor waiting for him, but proceeding on his own way homeward, too much absorbed in the joy of his conversion to think even of the instrument by whom it was effected. For a similar effect of an analogous cause, though not the same precisely, see above, on 1, 11. 12. In the case before us, the miraculous vanishing of Philip, if affirmed, must not be made to rest on an inexact translation.

40. But Philip was found at Azotus; and passing through, he preached in all the cities, till he came to Cesarea.

No stress is to be laid upon the *but*, which is the usual continuative particle (δέ), and might as well have been translated *and*, as it is in vs. 30, 31, 34, 36, 37, 39. *Was found* seems certainly to favour the conclusion that the separation between Philip and the Eunuch was produced in some extraordinary way. Those who deny this understand it to mean merely that *he was* there, or *was present* there, for which the usual equivalent in Hebrew is the passive of the verb *to find*. This analogy, however, is scarcely sufficient to explain the use of an expression so significant in this connection. And even if we take it in the stronger sense of being next seen in Azotus, this at once suggests that he had reached that place in some extraordinary manner. There is therefore a presumption, although not conclusive evidence, in favour of this ancient and most prevalent interpretation. *Azotus* is the Greek or Latin form of *Ashdod*, one of the five capitals of the Philistines (Josh. 13, 3. 1 Sam. 51, 6. 4), belonging nominally to the tribe of Judah (Josh. 15. 47.) It is still in existence as an unimportant village, under the slightly altered name of *Esdud*. Here Philip seems to have resumed his missionary labours, either because, as some suppose, he was transported thither through the air, or because the country between Ashdod and the place where he had left the Eunuch was a wilderness, affording no opportunity of preaching. *Passing through*, or *coming through*, is rendered in the older English versions (Tyndale, Cranmer, and Geneva), *and he walked throughout the country*, i. e. the country between Azotus and Cesarea. This last is not the Cesarea mentioned in the Gospels (Matt. 16, 12. Mark 8, 27), but an ancient seaport on the Mediterranean, formerly called Straton's Tower, rebuilt and beautified by Herod the Great, and named by him in honour of Augustus. Josephus calls it one of the great towns of Palestine, chiefly inhabited by Greeks. It was here the Roman governors resided after Judea had been taken from the Herods and annexed to Syria. (See below, on 9, 30.) To this important city Philip's course was now directed, at the end of a missionary tour, the length of which we have no means of determining. We only know that *passing through* (the intervening country) *he preached in all the cities*, or retaining the original expression, he evangelized them all, by publishing the good news of salvation. That Cesarea now became his permanent abode, or at least the centre of his operations, although not expressly stated, is extremely probable, because in the only other place where he is again mentioned, he is not only still at Cesarea, but surrounded by a family of adult children. (See below, on 21, 8. 9.)

CHAPTER IX.

This division of the text contains two narratives, both relating to the spread of the church after the martyrdom of Stephen, but entirely distinct from one another, and rather parallel than successive. The first (1–30) records the conversion of Saul, his early ministry, and subsequent return to his own country; the second (31–43) a visitation of the churches in Judea by Peter, during which he performed two signal miracles at Lydda and Joppa. These accounts, though thrown into a single chapter, are not to be read as one continued narrative, but rather as the record of two independent radiations from a common centre; the historian, at the close of the first, reverting to the point from which he had set out, to wit, the death of Stephen, the ensuing persecution, and the consequent dispersion of the church from Jerusalem in various directions. While the two parts of this chapter must be thus distinguished, the second (31–43) is connected, in the closest manner, with the narrative contained in Chapter 10, and in the first eighteen verses of Chapter 11, the subject of which narrative is the conversion of Cornelius, or rather the reception of the first Gentile convert into the church, without first passing through the vestibule of Judaism. To this important portion of the apostolical history, the latter part of the chapter now before us is directly introductory. A due regard to this relation of the chapters will not only show how injudicious the division often is, but aid the reader in obtaining a clear view of the historian's design and method, which may otherwise seem dark and doubtful.

1. And Saul, yet breathing out threatenings and slaughter against the disciples of the Lord, went unto the High Priest —

Yet or *still* connects what follows with the statement in 8, 1, to which point the narrative goes back, so that what intervenes may possibly have happened at the same time with the events about to be recorded. As if he had said, 'While Philip was thus occupied, Paul was still persecuting the disciples.' (See above, on 8, 4, and below, on v. 31.) *Breathing out*, or more exactly, *breathing in*, inhaling, i. e. as some explain it, living in an atmosphere of rage and murder; or, according to others, simply *breathing*, as the verb often means in classic Greek, the idea of expiration being then implied, though not expressed, with an allusion to the panting or snorting of wild beasts, or to flowers breathing odour. The Peshito renders the word *full*, and some critics suppose a corresponding Greek word, not unlike in form, to be the correct reading (ἔμπλεως for ἐμπνέων.) But no such change is either authorized or needed, as the common text conveys a strong and suitable, though somewhat indefinite idea, namely, that of passionate excitement outwardly exhibited in word and deed, i. e. by *threatening*, (not *threatenings*, as in all the English versions) and *murder*, either actual or meditated and intended. *The disciples of the Lord*, those who acknowledged the authority of Christ as their Master, in the twofold sense of an instructor and a sovereign. *Went*, literally, *going*, of his own accord, a strong proof of his sincerity and zeal. *To the High Priest*, the acknowledged head and representative of the theocracy, particularly since the abolition or suspension of the prophetical and regal offices in Israel. Who was High Priest at this time, can only be conjectured, as the time itself is far from being certain, the opinions of interpreters ranging through a period of ten years (from A. D. 31 to 41.) This uncertainty, however, has no more effect upon the clearness of the history than the similar question with respect to the nativity of Christ. Caiaphas, under whom our Lord was put to death, appears to have remained in office till the Passover of the year 37, when he was removed by Vitellius, the Proconsul of Syria, to whose province Judea was attached, and his place filled, first by Jonathan, and after a few weeks by Theophilus (see above, on 1, 1) who held it till he was displaced by Agrippa, A. D. 41. Both these were sons, as Caiaphas was son-in-law, of Ananus or Annas. One of them is probably the High Priest to whom Paul went on this occasion, as recorded here and afterwards acknowledged by himself, with an appeal to the High Priest and Elders, as witnesses of what he said. (See below, on 22, 5.)

2. And desired of him letters to Damascus, to the synagogues, that if he found any of this way, whether they were men or women, he might bring them bound unto Jerusalem.

The sentence is completed from the first verse. *Desired*, literally, *asked*, but in the middle voice, meaning *asked for himself*, or as a favour, showing his forwardness and zeal in persecution. (See above, on 3, 14. 7, 46.) *Of him*, literally, *from him*, not in his private but official capacity. *Letters*, like the Latin *literae*, may mean a single letter; but this construction is unnecessary, as *synagogues* is in the plural. With respect to these bodies, see above, on 6, 9. Those in foreign parts had probably more of a distinct organization. The power of the High Priest over these societies was merely moral and ecclesiastical, but not on that account less real, as we may learn from that of the Pope in many Christian countries. *Damascus* is perhaps the oldest city in the world, being mentioned in the history of Abraham (Gen. 14, 15. 15, 2.) It was afterwards the capital of a kingdom, which appears to have been raised up as a rival and a scourge to that of the ten tribes, with which it was destroyed by the Assyrians. (1 Kings 11, 23–25. 2 Kings 16, 9.) The city, however, still retained its importance, and is flourishing to this day. It is finely situated in a fertile plain, between the mountain-chains of Libanus and Anti-Libanus, at a point where several of the great caravan routes come together. The Jewish population of the place was very large, Josephus saying that ten thousand Jews were massacred there at one time under Nero.

The gospel may have been carried thither after the day of Pentecost or the death of Stephen. *If he found any* seems to imply a doubt, but according to Greek usage may mean, *whomsoever he there found*. *Of this way*, literally, *of the way*, i. e. the new way of life and way of salvation. (See above, on 5, 41.) The original expression is, *of this way being*, which last word is omitted in the English versions or connected with what follows, *whether they were men or women*. But the Greek construction is, *of this way being, both men and women*. (See above, on 8, 3. 12.) *Bound*, either literally tied, chained, or metaphorically, under arrest, in custody. In the absence of any reason to the contrary, the first is entitled to the preference. This commission seems to imply the connivance of the Roman government, so that the same conspiracy of Jews and Gentiles, which put Christ to death, (4, 27) pursued his followers even into foreign parts.

3. And as he journeyed, he came near Damascus, and suddenly there shined round about him a light from heaven.

As he journeyed, literally, *in the journeying*, in the very act of going forward. *He came near*, literally, it happened (came to pass) that he drew near, or approached. The omission of the first verb is confined to the authorized version; the older ones have *chanced*, *fortuned*, or *befell*. *Shined*, or more exactly, *flashed around him*, the Greek verb being properly applied to lightning. It is not, however, a mere flash of lightning that is here described, but a continued light from heaven, illuminating the place for some time. *A light*, or more simply and emphatically, *light*, without the article. *From heaven* not only indicates the apparent or visible direction, but implies the supernatural or celestial source of the illumination. (See above, on 2, 2.)

4. And he fell to the earth, and heard a voice saying unto him, Saul, Saul, why persecutest thou me?

The impression on the sense of sight is followed by one upon the sense of hearing. *Fell*, literally, *falling* or *having fallen*. *Saul* is here written in the proper Hebrew form, which agrees exactly with the statement elsewhere, that the voice addressed him in the Hebrew tongue (see above, on 7,

58, and below, on 26, 14.) The repetition of the name adds solemnity and earnestness. (Compare Luke 10, 41. 13, 25. 22, 31.)

5. And he said, Who art thou, Lord? And the Lord said, I am Jesus, whom thou persecutest. It is hard for thee to kick against the pricks.

Lord, not *Sir*, which would, in this connection, be incongruous. He seems to have some suspicion of the truth, or at least to be aware that he is in communication with some superhuman being. *The Lord*, i. e. the person whom he had thus addressed, and who was really the Lord Jesus Christ. *I am Jesus* (that Jesus) *whom thou persecutest*, or art persecuting. He thus identifies himself with his people, not as an aggregate body merely, but as individuals, according to the principle which he had formerly laid down, when teaching his disciples how they might indulge their feelings of attachment to him, even in his absence. "Inasmuch as ye have done it unto one of the least of these my brethren, ye have done it unto me." (Matt. 25, 40.) The situation here described may be compared to that of Balaam, when the Angel of the Lord said, " I have come out to withstand thee, because thy way is perverse before me." (Numb. 22, 32.) There is also a resemblance to the incident recorded in John 18, 4–6, where our Saviour says to those who came forth to arrest him, "Whom seek ye? They answered him, Jesus of Nazareth. Jesus saith unto them, I am he. As soon as he had said unto them, I am he, they went backward and fell to the ground." Common to both scenes, although not in the same order, is the sudden and violent prostration, and the solemn recognition of the Saviour's person. *It is hard for thee to kick against the pricks*, is found in no Greek manuscript at this place, but in several old versions, and is now commonly agreed to be an interpolation from 26, 14 below. It owes its origin, no doubt, to the practice of the ancient copyists, in making parallel passages complete each other. Nothing of course is lost by its exclusion from the verse before us, into which it seems to have been first introduced by Erasmus. The clause itself is a proverbial one, of frequent occurrence in the Greek and Latin classics, being found in Pindar, Æschylus, Euripides, Plautus, and Terence. *Hard*, not difficult but painful, dangerous; not hard to do, but hard to bear. *Pricks*, i. e. sharp points, specially applied to the stings of insects, and to the goads or pointed staves employed in driving. The idea meant to be conveyed is not merely that of vain resistance to the irresistible, but that of a resistance which incurs new injury or suffering. 'Cease thy vain resistance to my will and power, which can only render thee worse and thy condition more deplorable.' The sentence has no bearing on the doctrine of irresistible grace. It was not grace which Saul had been resisting, but authority and evidence. The first effect of grace was to subdue him.

6. And he, trembling and astonished, said, Lord, what wilt thou have me to do? And the Lord said unto him, Arise, and go into the city, and it shall be told thee what thou must do.

In all Greek manuscripts this verse begins with the word *arise*, and is a direct continuation of the previous address. The case is different, however, from that of the supposed interpolation in v. 5. There, the insertion of the words can be accounted for, by assimilation to another passage. Here, the inserted words are such as occur nowhere else, which makes it harder to account for their insertion, unless they existed in the oldest copies, now no longer extant. Their genuineness is also favoured by their appropriateness or congruity, and the absence of any thing to cause suspicion of a later forgery. The effect produced on Saul himself (*trembling and astonished*) is just what might have been expected, and the question put into his mouth (*Lord, what wilt thou have me to do?*) has been a formula of pious resignation and devotion for a course of ages. On the other hand, the absence of the words in all Greek copies, and their various forms in versions and quotations, have led some of the most cautious critics to regard them as a paraphrastic gloss.

7. And the men which journeyed with him stood speechless, hearing a voice but seeing no man.

Those journeying with him, his fellow-travellers, perhaps a caravan which he had joined, but possibly soldiers or officers of justice, who attended him to aid in the execution of his commission. *Stood*, i. e. stood still, stopped, as opposed to going forward, not to sitting down or lying prostrate. (See below, on 26, 14.) If we give the verb its strict pluperfect sense (see above, on 1, 10), the idea is that they *had stopped* or *stood still* when they saw the light, although they afterwards fell prostrate. *Speechless*, a word used in the classics to denote those deaf and dumb. (See the Septuagint version of Isaiah 56, 10, and compare that of Prov. 17, 28.) *No man*, no one, nobody; see above, on 4, 35.

8. And Saul arose from the earth, and when his eyes were opened, he saw no man; but they led him by the hand and brought him into Damascus.

The first indication of a moral change is that afforded by Saul's childlike obedience to the voice of his new master. *Arose*, or more exactly, was aroused or raised, implying passive rather than active obedience, and perhaps that he was in a kind of trance or waking-dream, but not that the incidents recorded were imaginary; for they were witnessed by others as well as by himself. *When his eyes were opened* does not mean merely, after he had opened them, but even when his eyes were open. *Saw no one*, does not mean merely, as in v. 7, that the speaker was invisible, but that Saul could see no one whatever, being blind. *Led him by the hand* is one compound verb in Greek, which might be rendered *hand-led* (compare *calf-made* in 7, 41), and is used by Anacreon and other classics, with particular reference to blindness. *They led* may either be indefinitely construed as equivalent to the passive form in 22, 11, or referred to *the men* of the preceding verse, who are expressly represented as the agents, in the parallel account just cited. *Into Damascus* may imply proximity; but see the same phrase in v. 2 above. Local tradition still identifies the scene of this transaction at a bridge not far from the city. The contrast between Saul's designed and actual entrance into Damascus, though susceptible of very high rhetorical embellishment, is left by the historian, with characteristic moderation and simplicity, to the imagination of the reader.

9. And he was three days without sight, and neither did eat nor drink.

The physical effect of this event was to be neither permanent nor momentary. He was not merely dazzled for an instant, nor was he blinded for the rest of life; but *he was three days without sight* (literally, *not seeing*.) *Ate not neither drank*, expresses total abstinence; nor is there any reason for extenuating the expression. According to the Jewish mode of computation, the *three days* may either have been three whole days, or one whole day and portions of two others. The fast or abstinence itself has been variously understood, as a natural expression of Saul's penitence and grief; or as a medicinal appliance for the restoration of his sight; or as the spontaneous effect of his abstraction from his ordinary thoughts and occupations, and his absorption in the care of his salvation. (See below, on 27, 21. 33.) *Three days* some suppose to have been chosen, in allusion to the history of Jonah, or to our Saviour's burial. (See Jon. 1, 17. Matt. 12, 39. 40.)

10. And there was a certain disciple at Damascus, named Ananias, and to him said the Lord in a vision, Ananias. And he said, Behold, I (am here), Lord.

As a new character is here introduced, the first words might be translated *now there was*. *A disciple*, i. e. of Christ, a believer, a converted Jew, as we know from ch. 22, 12. *A certain disciple*, see above, on 5, 1. *In Damascus*, where he may have taken refuge from the persecution at Jerusalem (8, 1), as it is not probable that all who fled remained within the limits of the Holy Land. It is equally possible, however, that he may have been a native of Damascus, or a Jew residing there, but present in the Holy City on the day of Pentecost; or afterwards converted by the agency of some one who had witnessed the effusion of the Holy Spirit, or been driven into exile on the death of Stephen. He is not here mentioned as the sole disciple in Damascus; and we know from v. 14 below, that there were others. *Named* (literally, *by name*) *Ananias*, precisely as in 5, 1. (See also, 23, 2. 24, 1.) *The Lord*, i. e. the Lord Jesus, as in v. 5. *In a vision*, either in the wide sense of a revelation, a divine communication, or in the strict sense of a divine or preternatural appearance. (See below, v. 12, and compare 7, 31. 10, 3. 17. 19. 11, 5. 12, 9. 16, 9. 10. 18, 9.) *Said in a vision* does not necessarily imply that there was only a verbal revelation, but rather that the words were uttered by a visible speaker. *Behold me* (Wicl. *lo, I*) is a close translation of the usual response in

Hebrew to a call by name, equivalent to saying *see me*, but usually rendered in the English Bible, *Behold I am here* (as in Gen. 22, 1. 27), but sometimes simply, *here am I* (as in Gen. 22, 11), although the idea thus omitted is the one really expressed, that of presence being only implied. When addressed to a superior, this formula suggests the accessory idea of readiness for service, or of promptness to obey.

11. And the Lord (said) unto him, Arise and go into the street called Straight, and inquire in the house of Judas for one called Saul of Tarsus; for behold, he prayeth.

The particle at the beginning is the same as in v. 10, and might here be rendered *so* or *then*. There is no need of assuming a grammatical ellipsis of the verb *said*. It is rather an abbreviated formula, like the names prefixed to the parts in a dramatic dialogue. *Arising go* is not an unmeaning pleonasm, but either a command to address himself to action (see above, on 8, 26. 27), or still more probably, a literal command to stand up or arise, i. e. from sleep or out of bed, if the vision was a dream, as in many other cases. *Arising go*, go away, depart, implying not mere motion, but entire change of place. (See above, on 1, 10. 11. 25. 5, 20. 41. 8, 26. 27. 36. 39. 9, 3.) *Street*, a Greek word corresponding to the Latin *vicus*, and denoting properly a lane or alley, as opposed to a wide street or broad way. (See above, on 5, 15.) This is the only street named in the New Testament, and by a curious coincidence, if nothing more, Damascus still exhibits what is rare in oriental towns, a long straight street, running through its whole length from east to west, and probably marking the direction of the one to which Ananias was commissioned. *Inquire*, literally, *seek*, as in all the older English versions. *The house* is more definite than the original, which strictly means *a house of Judas*, i. e. a house belonging to one Judas, who seems to be referred to as a person quite unknown to Ananias, although some consider it more probable that Judas was a Christian or converted Jew. It is no less probable, however, that he was an old friend or acquaintance, or his house one of public entertainment, or that Saul had made arrangements to reside with him before his actual arrival. *Judas, Jude*, or *Judah*, being a national name, was still more common than *Ananias*, there being four of that name mentioned in this book, besides several others in the Gospels. (See 1, 13. 5, 37. 15, 32, and compare Matt. 1, 2. 3. Luke 3, 26. 30. Mark 6, 3. John 6, 71. 14, 22.) *One called Saul of Tarsus*, literally, *Saul by name, a Tarsean*, i. e. a Tarsean named Saul. *Tarsus*, the capital of Cilicia, the southeastern province of Asia Minor, described by Xenophon as a great and flourishing city, and by Strabo as a seat of science equal or superior to Alexandria and Athens. Even allowing this to be extravagant, the truth which it exaggerates must be sufficient to evince that Paul's advantages or opportunities of early education were among the best afforded by the Roman Empire or Augustan Age, and to explain the frequent indications, in his writings and discourses, of familiarity with classical literature. *Behold*, or *lo*, as usual, introduces something strange and unexpected. *He prayeth* (or *is praying*) is not given as a proof that he would now be found at home; but either means that he was asking for the very thing about to be bestowed; or is descriptive of conversion, as in modern phrase a convert is often represented as a praying man. After his three days' struggle he begins to pray, which shows that he is ripe for restoration to his eyesight, and admission to the church by Christian baptism.

12. And hath seen in a vision a man named Ananias coming in and putting his hand on him, that he might receive his sight.

Some make this the beginning of a new sentence, containing a remark of the historian, that while Ananias was receiving this command, Saul saw it executed in a vision. But the only natural interpretation is the obvious and common one, which makes this a direct continuation of the reason given in the end of the preceding verse, why he should go in search of Saul; *for lo he prayeth, and hath seen in vision a man named* (literally, *by name*) *Ananias*. The whole vision being supernatural, the name could be as readily suggested as the rest. How often, in our ordinary dreams, do we seem to be aware, not only of a person's looks, but of his name and character. This expression seems to decide the question, whether Saul and Ananias were before acquainted; for if that had been the case, the natural expression would be, *and hath seen thee*, not *a man named Ananias*, which can only mean, without a forced construction, that he saw a man whom he had never seen before, but whom he knew at once to be named Ananias. The coincidence of two distinct communications, at or near the same time, and for the same purpose, but to different persons, while it served to prepare them for a subsequent meeting, tended also to preclude the supposition of an accident or mere imagination, which, though possible in one case, could not well occur in two, without a supernatural occasion and direction. Another instance of the same thing is afforded by the visions of Peter and Cornelius in the following chapter.

13. Then Ananias answered, Lord, I have heard by many of this man, how much evil he hath done to thy saints at Jerusalem.

It is a curious thought of Chrysostom, that this commission was intrusted to one otherwise unknown, that there might be no pretext for asserting Paul's apostleship to be dependent upon human teaching. This obscurity of Ananias makes it more surprising that, instead of catching at the offered honour, he declined it, or at least suggested difficulties which might serve as an excuse for doing so. It is worthy of remark how often this kind of resistance, on the part of God's most honoured instruments, occurs in Scripture. The most striking instances are those of Moses (Ex. 3, 11. 13. 4, 1. 10. 13) and Jeremiah (1, 6.) The motive of refusal, in the case before us, has been variously understood to be the fear of personal injury from Saul, which is absurd, since he had just been described to him as blind and praying; or indignation and a wounded sense of justice, that this cruel persecutor should be made the object of divine compassion, and himself the channel of communication (compare Jon. 4, 1–11); or, more probably than either, incredulity, a real incapacity to credit what he heard, or to believe that such a change was possible. Thus understood, the spirit of his answer is not, as an old Greek commentator paraphrases it—'See to whom thou art betraying me; I fear lest he take me to Jerusalem; why dost thou put me in the lion's mouth?'—but rather, 'Can it be that this arch-bigot and fanatic is approachable by me on such an errand?' As in other cases of the same kind, the resistance shows a childlike candor and simplicity, as well as confidential intercourse between the servant and the master. *By many*, literally, *from many*, i. e. many years, as some explain it, which, according to Greek usage, means, for many years (or for a long time) past. But the obvious construction supplies *men* or *persons*, as the sources of his information. This implies an interval of some length since the beginning of the persecution, and a considerable emigration of the exiles to Damascus, unless we suppose Ananias to have heard the news from others, or in other places. *Of* (about, concerning) *this man* is perhaps contemptuous. (See above, on 4, 10. 6, 14. 7, 40.) *How much evil*, literally, *how many* (or *how great*) *evils.* See above, on 2, 39. 3, 22. 24. 4, 6. 23, 28. 34. 5, 36. 37.) *He hath done*, or adhering to the strict sense of the aorist, *he did*, i. e. before he came here. *Saints*, or *holy ones*, is here used for the first time to describe disciples or believers. It is still disputed which of the two leading senses of the Greek word, and the corresponding Hebrew one, is the original, and which the secondary meaning, intrinsically pure and free from taint, or separated, set apart to sacred uses. But in both these senses it may be applied to Christians; as a consecrated or peculiar people, and as such required to be personally holy, or as actually sanctified, at least in part. Thus Christ himself is called "the Holy One of God" (Mark 1, 24), "whom the Father hath sanctified and sent into the world" (John 10, 36.) Thus too his followers are called "the sanctified" (20, 32) and "saints," not only here and in vs. 32. 41 below, but in the formal titles or original inscriptions of several apostolical epistles (Rom. 1, 7. 1 Cor. 1, 2. 2 Cor. 1, 1. Eph 1, 1. Phil. 1, 1. Col. 1, 1.) The derisive use of the word "saints" by irreligious men, as an ironical description of believers, rests on the false idea that it involves a claim to perfect holiness; whereas, even giving it the strongest sense, as an expression of intrinsic quality, it is descriptive, not of what God's people claim to be already, but of what they ought to be, and hope to be hereafter.

14. And here he hath authority from the chief priests, to bind all that call on thy name.

And (*even*) *here*, in Syria, in Damascus, in this foreign city. This seems to be expressive of surprise at Saul's far-reaching zeal, which could not be content to spend itself at home. (See below, on 26, 11.) The Greek adverb (ὧδε) in classical usage has the sense of *so* or *thus*, but the local sense of *here* is common in the later writers, and found by some philologists even in Herodotus and Homer. *Authority*, delegated right and power; see above, on 8, 19. *Chief priests*, see above, on 4, 23. 5, 24. *To bind*, arrest, imprison; see above, on v. 2. *All that call on thy name*, not those who are called (or call themselves) by thy name, which would be otherwise expressed, as in ch. 15, 17 below; but those who invoke thee, call upon thee for help and protection, and recognize thee as an object of worship. This is the true sense of the phrase in Greek as well as Hebrew, and may be distinctly traced in the usage of both Testaments. (See above, on 2, 21. 7, 59, and compare the Septuagint version of Gen. 13, 4. Deut. 32, 3. Ps. 98, 6. Joel 2, 32.) In answer to the question, how Ananias knew the fact here stated, some suppose that he had learned it from the Christians of Jerusalem, to whom the plans of so fanatical an enemy could scarcely be unknown. Others object that there was not sufficient time or frequency of intercourse between Damascus and Jerusalem, to render such communication possible; but this is mere conjecture. It is no less probable, however, and perhaps the simplest supposition, that the object of Saul's journey was divulged by his companions, especially if they were associated with him in his work of persecution, but unable or unwilling to pursue it after the defection of their leader.

15. But the Lord said unto him, Go thy way, for he is a chosen vessel unto me, to bear my name before the Gentiles, and kings, and the children of Israel.

His objection is entirely disregarded, and the command emphatically repeated. *Go thy way* (in modern English, *go away*) is another form of the same verb that is used above in v. 11. 'Go where I have sent thee, without doubt or apprehension; for this man, hitherto known only as a persecutor of my people, is a chosen instrument or vessel, by whom and in whom my name and doctrine are to be conveyed and upheld, in the presence of nations and their kings, as well as of the chosen people.' *Chosen vessel*, literally, *vessel of choice* (compare Rom. 9, 21–23. 2 Cor. 4, 7. 2 Tim. 2, 20. 21.) This idiom, although more common in Hebrew, is also found in classic Greek. The original noun (σκεῦος) corresponds both to *instrument* and *vessel*, or rather to *utensil*, or *implement*, including both. *Unto me*, not only chosen by me, but prepared for me and devoted to me. *To bear*, carry, the same verb that is used above in 3, 2, and below in 15, 10. 21, 35, in all which cases it means not only to convey, but to support or hold up, both which ideas are appropriate in this figurative application. Saul was chosen and commissioned, not only to diffuse but to maintain the gospel. The idea of exalting, glorifying, here assumed by some, is not expressed by the Greek verb, but may be considered as implied in this connection. *Before nations*, or according to the latest critics, before *both* (τε) *nations and kings*, indefinitely spoken of as two great ranks or classes, before whom Saul was to act the dangerous but honourable part assigned him, as the "Apostle of the Gentiles" (Rom. 11, 13), by way of eminence, but not exclusively, a qualification here suggested by the last words of the verse, *and* (also before) *the children of Israel*, considered as the ancient church or chosen people. As to the fulfilment of this promise, see below on vs. 20–22. 13, 46. 25, 23. 26, 32. 27, 24. 28, 17. Rom. 11, 13. 15, 16. Gal. 2, 8. 2 Tim. 4, 16. 17.

16. For I will show him how great things he must suffer for my name's sake.

The *for* has reference to something intermediate, implied but not expressed. Some suppose it to be 'fear not,' or 'fear nothing further at his hands;' but see above, on v. 13. The connecting thought may be, 'nor is he to be merely active in my service, but passive also.' The persecuting days of Saul were over, and the tables were now turned. He who had hitherto made others suffer for the truth, was now to suffer for it in his turn. There is an exquisite mixture of severity and tenderness in this disclosure; of severity in sentencing this "chosen vessel" to endure as well as labour; of tenderness in intimating that this purpose, though explicitly declared to Ananias, was to be more gradually made known to the sufferer himself. *I will show him* is in Greek a most expressive phrase, meaning, I will partly show him, or begin to show him, I am giving him a glimpse of what he is to suffer. The pronoun has more emphasis in the original, and may perhaps mean, I and not thou, i. e. do thy part, as it has been assigned to thee, and I will do mine, by disclosing to him what he is to suffer. *How great* (Genev. *how many*) *things* seems to be an allusion to *how great* (or *how many*) *evils* in v. 13, although the antithesis is obscured in English by the needless variation of the version. The sense may then be, 'Think no more how much suffering he has caused, for I am now about to show him how much he is to suffer in his turn.' *For my name*, for the sake of that religion and that master, whom he lately persecuted, even unto death (see above, on v. 2, and below, on 22, 4.) All this was to be shown to Saul, not merely in a providential way or by experience, but by prophetic intimations, such as those recorded in 20, 23 and 21, 11. (See also 1 Cor. 15, 30–32. 2 Cor. 1, 8–10. 4, 8–12. 6, 5. 11, 23–28. 12, 10.)

17. And Ananias went his way, and entered into the house, and putting his hands on him, said, Brother Saul, the Lord, even Jesus that appeared unto thee in the way as thou camest, hath sent me, that thou mightest receive thy sight, and be filled with the Holy Ghost.

Being satisfied by the divine assurance that the persecutor of the new religion had himself embraced it, Ananias now accepts and executes his singular commission. *Went his way*, i. e. *went away*, the strict translation of the Greek verb, which is not the same as that in v. 16. Another compound form of the same simple verb is that translated *entered*. *Then went away Ananias and went in*. *The house*, i. e. the house of Judas, spoken of in v. 11, and therefore definitely mentioned here, as something already known to the reader. This implies that he had previously sought for it, as commanded in v. 11. *Imposing upon him the hands*, as the Apostles did in Samaria, but with a solemn declaration of the authority by which he did it. *Brother Saul*, in Greek (and Wiclif's version) *Saul (my) brother*, by which address he recognizes him, not only as a fellow man, but as a fellow Jew, and, at least prospectively, a fellow Christian. *The Lord hath sent me;* this was his commission. *The Lord*, as in vs. 10. 11. 13. 15. It is here explained by Ananias himself, as meaning the Lord Jesus, that very Jesus who had appeared to (or been seen by) him (see above, on 2, 3. 7, 2. 26. 30. 35.) *As thou camest*, literally, *which thou camest*, i. e. to Damascus. (See above, on v. 3.) *Appeared*, i. e. as some explain it, revealed himself, declared his will, communicated with thee; while others regard it as a proof, that Saul saw the person of Christ, as well as heard his voice (v. 4). It is said indeed that *he saw no one;*

but this might mean that Christ had vanished; or rather, that after Saul arose, he could see no one, having lost his sight. That Paul did literally see Christ after his ascension, he affirms himself in one of his epistles (1 Cor. 15, 8), where the context relates, not merely to divine communications, but to actual appearances of the Lord's body. And if Paul saw him only once, it was most probably at this time; so that the strict interpretation of the words of Ananias (*the one seen by thee*) is, on the whole, entitled to the preference. The design of his commission is described as twofold, outward and inward, bodily and spiritual. The physical effect was to be the restoration of sight. The Greek verb primarily means to *look up* (as in 22, 13 below, and in Matt. 14, 19. Mark 6, 41. 7, 34. 8, 24. 16, 4. Luke 9, 16), but is used by Xenophon in the sense of opening the eyes again, and by Herodotus and Plato in that of recovering the sight, which is its common usage in the Gospels, even in speaking of one born blind (John 9, 11. 15. 18.) The other effect was, *that he might be filled with the Holy Ghost*, a stronger expression than *receive the Holy Ghost* (John 20, 22. Acts 8, 15. 17. 19; compare 2, 4. 4, 8. 31. 6, 3. 5. 7. 55.) It is therefore the more worthy of remark, that the instrumental agency employed was the imposition of the hands of one whom we do not even know to have been a deacon or evangelist like Philip, much less an apostle. This makes it still less probable that Peter and John were sent down to Samaria simply because Philip could not give the Holy Spirit (see above, on 8, 15–17.) That gift was so peculiarly divine, that the external medium was comparatively unimportant.

18. And immediately there fell from his eyes as it had been scales, and he received sight forthwith, and arose and was baptized.

The declaration of the purpose for which Ananias came is followed by the record of its instantaneous accomplishment, which, with the express divine command, shuts out the idea of a natural cure. *As it had been* (literally *as if*, see above, on 2, 3. 6, 15) is understood by some to mean, that Saul's sensations were like those which would have been produced by the falling of scales from his eyes; but as it is expressly said that something fell, the only question is whether it was scales or something like scales; and this is a point of no importance. The Greek word is applied, not only to the scales of fish but to egg-shells, and the rind or husk of plants, and even to metallic flakes or laminæ. *Received sight*, saw again, or looked up, as in v. 17. *Forthwith*, on the spot, the same word that is used above, in 3, 7. 5, 10. Only the bodily effect is explicitly recorded; but the other is implied, so that few readers probably observe the omission. As Saul had no doubt been looking forward to the restoration of his sight, as a final attestation of the truth or reality of what he had experienced, and consequently of the divine favour towards him and divine will respecting him, it put an end to his suspense, *and rising* (from his previous prostration and inaction) *he was baptized*, a sign both of his initiation into the Christian church, and of that spiritual renovation, without which mere external membership must be for ever worse than unavailing.

19. And when he had received meat he was strengthened. Then was Saul certain days with the disciples which were at Damascus.

As Saul's preternatural condition was now ended, he was once more dependent upon natural and ordinary means for his subsistence. To mark this transition, we are told expressly that he broke his fast, and *taking* (or *having taken*) *food, was strengthened*, or retaining the active form of the original, *became* (or *grew*) *strong*. *Then* (or and, so, but) *Saul was* (or literally, *Saul became*, implying change of character, as well as of relations) *with the disciples*, i. e. avowedly a member of their body. He did not simply continue with them, but became something to them that he had not been before. This implies, not only that there were disciples there besides Ananias (see above, on vs. 2. 14), but also the existence of an organized body, of which Paul now publicly avowed himself a member, and became, as stated in the next verse, a zealous and successful minister. *Certain days*, in modern English *some days*, an indefinite expression, suggestive of a smaller rather than a greater number. Some, however, understand it as including the three years preceding his return to Jerusalem after his conversion (Gal. 1, 18), while others introduce them between vs. 19. 20, or under the *many days* of v. 23, or after v. 25. This variation shows that the narrative itself does not contain sufficient data for the solution of the question, which may for that very reason be regarded as more curious than important.

20. And straightway he preached Christ in the synagogues, that he is the Son of God.

Straightway (or *immediately*, as the same word is translated in v. 18), i. e. without ceremonious delay or human instruction, but as soon as he had been baptized and relieved of his bodily infirmity. This verse relates not to the end but the beginning of the "certain days." *In the synagogues*, implying a plurality, as in v. 2; but see above, on 6, 9. This fact and the license given, even to strangers, to address the people (see below, on 13, 15), made the synagogues important means of access, not to the Jews alone, but to the more devout and serious Gentiles, who were often present at the Jewish worship, and appear to have regarded it with great curiosity, and often with an interest still deeper. *Preached*, in its primary sense, proclaimed or heralded, an idea not conveyed exactly by the first word, on account of its official and professional associations. The imperfect tense in Greek implies repeated or continued acts. He did not merely preach once, but was wont, accustomed, used to preach. *Christ* (the Messiah) was the subject of his preaching, and the doctrine which he taught was, that the promised Prophet, Priest, and King of Israel, foretold in the Old Testament, was to be a divine person. The reading adopted by the latest critics (*Jesus* for *Christ*) only makes the doctrine more specific by applying it, not merely to the office, but to the person, of the true Messiah. *The Son of God*, i. e. a partaker of his nature, a divine being. Some give the phrase a lower sense, as merely meaning the Messiah; but this confounds it with the *Son of Man* (see above, on 7, 56), and the subject of the sentence with its predicate.

21. But all that heard (him) were amazed and said, Is not this he that destroyed them which called on this name in Jerusalem, and came hither for that intent, that he might bring them bound unto the chief priests?

And amazed (2, 7. 12. 8, 13) *were all those hearing*, the natural effect of a change so sudden and complete. *And said*, as Chrysostom observes, not to Saul himself, whom they were afraid or ashamed to question, but to themselves or one another. The interrogation (*is not this*) implies a wonder rising almost to incredulity, as if they had said, 'No, this surely cannot be the same.' *Destroyed*, literally, *wasted*, desolated, like an enemy in war, a different word from that in 8, 3, but the same with that twice used by Paul himself, in speaking of this very subject. (See Gal. 1, 13. 23, where the English version needlessly employs two different verbs in translating the same Greek one.) *Those invoking this name*, i. e. in their prayers or worship, which had now become a distinctive mark, and therefore an expressive designation, of all believers or disciples. (See above, on 2, 21. 7, 59. 9, 14.) *And hither*, to Damascus; see above, on v. 14. *Came*, or according to the common text, *had come*, i. e. before this amazing change, implying that he had abandoned his design. *For that intent*, literally, *for this*, i. e. for this same purpose; an aggravating circumstance before alluded to, that Saul, not satisfied with persecuting the church at home, had volunteered to persecute it in Damascus. (See above, on v. 2, and below, on 26. 11.) *Bound*, as in vs. 2. 14.) *To the chief priests*, i. e. to their bar or judgment-seat, before the Sanhedrim, of which they were the leading members. (See above, on 4, 23. 5, 24. 9, 14.)

22. But Saul increased the more in strength, and confounded the Jews which dwelt at Damascus, proving that this is very Christ.

The more, in English, means that this effect was promoted by the very wonder just described; but the original expression simply means *still more*, (as in 5, 14), i. e. the more he preached the greater was his power and success. *Increased in strength*, literally, *was strengthened* or *made powerful*, a favourite verb of Paul's. (See Rom. 4, 20. Eph. 6, 10. Phil. 4, 13. 1 Tim. 1, 12. 2 Tim. 2, 1. Heb. 11, 34, and compare the uncompounded form in Col. 1, 11.) He increased not only in the strength of his convictions, but in the force of his defence and in the power of his persuasion. By some this clause is strangely understood as an allusion to Saul's sojourn in Arabia, as a time of intellectual and spiritual discipline, designed to strengthen him for after service. This would never have occurred to any reader, but for the supposed necessity of finding some allusion to that sojourn in this context, and the difficulty of determining at what point it shall be inserted (see above, on v. 19.) But without admitting ignorance on Luke's part, as to so important an event in the Apostle's life, the two accounts are perfectly consistent; and although the one before us would suggest to no mind the idea of his absence from Damascus, it contains nothing in the least at variance with that idea when suggested otherwise. All that is here expressed, however, relates directly to the time when he resided there, and makes a strong impression, not only of his diligence and courage in his new vocation, but of his success. It was not merely wonder that his public appearance in behalf of Christ excited. All were amazed (v. 21), and the Jews were *confounded*, a verb properly expressive of mixture by pouring together, but metaphorically applied to mental confusion, mingling and bewildering the thoughts, so as to prevent all clear perception and conclusive reasoning. *Proving*, literally, putting together or combining, i. e. various proofs and arguments, or prophecies with their fulfilment. The Greek verb is confined to Luke and Paul, who employ it in several different shades of meaning (see below, 16, 10. 19, 33. 1 Cor. 2, 16), besides the primary and strict one (Eph. 4, 16. Col. 2, 2. 19.) *Very Christ*, in Greek simply *the Christ*.

23. And after that many days were fulfilled, the Jews took counsel to kill him.

As days enough were filled, or being filled, an indefinite expression, which appears to be deliberately chosen, as best adapted to convey the knowledge which was meant to be imparted, and which no speculation or conjecture can make more determinate. (See above, on 7, 23. 30, and compare 2, 1, and Luke 9, 51.) *Took counsel*, or consulted, deliberated, plotted together. The idea of concert and collusion is expressed by the compound form; the simple verb occurs above, in 5, 33, followed by the one here rendered *kill*, and there *slay*. (See, also, 2, 23. 5, 36. 7, 28.)

24. But their laying await was known of Saul, and they watched the gates day and night to kill him.

But, as in vs. 21, 22, or *and*, as in v. 23. *Laying await*, in some editions *laying wait*, in modern English *lying in wait*. The simple meaning of the Greek, however, is conspiracy or plot. (Compare the kindred verb in v. 23.) *Known of Saul*, i. e. known by him, or made known to him (see below, on 23, 16), either by report or by divine communication. *They watched*, or more exactly, *they were watching*, i. e. when the incident recorded in the next verse happened. As if he had said, 'while they were actually watching the gates of the city, to seize him as he went out, he escaped in another way.' *Day and night*, not necessarily for many days and nights, perhaps for only one. It may mean simply that they watched the gates a whole day and night to seize him. We learn from the Apostle's own account in one of his epistles (2 Cor. 11, 32), that it was "the governor (or ethnarch) under (literally, of) King Aretas (that) kept (guarded or garrisoned) the city (of the Damascenes, a phrase omitted in King James's Bible, though expressed in all the older English versions) wishing to seize me." The only contemporary Aretas known to history is a king of Arabia Petræa, resident at Petra, whose daughter had been repudiated by Herod Antipas, for the sake of his niece and sister-in-law, Herodias (Matt. 14, 3. Mark 6, 17. Luke 3, 19.) This led to a war, in which Herod was defeated and his army destroyed. Vitellius, then governor of Syria, was ordered by Tiberius to help him; but while on his way to Petra, he received news of the emperor's death, and retired into winter quarters. It may have been during this inaction of the Roman forces, that Aretas gained possession of Damascus. This is at least more probable than that his deputy or viceroy simply happened to be there at the time; or that this ethnarch was a Jewish magistrate, appointed or confirmed by the Arabian king; or, most improbable of all, that *Areta* in Corinthians is the name of the ethnarch himself, 'Areta the ethnarch of the king,' i. e. of the Roman Emperor. The two accounts are perfectly consistent, and together teach us, that the agency of this Arabian chieftain in forbidding Saul's escape was instigated, if not purchased, by the Jews of Damascus.

25. Then the disciples took him by night, and let (him) down by the wall in a basket.

Then, as in vs. 13, 19. *The disciples*, or followers of Christ, who seem to be again referred to, both as numerous and as acting in concert or association. Some of them were no doubt Saul's own converts. *Took him*, taking him, or having taken him, *by night* relating equally to both words, a construction not so obvious in English. *Taking* may be a pleonastic expression, common in all languages, or may imply that some constraint was used by the disciples. *By the wall*, i. e. through the wall of the city, the strict sense of the Greek expressions (διὰ τοῦ τείχους), which are also used by Paul himself (2 Cor. 11, 32), with the additional circumstance, that he was let down through a window, i. e. through the window of a house upon the city wall. (See Josh. 2, 15, where the Septuagint version has the same Greek word for window.) The words translated *basket* in the parallel accounts are different, though no doubt interchangeable. By a curious coincidence, a similar diversity exists in the history of our Saviour's miraculously feeding the four and five thousand; the word for *basket* being different in all these cases. (See Matt. 16, 9. 10, and compare the parallel passages.)

26. And when Saul was come to Jerusalem, he assayed to join himself to the disciples; but they were all afraid of him, and believed not that he was a disciple.

Being come, or having arrived, the same verb that is used in 5, 21, and there explained. *Assayed*, tried, endeavoured, implying that he failed in his attempt. *To join himself*, the same verb as in 5, 13. *To the disciples*, as a body, as a church, not merely to their families or persons. *All feared him, not believing that he is a disciple*, thinking it impossible that he, who had so lately persecuted Christ in his disciples, should now be himself a convert. See above, on v. 13, and for the present tense (*he is*) on 7, 35. *All* may either mean all the individuals to whom he applied, or express the unanimous action of the church as such. This implies that Paul had not been constantly in public view since his conversion, and favours the opinion, that the greater part of the three years since that event had been passed in Arabia, and even there perhaps in retirement rather than in public labour.

27. But Barnabas took him and brought him to the Apostles, and declared unto them how he had seen the Lord in the way, and that he had spoken to him, and how he had preached boldly at Damascus in the name of Jesus.

From this embarrassing and mortifying situation Saul is freed by Barnabas, with whom the history has previously made us acquainted, as one of the earliest and most signal instances of liberality in the infant church. (See above, on 4, 36. 37.) The same Cyprian Levite, whose conduct was before contrasted with the selfish ambition and hypocrisy of Ananias, is here seen acting a no less noble part in behalf of this suspected, not to say rejected convert. Though not affirmed, it seems to be implied, that they had no previous acquaintance with each other. *Took him*, either literally by the hand (as in 23, 19. Mark 8, 23. Heb. 8, 9), or metaphorically, under his protection (as in Heb. 2, 16), or more probably than either, in his company, along with him, as when one friend takes another, to present or introduce him to a third, which is exactly the idea here. *To the Apostles*, not to *the disciples*, or promiscuous body of believers, by whom he had already been repelled, but to the twelve, who had both the official right and the spiritual gift to determine his true character, and who, it should seem, had not yet been consulted, although some suppose them to have joined or acquiesced in Saul's rejection, until satisfied by Barnabas that he was a true convert. *Declared* (related, or detailed historically) *to them*, (not merely *that* but) *how* (i. e. in what manner, under what circumstances, including those of time and place) *in the road* (by the way, on his journey to Damascus), *he saw the Lord* (i. e. the Lord Jesus Christ, as in v. 17 above), *and that* (not how, as in the other case, but simply that) *he talked to him* (i. e. the Lord to Saul.) This was enough to settle the whole question. He to whom the ascended and exalted Saviour had appeared and spoken was fit company for any man. But more than this; the man thus signally distinguished by receiving the Lord's personal instructions, had proved faithful to his trust by manfully obeying them. *In Damascus*, in the very city whither he was going with authority to seize all believers, whether men or women (see above, on v. 2.) *Preached boldly*, or spoke freely, the verb corresponding to the noun used above in 2, 29. 4, 13. 29. 31, and there explained. *In the name of Jesus*, as his disciple, by his authority, and in assertion of his claims as the Messiah. (See above, on vs. 14. 15. 16. 21.) The two reasons for receiving Saul, suggested by this narrative of Barnabas, were, first, his miraculous conversion, and secondly, his ministerial fidelity; the one attested by the visible form and audible voice of his ascended Lord;

the other by his public, plain, and fearless proclamation of that Lord, as his own Sovereign and Redeemer.

28. And he was with them, coming in and going out, at Jerusalem.

In consequence of this interposition, Saul was recognized by the Apostles, and in deference to their authority no doubt by the disciples also, as a convert and a minister, in which capacity *he was* (or continued) *with them*, not merely as a guest or a companion, but associated with them and taking part in their official labours. *Coming in and going out*, literally, *going in and going out*, a phrase synonymous though not identical with that employed in 1, 21 (*came in and came out*) and there explained. *In Jerusalem* seems to be added, to remove all ambiguity and prevent the reader's taking this as a continuation of what Barnabas related of Saul's labours at Damascus, whereas it is Luke's record of his labours at Jerusalem.

29. And he spake boldly in the name of the Lord Jesus, and disputed against the Grecians; but they went about to slay him.

Spake boldly (literally, *speaking freely*) is identical in Greek with the *preached boldly* of v. 27, and describes Saul as doing at Jerusalem precisely what he had done at Damascus. The construction of the words here is ambiguous, some manuscripts and printed copies joining them immediately with what precedes—'going in and going out at Jerusalem, and preaching boldly in the name of Jesus.' Others make them the beginning of another verse—'and preaching boldly in the name of Jesus, he both talked and disputed with the Grecians.' *Both* (τέ), not only discoursed in a didactic way, but reasoned and disputed. *Against*, literally, *to* or *at*, not in their absence or behind their backs, but in their presence, to their face. *The Grecians, Hellenists*, or foreign Jews (see above, on 6, 1, and below, on 11, 20), of whom Saul was himself one; the same class, and possibly some of the same persons, with whom Stephen had contended (6, 9), and by whom he was destroyed. A similar effect was now produced upon them by the arguments of Saul. *They went about*, an old English phrase meaning *sought, attempted*, which is also used in the authorized version of John 7, 19, Rom. 10, 3, to express a verb which means to *seek;* whereas the one employed here means to *take in hand* or *undertake*, and is confined in the New Testament to Luke. (See below, on 19, 13, and compare Luke 1, 1.) *To slay him*, the same verb that is translated *kill him*, in v. 23.

30. Which when the brethren knew, they brought him down to Cesarea, and sent him forth to Tarsus.

But the brethren knowing (or discovering it), *brought him down*, &c. *Which* and *when* are both supplied by the translators. *The brethren*, followers of Christ, believers in the new religion, called *the disciples* in v. 25. It is worthy of remark how promptly and unitedly the brethren or disciples acted in both cases, not as individuals, but as a body, no doubt accustomed thus to act in concert. *Brought him down*, the usual expression in describing motion from the inland to the seacoast, or in any direction from the Holy City. (See above, on 7, 15. 8, 15. 26.) *Cesarea* here is not, as some suppose, Cesarea Philippi, near the sources of the Jordan, but the seaport of that name, where Philip was left at the close of the last chapter. (See above, on 8, 40.) *Sent him forth* or *off*, or still more exactly, *sent him out away*, a favourite expression of our author (see above, on 7, 12, and below, on 11, 22. 12, 11. 13, 26. 17, 14. 22, 21, and compare Luke 1, 53. 2, 10. 11), the only other writer who employs it being Paul (Gal. 4, 4. 6.) It implies great distance, and is here applied no doubt to a voyage by sea. *Tarsus*, his native place, to which the history thus brings him back and for the present leaves him. (See above, on v. 11, and below, on 11, 25.)

31. Then had the churches rest throughout all Judea and Galilee and Samaria, and were edified, and walking in the fear of the Lord, and in the comfort of the Holy Ghost, were multiplied.

This is marked in some editions of the text, and explained by some interpreters, as the conclusion of the narrative of Paul's conversion, and as meaning that in consequence of that event, the churches of Palestine enjoyed repose from persecution, and an opportunity as well of outward as of inward growth. But Paul was not the only persecutor; nor could his conversion, especially if it were the only case, immediately give peace to all the churches, or save himself from being persecuted afterwards. (See Gal. 5, 11. Rom. 15, 31.) Besides, his new commission seems to have been limited to foreign cities (see above, on v. 2, and below, on 26, 11), and its termination could not therefore have afforded peace to all the churches of the Holy Land. This erroneous view of the connection has arisen partly from the use of the word *rest*, implying previous suffering or disturbance, to translate a word which is always rendered *peace*, except in this book (see above, on 7, 26, and below, on 24, 2); and partly from the use of the word *then*, to represent a phrase which properly means *so then*, and marks the resumption of a narrative before interrupted. (See above, on 8, 4. 25.) The point to which the writer here reverts is no doubt the dispersion consequent upon the death of Stephen. The verse is then introductory to a new subject, Peter's visitation of the churches after the first force of the persecution had been spent. Notwithstanding all that they suffered, the churches of Palestine were now highly prosperous. It is not necessarily implied that persecution had entirely ceased, nor need we assume a reference to the profanation of the temple by Caligula, as a reason for its ceasing. All that is here recorded is the growth and prosperity of the Jewish-Christian churches. What really implies that they were not now persecuted, is that Peter could be absent from Jerusalem. (See above, on 8, 1.) *Edified*, i. e. built up, a favourite figure in the New Testament, not for mere numerical increase and outward organization, but for internal growth and spiritual progress (1 Cor. 8, 1. 10. 10. 23. 14, 4. 17. 1 Thess. 5, 11.) *Walking*, not merely in the sense of living, habitually acting, but in that of advancing, making progress. *The fear of the Lord*, the spirit and practice of the true religion, with special reference to fear in the restricted sense. *Consolation*, exhortation, or instruction (see above, on 4, 36.) The Rhemish version (*replenished with the consolation of the Holy Ghost*), though not incompatible with classical usage, is at variance with that of the Hellenistic Greek, according to which the verb here used means only to *multiply*, in the active or passive sense. The construction is ambiguous, as we may either read, by the consolation of the Holy Ghost were multiplied, or, as in the common version, walking in the fear of the Lord and the consolation of the Holy Ghost, were multiplied. The essential meaning is the same in either case.

32. And it came to pass, as Peter passed throughout all (quarters), he came down also to the saints which dwelt at Lydda.

During this auspicious period of prosperity and growth in the infant churches of the Holy Land, an incident occurred, or *came to pass*, which was closely connected with subsequent events of great importance. This was a general visitation of the churches by the Apostle Peter, in the course of which, *passing through all*, i. e. through all parts of the country; or through all its cities; or through all the places where the church had been established; or, as some supply the ellipsis, through (i. e. among) all the saints, believers, or disciples in the Holy Land. (Compare the similar expressions used by Paul in 20, 25, and Rom. 15, 28.) In the course of this official journey, *he came down* (see above, on 8, 15. 26), not only to a multitude of other places not here named, but *also to the saints* (see above, on v. 13) *inhabiting Lydda*. This was the *Lod* of the Old Testament, built or rebuilt after the return from Babylon (1 Chron. 8, 12. Ezr. 2, 33. Neh. 7, 37. 11, 35), and afterwards known by the Greek name of *Diospolis*. Here Richard Cœur-de-Lion built a church to St. George, the ruins of which are said to be still visible.

33. And there he found a certain man named Eneas, which had kept his bed eight years, and was sick of the palsy.

Found, or met with, unexpectedly, as seems to be suggested by the use of this expression. The Greek form of the name (*Eneas*) has led some to the conclusion, that the sufferer, *who had kept his bed* (literally, *lying down upon a bed or couch*) *since* or *for* (literally, *from*, see above, on v. 13) *eight years*, was a Gentile; while others, with more reason although not conclusively, infer from the previous mention of the saints, that he was certainly a Christian. *And was sick of the palsy*, literally, *who was paralyzed* or *paralytic*. (See above, on 8, 7, and compare Luke 5, 18. 24.)

34. And Peter saith unto him, Eneas, Jesus Christ maketh thee whole; arise and make thy bed.

Calling him by name, in order to secure his attention and

identify the object of address, the Apostle solemnly assures him that he is already healed, and that the power by which the miracle was wrought is that of Jesus Christ. He does not even name himself as the instrumental cause, or invoke the name of Christ (as in 3, 6), but expressly represents him as the efficient and immediate agent. *Maketh thee whole*, or more emphatically and yet more exactly, *Jesus Christ is healing thee*, now, at this moment, even while I speak. This form of expression shows, in the clearest manner, the Apostle's full persuasion of the truth of what he says, which is also suggested by the following command. *Arise, stand up*, an act which a moment sooner would have been impossible, and the failure to perform which now would have covered Peter with confusion, and exposed him to contempt, if not to punishment, as an impostor. *Make thy bed*, literally, *spread for thyself*, which some have strangely understood of spreading a table or providing food; but which refers to the spreading of his couch, or the arrangement of the bed-clothes, both which, in the East, are comparatively simple operations. The command does not refer to future practice—'henceforth make thy own bed, and no longer be dependent on the help of others'—but to an immediate act, affording proof of his entire restoration, by performing, on the spot and in a moment, what for eight years he had not been able even to attempt. If he had not done it, how pitiable would have been the attitude of the Apostle! How complete the refutation of his claims to represent a divine person, by whose power the cure had been effected! But he was not to be thus disgraced. The success of the experiment was instantaneous, as appears from the concise but most expressive statement, that the paralytic *instantly arose*, and no doubt made his bed, as he was ordered.

35. And all that dwelt in Lydda and Saron saw him, and turned to the Lord.

There was nothing secret, either in the previous condition of this man, or in the change which he experienced. In both states he was a familiar object. *All saw him*, not once for all, or at the moment of the cure, but often, or from time to time. This statement comprehends, not merely the inhabitants of Lydda, where Eneas lived, and where the miracle was wrought, but those of the whole tract or region, here described by its ancient name of *Saron* (*Sharon*), meaning originally any plain, but specially applied to that along the Mediterranean coast between Cesarea and Joppa, once so famous for its fertility that it is sometimes joined with Lebanon and Carmel, as a proverbial type or emblem of luxuriant vegetation. (See Isai. 33, 9. 35, 2. 65, 10, and compare 1 Chr. 27, 29.) *And turned* (literally, *were turned*) *to the Lord*, is not the statement of an additional event, unconnected with the miracle except by chronological succession. Nor does it qualify the *all* of the preceding clause, and mean that all who had already been converted saw him after he was healed; for the verb is not in the pluperfect tense, and the sight of the restored paralytic could not well have been confined to the disciples; an objection only partially removed by saying that, although they could not be the only witnesses, they might be the only ones appealed to by a Christian writer. Besides, the terms here used are descriptive of new converts, which is the uniform and constant sense of turning to God, or to the Lord (Jesus Christ), the first form being chiefly used of Gentile and the last of Jewish converts. (Compare 15, 19. 20. 21, with 11, 21. 2 Cor. 15, 3. 16.) The true sense, therefore, is that the healing of Eneas was the occasion of a general conversion to the new religion in that part of the country. 'They saw the miracle and turned to God.' This is, no doubt, a reason for this one case being singled out from many of the same kind and particularly stated, not because it was intrinsically more important, but because it was connected with this progress of the truth, and with other great events about to be recorded.

36. Now there was at Joppa a certain disciple named Tabitha, which by interpretation is called Dorcas: this woman was full of good works and almsdeeds which she did.

The healing of Eneas was connected with another miracle, which led to similar results in that part of Judea, and immediately prepared the way for Peter's memorable visit to Cesarea, described in the next chapter. *Now*, not a particle of time but of narration; see above, on v. 10. *Joppa*, the Greek form of the Hebrew *Japho* (Josh. 19, 46. 2 Chr. 2, 16. Ezr. 3, 7. Jon. 1, 3) and the Arabic *Jaffa*, in all which names the initial letter is a vowel or a semivowel nearly equivalent to our *y* at the beginning of a word, although pronounced in

English as a double consonant. The place so called is a seaport on the Mediterranean coast of Palestine, described by Pliny as extremely ancient, and in Scripture as the point where materials were landed for the building both of the first and second temple (2 Chr. 2, 16. Ezr. 3, 7.) The harbour was a bad one, but the best upon the coast, until Herod the Great made an artificial port at Cesarea. (See above, on v. 30 and 8, 40.) Hence Joppa was conspicuous in history for ages, as well as for the changes which it underwent, having been repeatedly demolished and rebuilt. Since the first Crusade, it has been the landing place for Christian pilgrims, and visited by almost every traveller in the East. It was sacked by Napoleon in 1797, and witnessed the famous massacre of prisoners. The Hebrew name means *beautiful*, and probably alludes to its appearance at a distance. It occurs in the New Testament only in this narrative. (See below, vs. 38. 42. 43. 10, 5. 8. 23. 32. 11, 5. 13.) Here Peter was commissioned to perform a miracle still greater than the one at Lydda. The subject of it is described as a female convert or disciple. According to the custom of the age and country (see above, on 1, 13. 23. 4, 36), she had two names, one Greek (*Dorcas*) and the other Aramaic (*Tabitha*), both denoting a gazelle or antelope. The double name may possibly imply a mixed population, which is quite as probable in Joppa as in Cesarea, where we know from Josephus that it did exist. (See above, on 8, 40.) *Full of* (or *abounding in*) *good works*, an expression sometimes signifying virtuous or pious acts in general, and sometimes acts of charity and kindness in particular. (See above, on 4, 9, and compare Rom. 2, 7. 13, 3. 2 Cor. 9, 8. 1 Tim. 5, 10. 3, 17.) The latter meaning is required here by the specific statement following. *Alms-deeds*, or *alms*, as the same word is translated in 3, 2. 3 above. *Did*, in the imperfect tense, used to do, habitually practised.

37. And it came to pass in those days that she was sick and died, whom, when they had washed, they laid her in an upper chamber.

In the life of this exemplary person a remarkable event occurred, or *came to pass, in those days,* i. e. during Peter's residence at Lydda. *Having sickened* (or *been sick*) *she died. When they had washed,* literally, *having washed.* The form of the Greek word is masculine and plural, and describes the agents in the most general way without regard to sex. The masculine is thus generically used, not only in Hebrew, but in the best Greek writers, a striking instance being found in Xenophon. *In an upper room*, see above, on 1, 13. The Greek phrase may possibly here mean, *up stairs*, or in the upper story.

38. And forasmuch as Lydda was nigh to Joppa, and the disciples had heard that Peter was there, they sent unto him two men, desiring (him) that he would not delay to come to them.

Lydda being near to Joppa, to wit, ten or twelve miles, on the highway to Jerusalem. *The disciples* (of Christ), still acting as a body (see above, on v. 30.) *Had heard*, literally, *having heard*, as the report of the first miracle had spread throughout the plain of Sharon (see above, on v. 35.) *There*, literally, *in it*, i. e. Lydda. *Desiring*, exhorting, or entreating (see above, on 2. 40. 8, 31.) *Would not delay*, literally, *not to delay*, hesitate, or put off coming, applied in classic Greek especially to hesitation caused by fear or sloth. Instead of the infinitive *to delay*, the oldest manuscripts, followed by the Vulgate, have the second person, *do not delay*. *To come*, literally, *to come* (or *pass*) *through*, i. e. through the intervening space (see above, on v. 32, and on 8, 4. 40.) *To them*, as far as to them (see above, on 1, 8.)

39. Then Peter arose and went with them. When he was come, they brought him into the upper chamber; and all the widows stood by him, weeping and showing (the) coats and garments which Dorcas made, while she was with them.

Then, as in vs. 19. 25. *Arose*, put himself in motion, or addressed himself to action. (See above, on 5, 17. 34. 8, 26. 9, 11.) *Went with them*, whether simply to console the mourners, or with the expectation of restoring her to life, the narrative does not inform us. There is no such objection to the supposition of a previous divine communication, as there was in relation to the death of Ananias. (See above, on 5, 5.) *When he was come they brought him*, literally, *whom being come they brought* (or *led*) *up into the upper chamber*, mentioned in v. 37, where the body was laid out. *All the widows* may mean those of Joppa, as a class, having charge of the sick, like the deaconesses of the apostolical churches (compare 1 Tim. 5, 9. 10); or the widows for whom Dorcas had provided by her charities (see above, on 6, 1, and compare 1 Tim. 5, 16. James 1, 27.) In the latter case, the garments shown were those which they then wore; in the former, those which she had left for distribution. *Coats and garments*, or according to the strict sense of the Greek words, under and upper garments (see above, on 7, 58), the tunic and robe or gown, which still constitute the oriental costume of both sexes. *Which*, literally, *as many as*, but not necessarily denoting all (see above, on vs. 13. 16, and 4, 34.) *Made*, in the imperfect tense, which may either mean she used to make them, or was actually making them, when seized with her last illness. *While she was with them*, literally, *with them being* (i. e. when she still lived.)

40. But Peter put (them) all forth, and kneeled down and prayed, and turning (him) to the body, said, Tabitha, arise. And she opened her eyes; and when she saw Peter, she sat up.

In imitation of his Master at the house of Jairus (Matt. 9, 25. Luke 8, 51), where Peter was one of the three suffered to attend him, the Apostle now excludes all the rest from the chamber of death, and kneeling down (*placing the knees*, as in 7, 60), invokes the divine interposition, thus again, but in another form, acknowledging his own part in the whole transaction to be merely instrumental. (See above, on 3, 6. 16. 4, 10.) Then, instead of saying, as he did to Eneas (v. 34), "Jesus Christ is healing thee," he turns to the corpse and addresses it directly, in an authoritative tone, commanding the dead woman, by her Aramaic name, and no doubt in the Aramaic language of the country (see above, on 1, 19), to arise from the place where she was lying. *Turning*, in the primary corporeal sense, as distinguished from the metaphorical or moral, which occurs above in v. 35. Presumptuous or mad as this command might well have seemed, it is immediately obeyed, by a succession of acts showing the return of life. When she opened her eyes, which had been so long closed in death, they rested upon Peter, whom she no doubt saw to be a stranger and alone in the apartment. Roused by this unexpected sight, she finally sat up, thereby evincing the completeness of the miracle, and her own entire resuscitation. Nothing could be more natural and simple, or at the same time more graphic, than this narrative.

41. And he gave her (his) hand, and lifted her up, and when he had called the saints and widows, he presented her alive.

Having described the acts of the resuscitated woman, Luke describes those of Peter after her revival. *Gave her his hand and lifted her up*, not because she was too weak to rise without help or to stand alone, for the recovery, in all such cases, was complete and instantaneous; but rather in the way of welcome or congratulation. *Gave his hand*, implying that she took it, and was not therefore altogether passive. He then calls in the witnesses whom he had before excluded (v. 40), the saints (believers or disciples) in general, and the widows, previously mentioned (v. 39) as chief mourners, in particular. To these he now *presents her living*, the same expression that is used in 1, 3, and there explained. The whole account suggests the idea of deliberation and composure, as opposed to that of hurry and excitement on the part of Peter, or of possible delusion on the part of the spectators.

42. And it was known throughout all Joppa; and many believed in the Lord.

As in the other case at Lydda (v. 35), the historian now records the effect of this great miracle, first stating its publicity and notoriety. *It became known* (see above, on 1, 19, and below, on 19, 17) *throughout* (see above, on v. 31, and below, on 10, 37) *all Joppa*. This circumstance is introduced, not merely for its own sake, or to show the certainty of the event, but also for the purpose of suggesting an important providential end which it promoted. *Many believed in the Lord*, or rather on him, the Greek preposition suggesting the idea of reliance or dependence, as in 1, 17 above, and 15, 31. 22, 19 below. (Compare Rom. 4, 24.) It also denotes motion towards an object, and thus suggests the idea of conversion, as involved in that of faith, or inseparable from it. *The Lord*, i. e. the Lord Jesus Christ, as the wider sense of God would here be too indefinite. (See above, on v. 35.)

43. And it came to pass, that he tarried many days in Joppa, with one Simon a tanner.

Having shown how Peter came to be in Joppa at all, the narrative now explains how he happened to be still there, when the incidents recorded in the tenth chapter came to pass. Though suddenly brought thither in a great emergency, he had determined or consented, for some reason which is not explained, to stay there. *It came to pass* (or *happened*) may imply, that this was not his expectation or original intention; that he did not mean to stay there, yet it so happened or turned out. *Many days*, literally, *days enough*, as in v. 23. 5, 37. 8, 11. A strong impression of exactness and personal knowledge of the facts related, is made by the writer's introduction of an otherwise unimportant circumstance, to wit, the very house where Peter lodged at Joppa. *With*, in Greek a preposition which, when construed with the dative or accusative, denotes juxtaposition, by or alongside of (see above, on 4, 35. 37. 5, 2. 10. 7, 58, and compare Luke 9, 47.) In its more figurative use, it is applied especially to eating with a person (Luke 11, 37. 19, 17), or to lodging with him (see below, on 10, 6. 18, 3. 20. 21, 7. 8. 16, and compare John 1, 40. 4, 4.) The Apostle's host on this occasion was a namesake of his own, but distinguished by his occupation as a currier or tanner, which was regarded by the Jews as an unclean one, from which some have needlessly inferred, that Peter was already free from Jewish prejudice; while others argue, still more gratuitously, that he and his office were held in little honour by the people of Joppa.

CHAPTER X.

This chapter is entirely occupied with one great subject, the first reception of converted Gentiles to the Church, without passing through the intermediate state of Judaism. To this narrative, 9, 31–43 is an introduction, and 11, 1–18 an appendix. The narrative itself describes the providential means, by which the representatives of the Gentile world on one hand,

and the chosen instrument of their reception on the other, were prepared for their respective parts in this transaction. These means consisted of two visions or divine communications, one to Cornelius, assuring him that God had purposes of mercy towards him, and directing him to seek an interview with Peter (1–8); the other to Peter himself, informing him that the old partition between Jews and Gentiles was now broken down, and directing him to meet the advances of Cornelius (9–20.) In obedience to this order, he accompanies the messengers to Cesarea (21–24), and, after correcting the centurion's error as to his own person (25–26), avows the change which he had recently experienced (27–29), receives a formal statement of the message to Cornelius (30–33), and preaches Christ, as the Judge and Saviour both of Jews and Gentiles (34–43.) While he is speaking, the new converts are baptized with the Holy Ghost, and then with water (34–47), after which Peter still continues with them, no doubt to instruct them in the doctrines and duties of their new religion (48.)

.1. There was a certain man in Cesarea called Cornelius, a centurion of the band called the Italian (band) —

The beginning of this narrative is less abrupt in Greek, where the usual continuative particle (δέ) connects it closely with what goes before. Those who regard it as the commencement of an entirely new subject, overlook the bearing of the miracles recorded at the close of the ninth chapter on the history that follows. It was while Peter was still resident at Joppa, and therefore easily accessible from Cesarea, that the incidents recorded in this chapter happened. *Cornelius*, a familiar but honourable name in Latin, being that of a distinguished Roman family. *A centurion* was strictly the commander of a hundred men; but the title was applied, with some degree of latitude, to those who led the subdivisions of a legion. *The band* here probably means such a subdivision. *The Italian*, probably so called because composed of Romans, although stationed in the East, as the European officers and soldiers in India are distinguished from the native troops or *sepoys*. The *Italian legion*, spoken of by Tacitus, was subsequently organized by Nero, and would not have been designated by the term here used (σπείρα.) The same phrase is employed by Arrian, and an old inscription mentions "the cohort of Italian volunteers which is in Syria." The main facts here are the country, the profession, the rank, and the residence of the man who was to represent Gentile Christianity, in its first encounter, so to speak, with the Jewish type or aspect of the same religion.

2. A devout man, and one that feared God with all his house, which gave much alms to the people, and prayed to God alway.

His character and previous religious history. *Devout*, pious, reverent, not merely in the heathen sense, but as the fruit of divine grace. *Feared God*, i. e. the one true God, as opposed to the many gods of heathenism. *With all his house*, or household; not alone, or merely in his own person, but as the teacher and example of those dependent on him. *Which gave much alms*, or rather, *practising many charities*, not merely to the poor in general, but *to the people*, i. e. the chosen people, the children of Israel, among whom he lived and from whom he had learned the true religion. *Praying to God*, or asking of God, i. e. looking to Jehovah, or the God of Israel, and not to idols, for the supply of his necessities in general, and for spiritual guidance in particular. This is not the description of a proselyte, in any technical or formal sense, but of a Gentile whom divine grace had prepared for the immediate reception of the Gospel, without passing through the intermediate state of Judaism, although long familiar with it, and indebted to it for such knowledge of the word of God as he possessed.

3. He saw in a vision, evidently, about the ninth hour of the day, an angel of God, coming in to him, and saying unto him, Cornelius!

The means used to bring this representative of the Gentile world into contact with the new religion. *Saw* is construed directly with *a man* in v. 1. by the latest critics, who omit the verb in that verse, and make one long sentence of the three. ' A certain man in Cesarea, named Cornelius, a centurion &c. . . . . . devout and fearing God &c. . . . . saw.' *In a vision*, not a dream, which would be otherwise expressed (as in Matt. 2, 13. 19. 22), but **a** supernatural communication, addressed not merely to the mind, but to the senses. (See above, on 7, 31, 9, 10. 12.) *Evidently*, clearly, certainly, not doubtfully or dimly. *About* (literally, *as if*, i. e. as if it were) *the ninth hour* (after sunrise, see above, on 2, 15), not far from three o'clock in the afternoon. The object thus and then seen was *an angel of God*, a messenger sent by him from the other world, belonging to a race of superhuman spirits, but no doubt clothed in human form. The popular idea of winged angels is derived from the cherubim (Ex. 25, 20) and seraphim (Isai. 6, 2), but is never suggested by any of the narratives of angelic visits to this world and its inhabitants. *Coming in to him*, into his house and presence, like an ordinary visitor, and addressing him familiarly by name.

4. And when he looked on him, he was afraid, and said, What is it, Lord? And he said unto him, Thy prayers and thine alms are come up for a memorial before God.

Gazing (intently looking) *at him, and becoming fearful*, not afraid of personal injury, but awe-struck at the presence of a superhuman being, which must have been betrayed by something in the stranger's aspect. *What is (it)?* i. e. what is the occasion of your coming? *Prayers and alms*, the two kinds of religious service previously mentioned, as the proofs of the centurion's devout regard to the divine will and the true religion. *Come up*, ascended, in allusion to the vapour of the ancient offerings. *For a memorial*, to remind God, as it were, of the offerer's existence and necessities; another allusion to the ceremonial law, in which this name is given to a part of the burnt-offering. (See Lev. 2, 2. Num. 5, 21.) *Before God*, not merely in his judgment or his estimation, as in 8, 21, but in his presence, in the place where he manifests his glory. Intrinsic merit or efficacy is no more ascribed in these words to the good works of Cornelius than to the oblations from which the figure or comparison is taken. It was not as a reward of what Cornelius had thus done, that the Lord now favoured and distinguished him; but this distinguishing favour was itself the cause of those devotional and charitable habits, which had been recognized in heaven as being what they were, not meritorious claims to the divine blessing, but experimental proofs that it had been bestowed.

5. And now send men to Joppa, and call for (one) Simon, whose surname is Peter:

As this vision was not intended merely to astonish or to please Cornelius, but to prepare for his reception into the Church, the angelic assurance of the divine favour is immediately succeeded by directions as to his own duty. *And now*, since God has purposes of mercy towards thee, *send to* (or *into*) *Joppa*, where Peter had been left at the close of the last chapter (9, 43.) *Men*, and by implication, chosen men, or men fit for such a service (see below, on v. 7.) *Call for*, literally, *send for*, a compound form of the preceding verb. *One* before *Simon* is supplied by the translators. Both names are given to identify the person.

6. He lodgeth with one Simon a tanner, whose house is by the sea side: he shall tell thee what thou oughtest to do.

Minute directions how he should find Peter. *Lodgeth with*, or is entertained by; for it may have been a case of Christian hospitality. *A tanner*, see above, on 9, 43. *To whom there is a house by the sea*, perhaps on account of his occupation, and perhaps at a distance from the town, as the Mishna requires in the case of such employments.

7. And when the angel which spake unto Cornelius was departed, he called two of his household servants, and a devout soldier of them that waited on him continually.

As soon as the vision is concluded, he takes the necessary measures to obey the order which he had received, employing for this purpose three of his own household, two domestics, or, as the word originally means, two members of his family, and a military servant, who was his constant personal attendant, as, in some modern armies, officers are waited on by soldiers. This man is described as like his master or commander in religious character, and therefore peculiarly well fitted for the service now assigned to him. Although not affirmed, it seems to be implied, that the other two messengers were like-minded; so that we have here the interesting case of a whole Gentile household, brought by intercourse with Jews, and by the grace of God, to the very threshold of the true religion.

8. And when he had declared all (these) things unto them, he sent them to Joppa.

Such being their character, he does not send them blindfold, but states the whole case to them. *Declared*, expounded, or detailed, the verb from which *exegesis* is derived, but specially applied in Greek to historical narration. (See below, on 15, 12, 14, 21, 19, and compare Luke 24, 35.) *All these things*, including the vision, the divine command, and the expected revelation.

9. On the morrow, as they went on their journey, and drew nigh unto the city, Peter went up upon the house-top to pray, about the sixth hour:

While the centurion's messengers are on their way, the other part of this providential scheme is set in motion, by the vision of Peter, answering to that of Cornelius. *On the morrow*, or the next day, after they set out. *They journeying*, or moving onwards, *and approaching* (or *being near*) *to the city* (or town of Joppa.) *The house*, or, as some editions read, *the house-top*, the flat roof, to which the word (δῶμα) is applied in later Greek, while its English derivative (*dome*) denotes a peculiar kind of roof, and that not a flat one. *To pray*, a frequent use of the oriental roof, on account of its elevation and retirement. *The sixth hour* after sunrise, one of the three stated hours of prayer. (See above, on 2, 15.)

10. And he became very hungry, and would have eaten; but while they made ready, he fell into a trance,

Peter is prepared, in mind and body, for the extraordinary revelation which awaits him. *Would have eaten*, literally, *wished to taste* (*food*), an expression used in classic Greek, even of a full meal. *While they made ready*, literally, *they preparing*. *They*, i. e. his friends, the people of the house, a form of expression familiar to the dialect of common life. *Preparing*, either his noon-day meal, or in anticipation of it, and at his request. *He fell into a trance*, in Greek, *there fell on him an ecstasy*, a preternatural, abnormal state of mind, preparing him for the reception of the vision. (Compare the corresponding verb in 2, 7. 8, 9. 11, 13.) *Fell on him*, by a sudden influence or illapse from above, produced by a superior power. (See below, on v. 44.)

11. And saw heaven opened, and a certain vessel descending unto him, as it had been a great sheet, knit at the four corners, and let down to the earth:

The vision itself corresponds to his bodily condition. While his thoughts are running upon food, it is exhibited in great abundance and variety, but in an extraordinary manner, showing that something was intended, very different from the satisfaction of the appetite, or even the relief of an unusual hunger. *And saw*, or rather, *and beholds*, surveys, implying something strange and striking in the object of vision. (See above, on 3, 16. 4, 13. 8, 13. 9, 7.) *Heaven opened*, as in 7, 56, except that the number here is singular, not plural. *Sheet, sail*, or *cloth*, the Greek word denoting the material rather than the shape. *Knit*, literally, *tied*, bound, fastened. *Corners*, literally, *beginnings*, but in Greek used also to denote extremities or ends. It may here mean the ends of chains or cords by which the sheet seemed to be fastened to something above, or the ends of the sheet itself, which must then be conceived as gathered up and tied, so as to be capable of holding its contents.

12. Wherein were all manner of fourfooted beasts of the earth, and wild beasts, and creeping things, and fowls of the air.

The contents were as surprising as the vessel, comprehending all kinds of animals—beasts, birds, and creeping things—including therefore both the two great classes, which the Law of Moses and the Jewish practice recognized, the Clean and Unclean. (See Lev. xi. and Deut. xiv.) This is the grand idea meant to be conveyed, and it was therefore as indifferent to Peter as it ought to be to us, into how many classes a zoologist would have divided them, or what might be the strictly scientific application of the terms, *quadrupeds of the earth, beasts, reptiles*, and *birds of heaven*, or of the air. (See Gen. 1, 20.) The distinctive names might have been more numerous or less so, more precise or less so, without varying the essential fact, that the vessel seen by Peter in his trance or vision, contained *all manner* (i. e. all kinds) of animals, both clean and unclean. *Wild beasts* is a correct translation of a single Greek word, which is usually so applied.

13. And there came a voice to him, Rise, Peter; kill and eat.

Still more surprising than what Peter saw was what he heard. *A voice came*, literally, *became*, i. e. became audible, *to him*, not merely heard by him, but addressed to him. The voice may have proceeded from the open vessel, but more probably from the open heaven (v. 11.) *Rise* (literally, *rising*) may imply that he was on his knees, or lying down, or sitting. It may also be, however, a command to rouse himself from a previous condition of inaction or repose. (See above, on 9, 6. 11. 18.) *Kill* is in Greek a verb denoting sacrificial slaying, or the act of killing with a reference to some religious purpose. The use of this significant expression, which is not to be diluted or explained away without necessity, shows that the following command (*and eat*) refers not merely to the satisfaction of the appetite, but to those ceremonial restrictions, under which the law of Moses placed the Jews, both in their worship and in their daily use of necessary food. As if the voice had said, 'From among these animals select thy offering or thy food, without regard to the distinction between clean and unclean.'

14. But Peter said, Not so, Lord; for I have never eaten any thing that is common or unclean.

Peter responds to this command as any conscientious Jew or Jewish Christian would have done, by representing it as inconsistent with the whole previous tenor of his life. *Not so*, not at all, by no means. The emphasis and positiveness of this refusal is in curious contrast with the title of respect which follows, and which can scarcely be translated *Sir* in this connection, but must imply that he regarded the voice as that of a superhuman if not a divine speaker. (See above, on 9, 5. 6.) Even such authority was not immediately sufficient to break the force of prejudice and habit. The thought to be supplied between the clauses is, 'I cannot do it now, because I never did before.' *I have never eaten* (more exactly, *never did eat*) *any thing* (literally, *all* or *every*) i. e. all that came to hand, without discrimination. The reference is not to any personal peculiarity, but to that restrictive law of food, which constituted one of the most striking points of difference between Jew and Gentile, and one of the most operative means of separation, as it does to this day. *Common*, not appropriated, set apart, or consecrated, which some regard as the original or primary sense of *holy*. (See above, on 9, 13.) Others make the essential idea to be that of purity, the opposite of which is also here expressed (*unclean*.) Taken together, therefore, they exhaust the idea of *unholy* or profane, which was present to the mind of the Apostle. The general fact which he affirms is that he had always lived as a strict Jew, and therefore separate from other people. The particular sign of this seclusion here referred to—the distinction of food—served, at the same time, as a type or emblem of a moral difference, the Gentiles being to the Jews, in this respect, what unclean animals were to the clean.

15. And the voice (spake) unto him again the second time, What God hath cleansed, (that) call not thou common.

The voice, or more exactly, *a voice*, implying that the speaker still remained invisible. *Again, a second* (time), an emphatic reduplication, which seems intended to make the parts in this dramatic dialogue as distinct as possible. The same effect is promoted by the suppression of the verb (*said*); see above, on 9, 11. The literal translation of the last clause is, *What* (*things*) *God hath purified do thou not render common*, or treat as such, a phrase representing one Greek verb (κοίνου), which has no equivalent in English, unless we coin for the occasion some such form as *communify*. The two verbs in this clause correspond to the two adjectives in Peter's answer. *Call not common* is a version justified by the analogy of certain causatives in Hebrew, which are *used* in a declarative sense, and in a ceremonial application. (E. g. *to purify*, i. e. to pronounce pure; *to pollute*, i. e. to pronounce polluted, Lev. 13, 3. 6. 8. 11.) But the proper causative sense of *making common* or *unclean* is not only appropriate, but much more pointed. 'What God has hallowed do not thou attempt to unhallow.' This reply of the unseen speaker to Peter's true but proud profession of Levitical fidelity and strictness **must** have been surprising and at first confounding. Instead of recognizing his pretensions to the praise of ceremonial perfection, the person, whose authority he had just acknowledged by addressing him as Lord, denies the truth and value of the distinction altogether. It is not a mere precaution against error in the application of the ceremonial principle, but an abrogation of the principle itself. Peter is not simply put upon his guard against the error of regarding as unclean, according to the Jewish standard, what was really, according to that standard, clean. He is warned against the far worse error of continuing to recognize that standard as itself obligatory, after it had ceased to be so. Hitherto there had been a distinction between clean and unclean, both in meats and persons. Henceforth there could be none; for what had been unclean for ages by divine authority was now pronounced clean by the same; and what had thus been constituted clean could not be rendered common by the exercise of any human power or authority.

16. This was done thrice, and the vessel was received up again into heaven.

This, i. e. the whole scene, including sights and sounds, the vision and the dialogue. *Was done*, happened, came to pass; the same verb that is used with *voice* in v. 13. *Thrice* is in Greek a peculiar idiomatic phrase (ἐπὶ τρίς), the nearest approach to which in English is, for three times, or on three occasions. An analogous though different expression is, to the number of three. *Received up*, or taken back, or both, which seems to be the meaning of the same verb in the first sentence of the book. (See above, on 1, 1.) This repetition of the revelation, no doubt in precisely the same form, may have been intended partly to impress it on the memory, but chiefly to preclude the suspicion of its being a mere dream or fancy. *Again*, or according to the oldest manuscripts and latest editors, *immediately*, the former having probably been introduced, by assimilation, from 11, 10. (See above, on 9, 5.)

17. Now while Peter doubted in himself what this vision which he had seen should mean, behold, the men which were sent from Cornelius had made inquiry for Simon's house, and stood before the gate,

Now is the particle translated *but* in v. 14, and not translated at all in vs. 16,19. *While*, literally, *as ;* see above, on 1, 10. 5, 24. 7, 23. 8, 36. 9, 23. 10, 7. *Doubted*, was perplexed, or at a loss, the same verb that is used above, 2, 12, and there explained. (See also, on 5, 24.) *Should mean*, or more exactly, *what it was*, or *might be*. (See above, on 5, 24, where a similar though not the same expression is employed.) *Behold*, literally, *and behold*, a form of expression foreign from our idiom, but common in Hebrew and in Hellenistic Greek. (See above, on 1, 10. 8, 27.) *Which were sent*, literally, *those sent*, or *the (men) sent*. *From Cornelius*, not merely by him, but away from him, implying that he remained at home. *Had made inquiry*, literally, *having asked* or *inquired*. (See above, on 1, 6. 5, 27, where another compound of the same verb is employed.) Perhaps the full force of the one here used is, having ascertained or found out by inquiry. *Before the gate*, or at the porch or vestibule, the front side of an oriental house, through which is the entrance to the open court within. (See below, on 12, 14. 14, 13.)

18. And called, and asked whether Simon, which was surnamed Peter, were lodged there.

And called, literally, *calling* or *having called*, i. e. as some explain it, having called some one out to them; but the absolute sense of calling, i. e. raising the voice, shouting, as a substitute for knocking, ringing, and the like, gives an equally good meaning and is equally agreeable to usage, while it makes the syntax simpler, by assuming no grammatical ellipsis of the object. *Asked*, in the imperfect tense, *were asking*, at that very moment. The Greek verb is not the same with that in the preceding verse, but one employed above in 4, 7, and below in v. 29. 21, 33. 23, 19. 20. 23, 34. The form of the interrogation is the same as in 1, 6, and gives the very words of the inquirers, (tell us) *if Simon, the* (one) *surnamed Peter, lodges* (or *is lodged*) *here*. (See above, on v. 6.)

19. While Peter thought on the vision, the Spirit said unto him, Behold, three men seek thee.

Peter pondering (revolving, or turning it over *in his mind*, which last is the etymological import of the Greek verb) *about* (concerning, as to) *the vision* (the extraordinary sight which he had just seen), *the Spirit* (i. e. the Divine or Holy Spirit, see above, on 8, 29) *said to him, Behold* (or *lo*, implying something unexpected and surprising, see above, on 1, 10. 2, 7. 5, 9. 25. 28. 7, 56. 8, 27. 36. 9, 10. 11), *three men are seeking* (asking or inquiring for) *thee*. This coincidence of time, between Peter's anxious meditations and the inquiries of the men from Cesarea, brings the two parts of the providential scheme into conjunction and co-operation.

20. Arise therefore, and get thee down, and go with them, doubting nothing ; for I have sent them.

But arise (not *therefore*, which is never so expressed in Greek), i. e. while they are seeking thee, do thou, on thy part, *stand up* (from thy sitting or recumbent posture; or arouse thyself, address thyself to action, see above, on v. 13), *and go down* (of which *get thee down* is an old English equivalent), *and depart* (set off or journey, see above, on 9, 3. 11. 15. 31) *with them, doubting nothing,* i. e. as to nothing, asking neither who nor what they are. The Greek verb, in its active form, means first to separate or sever; then to distinguish or discriminate ; and then to determine or decide. (See below, on 15, 9, and compare 1 Cor. 4, 7. Matt. 16, 3. 1 Cor. 11, 29. 31. 14, 29.) The middle means to *differ*, either with others, i. e. to dispute, or with one's self, i. e. to hesitate and waver. (See below, on 11, 2, and compare Jude 9 with Matt. 21, 21. Mark 11, 23. Rom. 4, 20. 14, 23. James 1, 6. 2, 4.) Either the second or the last of these is here appropriate—'not at all hesitating so to do'—or, 'not distinguishing without a difference, making no gratuitous, invidious distinction between Jew and Gentile.' The latter seems entitled to the preference, as involving an allusion to the heavenly lesson he had just received. *For I have sent them*, not immediately, but through the Angel (v. 5) and Cornelius (v. 8).

21. Then Peter went down to the men which were sent unto him from Cornelius, and sa d, Behold, I am he whom ye seek ; what is the cause wherefore ye are come ?

Then (and, but, or so) *Peter descending* (going down stairs from the flat roof where he saw the vision) *to the men* (still standing in the porch or at the front door), *said, Behold,* (i. e. see me, here I am, as in 9, 10), *I am he whom ye seek* (or after whom ye are inquiring, compare John 18, 4–8.) *What* (is) *the cause* (reason or occasion) *wherefore* (i. e. for or on account of which) *ye are come,* (or more exactly, ye are present, ye are here.) Peter, as Chrysostom observes, shows that he had no thought of concealing himself from them, by first making himself known and then inquiring why they sought him. It is characteristic of the man and the apostle that he affects no knowledge which he did not possess, and notwithstanding the two divine communications which had just been made to him, acknowledges his ignorance of what had not been thus revealed. The words, *sent from Cornelius,* are wanting in the oldest manuscripts and versions, and supposed by modern critics to have been inserted from a lectionary or collection of lessons to be used in public worship, into which they had been introduced to make the narrative intelligible and complete.

22. And they said, Cornelius the centurion, a just man, and one that feareth God, and of good report among all the nation of the Jews, was warned from God by a holy angel to send for thee into his house, and to hear words of thee.

The centurion should be *a centurion,* as in Greek, referring to a person not yet known to Peter, but intended to be made known by this very description. The definite form is the less appropriate, as there were many Roman officers of this rank in the Holy Land. (See below, on 21, 32. 22, 25. 23, 17. 23. 24, 23. 27, 1, and compare Matt. 8, 5. 27, 54. Mark 15, 44.) For *devout* or *pious* in v. 2, we have here the more generic term, *just* or *righteous* (see above, on 3, 14. 4, 19. 7, 52.) *Fearing God,* literally, *the God,* i. e. the true God, or the God of Israel (see above, on v. 2.) *Of good report among,* or more exactly, *testified* (attested, certified, to be such as they had just described him, not only by his countrymen and fellow Gentiles, but) *by all the nation* (or the whole nation) *of the Jews,* a natural hyperbole denoting all the Jews of Cesarea, or more indefinitely, Jews in general, as distinguished from the Gentiles. *Warned from God,* the same verb that is used in Matt. 2, 12. 22. Heb. 8, 5. 11, 7. 12, 25, and originally meaning to transact business, more particularly money-matters, then, to negociate or confer on state affairs ; and then, to give an answer after such negociation, in which last sense it is used by Demosthenes and Xenophon. By a still further elevation and restriction of the meaning, it is applied to the responses of the oracles, and in the Scriptures to divine communications, more especially those made to individuals. The sense of warning is required by the context in Matthew and Hebrews; but in this place it may either have the general sense of a divine communication or instruction, or the more specific one of a divine response, i. e. to the prayers of Cornelius for divine direction. (See above, on v. 2, and for a very different use of the same verb, below, on 11, 26.) *From God* is supplied by the translators as really included in the meaning of the verb. *By a holy* (i. e. an unfallen) *angel*, as distinguished from "the devil and his angels" (Matt. 25, 41. 2 Cor. 11, 14. 12, 7. Rev. 12, 19.) *To send for thee*, not to come in person, which may be stated as a reason for the absence of Cornelius. *And to hear words of thee* (i. e. from thee, spoken by thee), an addition to the narrative in v. 6, the last clause in the common text of that verse being omitted by the oldest manuscripts and latest critics, as an unauthorized assimilation to 9, 6. (See above, on 9, 5.)

23. Then called he them in and lodged (them.) And on the morrow, Peter went away with them, and certain brethren from Joppa accompanied him.

Then, or rather *therefore*, i. e. because they came on such an errand. *Called them* (more exactly, *calling*, or *having called them*) *in*, which does not necessarily imply that they were still without and he within the house; for it may mean *inviting them* (in which sense Aristophanes employs the same verb), not to cross the threshold merely, but to take up their abode there for the night. *Lodged them*, or rather, *entertained them*, including all the rites of hospitality, which may be also meant in vs. 6 and 18. *On the morrow*, or the next day after their arrival, as the same phrase in the ninth verse means the day after they left Cesarea. *Went away*, literally, *went out*, i. e. from the house and from the city. *Certain brethren*, literally, *some of the brethren*, i. e. disciples or converted Jews (see below, on v. 45), whose names and number are not given here, although the latter is recorded in 11, 12 below. *From Joppa*, not merely belonging to it, although that idea is of course suggested, but coming from it upon this occasion. We are not told whether Peter took them with him by divine command; or as a wise precaution, the utility of which appears from the next chapter (see below, on 11, 12); or merely as companions and friends, their use as witnesses then forming no part of his own plan, though it did of God's. Wiclif adds expressly, *that they be* (i. e. might be) *witnesses to Peter*. But their errand may have been still more important. (See below, on v. 46.)

24. And the morrow after, they entered into Cesarea; and Cornelius waited for them, and had called together his kinsmen and near friends.

The morrow, the next day after leaving Joppa, which was thirty miles from Cesarea. *Cornelius was waiting for them*, perhaps implying that they were longer on the way than he expected. It may mean, however, nothing more than his anxiety to meet with Peter. *Having called together*, not merely to do honour to his visitor, but for their own instruction, *his kinsmen*, from which some infer that Cesarea was his native place, or at least that he had formed intimate connections in the country. *Near friends*, in the older English versions *special friends*, and in Greek *necessary friends*, which may either denote natural relations, not dependent on the will of the parties, or the closest intimacy, making their society essential to his comfort or his happiness. The main fact is the same in either case, to wit, that the centurion had gathered his most intimate acquaintances and friends, to share in the divine communication, which he expected to receive through Peter. As this would hardly have been done without some preparation or predisposition upon their part, it would seem to imply a previous work of grace among these Gentiles, leading them to Christ, even before they came in contact with his gospel or his ministers.

25. And as Peter was coming in, Cornelius met him, and fell down at his feet, and worshipped (him.)

And as it came to pass that Peter entered, i. e. just as Peter entered, *Cornelius, meeting him* (and) *falling at the feet* (of Peter), *worshipped*. Having been directed by an Angel to send for the Apostle, with a promise of divine communications from him, it is not surprising that Cornelius should have supposed him to be more than a mere man, or even a divine person. His feelings were perhaps the same as if he had been honoured with a visit from our Lord himself, while yet on earth. How could he be expected, without previous instruction, to distinguish so exactly between the Apostle and his Master, as both appeared in human form, and both exerted superhuman power? This seems more natural and satisfactory than to suppose that this Roman soldier simply meant to do obeisance in the oriental manner, which was not in common use among the Jews themselves, much less among the Romans.

26. But Peter took him up, saying, Stand up, I myself also am a man.

Took him up, literally, *raised him*, i. e. from his prostrate attitude. Some have understood Peter's words as meaning, 'I am a man, as you are, although of another nation, and I claim no right to such profound veneration, even from a Gentile.' But how can we imagine that Cornelius, who had long been well acquainted with the Jews, at least in Cesarea, could be so overwhelmed by the appearance of another Jew from Joppa? The obvious meaning of the answer is, 'I am a mere man like yourself, and therefore not an object of religious worship.' (Compare the similar expressions in Rev. 22, 9.) It has been well observed that Christ himself never disclaimed his title to such honours, although often offered. (See Matt. 8, 2. 9, 18. 14, 33. 15, 25. 20, 20. 28, 9. 17. John 9, 38.)

27. And as he talked with him, he went in, and found many that were come together.

Conversing with him, not in the restricted modern sense of talking, but in the Latin and old English one of keeping company, associating, holding intercourse, which is the only classical usage of the Greek verb in its simple form, and in the single instance of the compound which is cited in the lexicons. The sense of talking is moreover less appropriate, as it implies that something passed in conversation between Peter and Cornelius which is not recorded. This, though not impossible, would mar the beauty and completeness of the narrative, which seem at least in part dependent on the fact that we have here, upon divine authority, just what was said and done by all the parties to this great transaction. The ensuing dialogue would lose much of its interest, if preceded by another, of which we know nothing. Both the context, therefore, and Greek usage are in favour of interpreting the clause to mean, that Peter entered with Cornelius, showing by his whole demeanour, not excluding what he said, that he felt no scruple in associating with him upon equal terms. The last clause discloses the additional circumstance, that the friends of Cornelius, mentioned in v. 24, were numerous. It may also be implied, that Peter was surprised to find so many gathered to receive him.

28. And he said unto them, Ye know how that it is an unlawful (thing) for a man that is a Jew to keep company or come unto one of another nation; but God hath shewed me that I should not call any (man) common or unclean.

He appeals to their own experimental knowledge of the hindrances to social intercourse between the Jews and Gentiles any where, but more particularly in Judea. *Ye know*, or more emphatically, know well, know for certain, or are well aware, which is the usage of this Greek verb in the classics, although less distinctly marked in the New Testament, where it frequently occurs, especially in this book. (See below, on 15, 7. 18, 25. 19, 15. 25. 20, 18. 22, 19. 24, 10. 26, 3. 26.) *How that it is an unlawful thing* is an awkward version of a very simple phrase, *how unlawful it is*, or still more simply, *that it is unlawful*. The Greek adjective is used but twice in the New Testament, and in both instances by Peter (1 Pet. 4, 3.) According to its etymology and classical usage, it denotes what is contrary to ancient custom or prescription ($θέμις$), rather than to positive enactment ($νόμος$); and this agrees exactly with the case before us, where the prohibition does not rest upon the letter of the law, but either on its spirit, as interpreted in later times, or on some traditional addition to it. *A man, a Jew*, i. e. a Jewish man, a man who is a Jew. (See above, on 8, 27.) The use of both terms is not pleonastic, but equivalent to saying 'for any man, that is (or at least) for any Jew.' *To keep company*, literally, to stick fast, to adhere, a figure for the most familiar, intimate association. (See above, on 5, 13. 8, 29, and below, on 17, 31.) *Or* (even) *to approach, to come to* (i. e. into the society of) any alien, foreigner, here put, perhaps through courtesy, for a Gentile, an alien both in race and religion. (Compare the Septuagint version of Isai. 2, 6. 61, 5.) Although the terms immediately preceding this are properly expressive of association or companionship in general, the whole connection gives them a specific application to domestic intercourse, and more especially to that of the table, or participation in the same food. This has always been avoided by the Jews, even to the present time, as necessarily endangering the violation of their dietetic laws, at least when they are the recipients and not the givers of the entertainment. This practice, growing out of the provisions of the law respecting clean and unclean meats, was so connected with the common intercourse and courtesies of life, that Peter's hearers upon this occasion must have been all familiar with it, and could therefore understand his meaning, even when conveyed in general expressions. This removes the objection that the Jews had never practised such entire seclusion from the Gentiles as the strict interpretation of the words would naturally indicate. Some conjecture not improbably that these words were immediately occasioned by the sight of the provision which Cornelius had made for the refreshment of his visitors. *But*, literally, *and* (not δέ but καί), 'Ye know that, and I know this, for God, etc.' *Shewed me*, not merely told or taught me, but *caused me to see it*, in the strictest sense, i. e. revealed it by a vision. *That I should not call*, a needless deviation from the form of the original, which is, *no man common or unclean to call*, except that *man* in Greek emphatically ends the sentence. As if he had said, 'no one so to call, who is a man, a human being, a partaker of our common nature.'

29. Therefore came I (unto you) without gainsaying, as soon as I was sent for. I ask therefore for what intent ye have sent for me?

For which (reason), i. e. because he had received this revelation in correction of his error, *I came* (hither, or to you, is implied, but not expressed in the original) *without gainsaying* (contradiction or refusal.) This last idea is expressed in Greek by one word, a compounded adverb, similar in form and usage to our *undeniably*, but having here the active sense of *undenyingly*. The statement of this reason for his prompt compliance shows that the true meaning of his vision had not been withheld from Peter till he came to Cesarea, but was probably imparted to him, in relief of his solicitous perplexity, just when he heard the voice of the three messengers inquiring for him. (See above, on vs. 17. 18.) The communication of the Spirit then made, as to the arrival and the errand of the men from Cesarea, was most probably accompanied by a disclosure, perhaps less explicit, but not less convincing, of the truth intended to be taught by the symbolical spectacle, which he had just seen, and upon which he was still musing. *As soon as I was sent for*, though substantially correct, is stronger than the Greek, which is a simple passive participle, meaning *having been* (or *being*) *sent for*. *I ask then*, or *therefore*, not the particle used in the first clause, but that employed above in v. 23. Having given the recent revelation as a reason for his coming without hesitation or delay, he now gives this promptness as a reason for demanding further information, or rather a formal and authoritative statement of what he must have heard already from the messengers. *For what word* (λόγῳ), not thing or matter (see above, on 8, 21), but cause or reason (see below, on 18, 14, and compare Matt. 5, 32.) This use of the Greek word is not a Hebraism, being found in Herodotus, Xenophon, and Plato. *Ye sent for me*, the active form of the same verb, of which we have the passive participle in the first clause. (See above, on vs. 5. 22, and below, on 11, 13. 24, 24. 26. 25, 3.)

30. And Cornelius said, Four days ago I was fasting until this hour ; and at the ninth hour I prayed in my house, and behold, a man stood before me in bright clothing —

Cornelius now repeats the narrative contained in vs. 3- 6, with a few unimportant variations. *Four days ago*, literally, *from the fourth day*, which has been variously understood, as meaning that Cornelius had been fasting four days when he saw the vision ; or that he had been fasting four days when these words were spoken ; or that he had been fasting from the morning till the ninth hour of the fourth day previous. No one of these ideas is explicitly conveyed by the expression, which is certainly anomalous; but that adopted by the English version is in itself more natural than either of the others. The essential meaning, upon any of these suppositions, is the same, to wit, that the centurion's prayers were accompanied by fasting, which not only proved the earnestness of his devotion, but rendered him less liable to be deceived by false appearances or mere imaginations. It might also serve to show his conformity to Jewish usages, not only in respect to fasting, but to stated hours of prayer. (See above, on 2, 15. 3, 1. 5, 7. 10, 9.) This was important only as a proof of the sincerity with which he had abandoned heathenism and begun to seek the one true God. *In my (own) house*, in retirement, at home, as distinguished from all public places of resort, and showing that the prayers and fasting mentioned were of the private and unostentatious kind described and recommended by our Saviour (Matt. 6, 5. 6. 16. 17.) The centurion's account of the angelic visitation is entirely consistent with the one in v. 3, although somewhat different in form. What Luke calls an angel, Cornelius calls a man, because in human form, whether merely apparent, or belonging to a real body, worn for the occasion and then laid aside, perhaps dissolved. An additional circumstance here mentioned is the bright, effulgent dress, probably the same with the white raiment of the two men upon Olivet (see above, on 1, 10.) This may be regarded in both cases as an emanation or reflection of the divine glory (see above, on 7, 2), with which these messengers from heaven were invested, as a proof of their legation and a source of awe to the beholders.

31. 32. And said, Cornelius, thy prayer is heard, and thine alms are had in remembrance in the sight of God. Send therefore to Joppa, and call hither Simon, whose surname is Peter: he is lodged in the house of (one) Simon a tanner, by the sea-side; who, when he cometh, shall speak unto thee.

Omitting the preliminary statement in v. 3, he gives the substance of the Angel's words as there recorded, with some freedom as to mere form and expression. While the simple phrase, *have been remembered*, takes the place of the more figurative one there employed, the *prayers and alms* are here divided and construed each with a distinct verb. The singular form (*prayer*) may have immediate reference to his prayer on that particular occasion, which was no doubt for divine illumination and a clearer knowledge of the true religion. It may also, however, be referred, as a collective, to the whole series of his previous petitions, and as therefore equivalent to the plural (*prayers*) in v. 4. *In the sight of God* is perfectly identical in Greek with *before God* in the fourth verse. *Then* or *therefore* answers to the *and now* of the fifth verse, and expresses still more strongly the connection between God's purposes of mercy towards Cornelius and the revelations to be made by Peter. *Send* is here used absolutely without *men*, which is sufficiently implied. *Call hither*, call away, or call back, are the usual senses of the Greek verb, a different one from that in v. 5, which properly means *send for*. *In the house of Simon*, literally, *in a house* (to wit, that) *of Simon*, takes the place of the less definite expression *with one* (or *a certain*) *Simon*, in the sixth verse. *When he cometh*, literally, being come, arrived, or being near you, with you (see above, on 5, 21.) *Will speak* (or *talk*) *to thee*, not in general merely, but with special reference to the questions which then occupied his mind, as to the worship of the true God and the method of salvation.

33. Immediately therefore I sent to thee; and thou hast well done that thou art come. Now therefore are we all here present before God, to hear all things that are commanded thee of God.

Immediately, or as the Greek word etymologically signifies, *from that same* (moment.) (See below, on 11, 11. 21, 32. 23, 30, and compare Mark 6, 25. Phil. 2, 23.) *Then*, or *therefore*, as in v. 32, i. e. because of this divine command and promise. *And thou*, or *thou too* (σύ τε), hast been prompt as well as I. (See above, on 1, 1. 8, 13. 5, 14. 8, 38. 9. 15.) *Hast well done*, didst well, i. e. right, or as in duty bound, but with an implied acknowledgment of kindness also, giving to these words a pleasing tone of courtesy and friendliness, as well as of solemnity and reverence. *Now then* (or *therefore*), i. e. after all that we have both experienced, and in these strange and solemn circumstances. *We all* (or *all of us*) *are present before God*, i. e. under his omniscient eye and providential guidance, and with our thoughts and expectations fixed upon him, *to hear all the (things)*, without exception or invidious distinction, *ordered* (or *commanded*) *thee by God*. It is remarkable how clearly and explicitly Cornelius, twice in this short sentence, distinguishes the man whom he at first had worshipped (v. 25), and to whom he still looked up as an inspired instructor, from the divine authority by which he was commissioned. It was not before Peter (although several of the oldest manuscripts have *thee* instead of *God*) that they considered themselves now assembled, but before his Master; it was not Peter's own views and opinions that they waited and desired to hear, but his inspired instructions and communications, whatever they might prove to be, even all the things enjoined upon him, or entrusted to him, as a messenger from God. His claim to be such does not seem to have been questioned by Cornelius for a moment, because amply attested by the angelic message to himself. Both these divine communications carried with them their own evidence, excluding all doubt as to their infallible authority, on the part of those to whom they were addressed.

34. Then Peter opened (his) mouth, and said, Of a truth I perceive that God is no respecter of persons—

Opening his mouth suggests the idea of a regular discourse, as distinguished from a simple conversation. (See above, on 8, 35.) *Of a truth*, really, certainly, qualifies the proposition, rather than the preface or preamble, to which it is immediately attached. (See above, on 4, 27.) *I perceive*, or rather, seize, grasp, apprehend, comprehend, something unknown or imperfectly understood before. (See above, on 4, 13, and below, on 25, 25.) *Respecter of persons*, is a single word in Greek, which, with the cognate forms, *respect of persons*, and to *respect persons*, is of Hebrew origin, and relates to judicial partiality, or the preference of one party to another, upon other grounds than those of right and justice. The same thing is repeatedly denied of God in Scripture (Deut. 10, 17. 2 Sam. 14, 14. 2 Chron. 19, 7. 1 Pet. 1, 17), and prohibited to man (Lev. 19, 15. Deut. 1, 17. 16, 19. James 2, 1. 9.) What is here denied is not a sovereign and discriminating choice, but one founded on mere national distinctions. 'I now at length understand that although God bestows his favours as he will, he does not mean to limit them hereafter, as of old, to any one race or people.'

35. But in every nation he that feareth him, and worketh righteousness, is accepted with him.

This verse has sometimes been abused, to prove that the knowledge of the Gospel is not necessary to the salvation of the heathen; whereas it merely teaches that this knowledge is attainable by them, as well as others. The essential meaning is that whatever is acceptable to God in one race is acceptable in any other. *Feareth God and worketh righteousness* are not meritorious conditions or prerequisites to the experience of divine grace, but its fruits and evidences. He who possesses and exhibits these may know that God accepts him, whatever his descent or country. Peter is not expounding the divine mode of dealing with the heathen, but confessing and renouncing his own error in regarding the precedence of his own race as perpetual. As if he had said, 'Now I see that we have no right to require more than God himself; if he is satisfied with piety and good works in a Gentile, we are bound to be contented with the same.'

36. The word which (God) sent unto the children of Israel, preaching peace by Jesus Christ—he is Lord of all——

The construction of the first clause is exceedingly obscure and has been variously explained. *The word* is an accusative in Greek and may be governed either by a preposition understood, (*as to*) *the word which God sent;* or by the preceding verb, *I* (*now*) *perceive* (or *apprehend*) *the word which God sent;* or by the following verb, *the word which God sent to the children of Israel ye know.* The first, if not the most grammatically regular, is much the simplest; but the general sense remains the same, on any of these suppositions, and may thus be paraphrased. 'As to the word or doctrine of salvation (13, 26), which God has sent in the first instance to his ancient people, its joyful news of peace and reconciliation cannot be designed for them alone, since Jesus Christ, through whom it is proclaimed, is Lord of all men, not of the Jews only.' (Compare Rom. 3, 29. 10, 12.)

37. That word (I say) ye know, which was pub-

lished throughout all Judea, and began from Galilee, after the baptism which John preached—

'Ye know yourselves the word of which I speak, the one that has become (known) throughout all Judea.' *Word* ($\acute{ρ}ῆμα$) may be simply synonymous with *word* ($λόγον$) in v. 36, or may be meant to vary the expression, so as to render it intelligible to the Gentile hearers. As if he had said, 'by word I mean the new religion of which you must have heard as something talked of or reported throughout all Judea.' To the commencement of this process he assigns two limits, temporal and local. It began in Galilee (see Luke 23, 49), and followed the ministry of John, here called the baptism which he preached (see above, on 1, 22.) Both these facts are spoken of, as well known to the hearers, who indeed could hardly fail to know them, living as they did at the seat of Roman power in Judea.

38. How God anointed Jesus of Nazareth with the Holy Ghost and with power, who went about doing good, and healing all that were oppressed of the devil; for God was with him.

(*Ye know*) *Jesus the* (*man*) *from Nazareth, how God anointed him.* Even in addressing Gentiles, he employs peculiar Jewish forms of speech, but such as must have been familiar to them, from their intercourse with Jews, and from attendance at the synagogues. In describing the great subject of the Gospel, Peter uses the popular description of our Lord, derisive in its origin, but now become a title of honour. (See above, on 2, 22.) *Anointed him*, endowed him with extraordinary spiritual gifts for the performance of his mediatorial functions, and thus consecrated him to his great offices as the Messiah. *With the Holy Ghost and power*, i. e. with the power of the Holy Ghost, or with power as a necessary consequence of this endowment. (See above, on 1, 8, and compare the combinations in 6, 3. 11, 24. 13, 52. John 4, 23. 6, 63. 1 Pet. 4, 14.) The extraordinary powers which our Lord possessed, are here referred to as notorious to all residing in the country, whether Jews or Gentiles. Another fact, assumed as equally familiar, is the use which he made of these divine endowments. He did not use them for his own advantage, or in vengeance on his enemies. *He went about*, literally, *went through* (life), or *through* (the country), or *among* (the people), *doing good*, not merely doing right, but doing favours, showing mercy. One particular form of his beneficence is specified, as that most universally appreciated, and most likely to be heard of at a distance. *Healing all those oppressed*, overmastered, tyrannically treated, *by the Devil*. This name, which occurs but twice in Acts (see below, on 13, 10), originally means a slanderer or false accuser, and is specially applied to Satan, as the great adversary of our race. (See above, on 5, 3, and below, on 6, 18.) The reference here may be specially, but not exclusively, to demoniacal possession, since disease in general is elsewhere ascribed to Satanic influence (see Luke 13, 16.) *For God was with him*, both in a providential sense, appropriate to any prophet or apostle, and in a personal essential sense, appropriate to Christ alone. The same double sense belongs to the Hebrew name *Immanuel* or *God with us* (Isai. 7, 14. Matt. 1, 24.) This ambiguous expression was peculiarly adapted to the audience whom Peter was addressing, none of whom would have denied that God was with Jesus in the lower sense, and all of whom were to be taught that God was with him in the higher.

39. And we are witnesses of all things which he did, both in the land of the Jews, and in Jerusalem; whom they slew and hanged on a tree:

To Cornelius and his fellows these things were known only by report; but Peter and the body of Apostles which he represented were eye-witnesses, ordained by Christ himself to publish and attest them. *All things which he did*, i. e. in public or officially (see above, on 1, 1.) These are divided locally into two classes, what he did in Jerusalem, and what he did in the rest of Judea, which may here denote either the province or the whole country. (See above, on 1, 8.) The last clause should have been connected, in the division of the verses, with the next, as both together present the favourite contrast between Christ's treatment at the hands of God and man. (See above, on 2, 23. 24. 3, 15. 4, 10. 5, 30.)

40. Him God raised up the third day, and shewed him openly —

The first clause belongs to the antithesis already mentioned, and might therefore have been added to the foregoing verse, while the last clause is connected in the closest manner with what follows; so that this verse might have been dispensed with, in the conventional division of the text. *Him*, literally, *this* (*one*), or (*this man*.) *Raised up*, literally, *awakened* (i. e. from the sleep of death, see above, on 7, 60), or *aroused* (from its inaction), which are the senses of this Greek verb in the classics. (See above, on 3, 15. 4, 10. 5, 30.) *Shewed him openly* is not a version but a paraphrase. The strict translation is, *and gave him* (i. e. caused or suffered him) *to be* (or to become) *visible* (apparent, manifest.) This last word occurs only here and in Rom. 10, 20. The obvious meaning of the clause is, that our Saviour was not merely said to have arisen from the dead, but was distinctly seen alive by others.

41. Not to all the people, but unto witnesses chosen before of God, (even) to us, who did eat and drink with him after he rose from the dead.

The Apostle here anticipates and answers an objection, which has often since been made to the New Testament account of Christ's resurrection, namely, that he did not publicly appear when risen, but was said to have been seen only by the narrow circle of his friends and followers. This was sufficient to establish the fact, which most men must believe, after all, upon the testimony of a few. It was also well adapted to exercise the faith of true believers who were not eye-witnesses, and more in keeping with the dignity and glory of the risen Saviour, which would now have been degraded by the same promiscuous and unreserved association with men, that was necessary to his previous ministry. The very fact that no such public recognition of his person is recorded, though at first it might have seemed to detract from the evidence of his resurrection, now serves to enhance it, by showing how free the witnesses of this event were from a disposition to exaggerate, or make their case stronger than it was in fact. *Not to all the people*, i, e. to the Jews, as the word usually means in this book (see above, on 2, 47. 3, 9. 4, 2. 5, 20. 6, 12. 7, 17. 10, 2.) The office of attesting this event had been entrusted to a select few, who neither could be deceived nor had a motive for deceiving others; who were not self-constituted or selected after the event, but previously chosen by divine authority; whose knowledge of the fact was not obtained by hearsay, or at second hand, or founded on a few short distant glimpses, but derived from intimate although not constant intercourse with Christ in private after his resurrection. *Chosen before*, a compound verb in Greek, used in the same sense by Demosthenes and Plato. The primitive or simple verb means to *vote* by stretching out or lifting up the hand, and then more generally to *elect*. This verb and the one employed in 1, 17, are combined by Plato to express the two modes of appointment to office, by vote and by lot. *Before*, i. e. before the resurrection, the event to be attested. (*Even*) *to us*, his immediate followers, in whose name I now address you. *Ate and drank*, i. e. partook of the same meals, or, as we should say, sat at the same table. The words are not to be severally understood but jointly, as denoting the most intimate companionship, and therefore the most perfect opportunity of knowing or discovering the truth. There is no difficulty, therefore, arising from the fact that his drinking with them is not separately mentioned (Luke 24, 30. 43. John 21, 13), much less any reason for connecting the last words (*after his rising from the dead*) with the preceding verse, and reading all that intervenes as a parenthesis. *We who ate and drank with him* is not a natural description of his followers and friends in general; whereas their eating and drinking with him after his resurrection made them competent witnesses to that event.

42. And he commanded us to preach unto the people, and to testify that it is he which was ordained of God (to be) the Judge of quick and dead.

Commanded us, or peremptorily required us (see above, on 1, 4. 4, 18. 5, 28. 40), not leaving it to our discretion, but making it a part of our official duty. *To preach*, i. e. proclaim, publicly announce, as heralds did. See above, on 8, 5. 9, 20, and compare the cognate noun as used by Paul and Peter (1 Tim. 2, 7. 2 Tim. 1, 11. 2 Pet. 2, 5.) *To testify*, a Greek verb technically used in Attic law to signify rebutting proof or testimony, but in the New Testament a mere emphatic or intensive form of the common verb meaning to bear witness. (See above, on 2, 40. 8, 25.) It may here suggest the accessory ideas of incessant, thorough, and explicit testimony, or to use the ancient English formula, the act of speaking the truth, the whole truth, and nothing but the truth. What is chiefly remarkable in this verse is that Peter, in addressing these Gentiles, renders prominent our Lord's judicial character and office, just as Paul did long after in addressing those at Athens (see below, on 17, 31.) This coincidence would seem to show that to this class of inquirers that particular aspect of Christ's dignity and power was peculiarly important. *He is the one designated*, marked out or defined (see above, on 2, 23.) (*To be* or *as*) *the judge of quick* (i. e. living) *and dead*, not in the spiritual sense of saints and sinners, but in the literal one of all generations, past, present and to come. (Compare Rom. 14, 9. 2 Tim. 4, 1. 1 Pet. 4, 5.)

43. To him give all the prophets witness, that through his name whosoever believeth in him shall receive remission of sins.

As the Gentile hearers, although previously ignorant of Christianity, had probably some knowledge of the Jewish scriptures, Peter closes by a general appeal to these as likewise testifying of Christ, not merely as a judge but as a saviour. *To him*, to this same man whom the Jews had slain by hanging on a tree (v. 39), *all the prophets testify*, i. e. the whole drift of the prophetic scriptures is in this direction. (See above, on 3, 24.) The cavilling objection that this is not literally true of every prophet in the Hebrew canon, is scarcely more unreasonable than the effort to refute it by the citation of particular predictions. Instead of fortifying the Apostle's declaration, this enfeebles it, by quoting but a small part of what he referred to, which was not a few detached expressions in the Prophets technically so called, but the whole tenor of the whole Old Testament, as a prospective or prophetic revelation. By a beautiful and striking change, the view of Jesus as a judge, which had been just before presented, is exchanged, at the very close of the discourse, for that of a redeemer. What the whole body of prophetic scripture teaches, is not merely that he has been designated as the final judge of quick and dead, which could only excite terror and despair, but also that remission of sins (see above, on 2, 38. 5, 31) may be obtained through his name, not merely by professing it, but by means of all that it denotes (see above, on 2, 38. 3, 16. 4,

12. 5, 28. 40. 8, 12. 9, 27), by every one believing in him, i. e. trusting and relying on him.

44. While Peter yet spake these words, the Holy Ghost fell on all them which heard the word.

Peter still speaking, before he had finished what he meant to say, and therefore unexpectedly to him, and of course without his agency or intervention. *These words* might be referred to the whole discourse (vs. 34–43), but are more naturally understood of what immediately precedes (v. 43.) He was still uttering the last words recorded in the context. *Fell upon*, descended from above, implying suddenness and superhuman origin. *The Holy Ghost* may here denote the influence exerted, the effect produced by the operation of the divine agent; but as the personal meaning is the usual and proper one, it seems best to retain it, and to understand the words as a strong figure for immediate action on a lower or inferior object. (See above, on 1, 5. 8, 16, and compare the use of the same figure in v. 10 above.) *All those hearing* may be strictly understood, as including a fresh spiritual influence, even upon those who had before received the Spirit, not excepting Peter himself (as in 2, 4. 4, 8. 31. 6, 5. 7, 55); or as a relative expression, like that in vs. 39. 43 (see above, on 1, 1), meaning all whom it concerned, not all who actually heard, but all whom Peter was addressing, i. e. Cornelius and his company. *The word* may either be synonymous with *these words* in the first clause (though the nouns are different in Greek), or signify the whole speech, as distinguished from its last words, there referred to. This sudden illapse of the Holy Spirit without previous baptism or imposition of hands (as in 8, 17 above, and 19, 5. 6. below), was probably intended to confirm the impression made by Peter's vision (see above, on v. 28), and to justify him in administering baptism without previous circumcision. (See below, on v. 47.)

45. And they of the circumcision which believed were astonished, as many as came with Peter, because that on the Gentiles also was poured out the gift of the Holy Ghost.

Were amazed, the same verb that is used above in 8, 9. 11. 13, and there explained. *The faithful*, in the strict sense, i. e.

full of faith, believers, converts. The English word is still sometimes so used when believers are collectively referred to; but its usual sense is *full of faith,* i. e. fidelity (which is the meaning of the word in the phrases "good" or "bad faith," "keeping faith," etc.) This is also the predominant New Testament usage (see 1 Tim. 1, 12. Col. 4, 9. 1 Pet. 5. 12. 1 John 1, 9); but there are also clear examples of the other (see below, on 16, 1, and compare John 20, 27. Gal. 3, 9. 2 Cor. 6, 15. Tit. 1, 6.) These believers are here more particularly described as being *of* (i. e. belonging to, or derived from) *the circumcision* (i. e. the religion, of which it was the badge or the distinctive rite; compare the use of *baptism* in 1, 22 above.) The whole phrase therefore means *converted Jews,* as all the followers of Christ had hitherto been. *As many as came with Peter,* from Joppa to Cesarea upon this occasion (see above, on v. 23.) In addition to the reasons there suggested for his bringing them, may now be added, as perhaps the chief, that they were meant to serve as chosen representatives of Jewish Christianity, and as such to bring it into contact with the Gentile form of that religion, represented by Cornelius and his company. The junction between these two branches of the church was not consummated, either objectively or subjectively, i. e. in point of fact or in the judgment of these Jews, until they witnessed the astonishing event recorded here. *Also,* as well as on themselves, or on the Jews. *The Gentiles,* literally, *the nations,* i. e. all besides the Jews. This vast body was adequately represented by the small number present, because the principle established, even in a single case, extended equally to every other. Between these two representative bodies stood the great Apostle, who, though specially devoted to "the circumcision" (Gal. 2, 7. 8), was commissioned, for important reasons, to admit the first Gentile converts to the church directly, without passing through the vestibule or outer court of Judaism.

46. For they heard them speak with tongues, and magnify God. Then answered Peter —

There was no room for doubt as to the fact that the Spirit had been given, as there might have been in the case of mere internal, spiritual changes. These were likewise wrought, as in every case of genuine conversion; but besides these, there were other gifts imparted, which were cognizable by the senses, and thus served as incontrovertible proofs of what had taken place. (See above, on 8, 17. 18.) The one here mentioned is the gift of tongues, the same with that described in 2, 4, notwithstanding the omission of the epithet there used (*other*), which, so far from implying a difference between the cases, is a mere abbreviation, tacitly referring to the more complete description previously given. Here again it seem still more evident than in the other case, that the gift of tongues was not intended merely as a practical convenience, but as a miraculous token of God's presence, and a type of the reconciliation between Jew and Gentile, whose alienation had for ages been secured and symbolized by difference of language. They did not merely hear them say they had received the Holy Spirit; *they heard them* (actually) *speaking with tongues* (i. e. in foreign languages), not unintelligibly or at random, but like the disciples on the day of Pentecost, in praise of God (see above, on 2, 11.) What is there called *speaking the wonderful* (or *mighty*) *works of God*, is here more concisely expressed, *magnifying God*, i. e. setting forth his greatness. Hence this occasion has been not unjustly styled the Gentile Pentecost.* *Then*, in the strict sense, after witnessing this great event, *Peter answered*, to the praises of the Gentile converts, or to the wondering exclamations of the Jewish brethren, or to the voice of God, so audible in what had just occurred. Any of these suppositions is more natural than that of an unmeaning pleonasm. (See above, on 3, 12. 5, 8.)

47. Can any man forbid water, that these should not be baptized, which have received the Holy Ghost as well as we?

The form of interrogation here used (with μήτι) is equivalent to a strong negation. 'Surely no one will now venture to forbid, etc.' (Compare Matt. 7, 16. Mark 4, 21. Luke 6, 37. John 4, 49.) The same verb which, applied to persons, means *forbid*, when applied to things, is better rendered by *withhold*, as in Luke 6, 29, where *to take* is supplied by the translators. *Water*, or more exactly, *the water* (answering to *the Spirit*) i. e. the baptismal water, or the water necessary for the purpose. Although nothing can be proved from this ex-

---

* Colligi etiam potest ex hoc loco, non tantum necessitati datas fuisse linguas, ubi evangelium exteris et diversi idiomatis hominibus praedicandum erat, sed etiam in ornamentum ipsius evangelii et decus.—CALVIN.

pression, it is certainly more natural in reference to the bringing in of water, than to the act of going to it. *Which have received*, being such as have received, the same form of the relative with that in 7, 53. 9, 35, and there explained. The reason here assigned is, that they who had received the baptism of the Spirit must certainly be fit for that of water. Why should the sign be withheld from those who were possessed of the thing signified? If God was willing to accept them as converted Gentiles, why should man insist upon their coming forward as converted Jews? *As well* (*even as*, or *just as*) *we*, i. e. you and I, addressing those who came with him from Joppa; or we the disciples of Christ in general, i. e. such as had received the Holy Ghost. This is an argument *ad hominem*, equivalent to asking, What higher evidence have you and I, that God has chosen us and given us his Holy Spirit, than the evidence afforded by this company of Gentiles?

48. And he commanded them to be baptized in the name of the Lord. Then prayed they him to tarry certain days.

The sign might have seemed to be superfluous after the gift of the thing signified; but baptism is a sealing and initiatory no less than a typical ordinance, and is rendered necessary, not by utilitarian reasons, but by express divine command. It can scarcely be a mere fortuitous coincidence, that Peter, Paul, and Christ himself, should all have left this rite to be administered by others. "Jesus himself baptized not, but his disciples" (John 4, 2.) "I thank God that I baptized none of you, save Crispus, etc." (1 Cor. 1, 14.) "Christ sent me not to baptize, but to preach the gospel" (ib. v. 17.) As none of these expressions can be intended to detract from the value and importance of the rite in question, they may best be explained as warning us against the error of exalting this part of the Christian system to a disproportionate importance, which may be just as superstitious as the eucharistical corruptions of popery, or the hierarchical excesses of prelacy. One idolatrous extravagance cannot be corrected by another. The true corrective is to keep all parts of the revealed system, both of faith and practice, in their proper place. *In the name of the Lord*, i. e. of the Lord Jesus Christ, as several of the oldest manuscripts expressly add. This, though it may be no part of the true text, is undoubtedly the true sense, as a baptism simply in the name of God would be without either meaning or analogy. The idea meant to be conveyed is that of *Christian baptism*, as distinguished from all others or from none, and not the formula employed in the administration, which was no doubt that prescribed by Christ himself. (Compare Matt. 28, 19, and see above, on 2, 38.) *In his name*, by his authority, professing faith in him, vowing obedience to him, and entering into union with him. *Then*, when they had been baptized accordingly, *they prayed* (literally *asked*) *him* to tarry (or, as the compound Greek verb strictly means, to stay on, or stay over, remain longer than he had intended) *certain* (literally, *some*, or as the older English versions render it, *a few*) *days*. This request, expressive of their hospitable feelings and desire of instruction, was no doubt complied with.

CHAPTER XI.

HERE again the connection of the history is obscured by the division of the chapters, that before us comprehending two entirely distinct subjects, under the form of a continued narrative. The first part is the sequel of the story of Cornelius (1–18); the second an account of the introduction of the Gospel into Antioch, after the dispersion on the death of Stephen (19–30.) The former of these narratives contains Peter's statement and defence of his own conduct in receiving Gentile converts to the Church, without circumcision or other conformity to the ceremonial law. Besides a brief account of the objection made to his proceedings at Jerusalem (1–3), we have what seems to be a full report of his defence, consisting of a plain historical recital of the facts, for the most part in the same form as before, but with some variations and additions (4–15), winding up with an appeal to the authority of Christ and God, as having definitively settled the whole question (16–17), in which conclusion all the brethren, including those who had at first objected, seem to have cordially acquiesced (18.) The remainder of the chapter is filled with an account of a fourth great radiation from Jerusalem, collateral to those described in the three foregoing chapters, and terminating in the capital of Syria, which was to become, in due subordination to Jerusalem, the metropolis or mother-church of Gentile Christianity. The principal particulars included in this narrative are the first extension of the church to Antioch and its success there (19–21); the mission of Barnabas, with a commission from the mother-church (22–24); his reunion with Saul, and their joint labours for a year at Antioch (25–26); the origin of the Christian name (26); the prophecy of Agabus (27–28); and the mission of Barnabas and Saul to Judea (29–30), during which the events described in the next chapter took place at Jerusalem, and from which, at the close of that chapter, they return to Antioch (12, 25.)

1. And the Apostles and brethren that were in Judea heard that the Gentiles had also received the word of God.

Then (δέ) *heard the Apostles and the brethren* (to wit) *those being in Judea.* It was not to be expected that these singular occurrences at Cesarea could long remain unknown to the churches in Judea, which were all composed of Jewish converts, many of them zealous for the law. (See below, on 21, 20.) *Heard*, received intelligence, either by common fame or by official information. *The Apostles*, who were therefore still residing, either in the Holy City, or with some of the affiliated churches in Judea, and perhaps engaged in visiting them in rotation, after the example of Peter (see above, on 9, 31.) *The brethren*, i. e. the disciples or believers as in 1, 15, and often elsewhere; or, in a more restricted sense, the officers and teachers of the churches here referred to. Neither these nor the Apostles are said to have formed or expressed any judgment in relation to the course pursued by Peter, until his return recorded in the next verse. *The Gentiles*, or *the nations*, represented by Cornelius and his household, whose reception settled the whole question (see above, on 10, 45.) *The word of God*, the gospel, the new religion, as a revelation or divine communication. *Received*, i. e. obtained it, or were favoured with it; and more actively, accepted it, acknowledged it as true, and assented to its terms of pardon and salvation. Their own reception to the church, though not expressed, is necessarily implied.

2. And when Peter was come up to Jerusalem, they that were of the circumcision contended with him,

Went up, i. e. from Cesarea; see above, on 9, 30. *Contended*, literally, *differed* with him; see above, on 10, 20. There is no allusion here to a judicial charge, but only to colloquial or private disputation. *With him* is literally *to him*, at him, implying that their objections were addressed directly to him, having been apparently reserved till his arrival. *They of the circumcision* means essentially the same thing as in 10, 45, namely, Jewish converts or converted Jews, but with the accessory notion, here suggested by the context, of a circumcision-party, or of such as not only had been circumcised, but looked on circumcision as a duty not to be dispensed with.

3. Saying, Thou wentest in to men uncircumcised, and didst eat with them.

The substance of their charges is now given, as in many other cases, in the form of a direct address to Peter. Not that these very words were uttered upon any one occasion; but what they said on various occasions might be thus summed up. The charge expressly made is that of going into the society of the uncircumcised and eating with them. This, as we know from Peter's own lips, was considered by the Jews unlawful. It may seem surprising that this lower and more trivial offence against the Jewish usage should be specified, when Peter had been guilty of one far more heinous in the estimation of these Jewish Christians, namely, that of baptizing those who never had been circumcised. The argument suggested is *a fortiori*. If mere association with the Gentiles was unlawful, how much more their admission to the ordinance of baptism. Or the words of this verse may be looked upon as the beginning of their accusation, the first charge in their indictment. As if they had said, You have acted unworthily of your profession and your obligations as an Israelite; for, *in the first place*, you went into the company of Gentiles, and by eating with them either broke, or ran the risk of breaking, one of our most sacred precepts.

4. But Peter rehearsed (the matter) from the be.

ginning, and expounded (it) by order unto them, saying —

Peter's defence against this accusation consisted in a bare historical recital of the facts, with a concluding question, showing how they bore upon the point at issue. His narrative, though brief, was a complete one. He began at the beginning, and expounded or set forth the facts in order, i. e. in the order of their actual occurrence. The Greek word here used (καθεξῆς) is peculiar to Luke, who applies it to time, succession, motion, and arrangement. (See above, on 3, 24, and below, on 18, 23, and compare Luke 1, 3. 8, 13.) Nothing can less resemble a forensic or judicial vindication than this simple statement, although recorded with the same sort of technical formality, that leads to similar repetitions in the records of our courts and legislative bodies. (See above, on 10, 30.) The variations in this form of the narrative from those preceding, although unessential, are not unworthy of attention, as indicative of conscious accuracy in the writer, with a certain freedom from restraint, as to the mere form of expression or minute details.

5–10. I was in the city of Joppa praying: and in a trance I saw a vision, a certain vessel descend, as it had been a great sheet, let down from heaven by four corners, and it came even to me; upon the which when I had fastened mine eyes, I considered, and saw fourfooted beasts of the earth, and wild beasts, and creeping things, and fowls of the air. And I heard a voice saying unto me, Arise, Peter, slay and eat. But I said, Not so, Lord; for nothing common or unclean hath at any time entered into my mouth. But the voice answered me again from heaven, What God hath cleansed, (that) call not thou common. And this was done three times; and all were drawn up again into heaven.

The minute particulars of time and place are here omitted with the circumstance of hunger predisposing him to such a vision. The words *ecstasy* (or *trance*) and *sight* (or *vision*) are repeated here. *Bound* (or *fastened*) is omitted. Instead of simply *let down on the earth*, we have the more specific form, *it came as far as me*, or *reached to me*. From this we learn that it was not a distant but a near view that he had of the descending vessel, into which, we are here told, he *gazed intently* and *inspected* the contents, and saw that they consisted of the various kinds of animals, described precisely as they were in 10, 12. In his answer to the voice which summoned him to slay and eat, there is a slight variation as to form, not substance. *I never did eat* is exchanged for *never came into my mouth*. For *received up*, we have here the more expressive phrase, *was drawn up*.

11. 12. And behold, immediately there were three men already come unto the house where I was, sent from Cesarea unto me. And the Spirit bade me go with them, nothing doubting. Moreover these six brethren accompanied me, and we entered into the man's house.

Behold, as usual, denotes surprise at something unexpected. *Stood at* or *over*, *near* or *by*, this idea being suggested both by the compound verb and by the separate preposition. *Nothing doubting* or *hesitating*, differing with myself, or perhaps distinguishing without a difference, by needless scruples. (See above, on v. 2, and on 10, 20.) *Six brethren—these*, here present. Thus we learn the number of the men who went with him to Cesarea, and the fact that they accompanied him also to Jerusalem, perhaps as witnesses on this occasion. *And we came into the house of the man.* This definite expression, as Cornelius is not previously mentioned in this context, either shows that we have only an abridged summary of Peter's speech and not his very words, or else must be referred to the prevailing rumours, in which the centurion was no doubt a conspicuous figure. As if he had said: we came into the house of the man, of whom you have all heard so much. Or the allusion may be to the charge in v. 3, and the collective or indefinite expression there used. *And we came into the house of the man*, with whom (and his associates) you now accuse me of having eaten and kept company.

13. 14. And he shewed us how he had seen an

angel in his house, which stood and said unto him, Send men to Joppa, and call for Simon, whose surname is Peter, who shall tell thee words, whereby thou and all thy house shall be saved.

Here again, the definite expression (*the angel*) is not to be neglected, or gratuitously treated as indefinite, but considered as implying previous acquaintance with the story, on the part of those who were now hearing it. This shows that Peter was repeating these details, not simply, or at all, for information, but for argument. The same thing, indicated in the same way, has already been observed in Stephen's speech before the council, where the leading incidents of Jewish history are recapitulated, not as something new to such an audience, but as familiar premises from which he was about to draw an unexpected conclusion. See above, on ch. 7. *In his house*, or in *his own house*, not abroad, or in a strange place, where he might have been more easily deceived, but at home, in private, and with every safeguard and assurance against error or illusion. The word *men* is omitted in some critical editions, as a probable amendment of the text by assimilation to 10, 5. *Standing*, or still more exactly, *stationed*, as the participle here used has a passive form, although equivalent in usage to an active one. *Send away*, a stronger expression than the one employed in ch. 10, 5, and etymologically unconnected with the one that follows. *By which*, literally, *in which*, i. e. in the hearing, or rather in the doing of which. The words which Peter was to speak were not merely doctrinal or theoretical, but practical, preceptive, and imperative. They were to tell him what to do, and in the doing of it he was to be saved, in the highest and most comprehensive sense, that of deliverance from all the evils of his previous condition. *And all thy house* or *household*, who had been before described as sharers in his fear of God (see above, on ch. 10, 2), and no doubt in his prayers and alms and longing for salvation. To them, as well as to himself, it pleased God that the words of Peter should be savingly effectual.

15. And as I began to speak, the Holy Ghost fell on them, as on us at the beginning.

It is remarkable that Peter here gives no account whatever

of his own discourse at Cesarea, because it was not one of the facts on which he chose to rest his vindication. It was not what he said, but what God did, that furnished his apology. In consequence of this characteristic reticency, the account before us, taken by itself, would naturally leave the impression, that the illapse of the Spirit took place before Peter had said any thing. And yet the narrative is perfectly consistent with the one in the preceding chapter. *Began* should neither be explained away as a pleonasm or unmeaning superfluity, nor interpreted too strictly, as implying that he had just begun, or scarcely begun, but understood more freely as denoting after he began, without determining how long. The nearest approach that can be made in English to the form of the original is, *in my beginning*, i. e. as, when, or after I began. There is a double preposition in the next clause, as in v. 11, the verb itself meaning to *fall on*. The figure of falling, as in 10, 10, denotes an influence or impulse from above, i. e. from a superior power. It is also worthy of remark that in this baptism of the Spirit, the act described is that of pouring, not of plunging or immersing. *The Holy Spirit* is expressed in the original very emphatically and precisely, *the Spirit, the Holy* (*One*.) The words *as also* (ὥσπερ καί) mean *as really*, and *as evidently*, as on us, i. e. on the Apostles and first converts on the day of Pentecost. This is here called *the beginning* of the Christian dispensation or the Christian Church, which dates from the effusion of the Holy Ghost at that time, corresponding to the organization of the Mosaic church by the Theophany and giving of the Law at Sinai, which Pentecost, according to a highly probable tradition of the Jews, was partly instituted to commemorate. (See above, on 2, 1.) The Greek phrase (ἐν ἀρχῇ) is the same with that at the beginning of John's Gospel, and of the Septuagint version of Genesis. In itself it is indefinite or relative, and simply means *at first*. The *terminus a quo* must be determined by the context. The beginning here meant can be only that of the entire series of events, connected with the re-organization of the Church.

16. Then remembered I the word of the Lord, how that he said, John indeed baptized with water; but ye shall be baptized with the Holy Ghost.

The reference is probably to Christ's last interview with

the Apostles (see above, on 1, 5, and compare Luke 22, 61.) *John indeed* (μέν), a concession; it is true, the type has come, but not the antitype. These are constantly spoken of, as exactly corresponding. The associations in the minds of men with one of these would govern their associations with the other. If they were accustomed to think of the baptismal Spirit as poured out or down, they would naturally look for such effusion or affusion in the case of the baptismal water. *With the Holy Ghost*, not *in holy spirit*. (See above, on 1, 5.)

17. Forasmuch then as God gave them the like gift as (he did) unto us, who believed on the Lord Jesus Christ, what was I, that I could withstand God?

This is the argumentative part of the discourse, or the conclusion to which all the foregoing statements had been tending. The sum of all is, it was God himself who had determined the question. The illative particle (οὖν) at the beginning has respect to the preceding narrative. 'Since then it is evident from what I have related, that the question was determined by divine authority, and wholly independently of me, nay, in total opposition to my previous opinions and desires, I leave it to yourselves whether I could have done otherwise, and whether I am justly liable to censure.' *The like gift*, literally, *the equal gift*, i. e. the same. *Who believed*, literally, having believed. This may agree either with *them* or *us*, or both. *To them as to us*, both having believed alike. The position of the pronoun in the last clause gives it a peculiar emphasis. *I—who was* (*I*) (that I should be) *able to forbid God?* (Compare Ex. 3, 11.) To forbid or hinder God from doing as he pleased, which would be impious if possible, becomes absurd from its impossibility. The argument amounts to a *reductio ad absurdum*.

18. When they heard these things, they held their peace, and glorified God, saying, Then hath God also to the Gentiles granted repentance unto life.

The effect of Peter's argument appears to have been instantaneous and complete. They who heard it *acquiesced*, not merely held their peace, or ceased to speak upon the subject, but were satisfied, relinquished the position they had taken, and assented to the doctrine and the practice which they had so strongly censured. It might denote mere cessation from dispute, without conviction or a change of mind, as in Luke 14, 3 (4), where the stronger sense is inadmissible, and where, as here, the silence was produced by an unanswerable question. But that idea is precluded here by the additional statement, that *they glorified God and said, So then* (it is true after all, unlikely as it seemed beforehand, that) *even to the Gentiles* (or to the Gentiles also), *God has given repentance unto life* (or that repentance which is necessary to salvation.) To the Gentiles *also*, i. e. as well as to the Jews, and as directly, without any intermediate or preparatory process, in the one case more than in the other. These expressions, all implying joy at the event, determine the quiescence of the Jewish Christians after Peter's speech to have been acquiescence in his theory and practice, with respect to Gentile converts.

19. Now they which were scattered abroad upon the persecution that arose about Stephen travelled as far as Phenice, and Cyprus, and Antioch, preaching the word to none but unto the Jews only.

Now, or *so then;* see above, on 9. 31. The point to which the author goes back, both in this and in the other cases, is the death of Stephen, the ensuing persecution, and the consequent dispersion. As this disaster had been overruled for the extension of the Gospel to Samaria and other quarters, so it was made to have the same effect in this case. *Upon the persecution,* literally, *from the affliction* (or *distress*), not merely *after* it in point of time, or *from* it in the sense of springing from it, but with a distinct allusion to their fleeing and escaping from it. *About Stephen* has been variously understood to mean *over* his body, *after* his death, *during* his time. (Vulg. *sub Stephano;* but the translator probably read στεφανοῦ, which is found in some Greek MSS.) and *on account of* him or for his sake, which last is the most natural. *Travelled*, literally, *passed through* (the intervening country.) *As far as* indicates the limit of their mission, but without excluding intermediate places. *Phenice* is the Greek name, and *Phenicia* the Latin, of the narrow tract of sea-coast north of Palestine, including Tyre and Sidon, and famous in the ancient world for its extensive maritime commerce. *Cyprus* is the ancient and modern name of the large and fertile island off the coast of Palestine and Asia Minor, noted of old for the wealth and luxury of its inhabitants. *Antioch*, the capital of Syria, built by Seleucus Nicator on the south side of the Orontes, fifteen miles from its mouth, and named in honour of of his father Antiochus. If what is here recorded took place after the conversion of Cornelius, which is very doubtful, that event was probably unknown to these first missionaries to Phenicia, Syria, and Cyprus.

20. **And some of them were men of Cyprus and Cyrene, which, when they were come to Antioch, spake unto the Grecians, preaching the Lord Jesus.**

There are two important questions in relation to this verse, one critical or textual, the other more grammatical and exegetical. The first is, whether the true text is *Greeks* (ἕλληνας) or *Grecians* (ἑλληνιστάς), Gentiles or foreign (Greek-speaking) Jews. (See above, on 6, 1. 9, 29.) The manuscript evidence, though dubious and meagre, is in favour of the latter reading, which is that of the *textus receptus*. But the other has been commonly adopted, in the ancient versions and by modern critics, chiefly on internal evidence, namely, the supposed improbability, that Luke would have recorded, as something new or strange, the fact that these dispersed believers preached the Gospel to the Hellenists as well as to the Hebrews, when it had been preached to both from the beginning (see above, on 2, 5. 6, 1. 9, 29); whereas their preaching to the heathen Greeks was really a new thing, especially if previous to the conversion of Cornelius, or at least without the knowledge of that great event. This reading (ἕλληνας) is moreover found in two of the most ancient copies (A. D.), and is supposed to be required by the antithesis between *indeed* (μέν) in v. 19, and *but* (δέ) in v. 20. This last, however, is an argument of no weight, as the particle in v. 19 is not the simple one, so commonly opposed to δέ, but the compound one (μὲν οὖν), answering to *so then*, and employed in the resumptions of a narrative. (See above, on 8, 4. 9, 31.) To the manuscript authorities it may be answered, that the reading in one of them (D) is not original, but introduced by a later (though still ancient) hand; and that the other (A) has the same reading in 9, 29, where it is universally allowed to be erroneous. The remaining argument in favour of this reading rests on the assumption, that the writer must be stating something new or strange. But why may he not be simply understood as saying, that when the refugees arrived at Antioch, such of their number as were Hellenists or foreign Jews preached to the Jews of their own class whom they found there, as the Hebrew or native exiles had done on the way to their own countrymen? The sense obtained by this interpretation is so good in itself, and so consistent with the context, that there seems to be no need of any emendation. The other reading is preferred, however, by the great majority of critics and interpreters, who understand this as another instance of the Gospel being preached among the Gentiles, entirely independent of the one recorded in the preceding chapter. Of those who thus explain the last clause of the verse before us, some understand the first clause as relating to the Jews mentioned at the close of v. 19. The sense will then be that, although the exiles from Jerusalem, referred to in the first clause of v. 19, preached exclusively to Jews, their Jewish converts were more liberal or fearless, and extended their instructions to the Gentiles also. A more natural and usual construction refers *some of them* to the exiles themselves, and understands them to have either changed their method of proceeding when they got to Antioch, or to have differed from the first among themselves, some preaching only to the Jews, and others to the Gentiles likewise. All these questions are precluded by retaining the received text (ἑλληνιστάς), and supposing the essential fact recorded here to be that the first missionaries from Jerusalem in this direction preached exclusively to Jews, the Hebrews to the native and the Hellenists to the foreign class. The only serious objection to this view of the passage, over and above those which have been already set aside, is that it then contains no explicit mention of the first extension of the Gospel to the Greeks of Antioch, which is however necessarily implied in the existence of the church there, and its subsequent relation to the whole field of Gentile Christianity.

21. And the hand of the Lord was with them: and a great number believed, and turned unto the Lord.

The hand of the Lord, i. e. the manifest exertion of his power. The expression is an oriental and especially a Hebrew one. Precisely the same words occur in reference to John the Baptist (Luke 1, 66.) Very similar terms are applied to human influence in the Septuagint version of 1 Kings 17, 22 (compare 2 Kings 14, 19.) The cognate figure of the Lord's *arm* is employed by Isaiah (53, 1) and quoted by John (12, 38.) The power here meant is a spiritual power acting through the truth as propounded in the Gospel and tending to conviction and conversion, but not exclusive of miraculous attestations, which are primarily meant by the same figure in 4, 30. It is a curious illustration of the way in which the text was often unintentionally falsified, that three Greek mss. add to this clause the words "*to heal them*," evidently borrowed, by an error of judgment, or perhaps unconsciously, from Luke 5, 17. *With them* of course means with these preachers to the Gentiles, who are the subject both of the preceding and ensuing context. The manifestation of the divine power was a formal approbation of their having preached directly to the Gentiles, and a warrant for continuing to do so. *The Lord*, to whom the converts turned, was God as manifested in his Son. One ms. has *turned to the Lord Jesus*. *Much* is here coupled with a noun of multitude, where our idiom requires *great*. (Compare Mark 5, 24. John 6, 2. Acts 14, 1. 17, 4. Matt. 9, 37.) The conversion of Cornelius, whether first in time or not, was meant to be the type of all accessions from the Gentile world; but it was not necessary to this end that it should be superior, or even equal, to the case before us, in the multitude of converts.

22. Then tidings of these things came unto the ears of the church which was in Jerusalem; and they sent forth Barnabas, that he should go as far as Antioch.

These proceedings at Antioch, like those at Cesarea, could not long remain unknown to the mother-church in Jerusalem, which, partly from its seniority, partly from its local situation, and partly from its connection with the Apostles, still continued to be the centre of influence to the Christian world *Tidings*, literally, *the word*, not the gospel as in v. 1, but the report or news. *Of these things*, or rather, *concerning them*, i. e. the Gentile converts and their teachers. *Came unto* (literally, *was heard into*) *the ears*, a Hebrew idiom. *The* (*one*) *in Jerusalem* is added to explain and specify the absolute expression, *the church*, which, though not inapplicable in an emphatic sense, as we have seen, might not be universally intelligible. The representation of the body of believers in Jerusalem as one church is the more remarkable in this case, because it not only individualizes but personifies that body, speaking of its ears, etc. *Into the ears* does not imply a secret communication, as in Matt. 10, 27 (compare Luke 9, 44), where that idea is suggested by the context, and especially by the antithesis. Their hearing *of them* is supposed by some to exclude the idea of their hearing *from them ;* but the two are scarcely incompatible. The plural verb (*they sent*) refers to the collective term (*church*) preceding. The Apostles are not expressly mentioned, as in ch. 8, 14, which some regard as an important difference between the cases. But the church at Jerusalem included the Apostles who were there, as we shall see below (on 15, 2.) Another supposed difference is, that the person sent was not in this case an apostle. The high-church Anglican divines maintain that he was; but Archbishop Sumner merely says he was "considered as an apostle," and Alford admits that he was not one " in any distinctive sense." Barnabas may have been selected as a Hellenist or Greek Jew, and even as a Cyprian, as some of the first preachers of the gospel at Antioch were from that country. He may also have been chosen as a " son of exhortation " (see above, on 4, 36), and as such well qualified to do precisely what he did on his arrival, as recorded in the next verse. There was also reference no doubt to the moral and spiritual qualities there mentioned. He was not commissioned merely *to Antioch,* but *to pass through* (the intervening country) *as far as* (or until he came to) *Antioch*, plainly implying that he was to preach the gospel by the way as well as after his arrival. (See above, on 8, 4. 25, 40. 9, 32.)

23. Who, when he came, and had seen the grace of God, was glad, and exhorted them all, that with purpose of heart they would cleave unto the Lord.

Having arrived (or *got there*), not merely finished his journey from Jerusalem, but executed his commission by the way. *Seeing the grace of God,* i. e. the manifest effects of an immediate divine influence in the conversion of the Gentiles. The idea of benevolence or favour is essential to the definition of divine grace, but is not the prominent idea here. Some late interpreters regard it as implied in Luke's expressions, that the effect upon the mind of Barnabas was unexpected both by him and those who sent him; that he went rather for the purpose of correcting and controlling than approving and rejoicing in the work already going on in Antioch, but found the evidence too strong to be resisted, and with true Christian candor heartily rejoiced in what he saw; and instead of recommending any other method of procedure, simply *exhorted all* (who had believed or been converted) *with purpose of heart*, including the ideas of sincerity and constancy or perseverance, to *cleave* or *adhere, to stand by* or *continue with, the Lord*, in whom they had believed, without the slightest reference to the ceremonial law, as a necessary preparation for the gospel.

24. For he was a good man, and full of the Holy Ghost and of faith; and much people was added unto the Lord.

The connection between this verse and the context has been variously understood. Some suppose it merely to assign a reason for the choice of Barnabas as a commissioner to Antioch. But this requires the preceding verse to be explained as a parenthesis, and makes the causal particle (*because*) dependent on a verb in v. 22; both which constructions are unnatural. Another explanation makes the particle dependent on the verb (*exhorted*) in v. 23, and supposes this verse to assign the reason for the diligence of Barnabas in preaching. Intermediate between these, and more satisfactory than either, is the supposition that this verse is to be construed more directly with the verb *was glad* (or *rejoiced*), and assigns a reason for what might have appeared strange without it, namely, that Barnabas, instead of finding fault or doubting the reality of what he saw, *rejoiced* or *was rejoiced*, the form of the original verb being passive. This would seem to confirm the supposition that the actual effect was somewhat different from what had been expected, and required explanation. He acknowledged what he saw to be the work of God, and as such a subject of rejoicing, *because he was a good man*. There are two ways of explaining this description. One gives to *good* its widest sense as the opposite of *bad*, and as a general expression for moral excellence. The other makes it more specific and expressive of a distinct quality—not religious zeal as some imagine—but benevolence and gentleness of disposition, the negation of that envious malignity, or even that censorious asperity, which would have led him to suspect or question what he saw without sufficient reason. As these two senses are entirely consistent, one being really included in the other, it is not at all improbable that both were meant to be suggested, one as the primary, the other as the secondary sense of the expression. The connection of the clauses may be either that Barnabas was not only of a good natural disposition, but also under special divine influence; or that the very goodness here ascribed to him was not a natural endowment, but a fruit of the spirit and effect of faith. *Full of the Holy Spirit* does *not* always denote inspiration, but may signify the sanctifying influence exerted upon all believers. The last clause seems descriptive of the effects produced by the preaching of Barnabas himself, in continuation of that previous work which caused his joy. As to the form of expression, see above, on 2, 41. 47. 5, 14.

25. Then departed Barnabas to Tarsus, for to seek Saul :

If Barnabas took this step on his own motion and responsibility, his motives may be readily conjectured. It is easy to conceive that as soon as he was satisfied that God had called him to this field of labour, he would think of Saul of Tarsus as a suitable assistant. He could not have forgotten his miraculous conversion and his introduction to the Apostles by Barnabas himself (9, 27), the zeal with which he had opposed the Hellenists or Greek Jews (9, 29) at Jerusalem, and the proofs which he had given of superior wisdom and of dialectic skill in the defence of the new doctrine. He may also have known something of Saul's designation as Apostle to the Gentiles in a vision at Jerusalem (see below, on 22, 21.) All these are probable suggestions, on the supposition that Saul's call to Antioch was a simple call from Barnabas himself. But there are reasons for believing that it came to him from higher authority, even in the church, than that of his intended fellow-labourer. It is highly improbable that Barnabas, not claiming apostolical authority, and acting himself under a commission from Jerusalem, would undertake, upon his own responsibility, to share this delegated power with another. It is also worthy of remark, that when the mother-church, upon a similar occasion, sent a commission to Samaria (ch. 8, 14), it was not only one of apostolical rank, but composed of two persons, in accordance with our Saviour's constant practice (Matt. 21, 1. Mark 6, 7. 11, 1. 14, 13. Luke 10, 1. 19, 29.) This makes it singular, to say the least, that in the case before us, Barnabas was sent alone. Both these apparent difficulties are removed by the assumption, that Saul was really included in the apostolical commission, but not mentioned in the narrative, because he was absent from Jerusalem, and therefore was not actually sent with Barnabas, who was authorized however to associate Saul with him, as soon as he had satisfied himself that what was going on at Antioch was a genuine work of grace. This supposition also supersedes the necessity of assuming a written correspondence between Barnabas and his superiors or constituents, before he went in search of Saul; though it does not materially impair the force of Calvin's observation, that the character of Barnabas is set in an amiable light by the alacrity with which he called in the assistance of a person, whom he must have known to be his own superior, as well in fact as in the divine purpose. One of the latest writers cites, as a parallel from modern history, the conduct of Farel with respect to Calvin himself. How long Saul had been in Tarsus since he left Jerusalem (9, 30), can only be conjectured, as the ablest writers differ widely in their estimate, ranging from nine years to one, or even to six months. How Saul had spent this interval, is equally uncertain. Some suppose that he had been studying Greek literature and philosophy, in the cultivation of which Strabo represents Tarsus as surpassing even Alexandria and Athens (see above, on 9, 11); or meditating on the state of the Gentiles and the greatness of the work which lay before him; or enduring some part of that painful discipline described by himself to the Corinthians (2 Cor. 11, 23–27.) The only conjecture which has any historical foundation is, that during this interval those churches of Cilicia were planted, which are afterwards referred to, as already in existence (15, 23. 41), and to which the Apostle's declaration (Rom. 15, 20) may have been intended to apply. This supposition, while it fills a chasm in the history without forced or gratuitous assumptions, is moreover recommended by its perfect agreement with the energetic character and active habits of the great Apostle. The verb translated *seek*, in the only other place where it occurs (Luke 2, 44), denotes a diligent and anxious search, and may here suggest that Barnabas was doubtful where he should find Saul, and went to *look him up*, a phrase etymologically corresponding to the compound Greek verb. The idea that he had concealed himself, like Saul in the Old Testament, is quite gratuitous. The only natural assumption is, that he was not in Tarsus, and that Barnabas was under the necessity of seeking him. The same idea is suggested by the next phrase, *having found him*, which would seem to be unmeaning or superfluous, if he found him without search; and perhaps by the statement that *he brought* (or *led*) *him into Antioch*, in a sort of friendly triumph or compulsion. As to Paul's motive in complying, the necessity of ascertaining it is superseded by the double authority to which he yielded, that of God himself and of the mother-church. And yet it still remains true, as observed by Chrysostom, that in going to Antioch, he went to a wider field of labour, and with higher hopes of usefulness.

26. And when he had found him, he brought him unto Antioch. And it came to pass, that a whole year they assembled themselves with the church, and taught much people. And the disciples were called Christians first in Antioch.

It came to pass, as here used, is nearly equivalent, in modern English, to the phrase, 'it was (or is) a fact.' The Greek verb governs all the others in the sentence, so that the connection of the clauses is much closer than in English. As if he had said, several things happened now at Antioch, such as the ministry of Barnabas and Saul, and the application of a new name to the disciples. The first thing that is thus said to have come to pass or taken place, is that Barnabas and Saul, for a whole year, *were brought together in the church*. As the same Greek verb is used in the Septuagint version to translate a Hebrew one denoting hospitable entertainment, or the act of taking strangers in or home, some give it that sense here, as well as in Matt. 25, 35. 38. 43. 'They were entertained a whole year by the church.' But there is nothing in the context to suggest that meaning, as there is in all the other cases. Others understand it to denote the act of meeting or encountering the enemies of the new religion. (See Matt. 22, 34. 27, 37, and compare Rev. 16, 14. 16. 20, 8.) But in all the other instances of this use, the enemies are expressly mentioned. The best sense therefore, though expressed in an unusual manner, is that they met (or assembled) in (and with) the church, for worship and instruction. (See Matt. 13, 2, and compare Matt. 22, 10.) The effect was that they *taught much people*, or more exactly, *a sufficient crowd*, implying that their hearers were not only numerous, but of various classes and descriptions. (See above, on 1, 15. 5, 37.) *Taught* does not of itself imply conviction or conversion, although these ensued in many cases, but the communication of a knowledge of the true religion, as a necessary means to that result. The other thing that *came to pass* was the use of the name *Christian*. The connection of the clauses, which is very faintly indicated in our version, is expressed too strongly in some others, e. g. whence (Luther) so that (Vulgate) they were named Christians. The labours of the missionaries and the rise of this new name are not here spoken of as wholly unconnected, nor as sustaining a causal relation, but as coincident in time and place. It was during this year of missionary labour that the name was first applied. *The disciples*, i. e. as some understand it, they who were previously called disciples; but the new name did not necessarily supersede the old one. *Were called* is not a passive verb in Greek, but the active form of the one used above in 10, 22, and there explained. It does not here mean to be named by God or by themselves; for then the name would have occurred more frequently; whereas it is used only twice besides, and both times as a term employed by enemies or strangers. (See below, on 26, 28, and compare 1 Pet. 4, 16.) It means here (as in Rom. 7, 3), that they were so called by others; not by the Jews, for they would thereby have conceded the Messiahship of Jesus; nor by Greeks, for they would probably have used another termination (as in 1, 11. 10, 1); but by Romans, as the form is Latin, like *Herodians* (Matt. 22, 16. Mark 3, 6. 12, 13), and many others found in the contemporary classics (such as *Pompeiani, Mariani, Vitelliani.*) The name may possibly have been derisive in its origin, like others which have afterwards been gloried in as titles of nobility (e. g. Huguenots, Puritans, Pietists, Methodists.) All that it properly denotes, however, is that they were followers of Christ, whether those who first applied the name knew that it denoted the Messiah of the Jews, or regarded it merely as the personal name of a ringleader. Thus Suetonius says that Claudius expelled the Jews from Rome, on account of their frequent insurrections, prompted by one Chrestus (*assidue tumultuantes Chresto im-*

pulsore.) This may be a mere mistake for *Christo*, or the real name of some well-known Jew at Rome. The form *Chrestus* would be more familiar to the Greeks, and more significant than *Christus ;* and we find that Justin Martyr, and some other early writers, actually use that form and play upon its meaning (*good*) as descriptive both of Christ and Christianity. The fact recorded in this clause is one of the three grounds, on which Chrysostom claimed for Antioch the rank of a metropolis or mother-church.

27. And in these days came prophets from Jerusalem unto Antioch.

In these days may be either an indefinite expression (see above, on 1, 15. 6, 1), denoting merely a time subsequent to that of the events just mentioned; or a specific one, denoting the *whole year* spent by Barnabas and Saul in Antioch (v. 26,) which last is the opinion of the ablest modern writer on the chronology of Acts. *Came,* or more exactly, *came down,* the usual expression for departure from Jerusalem. (See above, on 8, 5. 15, 26. 9, 32.) The particular Greek verb here used is one of Luke's peculiar terms, being used by him fifteen times, and only once besides in the New Testament (James 3, 15.) *Prophets,* inspired teachers or expounders of the divine will. The prediction of futurity was only one of the prophetic functions, but the one exercised on this occasion. That the Prophets spoken of in the New Testament were the Seventy Disciples (Luke 10, 1), or the Presbyters of the Apostolical Church, is not only a gratuitous assumption, but at variance with the temporary office of the Seventy, who are mentioned only in a single passage, and with the language of v. 30 below. The visit of these prophets has been variously explained, as a second mission, similar to that recorded in vs. 19–21; or as a reinforcement of inspired teachers, to relieve and aid those who were there already; or as a proof of constant intercourse between the two mother-churches; or as a special mission sent to warn the church at Antioch of the coming famine, and secure its contributions to the poor saints at Jerusalem (Rom. 15, 26.)

28. And there stood up one of them, named Agabus, and signified by the Spirit that there should be great

dearth throughout all the world; which came to pass in the days of Claudius Cesar.

Stood up, or arose, implying that he spoke in public, and with some formality. (See above, on 1, 15. 5, 34.) *One of them*, or *from (among) them*, as they sat in the assembly. *Named Agabus*, literally, *Agabus by name* (see above, on 5, 1. 34. 8, 9. 9, 10. 11, 12. 33, 36. 10, 1.) *Agabus* seems to be a Hebrew name, with a Greek or Latin termination, perhaps the same with that in Ezra 2, 45. 46. Neh. 7, 48. This man is mentioned only here and in 21, 10 below, where he reappears as a prophet in the strict sense. *Signified*, a verb repeatedly employed by John in reference to disclosures of the future, and for the most part with an implication of obscurity or mystery. (See John 12, 33. 18, 32. 21, 19. Rev. 1, 1.) *By the Spirit*, i. e. by the aid or at the instance of the Holy Spirit. It is more usual to represent the Holy Ghost as speaking by the Prophet, i. e. through him, by his instrumental agency. (See above, on 1, 16.) *Should be*, was to be, or was about to be, the same verb that is used above in 3, 3. 5, 35, and there explained. *Great dearth*, a great hunger, famine, scarcity of food. (See above, on 7, 11.) *Throughout all the world*, literally, *on* (or *over*) *the whole inhabited* (*earth*.) This phrase, though strictly universal in its import, is often used in a restricted sense. The Greeks, in their peculiar pride of race, applied it to their own country; the Romans, in like manner, to the empire. A similar restriction of the term by Jews to Palestine would be perfectly analogous, though it may not be demonstrable in usage. If this sense were admissible, the prophecy of Agabus might be said to have been fulfilled in the fourth, fifth, and sixth years of Claudius, during which many died of famine at Jerusalem, as related by Josephus, Eusebius, and Orosius. There had been a previous scarcity at Rome itself, in the first and second years of this reign, to relieve which Claudius opened roads and a new harbour, and caused a medal with a corn-measure to be struck in memory of the event, as stated by Suetonius. In the ninth year of the same reign, Eusebius records a great famine which prevailed in Greece. In the eleventh, Rome was visited again by scarcity, in consequence of which the emperor was pelted by the people, as we learn from Tacitus and Suetonius. All these were local famines; but as they succeeded one another so rapidly, they may be considered as together constituting one continuous progressive famine, and correctly represented as a great dearth which came upon the whole empire (or the whole known world) under (or in the time of) Claudius. *Cesar* is omitted in several of the oldest manuscripts and versions, and rejected by the latest editors as spurious.

29. Then the disciples, every man according to his ability, determined to send relief unto the brethren which dwelt in Judea —

The effect of this prediction shows the intimate relation which existed between the affiliated churches and Jerusalem the mother of them all (Gal. 4, 26.) The original construction is, *and of the disciples as any one was prospered, they determined each of them,* etc. *The disciples* are of course the Christians of Antioch. *As,* in proportion as; see above, on 7, 17. *Was prospered* or successful, an expression not suggestive of great wealth, but rather of sufficiency or competency to relieve the wants of others. The same idea is expressed by Plato almost in the same words (καθ' ὅσον εὐπορεῖ τις.) The same rule or measure is prescribed by Paul in 1 Cor. 16, 2. *Determine* means originally to divide or bound; then to define bounds; then to define any thing; and lastly to determine or decide. It is used in the New Testament only by Luke and Paul, and elsewhere construed with a noun in the accusative (see below, on 17, 26. 31, and compare Heb. 4, 7), or as a passive participle (see above, on 2, 23. 10, 42, and compare Rom. 1, 4.) This is the only case in which it governs another verb in the infinitive. *Each* or *every* with a plural verb is no unusual construction. (See above, on 2, 6, and compare Matt. 18, 35. John 16, 32.) *Relief,* or more exactly, *for service* (or *administration*), i. e. charitable distribution, a frequent sense of the Greek noun (2 Cor. 8, 4. 9, 1. 12) and its corresponding verb (Heb. 6, 10.) If the famine was to be a general one, how could the church at Antioch relieve that at Jerusalem? Their undertaking so to do implies either a great difference of wealth, or an earlier visitation in Judea, or an entire exemption of the Syrian capital, or all these circumstances in conjunction. The churches of Judea seem to have been always poor, because, as some suppose, originally gathered from the humbler classes (but see above, on 6, 7, and compare Matt. 27, 57); or because, as others think, impoverished by the community of goods (but see above, on

2, 44. 45. 4. 32.) In this case the necessity is represented as arising from a special and a temporary cause. The motive of the church at Antioch, however, was not mere natural benevolence, or even Christian charity, but a sense of filial obligation to the mother church, analogous to that which led the Jews of the Diaspora, although beyond the reach of all coercion, to contribute largely to the treasury of the temple. (See Mark 12, 41. 43. Luke 21, 1. John 8, 20, and compare Rom. 15, 25–27. 1 Cor. 16, 1–4. 2 Cor. 8, 1–15. 9. 1–15.)

30. Which also they did, and sent it to the elders by the hands of Barnabas and Saul.

The purpose thus formed was promptly carried into execution. The affection of these Christians towards the mother church was shown not merely in their words but in their deeds. *Which* refers to the determination mentioned in v. 29. *Did* is in direct antithesis to *determined*. *Also* is emphatic, not only said but also did. The subject of the verb is of course the plural noun *disciples*. There is nothing to restrict it, though the act was probably performed by the church officers, (*the elders*) *sending to the elders*. These are by some understood to mean the elders of the Jews, or their hereditary chiefs and representatives under the Patriarchal system, who are so often mentioned in the Gospels as well as the Old Testament, and in the book before us (see above, on 4, 5. 8. 23. 6, 12, and below, on 23, 14. 24, 1. 25, 15.) This supposes the donation from the church at Antioch to have been intended not for the Christians of Judea in particular, but for any who might need it; and the same wide scope is assumed to have existed in Paul's later collections. (See below, on 24, 17.) Another explanation is that these were Christians, but still elders of the Jews by hereditary right. It is commonly agreed, however, that the reference is to office-bearers in the Church; some say the Apostles, because Peter and John describe themselves as Presbyters or Elders (1 Pet. 5, 1. 2 John 1. 3 John 1); others, the Bishops of Judea, who were to distribute the donation in their dioceses; others, the Seventy Disciples, whom they identify with the first Christian Presbyters, inferring their perpetual or permanent commission from the words of Christ in Luke 10, 19. This would certainly account for the extraordinary fact that, while the institution of the Apostleship and the Diaconate is given in the history, the Presbyterate or Eldership, considered as an office in the Christian Church, is here mentioned for the first time, and that only in an incidental manner. But this omission admits of a still more satisfactory solution, because not requiring any dubious assumption as to the commission of the Seventy Disciples. This solution is, that the office of Presbyter or Elder was the only permanent, essential office of the Jewish Church, and as such was retained under the new organization, without any formal institution, and therefore without any distinct mention in the history, such as we find afterwards in reference to the organization of the Gentile churches, where the office had no previous existence, and must therefore be created by the act of ordination (see below, on 14, 23.) This is a much more probable account of the institution of the Christian Eldership than that which derives it from the constitution of the Jewish Synagogue, which was itself probably of later date, and, as a separate organization, without divine authority. (See above, on 6, 9.) *By the hands*, literally, *the hand*, a common figure, more especially in Hebrew, for mediation, intervention, instrumental agency. (Compare the similar expression in Gal. 3, 19.) They did not merely avail themselves of the return of Barnabas and Saul at the expiration of their year of labour (see above, on v. 26), but appointed them expressly to this service, as we learn from 12, 25 below. The appointment shows the light in which these two men were regarded by the church of Antioch, and also the importance which they attached to the commission itself. It is worthy of remark that the highest qualifications were required in those who were entrusted with the charities of the church in apostolic times. As to the precedence here and afterwards assigned to Barnabas, see below, on 13, 1. 9.

CHAPTER XII.

During the visit of Barnabas and Saul to the churches of Judea, a new persecution of the Christians at Jerusalem was begun by Herod Agrippa, the first of the name. The history of this persecution is recorded in the chapter now before us

(1–19), with a supplementary account of Herod's death (20–24), and the return of Barnabas and Saul to Antioch (25.) The particulars belonging to the first head are the commencement of the persecution (1), the death of James (2), the arrest of Peter (3), his imprisonment (4), and the intercession of the church for him (5), his miraculous release (6–11), his appearance at the house of Mary (12–16), and departure from Jerusalem (17), the search for him and execution of the guards (18–19.) Under the second, we have Herod's last visit to Cesarea (19), his negotiation with the Tyrians and Sidonians (20), his public address to them (21), the blasphemous applause bestowed upon it (22), and his death by a judicial stroke (23); after which, or in the mean time, the church prospered (24), and the deputies from Antioch returned to those who sent them (25.)

1. Now about that time, Herod the king stretched forth (his) hands, to vex certain of the church.

This chapter is connected with the one before it in the closest manner, not only by the usual continuative particle, *now* (*and* or *but*), but by the phrase, *about* (or *at*) *that time*, which, although in itself indefinite, is here determined by the context to mean at the time of the official visit to Judea mentioned at the close of the last chapter. (See above, on 11, 30.) It is nowhere said that Barnabas and Saul were in Jerusalem at all, and as their errand was "to the brethren dwelling in Judea" (11, 29), some suppose them to have been deterred from visiting the Holy City by the very persecution here described; while others, with as much or as little probability, assume that they were witnesses of what is here recorded, and were even present at the meeting mentioned in v. 12 below. *Herod the king*, not the one so called in Matt. 2, 1. 3, nor the one so called in Mark 6, 14, but the nephew of the latter and the grandson of the former, and descended through his mother from the Maccabees or Hasmonean kings of Judah. He was brought up at Rome with the royal princes, Caligula and Claudius, by whom, on their accession to the throne, he was gradually repossessed of the dominions of his grandfather, Herod the Great. He bore the name of the famous Agrippa, which Luke applies, however, only to his son (see below, on 25, 13), while he calls the father simply by his family name, *Herod*. Notwithstanding his heathen education, he professed to be a zealous Jew, perhaps less from conviction than from policy (see below, on v. 3.) Josephus, the historian, describes him as a mild and liberal but ambitious prince, which, with due allowance for the flattery involved in the description, is by no means irreconcileable with what is here recorded. *Stretched forth his hands*, or more exactly, *laid his hands on*, an expression often used by Luke, and always in the sense of seizure or arrest. (See above, on 4, 3. 5, 18, and below, on 21, 27, and compare Luke 20, 19. 21, 12.) The marginal translation in the English Bible (*began*) is still less exact. *To vex*, an English word now chiefly used of petty annoyances, but in the translation of the Bible having a much stronger sense. (See for example Num. 20, 15. Judges 16, 16. 2 Chr. 15, 6. Job 19, 2. Ps. 2, 5. Isai. 63, 10. Matt. 15, 22.) The Greek verb here used strictly means to *make bad*, and is once applied to moral influence (see below, on 14, 2), but commonly to persecution or oppression (see above, on 7, 6. 19, and below, on 18, 10, and compare 1 Pet. 3, 13.) *Certain of the church*, or more exactly, *some of those from* (i. e. belonging to) *the church*. (See above, on 10, 23, and compare 10, 45. 11, 2.) It is worthy of remark, that the Christians of Judea, or at least those of Jerusalem, are still described as constituting one church. (See above, on 2, 47. 5, 11. 8, 1. 3. 11, 22.)

2. And he killed James the brother of John with the sword.

Killed, despatched, or made away with (see above, on 2, 23. 5, 33. 7, 28. 9, 23. 29. 10, 39.) *James*, the son of Zebedee, one of our Saviour's earliest followers and most confidential friends (see above, on 1, 13), never mentioned in the Gospels but with John, as whose brother he is here described, because of John's celebrity in later times. *With the sword*, most probably by decapitation. This martyrdom may be regarded as the fulfilment of Christ's words in Matt. 20, 23. John's sufferings were less acute but more protracted. It is remarkable that, so far as we know, one of these inseparable brothers was the first, and one the last, that died of the Apostles. This verse may be either a specification of the one before it (some of the church, among whom was James the brother of John), or an additional fact, forming a kind of climax (not only some obscure members of the church, but one of the most eminent Apostles.)

3. And because he saw it pleased the Jews, he proceeded further to take Peter also. Then were the days of unleavened bread.

Because he saw, literally, *seeing* or *having seen*. *Pleased*, literally, *is pleasing* or *acceptable*. The present tense calls up the scene as actually passing. (See above, on 7, 25. 9, 26.) *The Jews*, not merely the rulers, but the people, whose feelings towards the church had undergone a great change since the time referred to in 2, 47. 5, 13, during which interval indeed the previous persecution had occurred. (See 6, 12. 8, 1.) The motive here assigned was not necessarily the primary or only one. It rather seems to be implied that, having killed James for another purpose, he perceived that he had thereby pleased the Jews. This he may have done while gratifying some ambitious or malignant passion of his own. *Proceeded further*, literally, *added*, a Hebrew idiom, which Luke uses elsewhere. (Compare Luke 19, 11 and 20, 11.) *To take*, take up, seize, arrest. (See above, on 1, 16.) Whatever may have been the motive for destroying James, Peter was probably selected as the most conspicuous and best known of our Lord's disciples. It can scarcely be regarded as fortuitous, that Herod should have laid his hands on two of Christ's three most intimate and confidential friends and followers. The specification of the time when this arrest took place is a strong though incidental proof of authenticity. *Then*, not the adverb of time, but the continuative particle, translated *and* in v. 2, and *now* in v. 1. *The days of unleavened bread* (Luther and Tyndale, *sweet bread;* Wiclif, *therf loaves;* Rhemish version *azymes*), i. e. the festival week following the Passover, during which the use of leaven was forbidden in the Law. (See Ex. 12, 18. 27. Deut. 16, 3. 8, and compare Matt. 26, 17. Mark 14, 1. 12. Luke 22, 1. 7.) This festival began on the fourteenth day of the month Nisan, corresponding partly to our March and April. (See below, on 20, 6.)

4. And when he had apprehended him, he put (him) in prison, and delivered (him) to four quaternions of soldiers, to keep him, intending after Easter to bring him forth to the people.

Whom having also seized (or *apprehended*.) The Greek

verb is a Doric form of one which means to press or squeeze, but in the Hellenistic usage, to lay hold of, to hold fast. It is applied by John to the taking of beasts and fishes (John 21, 3. 10. Rev. 19, 20), but still more frequently to forcible arrest or seizure (John 7, 30. 32. 44. 8, 20. 10, 39. 11, 57.) *Put into prison*, or confinement; see above, on 5, 19. 22. 25. 8, 3.) *And delivered*, literally, *delivering*, committing, or entrusting, which is not a mere specification of the preceding phrase ('whom he put into prison by delivering' etc.), but an additional distinct act, showing the unusual precautions taken to secure a captive so important ('whom he not only put into prison, but delivered' &c.) *Four quaternions* is not a mere periphrasis for *sixteen*, as the Peshito renders it, but a technical expression borrowed from the Roman discipline or art of war, in which the night was divided into four watches (see above, on 2, 15), and each of these entrusted to four soldiers, who succeeded or relieved each other every three hours. These details are found, not only in the Jewish writer Philo, but in ancient military works, such as those of Polybius in Greek and Vegetius in Latin. In the case before us, four armed men appear to have been constantly employed, two in the cell and two before the door, to watch one unarmed and defenceless prisoner. *To keep*, i. e. to watch or guard, a stronger sense than that attached to the word *keep* in modern English. *Intending*, literally, *wishing* or *desiring*, but with the accessory notion of a plan or purpose. (See above, on 5, 28. 33, and for the usage of the cognate noun, on 2, 23. 4, 28. 5, 38.) *After Easter*, a singular confusion of the Christian with the Jewish festival, transcribed into King James's version from the older ones of Tyndale, Cranmer, and Geneva, while Wiclif and the Rhemish Version go to the opposite extreme of retaining the original without translation (*after pask* or *pasche*.) There is no imaginable reason why it should not be translated here, as in every other place where it occurs, by its exact equivalent, *the Passover*. (See Matt. 26, 2. Mark 14, 1. Luke 2, 41. John 2, 13. 1 Cor. 5, 7. Heb. 11, 28, and more than twenty other instances, to which the one before us is the sole exception.) The word properly denotes the sacrifice and supper on the fourteenth day of Nisan, but is here used, as in several of the places just referred to, for the whole festival, described in the preceding verse as *the days of unleavened bread*. *To bring him forth*, literally, *up*, as we speak of bringing a man up before a court or magistrate. (Compare

Luke 22, 66.) The Greek verb frequently occurs in Acts, but almost always as a nautical or sea-phrase (see below, on 13, 13, and compare 7, 41. 9, 39. 16, 34.) *To the people*, not as judges, but as spectators, in some great assembly, either for amusement, or to witness Peter's execution. (Compare the case of Samson, Judg. 16, 25.) Herod's motive for postponing this exposure of his prisoner may have been some scruple of his own, or a regard to the religious feelings of the people whom he wished to please, or quite as probably because he knew that during the paschal week their minds would be engrossed with its ceremonies and festivities, and therefore less fit to appreciate the treat which he proposed to give them.

5. Peter therefore was kept in prison; but prayer was made without ceasing of the church unto God for him.

Therefore, or rather *so then*, the same compound particle (μὲν οὖν) which we have had repeatedly before in this book, to denote the pauses and resumptions of the narrative, (See above, on 1, 6. 2, 41. 5 41. 8, 4. 25. 9, 31, 11, 19.) *Kept*, in the same strong sense explained above (on v. 4), though the verb is not the same, but one employed by Matthew (27, 36. 54. 28, 4) in the same sense, whereas in John it always means either to preserve or to observe. (See John 2, 10. 8, 51, and passim.) This is not a mere reiteration of a fact already stated, as the imperfect form of the Greek verb is equivalent to the modern phrase, *was being kept*, i. e. when something else took place, recorded in the next clause. There too, the literal translation is, *was being made*, the clauses forming an antithesis. While he was watched, they were praying. *Without ceasing* is a paraphrase of one Greek word, and that an adjective qualifying *prayer*, and originally meaning tight or strained, but in its figurative usage corresponding to *intense*, i. e. when applied to prayer, "instant and earnest," as it is well explained in the margin of the English Bible. *Of* (i. e. *by*) *the* church, still regarded as one body, however numerous its members or its subdivisions. (See above, on v. 1, and below, on v. 12.) *To God*, not to man, not to Herod, whom they might have hoped to influence in some way. *For him* concerning him, in his behalf; not merely for his liberation, but for a happy issue to this trial, both to him and to the cause for which he suffered. (See below, on vs. 15, 16.)

6. And when Herod would have brought him forth, the same night Peter was sleeping between two soldiers, bound with two chains, and the keepers before the door kept the prison.

Would have brought, or more exactly, *was about to bring*. Herod's plan was on the very eve of its accomplishment. *To bring forth* (or *forward*) is the true sense of the verb here used, a kindred form to that in v. 4, and in this book always applied to prisoners. (See below, on 16, 30. 25, 26.) *The same night*, or (*in*) *that* (*very*) *night*, the one preceding the day fixed for Peter's public appearance. His *sleeping* probably, but not necessarily, implies composure and serenity. *Bound with two chains*, to the arms of the two soldiers, a method of confinement spoken of by other ancient writers, especially by Seneca (*eadem catena et custodiam et militem copulat*) and Josephus, who describes this very Herod or Agrippa as having been so secured by order of Tiberius. *And the keepers*, or *the keepers also* (τε), i. e. the two remaining men of the quaternion (see above, on v. 4.) *Keepers*, in the strong sense of guards or watchers. *Before the door*, either the main entrance to the prison (see below, on v. 10), or the door of the particular ward, cell, or dungeon, in which Peter lay. *Kept*, in the imperfect tense, *were keeping*, guarding, watching. The correspondence of the verb and noun is lost in the translation, unless we read, *the gaolers kept the gaol.*

7. And, behold, the angel of the Lord came upon (him), and a light shined in the prison, and he smote Peter on the side, and raised him up, saying, Arise up quickly; and his chains fell off from (his) hands.

Behold, as usual, prepares the mind for something unexpected; see above, on 11, 11. *The angel* (or *an angel*) *of the Lord;* see above, on 5, 19. *Came upon him*, or *stood over him;* see above, on 4, 1. 6, 12. 10, 17. 11, 11, (Wicl. *stood nigh*. Tynd. *was there present*. Rhem. *stood in presence*.) *A light*, or simply *light* without the article; see above, on 9, 3. This light may have proceeded from the Angel, as a supernatural and heavenly effulgence; or it may have been a separate illumination, intended to facilitate the prisoner's escape. *In the prison*, literally, *in the house* or *dwelling*, a term used in Attic Greek, by a peculiar superstition, instead of the unlucky word which distinctly denotes prison. This singular usage is affirmed by Plutarch, and exemplified by Thucydides and Demosthenes. *And smote* (literally, *smiting*) *Peter's side*, or *pleura*, a term still used in anatomy. As the Greek verb elsewhere means to strike with violence, so as even to wound or kill (see Matt. 26, 31. 51. Luke 22, 49. 50), we have neither right nor reason to give it, in this one place, the diluted sense of striking gently. *Raised him up*, or rather *roused him*, the idea being not merely that of lifting (as in 3, 7) but of awakening from sleep, in which sense the verb is metaphorically used of resurrection or resuscitation. (See above, on 3, 15. 4, 10. 5. 30. 10, 40.) *Arise* (or *stand up*) *quickly* (or *in haste*.) *His chains*, literally, *the chains*, as the pronoun in Greek is not repeated. *Fell off from* (or, as the original expression strictly means, *fell out of*) *his hands*, as if he had been holding and not merely wearing them.

8. And the angel said unto him, Gird thyself, and bind on thy sandals; and so he did. And he saith unto him, Cast thy garment about thee, and follow me.

Gird thyself, or, according to the text adopted by the latest critics, *gird* (thy clothes) *around* (thee). *Bind on* (literally, *bind under*) *thy sandals*, which covered the sole of the foot only. (For the use of the corresponding noun, see above, on 7, 33.) *And he did so* marks a stage or pause in the proceeding. *And he says to him*, a second time, again, *cast about* or *throw around* (thee) *thy* (upper or outer) *garment* (see above, on 7, 58.) *And* (now that thou art fully prepared) *follow me*. This command to dress himself completely and deliberately, may have been intended both to show him the reality of what he witnessed and to assure him of immediate liberation. This is perfectly consistent with the call to arise quickly. Hesitation in arising would have argued unbelieving doubts; undue haste in departure unbelieving fears. Both were sufficiently precluded by the summons to stand up at once, and by the subsequent instructions to resume every article of dress which he had laid aside, before he left the prison.

9. And he went out, and followed him; and wist

not that it was true which was done by the angel, but thought he saw a vision.

And going (or *coming*) *out, he* (Peter) *followed* (or *was following*) *him* (the Angel), *and* (as he did so) *knew not* (was not certain) *that it is* (as if present to the writer or the reader, see above, on 7, 25) *true* (i. e. real, not imaginary), *the* (thing) *done by* (or happened, come to pass, by means of) *the Angel. But* (although uncertain as to this point) *he* (rather) *thought he saw* (or *seemed to see*) *a vision* (a miraculous sight or ideal spectacle), such as he had lately seen in Joppa (10, 11. 12.) That Peter should have been inclined to this conclusion, after what he had so recently experienced, was certainly most natural.

10. When they were past the first and the second ward, they came unto the iron gate that leadeth unto the city, which opened to them of his own accord; and they went out, and passed on (through) one street, and forthwith the angel departed from him.

And having past (or *come through*) *a first and second ward,* or subdivision of the prison, which is much more natural than to understand it of a first and second guard or watch. *The iron gate* is spoken of as something well known, or perhaps as something usual in prisons. *Leading into the city* from the interior of the prison, but not necessarily from without the walls. There is nothing, therefore, to be learnt here as to the position of the prison, with respect to which there have been various conjectures. *Of his* (in modern English, *its*) *own accord opened* (was opened) *to them* (i. e. for them, or before them) to afford them passage. *Coming out,* at the iron door, and therefore from the whole enclosure of the prison. *Passed on,* came forward or proceeded. *Through* is supplied by the translators. *Street,* the same Greek word that is used above in 9, 11, and there explained. *One street,* i. e. probably the length of one. The reference may be either to a particular street, or to a customary measure like our square, block, etc. *Forthwith,* as soon as they had gone this distance. *Departed* is in Greek the converse of the verb employed in v. 7, a relation which can only be expressed in English by some such combination as " appeared " and " disappeared."

11. And when Peter was come to himself, he said, Now I know of a surety, that the Lord hath sent his angel, and hath delivered me out of the hand of Herod, and (from) all the expectation of the people of the Jews.

Coming to himself is not the same phrase that is so translated in Luke 15, 17, but one that properly means, *being* (or *beginning to be*) *in himself*, i. e. in his natural or normal state, as opposed to the perplexity and doubt described in v. 9. *Of a surety*, truly, really, or certainly, the adverb corresponding to the adjective in v. 9. *Sent*, or more emphatically, *sent out*, sent away, implying distance (see above, on 7, 12. 9, 30. 11, 22.) *Delivered* is a cognate form in Greek to that translated killed in v. 2; an analogous antithesis to that already noticed (on v. 10.) While one apostle was put to death, the other was put at liberty. *The hand*, power or possession. *Expectation*, that which they expected, namely his exposure and most probably his execution. (See above, on v. 4.) *All the expectation*, the worst that he had reason to anticipate with dread, and they with pleasure. *The people of the Jews*, the Jewish people, not merely individuals, but the whole community, which seems to have acted with great unanimity, as well in showing favour as in manifesting hatred. (See above, on 2, 47. 4, 21. 5, 20. 6, 12.)

12. And when he had considered (the thing), he came to the house of Mary the mother of John, whose surname was Mark, where many were gathered together praying.

When he had considered the thing answers to one word in Greek which means *considering* (i. e. where he was, or where he would be likely to find Christian friends assembled); or *being aware* (of his position, and the place where he was standing); or *being conscious* (in a state of consciousness, as opposed to an ecstatic one.) This last is nearly synonymous with *being in* (or *coming to*) *himself* in the preceding verse. For the usage of the Greek verb, see above, on 5, 2, and below, on 14, 6, and compare 1 Cor. 4, 4. *Came to*, or *upon*, perhaps implying that he did so unexpectedly. *Mary* (or *Miriam*) being one of the most common Jewish names, the person here meant is distinguished by the mention of her son, who was no doubt therefore well known. *John* being also an extremely common name, the son is distinguished in like manner by a Latin surname (*Marcus*), which, according to the custom of the age, was added to his Hebrew one. (See above, on 1, 23. 9, 36, and below, on 13, 1. 9.) This *John Mark* is no doubt the same who is mentioned in v. 25, and reappears in 13, 13. 15, 37–39. He is also supposed to be the same whom Peter calls his son (1 Pet. 5, 13), i. e. his spiritual son or convert; whom Paul names in three of his epistles as his fellow-labourer (see Col. 4, 10. 2 Tim. 4, 11. Philem. 24); and to whom an old and uniform tradition ascribes the composition of the second gospel. *The house of Mary,* i. e. the house where she was living; but whether as a lodger or an owner we are not told, and are therefore not at liberty to use this as a proof that individual property was not abolished by the community of goods described in 2, 44. 4, 32, although this negative conclusion is highly probable for other reasons. *Many were gathered* (or *crowded*), perhaps according to custom, but more probably in reference to this emergency. (See above, on v. 5.)

13. And as Peter knocked at the door of the gate, a damsel came to hearken, named Rhoda.

And Peter knocking, or, according to the latest critics, *he knocking. The door of the gate,* or rather of the *porch,* the front or street-door. Several of the older English versions have, *the entry-door.* (See above, on 10, 17.) *A damsel,* maid, or girl, perhaps a member of the family, but most probably a servant, as the Greek word is clearly so used elsewhere (see below, on 16, 16, and compare Luke 12, 45. Gal. 4, 22), and as female servants seem to have performed this office, even in great houses (see Matt. 26, 69. Mark 14, 66. 69. Luke 22, 56. John 18, 17.) *Came,* literally, *came to* (*it,* or to the door) from within. *To listen,* or as the margin of the English Bible less exactly renders it, *to ask who was there.* The expression here might seem to have respect to some particular emergency or danger, were it not used in the classics to denote the ordinary act of attending or answering the door. Two of the verbs here used (*knock* and *come to*) are combined by Lucian, and two (*knock* and *listen*) by Xenophon. A similar Latin phrase is used by Plautus (*fores auscultato.*) *Named* (literally, *by name*) *Rhoda,* or rather *Rhode,* as the name is Greek, not Latin, and the latter form is given even in the Vulgate. The name denotes a rose-bush, not a rose, as sometimes stated, which in Greek is a related but distinct form (*rhodon*.) Similar names, derived from plants or flowers, are *Tamar* (palm), *Hadassah* (myrtle), and *Susanna* (lily.) For others borrowed from the animal kingdom, see above, on 9, 36. The preservation of this beautiful but unimportant name in the history before us is a slight but striking proof of authenticity.

14. And when she knew Peter's voice, she opened not the gate for gladness, but ran in and told how Peter stood before the gate.

And recognizing Peter's voice, which may imply that he was in the habit of resorting to the house, if not (as Matthew Henry says) that she had often heard him preach and pray. This incident resembles that in Matt. 26, 73. Mark 14, 70, excepting that in that case it was not his voice, but his provincial dialect, that made him known. (For the meaning of the Greek verb here used, see above, on 3, 10. 4, 13. 9, 30.) *For gladness,* or *from joy,* a lifelike incident, analogous to those in Gen. 45, 26. Luke 24, 41. *Told how,* or *reported that* (compare the use of the same verb in 4, 23. 5, 22. 25. 11, 13 above, and in v. 17 below.) *The gate,* twice mentioned in this verse, is properly the porch or front part of the building, as before explained (on v. 13 and 10, 17.)

15. And they said unto her, Thou art mad. But she constantly affirmed that it was even so. Then said they, It is his angel.

They, i. e. the people of the house, as in 10, 10, or rather those who happened to be there assembled (see above, on vs. 5. 12.) *Thou art mad,* thou ravest, corresponds to one Greek word, which is applied, in precisely the same sense, to Christ himself, and to Paul (26, 24. John 10, 20.) It is here a strong expression of their incredulity. *Constantly* (or confidently, steadfastly) *affirmed,* is also a single word in Greek, often used, in the same sense, by Plato and the Attic orators. *That it was even so,* literally, *so* (or *thus*) *to have,* i. e. to have itself, to be, the same Greek idiom that occurs above in 7, 1. *Then,* the same word that is translated *and, but,* in the two preceding clauses. *His angel,* i. e., as some understand it, *his messenger*, a messenger from Peter. This is the original meaning of the Greek word, and occurs in a few places (Matt. 11, 10. Luke 7, 24. 9, 52. James 2, 5.) But this idea would have been expressed more naturally by the phrase, a messenger from him, or one sent by him. Besides, a message from Peter, guarded as he was, would have been scarcely less surprising than his personal appearance. Most interpreters, therefore, are agreed that *angel* has here its usual and higher sense, in which it has repeatedly occurred before. (See above, on vs. 7. 8. 9. 10. 11, and on 5, 19. 6, 15. 7, 30. 35. 38. 53. 8, 26. 10, 3. 7. 22. 11, 13.) Some understand by *his angel* a preternatural apparition, supposed in the superstitions of some countries to announce the death of the person represented. It is a very ancient notion, that this text confirms the doctrine elsewhere taught, that every person has his guardian angel. But no such thing is really suggested, either here or in Gen. 48, 16. Ps. 34, 7. Eccl. 5, 6. Matt. 18, 10. Heb. 1, 14. The doctrine of angelic guardianship is clearly taught in Scripture, but not that of a particular angel guarding every individual. Even if this were the meaning of the words before us, it would only show that the primitive Christians were not wholly free from superstition. But the words necessarily denote no more than the mission of an angel, which was not more incredible in this case than in that recorded just before in this same chapter. (See above, on vs. 7–10.)

16. But Peter continued knocking, and when they had opened (the door), and saw him, they were astonished.

Continued is in Greek an emphatic compound, and might be translated, *still continued* or *continued on*. *Having opened they saw him*, may refer, as before, to the people of the house, or still more probably, to the assembled Christians, who would naturally come out in a body, on receiving the glad news of his arrival. *Were astonished*, the same verb employed above in 2, 7. 12. 8, 9. 11. 13. 9, 21. 10, 45. Their wonder has been sometimes represented as a proof of weak faith, since they could not believe the very thing for which they had been praying. But their prayers may not have been exclusively for Peter's liberation (see above, on vs. 5. 12); or they may, to use a natural and common phrase, have thought the tidings too good to be true. (Compare the case of Ananias, in 9, 13. 14.)

17. But he, beckoning unto them with the hand to hold their peace, declared unto them how the Lord had brought him out of the prison. And he said, Go show these things unto James, and to the brethren. And he departed, and went into another place.

Beckoning, literally, *shaking down* (or *downwards*), a verb found only in this book of the New Testament, and always of the hand, as a preliminary gesture used by public speakers to secure attention. (See below, on 13, 16. 19, 33. 21, 40.) *To hold their peace,* or to be silent, is in Greek a single word. The clause may have reference, either to the ordinary noise of conversation, or more probably to the unusual expression of their joy at Peter's liberation. *Declared,* or as the Greek verb primarily signifies, *led the way through* the matter, or went through it in the form of a circumstantial narrative. For another instance of the same verb and the same construction with *how* (see above, on 9, 27.) *The Lord,* i. e. God, or more specifically the Lord Jesus Christ (see above, on 1, 24. 2, 36. 9, 27. 35. 42. 10, 36. 48. 11, 21. 23. 24), by the agency or intervention of his angel. *And he said,* or, *and said,* which would make the following clause a command of the Lord to Peter, (*Report to James and to the brethren these things*), which he was now executing. But no such command is mentioned in the previous context, and to most interpreters and readers it has always seemed more natural to understand the words as those addressed by Peter himself to the Christians gathered at the house of Mary. As James the son of Zebedee had been already put to death (see above, on v. 2), and the only other person of that name who has been previously mentioned in this history is James the son of Alpheus (see above, on 1, 13), the reference must be to him, unless some reason to the contrary should be suggested by the subsequent history (see below, on 15, 13.) He may be particularly named here as the only other Apostle then in Jerusalem, or as the one to whom the care of the church there had been specially entrusted, or on whom it was now to be devolved by Peter. *And he departed* might, on the hypothesis already mentioned, be supposed to refer to the disappearance of the angel (see above, on v. 10.) But the literal translation (*going out*) is less appropriate to that event, and the words have been almost universally applied to Peter's own departure from the house of Mary, or the city of Jerusalem. *Went*, or more emphatically, *went away*, departed, journeyed (see above, on 1, 10. 11. 25. 5, 20. 41. 8, 26. 27. 36. 37. 9, 3. 11. 15. 31. 10, 20.) The use of this word seems to show that the clause has reference, not to his concealment in some other quarter of the Holy City, but to his departure from it. This agrees well with the fact, that he appears no more there as a resident apostle, but only as a member of the Apostolical Council, which he may have come expressly to attend. (See below, on 15, 7.) To what other place he now removed there is nothing in the text or context to determine. Several names have been suggested by conjecture, such as Cesarea (see the next verse), Antioch (see Gal. 2, 11), and Rome, in order to sustain the tradition that Peter was for many years the bishop of the church there, a tradition inconsistent with the absolute silence of Paul respecting him, in writing to and from Rome.

18. Now as soon as it was day, there was no small stir among the soldiers, what was become of Peter.

And (*it*) *being* (or *becoming*) *day*. *Small* is in Greek the singular number of the word for *few* (see below, on 17. 4. 12.) *Stir*, commotion, tumult. The same word is applied by Luke to a popular disturbance or riot (see below, on 19, 23), and a kindred form by Mark (13, 8) to the same object, and by John (5, 4) to a physical commotion of the waters. It here expresses the confusion and excitement naturally caused by the escape of an important prisoner, especially among those to whose keeping he had been committed. (See above, on 5, 22–25.) As no discovery was made till daybreak, when the guard would be relieved, Peter was probably delivered during the last or morning-watch. (See above, on v. 4, and on 1, 15.) *Among* (or *in*) *the soldiers*, of the four quaternions, to whom the king delivered Peter for safe keeping. (See above, on v. 4.) The thought to be supplied between the clauses is 'to know,' 'to discover,' or the like. *What was become of Peter*, literally, *what then Peter had become*. This has been strictly understood by some, as implying that the soldiers suspected or believed him to have been transformed by magic into some other form, and thus to have escaped,

This idea might have been sincerely entertained by heathen soldiers, such as Herod's guards perhaps were; or it might have been invented as a cloak for what appeared to be their own neglect of duty. But the Greek words probably mean no more than our version has expressed, a kind of indirect inquiry, what had befallen or become of Peter. The form of the original, though foreign from our idiom, agrees almost exactly with the French mode of expressing the same thing (*ce que Pierre serait devenu.*)

19. And when Herod had sought for him, and found him not, he examined the keepers, and commanded that (they) should be put to death. And he went down from Judea to Cesarea, and (there) abode.

Having sought for him, and not finding him, having examined the guards, he commanded, etc. *Examined*, judicially, a verb used only by Luke and Paul (see above, on 4, 9.) *That they should be put to death*, literally, *to be led away*, sometimes without reference to judicial process (see below, on 23, 17. 24, 7, and compare Luke 13, 15. Matt 7, 13); sometimes meaning to the bar, or the presence of a magistrate (as in Matt. 26, 57. 27, 2. Mark 14, 53. 15, 16. John 18, 3); sometimes to prison or a place of safety (see below, on 23, 10, and compare Mark 14, 44); sometimes to execution (as in Matt, 27, 31. Luke 23, 26. John 19, 16.) This last is a favourite euphemism in the classics (see above, on v. 7), as when Pliny writes to Trajan, of the Christians who refused at his tribunal to deny Christ, "those persisting I ordered to be led away" (*perseverantes duci jussi.*) This is not to be regarded as an act of extraordinary cruelty in Herod, but as a simple application of the Roman military law, with which he was familiar. It is not necessarily implied that the miraculous deliverance of Peter was known either to the king or to the guards; but as the latter could give no account of his escape, there seemed to be no doubt that they must either have connived at it, or slept upon their post, a capital offence in Roman soldiers. (See below, on 16, 27, and compare Matt. 28, 14.) The last clause is referred by some to Peter; but this construction, although not impossible, has never seemed so natural to most interpreters and readers, as that which understands the words of Herod. *From Judea*, i. e. from the inland or interior, *to*

Cesarea, which was on the sea-coast, and also near the northern limit of the province. (See above, on 8, 40. 9, 30. 10, 1.) As this had been the residence of the Roman procurators, so it now was of Agrippa (see below, on 23, 35.) *Abode*, not necessarily for the same time, but spent the time there before his death. The same Greek verb is elsewhere rendered *tarried* (see below, on 25, 6, and compare John 3, 22), *continued* (see below, on 15, 35, and compare John 11, 54), and in one case simply *had been* (see below, on 25, 14), but most frequently as here (see below, on 14, 3. 28. 16, 12. 20, 6.) Josephus tells us that Agrippa went to Cesarea for the purpose of celebrating games in honour of the emperor, which, though not here mentioned, is entirely consistent with the narrative before us.

20. And Herod was highly displeased with them of Tyre and Sidon; but they came with one accord to him, and, having made Blastus the king's chamberlain their friend, desired peace, because their country was nourished by the king's (country.)

Highly displeased, literally, *warring in mind*, i. e. as the margin of our Bible renders it, bearing a hostile mind, but not, as it is there added, intending war; for this the Romans would not have permitted between two of their dependents. The same objection lies, with still more force, against the explanation, *furiously fighting*, although justified by classical usage. *Them of Tyre and Sidon*, literally, *the Tyrians and Sidonians*, the people of the two great cities of Phenicia (see above, on 11, 19), from whose foreign trade the country derived all its wealth, being itself a narrow strip of sea-coast, without any rich interior, and dependent even for the most indispensable supplies upon its neighbours, and especially on Palestine, a mutual relation which appears to have existed from the time of Solomon, and is expressly mentioned by Ezekiel in his vivid picture of the trade of Tyre. (See 1 Kings 5. 11. Ezra 3, 7. Ezek. 27, 17.) On this account it was their wisest policy to live on good terms with Agrippa, who was now the sovereign of all Palestine, and may have been disposed to look upon Tyre and Sidon as commercial rivals of the new port which his grandfather had created at Straton's Tower, now called Cesarea. (See above, on 8, 40. 10, 1.) This temper he could easily indulge by checking the communication, and especially the export of provisions to Phenicia. *With one accord*, unanimously, by agreement, which may possibly imply that they had been at variance among themselves, but now united in a measure equally important to both cities, and indeed to the whole country. *Came* (or more exactly *were present*) *to him*, i. e. came into his presence, sought an audience. This they did not directly, but through *Blastus, the king's chamberlain*, or as it is more literally rendered in the margin, *that was over the king's bed-chamber*. In ancient courts, as well as in some modern ones, domestic officers controlled the sovereign, and if not his ministers of state, were really his confidential counsellors. (See above, on 8, 27.) *Having made him their friend*, literally, *having persuaded him*, perhaps by bribes, but no less probably by arguments, showing that the interests of Herod coincided with their own. (See above, on 5, 40, and compare Matt. 28, 14. Gal. 1, 10.) *Desired peace*, or rather asked it for themselves, which is the full force of the middle voice, as here used. (See above, on 3, 14. 7, 46. 9, 2.) *Peace*, not merely as opposed to war, but to alienation, rivalry, or conflicting interests. *Because their country*, literally, *for* (or *on account of*) *their country being nourished*, i. e. supplied with food, no doubt in exchange for the proceeds of their foreign trade. *The king's country*, literally, *the royal*, agreeing with *country* (or *territory*) understood, or repeated from the clause immediately preceding. They probably embraced the opportunity, afforded by Agrippa's public or official visit to a seaport, to negociate this reconciliation.

21. And upon a set day, Herod, arrayed in royal apparel, sat upon his throne, and made an oration unto them.

A set day, i. e. one fixed or appointed for the purpose. We learn from Josephus, that it was the second day of Herod's games, or public shows, in honour of his friend and patron, Claudius, perhaps with reference to his safe return from Britain, which about this time he had reduced to its allegiance as a Roman province. Herod may have reserved his answer to the Tyrians and Sidonians for this public occasion, from vanity and fondness for display, which were his characteristic foibles. *Arrayed in*, or rather, *having put on*, which is the true force of the middle voice, as in Luke 12, 22. (Compare the active, Luke 15, 22, and the figurative use, Luke 24, 49.) *Royal apparel*, or a royal dress, the Greek word denoting not a single garment, but the whole costume. (See above, on 1, 10. 10, 30.) Josephus describes it more particularly as a dress of silver, that is, richly adorned with silver lace and embroidery, or actually made of silver tissue. This circumstance is also characteristic of Agrippa's vanity. *Sat*, literally, *and having sat* (down), or assumed his seat. *Throne* is elsewhere rendered *judgment-seat* (see below, on 18, 12. 16, 17. 25, 6. 10, 17, and compare Matt. 27, 19. John 19, 13. Rom. 14, 10. 2 Cor. 5. 10.) The Greek word originally means a *step* or *footstep*, of which we have one instance in the book before us (see above, on 7, 5); then a *step* or *platform*, any place ascended to by steps, such as the rostrum or tribunal of a magistrate, the upper seats of theatres, etc. This last agrees well with the statement of Josephus, that the meeting here described was in the theatre at Cesarea, and with the general Greek practice as described by Valerius Maximus (*Legati in theatrum, ut est consuetudo Graeciae, introducti.*) *Made an oration*, or harangued the people, as the Greek word properly denotes. *To them*, i. e. to the Phenician envoys, who were no doubt formally addressed, although the speech was really intended for the people. If this were not the case, the statement in v. 20 would be quite irrelevant and superfluous.

22. And the people gave a shout, (saying, It is) the voice of a god, and not of a man.

The people, not the word so rendered in vs. 4, 11 above, and often elsewhere, and most commonly denoting the chosen people or the Jewish church, but one of rarer use in the New Testament and only in the book before us, but employed in Attic Greek to signify the people in their corporate capacity, the sovereign people of the Greek republics, more especially when actually gathered for despatch of business. (See below, on 17, 5. 19, 30. 33.) So here, it denotes not the populace or mob, but the assembled people, called together by authority, and in the presence of their civil ruler. *Gave a shout*, literally, *cried* or *called to* (him), i. e. responded to, applauded what he said, by their shouts and acclamations. (See below, on 22, 24, and compare Luke 23, 21.) The remaining nine words of the version correspond to five in Greek, and might have been expressed by five in English, *God's voice and not man's,* which is moreover the original collocation of the sentence. It is not a proposition, but an exclamation, an expression of pretended admiration, perhaps begun by the Phenician envoys, in acknowledgment of Herod's favourable answer to their prayer (v. 20.) No Jew could join in such a cry without being guilty of blasphemy; but probably the meeting was entirely composed of Gentiles, being held in a Roman amphitheatre, to celebrate a heathen festival. Josephus states the words of the people in a more diffuse and feeble form: "Be propitious! If until now we reverenced thee as a man, yet henceforth we acknowledge thee superior to mortal nature." He also represents the acclamation as called forth by the reflection of the rising sun from Herod's silver robe; but this is far less natural and likely than the statement in the text, which may however serve to complete that of Josephus.

23. And immediately the angel of the Lord smote him, because he gave not God the glory; and he was eaten of worms, and gave up the ghost.

Immediately, or on the spot, the same word that is so translated in 3, 7, but in 5, 10 *straightway,* and in 9, 18 *forthwith. The angel* (or *an angel*) *of the Lord,* is not a figure for disease as sent by him, nor does it here denote a visible appearance, but an instantaneous physical effect produced by the instrumental agency of a personal messenger from heaven, sent forth for the purpose. (Compare Ex. 12, 21. 2 Kings 19, 35. 2 Sam. 24, 16. 2 Chr. 32, 21. John 1, 52. 5, 4.) Josephus says that Herod saw an owl perched upon a cord above his head, which he remembered to have seen before when imprisoned by Tiberius, and to have been assured by some one, that although it was immediately a favourable omen, yet if it ever reappeared, he might expect to die within five days; and accordingly he represents him to have lingered five days in agonizing inward pains. This is not inconsistent with Luke's narrative, which only says that he was smitten, not that he expired, immediately or on the spot. *Gave not God the glory,* or more exactly, *glory to God.* (Compare Luke 17, 18. John 9, 24. Rom. 4, 20. Rev. 4, 13. 14, 7. 16, 9, in all which cases the article is wanting, while in Rev. 19, 7 it is expressed.) The meaning is not that he failed to thank God for his eloquence, of which he probably had none, but that he allowed divine honours to be rendered to himself, or as Josephus phrases it, "did not rebuke them, and repel the impious adulation." *He was eaten of worms,* literally, *being* (or *becoming*) *worm-eaten,* an epithet applied by Theophrastus to decayed wood, but according to its etymology referring to the worm which feeds upon dead bodies. (Compare Mark 9, 44. 46. 48.) A similar death is said to have befallen Antiochus Epiphanes, Herod the Great, and other ancient persecutors of God's people. That Josephus speaks only of intense pains in the bowels, while Luke says he was devoured by worms, may arise from the natural desire of the former to spare the memory of Herod and the feelings of his children, or from Luke's professional exactness as a physician, or from both combined. That Luke, on the other hand, says nothing of the owl, shows his freedom from all fabulous admixtures and embellishments, even such as a Josephus thought it worth while to record. *Gave up the ghost,* or more exactly, *expired,* i. e. breathed out (his life or soul.) See above, on 5, 5. 10. This event took place, according to Josephus, in the fifty-fourth year of Agrippa's age, and the fourth of his reign, during the last three years of which he ruled the whole of Palestine. The date assigned to Herod's death by the chronologers is the first of August, A. D. 44.

24. But the word of God grew and multiplied.

But, i. e. notwithstanding Herod's persecution; or *and,* i. e. after it had died with him. The Greek word is the usual continuative particle (δέ) and not necessarily more emphatic here than in the beginning of the next verse, where it is translated *and.* Perhaps the connection which it indicates is this, that in the mean time, while these changes, whether prosperous or adverse, were occurring, the true religion was advancing. *The word of God,* i. e. the Gospel or the Christian revelation, here put by a natural metonymy for the cause or enterprise of which it was the basis, or rather for the body of believers who embraced it, and of which it might be literally said, that it *increased* (or *grew*) both in extent and power, *and was multiplied,* i. e. received continual accessions to the number of its members. (Compare the similar expressions in 6, 7 above, and 19, 20 below.)

25. And Barnabas and Saul returned from Jeru-

salem, when they had fulfilled (their) ministry, and took with them John, whose surname was Mark.

Barnabas and Saul, who were previously mentioned last in 11, 30, as having been deputed by the church at Antioch, to bear its contributions to the brethren dwelling in Judea, in anticipation of the coming famine. The connection between that verse and the one before us makes it highly probable, if not entirely certain, that the intervening narrative records events which took place during this official visit to Judea. Whether they were in the Holy City during Herod's persecution, is disputed, some inferring that they were, because they are here said to have *returned from Jerusalem;* while others explain this as meaning, that although Barnabas and Saul had been during these occurrences in other places of Judea, *they returned from Jerusalem,* i. e. they came there before going home, or made that their last point of departure. There is nothing in the text or context to decide this question, which is happily of little moment. *Having fulfilled the ministry* (or *service,*) or more precisely, *the administration,* charitable distribution or communication, which had been committed to their trust. (See above, on 11, 27. 30.) *Barnabas and Saul* is still the order of the names, and so continues, until the public recognition or appearance of the latter in the character of an Apostle. (See below, on 13, 1. 9.) *And took with them* (literally, *taking with them also*) *John the* (one) *likewise called* (or *surnamed*) *Mark,* who had been previously mentioned, with his mother Mary in v. 12 above, and reappears in 13, 5. 13, as the companion of these men on their first foreign mission, thus imparting to the narrative a character of oneness and coherence, very far removed from that of accidental fragments, independent documents, or desultory anecdotes. With this return of Barnabas and Saul to Antioch may be said to terminate one great division of the book, containing the history of the planting of the church among the Jews, its first extension to the Gentiles, and the institution of a secondary source or centre, from which light was to be diffused throughout the empire, as recorded in the following chapters.

END OF VOL. 1.

www.ingramcontent.com/pod-product-compliance
Lightning Source LLC
Chambersburg PA
CBHW051231300426
44114CB00011B/700